BERNINI'S SCALA REGIA AT THE VATICAN PALACE

Bernini's Scala Regia
at the
Vatican Palace

T. A. MARDER

Rutgers University

CAMBRIDGE
UNIVERSITY PRESS

PUBLISHED BY THE PRESS SYNDICATE OF THE UNIVERSITY OF CAMBRIDGE
The Pitt Building, Trumpington Street, Cambridge CB2 1RP, United Kingdom

CAMBRIDGE UNIVERSITY PRESS
The Edinburgh Building, Cambridge CB2 2RU, United Kingdom
40 West 20th Street, New York, NY 10011–4211, USA
10 Stamford Road, Oakleigh, Melbourne 3166, Australia

First published 1997

Printed in the United States of America

Typeset in Cochin

Library of Congress Cataloging-in-Publication Data

Marder, T. A.
Bernini's Scala Regia at the Vatican Palace: architecture, sculpture, and ritual / T. A. Marder.
p.   cm.
Includes bibliographical references and index.
ISBN 0 521 43198 0 (hc)
1. Scala Regia (Vatican Palace, Vatican City)   2. Bernini, Gian
Lorenzo, 1598 – 1680 – Criticism and interpretation.   3. Architecture,
Baroque – Vatican City.   4. Sculpture, Baroque – Vatican City.   I. Title.
NA1123.B5M37   1996
728.8'2'0945634 – dc20   96-3031
                                                                 CIP

*A catalog record for this book is available from
the British Library*

ISBN 0 521 43198 0 hardback

Research and publication of this book has been assisted with grants from the Graham
Foundation for Advanced Studies in the Fine Arts and the Samuel H. Kress Foundation.

Contents

Illustrations

Acknowledgments

The Scala Regia lies on the southern edge of the Vatican Palace, between the Sistine Chapel and St. Peter's. Except to the few who know it well, the staircase is virtually invisible from the exterior of the palace, and the interior is not normally open to visitors. Without the extraordinary privileges that I have been granted to visit the site and its physical context, this study could not have been undertaken, much less completed in its present form.

My first thanks are therefore due to the administration of the Vatican City (Governatorato della Santa Sede) and its staff, whose efficiency and constant cooperation made my work possible. Mrs. Marjorie Weeke, delegate of the Pontifical Council for Social Communications, was crucial in arranging site visits and offering guidance in the Vatican City. Without her help, I could not have made contact with the authorities whose support was necessary for the research and photography in this book. Time and again, Mrs. Weeke arranged special visits to the monument or meetings with the officials under whose jurisdictions parts of it reside. The cooperation of Bishop Dino Monduzzi, prefect of the Papal Household, was also very helpful in these endeavors, with permissions and frequent concessions to see parts of building rarely open even to scholars.

For information on the structure of the Scala Regia, I wish to thank engineer Massimo Stoppa, director general of the Technical Services Office of the Governatorato, and his staff: Dr. Angelo Costantini, architects Egisto Ercadi, Giuseppe Facchini, engineer Pier Carlo Cuscianna, and Mr. Giovanni Lombardi. All of them facilitated my repeated inspection of Bernini's walls, dusty vaults, and hidden buttresses. The staff also very kindly shared with me the modern drawings made for purposes of maintenance, which were of great value in studying the historic structure. Msgr. Michele Basso, of the Archive of the Fabbrica di San Pietro, made the documentary material accessible for extensive study, even during the periods when the archive was being transferred after centuries in the same location.

Like everyone at the Biblioteca Apostolica Vaticana, I too was inspired by its enlightened prefect, Father Leonard E. Boyle O.P., and helped with various, more specific problems by Dr. Giovanni Morello, Dr. Gian Carlo Alteri, and Mr. Enzo Garofalo. The late Prof. Carlo Pietrangeli, director general of the Vatican Museums, has set a standard of excellence in his studies of the palace which I can only envy. Through his kindnesses and those of the late Dr. Fabrizio Mancinelli, I was able to visit and study many parts of the palace fabric not open to casual visitors.

Two other institutions in Rome deserve my special thanks. Under the direction of Joseph Connors, the American Academy in Rome became my oasis for planning site visits, preparing archival searches, and mounting photographic campaigns in the years between 1988 and 1991. The special welcome I enjoyed there, in the library and elsewhere, made it the ideal place for collating and scheming every step of on-site research. As only a handful of professional photographs of the Scala Regia existed at the time, I hired the remarkable Giorgio Vasari to make a new core collection of negatives. With these to hand, another great Roman institution, the Bibliotheca Hertziana of the Max-Planck Gesellschaft agreed to extend and complete the visual documentation. The approval of the codirectors Christoph L. Frommel and Matthias Winner, and the endorsement of Dieter Graf, director of the Fototeca, to carry out this broader photographic campaign was a significant extension of many years of scholarly hospitality and friendship. The second group of negatives was produced with great industry and good cheer by Gabriella Fichera. All of these friends and institutions have become collaborators in the course of my Scala Regia research, and without them, it simply could not have been completed in its present form.

In fact, the project began with a twenty-minute presentation at the College Art Association annual meeting in 1983, with material I hoped to incorporate in a book on Bernini's architecture. The opportunity to resume work on the Scala Regia came somewhat later, in 1988, during a sabbatical leave supported and extended by grants from the Graham Foundation for Advanced Studies in the Fine Arts, the Ailsa Mellon Bruce Senior Fellowship at the National Gallery of Art in Washington, D.C., and the Office of Research and Sponsored Programs at Rutgers University from 1988 through 1991. For the chance to work in Rome and Washington during this period, I am indebted to Carter Manny of the Graham Foundation and Henry Millon at the Center for Advanced Studies in the Visual Arts at the National Gallery. For the year 1990–91, Tilden Edelstein, then dean of the Faculty of Arts and Sciences at Rutgers University, agreed to an exceptional leave of absence, enabling me to finish the research in Rome.

As the outlines of a book began to emerge from the modest article originally envisioned, I enjoyed the wise counsel of William Loerke and Henry Millon. To them as to others who listened to my ideas and read early drafts go my deepest thanks, including Nicholas Adams, Malcolm Campbell, Christof Thoenes, and Mark Weil. John Pinto has my gratitude for helping to explore and measure dark and neglected corners over the vaulting. Patricia Waddy agreed to read the penultimate draft, and her corrections and comments have added immeasurably to the clarity and precision of the book.

Among many other friends and colleagues who helped with various sorts of information over the years, I would like especially to thank Maria Giulia Barberini, George Bauer, Allan Braham, Kathleen Weil-Garris Brandt, Lucia Cavazzi, Allan Ceen, Juliusz Chrościcki, Guido Cornini, Nicola Courtright, Peter Day, Diane DeGrazia, Sabine Eiche, Jesús Escobar, Marcello Fagiolo, Phillip Fehl, Jack Freiberg, David Friedman, Jörg Garms, Kenneth Gaulin, Dorothy Metzger Habel, Hellmut Hager, Ann Sutherland Harris, Elizabeth Hellman, Alice Jarrard, Richard Krautheimer, Irving Lavin, David Levine, Joseph Levine, Douglas Lewis, Børje Magnusson, Sarah Blake McHam, Elizabeth Parker McLachlan, Sarah McPhee, Karl-Heinz Mehnert, Domenico Minchilli, Leatrice Mendelsohn, Jennifer Montagu, Mieczysław Morka, Arnold Nesselrath, John Newman, Martha Pollak, Rudolf Preimesberger, Michael Putnam, Thomas N. Rajkovich, Louise Rice, Peter Schaudt, John Shearman, Thomas Gordon Smith, Luigi Spezzaferro, Stephen Tobriner, Maria Letizia Casanova Uccella, John Varriano, and Guy Walton. For the useful information and ideas in the book, the reader has to thank the inspiration of my teachers in New York a generation ago: Howard Hibbard, Richard Krautheimer, Milton Lewine, and Rudolf Wittkower. Their approaches to teaching, research, and writing remain as fresh and relevant to me today as they did upon first encounter. The combination of patience and persistence with which Beatrice Rehl, my editor at Cambridge University Press, pursued the Scala Regia material also remains in my mind a model of encouragement to academic authors. For their careful collaboration in production and copy-editing, respectively, Camilla Palmer and Maura High deserve my heartfelt thanks.

Finally, I have to thank Margaret Kuntz for observations and references that strengthened every chapter. Only couples working on closely related projects know how much substance was added to the project as a result. To my children I am likewise grateful. Because of them the book is infinitely more thoughtful than it might have been had they granted me the peace and quiet to write it more expeditiously.

Introduction

THE Scala Regia is a defining monument of the Roman Baroque and a textbook example of Bernini's art. It appears in surveys of the architect, of the period, and of art and architectural history in general as "the perfect Baroque synthesis of the arts."[1] The staircase, with its long, tunnel-like axis lined with columns, is familiar even to students with only a casual knowledge of Baroque art. Yet in many respects the Scala Regia is little known. Located deep in the fabric of the Vatican Palace and virtually invisible from the exterior, the stairs are not normally accessible to visitors. Even Rome-based art historians are sometimes unsure about its location in the palace and its relationship to St. Peter's and Bernini's piazza. Because of this, in turn, most scholars are only vaguely familiar with its function and the nature of its decoration. As a result, the Scala Regia has enjoyed an obscurity that is unique among Bernini's most famous works.

Due in part to these circumstances, only a handful of professional photographs of the Scala Regia exist, scores of others being the result of hit-or-miss opportunities that cannot provide a systematic record of the monument or its structure. In turn, there has been little inspiration to engage in the sort of archival research a monument of this prominence might otherwise merit; little to encourage a more broadly based investigation that would take into account the notoriously complicated histories of the Vatican Palace, St. Peter's, and Bernini's Piazza S. Pietro. The ensemble that composed the ceremonial entrance to the Vatican Palace and the principal link between the palace and St. Peter's has therefore remained seriously unstudied and somewhat mysterious.

The modern historiography on the Scala Regia begins with Erwin Panofsky's brilliant study of 1919. More often cited than read, it was largely influenced by his interest in perspective and was limited by his reliance on photographs, engravings, descriptions, and other second-hand information he could gather when writing from abroad. In a long article of 1922, Hermann Voss introduced a more methodical, less theoretical approach based on first-hand knowledge of the Scala Regia and on issues of structure and physical context rather than aesthetics. This dialogue was extended in 1931, in the magisterial catalogue of Bernini's drawings by Heinrich Brauer and Rudolf Wittkower, who published an extensive discussion of the Scala Regia (written by the latter), bringing together all available graphic and documentary evidence for the commission and placing it within the context of Bernini's work on Piazza S. Pietro.

The discussion of design process in Brauer and Wittkower's catalogue gave (and still gives) the impression of such complexity and thoroughness that it remained unsurpassed to our day. Yet many questions of structure, function, and meaning lay beyond the scope of the investigation. As a result, for example, the authors' treatment of Bernini's equestrian statue of Constantine hardly touches on the issue of its location at the foot of the Scala Regia. In the scholarly literature, the statue thus remained a work isolated in space and iconographic intention, a situation consolidated in Wittkower's later catalogue of Bernini's sculpture (first edition, 1955). Not surprisingly, Previtali's publication in 1962 of the early critique of the equestrian was handled as a sidelight in the history of the sculpture rather than as a new point of departure. Similarly, in 1967, H. G. Evers revived discussion of the issue of Bernini's perspective composition. Aiming to justify Panofsky's older arguments, the author presented new (to me inconclusive) evidence for the "medieval" shell within which Bernini was constrained to build the Scala Regia.

In short, neither the Scala Regia nor the equestrian statue of Constantine attracted the same dedicated discussion that Battaglia (1943) lavished on the Cathedra Petri or Wittkower (1961) orchestrated for Bernini's Louis XIV equestrian, although the same rich historical documentation was awaiting them. In 1981, Armando Schiavo brought out some valuable new archival material for the Scala Regia and the Constantine and, for the first time, considered the stairs and the equestrian statue as an ensemble. But this was only a signpost in its brevity. Still more documentation appeared in the monograph *Bernini architetto* (1981, English edition 1984) by Borsi and Quinterio, which of necessity left the job of individual studies to later research.

Missing in all of these contributions has been a consideration of Bernini's Scala Regia as a functional, ceremonial, and symbolic component of the Vatican Palace. Why was the Scala Regia built? What preceded the Scala Regia to serve the functions and symbols it embraced? When and how was Bernini's Scala Regia conceived and designed? How was it built? What meanings may be read in its form and decoration? How were they construed?

This book takes these issues as fundamental for a fuller understanding of the monument. My goals are therefore to set Bernini's achievement firmly within the context of the earlier history of the palace; to recreate the design and construction processes as we know them from graphic, documentary, literary, and archaeological evidence; and to interpret the results of these designs on the basis of patterns of use and iconographic intention.

My account of the Scala Regia differs from earlier discussions in its length, of course, but also in emphasis. First, I see the monument within the developing physical context of the earlier palace. Second, I emphasize the creation of the Scala Regia as a development of Bernini's schemes for Piazza S. Pietro. Third, I maintain that the design process offers impressive new evidence of Bernini's skill in manipulating structure for expressive, programmatic effect. Fourth, I consider both the statue of Constantine and the decorated staircase as polyvalent symbols related to the earlier history of the palace and basilica, to their seventeenth-century historiography, and to contemporary politics and church ritual. Finally, I interpret the Scala Regia as an architectural and figural ensemble intimately related to its functions as the main entrance to the Vatican Palace and its principal connection to St. Peter's.

Above all, I have tried to see the Scala Regia as bridging several streams of history pertaining to the basilica, the palace, and the piazza in a more thoroughgoing way than previous scholarship has attempted. By presenting an extensive complement of documents, drawings, and professional photographs, the book attempts to enrich our knowledge of the Vatican Palace, our understanding of Bernini's art, and our perceptions about his most active patron in architecture, Pope Alexander VII. To accomplish these goals, in turn, meant following in the footsteps of some of the greatest scholars of our time. This has been an exciting and humbling experience. It therefore goes almost without saying that my work is deeply indebted to the sturdy foundations laid in the writings of Ackerman, Brauer and Wittkower, Egger, Ehrle, Frommel, Kauffmann, Krautheimer, Lavin, Mancinelli, Martinelli, Panofsky, Pietrangeli, Redig De Campos, Shearman, Stevenson, Thoenes, and Voss, to name but a few.

As a result of my goals the material is divided into nine chapters. The first assumes the form of a descriptive tour of the Vatican Palace from Piazza S. Pietro, through the north corridor, up the Scala Regia, to the principal audience hall of the palace, the Scala Regia. This account is intended to help the reader understand the location of the Scala Regia, its physical character, and some of its subtleties. Knowing what is presently on the site also helps us to visualize the state of the palace before Bernini's work. Then, in the second chapter, I discuss the location and history of the southern entrance to the palace and the connections between the Scala Regia and St. Peter's from the later Middle Ages through the sixteenth century. Up to 1500, the development of the palace entrance responded to papal ambitions to rival foreign courts in grandeur and visual strength. Between 1500 and 1600, I suggest, the entrance and connections to St. Peter's depended on the building progress of the new basilica.

Chapter 3 introduces the changes to the southern portion of the Vatican Palace required by the nave and façade that were added to new St. Peter's in the early seventeenth century. The configuration of the palace entrance and the stairs to St. Peter's at this time provides the stage upon which Bernini's radical new schemes would make their appearance. In my opinion, it was a stage largely set, as so often elsewhere, by his illustrious predecessor, Carlo Maderno.

Chapters 4, 5, and 6 discuss the design process and construction of the Scala Regia from its inception as part of Piazza S. Pietro. At first, I deal with the introduction of the stairs into the program of the piazza. By reassessing Wittkower's analysis of the so-called counterproject drawings, I open the possibility that the notion of a new palace entrance was a contribution of Bernini's critics in the first instance, unforeseen by the architect or his patron Alexander VII. In the second part, I analyze the design and trace the execution of the corridors, which enables us to determine when and how Bernini and Alexander VII subsequently planned for the stairs. Among other contributions, this discussion provides additional documentation for portions of the palace that were demolished and others that were realigned above the corridor and staircase. Here, as in the following chapter, I consider all known drawings and many new documents for the enterprise. The third

part is devoted to the design of the staircase, where issues of structure and the challenges of construction are explained with reference to the eventual form of the architecture and its expressive content. Here Bernini resolved the problems that he himself considered the most difficult of his career.

Chapter 7 reviews the design and execution of the equestrian statue of Constantine, bringing together all known drawings and numerous new documents to explain the evolution of the sculpture, its pedestal, and its ornamental backdrop. Chapter 8 is a discussion of the iconographic meanings and intentions specific to the Constantine ensemble. Finally, in Chapter 9, I deal with the sculpture and architecture together within the contexts of palace and church traditions, ceremonial and ritual observances in the palace and the basilica, and the historical contexts of Alexander VII's pontificate. I here and throughout the planning stages maintain that Alexander played an active role in the configuration of the site and the composition of its programmatic intentions. As all accounts claim, the design is Bernini's, but this view is leavened by the contributions of his patron and even his capomaestro, aspects of the story that do little to compromise our traditional faith in his genius. In the end, my hope is to enrich our view of Bernini's creative processes, to document fully the last major addition to the Vatican Palace, and to understand from a variety of viewpoints the reciprocal influences of function and intention in a seventeenth-century ensemble of architecture and sculpture.

ONE

A Tour of the Monument

SEEN from the piazza in front of St. Peter's in Rome, the Vatican Palace rises majestically above the northern rim of Bernini's colonnade. Hovering above the grand sweep of the piazza, the masses of the palace advance and retreat in episodic measures, its projecting wings and reclusive inner courts creating silhouettes that suggest the ambitions of a myriad of building campaigns (Fig. 1). These were the contributions of various popes, architects, and epochs from the Middle Ages through the early eighteenth century. Formally, it is a confusing sight. The Palace of Sixtus V on the right, solid in proportion and detail, appears to float above unseen foundations. The façade of Bramante and Raphael's Logge recedes incongruously from the piazza and bears no clear geometric relation to the projection of Paul V's wing over the north corridor. From a purely visual analysis it is hard to appreciate this portion of the Vatican Palace and virtually impossible to grasp the history and topography that invests it with meaning and beauty. Fortunately, a good deal of that history and topography is encapsulated in the evolution of the entrance to the palace, culminating in Gianlorenzo Bernini's Scala Regia.

The staircase known as the Scala Regia was begun in 1663 under the patronage of Alexander VII Chigi (1655–67) (Fig. 2). Its purpose is to connect the piazza and the basilica of St. Peter's with the palace that towers about twenty meters above them. The staircase also served as the main entrance to the palace, bringing the visitor up to its principal audience hall, the Sala Regia. Here and in other rooms on this level, guests of distinction were received by the pope and his representatives. In the words of

Richard Lassels, writing in 1670, "these stairs render you up at the great Hall, called the Sala Regia, because the Pope receiveth here Embassadors of Kings in Their Embassies of state."[1] The Scala Regia that everyone knows from period engravings or modern photographs is lined with columns and decorated with marble and stucco sculpture that befit this and other functions performed by a passage that also links the palace with the basilica.

Despite this easily recognized image and its obvious functional importance, however, the precise location of the monument is hard to describe and its full character usually eludes attempts at illustration. For example, representations of Bernini's equestrian statue of Constantine at the foot of the staircase usually omit the architectural setting, and photographs of the Scala Regia rarely do justice to the statue. Yet these components were developed together to enhance the events and rituals that took place in their midst. To begin to understand the architecture, the sculpture must be considered, and vice versa. And both need to be seen literally and figuratively within the larger context of the Vatican Palace and the basilica of St. Peter's.

This book is therefore all about the Scala Regia in more ways than one. For if the principal argument advanced here is successful, we must grasp what stands in front, beyond, over, under, and to either side of the textbook image of the architecture and sculpture. Knowing where the monument is in relation to its neighbors becomes the first step in understanding its significance as a piece of the palace fabric and a symbolic statement about the edifice it ennobles. The Scala Regia therefore qualifies among

Figure 1. Piazza S. Pietro, St. Peter's, and Vatican Palace, painting, Giovanni Paolo Panini
(Toledo Museum of Art, acc. no. 1971, 157)

the highest ranks of those buildings that need to be visited and personally explored to be understood in any serious way. The purpose of this chapter is to describe that physical setting as an introduction to the history of the site. From this we may better grasp what lay there in the centuries before Bernini's appearance and how he manipulated both structure and tradition for evocative effect.

The Scala Regia is an extension of Bernini's design for Piazza S. Pietro, begun in 1656 for Alexander VII. Construction of the north colonnade was begun in 1657, and by 1661 it was virtually complete. As schemes evolved during these years, Bernini and his patron developed ideas for a palace entrance using an enclosed corridor to connect the piazza and palace. These circumstances explain the hurry to complete the northern colonnade, which

was finished before the southern colonnade was even begun. In these circumstances, the north half of the piazza assumed the second function of incorporating a principal entrance to the palace. Bernini excavated the foundations for the north corridor in 1660, and in 1663 construction of the Scala Regia was under way. The architecture of the staircase was largely finished by 1666, and the equestrian statue of Constantine's Vision of the Cross was unveiled in 1671.

Because the Vatican houses, protects, and symbolizes the spiritual and temporal leader of the Roman Catholic Church, the palace entrance must be understood as an ascent that is both real and symbolic. The visitor progresses from the terrestrial realm of the piazza, through the north corridor, to the base landing at the foot of the Scala Regia.

TABVLA 83. *PROSPECTVS SCALÆ REGIÆ AB EQVITE BERNINO EXTRVCTÆ SVB ALEXANDRO VII*

Figure 2. Scala Regia, engraving, Fontana 1694 (Princeton University, Marquand Library)

There, Constantine's Vision of the Cross identifies the divine source of the emperor's power. As visitors begin the stepped ascent, they become aware of the narrowing space between the columns of the lower stairs. After a pause at an intermediate landing, which separates the lower from the upper flight along the entrance axis, one arrives at a double landing. Here the visitor is required to make a 180-degree turn to continue along the upper stairs to the threshold of the Sala Regia, the largest audience hall of the palace. From the entrance portal on the piazza through the lower and upper sections of the stairs, the width of the space becomes ever narrower. In effect this sequence emphasizes the expansive space of the Sala Regia at the summit the Scala Regia, where the authority of the pope is presented in its full majesty. The following sections of this chapter will discuss each of these features in greater detail and provide a narrative that accompanies the plates at the end of the book. Our discussion begins where colonnade meets corridor at the north side of the piazza.

The Portone di Bronzo

Bernini's design for Piazza S. Pietro is dominated by two symmetrical colonnades cast over segments of an ellipse whose principal axis is perpendicular to the axis of the basilica (Fig. 3). The uniformity of the colonnades in plan is broken in the middle and at the ends of each segment by the wider intercolumniations of columns set out from the otherwise smooth curve of the scheme. Over each group of these projecting sections, an entablature bears the name of Alexander VII to mark entries into the shelter of the colonnaded perimeter. The entry on the northwest side of the layout also serves as a palace entrance, which is thus largely subsumed within the design of the entire piazza (Fig. 4). Any concern for exteriorizing the image of the palace is suppressed to favor the primacy of St. Peter's and its forecourt. Stendhal went so far as to suggest that the palace actually weakened the impression of the basilica. In a memorable phrase of 1828, he characterized the palace as a building of "ten thousand rooms and no façade."[2]

The entrance axis takes the twentieth-century visitor to a stepped ascent in front of the palace portal, the Portone di Bronzo (Plate 1). Set within a bay of the corridor, the portal is preceded by twenty steps organized in two flights. The steps are recent. On engravings from the seventeenth to the nineteenth century, the ascent is made by eleven treads pitched in ramplike fashion, as they are still at the entrance to the south colonnade (Fig. 5).[3] In fact, the entrance to the south corridor provides us with an idea of the original appearance of the north corridor (Fig. 6). To moderate the ascent, some of the treads extended into the colonnade. (A ramp of almost identical dimensions lay in front of the palace portal in the sixteenth century and may have been preserved in the structures that stood here early the following century; see Figure 21 below.)

At the entrance to the north corridor, details such as the awkwardly exposed plinths at the portal bases

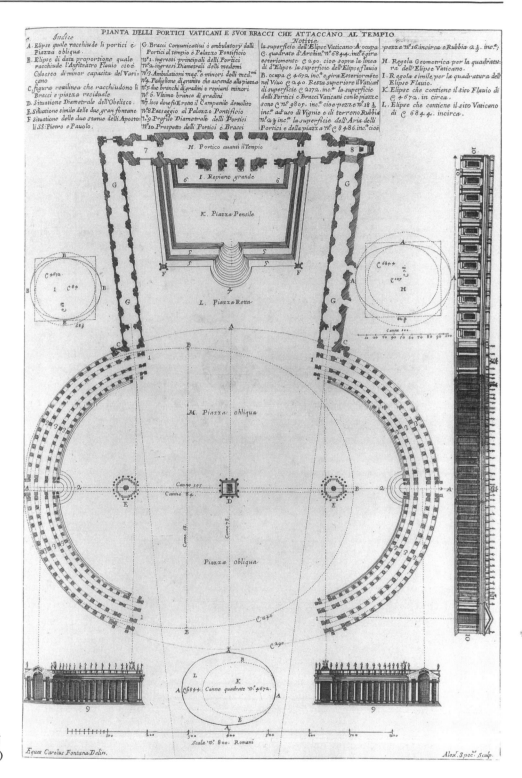

Figure 3. Plan of Piazza S. Pietro, engraving, Fontana 1694 (Bibliotheca Hertziana, D23753)

betray the modern origin of the first entry steps. The mincing stride necessary to climb the new stairs is entirely at odds with the smooth incline of the corridor beyond the portal and the stately pace subsequently enforced by the Scala Regia itself. Of course, much of the pageantry and ceremony that traditionally accompanied palace ritual has disappeared in modern times, and so too have complementary features of the architecture. One now-lost convention evident here is the use of an odd number

Figure 4. West end of north colonnade arm, Piazza S. Pietro (Marder)

Figure 5. East end of north corridor, engraving, Bonanni 1696 (Bibliotheca Hertziana, D21944)

of stairs, which is as old as the oldest surviving treatise on architecture (Vitruvius, book 3, ch. 4, 4), as seventeenth-century theorists were aware.[4] It insures that processors take the first step with the same foot that makes the first level stride at the top. In their number and abbreviated proportions, then, the present steps betray their modern character in contrast to the eleven inclined treads they replaced.

In the early eighteenth century, Taja summarized the function and significance of the Portone di Bronzo as the "primo ingresso nel Palazzo Apostolico."[5] The portal is composed of two huge bronze doors flanked by single columns, topped by a broken pediment, and ornamented with two marble angels and a mosaic depicting the Madonna enthroned with Sts. Peter and Paul (Plates 2–4). Bernini had salvaged and reused most of these components from the palace entrance commissioned by Paul V (1605–21) in the first decade of the century. The angels were carved by Ambrogio Bonvicino and Nicolò

Cordier, and the mosaic was executed by Giovanni Calandra on the design of the Cavaliere d'Arpino. With its broad divisions of studded surfaces and coffered panels, the Portone di Bronzo retains its original fortified aspect. Traditionally, a palace portal or gateway may symbolize the dwelling of a powerful, even godlike being, the seat of a government from which a state could be governed with divine wisdom, and this was certainly implicit in the meaning of the figures at the Vatican Palace entrance.[6]

To incorporate the preexisting components of the palace entrance, Bernini had to fit them under the groin vault of his new northern corridor in a constricted environment where they are not altogether comfortable. The angels, for example, were not designed to be perched so awkwardly on a raking cornice and placed as high as they are in relation to the mosaic. To incorporate the mosaic in the smaller dimensions of Bernini's architectural system, the frame was cut at the sides and made shorter.[7] Remains from an earlier era, these components were surely meant to recall the interventions of Paul V, as does the emphatic presence of St. Paul in the mosaic with his sword prominently displayed in the foreground.

While the entrance along with the rest of the north corridor was finished during the reign of Alexander VII in the period 1659–62, the south corridor was completed only much later, in 1667–69, by Clement IX Rospigliosi, whose coat of arms is displayed inside the portal. The much simpler decoration on the south consists of a mosaic representation of the calling of St. Peter executed by Pietro Spagna on the design of Ciro Ferri.[8]

The Corridor

The exterior of the corridor continues the scale of the colonnade with pilasters whose height and width are the same as the freestanding columns (Figs. 7, 8). But the pilasters are paired and the distance between the pairs is equal to half the height of the pilaster shafts, whereas the single columns around the piazza are arranged in radial fashion and more tightly spaced. In this manner, the rhythm of the vertical accents is slowed and redoubled in emphasis. A more ceremonious cadence replaces the rapid clatter of vertical accents from the colonnade. The effect is entirely appropriate to the palace entrance, although carriages were originally driven into the corridor to the foot of the Scala Regia. This fact is implied in the ornament where the pilaster bases, capitals, and entablature are inclined in response to the pavement of the piazza (Figs. 9, 10).

Although the pilasters of the exterior are larger than those within the corridors, this distinction is obscured by the Portone di Bronzo, which is a relatively small passage. In this way, the grand effect of the colonnade is maintained within the long enclosures of the corridors. Between the pilaster bays, windows are treated as rhomboids whose sills reflect the rising grade. On the north corridor, the windows have been partially infilled in modern times, presumably after the installation of artificial lighting. The windows along the shaded south corridor retain their original size.

The commanding width of the modern Via della Conciliazione (1934–50) absorbed roads like the

Figure 6. East entrance of south corridor (Marder)

Borgo Vecchio and Borgo Nuovo that led directly to the piazza. With their disappearance, relationships between the urban fabric and the palace have been obscured. Now largely forgotten, it was once possible to look back from the north corridor, through the Portone di Bronzo, across the piazza, and down the length of the Borgo Nuovo to Castel Sant'Angelo (Fig. 11).[9] Before the construction of Via della Conciliazione these relationships, captured in pre-1930s photographs, were commonly noted (Fig. 12).[10] Among recent historians, however, only Birindelli has adequately emphasized how Bernini aligned the portal and corridor with the axis of the Borgo Nuovo. This alignment can be imagined in a nineteenth-century photograph of the street at the end of which, on the far right, lies the palace entrance (Fig. 13). The location of the portal on this axis probably dates from the inception of the street itself around 1500, during the papacy of Alexander VI (1492–1503). Bernini's contribution was to maintain that correspondence and extend the axis west-

Figure 7. Vatican Palace from Piazza S. Pietro (Marder)

ward, literally into the palace via the new corridor and the Scala Regia. Given the circumstances we can imagine his patron, Alexander VII, taking special pleasure in extending the avenue originally known as the Via Alessandrina after its fifteenth-century creator.

Again, to read Stendhal is to obtain some glimmer of the original effect, predating the creation of the modern Via della Conciliazione. "This morning," he wrote, "when our barouche had crossed the Sant'Angelo bridge, we perceived St. Peter's at the end of a narrow street. Napoleon had announced the project marking his entry into Rome by the purchase and the demolition of all the houses that stand on the left side of this street.... We followed this straight street, opened by Alexander VI, and reached the Piazza Rusticucci, on which the pope's guard parades every day at noon with a fanfare of music and drums, but without ever being able to

keep step."[11] The width of the street is exaggerated but its path is otherwise faithfully recorded, full of pedestrians, by Cruyl in the later seventeenth century (Fig. 14).

Stendhal was not much enamored of the palace entrance, as we have seen, but if he had continued in the same direction, he would have enjoyed an equally impressive vista within the corridor. It includes the vaulted connection between piazza and palace, the brightly lit base landing of the Scala Regia, and the two flights of the lower staircase (Plate 5). At the end of the vista, there is a window lighting the southern half of the double landing. The subtle adjustments of the rising level of the corridor, the climbing path of the stairs, and the location of the window at the very end of this axis must have been carefully planned. Had the corridor been a level grade and the stairs steeper, for example, it would have been impossible to capture the entire distance

10

Figure 8. Exterior detail, bay of north corridor (Marder)

Figure 9. Exterior detail, pilaster bases of north corridor (Marder)

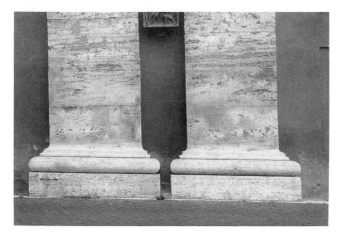

Figure 10. Exterior detail, pilaster capitals of north corridor (Marder)

in a single glance. More than any other evidence, this view suggests that Bernini and Alexander had the entire scheme of the palace entry in mind as the elevations of the respective components were settled. The Chigi escutcheons on the exterior above the west end of the colonnade, then inside the corridor above the Portone di Bronzo facing west, again at the foot of the Scala Regia, and finally in the window at the end of this extensive sequence establish Alexander VII's claim on the development of the axis that begins in the city itself (Plate 6).[12]

Within the bronze doors the corridor presents a vista of compelling uniformity punctuated by the intermittent presence of Swiss Guards and palace functionaries. A pair of pilasters and transverse bands of vaulting demarcate each of ten bays, their concave walls opening onto the south with the large windows we have described from the exterior. The formal effect of the vaulting is interrupted by electric lamps installed on iron ties. If we could remove these anomalous additions, it would be easier to appreciate the rhythmic alternation between the attenuated linear patterns arching across the grain of the dominant axis and the subtle chiaroscuro of the groin-vaulted sectors between them. This play of line and surface

11

Figure 11 (right). View from within Portone di Bronzo looking east down axis of the Borgo Nuovo (ICCD, G2375)

Figure 12 (below). View over Vatican Borgo and central spina (to the right of line indicating Borgo Nuova) (ICCD, D1721)

Figure 13 (left). View of St. Peter's and palace from Borgo Nuovo looking west (ICCD, G1856)

Figure 14 (below). View of Castel Sant'Angelo and St. Peter's with pedestrians on Borgo Nuovo, drawing, Cruyl (Ashmolean Museum, Oxford, neg. no. PI 121)

comes alive with the merest amount of light but would have been much stronger before the size of the windows was reduced.

The poetry of the scheme is based on the alternation of curved surfaces and pilaster pairs whose shallow projection composes the face of the massive piers upon which the vaults rest (Plate 7). In a more conventional composition, the piers might have been rectangular and the bays between them flat planes rather than gentle curves. Robert De Cotte may have had this in mind in the 1680s when he described the system of corridor vaults as "in bad taste."[13] In fact, a similar composition appears in a preliminary plan by Bernini that was later discarded for the present scheme (see Fig. 109). The problem with such a composition is that it would have revealed and emphasized all of the discomforting angles that the rising terrain imposes on vertical surfaces. In the revision, these rigid and static features were entirely avoided. The space between the pilaster pairs is spanned by concave surfaces and capped by shallow conches. Curved shapes incorporate and disguise the rising grade of the pavement, the subtle inclination of horizontal courses, and the geometric irregularities of the wall. The result is a pulsing image of movement.

The rhythmic swelling of forms between the sets of double pilasters transforms inert mass and surface into shapes whose indeterminant contours (not rectangular, not half-round) enforce the primacy of the main axis and effectively disguise the structural origins and aesthetic raison d'être of the double pilasters, to articulate the piers of a vaulted substructure buttressing the foundations of the palace. Understood in this way, the composition of the corridor is a kind of architectural *schiacciato* whose essential purpose is to modify and enliven the appearance of the groin vaults and inert wall mass.

The movemented aspect of the corridor's design is reflected in details as small as the pilaster bases. Here, in contrast to the conventional cushion shape used on the exterior of the corridor, Bernini employed the more sinuous profile: a quirked cima reversa (bulging below, curved in, then convex again) that is given added prominence by the indentation of a sunken fillet above the plinth (Plate 8). Against this soft, malleable form the gentle inclination of the pavement is entirely absorbed. The shape of the capitals is similar, with the echinus given a double cur-

vature on the interior of the corridor rather than the conventional single curve of the exterior pilaster capitals (Plate 9).

On the interior, the necking of the capitals continues behind each double pilaster unit, through the curve of each bay, to repeat the movement over the next pier mass. As a result the walls have a consistent "collar" for the vaults to rest upon, whereas the base moldings do not extend beyond the pilasters. Consistent with these details, the vaulting appears to be a continuous element of the interior, while the pavement level steadily ascends. At the west end of the corridor, thirteen steps rise to the elevation of the base landing (Plates 10, 11). The pilaster units of the corridor march into the steps, first burying their plinths, then the bases, and finally a portion of the pilaster shaft. That this solution was intended from the beginning is suggested by its presence in an early planning drawing in Munich, about which more will be said in a later chapter. The strategy was to transform the Doric pilasters into baseless wall strips to be conjoined to the Ionic order of the stairs without transgressing the customary distinctions between the different orders of architecture.

The original floor of the north corridor was paved with brick laid on edge in herringbone pattern. Letarouilly's engravings show that it survived into the nineteenth century, and the same paving is still in use in the south corridor (Fig. 15). The present stone pavement of the north corridor dates from the early twentieth century. A metal escutcheon embossed in the floor of the seventh bay includes an

Figure 15. Interior detail of south corridor with brick pavement (Marder)

inscription referring to the fifth year of Benedict XV's pontificate (1914–22) when the work was completed.[14] This may also have been the occasion for the installation of electric lamps in the corridor, at which time the windows onto the piazza would have been partially blocked up. Benedict XV's work provided the last opportunity to celebrate and embellish the relationship of the palace and the papacy to the Borgo and Rome before the Fascist era.

Before this time, lighting at night would have been provided by gas lamps and, before that, by candles and torches.[15] In the seventeenth century, pages were responsible for bringing torches to the foot of the stair for visitors arriving by coach and from there to the audience halls. Each gentleman of an entourage could be expected to hold a candle, but only one, in order to be prepared to make reverences along the way. Footmen helped fix the torches in the rooms and bring them back to the coaches at the end of the visit, while the *maestro di camera* was responsible for ensuring an appropriate provision of candles for such occasions.[16]

Among the structural details in Letarouilly's engravings, the progressive thickening of the north wall of the corridor is worthy of note (Fig. 16). The first two bays of this wall are relatively thin, for they support only their own vaults. At the fourth and succeeding bays, the wall becomes thicker where it serves as a foundation of the palace. These features correspond to the reinforced walls of the corridor depicted on the preliminary plan by Bernini to which we have already referred. Naturally, it is in this zone that the greatest structural difficulties occur, and we have evidence of leaks in the vaults here from 1840 and 1895 as proof.[17] The leaching due to dampness in the vault can still be seen in this area (1990–91).

An unexpected feature of the design is the expanding width of the corridor as it extends from the colonnade toward the Scala Regia. From inside the Portone di Bronzo at the east, the width of the corridor increases by just over a meter to the west end.[18] Birindelli explains the changing dimensions of the corridor with reference to the features it joins. He points out that the passage joining the corridor to the colonnade is less than seven meters in width, whereas the connection of the corridor with the narthex of the basilica varies between nine and 12 meters, calling for a wider dimension. He concludes

that the expanding dimensions of the corridor are intended to minimize the disjunction that might result in the union of these spaces.[19] This observation is certainly correct with respect to the visual effect of the structure, but the reason for the design also involves other considerations.

It should be emphasized that the expanding width of the corridor is almost imperceptible. It could be understood, for example, with reference to the rising terrain and the inclined pavement. As the width of the corridor increases, the span and height of the vaults also increase but maintain a relatively uniform profile. This would be important at the west end of the corridor, where the thirteen steps to the base landing at the foot of the Scala Regia might otherwise appear to constrict the space and compromise its unity. In fact, the increasing dimensions of the corridor were intended to provide the radius for carriages to turn around and leave the corridor after letting off their occupants (Chapter 5).

The Base Landing

The thirteen steps that bring the visitor to the foot of the Scala Regia have been replaced in modern times, probably also under Benedict XV; but unlike the ascent from the colonnade to the Portone di Bronzo their original character and dimensions have been preserved (Plates 10, 11). The deeper treads and lower risers encourage a deliberate pace in which forward motion is stronger than vertical rise.[20] Complementing the sense of appropriate pace is the uneven number of steps, enabling the visitor to arrive at the base landing with the stride that initiated the ascent.

At the base landing of the Scala Regia, the height of the vault dramatically increases, and a huge east-facing window admits vast quantities of light from a level above the roofs of the corridor (Fig. 17 and Plate 12). For the visitor entering the Vatican Palace by this route, there must have been a place where the transitional aspect of the corridor gave way to the palace precinct. From the visual evidence, it is clear that the corridor was treated as a ceremonial approach by virtue of its grand scale and formal homogeneity, which are metaphors of authority, but without the suggestive power of figural or decorative iconography. The transition to the palace precinct

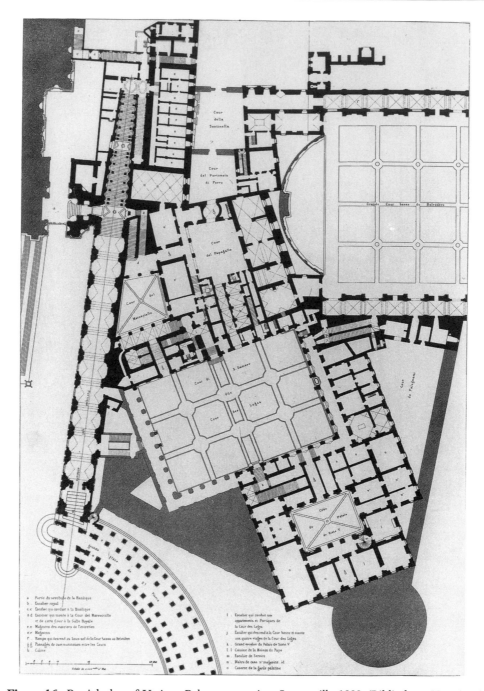

Figure 16. Partial plan of Vatican Palace, engraving, Letarouilly 1882 (Bibliotheca Hertziana)

took place at the base landing, where this iconography is introduced for the first time.

Most immediately conspicuous are the figures of fame that, like victories, bear the papal escutcheon of Alexander VII (Plate 13). They flank the Chigi arms like antique victories, their movement stabilized by the escutcheon rather than supporting it as is more generally true in Bernini's art. The figure on the left steadies herself with a hand clutching the escutcheon and a foot wedged with billowing drapery between the moldings of the extrados. Supported in this way, the figure appears poised to release the trumpet blast directed at the door of the basilica. The right-hand figure is posed more pre-

Figure 17. St. Peter's façade, north corridor, pointed peak of window over base landing (left), and buildings around Cortile del Maresciallo (right), with tympanum of Sistine Chapel in background (Marder)

cariously, with feet in midair and trumpet raised in anticipation.

The trumpeting fames are among the subtextual references to the site and its history that would have been understood by Bernini's contemporaries. In the sixteenth century, in the area located above the present base landing, there was a parapet known as the *Loggia dei Trombetti*. Here, by tradition, the palace trumpeters were sent to call the cardinals to consistory and announce the arrival of important persons. (The trumpeters are located in Fig. 41 to the right of the palace clock.) The *Loggia dei Trombetti* was destroyed in the rearrangement of the palace entrance in 1618, but a reference to the site in Bernini's trumpeting fames would have been unmistakable.

Although little noticed behind their modern glass counterparts, the original wooden doors of Paul V with their bronze heraldry and sculpture still separate the base landing of the Scala Regia from the narthex of the basilica. All other heraldic, dynastic, and ceremonial references in this portion of the palace, however, must be ascribed to Bernini's intervention. In the vault, pairs of sphinxes crouch within the fields of broad scrolls, and *ignudi* intertwined by oak leaf festoons raise relief medallions. The medallions depict, on the left (south), Constantine founding St. Peter's and, on the right (north), Pope Sylvester baptizing Constantine (Plates 14–17). These images, largely neglected in the literature on the monument, deserve extensive discussion (see Chapters 7 and 8). Suffice it here to note the location of the Founding of the Basilica over the door to the basilica narthex and the Baptism of the Emperor nearer the palace. It is precisely in these narratives that the origins of the basilica and the palace are subsumed and the "regal" character of the stairs confirmed.

Despite the lack of documentary evidence for the painting or gilding of these features, the medallions are clearly meant to recall the fictive bronze medallions on the Sistine Chapel ceiling. Similarly, the *ignudi* that bear the reliefs recall the painted *ignudi* in the Sistine Chapel, with the same variety of pose and gesture. There is a major difference, of course, and this is incorporated in the medium, for the figures in the Scala Regia are stuccoes, not paintings, and the medallions they bear are real reliefs. Moreover, the *ignudi* in the Scala Regia hold real reliefs set on the moldings of real architecture. The *paragone*, a comparison of the expressive potential of painting and sculpture, was a long-standing discussion in the Renaissance. Bernini appears to be contributing to it by reducing illusions to the very components whose reality seems most convincing, the medallion reliefs.

The principal sculpture of the base landing is the equestrian statue of Constantine (Plate 18). The statue is raised on a substantial pedestal set in a tall but shallow niche on the axis of the basilica's narthex. The horse rears violently and the gaze of the rider is cast upward in a direction reinforced by the upturned gesture of his hands. Wittkower maintained that the statue was calculated for a view from the narthex of St. Peter's, but the twist of the coffers over the niche urges an equally obvious viewpoint from the corridor, where the coffers appear undistorted (compare Plates 19 and 20).[21] Nevertheless, the subject of the equestrian group, Constantine's vision of the Cross, is not made entirely apparent until seen from within the area of the base landing, a point in which later critics found fault. At this close proximity the visitor is able to see the gilded cross in the upper reaches of the vault, revealing the instrument by which Constantine would triumph over his enemies at the Battle of the Milvian Bridge (Plate 25). It was here that the first Christian emperor vanquished the forces of Maxentius and made Christianity safe to practice in the empire.

A huge banderole located next to the Cross bears the words "IN HOC SIGNO VINCES" (in this sign you shall conquer), the motto that so often accompanies representations of Constantine's vision before the historic battle (Plates 12, 25). This is probably not the original banderole, for its turgid form has none of the fluttering grace of the banderoles on Bernini's crossing piers in St. Peter's.[22] When the statue of Constantine was officially unveiled, the inscription read as it does now, and so it is presented in the account of Domenico Bernini in 1713.[23]

The base landing is a major functional and symbolic nexus, where the palatial realm of the Scala Regia meets the terrestrial realm of the corridor and the ecclesiastical realm of the basilica. It is where ascent and descent conjoin, and the space is appropriately multidirectional and iconographically polyvalent, a fact that Bernini's critics did not adequately perceive when they complained that Constantine's surprised expression and gestures are largely unexplained when viewed from the narthex of the basilica (compare Plates 19 and 21). From the narthex one must climb nine broad steps to the base landing, where the enormous east-facing window transforms the eastern morning light into diagonal rays that activate and give formal sense and narrative meaning to the startled expression of the emperor, the spontaneity of his gestures, and the patterns of his drapery.

Behind the equestrian, a mass of drapery – slack, bunched, and clutched by an unseen force within the left zone of the arched recess – stretches diagonally to the right to serve as a foil and receptor of the divine light. The asymmetry of the drapery serves in part to disguise the asymmetrical location of the equestrian and its pedestal within the niche: horse and rider are displaced to the left of its vertical axis (Plate 20). The asymmetrical aspect of the pedestal is mitigated by the curves of its doors, which are the geometric equivalents of the drapery, since both features induce us to disregard the lack of strict alignment between figural group and enclosing niche. By these means, a view of the equestrian is perfectly framed by the door between the narthex and the base landing, even though the niche itself stands a bit to the east (right) of this axis.

Such adjustments as these and the variety of irregularly angled junctions of surfaces, moldings, and vaults express the discrete geometries that convene at the base landing. To articulate these components coherently, a distillation of priorities took place. In this process the decorative program featuring the statue of Constantine assumed a prominent place, inasmuch as the wall behind it is nonbearing. Like a real curtain that the stucco drapery emulates, the wall hides a staircase (the Scala di Costantino discussed below) that provides an alternate route to the upper palace. Ambiguities of form and a secondary path of ascent were thus disguised. A photograph of the vault over the base landing reveals how the surface angles and thicknesses of the corner piers are slurred to incorporate a union of the narthex, the corridor, and the stairs (Plate 25). In the early eighteenth century, A. M. Taja, in pointed contrast to Bernini's critics, particularly appreciated this achievement and Constantine's position in it.[24]

The First Flight of the Lower Stairs

The entire arrangement of the lower stairs is predicated on the convergent paths of the columns, their diminution, the gradual reduction of the radius of the barrel vault, and the converging paths of the outer walls. These features are illustrated in Carlo Fontana's plan and section (see Fig. 120). The columns are paired in three locations: next to the base landing, in front and behind the intermediate landing, and at the summit of the axis. The first and second flights, two groups of five bays, are separated by the intermediate landing. Together the ten bays and the landing correspond in number to the eleven-bay length of the corridor.

I have suggested that the pilasters of the corridor are transformed into baseless wall strips near the foot of the Scala Regia so that they can be set next to the columns over the lower stairs without awkwardly juxtaposing different moldings. On the lower stairs Bernini employed the Ionic capitals popularized by Scamozzi's treatise, their diagonal volutes emerging from an echinus of egg-and-dart and linked by swags (Plate 27). The column bases are also treated conventionally as the Attic type composed of a torus-scotia-torus combination (Plate 28). They rest on plinths of varying sizes adjusted to their location on the steps. Because the columns are positioned according to a perspective system of diminishing size and are thus ever closer together while the steps maintain a constant proportion along the ascent, the plinths must occupy varying positions over the treads and risers. It is said that some columns from Bernini's ill-fated campanili were reused

at the Scala Regia and elsewhere in Rome, but most would have been manufactured specifically for the stairs to provide the appropriate dimensions.[25]

The columns are components of a continuous serlian motif that tightens and focuses the passageway. Birindelli writes of a "sistema di pulsazioni," transmitted by successively widening and narrowing passages that also vary in height.[26] In addition to these "pulsations," the whole composition incorporates repeating dimensions and forms, of which the most prominent is the serlian motif, with the arched central passage and flat ceilings over the flanking passages, which recalls the vaulting over the colonnade arms. This relationship is strengthened by a similarity of dimensions, where the distance between the columns at the foot of the Scala Regia is virtually the same as the width of the central passage in the colonnade.[27]

The use of the serlian motif for the stairs was, as we shall see, a response to structural necessities. Nevertheless, it was a response laden with symbolic associations to a special place and ceremonial function. The serliana is an imperial motif and was known as such in seventeenth-century Rome. At the Scala Regia, it forecasts the serlian window that Julius II had installed in the Sala Regia above the papal throne and other, similar compositions in the palace (Fig. 18).[28] The ornate barrel vault of the stairs similarly recalls and "foretells" the huge barrel vault of the Sala Regia. These architectural prefigurations of imperial themes are consistent with the same set of references expressed in the *ignudi*, the medallions, the Constantinian iconography, and even the fames flanking the escutcheon, which are so close in composition to the winged angels flanking the throne wall of the Sala Regia embellished by Gregory XIII. These are more than gratuitous references, for they compose the essential unity of a ceremonial ensemble.

The choice of the Ionic order for the staircase speaks to this issue. Originally conceived with Corinthian capitals, the genus of the system must have been changed relatively late in the design process, and certainly after a nearly definitive composition had been achieved. We know this from the evidence of a project drawing in Munich and a later preparatory drawing for the foundation medal of 1663, both of which employ the Corinthian order (Chapter 6). At some point in the final design process, Bernini

Figure 18. North wall of Sala Regia (ICCD, E73637)

decided to change to the Ionic, and in so doing he related the stairs more closely to the basilica façade and the entry procession from the piazza. As executed, the Ionic order of the Scala Regia recalls the minor order Maderno employed at the three central doors of the basilica and on the fluted pilasters that appear around the interior of the narthex (Plate 19). At the Scala Regia, the Ionic columns are somewhat smaller and the design of the capitals differs, but the model in both cases is the Scamozzi type.

Moreover, for the visitor entering from the piazza, the use of the orders represents a progression from the Doric of the colonnade, to the Ionic of the Scala Regia's lower flights, to the Composite pilasters lining the final passage of stairs to complete a standard triadic sequence. It is perhaps significant that Bramante had introduced the progression of classical orders to the Renaissance in a spiral entrance ramp at the north end of the Cortile del Belvedere of the Vatican Palace. In this respect Bernini's design may refer in homage to the context of Bramante's precedent.[29]

Inspiring these expositions of the classical orders was the notion of a metaphorical ascent. Implied in

Bernini's change of design from Corinthian to Ionic for the capitals of the Scala Regia is the desire for a hierarchic progression between the piazza and the palace. The primacy of this approach over that from the basilica portico may be inferred from these circumstances, although the distinction cannot be pressed. The Composite of the upper flight also anticipates the pilaster order used by Antonio da Sangallo the Younger in the Cappella Paolina, the only one of the large ceremonial spaces in this area of the palace to employ a canonic order.

The use of paired columns next to the landings of the Scala Regia, mentioned above, may be explained with reference to the trabeation over the columns (Plate 29). As the stairs rise the trabeation must be inclined, too, while over the landings the trabeation must be horizontal. Over the columns next to the landings, the architraves and cornices (the omission of a frieze is neither original nor exceptional) are arranged horizontally. The architraves and cornices are then inclined over the second column on either side. As a result those parts must be sloped more steeply than the ascent of the stairs, since they must traverse the same height in a shorter distance. This intentional anomaly is virtually invisible, in part because the height of the architrave is progressively reduced to maintain a consistent proportional relationship with the diminishing size of the columns. These sorts of refinements were common in perspective illusions and follies but not to my knowledge in monumental architecture.

The columns diminish in size as the stairs rise, maintaining a consistent relationship with the constantly diminishing radius of the barrel vault. The proportion of width to height within the central passageway thus remains constant. On the stairs, the visitor will instantly perceive the process of diminution, for the closing radius is revealed in the barrel vault where the converging paths of the trabeation are all too obvious (Plate 30).

The vaults themselves are beautifully encrusted with stucco decoration. Flowered centers of apparently infinite variety impart the impression of organic profusion in a zone dominated by the geometry of the coffers. Bernini orchestrates this tension between the organic and the geometric components in part by covering the transverse ribs with leafy festoons (Plate 31). With these motifs, the vault is transformed into a bower, with a hint of

fleeting impermanence suggested in the wind-blown ribbon-ends overlapping the controlled rigidity of the coffers.

While the principal axis of the serliana is the main passage of the stair hall, no curious visitor would fail to investigate the aisles. These spaces have progressively diminishing widths that, at the summit, are impassable (Plates 32–35). Much has been made of Bernini's intentions in this aspect of the perspective scheme, an issue discussed at length in Chapter 6. It will suffice here to note that the columns converge more slowly than the walls, not, as generally thought, to slow the perspective but rather to maintain the proportions of the serlian motif from the bottom of the stairs to the top. If the lines of columns ran parallel to the walls, for example, the central arches would diminish in size while the spans over the flanking passages would remain constant, creating a discomforting consistency of lateral spaces flanking the diminishing central passage (Diagram C, middle, p. 137). As it is, the uppermost serliana (central arch and flanking openings) is already wider in proportion to its height than is the case at the base landing.[30] Even more awkward is a solution that would incorporate widening aisles flanking a rapidly converging central passage.

From Tessin's seventeenth-century plan we can be certain that the 41 steps between the base landing and the intermediate landing maintain the same dimensions as those of today, despite modern restorations (Fig. 119). From this it is reasonable to assume that the number of steps and the dimensions of treads and risers have remained unchanged since Bernini's day.[31] These dimensions average 11.5 centimeters high and 53.2 to 56.5 centimeters deep, respectively, varying from step to step particularly in depth. The incline of the ascent is uniform as is that of the second flight, where steps of comparable dimensions carry the visitor from the intermediate landing to a double landing at the summit of the principal axis of entrance.

The Intermediate Landing

The purposes of the intermediate landing are manifold. One of Alexander VII's complaints about the previous stairs was its low level of illumination. Another was its unrelieved pitch (see Appendix). Both problems were addressed at the intermediate landing, which provides a stopping place and a source of light to illuminate the treads at the middle of the ascent. Above all, it breaks the continuous rhythm of the stairs and offers a space for about seven strides before the steps recommence. In this regard, the composition again adheres to the convention by which processors would step off the lower flight and onto the upper flight with the same foot. By this means the papal sedan chair, for example, could be borne smoothly and predictably.

The intermediate landing also includes a south-facing window (Plate 36). In fact, the location of the landing was dependent upon the position of the window, which had to be placed where exterior walls permitted. A photograph taken from the exterior shows how closely the window is set against pre-existing walls (Fig. 123). The window and hence the landing are situated in the most easterly position possible. Even so, the landing breaks the ascent into unequal parts, with the second flight of thirty-seven steps and the first flight of forty-one. Although the size of the window was limited, its presence within the stairhall was magnified by a diaphragm arch. The same kind of arch is repeated for symmetrical effect on the opposite side of the landing, where there is no window (Plate 37). These moldings recall those used in earlier staircases and other monuments associated with Bernini and Maderno.[32]

In the vault above the intermediate landing, now equipped with a modern lighting system, an elaborate stucco frame encloses a smooth square field (Plate 38). This portion of the ceiling was undoubtedly meant to be painted but no physical or documentary evidence survives of the execution of such work. The crisply carved frame appears to lie over surrounding architectural decoration and to be held aloft by pairs of *ignudi* (Plates 39, 40). The crossed keys and papal tiara in the shallow spandrels below the *ignudi* also appear to rest upon architectural moldings. The papal presence is reinforced where clusters of the eight-pointed stars of the Chigi embellish the extrados of the lower and the upper serlian arches.

Along the walls of the stairhall, pilaster responds march up the steps in unison with the freestanding columns, but the effect of the pilasters is different from those of the corridor (Plates 41–43). In the corridor the pilasters are the faces of huge pier but-tresses, which are, in turn, part of a massive, rhythmic wall system. Along the staircase, the pilasters break the continuity of walls, and the niches between the pilasters perform the same aesthetic function. By these means, the columns of this section of the Scala Regia become more assertive. The molding of space in the corridor is developed into a free-standing cage defined by columns on the Scala Regia, where mass, surface and large scale are replaced by smaller, more sculptural elements.

The Double Landing

The principal entrance axis leading westward from the piazza terminates at a double landing. It is here that the visitor turns back 180 degrees to mount the last flight of stairs and enter the palace (Plates 44–47, 59). The interest of the double landing lies in its function as a connecting element whose location, dimensions, and shape were determined with reference to preexisting structures. The width (north–south dimension) of the double landing was based on the widths of the two flights of stairs arriving from above and below. Its depth was limited by a huge buttress supporting the south wall of the Sistine Chapel. The resulting east–west dimension was repeated at the base landing, probably in the interests of formal cohesion but also to help the processors and porters gauge their turning radius when ascending from or descending to the basilica narthex.[33]

Much of the fascination of the double landing lies in the treatment of the walls and corners, which emulate right angles without achieving them, and in the elevations, which resemble each other despite differing dimensions. Some examples will illustrate the situation. The upper flight of stairs has a precise east–west orientation, responding to that of the Sistine Chapel. Yet at the double landing the Sistine wall (the north wall of the landing) is angled back some thirty centimeters (Plate 46). With this small adjustment, the visitor arriving from the lower stairs will be faced with a wall parallel to the axis of ascent rather than a canted surface.[34] A sense of regularity is thus urged where it is not present. The acute and obtuse angles that result in all corners are disguised by freestanding columns.

The corner columns create a spatial cage within the area of the double landing. On the north and south, the columns bear arches set in front of the walls and hide the window (and false window) moldings. Over these arches, the same palmette and anthemion series seen at the foot of the stairs returns (Plates 44–46). Where the arches open above the two staircases, an elaborate play of moldings simulates the appearance of arches equal in size, although the radius above the lower stair is much greater than that of the upper stair (right on Plate 47). The arches around the double landing in turn support the ovoid fields of vaulting over which putti gambol. The west wall is a frank concession to the inequality of dimensions: the carved wooden doors of equal height differ in width (note the inscriptions), the portions next to the doors are of different widths, and the central pilaster dividing them thus appears uncomfortably asymmetrical in location (Plate 45). Similarly the west walls of the double landing are perpendicular to the respective axes of the upper and lower stairs but do not compose a single plane.

It is above all in the vaults over the double landing that the disparate dimensions of the space can be assessed. One vault is an elongated ellipse, the other a broader ellipse. Like the resolution of the domes over the twin churches at Piazza del Popolo, whose designs date to the same period, an image of paired equality results from dissimilar dimensions.[35] It is also in this zone that Bernini choreographed the most elaborate relations between figural and architectural elements. At the base landing, the figures kneel on real architecture, holding real relief medallions (Plates 14, 16). On the vault above the intermediate landing, the *ignudi* do much the same, but bear the frame of a two-dimensional surface (Plates 39, 40). This combination reestablishes the traditional dichotomy between pictorial illusion and sculptural reality, with the sculptural reality intended also to embrace the decorative reality of the architectural moldings. Over the double landing, these realms are united. The putti fly through the motifs of the decorations, climbing over and occasionally perching upon them.

We can be certain from documents that the framed surfaces over the double landing, unlike the vault over the intermediate landing, were painted. They were transformed into fields of azure, highlighted by gold stars – no doubt the eight-pointed Chigi stars – intended to represent the sky. The same combination was evident on the Sistine Chapel ceiling before Michelangelo replaced it with episodes from Genesis. Again, therefore, the notion of a reference to the site and its history, even destroyed parts of its history, is consciously manifest. At the same time the stuccoes help to complete the progressive composition of the stairs.

In the reliefs that the arriving visitor is likely to see first, the putti are depicted illusionistically within the real architectural confines, where their limbs overlap or rest upon decorative moldings (Plate 48). The figures are represented in illusionistic space but lean upon real architectural details. The conceit is developed to express solecistic intentions. In some instances the putti reach into and out of the illusory space on the vaulted field, while in other instances they appear to support the frame of that space (Plates 49–51). The result is a *quadro riportato* in two media. It must have fascinated many a visitor.[36]

There is even the possibility that the putti are depicted in the process of arranging the decoration over the double landing. This process has been mostly finished on the east and is being finished on the west. On the west, the last of four Chigi stars is set upon its pendentive, and the putto who holds its upper tip also points to an acorn of the Chigi oak that lines both of the vaults (Plate 52). The depiction of these decorations-in-progress is made explicit in the north vault where a putto is placing a star above the Chigi monti but has not yet adjusted it to conform to the other stars of the vault (Plates 53, 54). The same may be said of a putto who appears to be forming rather than merely carrying some of the moldings, while below, his companion hovers behind the monti (Plate 55). Perhaps these monti, like those of another corner, have just been assembled (Plate 56). Might we be dealing here with a punning reference to the hurried pace of Bernini's execution of the decoration?

The putti themselves have ample precedent in Bernini's work as, for example, where two putti over Urban VIII's tomb in St. Peter's actively adjust the Barberini escutcheon and the papal tiara.[37] But the effect there is not as direct and meaningful as it is in a space of procession like the Scala Regia, where the figures suggest a more complex movement and their palm fronds symbolize entry and salvation (Plates 57, 58). Palms symbolize resurrection, and they accompanied Christ's entry into Jerusalem. In these regards Palm Sunday pageants have been related to royal entries.[38] In some generalized way, then, the entry into the palace becomes an ascent into a celestial realm in the same way that the fronds in the dome of S. Ivo alla Sapienza (finished under Alexander VII) suggest the beckoning to a heavenly realm. At both S. Ivo and the Scala Regia, the allusions are enhanced by a prominent display of stars, double references to heaven and to the papal family emblems.

The palms may, like the conspicuous acorn, allude specifically to the patron. The conclave in which Alexander VII was elected was a particularly long and difficult one, extending from January 20 to April 7, 1655.[39] For various reasons, the successive scrutinies (voting sessions) had taken place in both the Sistine Chapel and the Cappella Paolina. On Palm Sunday (21 March) the Holy Sacrament was displayed in the Paolina, and divine help was implored in resolving the election. In the following scrutiny, also held in the Cappella Paolina, the conclave produced the election of Cardinal Fabio Chigi.[40] Using the staircase at every anniversary of the pope's election, as was usual (see Chapter 9), Alexander and his court would have been reminded of the connection to the holy feast that presaged his elevation.

The Third Flight

The path of the upper staircase, connecting the double landing to the Sala Regia, was inherited from the sixteenth century (Plate 59). Bernini raised and redecorated the barrel vault, and he provided new ornament for the walls, but he did not change the essential dimensions of the forty-six steps that rise without interruption along the outside of the south wall of the Sistine Chapel. This will explain why they are somewhat larger than those of the lower two flights.[41] To have changed the uppermost flight would have required extensive demolition and rebuilding. By maintaining the preexisting arrangement, Bernini could leave the portal connecting the stairs to the Sala Regia in place; the wall between the lower and upper runs of stairs could be retained intact; and the pavement of the double landing would maintain its correspondence with the floors of the rooms directly below the Sistine Chapel.

The mural character of the processional approach, so insistent in the corridor, returns in the upper staircase. In this case the explanation lies in Bernini's use of the preexisting stair width, whose walls he redecorated with pairs of remarkably flat Composite pilasters (Plates 60–62). The rhomboid wall panels recall the motif used on the corridor exterior, where it also separates pilaster pairs. In the upper staircase, however, the panels produce a jarring rhythm between the pilaster bases, as the inclined sills of the panels clash with the horizontal bases. The horizontal bases and capitals are possible because Bernini has inserted plinths below the former and dosserets above the latter to absorb the inclination of the stair. Such features were unremarkable in the seventeenth century – they appear in the staircase of Palazzo Barberini, for example – but earned the censure of neoclassical criticism in a subsequent era.[42]

Uneven quality in the design of these details belies the delicacy of stucco work on the vault and the complexity of its composition (Plate 63). Two transverse bands rimmed with egg-and-dart and bead-and-reel join the pilasters over the vault, and these are separated by the same oak garland used over the lower stairs. The vault is gridded by coffers whose decoration also recalls the lower stairs, but lying over the coffered grid are six large frames enclosing blank fields and skylights. All six compartments originally opened with skylights, as Taja reported in the eighteenth century, although only two survive today. The glazing must have raised the level of illumination on the upper stairs to a remarkable intensity and provided a luminous quality that compensated for any sense of lateral constriction in this portion of the ascent.

Much of the design of the entire Scala Regia derives from structural considerations bearing on matters of economy and design coherence. Yet the composition also facilitated various functional and ceremonial patterns. In the progressive reduction of width from the base landing to the top of the third flight, the stairs may have served to enforce the usual courtly procedure of leaving ever more attendants behind as a ceremonial entry proceeded. And as the order changed from Doric to Ionic to Composite, the visitor was drawn along by an ever increasing level of illumination. In other words, the ascent was invested with metaphorical significance, complemented by the scale of the environment, the nature of the decoration, and the level of illumination.

The carefully controlled infusion of natural light is an effect that deserves emphasis in view of previous assumptions about the current state of the monument as an accurate indication of Bernini's intentions. The two skylights in place today are modern replacements and only weakly suggest the dazzling result that must have been produced in the original scheme. The documents indicate that Bernini required a good deal of trial and error successfully to complete this aspect of the design, whose inspiration is to be found in the unexecuted skylights that Michelangelo planned for the Laurentian Library vestibule (see Chapter 6). Even the use of skylights in the context of stairs was not unprecedented in the seventeenth century.[43] Their special significance pertains to the way they were deployed.

Bernini's hard-won solution to the skylights contributed to the formal integrity of the whole staircase. In the vaults over the base landing and the intermediate landing, *ignudi* support the frames for carved and painted representations, respectively. The expansion of the representational environment on the intermediate landing is then adumbrated in the double landing, where the celestial vision of stars on a blue ground is conjoined to the terrestrial imagery by the frolicking putti. In the final flight of the stairs, the conjunction is made real and explicit where views of the sky and wind-driven clouds blanketed the space. The result is a pictorial metaphor that recalls Brunelleschi's famous perspective panels, where real sky concluded the analogy between celestial perfection and the construction of its harmonic equivalent by pictorial means.[44] At the same time, an allusion to the imperial palace on the Palatine, where ceilings opened to celestial imagery as described by Dio Cassius, may have been intended.[45]

The view to the heavens is, of course, the generative theme of the oculus in the Pantheon, whose interior becomes the medium between the earth and the heavens. In this context, we should remember that Alexander VII had intended to glaze the oculus of the Pantheon. Although Bernini was not responsible for this project, he was profoundly aware of the effects of light falling from above, which he claimed made everything more beautiful than it would otherwise be.[46]

The incorporation of skylights, therefore, has special resonance along the path leading to the presence of the pope. The effects they produce imply both a deeper and a visually more apparent meaning to the metaphor of ascent, which is characterized by a progressively ennobling ambience. That the skylights were understood in such broad contexts in the seventeenth century is suggested by Falda's representation of a grand oculus over the base landing of the Scala Regia (Fig. 193). When Falda's engraving was published in 1665, the construction of the stairs had not been completed. I think it unlikely that he had access to the monument, relying instead on his imagination and shreds of information from workers (see Chapter 7).

At the top of the stairs, the last pilasters abut the west wall of the Sala Regia, whose thickness is only partially disguised by a papal escutcheon and frolicking putti (Plates 64, 65). Here again, the sculptor investigates the possibilities for demonstrating how feet and legs can disappear behind the decorated surface or extend forward in real space. From the visitor's vantage point about halfway along the upper steps, tall wooden doors at the Sala Regia open to frame a view of the representation of Charlemagne frescoed on the east wall of the Sala Regia (Plate 66). This vista was no doubt planned in the sixteenth century in conjunction with the inclination of the stairs and the uniform proportions of the Sala Regia portals. The image of the enthroned monarch, like others in the Sala Regia, recalls the reciprocal importance of rulers and the authority of the popes, and reminds visitors of that other regal figure, Constantine, located where the steps of the Scala Regia begin.

Related Features

To the description of the main ceremonial entrance, we need to add a few comments about the structures and spaces that Bernini worked around, remodeled, or created anew in connection with the Scala Regia. In the sixteenth century, a stepped ramp, or cordonata, joined the palace entrance on the piazza with the Cortile di S. Damaso. The cordonata was later attached to Bernini's north corridor. In 1860 under Pius IX (1846–78) a new staircase was built to serve the same purpose. In the process, the old cordonata was almost entirely demolished. The Scala Nuova, as it was called, opens through a large marble frame from the second interior bay of the north corridor

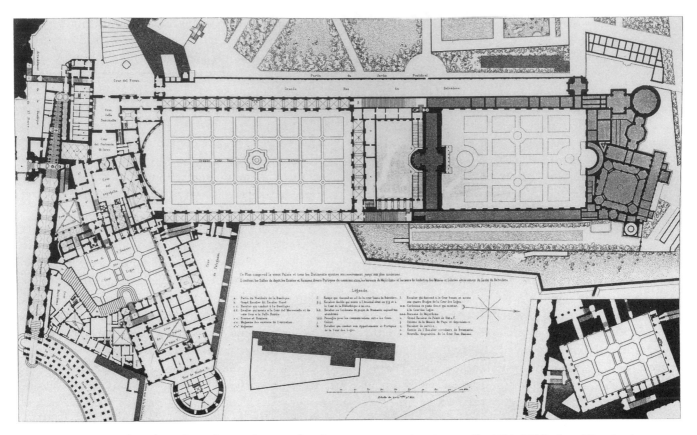

Figure 19. Plan of Vatican Palace with inset of Scala Nuova, engraving, Letarouilly 1882 (Bibliotheca Hertziana)

(Plate 5). The respective positions of the present Scala Nuova and the old cordonata can be seen in an engraving of Letarouilly, where an inset illustrates Pius IX's new stairs (Fig. 19).[47] Although the cordonata was therefore ruined in the nineteenth century, bits of it still remain behind a small door in the fourth interior bay of the corridor. These short sections of travertine-edged, brick steps confirm the union of the cordonata and Bernini's construction.

The new neoclassical staircase (designed by the palace architect, Filippo Martinucci) is an entirely enclosed ascent, whereas the old cordonata was largely open to the sky.[48] Gas lamps were installed in the Scala Nuova, and at the level of the Cortile di S. Damaso a protective portico was enclosed in glass. Pius IX also had the windows of the north corridor glazed, and it is my guess that he was responsible for installing the twenty travertine steps leading from the piazza to the corridor.[49]

By the end of the nineteenth century, Pius IX's Scala Nuova had become so heavily used that repairs were already necessary. In organizing them the palace architect at the time, Francesco Vespignani (1842–99), went so far as to propose the construction of service stairs nearby to separate the more dignified visitors from the workmen and "mascalzoni" in shirt sleeves, scullery boys, servants laden with correspondence, eager students of the library, and palace employees who habitually smoked cigars and spat tobacco. Alternative sites for the new stairs were suggested, but in the event, the repairs initially projected were pursued instead.[50] A drawing records these proposals and serves to illustrate the location the old cordonata behind the staircase of Pius IX (Fig. 20).

A second staircase in the vicinity of the corridor is located behind the pedestal of the Constantine statue. Bernini excavated and vaulted this staircase, called the Scala di Costantino, to maintain a direct connection between the base landing and the Cortile del Maresciallo. The lower end of the stairs issues onto the landing through the doors on either side of Constantine's pedestal. Narrow and virtually undecorated, the Scala di Costantino was a utilitarian passage not unlike the "back stairs" of monumental palaces and country houses. A groin-vaulted bay located behind the statue leads to the first eight steps, a corner landing, and the subsequent 41 steps to the level of the Cortile del Maresciallo (Plates 67–69).

Emerging through a small arch on the Cortile del Maresciallo the visitor may chose to continue the ascent by way of a larger stair to the Sala Regia, called the Scala del Maresciallo (Plates 70, 71). Like the uppermost flight of the Scala Regia, it was laid out during the pontificate of Paul III (1534–49). The staircase is therefore similar to the uppermost flight of the Scala Regia, although the dimensions of the Maresciallo's 47 steps are slightly steeper than the third flight of the Scala Regia.[51] The Scala Regia incorporates 124 steps from the base landing to the Sala Regia, whereas the Scala di Costantino and the Scala del Maresciallo together make the same rise over 96 steps.

The Scala del Maresciallo provides an eastern en-trance to the principal audience hall of the palace. This function became far less important after Bernini's elaboration of the new Scala Regia, however, and his efforts to modernize the older access were modest. There are single Doric pilasters at the foot and summit of the stairs and vertical strips along the walls. The pilasters have unremarkable bases and capitals, although the magnified scale of the architrave betrays some ambition for the design (Plates 72–74). The linear quality of these moldings is echoed in the transverse ribs and compartments of the vault.

The lunette at the foot of the stairs bears a fresco depicting Christ washing the feet of the Apostles, the event annually reenacted in the Sala Ducale when the pope washed the feet of paupers (Plate 75).[52] In the seventeenth century, before Bernini's intervention, a now-lost fresco of Christ and Peter walking on the waves was to be found in the corresponding location on the Scala Regia. Its presence there is

Figure 20. Project for new staircase at north corridor, drawing, Vespignani, 1890 (Archivio Segreto Vaticano)

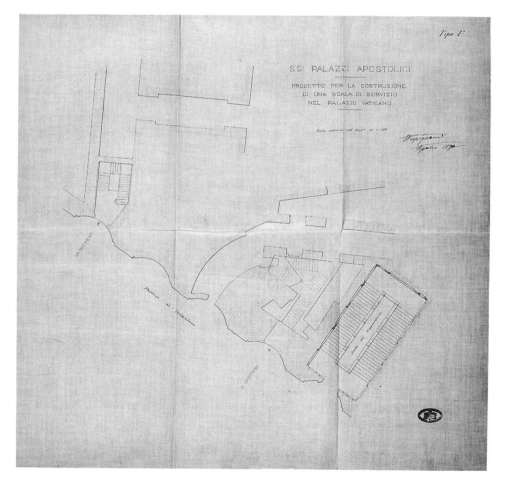

attested as late as 1663 by Giovanni Battista Mola.[53] Mola follows Baglione in attributing both frescoes to Donato da Formello, who seems to have been something of a staircase specialist at the Vatican Palace from the time of Gregory XIII.[54] (Whether a scene like the Calling might have been intended for one of the stucco-framed vaults of Bernini's Scala Regia must remain a matter of speculation.)

The lower end of the Scala del Maresciallo issues into a vaulted portico also built under Paul III. From the foot of the stairs the modern visitor can look eastward through an arch into the Cortile di S. Damaso and imagine the entrance planned by Paul III. Both the western and eastern sides of the Cortile del Maresciallo are bordered by the arcades that were built in this period (Plates 76, 77). The arcades were constructed of octagonal piers salvaged from a similar loggia that stood on the site in a different configuration from the fifteenth century. In the early seventeenth century, these piers were reinforced so that apartments could be built over the east and west sides of the court. One arch, on the south side of the western arcade, bears witness to the modest demolition necessary to complete Bernini's northern corridor (Plate 76). In fact, the corridor defines the southern boundary of the Cortile del Maresciallo and the whole palace. The roof of the north corridor is now partly occupied by metal bleachers providing favored viewing seats for important liturgical festivities. In the 1840s, the role of these bleachers was fulfilled by a brick loggia.[55]

At the west end of the corridor stands the huge window that lights the base landing (Plate 78). Its upper profile is readily visible from the piazza and constitutes one of the most extraordinary gestures in the architecture of the Scala Regia, not least because its sharply pointed profile nudges over the horizontal moldings that divide two stories of the palace (Fig. 17). The rim of the window molding is in fact so high that the vault behind it appears to push through the floor above it. In this instance, the appearance is the reality. Within the room nearest the peak of the window, the floor level was stepped up toward the outer wall in order to accommodate the top of the vault. Unfortunately, these features are no longer visible, for the room was recently transformed from an infirmary to a lavatory, and the irregularities of the walls have been encased in tile and new masonry. The chief advantage in studying the

window from the height of the corridor roof is to see the upward tilt and funnel-like shape of the vault over the base landing, which the stucco decoration of the interior effectively hides when observed from the base landing.

The Term "Scala Regia"

In preserving a major entrance to the Vatican Palace on the piazza, Bernini maintained centuries of historical precedent. In his construction of the Scala Regia, as we shall see, he even followed the path of a preexisting staircase. Before Bernini's time, the old staircase led from the palatial halls of ceremony to the narthex of St. Peter's, behind the Constantinian atrium and far removed from the piazza. After the destruction of the atrium and the construction of the new façade and nave of St. Peter's in the early seventeenth century, the stairs still descended to the basilica narthex without any direct connection to the piazza. Where Bernini departed from precedent was in conjoining the old path of the stairs, formerly isolated far behind the façades on the piazza, with a principal entrance to the palace.

In these respects, it can be said that Bernini transformed the old Scala Regia even before he had redesigned it. By arranging Piazza S. Pietro so that its north corridor extended to the foot of the staircase, he incorporated the stairs in an entrance path from the city, as well as from St. Peter's. The north corridor, built between 1661 and 1662, extended the palace entrance eastward to the piazza and the newly built colonnade. The subsequent reconstruction and redecoration of the stairs beginning in 1663 became the final installment in the campaign to modify and embellish the entrance and to complete the new circulation patterns. Crystallizing this campaign was Bernini's equestrian statue of Constantine, placed at the foot of the staircase. Although work on the sculpture went slowly – the figure was unveiled only in 1670 – the stairs were largely finished by 1666.

Perhaps because Bernini's Scala Regia appears to be the very embodiment of a "regal" or "royal" staircase, one naturally seeks the origin of the term in the literature and documents for the Vatican Palace. Did the expression predate Bernini's intervention or become more common subsequently? Is there any chance that the term itself became either a generating idea for the design or, alternatively, a neat way of summarizing its formal intentions? The answer to these questions is both yes and no. Given the fact that sixteenth-century documents and drawings refer to the Sala Regia as such, it is likely that the staircase rising to it was similarly referred to at the time as a Scala Regia.[56] Having found no document to support this assumption, my suspicion is that the evidence has simply eluded me, yet the term cannot have been generally known or widely used. In any case its derivation would have to be sought eventually in the origin and changing program of the Sala Regia, which is beyond the scope of this study.

This much we do know. Before and immediately after the creation of Bernini's Scala Regia, the staircase was referred to as the great staircase ("scala magna") of the palace. This was the term used by the papal masters of ceremony in January 1655 to describe the staircase down which the corpse of Innocent X was carried into the basilica.[57] And it is a variant of the term used by Carlo Fontana to describe the preexisting stairs, the "scala maestra," upon which Bernini's refashioning of the fabric took place (Appendix). Even when the masters of ceremony described the first use of the stairs by Alexander VII, for the Easter celebration on 13 April 1664, they described it as the "schala magna."[58] Again, in 1666 to record preparations for Corpus Christi in 1664 and 1665, feasts of great importance to Alexander VII, the notations of the Congregation of the Fabbrica di S. Pietro (administrators of the building) refer simply to the "scala nuova."[59] In October 1676, for the coronation of Innocent XI – fully ten years after Bernini's Scala Regia was in use – the masters of ceremony still described the train from the Sala Regia into the basilica as taking place "per scalam magnam."[60]

Most often, the early stairs were simply indicated in reference to their location within the palace complex. This was the case in the account of the exequies for Alexander VI in 1503, when the procession descended "by the stairs across from the main gate of the palace."[61] It was also true upon the election of Urban VIII in 1623, when the stairs were still characterized as located across from the principal portal of the palace and next to the lodgings of the

Vatican druggist (in rooms now occupied by the palace sacristan).[62] In the account of Alexander VII's coronation in April 1655, the master of ceremonies described a wooden stage erected in the narthex of the basilica as being "next to the Palace stairs."[63] Building documents for the monument itself refer to the "stairs that lead to the Sala Regia," "stairs that lead to the Paolina," or the "great stairs where the pope descends to go into the church."[64] Many of the building documents from Bernini's era also refer to the "Scala Regia."[65]

There is a suggestion that the concept of a "regia scala" at the Vatican immediately predated Bernini's activity. This is located in Lualdi's manuscript account of the palace, written around 1644 to 1653. The account refers to the "due reggie scale," describing the two stairs that rose from the basilica to the Sala Regia and to the Cortile del Maresciallo before Bernini's work.[66] And from the period after Bernini's work there are innumerable examples of references to the "Scala Regia." Carlo Fontana scrupulously uses the term to refer to the results of Bernini's design at the end of the century (again, Appendix), as does the writer Alveri as early as 1663.[67] It is therefore puzzling that Falda's engraving of the monument, part of a suite meant to record Alexander VII's greatest works in Rome, is so prosaic: "interior staircase that leads to the papal chapel in the Vatican" (Fig. 193).

Given this background, perhaps the only pressing question is whether the notion of a "royal staircase" was employed consciously to shape the whole program and general intention of the design. To this our answer must be that, if true, this idea remained one of the better kept secrets of an era notably proud to demonstrate exactly such relationships between conception and expression. On the other hand, as I will suggest in the last chapter of this book, the inclination to embrace regal, monarchic, or imperial imagery in his building campaigns was a general, overriding concern of the papal patron, who sought at every turn to transform palace life into an exemplary reflection of his spiritual and temporal dominion. Thus, it is not a matter of terminology but rather the historical, artistic, political, religious, and cultural contexts that ultimately give the Scala Regia its fullest meaning.

TWO

The Palace Entrance and Stairs During the Renaissance

THE Tiber enters the city of Rome with a sweeping curve from east to west and then to the south. Outside this elbow, far up the west bank, rises the Mons Vaticanus with the basilica of St. Peter's at its foot. The geography of this area is typical of Rome, whose large and small hills and dales have shaped the history of the city, its urban development, and its monuments. St. Peter's and the Vatican Palace are part of this process, defined as much by their mutual dependence as by the abrupt shifts in terrain upon which they are built.

The broad view of St. Peter's and the Vatican Palace drawn between 1532 and 1536 by Martin van Heemskerck offers a convenient orientation to the Renaissance aspect of the site (Fig. 21).[1] The view represents the façade of the basilica on the left and the palace on the right, seen from the irregular space of Piazza S. Pietro looking west. As it is preserved, the drawing has captured a dramatic expanse from the Palace of the Archpriest on the extreme left to the north tip of the Cortile del Belvedere. In the foreground on the right stands the Porta S. Petri, an arched gate flanked by massive square towers protecting the Vatican precinct. The gate was built along the Leonine Wall which, from the Middle Ages, connected the elevated palace to Castel Sant'-Angelo and the Tiber. Located in the center of the drawing and receding into the distance in sharp perspective is the three-storied Logge built by Bramante and Raphael. Peeking out from behind the Logge is the roof of the Sistine Chapel.

On the left of the drawing, to the south of the basilica, the arcades of the Palace of the Archpriest adjoin portions of the brick and stone façade of the Constantinian atrium, which stood in front of the venerable basilica. Part of the atrium was fronted by the four bays of arches in three stories that incorporated the Benediction Loggia. Behind all of this rose the pediment of the old basilica, whose nave was terminated by an arch of the incomplete crossing of new St. Peter's. To the right of the Benediction Loggia, a prominent entablature and flanking columns framed an impressive portal. Two rows of Swiss Guards presided over a stepped ramp that led up from the piazza to this, the principal entrance to the Vatican Palace.

From the beginning the palace was situated next to the basilica, on the north side of the old Constantinian atrium. As the importance of the papacy grew in the Middle Ages, a group of large ceremonial rooms were needed. These were built on a rising scarp of land, the Mons Saccorum, overlooking the church to its south and the Vatican Borgo (or "burg") that stretched eastward toward the river.

The plan composed by Tiberio Alfarano in 1571 illustrates the situation (Fig. 22).[2] Behind the Benediction Loggia (labeled "ii") stood the foundations of the campanile and the north wing of the church atrium ("L"). Beyond the entrance portal of the palace ("kk") lay the palace atrium, whose contours were lined by porticoes on the south and west. Since the Swiss Guard were stationed here, the court became known as the *atrium helvetiorum*. Its irregular plan betrays its function as a buffer between the tight geometry of the basilica and the looser composition of palace structures on higher ground to the north (right). Stairs in the northwest corner indicate the changing elevation of the terrain. The staircase

Figure 21. View of St. Peter's and Vatican Palace from Piazza S. Pietro, drawing, Heemskerck (Albertina, 49.897 c)

with a north–south orientation ("bb" = Gradus Palatii Apostolici) rose from the narthex of the basilica to a landing where the ascent divided to converge again at the principal audience hall of the palace, the Sala Regia ("122" = Aula Regia Sacri Palatii).

The rectangular Sala Regia lies perpendicular to the basilica and the Sistine Chapel, which the Sala Regia adjoins. Other parts of the palace are only loosely related to this geometry, where orientations respond more firmly to the local geography. On the side of the Sala Regia opposite the Sistine Chapel, for example, rooms that became the Sala Ducale diverge from the grid of the larger structures. The Cortile del Maresciallo (labeled "Q," with porticoes on facing sides) merges these disparate orientations and provides a transition to the Logge of Bramante and Raphael. The upper portions of the palace, built on the Mons Saccorum for both symbolic and defensive concerns, thus encompassed a group of irregularly oriented ceremonial rooms. These features are also illustrated in a diagram of portions of the palace located near St. Peter's (Diagram A).

As the Alfarano plan and our diagram make clear, the staircases that joined the basilica and the palace were located deep within the building and without any direct connection to the piazza. On the public fronts, the entrances to the palace and the basilica

were quite separate, having been shaped by different but related histories and functions. Bernini's Scala Regia would modify the connection between the basilica and the palace by extending that connection to the piazza. To put the matter succinctly, Bernini made a single palace staircase the principal route of access from both church and city, but the subtlety of his achievement can only be appreciated in the context of a long historical development.

Early History of the Palace

In Bernini's time the Vatican Palace was generally thought to have been founded by Constantine.[3] But the literary evidence upon which modern research depends has identified Pope Symmachus as builder of the first papal residence at the Vatican around the year 500.[4] This residence, referred to as the *episcopia* because it served the pope as bishop of Rome, stood beside or was incorporated in the fabric of the Constantinian basilica, perhaps in the façade towers.[5] Charlemagne is credited with the expansion of a *palatium Caruli* during his visit to Rome in 781, and by the pontificate of Leo III (795–816) the *episcopia* stood at the north side of the atrium of the basilica.[6] This wing of the atrium formed the core of the so-called lower palace (*palatium inferiore*). To this lower

31

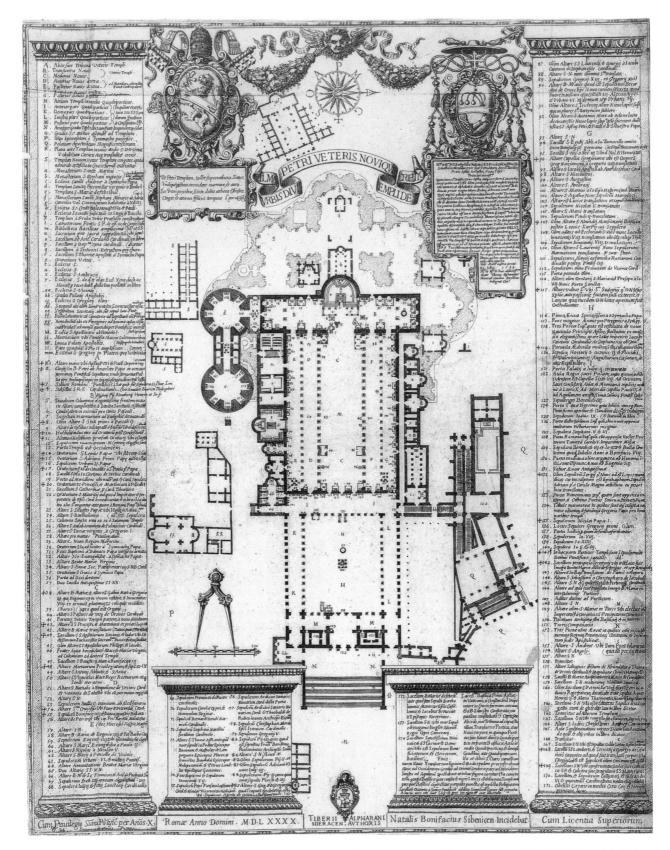

Figure 22. Plan of old and new St. Peter's and Vatican Palace, engraving, Alfarano (BAV, Chigi P VII, 9, fol. 38r)

32

Diagram A. Schematic plan of the Vatican Palace before 1534, showing (a) old St. Peter's, (b) basilica narthex, (c) basilica atrium, (d) Benediction Loggia, (e) Prima Porta, (f) Atrium Helvetiorum, (g) Curia Innocenziana, (h) old Scala Regia/Via Iulia Nova, (i) Turris Scalarum, (j) Aula Prima or Sala Regia, (k) Scala del Maresciallo, (l) Cortile del Maresciallo, (m) Capella Parva, (n) Aula Secunda, (o) Aula Tertia or, with the preceding, the Sala Ducale, (p) Sistine Chapel, (q) Bramante/Raphael Logge, (r) Cortile di S. Damaso, (s) Loggia dei Trombetti, (t) Porta S. Petri (drawing by Nora Onorato)

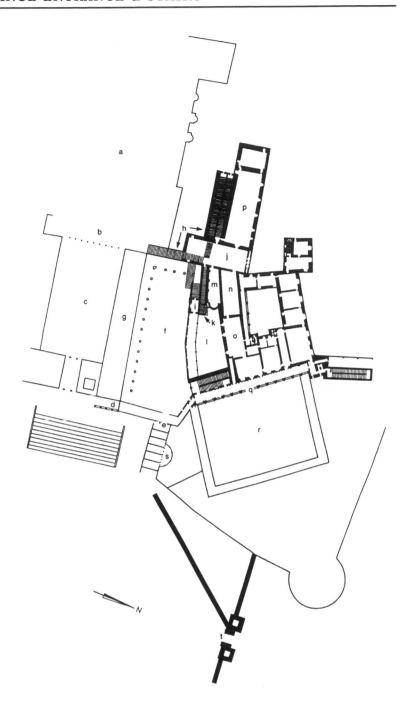

palace a second floor may have been added by Gregory IV (827–844) in the early ninth century. Over time, it evolved into a three-story building, usually known as the Curia Innocenziana because of the renovations of Innocent VIII at the end of the fifteenth century.

The construction of the great Leonine Wall by Leo IV (847–855) protected the Vatican and encouraged the expansion of the palace.[7] The exact location of the *palatium novum* of Eugene III (1145–53) is still debated, but all scholars presume it to have been positioned on the low ground next to the basilica and thus as an extension of the lower palace. Only under the pontificates of Innocent III (1198–1216), Innocent IV (1243–54), and Nicholas III (1277–80) did the palace begin to occupy the Mons Saccorum north of St. Peter's. This became the site of the upper palace (*palatium superiore*).

Precisely where Innocent III began monumental building on the Mons Saccorum is a debated issue. The older literature suggests that he built a tower and the two rooms that compose the present Sala Ducale.[8] A more recent theory, which has the weight of archaeology and historical comparanda supporting it, holds that Innocent III instead built the double-nave hall with groin vaults that is the substructure directly below the Sala Regia. This hall is still in active use as room 32 of the Vatican's Gallery of Modern Religious Art. It appears to the north (right) of the Scala Regia in Fig. 16. The medieval documents refer to it as the *marescalcia*, or stables, that we know Innocent III built at the palace. Its double nave, with groin vaults supported by Ionic capitals and abacus, finds precedent in the nearly contemporary Sala Capitolare at the Tre Fontane.[9]

To this vaulted structure were added the two separate rooms that now compose the Sala Ducale. These rooms abutted a defensive tower to the east, which is now believed to belong to Innocent IV's pontificate in the thirteenth century. A medieval chronicle mentions the pope's work on a tower and attached rooms, and the masonry and typology of the tower conform to the period, especially in the use of *opus sarracinescum* and the *sedilia* incorporated below windows. The construction would have taken place after Innocent IV's long stay in north Italy (1252–53), where such towers commonly appear in civic palaces. The Vatican tower in turn would have served as a model for Roman buildings such as the Palazzo Senatorio (c. 1260).[10]

The rooms of the Sala Ducale on separate axes bear witness to two building campaigns and to the influence of the irregular terrain that discouraged a cohesive axial arrangement of the palace.[11] The medieval stronghold on the Mons Saccorum rises almost twenty meters above the piazza and at least twelve meters over the floor of the basilica.[12] The Sala Ducale was unified in the seventeenth century when Bernini removed a dividing wall between the angled components and replaced it with rich swags of stucco drapery hiding the irregularities of structure (Chapter 9).

The citadel on the Mons Saccorum was largely completed by Nicholas III, who built a grand reception hall over the vaulted, double-nave *marescalcia*.[13] The hall of Nicholas III became known as the Aula Prima and the rooms of the Sala Ducale adjacent to it were subsequently referred to as the *aula secunda* and *aula tertia* ("j," "n," and "o" on Diagram A).[14] The grand *aula* of Nicholas III may have been built to celebrate the withdrawal of the Angevins from Italy and to herald the role of the pope as an independent ruler with sole jurisdiction over temporal affairs in the Papal States.[15] The present appearance of the Sala Regia is the result of changes ordered by Julius II and Paul III. In the early sixteenth century, Julius II remodeled the hall by inserting serlian windows in the ends. Several decades later, Paul III ordered Antonio da Sangallo the Younger to build its walls higher and span them with a commanding barrel vault. By the end of the sixteenth century, Vasari, Sabbatini, Salviati, the Zuccari, and others had frescoed the walls with scenes that constituted a history of the obedience that emperors and kings rendered to the pope.[16]

Here, the popes would receive their most important visitors, such as emperors, kings, and their representatives, and perform the most conspicuous acts of governance. The *aula secunda* and *aula tertia* provided the setting for the reception of princes and representatives of the republics, the proclamation of new cardinals, public consistories with papal legates, and a host of lesser functions that over time were shared with other offices in the palace.[17] This was the information that visiting foreigners were aware of even in Bernini's day for, as Skippon wrote, "in the Sala Regia kings embassadors have audience," and "in the Sala Ducale are Dukes embassadors receiv'd."[18]

East of these halls, along a front of the palace facing the city, Nicholas III built a loggia that overlooked a secret garden and much of the Borgo. The loggia was later incorporated into the Logge of Bramante and Raphael, represented in Heemskerck's view, and the garden immediately below it was eventually transformed into the present Cortile di S. Damaso ("q" and "r" in Diagram A).[19] The courtyard takes its name from St. Damasus, who discovered a spring here that enabled Pope Liberius (352–66) to baptize a multitude of the faithful during the Whitsun holidays.[20]

From the foregoing discussion, it is obvious that good communications must have existed between the lower and upper palaces. Yet the connections between them must be pieced together from a variety of data. A tower stair, the *turris scalarum*, stood at one side of the *atrium helvetiorum*, next to the Sala Regia ("i" in Diagram A). It appears as a battlemented tower in Schedel's fifteenth-century woodcut (Fig. 23).[21] The foundations of the tower also appear on sixteenth-century plans (Figs. 27 ["torre"], 28). The date of these stairs, previously unknown, can be determined by understanding them in relation to nearby structures.

Steinke and Shearman have independently identified the *capella parva S. Nicholai* that extended from the east side of the Sala Regia as the chapel built by Nicholas III and mentioned in a medieval inscription ("m" in Diagram A). This interpretation makes good sense: it offers a date, previously uncertain, for the *capella parva* (1277–80) and handily explains its dedication.[22] The "little chapel" served principally as the sacrament chapel of the palace and as the place where cardinals met in conclave to cast their votes for a new pope.[23] From these facts some new conclusions may be deduced about the medieval palace stairs.

The *capella parva* has a tapered, asymmetrical plan whose width increases toward the apse (Figs. 27, 28). To explain its unusual shape, we must conclude that it was inserted within a space limited by pre-

Figure 23. View of Rome, woodcut, Schedel 1493 (The Metropolitan Museum of Art, Rogers Fund, 1921; 21.36.145, fol. 57v, neg. no. MM 13265 B)

existing structures, namely the *aula secunda* and the *turris scalarum*. In my view the *turris scalarum* therefore predates the *capella parva*. The fortified tower stair would have been built to connect the upper and lower palaces certainly before the end of the thirteenth century, presumably during the formation of the citadel under Innocent III, at the end of the twelfth century.[24] The *turris scalarum*, the only major connection between the lower and upper palaces of which we have notices from the Middle Ages, would have been contemporary with the *marescalcia*, providing a horse ramp leading up to these stables. A flight of stairs, continuing those of the *turris scalarum* from the Cortile del Maresciallo to the Sala Regia, would then have been built nearly a century later by Nicholas III to provide access to his new reception hall and the adjoining *capella parva S. Nicholai*.

The construction of a *capella magna*, on the other hand, is now thought to have been built on the site of the later Sistine Chapel ("p" in Diagram A). Of nearly the same dimensions as its successor, the original construction of the main palace chapel took place sometime before or immediately after the exile of the popes in Avignon (1305–77).[25] The existence of this important addition to the west side of the Sala Regia would, in turn, suggest the utility of a second medieval staircase to give access to it from the west. In fact, newly discovered archaeological evidence suggests that a staircase did exist to serve the *capella magna*. The evidence, uncovered during the current Sistine restorations, consists of a door immured in the southeast corner of the chapel. It is assumed the door was covered up during the restructuring of the chapel under Sixtus IV (1471–84). Pagliara argues persuasively that the original door opened to a staircase connecting the old chapel to the floor below it and perhaps to the narthex of the basilica.[26] Such a connection would be the direct ancestor of Bernini's Scala Regia.[27]

Because the date of the *capella magna* is uncertain, we can only suggest a generic fourteenth–early-fifteenth-century date for the western stairs. They must have been altered by Sixtus IV to correspond to the new elevation of the chapel and perhaps again by Innocent VIII (1484–92), who built a *magna porta* that led from the basilica narthex up to the palace.[28] Another piece of evidence for the stairs is a notice describing how this passage to the Sala Regia had to be temporarily bricked up at the end of Alexander VI's pontificate (1492–1503) to secure the conclave that elected his successor.[29] All of these notices provide a background for the staircase that Julius II had Bramante build between the basilica narthex and the Sala Regia in the early sixteenth century, discussed later in this chapter.

The entire division between the lower and upper palace was enforced by a medieval retaining wall positioned between the northern edge of the *atrium helvetiorum* and the southern border of the Cortile del Maresciallo ("f" and "l" in Diagram A).[30] This wall continued to exercise a significant influence on the palace entrance from the sixteenth century to Bernini's day. The *atrium helvetiorum* itself had taken shape well before the mid-twelfth century, the porticoes on its south and west sides dating from the pontificates of Eugene III and Innocent III.[31] The origins of the lower courtyard of the palace were no doubt related to the need for defending the palace entrance and especially for protecting the integrity of the conclaves during the election of a pope. The upper or second courtyard of the palace, the Cortile del Maresciallo, derives its name from the apartments of the conclave marshal whose job was to ensure the isolation of the cardinals ("con claves" = with keys) whenever they gathered to elect a pope.

These features of the palace complex suggest how one entered from the piazza during the Middle Ages. The first gate of the palace, the *porta prima* or *porta curie palatii*, faced east, and it led into the first courtyard, the *curia prima* or *atrium helvetiorum*, surrounded by curial offices.[32] This area and the principal entrance to the palace were heavily guarded.[33] Within the *atrium helvetiorum* cellars were excavated from the north side of the court.[34] At the foot of the *turris scalarum* in the northwest corner of the courtyard was the "second gate" of the palace, which led to the staircase that rose through the tower to the upper palace.[35] At the end of this ascent one arrived at the *curia superior* that is, the Cortile del Maresciallo, an outdoor vestibule with a staircase, the Scala del Maresciallo, rising to the Sala Regia ("k" in Diagram A).[36] The documentation published in the eighteenth century by Catalano and in our century by Ehrle and Stevenson indicates the locations of the *secunda custodia* at the foot of the *turris scalarum*, the *tertia custodia* at its summit, and finally a *quattuor custodia* positioned outside the portal into the Sala Regia.[37] These posts ensured the isolation of the upper palace.

The Palace Entrance from Nicholas V to Alexander VI

From the pontificate of Nicholas V (1447–55) there survives an impressive scheme for revitalizing Rome, including the Borgo, St. Peter's, and the Vatican Palace. This scheme, mostly unexecuted, is part of an account of the life of Nicholas V written by the Florentine humanist Giannozzo Manetti. Manetti composed his account immediately after the pope's death in 1455. Although we cannot be certain about the date of the projects or the identity of their author or authors, scholars frequently mention Leon Battista Alberti in this context.[38]

Among these proposals were suggestions for replanning the Borgo to complement the refurbishing of the basilica and the palace. The Borgo was to be organized around three major streets that ran from the Tiber to the Mons Vaticanus. On the south the Borgo S. Spirito would be regularized to lead to the obelisk on the flank of the basilica where a "dormitory" for the canons of St. Peter's was to be built. The middle street, the Borgo Vecchio, would have been realigned to lead directly to the central door of St. Peter's. A northern street would be cut to lead directly to the door of the palace.[39] The three streets were to be lined by porticoes with shops below and housing above them.[40] To mark the palace entrance, a huge triumphal gate was to be erected.[41]

The triumphal *fornix* was to be flanked by two large towers. On the basis of comparable monuments, Magnuson and Westfall have suggested that the gate consisted of a round-arched passage between squat turrets. Examples of this composition include the thirteenth-century gates at Capua and Castel del Monte built by the emperor Frederick II, the triumphal Gate of Alphonso of Aragon at Castel Nuovo in Naples (1443), and the Porta S. Petri built by Alexander VI (1492–1503) on the north side of Piazza S. Pietro (Fig. 21).[42] The triumphal gate may have been projected to replace an existing entrance at the site of the *porta prima* or for a site further east where it would have served as the terminal feature for a defensive wall built by Nicholas V.[43] This new wall joined the round tower of Nicholas V with a larger defensive *enceinte*, as can be seen on Figure 30. Through the principal *fornix* a series of steps would have led into the *atrium helvetiorum*, which was to be embellished by porticoes replacing those from earlier times.[44] A spiral staircase would have connected the entrance level to the upper palace.[45]

Westfall and Fagiolo have emphasized the notion introduced by Manetti of a comparison between the palace of Nicholas V and Solomon's palace as described in the Bible. The entrance portal is included in this association, and there is little doubt about the parallel Manetti intended to draw between the palace of the popes and that of their Old Testament forebear.[46] Both, for example, include a spiral staircase at the entrance. Moreover, the Sistine Chapel has been likened to the Temple of Solomon, which makes good sense in this larger context.[47] Fifteenth-century planners also may have intended to draw architectural analogies with the Imperial Palace at Constantinople, which again had a spiral staircase, or *cochlea*, leading to the emperor's box, from which he would appear to the general public.[48]

The triumphal gate projected by Nicholas V is important in the Renaissance history of the Vatican as the first recorded attempt to magnify the architectural importance of the palace entrance. The project would have had both symbolic and real significance, heralding the revival of the apostolic residence at the Vatican after the return of the papacy from Avignon and providing for its defense. Concern for matters of defense are generally overlooked in discussing the entrance to the Vatican Palace, but it was a significant issue for Nicholas V. It is a telling fact that of his grand plans, only the portions related to fortifications were largely executed.[49] In truth, defensive concerns and defensive imagery dominated all schemes for the Vatican Palace entrance from the construction of the *turris scalarum* until the mid-seventeenth century, by which time the possibility of armed conflict in the vicinity was quite remote.

During the pontificate of Pius II (1458–64) the façades of St. Peter's and the Vatican Palace assumed an aspect distinct from their medieval vestiges. Pius II's most conspicuous contribution was the Benediction Loggia, a documented work of the architect Francesco del Borgo ("d" in Diagram A). According to Frommel's reconstruction, the Benediction Loggia was to have extended across the full expanse of the basilica façade and the palace. The

four bays that were constructed mask only the west end of the lower palace and should therefore be considered an integral element of the palace as well as the basilica. The relevant chronologies bear out this notion, for the Benediction Loggia was begun in 1461, and in 1462 a new tower entrance was begun at the existing palace entrance. Payments to a stonemason in 1463 refer to a new "frontispitio," a marble door, merlins, and battlements, and to a marble portal on the inside of the passage.[50]

At this time the stepped ramp from the piazza to the portal was constructed, or perhaps reconstructed from earlier foundations ("e" in Diagram A).[51] The ramp extended the axis of the palace entrance into the piazza, as depicted much later by Heemskerck. This axis would have been punctuated by a fountain mentioned in documents of 1462 and 1463, and later altered during the pontificates of Innocent VIII, Alexander VI, and Paul V (Fig. 24).[52] Similar ramps were incorporated into the palace entrance under Paul V and Alexander VII, while the much remodeled fountain was also used in Bernini's piazza. As Thoenes has observed, the original fountain marked the middle of the north–south dimensions of the piazza before its enlargement in 1564.[53] In other words the entrance axis to the palace had once been a controlling feature of the piazza, a fact that may explain why relatively little additional attention was lavished upon it.

The palace portal constructed by Pius II had a square-headed opening, as depicted in Benozzo Gozzoli's fresco in the church of S. Agostino, S. Gimignano, in 1464–65 (Fig. 25). The portal was finished in January 1464, its doors painted a striking azure and decorated with gilded nail heads and the glistening moon shapes of the Piccolomini arms of Pius II, whose bust, also gilded, was installed over the entrance.[54] As suggested in Chapter 8, the image of a ruler presented at his palace entrance has a long and venerable tradition that culminates at the Vatican with the equestrian statue of Constantine. The portal was built in a wall projecting beyond the plane of the Benediction Loggia, and so must have had its own foundations (Fig. 26). At the end of the fifteenth century, under Innocent VIII, the portal was given a round-headed opening, as this and all later drawings show.[55]

The entrance wing of Pius II was a single story in height, as the S. Agostino fresco shows. The ele-

Figure 24 (above). View of St. Peter's and Vatican Palace from Piazza S. Pietro, drawing by the anonymous artist B (Devonshire Collection, Chatsworth, 839 A. Reproduced by permission of the Chatsworth Settlement Trustees; photograph Courtauld Institute of Art neg. no. 307/62, 31).

Figure 25 (right). View of St. Peter's and Vatican Palace, fresco detail, Benozzo Gozzoli, church of S. Agostino, S. Gimignano (Marder)

vation corresponded to the ground story of the Benediction Loggia, both enterprises being completed in subsequent pontificates. Thus, it was Paul II (1464–71) who constructed the wing over the palace portal connecting the upper stories of the Benediction Loggia to the upper palace.[56] This addition offered a direct passage between the Benediction Loggia and the Cortile di S. Damaso and brought the upper palace into a cohesive relationship with the basilica fa-

çade. Yet Paul II's contribution was more than a simple passageway on two stories, for the room over the portal was referred to as an "aula," and the floor above it included a "second room above the palace entrance," hence presumably a space of similar dimensions.[57] The evidence is consistent with Vasari's assertion that Paul II was responsible for the east wing of the *atrium helvetiorum*, a three-story loggia facing a similar loggia on the west.[58] Both the east

Figure 26. View of entrances to St. Peter's and Vatican Palace, drawing (Staatlichen Kunstsammlungen Dresden, C 550; neg. no. 13696)

and west sides of the passage above the entrance portal had large arched openings.

Later, in the sixteenth century, the wing would be modified to accommodate two private apartments, which belonged to lay members of the palace staff. These apartments each consisted of three rooms and a kitchen. Above each of them were three smaller rooms for servants, in sum four living units. These would account for the four chimneys visible on the roof of the wing above the palace entrance in Figure 26. The necessary connection between the palace and the Benediction Loggia, the corridor above the portal, was nevertheless maintained.[59]

On the exterior of the entrance, Paul II commissioned the clock that stood over the entrance portal until it was reinstalled in the early seventeenth-century clock tower of Paul V.[60] Finally, in 1470–71, Paul II erected an arcade along the top of the wall dividing the Cortile del Maresciallo and the

atrium helvetiorum. This arcade appears on two sixteenth-century drawings showing the columns that supported arches and vaults on the south side of the Cortile del Maresciallo, overlooking the *atrium helvetiorum* (Figs. 27, 28).[61] Paul II thus constructed a system of covered passageways to connect the lower and upper palaces at the east and the west.[62] Although the drawings show an unbroken wall behind the arcade, another plan illustrates windows overlooking the lower courtyard (Fig. 29). Because the windows are not precisely aligned with the bays of Paul II's portico, they may predate it. A medieval origin for this screening wall is also suggested by the one window that is centered on the *turris scalarum*, which would have illuminated the ascent from the lower courtyard. Recollections of the portico survived in Ferrabosco's unexecuted palace loggia overlooking the piazza in the early seventeenth century (Chapter 3).

Sixtus IV (1471–84) is best known for rebuilding

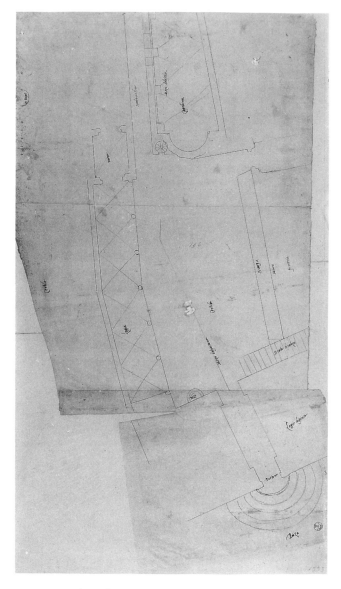

Figure 27. Plan of Cortile del Maresciallo, drawing, Antonio da Sangallo the Younger (Uffizi 1333A)

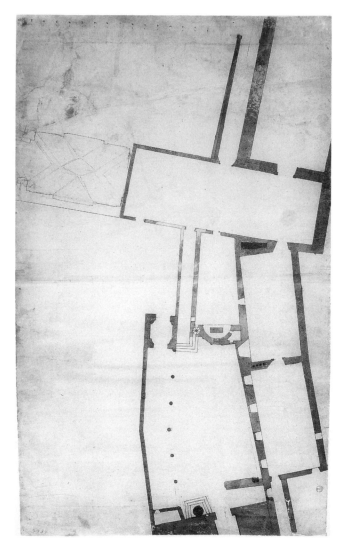

Figure 28. Plan of Cortile del Maresciallo, Sala Ducale, Sala Regia, and Cappella Paolina, drawing, workshop of Antonio da Sangallo the Younger (Uffizi 3989 A)

the principal chapel of the palace, but under his auspices the lower palace was also embellished. On the south and west borders of the *atrium helvetiorum*, new porticoes were constructed on three stories, complementing the work of Paul II discussed above ("f" in Diagram A). These additions completed a circuit by which the lower and upper palaces were firmly connected on the west and east and along passages to the north and south, at least partially obscuring the discrepancies of the natural terrain. According to a contemporary account the porticoes were built hurriedly and eventually left incomplete. This will help

to explain why they had to be finished by his successor, Innocent VIII.[63]

Innocent VIII (1484–92) is remembered today for constructing the Villa Belvedere that Bramante would link to the palace in the early sixteenth century. In the fifteenth century, however, he was best known for work on the lower palace that subsequently bore his name ("g" in Diagram A).[64] Here we need only mention his remodeling of the "prima porta" depicted in Heemskerck's view. It shows an arched portal flanked by columns on prominent socles supporting the projecting sections of a full entablature over the portal. Frommel has suggested

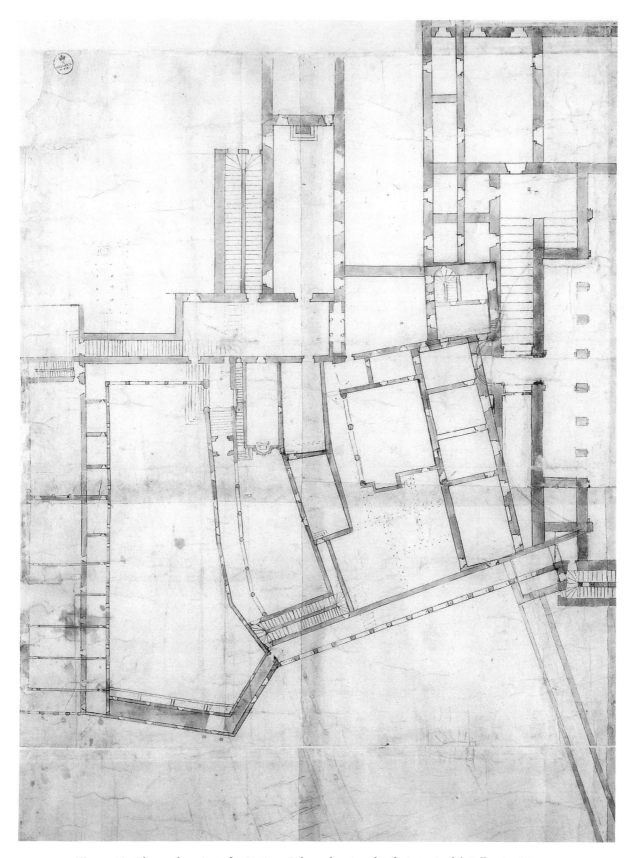

Figure 29. Plan and projects for Vatican Palace, drawing detail, Antonio del Pellegrino(?) (Uffizi 287 A)

that a drawing of the "porta del palazzo del papa" of about 1520 records these ornaments.[65] If, in fact, the drawing does depict the Vatican Palace portal in the late quattrocento, it gives evidence of an exceedingly precocious use of the classical orders in late-fifteenth-century Rome.

In developing patterns of circulation within the Vatican Palace, it would appear that planners after Nicholas V's time took no account of the urban context, but this is not quite correct. Nicholas V had already projected an entrance that would have been aligned with a major east–west street, the Borgo Nuovo, and this notion probably survived his reign. Evidence for this can be found on Figure 30 in the previously unexplained angle of the wing between the Benediction Loggia and the Bramante and Raphael Logge. The wing does not respond to the dominant orientations of the terrain, the palace, or the basilica. I believe the wing, which incorporated the palace entrance, was angled to set the entrance portal squarely on the axis of the street that later became the Borgo Nuovo.

The importance of this arrangement was forecast under Pius II (or earlier?) before it was fully exploited in the creation of the Borgo Nuovo during the pontificate of Alexander VI (1492–1503).[66] Fig-

ure 30 shows that a defensive wall of Nicholas V ended where a new portal attached to it would have maintained this orientation. When Alexander VI systematized the Borgo Nuovo in preparation for the Holy Year 1500, he was, in effect, amplifying the connection between the street and the entrance to the palace in the manner that Manetti had forecast and that Bernini would later take considerable pains to respect. When the Borgo Nuovo disappeared with the clearing of the spina in the twentieth century, these connections were lost. Today the effect can be imagined in a similar situation, where the Borgo Pio leads directly to Bramante's Porta Iulia in the lowest section of the Cortile del Belvedere. Bramante built that portal for Julius II, although the street was realized only in the period 1559–65.[67]

Julius II and the Via Iulia Nova

The ambitions of Julius II (1503–13) for the Vatican Palace are incorporated in the huge drawing now attributed to Antonio del Pellegrino, dated circa 1505–7, and long considered a product of Bramante's workshop (Fig. 30).[68] The plan depicts the state of the palace at the beginning of the sixteenth cen-

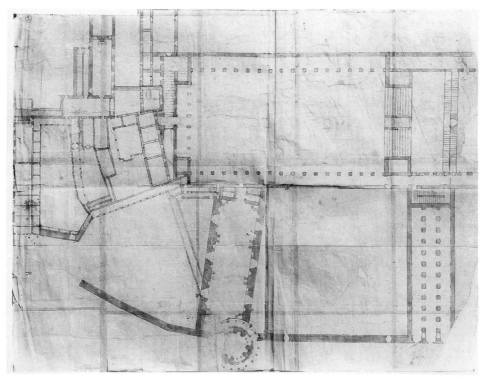

Figure 30. Plan and projects for Vatican Palace, drawing, Antonio del Pellegrino? (Uffizi 287 A)

tury and incorporates several projects. The grandiose tenor of these schemes and the large size of the drawing (1.03 m. × 1.34 m.) explain why Frommel has identified this plan as the "disegno grandissimo" described in Vasari's *Life of Bramante*.[69] Included in the drawing is the staircase begun by Bramante in early 1506 and finished in 1508, where the earlier stair had been and where Bernini would build his Scala Regia.

Because the drawing shows no stair landing at the door into the Sistine Chapel, the stairs on the drawing have been assumed to be a project.[70] Positioned along the south wall of the Sistine Chapel, the stairs turn at a double landing to continue down, passing under the Sala Regia. Under the Sala Regia where the stairs are drawn in pencil, they make a right-angled turn to join the flight of steps rising from the narthex of the old basilica. With the information available, it is presently impossible to determine whether the drawing records a Bramante project or the situation before his time.

We do know that a new staircase in this location was Julius II's major contribution to the old fabric of the palace ("h" in Diagram A).[71] It was built during the period 1506–08, when he sponsored the foundations of new St. Peter's. (This coincidence of events would support the current notion that Julius II initially planned a longitudinal rather than centralized scheme for the new basilica, which would be connected to the new stairs.)[72] The preexisting stairs were demolished in May 1505, about a month after the cornerstone of the new basilica was laid. Julius used portions of the new staircase just a year later, at Pentecost in 1506 (31 May), when it was referred to as the "Via Iulia Nova," as it was again at Easter (April 4) 1507.[73] Documents of 1508 for the stonemasons' work at the stairs confirm the chronology.[74] The stairs were still referred to by the name of their builder in 1536, when Charles V and Paul III ascended from the basilica to the upper palace "per scalas novas Iulii ad Salam Regiam."[75]

The Via Iulia Nova must have significantly improved the connection between the basilica and the halls of reception, as well as between the lower and upper palaces. The ascent began at the north end of the basilica narthex, at the *porta palatii* or *magna porta*, built by Innocent VIII but remodeled by Julius II and still identified with him in the late sixteenth and early seventeenth centuries.[76] The stair-

case rose to the north, encompassed within the west wing of the *atrium helvetiorum*.

The stairs are depicted in a number of plans, such as Peruzzi's sketch of the northeast portion of St. Peter's (above the "palazo di pp. Innocentio VIII"), Sangallo's drawings of the area between basilica and palace, Mascarino's detailed record of the same area, and Alfarano's engraving of 1590 (where the portal is labeled "Porta Palatii a Iulio II restaurata") (respectively Figs. 22; 31; 32 and 33; 34 and 35). The engraving published by Ferrabosco and Costaguti, which derives from Alfarano's plan, includes a reference (no. 122) to the "Adito per entrare nel Palazzo Pontificio" (Fig. 36). From the Ferrabosco-Costaguti engraving, it would appear that the lowest landing of the Via Iulia Nova was also accessible from the southwest corner of the *atrium helvetiorum*

Figure 31. Partial plan of old St. Peter's, atrium, narthex, and Via Iulia Nova, drawing, Peruzzi (Uffizi 11 A)

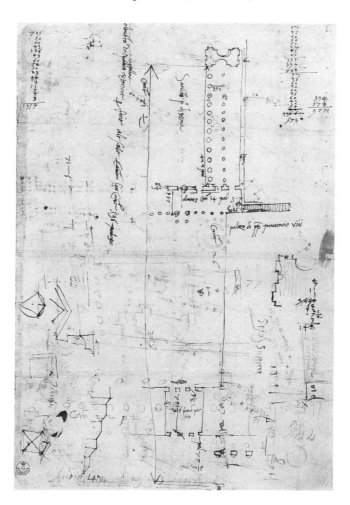

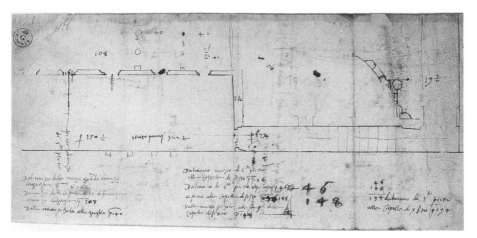

Figure 32. Partial plan of old St. Peter's, narthex, and Via Iulia Nova, drawing, Antonio da Sangallo the Younger (Uffizi 119A r)

and from a passage flanking the basilica. Since these connections do not appear in the earlier graphic evidence, they may represent later changes to the fabric.

In Sangallo's drawings the *porta palatii* between the old narthex and the palace stairs is 12 palmi wide (Figs. 32, 33). The portal opens to a staircase rising toward the north for a length of 172 palmi (38.42 m.) before making a 90-degree turn to the left (west). Then, rising toward the west, the stairs are some 19½ palmi (4.36 m.) in width, narrowing gradually to 16 palmi (3.57 m.) at the double landing where the ascent makes a turn of 180 degrees. From the double landing, the stairs continue up to the Sala Regia along the south wall of the Sistine Chapel, maintaining a constant width of 15½ palmi (3.46 m.).[77] Thus, the lower portion of the staircase tapers towards the top, whereas the uppermost leg of the stairs remains constant in width.

We cannot be certain whether the drawing rep-

resents Bramante's stairs, or a Sangallo proposal to remodel them, or Sangallo's actual remodeling. Whatever the case, the narrowing passage of the ascent, particularly the taper of about three-quarters of a meter along the main east–west flight, represents a previously unrecognized precedent and possible catalyst for Bernini's design, to which the dimensions bear an uncanny resemblance.[78]

Julius II was obviously aware of the symbolic and functional advantages of palatial stairs. In Bologna, where the present Palazzo Comunale once served as an apostolic residence, he built a staircase resembling the Via Iulia Nova. Significantly, the work was designed by Bramante, probably in 1507.[79] Not long thereafter work began on the stairs at the south end of the Bramante-Raphael Logge ("q" in Diagram A). The construction of the lowest flights was begun in 1509, and the upper flights were under construction from 1513 until 1517. Julius II died in 1513, and after Bramante's death the following year, the

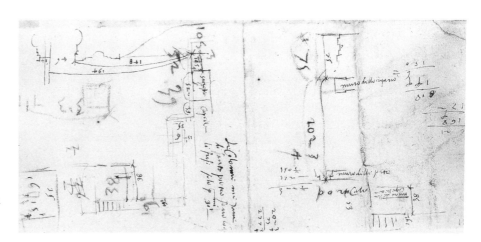

Figure 33 (right). Partial plans of Via Iulia Nova, drawing, Antonio da Sangallo the Younger (Uffizi 119A v)

work was taken over by Raphael, who composed a wooden model of the stairs and the Logge "con maggior ordine ed ornamento che non aveva fatto Bramante." Sources make clear that the Logge staircase and the staircase in Bologna were composed of a stepped ramp, or cordonata, negotiable by horses.[80] In this regard they followed the precedent set by yet another Julian stair, Bramante's spiral cordonata at the Cortile del Belvedere.[81]

Given the historical contexts it is quite likely that the Via Iulia Nova was also a cordonata, negotiable on horseback rather than stepped for the exclusive use of pedestrians. And while it is hard to imagine horses in the narthex, we have an unimpeachable reference to Julius II leaving St. Peter's for the palace on horseback.[82] It was no doubt more usual to arrive on horseback from the city and gain access to the upper palace by way of the *turris scalarum*, but the problem is complicated by the ambiguity of the sources.[83]

Perhaps Julius II's ultimate goal was to construct an entirely new palace entrance at the south end of the Cortile del Belvedere. In Figure 30 there are a group of buildings projected east of the Belvedere, including an enormous conclave hall, a square court, and a triple-nave building of uncertain function. These buildings would have composed an entrance sequence continuing in the southwest corner of the lower Belvedere at a staircase of extraordinary proportions, its 33-palmi (7.37 m.) width more than double that of the usual palatial stair in this period.[84]

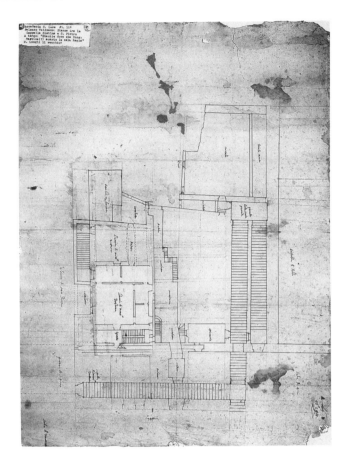

Figure 34. Plan of Vatican Palace between Sistine Chapel and St. Peter's, lower levels, drawing, Mascarino (Accademia di S. Luca n. 2488, formerly G. 108)

Figure 35. Plan of Vatican Palace between Sistine Chapel and St. Peter's, upper levels, drawing, Mascarino (Accademia di S. Luca n. 2489, formerly G. 111)

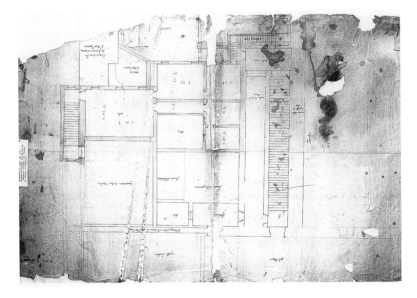

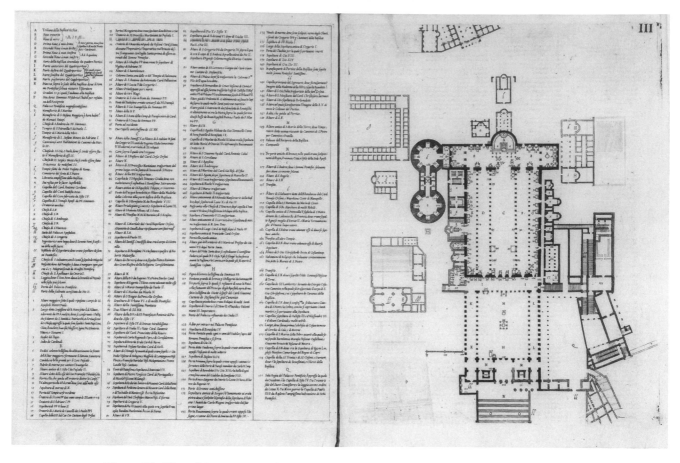

Figure 36. Plan of St. Peter's and Vatican Palace, engraving, Ferrabosco and Costaguti 1684 (BAV, Capponi S. 9, III)

This new entrance to the upper palace would have been accessible on horseback, but neither it nor the massive buildings projected on the drawing were ever begun. In their stead, Bramante built the Porta Iulia into the lower Belvedere for papal courtiers.[85]

Finally, the "disegno grandissimo" bears a number of pentimenti in red and black chalk, some of which may be in Bramante's hand. Among these are the square contours anticipating the shape of the future Cortile di S. Damaso, the sketch of a portal similar to the Porta Iulia to be built at the foot of the Logge, and some lines that Frommel suggests may render a staircase leading from the piazza up to the cortile.[86] Whether these sketches are Bramante's and whether they really include a staircase are questions that must remain open. Given the absence of conclusive evidence, the most we can say is that such a scheme would have anticipated future developments and otherwise unexplained features in a most reasonable way. For the Cortile di S. Damaso would

soon have its own access to Piazza S. Pietro; and the massive rusticated portal at the base of the Logge, executed by Bramante's successors (discussed in the next paragraph), brought visitors from the Cortile di S. Damaso into the Cortile del Maresciallo where stairs led up to the Sala Regia (Fig. 37).

The Works of Leo X and Clement VII

Under Leo X (1513–21) and Clement VII (1523–34) the Logge were capped and embellished on the west side by the so-called Loggetta of Raphael and the Stufetta of Cardinal Bibiena.[87] Unlike the Logge, however, these buildings overlook the core of the palace toward the west. From the southern end of the Logge, Leo X also built a short wing projecting eastward to form the beginning of a southern boundary for the Cortile di S. Damaso. Today this wing

Figure 37. Rusticated portal, Cortile di S. Damaso (Bibliotheca Hertziana, D21262)

the basilica and proceed to the upper palace by way of the Via Iulia Nova. By contrast, the Porta Pertusa and Porta Vaticani, indicated on Bufalini's map, were located on the extreme west side of the palace gardens, removed from the major urban approaches (Fig. 38). These could be used for inconspicuous arrivals from western arteries into the city. A differentiation according to rank and purpose is made evident in 1510, when Albertini explained that the doors of Bramante's Porta Iulia at the lower Belvedere were intended "not for general use, as are the others, but rather are opened for the convenience of the Pope and members of the Curia."[90]

Thus far, it has been possible to consider all but one component of the eastern palace entrances, namely the cordonata that led from Piazza S. Pietro to the Cortile di S. Damaso. Letarouilly recorded the plan of the cordonata, Rossini depicted a view of the lower portion, and Francesco Panini illustrated the upper portion on the Cortile di S. Damaso (Figs. 19, 39, 40 respectively). Maderno shows the cordonata on his projects for the palace entrance, and Bernini incorporated it in the systematization of the north

Figure 38. Plan of St. Peter's and Vatican Palace, woodcut, Bufalini, 1551 (Bibliotheca Hertziana, C5640)

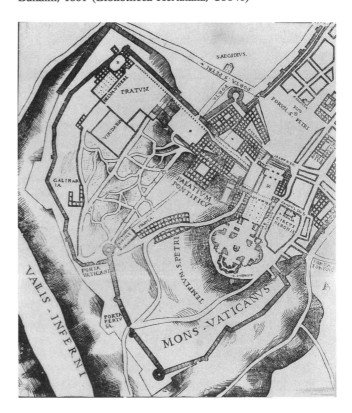

is enclosed in later construction.[88] The increasing importance of the eastern orientation of the palace was signaled by the construction of the massive rusticated portal sketched on Figure 30. Although the design has been attributed to Bramante, the portal is generally thought to have been built by his successor, Antonio da Sangallo the Younger.[89]

The conspicuous size and texture of the portal, which seems otherwise out of place, complement the entrance route from the piazza, to the Cortile di S. Damaso, to the Cortile del Maresciallo (Fig. 37). It was, of course, still possible to arrive at the Cortile del Maresciallo by crossing the *atrium helvetiorum* and climbing through the old *turris scalarum*, but this route lacked grandeur. It did not offer the majestic view of the Logge towering over a broad and airy Cortile di S. Damaso, nor the panorama over Piazza S. Pietro and the rest of Rome.

In fact, there were a number of entrances from the city into the Vatican Palace in the sixteenth century. The time-honored one, through the *turris scalarum*, provided a direct route to the core of the upper palace. A more formal arrival would begin at

Figure 39. Cordonata di S. Damaso, engraving, Rossini (Bibliotheca Hertziana, D20229)

"s" in Diagram A).[91] This portico was known as the Loggia dei Trombetti, from which the papal trumpeters announced the arrival of the pope, signaled the entrance of important dignitaries, and summoned the cardinals to consistory. Gregory Martin described trumpeters in 1581: "At the Palace gate stand on high from the ground the Trompeters. . . . At the very appearing of him [the pope] in the Palace gate to come forth the Trompeters play their part with melodious blastes."[92] The players are shown in action on the right side of Faletti's engraving of 1567 (Fig. 41). From Vasari we learn that Giulio Romano designed the Giberti apartment, which must have preceded the artist's departure for Mantua in 1524. Especially relevant to our discussion is Vasari's description of the entrance to the apartment "by a slope of commodious stairs that one can climb on horseback or on foot," in other words, a cordonata.[93]

In the past the Giberti apartment has been only casually related to the palace entrance, although some significant relationships did in fact exist.[94] They are clarified in two late-sixteenth-century descriptions of the Vatican Palace. The descriptions enable us to locate the apartment and its entrances, and these are positioned in close proximity to the entrance portal of the palace. One of the descriptions provides an entrance itinerary as follows: "Having passed this [the *porta prima*] one enters the first court [*atrium helvetiorum*] where on the right there is an arch where the *salita* begins to go up to the Cortile della Conserva or Dispensa [Cortile di S. Damaso]." The itinerary proceeds along this *salita*, past various doors, rooms, and stairs, until one arrived at a *sala pubblica* that led to an apartment of six rooms, a small chapel, a gallery, and an overlook onto the piazza, which can only be the Loggia dei Trombetti.[95]

This and a second, exactly contemporary description of 1594 make it clear that the apartment also had a back stairs in the form of a small spiral ascent, a "lumaghetta," that extended from the *porta prima* to the Loggia dei Trombetti.[96] Nicholas V's proposal for a spiral staircase, with its Solomonic and Constantinopolitan associations, perhaps inspired this feature, which, in turn, may have influenced Bramante's famous spiral stairs at the Belvedere. Yet a passage invariably described in the diminutive in the sixteenth-century sources must have been a private, not a public, entrance. Its restricted size will explain

corridor (Figs. 50, 109). At what moment was this route of access established between the piazza and the upper palace? A likely answer would involve Julius II and Bramante, who had begun the Logge and projected the rusticated portal at its base. But there is no evidence for their work on such a scheme. The first bit of graphic evidence for the cordonata appears on Bufalini's map of 1551 (Fig. 38). The map shows an L-shaped passage leading from the *porta prima* to the foot of the Logge.

I believe that earlier evidence of the cordonata can be construed in notices about an apartment built for Clement VII's datary, Giammatteo Giberti. Destroyed in the early seventeenth century for the new entrance complex of Paul V, the Giberti apartment overlooked the *prima porta* and Piazza S. Pietro. The apartment was crowned by the Doric hemicyclical portico recorded on Heemskerck's view (Fig. 21 and

Figure 40. Cortile di S. Damaso, engraving, Francesco Panini (Bibliotheca Hertziana, B5957)

Figure 41. Piazza S. Pietro, Pius V's blessing from Benediction Loggia, engraving, B. Faletti, 1567 (Musei Vaticani, XXXIV.5.15)

why it does not appear on Bufalini's plan and why the *lumaghetta* cannot be confused with Vasari's description of a *salita di commodissime scale* serving the Giberti apartments.

While explicit documentation is lacking, it nevertheless seems reasonable to identify Giulio's staircase with the cordonata that provided a major avenue of approach to the upper palace during the sixteenth century. This hypothesis would explain the genesis of a palace entrance that is otherwise unaccounted for. Moreover, these circumstances would clarify the reason for Giulio's close association with the site more than a century after his activity there. In the 1660s, when Bernini was working on the northern corridor and recollections of the Loggia dei Trombetti and the ramped entrance were still fresh, Giulio's responsibility for them was still remembered. At the time, Cardinal Antonio Barberini and then Cardinal Rospigliosi occupied Giberti's apartment.[97]

This picturesque and stirring route of entrance was described by the English traveler Fynes Moryson, who visited the Vatican Palace in the last years of the sixteenth century. He marveled how "the Pallace is of great circuit, and the staires are so easie, that Horses and Mules may goe up to the top of the Mountaine, and with easie ascent and descent beare the Popes carriage." And he confirms the prominent appearance of the Logge as an entrance feature: "At the enterance there be three galleries one above the other . . . all fairely painted and guilded."[98] Even after the construction of Bernini's Scala Regia, this would remain a usual palace entrance, as we know from an anonymous French traveler of about 1676–89, from Keyssler's mid-eighteenth-century account, and from reports of the late nineteenth century.[99]

An early-seventeenth-century source described the entrance experience as a passage through a "pleasant old cordonata" located inside the main palace entrance. This source also indicates that the cordonata opened on the *atrium helvetiorum* with a "rustic and magnificent portal."[100] We can only presume that this portal was designed to correspond to the rusticated portal at the Cortile di S. Damaso. Such a design would have been completely consistent with Giulio's interest in rusticated gates and may well have been his.[101] The architectural imagery on the lower court would thus have projected a continuous path of entrance to the ceremonial core of the palace.

The Work of Paul III

The achievements of Paul III (1534–49) demonstrate a continuing commitment to the realization of a new eastern entrance to the palace. Under Paul III's bold orders, the *capella parva S. Nicholai* was demolished and the upper parts of the *turris scalarum* were dismantled. These operations permitted the widening of the Scala del Maresciallo to dimensions equaling those of the Via Iulia Nova, as would befit the ceremonial entrance to a major sixteenth-century palace. Coupled with this project was the enlargement of the Sala Regia, its reinforced walls raised higher, covered by a barrel vault and splendid coffers, to complement and terminate the new processional grandeur of the entrance. To house the traditional functions of the old *capella parva*, the pope ordered the construction of the Cappella Paolina on the south end of this impressive hall. (These functions remained in effect through the era of Bernini's interventions, as we know from a visitor's account.)[102]

All of this work was begun in 1537 under the direction of Antonio da Sangallo the Younger, as is generally known, but its relationship to patterns of circulation into and through the palace have not been adequately assessed.[103] In general, the destruction of the *capella parva* and widening of the Scala del Maresciallo, the construction of the Cappella Paolina, and the enlargement of the Sala Regia have been viewed by historians as campaigns to enhance the magnificence of the palace at its ceremonial core. A major component of these activities was the operation necessary to realize the early-sixteenth-century plan for an entrance route that would traverse the Cortile di S. Damaso and the Cortile del Maresciallo directly into the principal halls of ceremony.[104] The results of this plan deeply affected the history and shape of the palace.

With the new entrance, for example, the Cortile del Maresciallo gained special importance. To regularize its haphazard contours – the result of centuries of growth influenced by considerations of topography, defense, and magnificence – Paul III ordered the loggia built by Paul II on the south side of the Maresciallo to be dismantled and its parts reused to construct porticoes on its east and west sides. The changes can be seen by comparing the old state in Figures 27, 28, and 29 with the new state

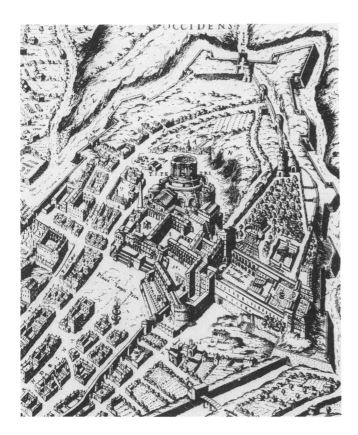

Figure 42. St. Peter's and Vatican Palace, engraving, Duperac and Lafrery, 1577 (Bibliotheca Hertziana, C5619)

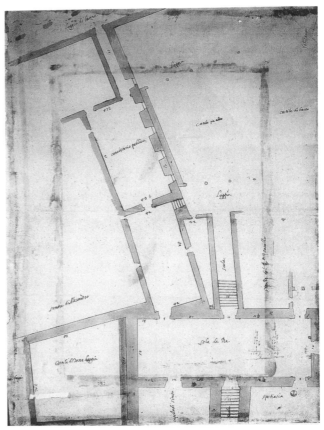

Figure 43. Sala Ducale, Sala Regia, and Cortile del Maresciallo, drawing, De' Rocchi (Uffizi 1979A)

of the courtyard in Figures 42 and 43 (where both porticoes are labeled "loggia"). Four arches were erected on the east and at least three arches on the west side of the Maresciallo (Fig. 42).[105] This operation maintained the tradition of covered passages on the Maresciallo and, by the reuse of fifteenth-century components, its early Renaissance Pauline associations. To commemorate the alterations, the Farnese arms of Paul III were carved on keystones in the vaults of both porticoes (Fig. 44).[106]

The new arrangement of piers and arches across the west and east sides of the Cortile del Maresciallo softened the effect of its irregular contours. Shadows engulfed the previously jarring combinations of acute and obtuse corners, and the sides facing the arriving and departing visitor now could be scanned as a uniform rhythm of arches (Plates 76, 77). In this arrangement the east portico would cover an exposed entrance to the cordonata of the Logge, and the west portico would incorporate the *turris sca-*

larum. The arches and octagonal piers of Paul II, deliberately reused for their archaizing effects, encouraged a perception of regularity that was contradicted by the geometric realities. A progressive-seeming arrangement of clean angles and unobstructed lines was teased out of the old, irregular space.

The lines and inscriptions on Figure 27 capture Paul III's intentions where new alignments are superimposed on the earlier state of the Cortile del Maresciallo. The entrance axis from the Cortile di S. Damaso through the rusticated portal is determined by the "mezo del portone" that passes under the Logge from the "piazza" in front of it. Five concentric steps arranged in semicircular fashion emphasize the importance of the portal on the Cortile di S. Damaso and betray a sloping terrain. The entrance axis makes a turn in the middle of the Maresciallo and continues as a dotted line through the *capella parva* ("capellina") to be demolished. The line

Figure 44. Ornamental keystone in groin vaulting of west loggia, Cortile del Maresciallo (Bibliotheca Hertziana, D36919)

labeled "mezo dela scala" identifies the axis of the new Scala del Maresciallo, which would replace the "scala vecchia" indicated on the plan.[107]

Before Paul III's work the main door to the *capella parva* stood opposite the Via Iulia Nova (Fig. 28). In the new configuration the broadened stairs took the place of the chapel, facilitating their location directly opposite the old Scala Regia. The doors to the staircases were aligned and their axes coordinated, although the entrance from the east had to incorporate a turn at the Cortile del Maresciallo to join the passage from the Cortile di S. Damaso. Here again, however, the perception of geometric coherence is urged where the porticoes of the Maresciallo were arranged perpendicular to the axes of entrance.

These formal effects complemented the larger reorientation of the palace entrance. For perhaps three decades an eastern entrance to the palace had been under discussion, and this was certainly a response to progress on new St. Peter's. In anticipation of a design requiring the demolition of the lower palace, new facilities had to be constructed. One guess is that Charles V's visit in 1536 emphasized the difficulties of hosting receptions at the palace on a truly imperial scale. But the overriding consideration was

embodied in the need to reconfigure the palace. During the reign of Paul III, the execution of a centralized design for St. Peter's was by no means assured, and Sangallo's extensive wooden model survives to illustrate how seriously the option of a longitudinal scheme was taken. While the demolition of the lower palace was not imminent, the need for an eastern palace entrance was inevitable, and Paul III acted upon these facts. From Vasari's perspective in 1550 and 1568, Paul III had virtually rebuilt the palace. The new basilica entirely justified this campaign.

Vasari lavished extraordinary praise on Sangallo's accomplishments at the Vatican Palace. Among them, Vasari mentioned the gentle declivity of the stairs that descended from the Sala Regia to St. Peter's, "so commodious and well done that among the ancients and moderns one has not seen better."[108] Because Bramante was responsible for the Via Iulia Nova, it has been thought that Vasari must have been referring to the new Scala del Maresciallo.[109] In my opinion, however, Vasari should be read literally when he explicitly describes the staircases (he uses the phrase "alcune scale," which is plural) that Sangallo built to the basilica. One was the Scala del Maresciallo, which led to the basilica by virtue of its connection to the base of the old Julian stair. The other was the Julian staircase itself, which Sangallo must have remodeled in the course of his work on the Sala Regia. This reading of Vasari's text makes sense of all the data presently at hand. It would explain why the dimensions of the Scala del Maresciallo and the upper flight of the Scala Regia are comparable and were left essentially unchanged by Bernini.

Sernini's statement in 1538 that the Maresciallo was where the cardinals traditionally dismount was correct – one recalls the *marescalcia* here – but his assumption that Sangallo's new stairs would permit a horse to be ridden into the Sala Regia was mistaken. Writing well before Sangallo had finished his work, Sernini may have known that the two major stairs to the Sala Regia would be made commensurate with each other (the smaller one enlarged) and incorrectly assumed that both would be ramped (as the larger had been) rather than stepped.[110] Our late-sixteenth-century accounts state explicitly that the Cortile del Maresciallo was still the place to dismount and approach the Sala Regia on foot.[111] Even in the early seventeenth century, arriving or departing princes and ambassadors still mounted or dismounted at the Maresciallo below the Sala Regia.[112]

If, as Vasari suggests, Sangallo was responsible for structural interventions on more than one staircase, he must have been occupied with Bramante's Via Iulia Nova. In this case, I suspect, he transformed it from a cordonata into conventional steps. This forced the visitor to ascend to the Sala Regia on foot, instituting a new formality in the approach to the upper palace that is consistent with the changed size and configuration of the ceremonial rooms. Sangallo's operations made the Sala Regia a more impressive space and the location of the Cappella Paolina Chapel symmetrical on it. In sum, geometric regularity and ceremonial formality were mutually enhanced.

Vasari alluded to the fact that Sangallo had to shore up the walls of the Sistine Chapel in anticipation of the changes to the Sala Regia, whose walls were made higher and thicker to carry an imposing barrel vault. Part of the old Julian stairs was built directly under the Sala Regia, and were attached to the south wall of the Sistine Chapel; and immediately south of the stairs, Sangallo constructed a group of vaulted rooms to support the floor of the new Cappella Paolina. Given these facts, it is almost impossible that Bramante's staircase could be left unchanged. These changes would have been structurally and aesthetically motivated. The knowledgeable certainly understood the history of the Scala Regia this way.[113]

A good deal of Pauline masonry, most of which has not been studied, survives above and around Bernini's Scala Regia, confirming the accuracy of Vasari's account (see Chapter 6). The location of this masonry is perfectly consistent with the appearance of the stairs in graphic evidence, such as Mascarino's drawings. After Sangallo, the principal staircase of the palace is not referred to as the Via Iulia Nova, and no changes are recorded until the time of Bernini. Indeed, the structural integrity of the staircase and the walls of the Sala Regia above it presented Bernini with the most difficult architectural challenges of his career.

Paul III's work was the last stage in transforming a medieval citadel into a Renaissance palace and the first step in molding the Renaissance palace to new

St. Peter's. Henceforth, there would be a clear distinction between a palace entry by way of the basilica and an entrance made directly from the piazza. The new arrangement presupposed the destruction of the lower palace by instituting an entrance on the piazza in front of it while maintaining the older connection to the basilica. Visitors from the city could avoid the *atrium helvetiorum* and proceed directly to the upper levels of the palace to be greeted by the towering Logge and the spacious Cortile di S. Damaso before entering into the smaller Cortile del Maresciallo. The notion of a real and symbolic ascent was made immediate, and it was complemented by symmetrically and axially regulated structures and spaces. Bernini concluded this process with the design for Piazza S. Pietro and the Scala Regia, which finally and thoroughly welded the new basilica to the palace and its entrances.

Palace Entrance and Stairs in the Later Sixteenth Century

For the balance of the sixteenth century, there were no significant changes to the entrances to the Vatican Palace from the piazza, and little was done to affect the character of the stairs between the narthex of St. Peter's and the Sala Regia. During the pontificate of Gregory XIII (1572–85) the Cortile di S. Damaso was formalized, and to the east a massive new palace was begun. To this new palace block, Domenico Fontana added a full story at the direction of Sixtus V (1585–90), by whose name the Palace of Sixtus V is still known.[114] These developments gave new emphasis to the eastern palace entrance.

Sixtus V also had Domenico Fontana build a staircase between the sacristy of the Sistine Chapel (behind the altar wall) and the still unfinished new St. Peter's. This staircase allowed the pope to descend to the recently finished Cappella Gregoriana built under Gregory XIII. The Cappella Gregoriana occupies the northeast quadrant of new St. Peter's, the closest and most accessible portion of the new basilica, and therefore the most obvious place for a direct link to the palace. Steep and narrow, the staircase enables the pope to arrive at and depart from the basilica in the exclusive company of his personal retinue.[115] The private aspect of the Sistine staircase thus complemented the public nature of the Scala Regia, which led to the narthex of the Constantinian church and required a procession down the nave to arrive at a given altar.

Sixtus V built a short corridor to connect his stair with the Scala Regia at the double landing, thus permitting the papal entourage to descend from the Sala Regia or the Sistine Chapel to the narthex or the nave of St. Peter's. A papal escutcheon and an inscription, both lost after Bernini's interventions, bore witness to Sixtus V's achievement.[116] These were located over a large door on the double landing that opened to the corridor.[117]

At the double landing the principal ornament was a fresco of Christ and Peter walking on the waves.[118] The image was accompanied by another inscription, in Greek, undoubtedly conceived by Sixtus who studied the language himself. The fresco is usually overlooked in the Vatican Palace literature, although Evelyn confirms its presence well into the seventeenth century: "Going up these stayres there is painted st. Peter walking on the sea towards our Saviour."[119] As mentioned earlier, Mola and Baglione attributed the work to the sixteenth-century painter Donato da Formello, who was also responsible for the fresco of Christ washing the feet of the apostles, which is at the foot of the Scala del Maresciallo.[120] At the double landing of the Scala Regia the image would have reminded the pope of his charge, inherited through Peter directly from Christ. For visitors to the palace, the fresco was a reminder of the origin of papal authority, derived through Peter from Christ. Similarly, the representation at the Maresciallo underscored the reciprocal relations of apostles to their leader at the palace entrance most frequented by cardinals.

By the end of the sixteenth century, the disposition of the palace and its entrances combined features that existed for centuries with those that anticipated the destruction of the old basilica, whose nave and atrium nevertheless remained intact as did the lower palace. In front of the main palace portal was a guard house and small armory for the Swiss Guards assigned to protect the entrance.[121] The principal gate of the palace, labeled "kk" on the Alfarano plan of 1590, is called "Ianua Palatii Apostolici" (Fig. 22). Leading up to it, a stepped ramp brought the visitor from Piazza S. Pietro to the palace entrance. Through the principal gate, the full extent of

the *atrium helvetiorum* opened up. The engravings make its contours neater and more regular than they truly were, but perceptions of visitors on the site cannot have differed much from Alfarano's.[122] Although the buttress wall on the north cut diagonally inward, the space was controlled by the right angles formed by banks of porticoes on the south, east, and west. Behind them were the main offices of the curia.[123]

A few paces into the *atrium helvetiorum*, the visitor arrived at a second portal on the right, "rustic and magnificent, that renders an admirable visual strength and grandeur followed by the gentle old ascent" by which one still rose in the early seventeenth century to the Cortile di S. Damaso.[124] The cordonata was partially covered and only at the lower end, just as Quarenghi and Rossini depicted it in the eighteenth century (Fig. 39).[125] The upper portions were open to the sky, so that the alternation of light and darkness through the entrance from the piazza to the breadth of the *helvetiorum*, to the dark and narrow passage leading to the sky-lit breadth of the cordonata conforms to Partridge and Starn's characterization of the sixteenth-century palatial entrance.[126] Visitors who were to be formally received would have made their way across the Cortile di S. Damaso to the rusticated portal built by Sangallo to Bramante's design. This portal led into the Cortile del Maresciallo, where one proceeded up the Scala del Maresciallo and into the Sala Regia.

This route was accessible on horseback up to the Cortile del Maresciallo where the visitor dismounted and made the final ascent on foot. This is, for example, what the cardinals did on the feast days requiring their presence. Gregory Martin described how "al the Cardinals come in Coches mo or lesse according to the fest, and to theyr abilitie, none under two, the great ones with twentie, and so forth unto thirtie."[127]

Alternate routes were possible, and the visitor entering the palace on horseback might still have traversed the *atrium helvetiorum* and then walked or ridden through the old *turris scalarum* to the Maresciallo. From the northwest corner of the *atrium helvetiorum*, horses could be taken through the west loggia, crossing underneath the north–south portion of the Via Iulia Nova and continuing on a westward path under a covered passage that is indicated on Figure 45. This path led to the sixteenth-century lo-

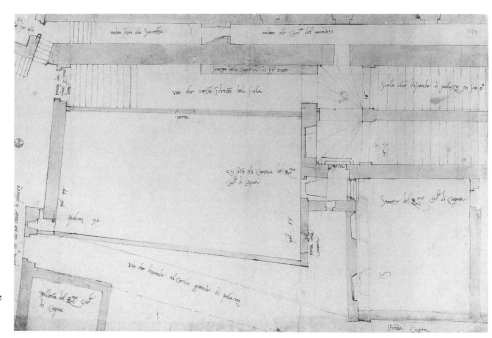

Figure 45. Plan of Vatican Palace between Sistine Chapel and St. Peter's, drawing (Uffizi 572A)

cation of the palace stables (indicated on Bufalini's plan), as well as to the Cortile del Belvedere (Fig. 38).[128] From the Cortile del Maresciallo, horses would have been led down to the stables through the Cortile del Pappagallo and Cortile della Sentinella.

The stairs of the old *turris scalarum* were also useful to pass between the offices of the upper and lower palaces. Indeed, since the formal entrance from the city was now a separate cordonata, the *turris scalarum* must have become ever more devoted to internal circulation. A passage cut between the Scala Regia and the medieval tower

stairs expresses the increasing need for efficient circulation routes. To this degree the path of the original Via Iulia Nova may have become more flexible in function, lending itself to the progress of visitors entering from the main gate as well as St. Peter's. This route was described in the last years of the sixteenth century.[129] We may understand Bernini's operations on the Scala Regia as a continuation of this evolution by providing a direct axial path between the stairs and the piazza entrance. The immediate context of his scheme, however, was the entrance reconfigured by Paul V in the early seventeenth century.

THREE

Paul V's New Palace Entrance

Ahundred years after its foundations were laid in 1506, the fabric of new St. Peter's remained an incomplete, hybrid complex. It consisted of a newly vaulted and domed crossing attached to the old Constantinian nave and medieval atrium with the lower palace on its northern wing. In September of 1605, the Congregation of the Fabbrica appointed by Paul V (1605–21) resolved to demolish what remained of the late antique basilica, finally ending the long-standing debate about preserving or replacing the venerable structure. During the following year, 1606, a number of projects for completing a new nave were submitted in competition, but no design was chosen. Even when the nave foundations were begun in March 1607, the design was not fixed. Eventually, in 1608, the decision was made to follow a model by Maderno.[1]

The model no longer exists, so it is impossible to know whether it included the ideas Maderno must have had for joining the palace to the basilica. Very likely it did, for by this time the destruction of the lower palace was under way to prepare for the new façade. Demolitions at the atrium of the basilica, or Cortile della Pigna as it was called, were begun as early as September 1607. The first portion of the old Curia Innocenziana to be taken down was the datary. By 1609 much of the lower palace must have been destroyed.[2] By 1610 the old Benediction Loggia was pulled down and the following year on Ascension Day, 12 May 1611, Paul V gave his benediction from the new façade.[3]

In spite of these demolitions, Paul V ordered the palace entrance to be maintained and even embellished where it stood, eventually adding a new wing behind it (Fig. 46). This work took place over the course of ten years. By 1618 the campaign on the basilica was completed and the entrance had been almost completely rebuilt. The new southern wing of the palace stood over the area previously enclosed by the *atrium helvetiorum* and overlooked Piazza S. Pietro. The new palace entrance featured a clock tower and a display of supporting structures and ornaments. Behind it was a small courtyard and, behind that, an armory. The little court gave access to the cordonata rising to the Cortile di S. Damaso. The design is generally attributed to the architects Martino Ferrabosco (died 1623) and Giovanni Vasanzio (died 1621), with Ferrabosco receiving the fuller credit.[4] The transfer of curial offices to spaces in the upper palace was accomplished under the guidance of the majordomo, Monsignor Giovanni Battista Costaguti. It was Costaguti who undertook a posthumous edition of Ferrabosco's designs for St. Peter's and the Vatican Palace that still serves this study.[5]

The structure served as the entrance to the palace for four decades, up to the time of its destruction by Bernini, and yet the circumstances and nature of the design are poorly understood. Most scholars have treated the façade as a purely decorative confection without considering its structural organization or its impact on the rest of the palace. And while its attribution to Ferrabosco has never been seriously questioned by modern scholars, no clear explanation has been given for Maderno's exclusion from this conspicuous commission. For all of these reasons, its history deserves review.

Figure 46. Project for Paul V's entrance tower, engraving, Ferrabosco and Costaguti 1684 (BAV, Capponi S. 9, XII)

The Provisory Entrance

The changing appearance of the palace entrance and plans for its transformation from the early seventeenth century until Bernini's operations around 1660 can be traced in drawings, engravings, and documents, which together create a consistent account of an evolving situation. During the period after the demolition of the lower palace but before the construction of Ferrabosco's monumental entrance wing, the entrance looked much as Maggi depicted it in the engraving of 1615 (Fig. 47).[6] Egger recognized in Maggi's view the remains of the old Paul II entrance, which was sheared from its connection to the former Benediction Loggia on the south to form a short entrance front. Egger made the process clear by juxtaposing Maggi's engraving and the relevant detail in the sixteenth-century drawing by Heemskerck (Figs. 48, 49).[7] The comparison shows how the three-story entrance wing was simply truncated and embellished in the zone between the portal and the clock. Egger dubbed this ensemble the "provisory solution" because it was destined to be replaced by a new entrance within a decade.

To be sure, Maggi's engraving is not a consistent visual record of executed works. The piazza was not paved as had always been hoped, although he showed it so; the flights of steps he illustrated in front of the basilica were not yet built, though they soon would be; and the bell towers that appear on the façade of St. Peter's indicate Maderno's intentions, already publicly circulated in the Greuter engraving of 1613, that were never realized. Nevertheless, the unfinished character of the entrance wall and the irresolution of the walls behind it argue for Maggi's reliability in this detail, as does a substantial body of additional documentation. The entrance façade on Maggi's engraving would have been completed by a new wall extending back toward the basilica to enclose the entrance to the cordonata and thus regulate access to the Cortile di S. Damaso.

Egger dated the provisory solution to the period after 1609–10, yet aspects of the design must have been settled somewhat earlier, judging from the chronology of payments for its decorative features. Chief among these was the mosaic of the Madonna and child with Sts. Paul and Peter, which is indistinctly represented between the portal and the clock in Maggi's engraving. Between February and April 1608, Cavaliere Cesare d'Arpino received payments for the cartoon guiding the composition of the mosaic. In March 1608, even before the cartoon had been fully paid for, the mosaicists Ranuccio Semprevivo and Cesare Rossetti were busy implementing the design. (Although the cartoon does not survive, an autograph copy of the composition by d'Arpino was recently purchased by the Nelson-Atkins Museum of Art.)[8] Earlier still, in November 1607, Ambrogio Bonvicino and Nicolò Cordier presented a bill for the marble angels designed to flank the mosaic above the portal. A final bill was registered in February 1609 and payment made in March 1609.[9] Thus, it would appear that the decorative ensemble of mosaic and sculpture dates back at least to 1607, and there is no reason to suppose that the origins of the provisory scheme for the architecture is any later. Indeed, the date of 1607 for a provisory entrance scheme accords with the chronology of the

VATICANVM S·PETRI TEMPLVM TOTO TERRARVM ORBE CELEBERRIMVM CVM ADIVNCTIS PONTIFICVM AEDIBVS HORTIS

Figure 47. View of St. Peter's and Piazza S. Pietro, engraving, Maggi 1615 (Musei Vaticani, XXX.28.13)

earliest demolitions in the Constantinian atrium and the lower palace.

Since the fifteenth century, statues of Peter and Paul had flanked the entrance to the basilica, and as the patrons of the apostolic mission their presence at the entrance to the palace is not surprising. The fact that Paul V held the Virgin in special veneration may account for St. Paul's favored position on the Virgin's right.[10] Otherwise, the aesthetic character of these works is unexceptional, their form and iconography corresponding to the taste and artistic conventions of the early years in the pontificate of Paul V. A similar but smaller pair of angels by Bonvicino and Cordier were executed in 1607 for the sacristy at S. Maria Maggiore.[11] Similarly, the same mosai-

cists worked together under d'Arpino's superintendence on the dome of St. Peter's.[12] With regard to the imagery, the devotion of Paul V to Marian cults is attested by the dedication of the Cappella Paolina in S. Maria Maggiore.[13]

The significance of the decorations for the portal at the Vatican Palace therefore lies less in their formal or iconographical aspect than in their early date. No other entrance scheme is known for the palace at this time, and these commissions affirm the intention of retaining the existing palace portal in a modified state. With the new demolitions for the basilica, many options and design alternatives were possible. By maintaining the existing location of the entrance, rather than turning it to face the south to have visitors enter the cordonata directly, planners reinforced the traditional approach to the palace entrance on the axis of the Borgo Nuovo. This was also the effect of retaining the columnar portal.[14] As late as 1 November 1610, demolition work at the portal of the palace prevented the use of this entrance for the procession on the feast of the Assumption.[15] I suspect that these demolitions damaged the mosaic, for repairs are recorded from about this time. Most important, however, is the preservation and enrichment of the traditional site of the old palace entrance.

That the provisory portal in Maggi's engraving was actually used is proved in a notation regarding the visit of the bishop of Bamberg. On 8 January 1613, he came to the palace from his residence on the Borgo Vecchio, near Piazza Scossacavalli, to of-

fer the *obbedientia* of the Holy Roman Emperor. His route began on the Borgo Vecchio then quickly switched to the Borgo Nuovo, leading to the provisory portal. This would have taken him to the cordonata and the Cortile di S. Damaso, through the rusticated portal and the Cortile del Maresciallo, and finally up the Scala del Maresciallo to the Sala Regia.[16]

Maderno's First Scheme

The design for the palace portal shown on Maggi's engraving proved to be temporary. Even as it was under construction, Maderno was probably at work on a more thoroughgoing transformation of the palace entrance that would resolve a host of problems

Figure 48. Vatican Palace entrance portal, drawing, Heemskerck (Egger 1929)

Figure 49. Vatican Palace entrance portal, engraving, Maggi (Egger 1929)

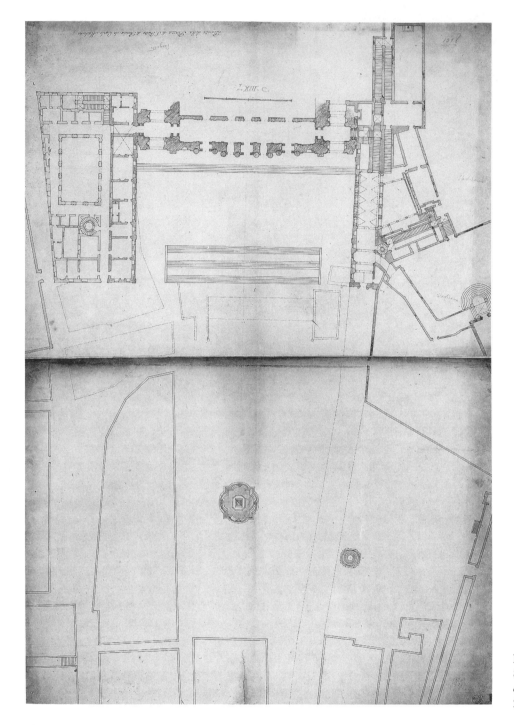

Figure 50. Project for Piazza S. Pietro and Vatican Palace, drawing, Maderno (Uffizi 263A)

posed by the advancing demolitions. Chief among these problems was a formal solution to the connection between the palace entrance and the new façade of the basilica. In addition, the narthex of the new façade had to be connected to the old Scala Regia, and new locations had to be found for the offices displaced from the lower palace.

The response to these and other problems is re-corded on a plan attributed to Maderno by Ferri and Pini in the nineteenth century (Fig. 50).[17] The plan includes the façade of St. Peter's rendered in hatched lines and the piazza in front of it. The obelisk on the piazza is surrounded by a large basin in a configuration typical for late-sixteenth-century Rome.[18] City blocks in the area of the future piazza are represented in solid lines and, where their removal is projected, in dotted lines. Existing parts of the palace to the north of the basilica façade are drawn in a blue/gray wash, and proposed additions to it are drawn in red ink. On the south side of the basilica, Maderno drew the plan for an enormous new palace, presumably to replace the palaces of the archpriest of St. Peter's and the confraternity of the Penitenzieri, the former destroyed for the new façade and the latter's destruction projected on this drawing.[19]

This scheme is usually discussed in relation to the piazza, which does indeed occupy most of the space of the drawing.[20] Maderno molded the space in front of the basilica by designing a south palace with an exterior symmetrical to the existing palace on the north side of the piazza. His impetus was the pressing need to formalize the palace entrance and resolve the appearance of the palace where it had been disrupted by the recent demolitions. Given these requirements, the piazza was a lesser concern. In truth, the principal intentions of the drawing depend upon the features Maderno proposed for the south edge of the palace. Here considerations of function and tradition had to coalesce. This is why the catalytic agent in Maderno's plan, the entrance wing of the palace, was not coaxed into a perfect rectilinear relationship with neighboring structures. As Thoenes observed, the entrance wing extends into the piazza at a slight angle to maintain the traditional alignment with the Borgo Nuovo.[21] The palace portal retained its relation to the urban context, while the palace structure on the south extends toward the piazza from the basilica at a strict right angle.

Wittkower pointed out that Maderno's plan for the entrance wing represents not one but two stories in elevation, a ground floor and the floor above it. The ground-floor plan has twelve windows facing Piazza S. Pietro, corresponding to the twelve windows drawn in the palace projected opposite it. A groin-vaulted, second-story loggia opened inward onto the Cortile del Maresciallo and out over the piazza. Maderno also envisioned a third and fourth story for the wing, projected on plans hinged as flaps to the drawing (Fig. 51).[22]

Maderno's loggia at the level of the Cortile del Maresciallo was surely meant to recall the old Paul II arcade that stood at the same location above the north side of the *atrium helvetiorum*. These features might have had a common source in the ceremonial

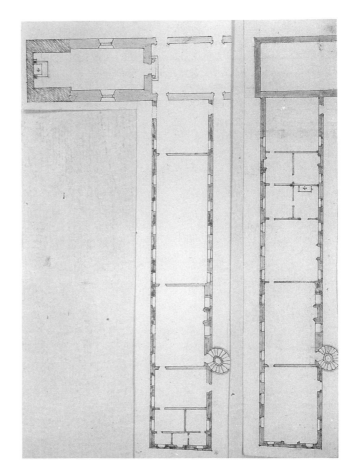

Figure 51. Project for Piazza S. Pietro and Vatican Palace, details of third and fourth stories, drawing, Maderno (Uffizi 263A)

galleries of royal appearances in Roman, late antique, and medieval palaces, "a characteristic feature of the *Sacrum palatium* with all its celestial implications," according to Smith.[23] In the new wing, Maderno also incorporated a spiral stair behind the cordonata in order to connect the four levels of the new wing to the Bramante-Raphael Logge.[24] In the palace on the south side of the basilica, Maderno drew a large circular stair resembling Bramante's spiral cordonata for the Cortile del Belvedere. Spiral stairs are to be found elsewhere in the Vatican Palace and in other buildings in which Maderno had a part, but without the same conspicuous presence as in this drawing.[25]

The third story of Maderno's project would have been located at the level of the Sala Regia. This observation is confirmed where a door connects the wing on this level to the Sala Regia near the entrance to the Cappella Paolina (Fig. 52).[26] Here, at

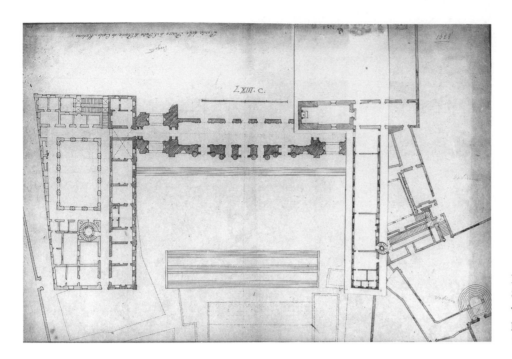

Figure 52. Project for Piazza S. Pietro and Vatican Palace, with detail of third story in place, drawing, Maderno (Uffizi 263A)

the extreme west end, Maderno drew two additional doors giving access to the new Benediction Loggia to the south and to the Scala del Maresciallo to the north. Maderno thus incorporated circulation paths between newer and older structures.

The fourth floor of the new wing was composed of three large chambers, a chapel, three small rooms, and a large private chamber at the back (Fig. 53). This arrangement includes the usual features of a private seventeenth-century apartment, and this association is strengthened by the location of three fireplaces on the north side and one on the south. Indeed, Maderno's audacious style as an architect can be recognized here, as at Palazzo Borghese (1611–14), in the positioning of walls over the space of rooms on the floor below; most architects would have set wall above wall on succeeding stories.[27]

Maderno may have intended the *maestro di casa* to live and work in these rooms on the fourth story, which resembled the rooms serving the same function at the Curia Innocenziana. This apartment was also known as the "camera imperatoris," because it was used as an apartment for the most distinguished papal guests on special occasions during the fourteenth and fifteenth centuries.[28] As we know from the contemporary records of Grimaldi, the memory of the "camera imperatoris" was not lost in the early seventeenth century.[29] At the time of the destruction

of the lower palace, the third floor included an impressive audience hall with painted representations of the tributary princes of the church.[30] Perhaps Maderno envisioned a similar iconography for the decoration of the large room (of reception?) on the third floor of the new wing, which led directly into the main reception hall of the palace, the Sala Regia, with its own decorative cycle of beneficent rulers.

The two upper floors of Maderno's project have not attracted much scholarly comment. Their interest for us lies in the relationship to the curial offices they were intended to replace. By designing a wing that is some 50 palmi wide, Maderno emulated the width of the old Curia Innocenziana and extended its length significantly to restore at least some of the space that had been lost in the demolitions for the new nave and façade.[31] This explanation would help account for the otherwise unnecessary width of the new wing, which would have required the reduction of the three-bay Farnese arcade (to two bays) on the west side of the Cortile del Maresciallo.

Because Maderno conflated the first two stories on his drawing, many of its features remain unclear. Could one have walked from the palace portal to the foot of the Scala Regia, or could the stairs be reached only by way of the portico of the basilica? In either case, while Maderno surely established a model for Bernini's later thinking, this model did not

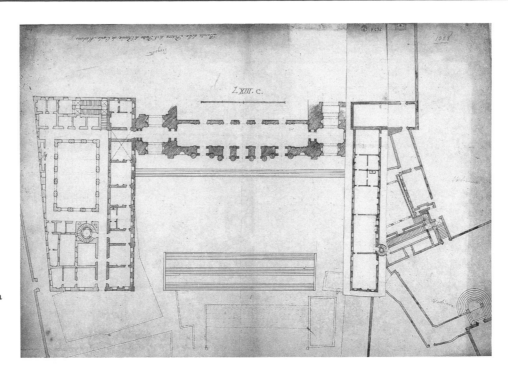

Figure 53. Project for Piazza S. Pietro and Vatican Palace, with detail of fourth story in place, drawing, Maderno (Uffizi 263A)

include the notion of an axial relationship between the entrance portal and the ascent by which one arrived directly at the principal hall of state.

Hibbard tentatively dated Maderno's project to the period around 1613–14 on the basis of its relationship to details in the famous Greuter engraving of St. Peter's façade of 1613, to the fountain depicted on the north side of the piazza that was rehabilitated in 1614, and to the inscribed date (tenth year of the pontificate, 1615–16) on the portal of the narthex leading to the Scala Regia.[32] This conclusion is consistent in a general way with Thoenes's observation regarding the shape of the north tower, begun in 1613 according to a design that was slightly different from that of the south tower.[33] On the other hand the comparison by Thoenes to G. B. Ricci's fresco of 1611 provides striking evidence that many aspects of the Maderno scheme existed *in nuce* from that earlier date (Fig. 54).[34]

The fresco is located in the Sale Paoline of the Vatican Palace. It shows a four-story palace wing with an entrance portal surmounted by angels who flank Cavaliere d'Arpino's mosaic composition. In both Maderno's plans and the fresco, the third story of the palace corresponds to the level of the Sala Regia and the Cappella Paolina, which is supported by an arch connected to the basilica. Despite these correspondences, the concept of a matching palace

on the south side of the piazza has not yet been proposed. The idea of setting up Giotto's Navicella on the exterior of the new palace wall, as depicted in the fresco, had been suggested as early as 1610, but Maderno appears to have rejected this idea in his drawing, preferring to incorporate windows where the venerable mosaic would eventually be hung.[35] The scheme depicted in Ricci's fresco of 1611 is therefore less developed and probably earlier than Maderno's drawing with its matching palace to the south of the basilica. Newly discovered documents of 1614–15 for systematizing the Scala Regia and the lower part of the Scala del Maresciallo provide a *terminus ante quem* for Maderno's sheet, which can therefore be dated between 1611 and 1613, just a little earlier than Hibbard indicated, but very much in keeping with the progress of related building campaigns and planning schemes.

Maderno's Changes to Sangallo's Staircases

Maderno's façade for the basilica was begun in late 1607 and largely finished by 1613.[36] In March 1613, having arrived from the Quirinal and participated in services in St. Peter's, the pope made his way back to the upper palace by way of the Porta S. Marta on the southwest side of the basilica.[37] This meant

Figure 54. Façade of St. Peter's and projected Vatican Palace entrance, fresco by G. B. Ricci, Sale Paoline, Vatican Palace, 1611–12 (BAV, Archivio Fotografico)

circling around the south side of the basilica, a route that was probably made necessary because the traditional connection between the narthex and the palace was out of service. The reason is clear. The new façade was located to the east of the old one, and the process of construction had required the adjustment of the old Scala Regia.[38] Because of the more easterly location of the new narthex, the old staircase had to be extended towards the east. Moreover, its steps had to be adjusted to the new level of the narthex pavement. The new configuration appears on the plan by Ferrabosco and Costaguti, where the stippled outline of Maderno's façade is drawn over the Constantinian basilica (Fig. 55).

Newly discovered documents enable us to date the renovation of the stairs to the period 1614–15, when 72 steps of the Scala Regia were replaced. The payments specify treads that were 16¼ palmi wide, identical to those of the earlier staircase and therefore set within the confines of preexisting walls.[39] We cannot be absolutely certain how the ad-

ditional length of the new stairs was bridged, whether by increasing the number of steps, increasing the depth of the treads, or some other solution that might have combined the two procedures and reduced the height of each riser. Most likely, the number of steps was increased, but whether the proportions of the individual steps were changed by Maderno from those built by Sangallo is impossible to say.[40] Because the depth of the new treads (3¼ palmi = 72.6 cm.) was notably greater than that of the present steps (ranging between 53 and 56.5 cm.), we can be certain that the ascent was long and unrelieved, just as Carlo Fontana described its condition before Bernini's intervention.[41] According to a description of about 1620, the vertical distance from the narthex of the basilica to the Sala Regia was around 94 meters (420 palmi).[42] From the double landing, 30 steps rose to the threshold of the Sala Regia, above which was an inscription commemorating Paul V's work.[43]

Under Paul V, 37 new treads were also installed

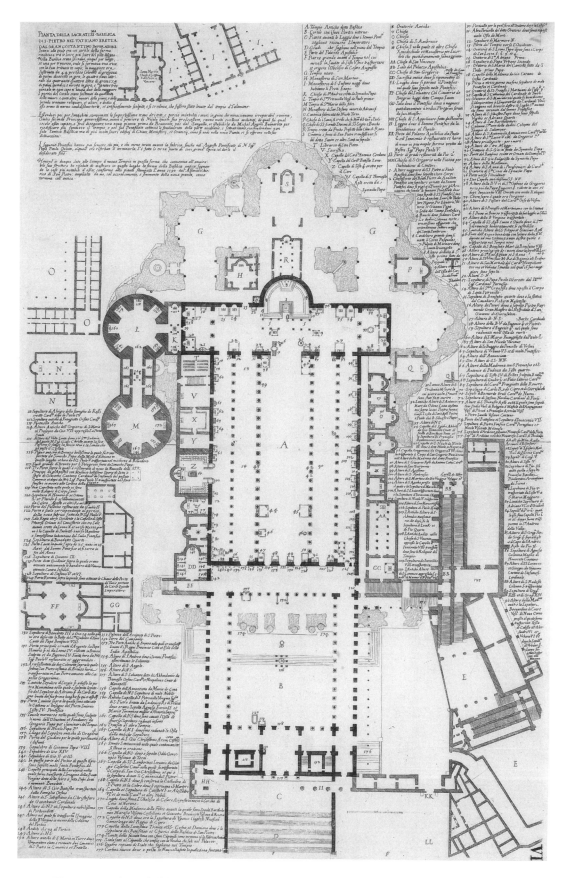

Figure 55. Plan of old and new St. Peter's and Vatican Palace, engraving, Ferrabosco and Costaguti 1684 (BAV, Capponi S. 9, VI)

in the old staircase rising through the former *turris scalarum*, presumably as replacements. These treads were cut to the same width as those for the Scala Regia, although the risers would have been much higher and the ascent steeper than the Scala Regia, whose length was so much greater. When Bernini rebuilt this stair as the Scala di Costantino, he increased the number of steps to a total of 49 and made their treads less deep.[44]

The cost of these works amounted to 6,094 scudi, but this reconstruction was only the larger part of the process of rehabilitating the connection between the palace and the narthex of the basilica. The documents also record the provision of 24 steps to connect the narthex of the basilica to the base landing common to the Scala Regia and the stairs rising to the Cortile del Maresciallo. In short, a new north–south flight of steps was necessary to bring the visitor from the pavement level of the narthex to the foot of the palace stairs. The Fabbrica spent an additional 200 scudi on this short flight of steps, including the cost of the rounded, projecting ends (*cavalcatori*) traditional at palatial entrances.[45] The stairs documented in the newly found payments are depicted on the plan by Ferrabosco and Costaguti.[46] The stairs are illustrated with still greater precision in an engraving where even the *cavalcatori* for the 24 steps are rendered (Fig. 56).[47]

Paul V completed the modifications of the old Scala Regia by ordering a statue of St. Peter to be placed at its base, exactly where Bernini's Constantine would later be located. Although rarely discussed in the palace literature and never with respect to its successor, the statue of St. Peter was a conspicuous presence at the entrance to the palace where it joined the basilica. The statue is mentioned in the palace description of around 1620, and in 1639 Baglione described it as a "marble statue of St. Peter the Apostle with keys in his right hand and a book held in his left."[48] The statue remained in this location through the 1650s and into the early 1660s.[49] Alexander mentioned it in the present tense in a diary entry of July 1664, when he was pondering the accommodation of the Constantine.[50] And Martinelli, who is thought to have written his guide in the early 1660s, recalled the statue destined to be removed by the pope.[51] Even at the turn of the century, the statue of St. Peter was recalled by Bonanni.[52]

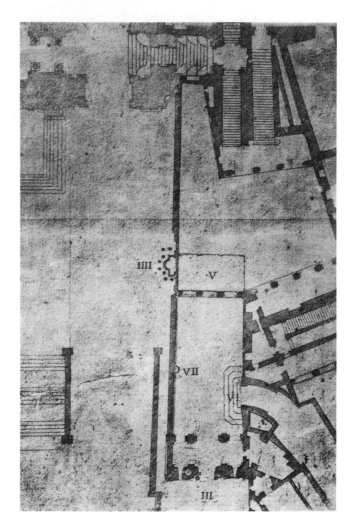

Figure 56. Plan of Paul V's palace entrance, detail, proof-engraving, Ferrabosco (Egger 1929, courtesy J. Freiberg)

The placement of the statue of St. Peter in conjunction with the narthex of the basilica recalled a tradition at the basilica that can be traced to the fifteenth century and perhaps as early as the eighth century.[53] The *Liber Pontificalis* records a donation of Leo III (795–816) of a gold urn with gems that was displayed before the "image" of the apostle at the entrance to the basilica; and in 1430 Giovanni Rucellai recorded a seated bronze figure of St. Peter in front of the portico.[54] The location of a statue of St. Peter at the narthex was also recalled by Alfarano and Grimaldi, and noted in the Ferrabosco and Costaguti plan.[55] In placing a statue of St. Peter at the foot of the Scala Regia, Paul V reinforced the newly forged union of basilica and palace by emphasizing the Petrine authority that governed both of them.

This connection was emphasized by the figural program of the narthex, which featured thirty-six of the earliest popes.[56]

Maderno's Economical Solution

From the foregoing information it is clear that Paul V was inspired like his Renaissance predecessors to embellish the entrances to the Vatican Palace, and particularly the works of his namesakes Paul II and Paul III, who had done so much to improve the eastern circulation patterns of the palace. Yet the resolve of the pope was compromised by his abiding wish to live and work at the apostolic palace on the Quirinal Hill.[57] Here Paul V found a more congenial setting for his daily activities and spent a good deal of money making it more grandiose. My guess is that Maderno's ambitions for the Vatican Palace, included in the drawing in Figure 50, outstripped Paul V's will to finance them. Far more humble is the subsequent proposal that Maderno initiated for the completion of the southern flank of the Vatican Palace (Fig. 57). This drawing offers the key to understanding Maderno's role in designing the new wing of the palace built by Ferrabosco.

The drawing was attributed to Maderno by Ferri and Pini, and first discussed in the modern palace literature by Egger.[58] As in the previous design, here too the principal walls of the palace as proposed are rendered in red wash. They extend from west to east, incorporating a south-facing portal for the cordonata and a gate to the barracks of the Swiss Guard. At an east-facing opening, a defensive tower is projected in black chalk. To date no one has proved the connection of this tower to Nicholas V's plan for a massive double-tower palace entrance, yet the formal relationship is evident from the placement of the structure on the path from Castel Sant'Angelo through the Borgo Nuovo. Even the position of the south-facing portal to the cordonata could be said to respond to old thinking in that its location coincides, at an oblique angle, with the central axis of the Borgo Nuovo.

The round tower depicted in Figure 57 is part of a set of chalk lines drawn over the inked portions of the drawing that represents a second phase in the development of the scheme. An entrance portal rendered in chalk appears in two different positions. In the darker of the alternatives, the portal is coupled with a long rectangular vestibule whose composition (entry, atrium, rear porch) strongly resembles what Ferrabosco would subsequently build. The door to an armory behind the rear porch is also indicated. This scheme would have cut into the thick diagonal buttress wall that separated the lower from the higher terrain, the former *atrium helvetiorum* from the upper palace. In the more lightly drawn lines can be seen an alternative design, with features only slightly changed in position. (Some of these details are almost invisible in photographs.) A faintly drawn portal has been moved east (down) to coincide with a slight angle in the buttress wall. The lighter scheme also includes a row of windows overlooking the piazza and, in their midst, a small basin marking the intended location of the Navicella. Evidently the plan for the mosaic, mentioned in 1610 and depicted on Ricci's fresco, was being put into effect.

These features anticipated the composition of Ferrabosco's entrance tower and the new wing built behind it in 1617–18. There we shall find the same footprint for the new additions and the same rectangular entrance complex, with column screens at the front and back of the entrance vestibule and an oddly angled space behind it, which would become Paul V's armory. The superimposition of this design, drawn in chalk over a retaining wall indicated in red ink, leads us to question the date, authorship, and function of the scheme. Should it be considered a drawing for the provisory solution, as Egger and most other scholars have thought? An early alternative to the provisory solution? A later, economical proposal for the swift completion of the palace and its entrance? An early design in ink upon which later proposals were drafted in chalk? Sketches by Ferrabosco over inked lines by Maderno?

Egger dated the drawing only loosely to the years 1610 to 1617, and few scholars have done more with the problem.[59] Hibbard proposed a date close to 1616, because the drawing shows the north campanile of the basilica as built (unlike and therefore later than Uffizi A 263), because the eastern steps are shown as built in 1616 (although they are shown this way in Uffizi A 263), and because the corner bevels of the steps in front of the façade are squared in chalk, as built in 1617.[60] From Hibbard's analysis two useful conclusions emerge. First, we have every reason to credit Maderno with all aspects of the

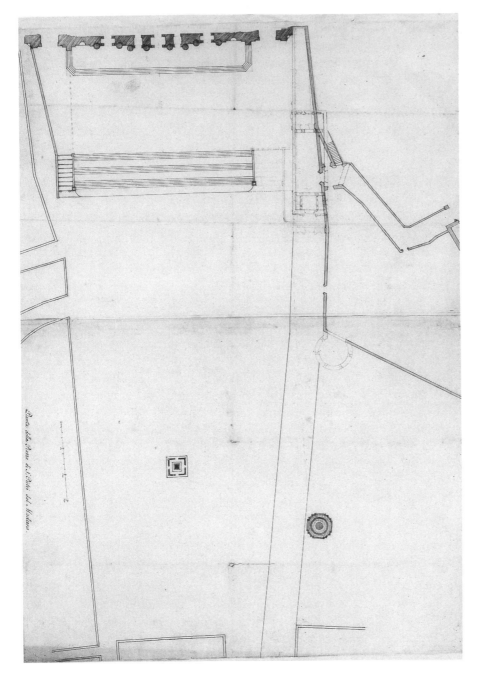

Figure 57. Project for Piazza S. Pietro and palace entrance, drawing, Maderno (Uffizi 6728A)

drawing and no compelling reason to attribute any of its features to Ferrabosco, since Ferrabosco had no part in the design or construction of Maderno's façade for St. Peter's or the two sets of steps whose details are shown so knowledgeably. Second, given the similarity of the plan as drawn in chalk to the entrance wing as executed, the chalk overdrawings must precede the construction of the entrance wing by a very short time.

Whether the original, inked portions on Figure 57

were intended as an economical provisory scheme of early date or an economical permanent scheme of later date cannot be determined. In some sense, however, this question is less important than the authorship and date of the chalk overdrawings. Indeed the darker lines bear a striking similarity to the dimensions of the entrance wing as recorded in a document and in a preparatory study by Bernini (Fig. 109).[61] The wall extending from the basilica to the clock tower was recorded as 289½ palmi long in our document, 293 palmi in Bernini's drawing, and 300 palmi in Figure 57. The width of the entrance wing appears as 57 palmi in both the document and Bernini's drawing, and 65 palmi in Figure 57. The distance from the entrance portal to the cordonata entrance measures 66 palmi on Bernini's drawing and 65 palmi on Figure 57. Given the essential correspondence of these measurements, the drawing in Figure 57 may be said to have forecast the composition, proportions, location, and alignment of the new entrance wing.[62]

This evidence indicates that Maderno was largely responsible for the design of the new entrance wing of the palace. While it is possible to imagine the intervention of Ferrabosco, Vasanzio or others on the drawing we have just considered, there is no reason to do so on the basis of documented circumstances or drawing style.[63] And if there is no reason to do so, there is also no reason to continue to exclude Maderno from the planning process of the new entrance as the literature on the palace usually has. Among its many attractions this argument corrects the mystifying omission of Maderno's presence in the design of the new wing, which took place during his hegemony over the renovation of the basilica. Circumstances suggest that he must have been involved in designing portions of the palace adjoining St. Peter's, and the drawings and documents agree with this conclusion.

Ferrabosco's Superintendence of the Entrance Tower and Portone di Bronzo

Between 1617 and 1619, the elaborate towered entry to the palace and the new palace wing behind it replaced the provisory entrance. Payments to the *capomastri muratori* for the new building appeared in June 1617, and there were payments for bronze and brass fittings as late as 1619. The record of an inscription that hung inside the entrance provides the date of 1618 for the completion of the new wing, and this is confirmed in the inscription that is still visible on the exterior of the Portone di Bronzo from the fourteenth year of the pontificate (May 1618 – April 1619). The entire cost of the new wing, the tower, and the portal amounted to 33,997.38 scudi.[64]

When the provisory entrance was devised, it utilized existing elements of the earlier palace entrance,

including the old doors of Pius II that had been renovated by Innocent VIII and the architectural members flanking them. With the construction of the new entrance tower, the recent additions of the marble angels and the mosaic of the enthroned Madonna and child were complemented by the addition of newly made bronze doors. Constructed of bronze laid over a wooden core, the Portone di Bronzo was being fabricated in March 1617, and in July the pope came to visit the site.[65] At this time Paul V would have found the carpenter Giovanni Battista Soria at work on the wooden portions of the portal and Orazio Censore attending to the casting and hammering of the metal components.[66] Soon, the Cavaliere d'Arpino's mosaic and the flanking angels by Bonvicino and Cordier were reinstalled with a new inscription over them: "PAULUS V PONT. MAX. ANNO 13" (that is, 1617–1618).[67]

The literature on the palace has paid little atten-

Figure 58. Bronze doors between narthex of St. Peter's and base landing of Scala Regia (Marder)

Figure 59. Project for Paul V's entrance tower, drawing, Ferrabosco (Albertina, AZ Rom, N7793)

Figure 61. Project for Paul V's entrance tower, drawing, Ferrabosco (Albertina, AZ Rom, N7793b)

Figure 60. Project for Paul V's entrance tower, drawing, Ferrabosco (Albertina, AZ Rom, N7793a)

Figure 62. Project for Paul V's entrance tower, drawing, Ferrabosco (Albertina, AZ Rom, N7793c)

70

Figure 63. Project for Paul V's entrance tower, engraving, Ferrabosco, in Bonanni 1696 (Princeton University, Marquand Library)

tion to the significance of the Portone di Bronzo and virtually no attention to a second set of bronze doors, still *in situ*, between the narthex of the basilica and the base landing of the Scala Regia (Fig. 58). Both sets of doors bear the name and the escutcheon of Paul V and leave no doubt about their origins in the Borghese pontificate. The use of bronze doors in ecclesiastical and palatial contexts has a venerable tradition, with which those of Paul V must have been consciously allied.[68] An example that Paul V surely emulated was the Bronze Gate of the Imperial Palace in Constantinople. It was upon this portal, according to legend, that the emperor Maurice (582–602) had seen a vision of Christ, which was later replaced by a painted image. This image was in turn replaced by a cross in 726, during the Iconoclastic Controversy.[69] The obvious connection with Bernini's imagery of Constantine and the cross at the foot of the Scala Regia is a matter for discussion below. Here it will suffice to relate the mosaic image of the enthroned Madonna and child with Sts. Peter and Paul to the same tradition. An analogy with the vestibule of the Imperial Palace at Constantinople must have been invested in these images.[70]

Exactly when Maderno's participation ended and Ferrabosco's began is still vague, but a group of studies for the elevation of the entrance tower offers a basis for speculation. Of the four drawings in the Albertina, three are finished presentation drawings with differing solutions to the main front; the fourth is a side elevation (Figs. 59, 60, 61, 62).[71] Of two additional projects recorded by Bonanni, one is interesting for entirely preserving recollections of the old portal at the foot of a slim, three-tiered bell tower capped by an onion dome (Fig. 63).[72] The other project in Bonanni includes a sturdy base story with battered walls and corner quoins and ports for gun emplacements, like the drawings (Fig. 64). Given the narrow proportions of features above the base story in the engravings, it is likely that these two schemes were drawn up when the projected loggia, visible in Figure 46, was eliminated from the program, as seen in Figures 66, 67, and 70. (The loggia would have stood awkwardly over the little open courtyard visible in Fig. 66.)

Figure 64 (left). Project for Paul V's entrance tower, engraving, Ferrabosco, in Bonanni 1696 (Princeton University, Marquand Library)

Figure 65. Piazza S. Pietro, St. Peter's, and palace entrance, engraving, I. Silvestre (by kind permission of the Istituto Nazionale per la Grafica, Rome; FC66912)

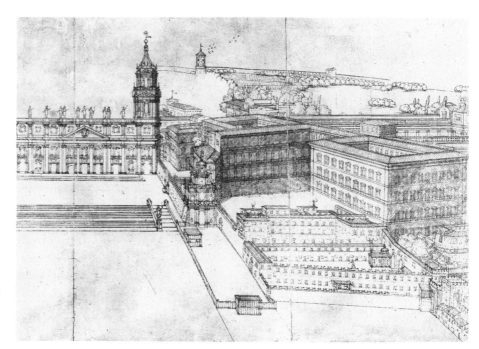

Figure 66. View of St. Peter's and Vatican Palace, drawing, Ferrabosco? (Kunstbibliothek, Staatliche Museen Preussischer Kulturbesitz, Berlin, Hdz 3840)

As a group the projects are strikingly similar but for the manner in which they reconfigure a common stock of decorative motifs. In one proposal, for example, the angels by Cordier and Bonvicino flank the clock on the third story of the tower, while in another their positions are maintained on the second story on either side of the mosaic of the Madonna and child with Sts. Paul and Peter. A project bearing an inscription on the frieze refers to the thirteenth pontifical year (beginning May 1617), suggesting a date for the entire group (Fig. 59). This date is con-sistent with the documentary evidence for the beginning of the building campaign in July 1617.

Graphic representations of much later date confirm that the tower was built upon a battered base with prominent corner quoins and a heavily rusticated, arched portal (Figs. 65, 66, 67).[73] The portal was flanked by Doric columns and capped by a triglyph-and-metope frieze supporting a broken pediment with the papal escutcheon inserted at its peak. The second story was divided into three bays, with the central one accommodating the marble angels

Figure 67. View of Paul V's entrance tower and Borgo Nuovo from façade of St. Peter's, drawing, Stefano Della Bella (Département des Arts Graphiques, Musée du Louvre, Paris; copyright R.M.N., inv. no. 293/2)

Figure 68. Panorama of Vatican from dome of St. Peter's, drawing, I. Silvestre (by permission of the President and Fellows, Harvard College; Harvard University Art Museums, 1961.7)

and the mosaic of the Madonna and child with Sts. Peter and Paul transferred from the provisory entrance. The clock was installed in the third story, which was a single bay in width. A bell set within ornamental braces sprang from the corners of the tower to cap the progressively narrowing elevation. While none of the projects forecasts the precise form of the executed tower as we know it from the graphic evidence that survives, one drawing bears a close resemblance to this scheme (Fig. 61).[74]

The tower, though unremarkable in its design, incorporated several important references to Vatican tradition. The clock was probably the same as the one that had stood at the palace entrance since the

fifteenth century. Now, however, a bell tower was conjoined to it. In effect, it recalled the old campanile of the basilica, which was pulled down beginning in 1610.[75] Shortly thereafter, a specialized study of bells was published, no doubt lamenting the loss of this notable monument to the original basilica.[76] The new tower may also have been intended to recall the *turris scalarum*, the medieval tower gate that was the principal entrance to the upper palace from the twelfth to the sixteenth century. Finally, the position of the entrance was located on the axis of the Borgo Nuovo, as can be seen in a view drawn in 1641 from the dome of the basilica by Israel Silvestre (Fig. 68).[77] In these ways the new structure preserved memories of the earlier entrances to the palace. Issuing its sonorous tones every quarter-hour and hour, Paul V's tower was a memorable feature of the palace, not least because of the rare use of bells in Rome at this time.[78]

The elevation projects for the bell tower have traditionally been attributed to Ferrabosco, and there is currently no reason to question his authorship. The style of the Albertina drawings is not Maderno's, nor can the formal vocabulary be related to his oeuvre. Moreover, the early sources consistently credit Ferrabosco with the new bell tower. This situation can, I think, be explained if we assign to Ferrabosco the principal responsibility for design and construction of the palace entrance and the new wing behind it, built over the footprint anticipated by Maderno.

Ferrabosco's Superintendence of the New Wing behind the Entrance Tower

Two papal annual medals issued by Paul V document the importance of the new entrance tower and the wing built behind it.[79] The first medal features the elevation of the entrance portal (Fig. 69). Since the inscription on the obverse refers to the thirteenth regnal year, the medal can be dated to June 1617, for the medals were traditionally issued on the feast of Sts. Peter and Paul. The medal was surely intended to commemorate the beginning of the building campaign. A year later, 1618, the second medal was issued, bearing a more developed image that is consistent with its later date. Rather than an elevation, the second medal presents a perspective view of the palace that includes the wall in front of the portal, the new wing behind the tower, an indication of the Navicella, and portions of the Cortile di S. Damaso and the Cortile del Maresciallo (Fig. 70). Presumably, the second medal commemorated the completion of construction.

To study the interior layout we must refer to the engraving that served as a proof for Ferrabosco's book, a plan by Virgilio Spada of 1651, and Bernini's plan of 1659–60 (Figs. 56, 71, 109).[80] These plans, read in conjunction with the literary evidence, enable us to re-create the entrance sequence that began at the portal marked "III" on the Ferrabosco's engraving.[81] Within the portal was a small atrium open to the sky, depicted in Figure 66. Grimaldi referred to this open-air space as the *atrium helvetiorum*, an obvious reference to its predecessor that also sug-

Figure 69. Paul V's entrance tower façade, engraving of foundation medal by G. A. Moro, cast 1617, Bonanni 1706 (Bibliotheca Hertziana)

Figure 70. Paul V's entrance tower façade, engraving of annual medal by G. A. Moro, struck 1618, Bonanni 1706 (Bibliotheca Hertziana)

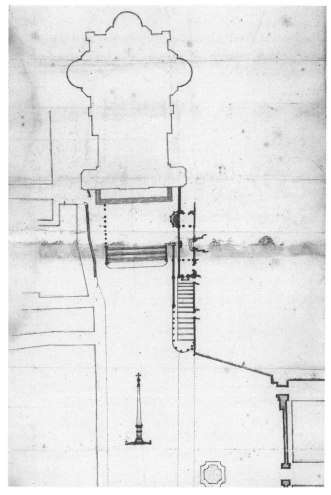

Figure 71. Plan of Piazza S. Pietro and St. Peter's, drawing, Virgilio Spada, 1651 (BAV, Vat. lat. 11257, fol. 6)

gests the continuing presence of the Swiss Guard at this location.[82]

Egger and most others treat the tower and entrance of the palace as a decorative confection whose derivation should be sought in temporary architectural settings of impermanent materials.[83] Nevertheless, there is compelling evidence for the fortified aspect and defensive function of the new wing. Even in 1581, Gregory Martin made note of "the twelve peeces [cannons] that lie alwayes before the Palace gate."[84] Later, in Maggi's engraving of 1615, cannons are shown in defensive positions on both sides of the provisory entrance, and bollards created a barrier from the rest of the piazza, forcing visitors to leave their carriages outside the palace grounds. Moreover, four of the six preparatory designs for the tower include gun emplacements that manifest the

need for defense. Payments of February 1618 included reimbursement for work on "the two pieces of artillery located at the cannon ports of the portal of the Vatican palace." Thus, the use of a new atrium behind the portal "pro custodia Portae Palatii et tormentis bellicis" had serious military implications.[85]

Whether it was for display or was adequate to repel an attack, the presence of artillery flanking the portal was conspicuous enough for Lualdi to make prominent mention of it in the mid-seventeenth century.[86] By then, the "piazza d'arme" described by Martin in front of the portal had seriously deteriorated, an indication of the lack of concern for defending the main palace portal by force in Bernini's era.[87]

These facts correspond with the presence of the armory couched within the sturdy walls to the west of the new *atrium helvetiorum*, located behind the numeral "V" on Ferrabosco's proof engraving.[88] The armory was housed in the irregular, pie-shaped space between the new battered wall overlooking the piazza and the diagonally oriented buttress wall that had previously divided the lower from the upper palace. Here it corresponded to Cortesi's recommendations for the ideal cardinal's palace.[89] An inscription in the atrium referred specifically to the first defenses of the palace and its armory housed in the new tower. The inscription bore the date 1618.[90] During the pontificate of Urban VIII (1623–44), the armory was transferred to a new, more spacious location within the Cortile del Belvedere and later enlarged by Alexander VII.[91] But even in these later years, it was recalled how Paul V had stored enough material "to arm many thousands of people."[92]

In retrospect, it is interesting to observe how Bernini's north corridor eliminated these provisions for defense. In truth, by the mid-seventeenth century the Vatican Palace was no longer prepared to deal with military assault, which in turn reflects the changing role of the papacy in European politics, which, more than any other single historical fact, influenced the commission for Bernini's Scala Regia.

A marble fountain emblazoned with Borghese heraldry stood against the south wall of the new entrance atrium. In Spada's plan the fountain is drawn directly opposite the cordonata, while in Ferrabosco's proof-engraving the features are offset so that the fountain would mark the middle of the open atrium. In either case there can be little doubt that the fountain was intended as an introduction and terminus to the ramped stair that brought the visitor up to the Cortile di S. Damaso. Egger knew the fountain from the proof engraving and from an engraving of the fountain itself by Parasecchi.[93] The fountain was preserved after the tower was demolished, and has recently been rediscovered by Freiberg in the Palazzo del Commendatore of the Ospedale di S. Spirito, where it had been transferred in the 1660s (Fig. 72).[94]

Carved by Cordier in 1609 for a garden entrance to the palace, the fountain was removed to the main palace entrance in 1618.[95] The ensemble consists of a winged Cupid standing on an elaborate basin set within a niche that is flanked by Ionic pilasters and capped by a segmental pediment broken at the top. In the absence of other information, we can only surmise that the rush to complete the new wing of the palace induced Paul V to order an existing fountain sculpture transferred to a more conspicuous location. In its original location the figure of Cupid alluded to the aqueduct that fed the Vatican Gardens, the "Acqua di Venere di Bracciano," for Cupid was the son of Venus. As Freiberg explains, the aqueduct was identified in the seventeenth century with the Acqua Alsietina built by Augustus. According to Virgil's *Aeneid*, Augustus was descended from the Julian family that traced its origins to Venus and Cupid by way of Aeneas, legendary founder of Rome. As Paul V restored the Augustan conduit, the little garden fountain offered a veiled claim for renewing this glorious heritage. Thus, on several levels from the superficial to the arcane, the fountain represented Paul V's custodianship of the ancient imperial heritage.

After the transfer to the atrium of the main palace entrance, the fountain was embellished with colored marble revetments, a scalloped shell at the top of the niche, an eagle, and a dragon.[96] A trident held by Cupid signified the ruler's power and dominion, evoking the ideals of martial power and affability that characterized the goals of Paul V's reign.[97] Cordier's fountain may even have been conceived in the new location as something like a lavacrum, a place for the ablution and sanctification of rulers at the entrance to a palace.[98] Such a reference would be consistent with the jurisdiction of a heavenly authority as symbolized by the iconography of the Portone di Bronzo and its mosaic representations.

Figure 72. Cupid Fountain, formerly within Paul V's entrance wing at Vatican Palace and presently located at Ospedale di S. Spirito, Palazzo del Commendatore, Rome; Nicolò Cordier (J. Freiberg)

Conduits behind the fountain connected it to another located below the Navicella on the other side of the new brick wall below the palace. Both of the fountains were operating by May 1618.[99] Perhaps they were finished in time for a dedication of the new wing on the feast of Sts. Peter and Paul in that year, accompanied by the medal we have discussed and by an inscription in the new *atrium helvetiorum*.[100]

The Navicella

The long wall that connected the façade of the basilica to the clock tower and the palace portal was a battered mass of brick capped by a travertine course and punctuated by stone openings for cannon emplacements.[101] The chief ornament in this portion of the Vatican Palace was Giotto's Navicella mosaic above a south-facing fountain. During the demolition of the basilica in 1610, special care was taken to remove the Navicella in three pieces from the Constantinian atrium, where it hung on the inner side of the eastern arm.[102] The display of the Navicella in front of the basilica façade, on the new flank of the palace, had been planned from July 1610 and anticipated in the Ricci fresco of 1611.[103] Between August and October 1610, the mosaic was detached, crated, and transported to the "cortile de' Todeschi," that is the *atrium helvetiorum*, for storage.[104] The protection afforded the mosaic in transport must have been extensive, for in 1612 the *atrium helvetiorum* was described as full of wood from the old basilica and the crated mosaic.[105]

Despite these precautions, the transfer of the fragile mosaic was not accomplished without damage, and when it was set in place on the new wing of the palace by October 1617, Paul V ordered its cleaning and restoration.[106] This work required several months to complete, and not until 10 March 1618 was the Navicella unveiled. For this occasion, Paul V came to the Vatican Palace from the Quirinal, descended to the basilica, and exited onto the piazza where the Navicella was first revealed since its removal from the Constantinian atrium.[107] In effect, the Navicella transformed the space in front of Maderno's new nave and façade into a surrogate for the Constantinian atrium. Interested visitors would have been keen to see the venerable mosaic, whose new location was immediately incorporated into the guidebook literature.[108] A drawing by Bernini or his workshop shows the mosaic with its decorative framing features as they looked at this time (Fig. 73).[109] The semicircular niche shown in plan directly behind the Navicella indicates the location of the Cupid Fountain within the entrance atrium.

Although an inscription of 1618 claimed that Paul V saved the mosaic "from the ruins of the atrium of the Vatican basilica," paradoxically, his choice for the location of the great work would itself be considered ruinous by his successors.[110] Indeed, over the subsequent decades, Giotto's Navicella led an extraordinary existence that deserves fuller recognition. In 1628–29, under Urban VIII, Bernini directed the return of the mosaic to the basilica to be installed on the inside of the entrance wall to the nave as recorded in drawings and mentioned in av-

visi, documents, and secondary sources.[111] The reason for the transfer was to preserve the mosaic from the damage caused by "rain, wind, ice, and other threats." Many studies were made, and to illuminate the work in the most favorable way, new windows were eventually cut in the fabric of St. Peter's.[112] Yet within two decades the Navicella would be moved again.

Almost unremarked in the literature is the episode of 1648–49, during the reign of Innocent X when, after considerable debate, the mosaic was removed from the interior of the entrance wall of St. Peter's to be hung once again at the palace entrance.[113] The motivation for this third transfer is not entirely clear. To be sure, there were some who considered the placement of the mosaic overlooking the nave to be

Figure 73. Giotto's Navicella and fountain, Paul V's entrance wing at Vatican Palace, drawing, Bernini, 1623–28 (Museum der bildenden Künste Leipzig, inv. 7829)

too high and poorly illuminated, while others argued strenuously for preserving the association with the basilica.[114] Yet the debate hardly accounts for the expense and risk involved in the effort. It should probably be explained with reference to the program for redecorating the interior of the basilica under Bernini's supervision in preparation for the Holy Year 1650.[115]

Gigli recorded the transfer of the mosaic in 1648 to its new location, "in the first court opposite the portal of the papal palace where the modern mosaic images of St. Peter and St. Paul are, which Paul V ordered."[116] Paeseler has emphasized that Gigli's report is consistent with a guidebook description of 1652, which mentions the Navicella "nell'ingresso del Palazzo Pontificio, dove hora si vede."[117] To this we can add the account of Giovanni Battista Mola of about 1660, who refers to the Navicella "again moved" to a position behind the entrance portal of the palace.[118] Unfortunately, there is no visual documentation of the Navicella for the period 1648–1660, but Paeseler concluded that the Navicella would have been hung in the little atrium of the entrance in front of the armory, that is, within the open-air court beyond the tower entrance, and not on the wall of the new wing overlooking the piazza as generally thought.[119]

Paeseler's conclusion can now be supported with documentary evidence to prove that indeed the Navicella was placed within the new *atrium helvetiorum* during the pontificate of Innocent X. An informed account of works undertaken by Alexander VII for Bernini's Scala Regia describes "the arsenal of artillery [the armory] with a little portico in front, above which was the Navicella in mosaic."[120] The account goes on to describe the open-air court and the marble Cupid fountain opposite the cordonata, so that we can be certain the writer is inside, not outside, the entrance wing. No illustration includes all of those features of the Navicella in this setting, but the account of the dismantling of the entrance wing, including the removal of Innocent X's escutcheon over the mosaic, cinches our information. The escutcheon complemented the Barberini bees that were set below the mosaic as seen on Bernini's (workshop?) drawing.[121] In August 1662, after Bernini had demolished the wing of Paul V to build the north corridor, "the portal of the Arsenal of the Ar-

tillery, which was located under the Navicella," was donated to Cardinal Ginetti.[122]

A decade after the transfer of the Navicella to the entrance wing under the auspices of Innocent X, Alexander VII authorized the demolition of the entire entrance wing of Paul V to make way for the northern corridor. Perhaps in preparation for its dismantling, Cosimo Bartoli made drawings of the Navicella, for which he was paid some years later.[123] During the early planning stages for Bernini's Piazza S. Pietro, a suggestion was made to relocate the Navicella on the façade of St. Peter's once again to overlook the piazza, but nothing came of this proposal.[124] Later, in 1671, Bernini presented a plan in which the Navicella would be placed at the south end of the narthex of the basilica, opposite the newly unveiled statue of Constantine. The plan was well received in the Fabbrica, possibly encouraged by an oil cartoon hoisted into place on Bernini's orders.[125] But the poor reception of his Constantine undermined the proposal, for it was thought improper to have "so old and worthy a work" located opposite a "heap of errors" seen in the Constantine.[126] Only in 1673–75 was the Navicella set in its fifth and final destination in the central lunette on the inside of Maderno's façade, where it recalled the original situation on the west-facing wall of the Constantinian atrium.[127] Under the protection of the narthex, the much restored image is safe from wind, rain, and frost, but is hardly visible in the darkness.

Additions to the Cortile del Maresciallo

The work of Paul V extended to the buildings on the east and west sides of the Cortile del Maresciallo. Here, Paul V reinforced the arcades that had been built by Paul II and rearranged in their present location by Paul III. The original fifteenth-century octagonal columns were encased in masonry leaving only one of their faces and their capitals exposed, as can be seen in Figure 74. Reinforcing arches (now restored) were inserted to sustain a new floor and mezzanine raised on both sides of the court. In this process, which Egger dated to 1617–18, the Loggetta of Leo X was enclosed in new buildings on the east side of the courtyard. The composition resulted in a pie-shaped projection of the palace that juts

from the south end of the Bramante-Raphael Logge.[128] To commemorate the work, Borghese escutcheons were hung on the west side of the courtyard and on the east apartments overlooking the piazza.

Ferrabosco and, later, Bonanni depicted the new entrance wing with a second-story loggia overlooking the piazza, but the upper portion of the design was never constructed (Fig. 46). The loggia, we have suggested, was inspired by Maderno's earlier project, and his inspiration, in turn, was no doubt the portico of Paul II over the south side of the Cortile del Maresciallo. But because none of this had been executed, the battered wall of the south palace wing was topped only by a balustrade lining a terrace that extended to the Cortile del Maresciallo. The drawing in Berlin illustrates this state of the monument, as do the drawings and the engraving of Della Bella and the medal commemorating the completion of the entrance wing and tower in 1618 (Figs. 66, 67, 70).

Without its second-story loggia, the new wing was easily connected to the north end of the basilica façade, the substructures of the palace, and the buildings around the Cortile del Maresciallo. The battered ground-story addition joined but did not interrupt or cross any existing fabric. On the other hand, if the full height of the new wing had been built – in four stories as Maderno planned or with the second-story loggia that Ferrabosco projected – many complications would have arisen. Had the upper levels of the new wing been built up to the basilica, they would have interrupted the portico on the west side of the courtyard. Maderno recognized this situation: in his earlier scheme, the number of arches on the west side of the Maresciallo is reduced to two (compare Fig. 50 to the original number of arches shown in Fig. 42). In the event, it was decided not to sacrifice any portion of the west side of the courtyard, but rather to build upon it.

The potential collision of the projected upper stories of the new wing with the arches on the west side of the Cortile del Maresciallo highlights the de-

Figure 74 (left). Pier on east side of Cortile del Maresciallo, dating from pontificate of Paul II but reerected and reinforced under Paul V, with modern restoration (Bibliotheca Hertziana, D36921)

XII

Figure 75. Elevation project for Piazza S. Pietro with façade of St. Peter's and flanking palaces, engraving, Ferrabosco and Costaguti, 1684 (BAV, Capponi S. 9, VI)

cision not to build the upper stories of Maderno's scheme or even the loggia anticipated by Ferrabosco. This decision establishes the priority of much-needed offices and apartments at the courtyard over the more obviously rhetorical schemes for the new entrance wing. The same set of considerations would be posed with different results under Bernini's aegis when, returning to Maderno's design, he made the north corridor the terminal element of the palace. Projecting this axis to the Scala Regia, he demolished a portion of the west side of the Cortile del Maresciallo leaving it with just two arches, exactly as Maderno had anticipated (Plate 76).

Paul V's Contributions

Paul V's contributions to the palace entrance responded to a long evolution of plans that relate the development of St. Peter's to that of the palace. As

work on the basilica advanced, the palace was enlarged. The new Logge of Gregory XIII, the Palace of Sixtus V, and renovations of existing buildings provided new rooms to absorb the functions of the curia that were displaced by the progressive demolition of the lower palace.[129] These transfers occurred quickly.[130] And while it has been thought that Maderno was not actively involved in this process, our study of the drawings suggests otherwise.[131]

Evidently, the palace entrance was largely Maderno's invention, adjusted and embellished by Ferrabosco to Paul V's taste and his preference for limiting the growth of the palace beyond its historic core. This will explain why Bonanni discussed the commission with reference to Ferrabosco and Vasanzio working together under Maderno's direction.[132] Maderno's career was tied to the Vatican, and to this day his reputation is still based largely on his work at St. Peter's. Little wonder that he did not stop designing where the basilica and the palace were

80

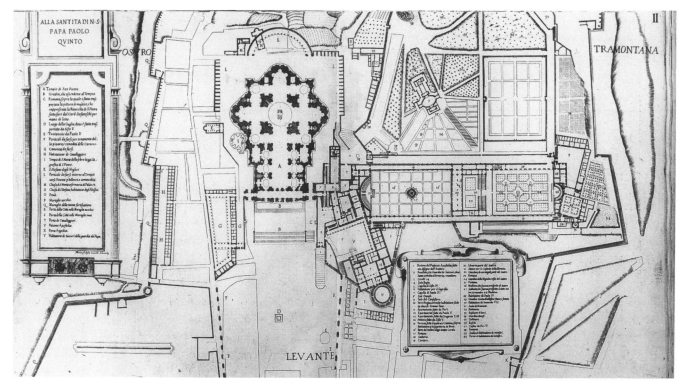

Figure 76. Plan project for Piazza S. Pietro and flanking palaces, engraving, Ferrabosco and Costaguti 1684 (BAV, Capponi S. 9, VI)

conjoined. Whether he designed or even intended a tall tower at the entrance cannot be determined with certainty, but the evidence of the drawings in the Albertina and the alternative schemes published in Bonanni suggests that Ferrabosco was here entirely in charge.

The legacy of Maderno's ambitions survives in Ferrabosco's proposal for twin palaces to flank the forecourt of the basilica, which is among the projects that Ferrabosco claimed as original in his posthumous book (Figs. 75 and 76). Here he simply repeated on the southern palace the tower he had built on the north wing, adding porticoes that extend from both ends of this forecourt into the streets of the Borgo in recollection of Manetti's plans. Much

later, to satisfy Alexander VII's intentions for Piazza S. Pietro, Bernini returned for inspiration to both Maderno's drawings and Ferrabosco's engravings. Bernini's goal was to solve the problem that Maderno had faced most directly: to bring order to the forms of the piazza and the palace in the crucial zone between St. Peter's and a palace entrance aligned with the Borgo Nuovo. Eventually, Bernini surpassed his predecessors by envisioning a route that penetrated and unified the essential entrance features. Unlike Maderno, Ferrabosco, or any earlier architect, Bernini literally saw through obstacles, tunneling a controlling axis all the way to the foot of the Scala Regia.

FOUR

Bernini's Designs from Colonnade to Corridor, 1656–1659

AS we have seen from the description of the monument in Chapter 1, Bernini was able to unify the entrance axis of the palace from the Borgo Nuovo and the end of the north colonnade arm, through the north corridor and the lower portion of the Scala Regia. This sequence of spaces is disposed over rising terrain, yet from the west end of the northern colonnade the entire length of the axis is visible, from the Portone di Bronzo across the gently sloping pavement of the north corridor, past the brightly lit base landing of the Scala Regia, and beyond it to the more steeply rising steps of the staircase. Such a view is possible because the heights of the vaults in each section of the entrance have been ruled by the same concern for a continuous aspect, as has their axial development. For more than 100 meters along the corridor, and for another 30 meters up the staircase, the plan and elevations of the portal, the corridor, and the stairs were calculated with an almost symbiotic consistency.

To the unsuspecting visitor, then, the design of the Scala Regia would appear to be the inevitable sequel to the colonnades, the result of a scheme firmly settled early in the design phases of Piazza S. Pietro. The axis of entrance would have been carefully worked out as an extension of the Borgo Nuovo, so that the corridor and stairs would reveal a continuous path of approach from the piazza to the foot of the steps, and from these into the palace itself.

By contrast with these impressions, the historical evidence offers a surprise. For when all of the drawings, building documents, and other written testimony are read together, the result indicates that the design of the Scala Regia was arrived at by means of an eccentric process, in which all of the components we have mentioned were incorporated progressively and sequentially into a single, one might almost say unpremeditated, ensemble. Thus, when the design for Piazza S. Pietro was initially taken up, Bernini was little concerned about the eventual connection with the palace. Even after the corridors were conceived and their foundations dug, the details of their design remained unsettled for a time. When construction did begin on the north corridor, the design of the Scala Regia in turn could have been foreseen only vaguely. When the corridor was essentially complete, we find Alexander VII calling for drawings for the Scala Regia.

Surely some of our perceptions are colored by accidents of survival. Yet when the remaining evidence is read as a whole, we learn that the entire building sequence had certainly been approved and probably planned incrementally, without the assurance of a binding design anticipating a precisely calculated visual effect.

Instinctively, one searches for evidence to the contrary. After all, the design would itself offer persuasive evidence of an all-embracing scheme. Yet every document, drawing, and contextual circumstance supports the contrary conclusion. In the earliest design stages for the piazza, Bernini's primary concerns involved the composition of the colonnades in plan and elevation, but not their connections with the palace or St. Peter's. These matters of composition in elevation and plan were debated with fervor, and only when they were settled and the construction of the piazza was under way do we find evidence for a design process pertaining to the north corridor. Even then, drawings demonstrate how a large part of that process was undertaken with the assumption that the old Scala Regia would be preserved rather than rebuilt. Later, the notion of creating an entirely new staircase was introduced with spectacularly successful results, which, again, were won incrementally as the expanded version of the project developed in response to structural necessities and aesthetic and functional concerns.

This process of piecemeal planning and construction seems odd and unsettling to the modern mind, and while it may have been more familiar in the seventeenth century, it surely caused some unease among those responsible for providing materials, hiring and directing workers, paying them, and countless other administrative matters. On occasion, as we shall see, there were major disagreements over practical issues, although in the end the extraordinary character of the piazza and the ambitions of the pope, his architect, and their closest advisers prevailed.

The principal concern of this chapter is to determine how the monumental entrance to the palace was incorporated into the piazza scheme. This matter has never been seriously investigated, and to do so it is first necessary to recognize that the north corridor is not a mere link between the colonnade and the narthex of the basilica, but an integral component of the ceremonial entrance to the Vatican Palace. If we accept this assumption, our first job must be to determine how and when the corridors were introduced into the larger scheme for Piazza S. Pietro.

From that point of departure we will be in a position to evaluate the subsequent development of designs for the corridor, which is the topic of the next chapter of this book. Finally, through careful analysis we should be able to see the extent to which these stages in the design process anticipated the configuration of the Scala Regia within the confines of the preexisting palace structure. This will compose the third portion of the design process.[1]

The essential data pertaining to the design and construction of Piazza S. Pietro, the northern corridor, and the Scala Regia are well known, and recent research has fine-tuned a chronology that is hard to improve except in the most minute details. In the previous literature, however, the focus of

study has been the achievement of the piazza, whereas the present overview is meant to create a context for the achievement of a crucial but overlooked aspect of the work, the new entrance to the Vatican Palace. This function has no place in Bernini's earliest designs, insinuating itself only in a subsequent moment in response to critics and rivals. Even after the inclusion of the corridor, an important phase of design would be devoted to consolidating it and completing the processional network along a new staircase.

From a modern perspective, this process will seem appallingly casual, yet it was not. At each step of the way, choices were bound by circumstances, options were circumscribed by physical realities, and designs were modified by structural necessities. In truth, the genius of the design in all its parts is to be found in its expression of aesthetic values generated by prosaic constraints.

Piazza Projects Before Bernini

Unlike Bernini's work from 1656, the earlier piazza projects are not thoroughly studied, although they constitute the history against which the executed scheme must ultimately be understood. In the mid-fifteenth century, Manetti described a piazza measuring 100 × 500 braccie that must have been related to the urban scheme for the Borgo and the monumental entrance to the palace projected by Nicholas V, but we do not know exactly how.[2] The porticoed streets projected through the Borgo would have recalled the covered walks along the medieval Via Cornelia, which ran from the Tiber to the portals of St. Peter's. Bernini's design ultimately reflected the connection of a covered approach to the palace entrance, a relationship obviously facilitated by the opening of the Borgo Nuovo under Alexander VI (see Chapter 2).

Under Pius IV in 1564 the Mantuan ambassador reported a plan to surround the piazza with porticoes, and some demolitions followed. It has not been determined whether these activities were related to the broad scope of an idealized view of Michelangelo's St. Peter's shown in a fresco in the Vatican Library.[3] While the notice of 1564 does not specify the contours of the piazza, the fresco presents the basilica in the midst of a vast, paved piazza bordered

Figure 77. Plan and elevation project for Piazza S. Pietro, engraving, Matthaeus Greuter for Papirio Bartoli (BAV, Chigi P. VII, 9, fol. 43)

by porticoes whose construction would have required the removal of much of the existing palace.

Maderno apparently broke with the tradition of a portico enclosure, for both of his projects take up the problem of the palace entrance without connecting it to a covered approach (Figs. 50, 57). Perhaps for reasons of defense, a second-story loggia was preferable to porticoes; in any case this model was followed by Ferrabosco in the design of the new entrance wing (Fig. 46). In a later project Ferrabosco formulated a trapezoidal piazza flanked by porticoes, whose northern edge leads directly to a stair ascending to the Cortile di S. Damaso (Figs. 75, 76). In the event, no stair was ever built on this side of the palace, although the trapezoidal shape of the piazza and the direct connection between portico and palace entrance would later influence Bernini's thinking in separate stages. Most interesting is the fact that Maderno had evidently anticipated this en-

trance in an opening at the southeastern corner of the palace, behind a defensive tower drawn in chalk, demonstrating as before Ferrabosco's dependence on his older colleague (Fig. 56).

Among the more problematic piazza schemes of the early seventeenth century is the engraving produced for Papirio Bartoli (Fig. 77). Because it was engraved by Matthaeus Greuter (d. 1638), Voss dated it to the 1620s or 1630s.[4] Wittkower, on the other hand, considered the engraving to reflect an earlier project datable between 1613, when Maderno rebuilt the fountain on the piazza (as shown in the scheme), and 1617, when Ferrabosco began the new entrance wing.[5] Wittkower's argument makes good sense also because the scheme appears to provide new space for offices displaced by the ongoing demolitions of the lower palace, as did Maderno's scheme of around 1611–14, composed before a new, more economical solution was proposed.

The Bartoli scheme is responsive to the palace in previously unremarked ways that are directly related to the various entrances. The dog-leg stairs along the right side of the engraving would have assumed the functions of the principal cordonata, carrying up to the level of the Cortile di S. Damaso. As we shall see, this feature anticipates one prominent aspect of the so-called counterproject critical of Bernini's plans. Even more important, indeed prescient, is the connection between the northern portico and the double opening at the foot of the Scala Regia. The shape of the double opening is entirely comparable to Bernini's sketches of it and so is its 16-palmi width (Figs. 108, 109, 112, 113, 114). Thus the Bartoli scheme anticipated Bernini's all-important invention, the axial alignment of the Scala Regia with the northern border of the piazza.

That Bernini had studied the Bartoli scheme is implied by the copy of the engraving preserved in the Chigi Archives.[6] It is also indicated by compositional similarities that have nothing to do with the palace entrance: the division of porticoes into one end and two side sections, the connection of the sides to the flanks of the narthex, and the central placement of the fountain and obelisk. These aspects of the composition reappear in Bernini's foundation medal, Figure 84, where so much of the executed design is incorporated.

By contrast, the connection of piazza and palace in a scheme of the early 1650s made for Innocent X

Figure 78. Elevation project for Piazza S. Pietro, drawing, Carlo Rainaldi (BAV, Chigi P. VII, 9, fol. 40v–41)

(d. 1655) and generally attributed to Carlo Rainaldi reverts in large measure to Ferrabosco's mechanical replication of the entrance tower motif on the south (Figs. 78, 79).[7] Rainaldi's solution was therefore simply to maintain the existing palace entrance and to extend from it a line of porticoes attached to the front of buildings in much the same way that Ferrabosco had also anticipated. For reasons I will indicate below, this appears to have been an initial inspiration for Bernini as well. Other plans by Rainaldi may also reflect his work under Innocent X, but I believe they were redrawn to respond to the challenge of Bernini's designs and should thus be considered at the end of this chapter.[8]

Early Design Chronology

Alexander's intentions for Piazza S. Pietro were announced in a meeting of the Congregation of the Reverenda Fabbrica di S. Pietro on 31 July 1656.[9] In the meeting it was revealed that the piazza would be formed by a portico (*porticus*) and that Bernini (the pope's favorite artist) would provide a design for the purpose of further discussions.[10] These decisions were made by papal fiat, and Alexander VII delegated the administration and supervision of the enterprise to the congregation of prelates who composed the Reverenda Fabbrica di S. Pietro, the administrative body responsible for overseeing the maintenance and embellishment of the basilica.

Figure 79. Plan project for Piazza S. Pietro, drawing, Carlo Rainaldi (BAV, Chigi P. VII, 9, fol. 42)

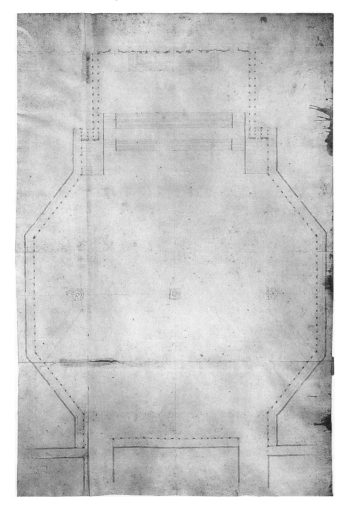

By entrusting the work to the Fabbrica, Alexander expressed his own view of the piazza as an extension of the basilica rather than the palace. Unremarked in the literature on the topic, this notion represents a basic departure from all earlier piazza projects. Previously proposed schemes for Piazza S. Pietro were always connected with enlargements of the palace, usually including new accommodations for the Chapter of St. Peter's and space for the conclaves. Inevitably, Alexander's position could not be strictly maintained: the piazza, even if it did not embrace an extension of the palace, would necessarily have a specific relation to it, as well as to the urban matrix. As a result of this fact, and quite paradoxically, the ceremonial entrance to the palace would be constructed under the Fabbrica's aegis – an unlikely event in any other scenario.

The Congregazione della Reverenda Fabbrica di S. Pietro was established in the sixteenth century for the construction of new St. Peter's. It was not until 1605, during the short-lived pontificate of Leo XI, that the congregation was institutionalized by the appointment of eleven cardinals. Alexander VII was also keen on formalizing the activities of the Fabbrica, issuing a series of protocols that prescribed weekly meetings of a "congregazione piccola" including the architect and representatives of the Fabbrica, meetings of the full body every two weeks, formal use of an agenda, and a method of reporting and recording minutes for every meeting.[11]

The project for the piazza was presented in a "congregazione piccola" by Virgilio Spada, who must have known of the pope's intentions at least some time before the meeting. He was probably selected to make the announcement because of his previous interest in developing the piazza. In 1651 Spada had proposed a scheme to open the "spina" from Piazza S. Pietro to Castel Sant'Angelo by demolishing the city blocks between the Borgo Nuovo and the Borgo Vecchio. Bernini supported this initiative, which included a piazza that was rectilinear in shape and called for a two-story loggia "with mezzanine." The lower portico would have included passages for carriages, and the upper portions would have provided living quarters for the canons of the basilica.[12]

From the notices following the announcement of Alexander's project, we learn that the pope had a clear vision of the general character of "the portico"

for the piazza, but only a foggy notion about its layout and relationship with existing buildings, including the Vatican Palace. Within ten days of the announcement, and through his nephew Flavio Chigi, Alexander conferred with Bernini.[13] Shortly after that, Alexander made his desires more explicit. The portico should be detached from the basilica but form angles at the ends, presumably to create a sense of spatial enclosure. The porticoes were to be laid out as close to parallel as the site would permit. They

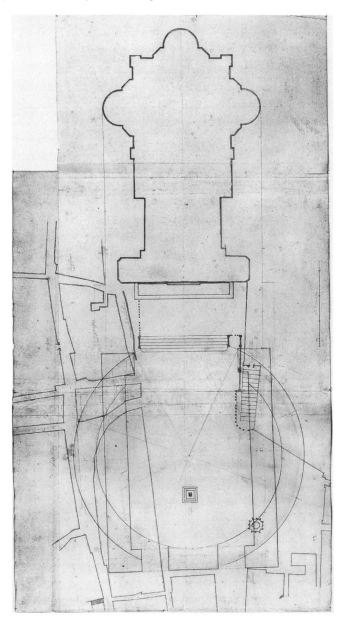

Figure 80. Circular and rectangular projects for Piazza S. Pietro, drawing (BAV, Chigi P. VII, 9, fol. 32v–33)

were to have no buildings over them and were to be capped with balustrades and statues ("senza fabrica sopra ma co' balustri e con statue ad ogni pilastrino"). These features are described in notations in Alexander's diary for 13 August 1656.[14]

Since the porticoes were to be arranged as close to parallel as possible, we can assume that existing buildings confined early projects to trapezoidal shapes, suggesting in turn a reliance on the precedent set by the porticoes in Ferrabosco's scheme of the early seventeenth century that had also influenced Spada's plan.[15] This deduction is confirmed in the Congregation minutes of 19 August 1656, when the greater width of the piazza near the church was criticized for its lack of correspondence with the narrower east side.[16]

One of the interesting features of Ferrabosco's piazza scheme is the way that his porticoes, attached to the façades of preexisting buildings, sought to connect essential features of the local topography. In particular, we can see how the north portico would have run from the Borgo Nuovo to the walls of the Vatican Palace, where a new entrance was intended to provide a link between the piazza and the Cortile di S. Damaso.[17] By contrast, we simply do not know whether Alexander VII or Bernini anticipated any changes to the palace entrance in the early stages of designing the piazza in 1656.

In fact, it is hard to determine exactly when considerations of the palace entrance first entered the design process. The first graphic evidence of these concerns appears on a drawing where the words "Ingresso del Palazzo Pontificio" were inscribed at the Portone di Bronzo (though hardly visible in Fig. 80). The drawing presents alternative plans for a piazza, one rectangular and the other circular. Very light chalk lines, almost invisible in photographs, show the width of the Borgo Nuovo traced up to the portal. Yet the alternative schemes for the porticoes surrounding the piazza do not defer to the presence of the portal or the street axis, and this means that the entrance was still not part of the discussions. Since one of the schemes on the drawing is a rectangle with nearly parallel sides, we may presume that this drawing postdates the 19 August meeting, when the trapezoidal shape of the piazza was rejected.[18]

Late in August 1656, Alexander consulted the learned Lucas Holstenius, librarian at the Vatican,

regarding his report "On Ancient Porticoes and Their Diversity." The report emphasized the prevalence of porticoes with double and triple, as well as single passages ("portici semplici, doppi, triplici") in ancient Greece, although the pope took particular interest in double porticoes.[19] In October 1656, Bernini presented Alexander with a design for "portici doppi," so that they might consider an alternative to the single portico that the artist had been studying. Ideas about both single and double porticoes remained current for a time. A drawing in the Chigi Archives that may be dated as late as March 1657 shows transverse sections of a single and a double portico and how each might provide shelter from the sun at different times of year (Fig. 81).[20]

The turning point in the design of the piazza occurred on 17 March 1657, when Bernini presented a scheme "in ovata forma," that is, an oval plan. He credited the scheme in part to Alexander, and, de-

Figure 81. Studies for angles of sun and alternative transverse sections for Piazza S. Pietro, drawing (BAV, Chigi P. VII, 9, fol. 34)

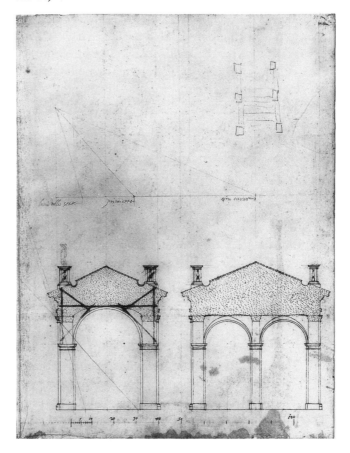

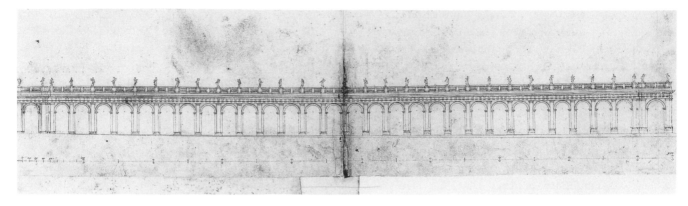

Figure 82. Proposed elevation for Piazza S. Pietro, drawing (BAV, Chigi P. VII, 9, fol. 35)

spite the obvious flattery embodied in the gesture, there may be considerable truth to the statement.[21] Alexander claimed to have studied architecture as a youth, and some drawings are now attributed to him.[22] The statement finds independent support in the not always flattering papal biography of the contemporary Sforza Pallavicino, which was published posthumously.[23] Moreover, the close communication between the artist and his patron would support a joint attribution. On the subject of the piazza they had communicated no fewer than five times from the beginning of the enterprise to a period of days before the presentation of the oval plan.[24] The involvement of the pope would also explain why previous designs had elicited repeated objections whereas the Fabbrica was unanimous in agreeing to this proposal. As it turned out, the design would change drastically in succeeding months.

At this stage the porticoes were composed as a system of arches with applied Doric pilasters and entablature facing the exteriors and crowned by balustrades and statues. These features are faithfully rendered in a broad workshop drawing (Fig. 82).[25] To study the effect of the scheme, a full-scale model was begun and finished by 14 April 1657. It consisted of three arches between four single pilasters with Doric capitals and full trabeation, including a triglyph-and-metope frieze.[26] Of the plans for connecting the piazza to the palace, we know only that the north portico was to be terminated at the "porta della Guardia dei Svizzeri," which might refer to the old Portone di Bronzo or to a portal leading to the barracks of the Guard.[27] In any case, it is generally assumed that at this time the Ferrabosco clock tower

entrance to the palace was to have remained intact on the site.[28]

To the oval design presented to the Congregation of the Fabbrica on 17 March 1657, Spada provided a prompt and lengthy response. In a memorandum dated 19 March, he praised the oval configuration but criticized the "puny" appearance of the single pilasters that looked like just "so many straws." He recommended doubling them. Spada also opposed the single portico, which would not provide adequate protection from sun, rain, and wind. The ancients, he said, used single porticoes only when they were attached to buildings; isolated, the single porticoes did battle with two enemies, one on each side. (This would have been an issue to study in the drawing comparing the sections of single and double porticoes.) He also found the dimensions of the single passage too narrow, recommending a width no less than the 19–20 palmi of the porticoes at the Quirinal Palace, and more properly 24 palmi to accommodate two carriages abreast. Moreover, in a sentence that I believe deserves special emphasis, Spada offered the means to realize Holstenius's "portici triplici" with a continuous annular vault over the central passage and flat ceilings over the side sections. This is the configuration that Bernini soon adopted and ultimately built.[29]

Spada's comparison to the Quirinal Palace, Alexander VII's favored residence, is telling. It suggests that Spada was thinking about the porticoes of the piazza in relation to the papal residence, and the point is made explicit when he remarked upon their function as routes of approach to the Vatican Palace. For in the memorandum, Spada reminded Alexander of the need to accommodate both the canons who came to the Vatican in rain and hot sun "all year 'round, twice a day" and the "cardinals, prelates, princes, and courtiers who meet there when His Holiness is in residence."[30] It is the first explicit acknowledgment that the portico around the piazza was intended to lead to the palace as well as St. Peter's. Even the foreign travelers were aware of this, as Skippon's notes of 1663 make clear. "Round the piazza," he wrote, "this pope Alexander VII is building a most stately portico (Cavaliere Bernini being architect), having four rows of great pillars, in the middle a coach may drive, and on each side people may walk; a balcony round the top."[31]

The need for protection from the elements was a point also made in Sforza Pallavicino's papal biography.[32] It was a theme almost instantly picked up for criticism by the Venetian ambassador in a letter of 9 July 1660, who wrote how "the pope claims, and he told me himself many times, that the porticoes must serve as protection for the carriages from the sun and the rain . . . but since the construction was not done in a manner that could ever entirely

fulfill the intent, it becomes universally considered to be a superfluous work and expense, especially since he has abandoned the *stanza* of St. Peter for that of the Quirinal."[33]

Spada's criticism, pertinent but colorful and expansive in tone, took quick effect. Less than a month after the full-scale model was completed in April 1657, Bernini responded with a plan and elevation that Alexander confirmed, apparently with relief ("e lo concludiamo così"), on 20 May 1657.[34] The nature of the plan and elevation at that time is made clear in the evidence for subsequent events. On 3 August 1657, the pope ordered the foundation medal for the cornerstone ceremony and specified the inscription that would appear on the medal.[35] These words had been provided by Holstenius in response to Alexander's request: asking for suggestions for the inscription, Alexander made a sketch of the piazza, which he described as a "portico triplice trionfale" (Fig. 83).[36] The triple portico therefore predates August 1657. Because Alexander was so emphatic in accepting Bernini's new plan and elevation on 20 May, it is reasonable to conclude that the pope's en-

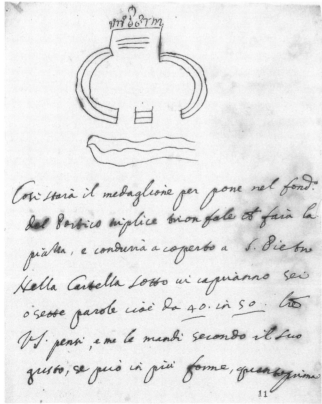

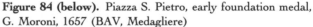

Figure 83 (left). Sketch and text for Piazza S. Pietro foundation medal, drawing, Alexander VII, 1657 (BAV, Chigi R. VIII, C, fol. 11)

Figure 84 (below). Piazza S. Pietro, early foundation medal, G. Moroni, 1657 (BAV, Medagliere)

thusiasm was due to the appearance of the new scheme, one that embraced Spada's arched central passage and side aisles with flat ceilings.

Exactly how Spada's influence was exercised over the design may have been forecast by his own wiles. In the passage that immediately follows his proposal for a triple portico, Spada suggested that if Alexander approved the idea, it would "not be difficult to find the means to make Cavalier Bernini appear to be its author, so that he will not be annoyed that others want to improve his designs."[37] In this, too, Spada was evidently successful, having communicated the idea and hidden his own role as its inventor both to the artist and to most of posterity.

The foundation medal was produced in a hurry for the ceremonial laying of the cornerstone of the project. Hastily organized, the ceremony took place on 28 August 1657, and a low mass was said in St. Peter's. From later correspondence we know that the medalist Gaspare Moroni had no time to strike the medals and therefore simply cast them, in a procedure not common since the papacy of Paul V.[38] The scheme on the medal reverse shows the piazza enclosed by freestanding colonnades on the north, south and east of the open space (Fig. 84). On the axis of the basilica the obelisk appears with a single fountain. The colonnade is articulated with pairs of columns, no doubt the response to Spada's criticism about the visual weakness of earlier vertical membering, and is trabeated with a continuous horizontal entablature, with its balustrade and pairs of statues. In my analysis, the elevation represented on the medal must have incorporated three passages like the executed monument. Most important, the line of trabeation is firmly joined to the basilica by the "arms" (bracci in the documents) that became the enclosed corridors.

It is fitting that the design on the foundation medal, influenced in so many ways by Spada's criticism, shows the corridors juxtaposed to the palace. Indeed, the medal provides our earliest securely dated indication that the tower entrance to the palace would be demolished and replaced.[39] At this stage, with the series of paired statues continuing west over both the inner and outer edges of the piazza, the north corridor appears to stand free of the palace. Yet from what we have learned of Spada's opinions, a functional connection with the palace was clearly of concern.

Later Phases of the Piazza Design

The scheme on the medal was but one of the designs under consideration at the time of the foundation ceremony. Just days after the cornerstone was laid, Bernini proposed to substitute single columns of larger diameter for the smaller double columns that appear on the medal. This proposal was recorded in Alexander VII's diary on 2 September 1657, with the following words: "Audientia al . . . cav. Bernini col disegno ultimo di colonne più grosse e non doppie."[40] By 15 September 1657, Spada reported in a letter to a Sienese correspondent that three plans had been discussed and (exaggerating somewhat) that nothing but their oval contours and general dimensions had been decided. Then he rehearsed the history of the design process, providing some important new details as he did so.[41]

The first design, Spada wrote, was composed of a single passage with arches and pilasters. But Alexander wanted a double passage and reiterated his insistence that there be no buildings atop it and that it serve the palace and the basilica exclusively. This decision disappointed those who foresaw a chapter house and conclave spaces over the porticoes.[42] Departing for a moment from Spada's account, we should note the association of the double portico with the need to serve the palace and the basilica. The double portico that Bernini presented in October 1656 may indeed have been inspired by the requirements of traffic to and from the palace.

Spada then described a second design characterized by a trabeated system borne on pairs of columns replacing the arches and pilasters. The column pairs were to be uniformly spaced, so that there would be a greater number of columns on the exterior circumference than on the interior. A third design consisted of a triple portico, whose center passage would be 25 palmi wide and barrel-vaulted, and the side passages 12½ palmi wide with architraves. It remained undecided whether the columns would be single or paired, the ends being located at the "porta della guardia dei Svizzeri" and the Borgo Nuovo.[43]

Spada's correspondent was Leonardo Agostini, an agent of Cardinal Leopoldo de'Medici; and with a letter to the cardinal dated 3 November 1657, Agostini sent a drawing that must date from the period Spada had described in the previous month. The drawing depicts the west end of the colonnade,

Figure 85. Plan and elevation of Piazza S. Pietro, drawing (by kind permission of the Ministero per i Beni Culturali e Ambientali; Archivio di Stato, Florence, Carteggio artisti, 17, fol. 41)

which is shown as a paired column system in the Doric order with a blank (nontriglyphic) frieze (Fig. 85). In essence, the drawing provides evidence that the entrance to the palace was under careful scrutiny. The drawing is from Bernini's studio but intended for a Florentine because the scales refer to "palmi romani" and "braccie fiorentine."[44]

The ambivalence with regard to the system of paired or single columns was embodied in a new full-scale model erected between September and November 1657.[45] The model consisted of six fluted Doric columns, again with a blank frieze. The fluting was surely intended to compensate for the fact that the columns would be pieced rather than monolithic, and the blank frieze accommodated the radial arrangement of columns of increasing size that would otherwise have required increasing the number and

size of triglyphs and metopes from interior to exterior elevations. (It is commonly thought that Bernini inserted an Ionic frieze in a Doric system, but the size and the features of the entablature adhere to the Doric order without triglyphs and metopes, similar to the system Peruzzi used at Palazzo Massimo alle Colonne [1533–36] to cite a conspicuous example.)[46] Documents indicate that each of the six columns was provided with just ten of the twenty flutes that complement a Doric column shaft.[47] The model must therefore have been intended primarily for a study of its exterior effect.

The second full-scale model was finished by 6 November 1657, when the accounts of the woodworkers were submitted. On 10 November, Alexander visited the site and was reportedly disappointed with the result. The nature of his objections is not entirely clear from the avviso recording the visit, but one concern was expense. Another problem, pointed out by observers, was the lack of correspondence with "the design of the façade of St. Peter's."[48] Because the scale represented by the model remained unchanged through final construction, it is possible that the "errors in good architecture" mentioned in the report of his visit had to do with conjoining two distinct systems of architecture.

By January 1658, the model was being dismantled and the purchase and transport of travertine arranged.[49] In March, on the feast of the Cross, Alexander arrived in procession at St. Peter's, and before returning to the Quirinal, he viewed "the first foundations and results" of the porticoes in the form of four column bases at the middle of the north colonnade.[50] By 20 September, the colonnade had begun to assume impressive dimensions, with 24 columns erected.[51] Discussion about the design of the piazza had been resolved to the extent that building activity could replace the proposals and debates that had dominated the enterprise up to this time. The project had become a reality, as yet fragmentary but clearly under way.

The Counterprojects

From the first announcement of the piazza in the meeting of the Fabbrica on 31 July 1656, Alexander's visionary scheme drew opposition. Cardinal Pallotto objected to the possibility of releasing infection by digging in the Vatican soil, he objected to the expense of demolitions that would be entailed, and he raised the matter of propriety in pursuing such an expensive enterprise at a time of "calamity and financial difficulties" for the church.[52] Within two months, the project was also "troubled" by a design promoted by Bernini's detractors who wished to do him a bad turn.[53] Thus, there were objections to both the project and its architect. The situation was encouraged by the initial vagueness of the project. Alexander was obviously open to considering design options inflected by ancient sources and iconographic meanings, as the discussions with Holstenius prove. Spada's memorandum following the presentation of the oval plan exemplifies the intense scrutiny of Bernini's proposals. Yet again, after the construction of the second full-scale model, there were "many" who came to identify various "eccettioni et errori di buona architettura" in the latest configuration. Under the circumstances it is easy to understand why Bernini jealously guarded the commission for the piazza and was loath to see developments in design to which he could lay no claim.

In addition to these notices, there is another body of evidence to suggest that the schemes of Bernini and Alexander VII were open to criticism: a group of drawings now gathered as a suite that Wittkower termed the "counter-project." The counterproject consists of some 25 drawings on 14 leaves bound together in the late nineteenth or early twentieth century. The drawings were first published by Andrea Busiri Vici in 1893 as original works by Bernini.[54] At the time Busiri Vici was their owner. They subsequently passed through several hands into the Brandegee Collection, Faulkner Farm, Massachusetts. There are numerous references to them in the older literature on Bernini, but in 1931 Wittkower was the first to recognize the designs as criticisms of Bernini's plans for the piazza rather than autograph works.[55] In 1963, the bound set of drawings was donated to the Holy See by the Rev. Wilfred A. Tisdell, Winchester, Massachusetts. The set is now located in the Vatican Library.[56]

Although the counterproject drawings have never been studied for this purpose, they provide our most extensive evidence for the earliest thoughts about the palace entrance. It is therefore important to review their character and contents. Wittkower believed that the drawings composed a suite intended to illustrate a now-lost treatise critical of Bernini's schemes.[57] According to this thesis, the drawings were sponsored by a single patron or critic and produced as "a last powerful appeal to the Congregation [of the Fabbrica] before construction of the piazza was started in the Spring of 1659."[58] Without the treatise, Wittkower was forced to rely on historical and iconographic analysis to clarify the significance of each drawing. Responding to the numbers inscribed in the upper right of many (but not all) of the sheets in what he took to be a seventeenth-century hand, Wittkower discussed the drawings in a manner that supposedly reflected their original order.

To this day, Wittkower's iconographical analysis has never been surpassed or refuted, nor have other aspects of his argument been significantly developed. Most recently, Menichella has proposed dating the counterprojects to late 1657 or early 1658, and attributing the work to someone "in the ambience of the Fabbrica" and elsewhere to "an observer outside of and in opposition to the creative debate" guiding Bernini's plans. She also doubts their influence on Alexander's thinking, given the longer course of events in the design process.[59] Del Pesco dates the counterprojects to the period before 21 June 1659, when the Fabbrica heard arguments "against Cav. Bernino" which were relayed to the pope by Spada.[60] A careful review of the evidence reveals new aspects of the counterproject drawings and may encourage a rethinking of their nature and importance.

If we recognize that the old numeration is not necessarily the original one, and perhaps not even from the seventeenth century, we are free to consider the drawings in relation to architectural themes. To go a step further, it might be suggested that, in the seventeenth-century context, the clarity of their purpose may have been apparent to anyone familiar with the project and that no text was needed to explain them. Many of the drawings are presented in pairs contrasting the weaker solution of Bernini's scheme with the superior solution of the critic, a method well known from later epochs.[61] In these cases an explanatory text is superfluous.

To be sure, not all of the drawings are conceived as comparisons, and for those that are not, Wittkower's iconographic analysis is entirely convincing. Yet the variety of design alternatives and iconographic presentations encompassed by the drawings, whether presented singly or in pairs, makes it unlikely that they were produced at a single moment in the design campaign or that they accompanied a written statement, unless that statement was itself a progressive account of the ongoing design process. In my opinion, the drawings reflect projects and critiques forwarded at different moments during the design procedure that were later redrawn as a record of various criticisms after the entire design was settled. Bernini certainly had rivals and detractors, as we have indicated, and they were undoubtedly capable of gathering for posterity the cumulative objections to his designs registered during the long *iter* of the project, if only to prove that the genius of the final scheme was not without its flaws and did not spring full-blown from the architect's head.

Indeed Spada's criticism of the pilasters ultimately resulted in the use of columns on a grand scale, and his scheme for a triple portico, like the ancient "portici triplici" described by Holstenius, was also adopted. It may even be that Spada or another contemporary wished to illustrate how some of the final features of the design were in fact borrowed from the critical responses that Bernini had to shoulder. But the only sensible way to understand the counterproject schemes as a group is to view them as a running critique of Bernini's ideas that points out his lapses and offers solutions to them.

From the drawings it becomes clear that the author or authors of the counterprojects hammered at three essential weaknesses of Bernini's piazza schemes: the lack of a graceful connection between the arcades and the basilica, the lack of symbolic form, and the lack of concern for an entrance to the papal palace. Of these considerations, the first two may be illustrated in a counterproject juxtaposing two ground plans (Fig. 86).[62] On the left of the sheet the critic presents the figure of Christ superimposed

Figure 86. Counterproject plan for Piazza S. Pietro (left) and critique (right), drawing (BAV, Vat. lat. 14620, fol. 3)

Figure 87. Counterproject scheme for Piazza S. Pietro looking west, drawing (BAV, Vat. lat. 14620, fol. 2)

on the plan of the basilica. The figure stands upon the "mounts" of the Chigi family, whose armorial symbols fit neatly within the configuration of the piazza in front of St. Peter's. The illustration is a punning reference, as Wittkower explained, to the notion of Peter's church founded *super hanc petram*, the rock referring also to the Chigi "monti" which formed part of Alexander's escutcheon. From Bernini's plan, shown on the right, no such interpretation can be read, and his critic pointed out an additional problem by tracing a dotted line behind which the visitor on the piazza could not have seen the Benediction Loggia on the façade of St. Peter's.

While a full reconsideration of the counterprojects must be undertaken elsewhere, for present purposes it must suffice to examine those drawings pertaining to the first and third points for the arranging of a palace entrance within the context of the new piazza. The leitmotif of the earliest counterprojects is a piazza laid out in a circular configuration, with the circle broken where it joins the basilica façade and at the Piazza Rusticucci, which opens up to the Borgo (Figs. 87, 88).[63] The principal architectural motif is a two-story serlian arcade lining the fronts of buildings that would have served as offices for

the curia and perhaps space for conclaves. What was already built on the north of the piazza was to be exactly replicated on the south.

In all these respects, it is obvious that the counterproject and its variants are pastiches drawn from projects of the earlier seventeenth century, all of which sought to extend the papal palace eastward over the structures that would border the piazza. The notion of articulating the fronts of buildings on major urban spaces with serlian arches can be associated with a number of conspicuous precedents, such as Sansovino's Libreria in Venice (1537) and Palladio's Basilica in Vicenza (1545). The importance of arcades lining the streets and piazze obviously survived from the time of Nicholas V and Pius II. If the Emilian Spada exercised some influence, it is also possible that the image of Bologna's arcaded streets may be perceived in these schemes. Unfortunately, the critics or patrons who drew the counterprojects remain unknown.[64]

A date early in the design process is likely for the genesis of these early counterprojects because the buildings over and behind the arcades were expressly rejected by the pope on 13 August 1656, when he clearly stated that the porticoes be free-

Figure 88. Counterproject scheme for Piazza S. Pietro looking east, drawing (BAV, Vat. lat. 14620, fol. 14)

standing and have no buildings upon them. At the same time, Alexander VII insisted on crowning features composed of balustrades with statues, which are not present in these counterprojects.[65] Although Spada still regretted these constraints upon the design a year later, there is no reason to suggest his continued promotion of drawings with these features.[66] Rather, it is more reasonable to presume that the early counterprojects had their origins in ideas discussed before the medal was cast for the foundation ceremony on 28 August 1657, because the design upon the medal incorporates the definitive contours of the piazza and many of the principal features in elevation.

Criticism of the piazza's contours had been developed in a well-known elevation in which the arms of the piazza are likened to the arms of the church (Fig. 89).[67] Here the point was to demonstrate again that in Bernini's oval scheme the colonnades do not join the basilica in a "natural" way. To illustrate the point the critic has drawn full-length figures of St. Peter superimposed on the basilica and Bernini's oval piazza (left), and contrasted it with a schematic vision of the circular counterproject (right). Whereas the outstretched arms of St. Peter embrace the contours of

the counterproject in a perfectly coordinated manner, Bernini's oval project requires the arms of St. Peter to be awkwardly double-jointed. The announcement of Bernini's oval scheme in the minutes of the Fabbrica for the meeting on 17 March 1657 would serve as a *terminus post quem* for dating this counterproject.[68]

The "human analogy" proposed in the counterproject criticism was undoubtedly inspired by the characterization of the oval scheme as representing the church with arms open to confirm the faith of the pious and to welcome heretics and disbelievers.[69] Both the justification and the illustrations are different from the analogies based on number and proportion that Renaissance architects relied on, of course, but the power of the contrast would have carried no less conviction in the seventeenth century. The pained face and contorted pose of St. Peter on the left of the drawing, in contrast to the serenity of his expression and graceful pose on the right, conveyed in a literal manner the objections to Bernini's intentions that would have disturbed the Prince of the Apostles himself.

Architectural traditions at St. Peter's are long-lived, and I suspect that the counterproject featuring the apostle was meant to recall the famous story of

Figure 89. St. Peter's counterproject critique of Piazza S. Pietro (left) and alternative (right), drawing, (BAV, Vat. lat. 14620, fol. 1)

Bramante, who was rejected from the gates of Heaven by no less than St. Peter himself because the architect had ruined the venerable basilica with his changes to it. It is as though the worst offenses of "Bramante ruinante" were being revisited upon the basilica by Bernini, with the response registered in St. Peter's contorted pose and anguished expression.[70]

From these sheets, the straight connection between the colonnades and the basilica can be identified as the offending aspect of Bernini's design that necessitated the break in the outstretched arms of St. Peter and a compromise in the visibility of the basilica façade.[71] In consequence, we must conclude that Bernini, in presenting his ideas to the Fabbrica, cannot have provided a convincing raison d'être for this portion of his scheme.

As generally believed, one of Bernini's initial solutions for the oval plan probably called for attaching the colonnades to the preexisting clock tower entrance (Fig. 90).[72] Here the oval is represented by a compact curve removed from the Ferrabosco tower. The connection is made by a series of arches at a level that is a story below the level of the clock. The colonnade is composed of a single passage, free-

standing and surmounted by a balustrade and statues, in accord with the pope's dicta. Nevertheless, essential features are still under discussion as is indicated by the ambiguous combination of columns and serlian arches.

Wittkower has suggested that in this drawing the critic "obviously wishes to show that it was not too late at this stage to alter Bernini's plans and adapt them to his own scheme."[73] In point of fact, the ambiguous rendering of the elevation with isolated columns and with arches indicates a moment of transition in the design process between the arches originally suggested and the columns that would ultimately be employed. What links this drawing with the counterprojects discussed above are the dotted lines that indicate a taller, broader circumference for the piazza that would be shaped as a single imposing curve. The contour of the dotted lines may be traced from the end of the colonnade on the right, through the tops of the balustrade figures in front of the Palace of Sixtus V, and across the entablature below the clock on Ferrabosco's tower. The revised form of the scheme would thus resemble the curve of the earlier counterprojects in which the border elements of the piazza were attached directly to the basilica,

Figure 90. Counterproject scheme for Piazza S. Pietro (left) and critique (right), drawing (BAV, Vat. lat. 14620, fol. 10)

except that here they are attached to the palace entrance.[74]

In the broad counterproject view toward St. Peter's, a perfectly symmetrical composition is dominated by a two-story loggia overlooking the piazza. Behind the serlian arches on the north rise the Palace of Sixtus V and the Logge and, on the south side of the piazza, the symmetrically corresponding buildings reproduced in Figure 87.[75] Apart from the enormous amount of new construction envisioned, this conception would have necessitated the demolition of significant parts of the existing palace, including the whole Ferrabosco wing, the clock tower, and the wedge-shaped building of Paul V that led to the end of the Logge. Recollections of the clock tower, whose origins went back to old St. Peter's, would have been preserved in the pairs of campanili incorporated into the loggia system on both north and south sides.

The campanili in the early counterproject views may have been intended also to serve as stairwells, as suggested by the steps located behind and in front of them (Fig. 86). Stairs behind the tower in front of the Cortile di S. Damaso would have brought the visitor directly into the heart of the palace. The destruction of the Ferrabosco wing would therefore re-

quire not relocating the palace entrance but rather reshaping it. Statues flanking the stairs on the piazza signaled the importance of the new stairs.

The details of the entrance were worked out on three counterproject drawings that modify and elaborate the scheme in a daring manner. One of them shows a view into the colonnade and up the stairs that lead to the Cortile di S. Damaso (Fig. 91).[76] The second drawing is a plan (Fig. 92).[77] Finally, a third drawing shows the Cortile di S. Damaso, with the stairs in its midst and the campanile on axis with the stairs; the Palace of Sixtus V is depicted on the left and the Logge on the right (Fig. 92).[78]

The perspective view from the portico shows the weapons of the Swiss Guard, a small arsenal that would have been kept at the palace entrance. The plan and perspective of the courtyard are consistent in showing that the thirteen bays of the Logge would be reduced to eight, by the loss of the five southernmost bays. The designer was clearly no partisan of Raphael, whose Logge frescoes would have been amputated. The stairs were to rise from the piazza to a landing where the visitor could turn left or right and follow the steps up to the courtyard level in a composition well known in palace architecture.[79] The Chigi emblems (monti and star) appear on the

Figure 91. Counterproject scheme for porticoes and palace stairs, drawing (BAV, Vat. lat. 14620, fol. 7)

campanili towering over the piazza like a signpost in front of the staircase entrance. There was, as we have seen, a long tradition for the presence of an entrance at this location, but given the absence of other evidence for Bernini's thoughts about the palace entrance, it is likely that these features predate his design for the corridors that would link the piazza to the palace, and may in fact be a criticism of his lapse in this regard, as Wittkower suggested.[80]

A variant of the proposed palace entrance is provided on yet another counterproject, which sought to preserve the famed Logge (shown as 12 rather than its full 13 bays) while retaining the essence of the composition already proposed for the piazza (Fig. 93).[81] In this scheme, the terminal bays of the Logge overhang the portico of the piazza, borne on a projecting serlian motif. The motif reiterates the main theme of the portico and creates a prominent distinction between the palace and the basilica, which are connected only by two low arches. In this composition, the author seems intent upon salvaging the earlier scheme, which was destined for instant rejection because of its disregard for the integrity of the Logge. The earlier schemes (Figs. 87, 88, 89, 91, and 92) undoubtedly date from the brief period – perhaps no more than two weeks – before 13 August 1656, when Alexander VII ordered that the porti-

coes have no buildings over them but rather be surmounted by balustrades and statues. Figure 93 on the other hand, with its single story, balustrades, and statues, must postdate that papal order. The lightly drawn building projected behind the portico on the right side of the same drawing suggests some lingering hope for enlarging the palace behind the new contours of the piazza. This possibility would not have been ruled out until the pope accepted the plan "in ovata forma" on 17 March 1657, which serves as a *terminus ante quem* for this drawing.

Two responses to the oval plan were, as we have seen, the drawings on Figures 89 and 88. A related response was presented on yet another counterproject, which concerns the view of the piazza from the Borgo Nuovo (Fig. 94).[82] We may think of all three of these counterprojects as last-ditch efforts both to call Bernini's stewardship into question and to oppose the oval scheme.

In the views from the Borgo Nuovo, Bernini's solution on the right is contrasted with the counterproject solution on the left. Bernini's solution preserves the Ferrabosco tower, the wedge-shaped wing of Paul V, and the Logge hovering over it. By contrast, the counterproject proposes remodeling the wedge-shaped wing of Paul V, whose eastern face would become a double-bay unit capped by a pedi-

Figure 92. Counterproject scheme for palace stairs from Piazza S. Pietro in plan (left) and perspective looking south (right), drawing (BAV, Vat. lat. 14620, fol. 8)

Figure 93. Counterproject scheme for porticoes and hanging Logge, drawing (BAV, Vat. lat. 14620, fol. 9)

99

Figure 94. Counterproject critique of Piazza S. Pietro (right) and alternative (left) seen from Borgo Nuovo, drawing (BAV, Vat. lat. 14620, fol. 6)

ment. Wittkower drew special attention to the motif in the upper right of the drawing, where a snake biting its tail symbolizes eternity. The symbol is an emblem of the formal continuity established by the circular piazza proposal. By contrast, the diagram above the rendition of Bernini's project is meant to remind the viewer of its episodic aspect, and how little the presence and character of his piazza is suggested by a view from the Borgo Nuovo. (That the view from this vantage point was important enough to be critiqued supports my reading of Bernini's eventual design.)

We must proceed a step beyond Wittkower's analysis to recognize that the concern of the drawings is not only, or even primarily, the composition of the piazza but rather the reciprocal relationships of piazza, basilica, and palace. In Bernini's scheme, the divisions between these components are, at best, slurred by the jumble of palace rooflines and their relations to the clock tower and the basilica façade. In the counterproject, the skyline of the palace is consolidated, and it is conspicuously separated from the basilica. As in the earliest counterproject design (Figs. 87, 88,) and the later scheme for a new palace entrance (Fig. 93), the terminal bay of Maderno's attic is transformed into a volute that serves formally to pull the basilica away from the palace.[83] For the critics, two low arches surmounted by statues form

the connection between the palace and basilica. Thus, in my opinion, the snake biting its tail symbolizes the formal integrity the critic hoped would inform the piazza and also the palace in relation to the basilica.[84]

The latest in the series of counterprojects still concerns the north side of the piazza (Fig. 95).[85] At this stage in the design process, which must be sometime after fixing the oval plan as a triple passageway supported on single columns, hence after the diary entry on 2 September 1657, the major issue must have been a matter of establishing the scale of the colonnade and the definitive form for the corridor.[86] The corridor is depicted as a continuation of the colonnade, that is, an open portico rather than the enclosed passage that was finally built. (We don't know whether this was a reflection of Bernini's plan or a counterproject.) Chalk lines indicate that the corridor would continue the axis of the Borgo Nuovo.

The drawing also points out potential problems of sight lines from the piazza where it was desirable to see the basilica façade and the palace, especially on those occasions when the pope offered public benedictions. The fact that this was not possible was obviously considered a significant flaw in the scheme.[87] Yet to emphasize this weakness of the composition at such a late moment in the design pro-

Figure 95. Counterproject critique of sight lines, drawing (BAV, Vat. lat. 14620, fol. 11)

cess can only have been an act of desperation on the part of those advocating the circular plan, which would have resolved the issue. In retrospect, it is more significant that this flaw in Bernini's design was accepted as a necessary defect and ultimately incorporated in the final design.

Later Chronology and the Beginning of Construction

The foundation medal of 28 August 1657 is the first certain indication that a corridor would replace the tower entrance to the palace. Because the medal shows crowning statues on both sides of both the north and south corridors, it is at least conceivable that the passages were intended to be freestanding, with the north corridor removed from the palace. This is consistent with the possibility, hinted at in the latest counterproject drawing, that the tracts below the corridors were initially planned as open porticoes rather than enclosed corridors. The freestanding character of the north corridor is underscored by the pilasters drawn on its north-facing exterior in later schemes.

The solution on the foundation medal left little to sustain critics' carping. The most serious deficiency

that could be pointed out was the problem of visibility: with Bernini's colonnade and corridor, much of the Palace of Sixtus V and of St. Peter's itself was invisible to the viewer standing in the northern half of the space. Thus, the critic of the late counterproject drawing had to retreat to a restatement of the objections originally made against the earliest transverse "oval" plan.

On 2 September 1657, as we have seen, Bernini produced a "disegno ultimo di colonne più grosse e non doppie."[88] This was not a "final" design but merely the most recent, introducing the scheme of single columns for the colonnade rather than the pairs that had been represented in the original medal. By the early fall, the size of the piazza and the location of the colonnade ends was established, according to Spada's letter of 15 September 1657.

That the north corridor was meant to lead to the old Scala Regia, as well as the narthex of St. Peter's, is subsequently made explicit in Alexander's diary notation for 29 October 1657, which mentions the "covered entrance to the stairs of the palace from the portico of the piazza."[89] It is Alexander's first statement about the connection of piazza and palace. Del Pesco may be correct in using this information to date a drawing that shows the path of the Borgo Nuovo across the piazza, although the sketch does not illustrate what interested Alexander in the diary entry, which is the tract from the piazza to the stairs (Fig. 96).[90]

Planning the porticoes continued from September through December 1657 with the aid of the full-scale models and with drawings made on walls of buildings on the site.[91] Despite the fact that the palace was now a consideration in planning, none of this work involved the design of the corridors, as far as we know. In 1658, as mentioned already, the construction process began. During the following year, 1659, construction on the northern colonnade proceeded "in a fury."[92] By July 1659, Bernini had completed one section of the colonnade elevation in its entirety, rising in the midst of 47 columns erected

for the north colonnade by the end of the month.[93] The number was less than half of the 128 columns eventually composing this quadrant of the scheme, whose general plan was not yet common knowledge, as the observations of Francis Mortoft indicate.

From his travels of 1658–59, Mortoft recalls, "Before a man enters into this Church we may behold a very fine fountaine in the same place wherein a Prince [sic] is building a very stately and magnificent walke, for the Building of which the Pope hath given him 7 yeares tyme."[94] Nothing in this statement betrays an awareness of the shape of a piazza. On the other hand Mortoft clearly understood the grandeur of the design in nuce and grasped its essential nature as a path associated with the basilica. Moreover, he

Figure 96. Study of clock tower and plan of Piazza S. Pietro with approach route, drawing (BAV, Chigi a. I. 19, fol. 26)

was aware of a kind of sabbatical time frame that anticipated the completion of the work in 1663, exactly the year in which the north corridor was finished and the Scala Regia begun.

Piazza and Palace Entrance

The early design history of Piazza S. Pietro takes on new significance when reconsidered in light of the relationship to the Vatican Palace. Above all, Bernini's very earliest thoughts about the piazza design in 1656 were not influenced by, and probably not adequately conscious of, the relation to the palace. Particularly striking is the initial lack of concern for coordinating the piazza with the principal entrance to the palace. We do not know how long such fundamental concerns could be ignored; in all probability it was a matter of weeks and days, not months. Nevertheless, we have to repeat that the enterprise did not embrace a revision of the palace fabric in the first instance, and certainly did not include thoughts about a new ceremonial entrance. It would be eight months, between July 1656 and March 1657, before the oval scheme was presented and, with it, the much criticized connection to the existing Ferrabosco wing.

During this interval, a group of counterprojects offered detailed solutions to the problems of connecting a uniformly curved piazza to the palace and incorporating a new entrance to the Cortile di S. Damaso. The earliest counterprojects follow the pattern of proposals presented during the first half of the seventeenth century, for they are characterized by the idea of expanding the papal palace over and behind arcades fronting the piazza and by the projection of palace buildings on the south to match symmetrically those on the north.

Alexander VII had an entirely different vision. It included freestanding porticoes surmounted by balustrades and statuary. But this difference did not discourage the authors of the counterproject, who altered the scheme of serlian arches to conform more closely to the pope's intentions. In these alterations a kind of dogged conservatism may be detected. It is certainly the mentality behind the invention for preserving the Logge upon a structure that projects into the piazza while maintaining the regular contour of the curved arcades. Such a plan may well have encouraged Alexander VII and Bernini to consider more radical changes to the piazza design without altering their intention of leaving the palace intact.

Possibly the most striking aspect of the counterproject proposals for a palace entrance is the retrospective nature of the critics' suggestions, despite the radical demolitions they entail.[95] In retaining the Cortile di S. Damaso as the main access to the papal palace, marked as before by a clock tower, the critics followed precedent in two regards. First, they would have preserved the place of entrance established under Paul III and monumentalized by Ferrabosco. Second, the critics would have resolved the episodic nature of the palace by extensive demolition and reconstruction, much as earlier architects (e.g., Maderno, Ferrabosco) had proposed. This synthesis of destructive conservatism may well have been the challenge that induced Bernini to invent a corridor whose audacious design pushed past the existing access of the Cortile di S. Damaso and through the Ferrabosco tract to unite the piazza directly with the old Scala Regia, just as Wittkower had intuited.[96]

The great turning point in the early design phase was the presentation of the layout "in ovata forma" on 17 March 1657. It provoked objections based on aesthetic judgment, symbolic content, and practicality. For the critics, it was not graceful or expressive, it did not carry obvious symbolic associations, and it compromised lines of sight toward the Benediction Loggia on the façade of St. Peter's. These objections did not focus on the oval per se, but rather on the necessity of imposing long, straight connecting links to the basilica. One answer to this dilemma was to change the contour of the oval, as is proposed on a rough, rather amateurish scheme signed by "P. Chircan," the pseudonym for Athanasius Kircher (Fig. 97).[97] The "visuali" on this design leave little to object to, but the price is a compromise in the regular contours of the porticoes, as well as the removal of the clock tower in favor of a new, vaguely indicated entrance to the "Palazo."

In Kircher's proposal the porticoes of the piazza continue down the Borgo Nuovo and Borgo Vecchio, but the alignment of the streets with basilica and the palace is imprecise. More precise diagrammatically, if less accurate topographically, are two projects by Carlo Rainaldi (Figs. 98, 99). Both of them are pastiches that combine features from the early and later phases of the design process.[98] The

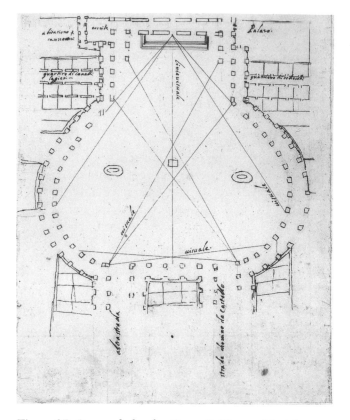

Figure 97. Proposed plan for Piazza S. Pietro with sight lines, drawing, Kircher (BAV, Chigi P. VII, 9, fol. 36)

drawing with the circular piazza, for example, would seem less advanced than the one with the oval plan; but the former includes two fountains on a cross axis (a relatively late feature), while the latter has a single fountain next to the obelisk, as depicted on the foundation medal. Notable on the oval plan is the lack of alignment between the streets of the Borgo and the western features of the piazza, while on the circular plan the streets of the borgo are perfectly aligned with corresponding features in front of the basilica. Finally, we should note that the oval plan does away with the Ferrabosco clock tower, whereas the circular plan has cleverly adopted the ground plan of the tower to generate a connecting link to the Scala Regia. These features suggest that an architect was reutilizing existing ideas in combinations that would give the patrons a variety of choices.

The stairs at the north end of the basilica narthex on Rainaldi's circular-plan scheme must have been an afterthought, for they are added free-hand in chalk. They appear to suggest that the axis of the Ferrabosco entrance could be made to join the steps

built by Paul V connecting the narthex of the basilica with the old Scala Regia. Whether Rainaldi invented this idea or picked it up from another source (Bernini?) will never be known. What can be inferred from circumstances, however, is the process by which Bernini arrived at a similar notion.

Like Kircher's sketch, all of the counterproject schemes entailed the demolition of the Ferrabosco clock tower. From the evidence of the counterprojects, Bernini was not ready to accept that, and his reasons may have been more than purely financial and practical. The clock tower represented the terminus of an axis that led down the Borgo Nuovo to Castel Sant'Angelo. Bernini must have known many examples of towers that terminated important street axes, and none was more laden with historic relevance than this one. For Bernini and Alexander VII, the tower linked the palace entrance to the Borgo and gave the appearance of a street generated by the palace. The same effect was created some years later in the composition at the back of the church at Ariccia (1662–65), where twin campanili mark the ends of medieval streets and seem actually to generate the urban tissue rather than respond to it.[99]

By contrast, the counterproject view looking west from the Borgo Nuovo offered a different set of values. The integrity of the piazza, symbolized by the snake biting its tail, was consistent with the emphatic separation of the basilica and the palace. The axis of the Borgo Nuovo would have dissipated in the void between palace and church. All three units – piazza, basilica, and palace – are thus conceived as removed from each other and from the street pattern surrounding them. This analysis indicates that Bernini, rather than an earlier or even a contemporary architect, should be credited with the conception of driving an axial entrance through the Portone di Bronzo to connect the piazza with the preexisting Scala Regia, which would thus be transformed into the main access route to the papal palace. Paradoxically, it is the counterproject drawing made early in the design process and showing the view toward the Borgo and Castel Sant'Angelo that illustrates the compelling logic of Bernini's invention (Fig. 88).[100]

The axis of the Ferrabosco wing behind the clock tower did not continue the line of the Borgo Nuovo beyond the Portone di Bronzo, nor did Bernini's critics imagine it to do so. The actual path of entry discouraged such a perception by enforcing a turn

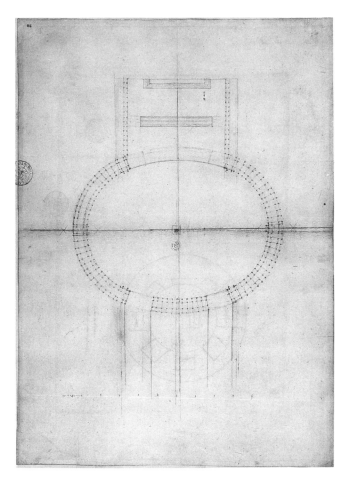

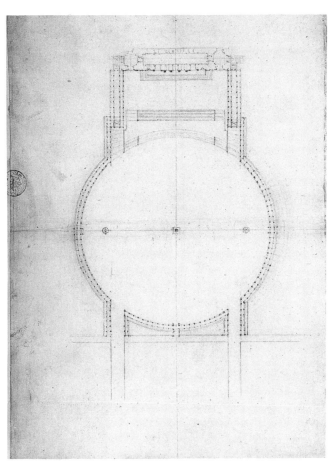

Figure 98. Proposed plan for Piazza S. Pietro, drawing, Carlo Rainaldi? (BAV, Vat. lat. 13442, fol. 29)

Figure 99. Proposed plan for Piazza S. Pietro, drawing, Carlo Rainaldi? (BAV, Vat. lat. 13442, fol. 28)

at right angles to the portal in order to ascend along the cordonata to the Cortile di S. Damaso. Had the critic of the counterproject viewed the Borgo Nuovo as a processional axis that penetrated into the heart of the palace, he would surely have developed this alignment. By contrast, the critic interpreted the axis as a void, a caesura that clarified the separation of buildings, street, and space.

Against the "classicistic" separation of components in the counterproject, Bernini advocated the messier vitality that represents the historic unity of street, piazza, and palace, as well as that of palace and basilica. At the same time, and unlike his critic, Bernini was able to preserve nearly all parts of the venerable palace other than the early seventeenth-century entrance. The fact that he did not surrender these considerations in the subsequent development of the piazza indicates a willingness to develop aesthetic and historic potentials for renewed expressive purposes. This decision, which may have been instinctive rather than conscious, led directly to the conception of the corridor and, almost as directly, to the invention of the new Scala Regia.

FIVE

Bernini's Designs for the North Corridor, 1659–1662

THE north corridor is the middle child of the entrance ensemble at the palace, neither as conspicuous as the colonnade nor as precocious as the Scala Regia. Most histories of Piazza S. Pietro pay scant attention to this phase of the enterprise, which has been overlooked as the crucial link to the development of the Scala Regia. In truth, the design and construction of the north corridor was the single most important phase in realizing a new entrance to the Vatican Palace by re-forming its southern border and reorienting its major staircase.

Bernini realized the corridor by accommodating the traditional site of entrance and accentuating it with an axial prolongation to the foot of the old Scala Regia. Implicit in the new scheme was the acknowledgment, characteristic of the age, that axiality enhances stateliness. Yet to achieve a thorough realization of the concept meant unforeseen and burdensome sacrifices of labor, time, and money. The substructures along the southern borders of the palace would have to be relocated, the entrance levels would have to be entirely modified, and a system of architecture would have to be invented that could be replicated on the south side of the piazza to suggest the symmetry that had been a goal of planners since the time of Nicholas V.

The notion of symmetry was of particular interest in the seventeenth century. Ferrabosco, Bartoli, Carlo Rainaldi, and the counterproject architect(s) all envisioned a symmetrical space in front of the basilica, whose façade would be framed by identical palace elevations. To build a second palace south of the basilica was, of course, prohibitively expensive in an age that could complete St. Peter's itself only

with difficulty. In the context of earlier solutions to this problem, Bernini and Alexander VII charted a radical course by resolving to continue the scale of the colonnade up to the basilica by means of a corridor that would also serve as the southern border of the palace. By replicating the corridor elevation on the south side of the piazza, they effected a subtle shift of emphasis. There would be no "matching palace" on the south side of the piazza. The desire for symmetry was to be satisfied instead by the shape of the piazza and its matching borders. A careful study of the corridors reveals that their eventual appearance was largely generated by a structural sleight of hand that provides the aspect of symmetry that is real and measurable only on the façades.

Physical Context for the Design of the Corridor

The physical context for the fabric that Bernini built is the subject of Chapters 1, 2, and 3. The entrance wing of the palace, built under Paul V, consisted of a portal at the base of a clock tower, behind which stood a brick wall that extended some 340 palmi (75.95 m.) to the end of the basilica façade.[1] Plans in an engraving by Ferrabosco, a drawing of Virgilio Spada, and a drawing from Bernini's shop illustrate the early seventeenth-century fabric. Bernini's plan studies the new corridor over the outlines of earlier buildings (Figs. 56, 71, 109).

In Bernini's plan, the most conspicuous outlines on Paul V's wing compose a thick, diagonal buttress wall that remained all but invisible to most palace visitors. In the fifteenth and sixteenth centuries, this wall had formed the northern edge of the *atrium helvetiorum*, defining and dividing the upper from the lower palaces. In the early seventeenth century, after the destruction of the lower palace, the wall was concealed within the new entrance wing, forming a wedge-shaped armory for the Swiss Guards. Later, under Urban VIII, the "armeria" was transferred to the east flank of the Cortile del Belvedere, where it was modified and refurbished under Alexander VII. We have no indication about the use of the armory space between the time of Urban VIII and Alexander VII, but one point is certain: there survives no evidence of a viable passage through it. Thus, there was no direct axial passage between the palace entrance and the old Scala Regia, the pavement levels of which differed significantly in elevation.

The old Scala Regia still stood in the state that Paul V had left it. It will be remembered from Chapter 3 that he had ordered changes to the staircase to accommodate the new façade of St. Peter's. The construction of the new façade and nave of the basilica also resulted in modifications to the rooms of the palace on the south side of the old staircase. The situation of these rooms around 1585, before Paul V's demolitions, can be seen on Mascarino's plans (Figs. 34, 35). The arrangement of the rooms after the interventions of Paul V but before the construction of Bernini's Scala Regia can be imagined on the basis of the wall system depicted in Letarouilly's engravings next to the new staircase (Fig. 16).

Drawings and the Design Process of the North Corridor

In July 1659, a portion of the colonnade was erected to full height for the pope. Before then, the successive models erected on the site and the staking of foundations must have piqued the curiosity of visitors and Romans alike. A print by the engraver Giovanni Battista Bonacina, made to Bernini's design and paid for in July of 1659, publicly revealed the entire scope of the enterprise for the first time (Fig. 100). The Bonacina engraving consolidated the arduous design process for the colonnades.[2] It also provides the first securely datable evidence for the corridors in plan.

In the Bonacina engraving and the preparatory drawing, the corridors are shown in a generic manner as straight passages (Fig. 101).[3] The north corridor consists of 19 bays on the drawing, and there are 18 bays in the same detail on the engraving. The width of the corridors is slightly smaller than the central passage of the colonnades and slightly greater than the aisles. My guess is that the piers of the corridors were to be fitted with large windows, like glazed versions of the colonnade.[4] The Bonacina engraving offers no more than a provisory solution for the corridors whose elevations are not revealed in the bird's-eye view of the piazza in the middle of the sheet. Like the representation on the foundation medal, the corridors are freestanding, and the palace was not yet part of the presentation.

A ground plan of the entire piazza and the corridors, which Wittkower dated to the months after the completion of the Bonacina engraving, represents a later stage of design (Fig. 102).[5] The drawing, which Kitao referred to as the "Vatican Plan," depicts the piazza design with its closing arm to the east, the so-called *terzo braccio*, but other features of the colonnade were drawn much as they would be executed.[6] Maderno's fountain is lightly depicted in its original location, east of the place where Bernini would relocate it to correspond with a newly built twin on the south. A sheet pasted over the front of the basilica offers the possibility of adding a tetrastyle portico to Maderno's façade (Fig. 103).

Wittkower's date of autumn 1659 for the Vatican plan, after the publication of the Bonacina engraving, is consistent with the evolution of the corridors.[7] The number of bays along the length of the north corridor has been reduced from the 18 and 19 depicted by Bonacina to 12 in the Vatican plan. As Wittkower noted, the narrowing of the corridor passage between the third and fourth bays in the Vatican plan represents an effort to incorporate the Portone di Bronzo without moving it. (Eventually it would be moved east, nearer the colonnade.) The interior and exterior of both corridors are lined by pairs of pilasters instead of single pilasters, and the bays between them are larger. Pilasters indicated on the northern exterior wall of the north corridor maintain the appearance of a freestanding structure, but the obvious proximity of the Vatican Palace suggests that Bernini had not yet confronted the problem of uniting it with the piazza.

In the Vatican plan, the north and south corridors

Figure 100. Half-plan and elevation with details of Piazza S. Pietro, engraving, G. B. Bonacina, 1659 (BAV, Chigi P. VII, 9, fol. 19v–20)

have identical dimensions. The interior width of the corridors, 22 palmi, is essentially uniform throughout the 12 bays from east to west. This dimension had been adjusted to correspond to the width of the middle passage of the colonnade.[8] (The exception occurs where the north corridor narrows to 18 palmi to accommodate the old Portone di Bronzo in its original location.) If incorporated within the larger structure in its original location, the Portone di Bronzo would not have required a newly graded access to be joined to the piazza. The three bays of the corridor to the east of the portal would have covered the same ramped ascent that stood before it for almost a half century, preserving its alignment with the Borgo Nuovo as depicted in Heemskerck's view. A marriage of tradition and convenience thus conspired in the early composition of the northern corridor.

For our concerns the Vatican plan is most notable for its vagueness in the western portion, near the

basilica. On the right there is no indication of a connection with the Scala Regia, although light chalk lines continue the axes of both north and south corridors beyond the inked portions. For all practical purposes it would seem that the northern corridor was still envisioned in isolation; yet this impression is false.

Using the scale on the Vatican plan, we can determine that the northern wall of the north corridor was positioned about 70 palmi from the north end (inner face) of Maderno's narthex. Looking ahead for a moment to Bernini's later corridor plan, which also has a scale, we discover the same dimension between the two features, that is, between the inner face on the north side of the narthex and the northern wall of the old Scala Regia (Fig. 109).[9] Given these relationships, we may conclude that the axis of the corridor in the Vatican plan would have coincided exactly with the path of the old Scala Regia that is not depicted. In sum, the Vatican plan gives

the façade" of St. Peter's.[10] In hindsight, we now see that the clarity of the façade in this scheme would have been the result of functional considerations, maintaining an alignment with the stairs and continuing the width of the colonnade. These points mark the beginning of a long process with significant changes. Throughout all of them, however, the position of the northern wall of the corridor remained constant in relation to Maderno's façade for the basilica.

Before continuing a review of the graphic evidence, it is important to establish that only the main lines of the scheme appear to develop in predictable sequential fashion. Various features of the design, while important, are less easily accounted for in the drawings. A sketch of the corridor that Wittkower supposed was from about the same time as the Vatican plan has single pilasters separating bays whose walls are broken by rectangular windows (Fig.

Figure 102. Plan of Piazza S. Pietro, drawing, 1659 (BAV, Chigi P. VII, 9, fol. 17v–18)

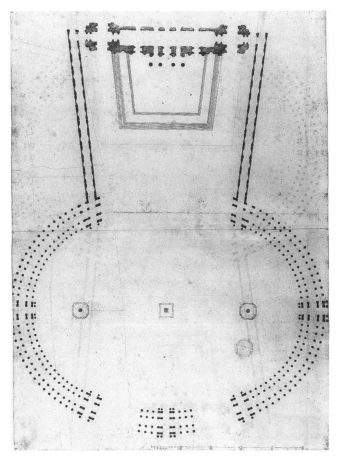

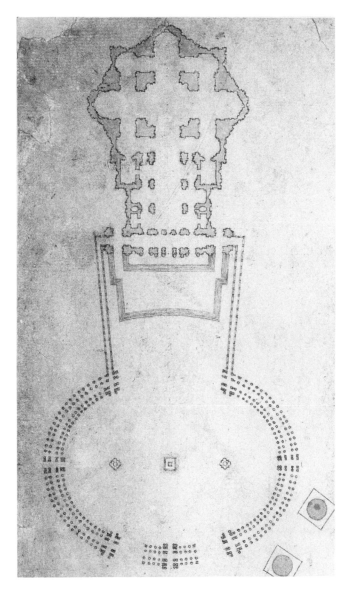

Figure 101. Plan of Piazza S. Pietro, detail of preparatory drawing for engraving, G. B. Bonacina, 1659 (British Museum, Payne Knight Oo 3–5)

evidence that the north corridor was already destined to arrive at the foot of the old Scala Regia. The ambiguous relationship of the corridor to the palace on the Vatican plan may therefore be explained by the desire at this time to emphasize the visual unity of the piazza and perhaps to uncertainties about the connection to the palace.

This phase of the planning process clarifies Wittkower's account, which ascribed the position of the corridor and its distance from the basilica to the necessity for establishing "the architectonic clarity of

Figure 103. Plan of corridors, detail, drawing, 1659 (BAV, Chigi P. VII, 9, fol. 17v)

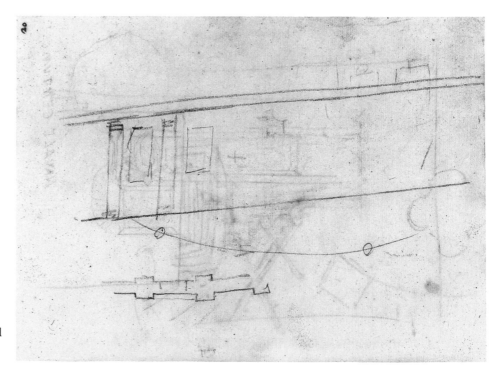

Figure 104. Partial elevation and plan of south corridor, drawing (BAV, Chigi a. I. 19, fol. 20)

104).[11] The same configuration of single pilasters and rectangular windows is recorded on an engraving of the piazza by Falda (Fig. 105).[12] A later version of the Falda engraving has no "terzo braccio," the Piazza Retta is stepped more simply in two increments, and double pilasters are substituted for the single units along the length of the corridor exterior (Fig. 106). These features would suggest that the window design was settled before the configuration of the pilasters was determined. Yet this conclusion is contradicted by the appearance of round-headed windows on a drawing of the corridor (discussed in the next paragraphs) bearing the double pilaster motif.[13] With this conundrum we return to the ruled drawings bearing scales and some legends.

An elevation representing the south-facing exterior of the northern corridor illustrates the relationship to the piazza and the old Scala Regia (Fig. 107).[14] Steps and inclined lines ascending from right to left illustrate how the interior connections of these components could be achieved. The lowest level of terrain is the grade on which the colonnade is set. The line at the letter "B" indicates the inclination of the piazza in front of the basilica. The letter "A" indicates the level at which carriages could pass under the arches of the façade on the flanks of the basilica. (Only the south arm, the Arco della Campana, is open today.) Directly above "A," the letter "C" is drawn over the pavement level of the narthex of the basilica. The narthex is joined to the higher level of the base landing by a flight of stairs. Finally, a dotted line shows the projected level of the pavement inside the corridor, which climbs steadily from the piazza to a level just below the sill of the westernmost window. The pavement then rises steeply to the level of the base landing at the foot of the Scala Regia.

The corridor elevation must have been drawn after the old location of the Portone di Bronzo was abandoned, for the threshold of the portal cannot have coincided with the gentle grade of the rising pavement depicted here. In the earlier projects such as those illustrated on the foundation medal (Fig. 84), the piazza is graded so that the oval area (the Piazza Obliqua) is separated by a group of steps from the trapezoidal area (the Piazza Retta) in front of the basilica. In the corridor elevation, the piazza is graded continuously without the separation of different levels, and this process of unifying the corridor and piazza was enhanced by removing the pediment depicted on the drawing at the western terminus of the colonnade.[15] These modifications would have taken place by 1661, the date of the completion of the north colonnade. As a result, 1661 may be taken as the *terminus ante quem* for the drawing of the corridor elevation. In my opinion the drawing was probably made a year earlier, as I will argue in the paragraphs below.

Between the Vatican plan of autumn 1659 and the later corridor elevation, the number of bays was reduced from 12 to 11 bays. Wittkower suggested that this change served to minimize the impression of length that repeating units tend to impart. Because the distance between the colonnade and the basilica remained constant, there would be another important result of such a reduction. Assuming a constant dimension for the pilaster pairs, the distance between them would have been increased. This, in turn, permitted the installation of larger windows offering more light within the corridor.

The luminous effect of large windows would have been amplified if the pavement level of the corridor rose as depicted in the elevation drawing. For the visitor's position would have been increasingly dominated by the windows until they sprang almost from the level of the pavement itself. As a result the presence of light would have progressively increased along the path of entry. Sometime shortly after the corridor elevation was drawn, the round-headed windows were changed to square-headed windows, which further increased the level of illumination and avoided the awkward appearance of a semicircular window head skewed to respond to the sloping terrain.

The left side of the corridor elevation illustrates the connection to the narthex of the basilica and, for the first time in these drawings, between the corridor and the preexisting Scala Regia. Steps rise from the narthex ("C") to the base landing within the last bay of the corridor. A niche on the north wall of the base landing measures 24 by 10 palmi (5.36 by 2.22 m.). The base landing measures 29 palmi (6.47 m.) in its east – west dimension. The height of the staircase vault is about 44 palmi (9.83 m.). The height of the vault over the base landing is 57 palmi (12.73 m.), a dimension no doubt established to conform to the

i Basilica di S.Pietro.
2 Portici fatti da N. Sig.
3 Palazzo Apostolico.

PIAZZA E PORTICI DELLA BASILICA VATICANA FATTI DA N.S.PAPA
ALESANDRO SETTIMO.
Per Gio Iacomo Rossi in Roma alla Pace 65 P. del S.P.   Gio Batta Falda diss.f.

4 Obelisco del Circo di Caio, è
Nerone.
5 Palazzo del Sant'Officio.

3

Figure 105 (above). Piazza S. Pietro from an early design, engraving, G. B. Falda (Bibliotheca Hertziana, D19853)

Figure 106 (below). Piazza S. Pietro from a late design, engraving, G. B. Falda (Bibliotheca Hertziana, D19905)

VEDVTA DI TVTTA LA BASILICA VATICANA ARCHITETTVRA DI MICHEL ANGELO BONAROTI LA FACCIATA DI CARLO MADERNI LI
Portici del Caualier Bernini la Cupola inalzata da Iacomo della Porta et la Guglia del Cau. Fontana.

i Palazzo Pontificio.   3 Sagrestia uecchia doue staua la guglia in mezzo   4 Palazzo del S. Officio.
2 Chiesa di S.Marta.   Gio Batta falda dis. et fec.   il cerchio di Nerone.   Per Gio Iacomo Rossi in Roma allà pace 65 pria S.Pour.   5 Corridore di Castello.   3

height of the Doric order of the colonnade and corridor (57½ palmi).[16] These dimensions are useful to issues raised later in this and succeeding chapters.

In the Chigi Archives there is a corresponding elevation of the basilica façade made on a slightly smaller scale and hence perhaps at a somewhat different moment, but the two elevations are otherwise closely related and, I believe, represent essentially the same stage in the design process (Fig. 108).[17] The façade elevation includes transverse sections of the corridors where they join St. Peter's. The corridors are connected to the façade by a pair of pi-

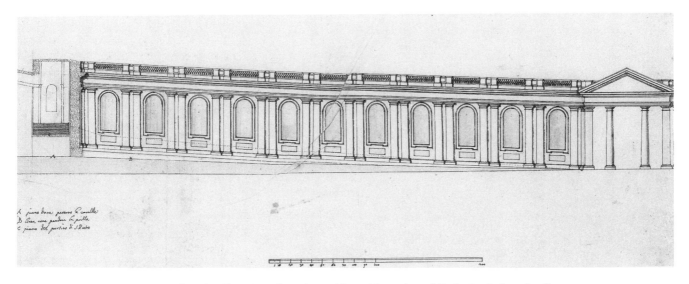

Figure 107 (above). Elevation of north corridor with section of Scala Regia base landing, drawing, 1660 (BAV, Chigi P. VII, 9, fol. 24 sup.)

Figure 108 (below). Façade elevation of St. Peter's with elevation of base landing, drawing, 1660 (BAV, Chigi P. VII, 9, fol. 24 inf.)

lasters couched in a space of some 11½ palmi between the ends of the façade and the corridors. This dimension signals a change in the design after the Vatican plan of autumn 1659, when the corridors were positioned about 22 palmi from the façade. As we have already established that the position of the outer walls of the corridors had been fixed in the Vatican plan, we must conclude that the passages within the corridors have been widened.[18] In addition, the widths of the corridors have been differentiated.

In Figures 107 and 108, the height of the steps rising from the corridor to the base landing is 11 palmi, the height of the vault over the stairs is 44 palmi,[19] and the height of the vault above the base landing is 57 palmi. It is crucial to establish the correspondence of these drawings, for I believe they represent the "disegno del braccio e dela facciata di S. Pietro" that Bernini presented to Alexander VII on 29 August 1660.[20] The "braccio" and the "facciata" are the corridor (in elevation) and the façade of the basilica (also in elevation but with sections of the corridors).

In the case of the north corridor it is obvious that the enlargement in width was prescribed in part by the width of the two sets of stairs (together, 37 palmi across the opening of the stairs) shown on the drawing. Although it has been thought that the stairs to the left of the old Scala Regia were designed by Bernini, they were on the site before his interventions. They apparently led to rooms south of the Scala Regia. The width of the south corridor was expanded to only 28 palmi.[21]

The evidence indicates that Bernini had now considered a width for the north corridor that would embrace both staircases at the west end of the entrance axis, and not just the width of the old Scala Regia. This fact is confirmed by a plan usually attributed to Bernini and certainly from his workshop (Fig. 109). It shows the new corridor in dark wash superimposed on the light lines of the preexisting Ferrabosco structures.[22] As in the basilica elevation, the width of the corridor next to the stairs is 37 palmi. The plan shows 11 bays (not 12, pace Wittkower) and a double-pilaster scheme facing the piazza, thus corresponding to the corridor elevation drawing in that respect. In all probability, the date of the plan is therefore close to that of the elevations of 1660.

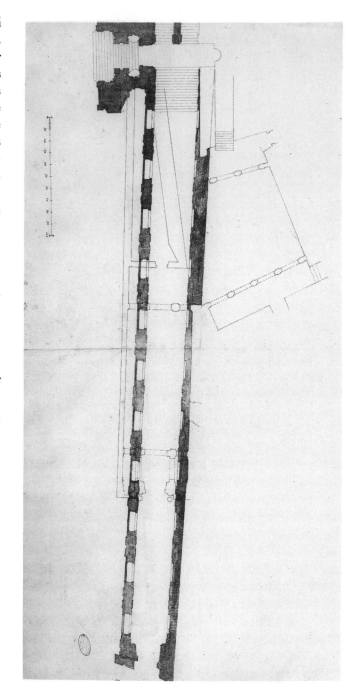

Figure 109. Plan of north corridor over plan of Paul V's entrance wing and Cortile del Maresciallo, drawing, 1660 (wash over pen) (BAV, Chigi P. VII, 9, fol. 25v–26)

A comparison of the new corridor plan with the Vatican piazza plan of a year earlier reveals important developments. Unlike the plan of 1659, there are no pilasters indicated on the side of the corridor destined to abut the palace. Most significant is the shift in vision from a corridor of a uniform width of 22 palmi aligned to meet the old Scala Regia (with a width of 16 palmi) to a corridor with a width expanding to 37 palmi that would have embraced both the old Scala Regia and the stairs next to it. To understand the creation of the expanding (or tapering) width of the north corridor, one must imagine its southern wall pivoted to bring its western end closer to the basilica while the eastern end of the wall remained stationary.

The widening of the corridor from east to west can be seen also on three autograph chalk sketches, so there can be little doubt of Bernini's intentions in this regard. On one sheet, above the tapering form of the corridor, the draftsman has also experimented with a corridor composed of parallel walls that are stepped wider in the middle of their length (Fig. 110).[23] On a second sketch the tapering of the corridor passage is depicted in the context of the larger piazza (Fig. 111).[24] In this drawing Bernini shows how the angled ends of the north colonnade have been adjusted to accommodate the Borgo Nuovo, which results in an asymmetrical colonnade.[25] Finally, on a third sketch the tapered width of the corridor is shown leading to the base landing of the stairs, while below it the elevation of the corridor is shown as a schematic extension of the colonnade (Fig. 112).[26]

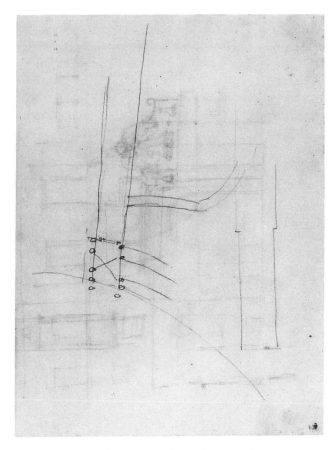

Figure 110. Plan of north corridor and colonnade, drawing (BAV, Chigi a. I. 19, fol. 17v)

Figure 111. Plan of north corridor and colonnade with Palazzo dei Penitenzieri (?), drawing (BAV, Chigi a. I. 19, fol. 28)

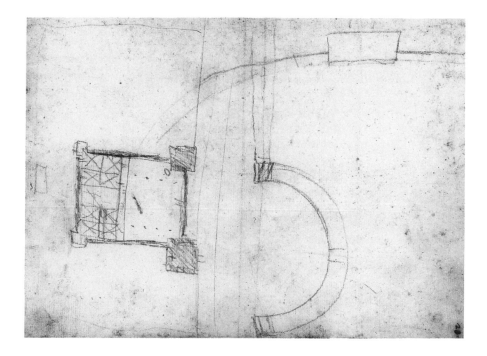

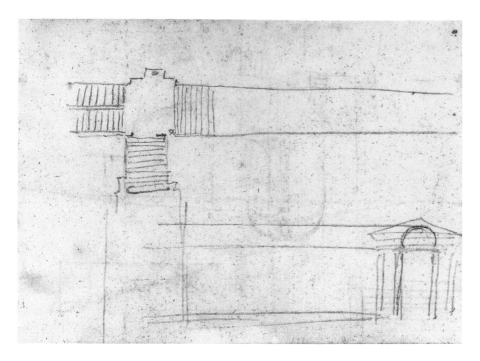

Figure 112. Elevation and plan of north corridor with connecting steps at base landing, drawing (BAV, Chigi a. I. 19, fol. 8v)

In each instance the widening passage provides a smooth transition from the dimensions established by the colonnade arm to those embracing the two staircases at the west end of the corridor. It is also possible to imagine that, above the gradually ascending level of the pavement, the ever broader corridor supported a vaulting system of increasing height from east to west. As a result, the visitor would seem to be walking under a vault of constant height and shape. In reality, only the proportions of the space remain constant within an ever expanding set of vertical and horizontal dimensions.

On the assumption that expanding walls operate perceptually in a manner contrary to that of an accelerated perspective, Wittkower suggested that the widening of the north corridor was intended to minimize the effect of the great length of the passage.[27] He believed that this intention was confirmed by the progressive reduction of bays in the successive plans. This explanation is consistent with his emphasis, influenced by Panofsky, on the purely visual aspects of the composition. In fact, it can be demonstrated that considerations other than purely aesthetic generated the essential dimensions of the north corridor in the first instance.

On the south, after all, there was no palace to limit the width of the corridor, which is smaller than its counterpart on the north. Wittkower did not rec-

ognize that the combined width of the preexisting Scala Regia and the staircase south of it (37 palmi or 8.26 m.) is virtually the same as the width between the walls of Bernini's new Scala Regia at the base landing (8.29 m.). In other words, at the stage represented on Bernini's corridor ground plan and related drawings (including the two elevations and three sketches discussed above), it is likely that the artist and his patron were thinking about a corridor wide enough to embrace the dimensions of a new Scala Regia (Figs. 107, 108, 109). Yet I do not believe this to be the impetus for the new dimensions.

In truth, the tapering width of the corridors is a functional issue. On the east, there had to be some parity with the width of the central passage of the colonnades. The dimensions of the colonnades in turn had been predicated on the necessity of carriage traffic, as we have seen in the previous chapter. Thus, the 22-palmi width of the corridors in the early scheme. But there is more.

We know that coaches could and did pass through the Portone di Bronzo in the seventeenth century, for in the 1680s the visiting French architect Robert De Cotte described the hairpin turn subsequently encountered on the cordonata between the north corridor and the Cortile di S. Damaso.[28] Presumably the 22-palmi width of the early corridor scheme was based on the accommodation of coaches, which in the seventeenth century could negotiate a passage as narrow as 11½ palmi, as Waddy has indicated.[29] From her study of reception areas and the architectural members around them, we know that 22 to 23 palmi are necessary for coaches to pass abreast. An adequate turning radius in the sixteenth century was 28 palmi, and in the seventeenth century it required 33 to 34 palmi.[30] A width of 37 palmi provided ample space for carriages to arrive and turn around to leave the corridor by the avenue they had entered.

Since it was customary for a dignified arrival to take place at the foot of a palace stair, the 37-palmi width at the western end of the corridor was necessary to provide the space for coaches to arrive, let off passengers, and turn to exit. Hence the tapered plan of the corridor. These considerations, lost in the early corridor plans, may have been stimulated by the Bartoli engraving (Fig. 77). Bartoli's double aisles are each 16 palmi in width and together offered a turning radius (without a dividing pier) of 36 palmi, as labeled on the engraving. It remains only to note that similar dimensions influenced urban plans of the era as well as palace plans. Relying on documents published by Ost, Krautheimer has emphasized how the dimensions necessary for carriage traffic helped to fix Alexander VII's plans for Piazza S. Maria della Pace.[31] In fact, the dimensions required for carriages appear to have influenced Roman planning well into the eighteenth century, if the development of Piazza S. Ignazio is a representative example.[32] It should come as no surprise that the corridors of Piazza S. Pietro responded to the same functional necessities.

These necessities were understood by a seventeenth-century contemporary, who noted that the Vatican Palace had no conveniently located courtyard accessible by coach that was close to a staircase, and no means for avoiding the harmful effects of sun and rain on the vehicles.[33] The Quirinal Palace, on the other hand, had a staircase positioned close to a courtyard with this capacity for protecting carriages, and thus the building earned Spada's consideration as a model for the dimensions of the colonnade (Chapter 3).

The shape of the base landing on a Chigi drawing (Fig. 112) is much more nearly square than the pronounced rectangular shape depicted on the corridor plan (Fig. 109), and is much closer to the executed

proportions (about 5.54 m. × 8.29 m.). The depth (east–west) of the landing is 29 palmi on the corridor elevation, while the width is 38 palmi on the basilica elevation (6.47 m. × 8.48 m.). On Bernini's corridor plan the depth is just less than 20 palmi, while the width is about 63 palmi (4.46 m. × 14.07 m.). These dimensions suggest that the corridor plan, having a base landing less like those executed, is earlier than the elevation drawings or the sketch in question. If the elevations date to late August 1660, how early can the plan be? At what moment do we have firm evidence of the desire to connect the corridor to the palace stairs?

I believe the answer is provided by notations in Alexander's diary for early 1660. On 19 February, he records a visit by Bernini "per sfilar quello corridoro." On 10 March, the diary makes reference to a consideration of "il modello pel corridore de' Portici, se incontra la scala," for which purpose the pope visited St. Peter's.[34] Because the term "sfilar" exactly describes the effect of the widening corridor, I would date Bernini's corridor plan to February to March 1660.

Bernini's corridor plan is the first finally to depict the north wall in contact with, that is to say, abutting the palace, and there is other evidence that the drawing helped to resolve problems of construction. Indeed, the general purpose of the plan is to distinguish the parts of the older structure that could be reutilized from those destined for demolition. This was timely information in early 1660, for by April of that year the demolitions had begun on the Ferrabosco wing. Because the Portone di Bronzo could not be in the center of the corridor, its transfer to the east was probably planned at this time. More daunting was the work at the west end of the corridor, where the massive diagonal buttress wall would have to be torn down and replaced by a wall nearly as large bordering the Cortile del Maresciallo. These foundations would be stabilized by the vaults of the corridor.

By relocating the buttress wall to make room for the axis of the north corridor, Bernini would have to sacrifice a precious portion of the palace. Like Maderno's project earlier in the century, Bernini's scheme called for demolishing a southern bay of the Cortile del Maresciallo. This operation and the imposition of a new buttress wall were the most radical steps in the process of designing the corridor and

Figure 113. Interior elevation of north corridor at west with section of steps at base landing, drawing (BAV, Chigi a. I. 19, fol. 8)

Figure 114. Interior elevation of north corridor at west with plan of center pier, drawing (BAV, Chigi a. I. 19, fol. 9v)

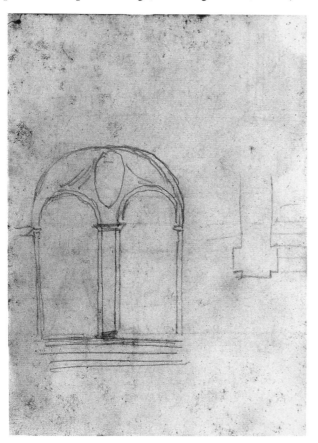

the most decisive in the course of its construction. The purpose in both cases was to facilitate the widening of the corridor to embrace the width of the two staircases at the base of the palace and permit an adequate turning radius for arriving coaches.

In two autograph sketches, Bernini illustrated the double arch that encompassed the two stairs at the west end of the corridor (Figs. 113, 114).[35] Wittkower was under the impression that Bernini had built the staircase immediately to the south of the old Scala Regia and designed the double portal with papal arms to serve as a symmetrical termination to the west end of the corridor.[36] For these operations, however, there is no documentary evidence among the copious building records. Wittkower's thesis is also unlikely because it does not explain why the design of the corridor on the Vatican plan, where the corridor was already aligned with the old Scala Regia, should have been superseded. Nor does this account for the striking similarity of the double portal in Bernini's drawings and the Bartoli engraving discussed in Chapter 4 (Fig. 77). In fact, it would be more in keeping with all of this evidence to regard the portal with double arches as the contribution of Paul V.[37]

The stairs in question appear on the façade elevation drawing, Bernini's plan, and two of the smaller sketches. In Figure 113, in the upper left, Bernini illustrated the profile of ten steps that led up through the left arch. The other sketch, in Figure 114, features a more focused view of the double portal and the wall that divided the two stairs. In this second sketch, or one like it conceived between March and August 1660, Bernini may have presented the crowning contribution to his plans for the palace entrance.

In recognizing that the breadth of the double arch at the old Scala Regia corresponds to the present dimensions of the base landing, we open the possibility that this moment in the design process led to the decision to rebuild the Scala Regia along the same path. If this hypothesis is tenable, it would be reasonable to conclude that from early 1660, Bernini and Alexander may have been speculating about a newly widened palace stair to prolong the axis of the corridor. This notion would have occurred to them during the process of defining the shape of the base landing to accommodate visitors arriving by coach.

Much would have preceded this decision. From early 1660 to the last months of 1662, the corridor would have to be built, and it would not be an easy or inexpensive task. Money was in short supply, the south colonnade had not yet been started, and Alexander was already advanced in years. Had the necessary will or money evaporated or other circumstances intervened, Bernini and Alexander would still have achieved a magnificent entrance corridor that brought visitors from the monumental colonnades to the very foot of the old palace stairs. That was an enormous innovation, changing forever the essential patterns of circulation and ceremony within the palace, but that was not the limit of their ambitions. From the very moment the new corridor was designed with its ever broadening contours, the die had been irrevocably cast for the future reconstruction of the Scala Regia.

We cannot know when during the years 1660, 1661, and 1662, Alexander and Bernini looked at the terminal motif of the corridor, a relic of the Borghese era, and began to envision a new Scala Regia. Judging from the small number of drawings from the next stage of the design process, the decision may have come later and more precipitously than we would prefer to imagine. We can be sure in any case that when the decision was made, the challenges of constructing the corridor had already filled many waking hours.

Beginning the Construction of the North Corridor

The construction of the north corridor can be closely followed in documents. These documents reveal a good deal about the preexisting state of the palace and the considerable challenges it posed to realizing the new corridor. Above all, we gain a clear sense of the construction process of the corridor, enabling us to see the extent to which it forecast the new Scala Regia. To do all of this we have the help of a precious compilation, the "diario dei lavori."

The "diario dei lavori" covers the period 4 September 1659 through 13 December 1662 in a daily account of 830 pages.[38] It consists of brief notices that indicate the nature of the work undertaken on a given day and can be used to trace the order of building events, to estimate the length of time spent on most facets of the work, and to learn how technically challenging tasks were accomplished. The "diario" was consulted by Haus and more recently by Martinelli in the effort to establish a firm chronology for the construction of Bernini's colonnades but, curiously enough, it has never been read to explain the process of design and construction of the north corridor, which it documents more fully than any other component of the entire piazza enterprise.[39] In addition to the indications in the "diario," there are misure e stime recording exactly what was done in a quantitative way: how much earth was moved, how much masonry was built, and how much each operation cost. These archival sources are also known but little studied. Finally, there are a host of other archival sources, some previously known and others not, that complete our picture of the construction process.

Although some parts of the north colonnade were still unfinished in the later half of February 1660, the massive pilasters terminating the west end were reaching completion.[40] By 19 February 1660, Bernini and Alexander were already conferring on the matter of aligning the corridor with the staircases at the foot of the palace walls.[41] By this means, the traditional alignment of the palace entrance and axis of the Borgo Nuovo was to be extended to the old

Scala Regia. The discussion continued into the following month, March 1660, with the help of a model.

Three-dimensional models built in small and full-scale dimensions were used to study the piazza and, in at least this case, the corridor. A wooden model, begun in April 1659 and finished at the end of January 1660, is undoubtedly the one mentioned in the pope's diary for 27 January, which depicted "tutto della mezzaluna sinistra."[42] The "mezzaluna sinistra" means the north colonnade, for in the documents "sinistra" consistently refers to the north side of the piazza, the left when viewed from the church. In addition, the model probably included the corridor, because Alexander consulted "il modello pel corridore de' portici, se incontra la scala" on 10 March 1660, and we have no notice of a separate model for this portion of the scheme.[43] From the available information, however, there is only a general indication of the nature of the model or the study it might have facilitated. Evidently it did not include a specific resolution of the relationship between the corridor and the Scala Regia, where Bernini's plans had been left intentionally vague.

Alexander's concern about the alignment of the corridor and the stairs indicates his active involvement in the planning process. On Easter Sunday, 28 March 1660, he met with Bernini and "ordered" the corridor, after which he met with Spada and Cardinal Flavio Chigi.[44] This must indicate the pope's approval of the scheme recorded on the corridor plan. Two days after that he discussed the "portoni" with Bernini, probably the design of the ends and the middle of the colonnade arms.[45]

To achieve an axial relationship between the colonnade and the Scala Regia, the old buttress wall, as well as the outer curtain wall built by Ferrabosco, had to be demolished. The second task was easy, but the first required a complicated sequence of demolition and reconstruction, for the wall was essential to the stability of the upper palace. Sections of the diagonal buttress could be removed only as replacements could be built up. Here, problems of logistics and structure had to coalesce in a procedure as rapid as practicable and with a result whose strength and stability would be assured.

From the corridor plan of early 1660, it is evident that the stability of the new buttress wall was enhanced by the vaulting over the corridor. The vaults would rest on piers composing the south side of the corridor to provide a counterthrust to the palace buildings on higher terrain to the north. Ferrabosco's unbroken curtain wall to the south would be replaced by what is, in effect, a line of regularly spaced piers joined in an east–west direction by thin sections of wall interrupted by windows.

Bernini's corridor plan indicates that the thickest part of the new buttress wall would be located next to the Cortile del Maresciallo. At the west and east ends of the corridor, the thickness of the wall is significantly reduced. Where Bernini's wall follows Ferrabosco's structure to the east, a strength of only moderate proportions was called for, because the palace buildings in this area spring from their own foundations. The new wall dissipates rapidly in thickness at the west where it joins preexisting masonry rising through the full height of the Scala del Maresciallo. This preexisting wall supports the south side of the Scala del Maresciallo.[46] On the other hand, the Cortile del Maresciallo is something like a hanging garden, whose grade lies well above the piazza and hence requires more substantial lateral support. The transverse vaults of the corridor would spring from double pilasters to provide counterthrusts exactly at the middle and the east and west ends of the cortile.

In addition to the walls of the Ferrabosco wing, two other features of the palace had to be demolished before the corridor could be built. One was the staircase that had connected the Cortile del Maresciallo to the narthex of the basilica. In some form, this staircase had been a part of the palace since the Middle Ages connecting the atrium of old St. Peter's to the *turris scalarum* at the southwest corner of the Maresciallo.

The other part of the palace to be removed was located at the southwest corner of the Maresciallo, near the façade of St. Peter's. Here Bernini excised a whole bay to make room for the path of the corridor. We discussed this operation at the end of Chapter 3. A comparison with earlier representations, such as the Duperac-Lafrery map, shows that the west apartment rose above at least three arches. The corridor plan prescribed their reduction to two, and the present state of the palace affirms that this was carried out. In this process, four rooms were lost on each of two floors, in addition to their mezzanines and connecting corridors.[47]

Given these challenges, it is not surprising that work on the corridor began with the necessary demolitions at the west end of the Ferrabosco wing and proceeded in a conventional manner from top to bottom. This permitted the most daunting obstacles of the whole operation to be overcome quickly, it allowed the portal under the clock tower to continue functioning as the main palace entrance, and it facilitated the completion of the north colonnade by allowing work there to proceed without interruption.

The first order of business was to pull down the south bay of the Maresciallo apartments. While a crew set to work there, others worked on the colonnades, although temporary shortages of stone and other interruptions, such as rain, occasionally permitted the transfer of additional workers to the demolition procedure.[48] As with modern construction, the work involving existing structures was slower and more tedious than the new construction, and large numbers of workers were usually not needed.

The demolition of the west apartments closest to the basilica was carried out predictably. First the rooms were stripped of their roofs.[49] Then came the demolition of their walls.[50] These events took place in the latter half of April 1660. In May and June 1660 the stairs that connected these apartments and continued down to the base landing of the old Scala Regia were dismantled.[51] How much of the palace it was necessary to destroy was largely a practical matter throughout the entire operation. Where necessary, as for the buttress wall, enormous masses of masonry were demolished and rebuilt. Where possible, structures on the site could be incorporated, as was the preexisting wall on the north side of the old Scala Regia and the south side of the Scala del Maresciallo.[52] On at least one occasion, described below, the demolitions yielded an unexpected dividend.

Before Alexander's interventions, the façades of Paul V on the east and west sides of the Cortile del Maresciallo did not compose a unified plane. As the sides of the courtyard were not parallel, the façades over the piazza formed a slight angle to each other.[53] After the necessary demolitions, these façades could be aligned on a single plane to suggest a regularity in planning that had not previously existed. Like a skim coat of plaster that hides underlying irregularities, the brick sheathing over the partly demolished western apartments was rebuilt to correspond with the façade plane of the eastern apartments. This operation explains why the east and west apartments overlooking the piazza correspond so exactly in appearance, despite the fact that Bernini's crews intervened on only one of them.

Very likely, the aesthetic advantage of these features was recognized only after the demolitions had occurred. Initially, the west apartments were cut back considerably more than necessary. The remaining portion of the arch on this side of the courtyard still bears witness to this operation, for its profile is amputated well back from the new corner of the building (Fig. 115). The curve of the arch was cut behind the plane of the balustrade that defines the northern wall of the corridor below. Builders must have first thought of demolishing the west apartments to correspond with this plane, which explains why a section of cornice for the balustrade extends

Figure 115. Southwest corner of Cortile del Maresciallo (Bibliotheca Hertziana, D36920)

under the west porch of the Maresciallo (Fig. 116; see also Plates 70, 76).

The change in masonry from the brick of the Borghese period to that of the Chigi pontificate can be identified in a vertical seam above the broken arch at the Cortile del Maresciallo. The newer brick surfaces continue across the south-facing walls of the western apartments and onto the façade that surrounds the east-facing finestrone. New masonry joins old at another vertical seam, located 5.6 meters north of the basilica façade, between it and the finestrone (Plate 78). This masonry suture indicates the extent of the west apartments before Bernini's intervention.

The stairs near the old *turris scalarum* also had to be sacrificed if the axial alignment of the palace portal to the Scala Regia were to be achieved.[54] The long tradition of a connection between the Cortile del Maresciallo and the portico of St. Peter's was temporarily broken in the first week of June 1660. It must have been apparent that new traditions were being forged in these operations when excavators on the Cortile del Maresciallo came upon medals dating from the pontificate of Paul II.[55] A replacement staircase, the Scala del Costantino, would later be built, but its form, location, and function made it something of a service stairs rather than a principal link between palace and basilica.

The documents for the chronology impart a pervading sense of deliberation, as though a controlling scheme had not been provided with all attendant dimensions. In late June 1660, Alexander continued to confer with Bernini about the demolitions for the corridor, and there follows a lull in activity for two and a half months.[56] During this time, Bernini and his team pursued the last work on the north colonnade. The architect was evidently also finalizing the plan of the corridor. On 18 August 1660, excavations were begun for its foundations.[57] Ten days later, the pope reviewed the elevations of the corridor and the basilica façade. Construction was initially arranged on a piecework basis, and continued in this manner through the first week of September, after which the work went forward under contract.

In the first week of September 1660, Alexander ordered Bernini to begin the appropriate foundations.[58] Thus, the excavating process was continued up to 6 September 1660.[59] The process of digging and "filling" the foundations henceforth proceeded together and lasted through the end of November 1660.[60]

By this time, the painstaking campaign to remove

Figure 116. Travertine molding under west portico of Cortile del Maresciallo (Bibliotheca Hertziana, D36917)

Giotto's Navicella mosaic from within the little *atrium helvetiorum* was under way. First came the construction of the appropriate scaffolding in October and November 1660, then the removal of the mosaic in November and December, and finally, from November 1660 to January 1661, the removal of the ornament that surrounded it.[61] The documents relevant to the destruction provide new sources of information about the state of the venerable mosaic and its context in the seventeenth century, as discussed in Chapter 3. The fountains in the little *atrium helvetiorum* and on the wall facing the piazza were dismantled later, in October 1661, suggesting the priority of removing the mosaic from harm's way.[62]

Meanwhile, from November 1660 to January 1661, building operations on the north corridor were reaching their most ambitious stage. Caissons were built into the foundations directly against the scarp of land south of the Cortile del Maresciallo. The excavations were filled with masonry, and huge niches were constructed to hold back the terrain.[63] The structure of the armory was finally dismantled only months after these operations had begun.[64] To some extent, these and later operations may have taken place behind the veil of the new exterior corridor wall, whose foundations were set in January 1661.[65] By May 1661, all excavations for the foundation walls were complete, save those under the clock tower, and efforts concentrated on the process of building walls.[66]

In all of these operations, we have evidence of three major changes in design since the project was presented on Bernini's corridor plan (Fig. 109). One was the restitution of the old cordonata leading up to the Cortile di S. Damaso, which was once thought unnecessary. Another was the reconstruction of a staircase between the Cortile del Maresciallo and the narthex of St. Peter's, excavated behind the equestrian statue and hence called the Scala di Costantino. In both of these contexts, the traditional connections between the upper and lower zones of palace, piazza, and basilica were judged useful enough to be preserved. The third important departure from Bernini's corridor plan, induced by structural considerations, called for the walls of the passage to be constructed as a series of broadly curving niches. Because existing walls made it impossible to erect piers, vaults, and a new buttress wall in a single conventional operation, work would have to advance piecemeal in self-supporting units. The bays of the corridor were therefore recast as self-sufficient buttresses for the vaulting over the corridor. The process was laborious. Each niche had to be individually excavated, the niche itself had to be built with the help of the usual scaffolding, and the masonry had to cure before workmen could continue with confidence.

It was a tedious procedure that neither additional men nor money could hurry. The spirit of the operation was captured by Virgilio Spada in a letter of 14 October 1660, addressed to Alexander VII. In it, Spada recognized the pope's desire to see the corridor finished, but reminded him of the risks to the stability of the palace should the campaign be hurried: "One has to think of the construction of the corridor as a slow fever," he suggested, "and have the patience to nurse it along little by little." For this reason he proposed strong arguments for beginning the excavations at the south colonnade, contrary to the inclinations of both Alexander and Bernini, even while the north side was being completed.[67] Eventually Spada got his way, although this was not always the case. On 18 November 1660, there appears the first notice of excavations on the south side of the basilica and of the demolitions of walls at the archpriest's palace.[68] Two days earlier, on 16 November 1661, the contract for the south colonnade had been advertised by edict.[69]

Contractual Difficulties

Until late 1660, all of the masonry for the piazza had been hired out *a cottimo*, that is, as piecework. This method allowed the supervising architect, whether Bernini or one of his assistants, to assess the quality of the result and base payments upon it. Each portion of the work could be evaluated and paid for individually, and if disagreements arose regarding its value, second and third estimates could be solicited.

The alternative to this process was to write a contract that would bind a capomastro to perform specified duties within a stated period at prearranged fees. The contract method did not permit the architects to revise payments for masonry on a task-by-task basis, but it did insure that a task was brought to completion with a minimum of delay and without the possible distraction of more lucrative employment. In November 1660, Alexander VII and Bernini decided to issue a public edict advertising the contract for the masonry of the south colonnade, which would come to include the corridors as well.[70]

This decision was seen as something of a surprise in view of Bernini's opposition to contract work, and the explanation may surely be found in the nature of a project whose magnitude made a commitment on the part of the capomastri a means of insuring successful completion.[71] After all, professional and financial risks were involved. On one hand, an inconstant arrangement with workers might have left the Fabbrica with no more than a partial piazza. On the other hand, a poor decision by a capomastro willing to abide by a contract could lead to his financial ruin. Of these hazards the most immediate was the second, and the proof is to be found in the lack of response to the edict. No capomastro was willing to assume sole responsibility for the enterprise.

Eventually, Bernini resolved the impasse by organizing a group of four capomastri to work as a team at prices that would be "judged reasonable." The group was led by Simone Brogi and included Giovan Albino Agustone, Giacomo Pelle, and Pietro Ostini. The prices, evidently more attractive than those initially advertised, would have to be approved by the Fabbrica, as would the entire contract, and this is where the trouble started. Spada found the proposed table of fees excessive, and a consultation with another capomastro confirmed his suspicions. Finally, Spada had a new cause, and he pursued it zealously.

The unnamed capomastro that Spada had consulted was not himself a viable choice ("non haveva polso") and referred Spada to others who might serve ("che havessero polso") and had worked with Bernini in the past. It was a clever gambit and no doubt well intentioned, but it underestimated Bernini's leverage in the Roman building industry where capomastri depended on the architect's trust and goodwill. Rivalries were the occasional pleasure and the exclusive preserve of patrons and architects but were the anathema of skilled and unskilled laborers. These facts became clear during a fortnight of swift negotiation that pitted Bernini's stature in the trade against Spada's power in matters of patronage. Behind this test of professional knowledge

and experience, one may imagine a clash of strong wills and equally intense politiking. Events of the next days and weeks progressed as follows:

13 December 1660: Spada consults the anonymous capomastro and learns of the high prices Bernini is offering.

20 December 1660: The Fabbrica orders Bernini to ask for a more competitive price from his capomastri.

3 January 1661: The Fabbrica learns that Bernini's capomastri would actually ask for more, not less, than the agreed prices.

10 January: The Fabbrica tentatively agrees to half the increase requested by the capomastri and simultaneously seeks bids from another group.

13 January: Spada meets with two of a group of four alternative capomastri, Sorrito and Ferrari, who promise to submit a competitive bid in writing.

14 January: Spada meets with his group again, this time with a third member of the team, Fonte, and receives their signed bid. The absence of the fourth member (the capomastro initially consulted) was an omen that Spada was slow to recognize. Responding to the new competition, Bernini's group offers a price reduction just ten days after their request for an increase. On this basis Spada claims *in congregazione* that his "medicine" was beginning to take effect ("vedesimo che la medicina operava").

15 January: Bernini dispatches his brother to Spada with the message that the new contract contained an "equivoco," a mistake compromising the challengers' position. No doubt embarrassed that he has obviously neglected to read their contract, Spada sends for his capomastri.

16 January: Spada meets with Ferrari and Sorrito. The former is getting cold feet ("freddo e poco volenteroso, d'applicare l'opera") and the latter asks Spada to withdraw their candidacy. Spada temporarily dissuades them from succumbing to the pressure, folding their tents, and withdrawing ("di piegare all'accettare"). In the meantime, for the benefit of the Fabbrica, Bernini compares the capomastri Brogi and Sorrito. As to their professional competence, Bernini respects both, the former for his ingenuity and the latter for his greater experience, but ultimately prefers Brogi. Sorrito is to be preferred on a strictly financial basis, with a bid 5,000 scudi lower than his competitor's. With re-

spect to fiscal reliability, Bernini considers Brogi only marginally superior to Sorrito. As the session closes, Spada senses that his team has won.

17 January: Bernini pays Spada an early morning visit personally to announce that Ferrari is in serious debt, that future payments from the Fabbrica can only be expected to liquidate these debts rather than pay the costs of current work.

18 January: Sorrito is given the opportunity to revise his proposal without his partners, who have suddenly evaporated. To parry the thrust of these compromising developments, Spada indulges in a kind of counterinsurgence. He urges Pelle to withdraw from the first team, but unsuccessfully, and he contacts the able Carlo Fontana ("buono di polso"), who wisely refuses to become a part of the proceedings. Such professionals did not mistake the drift of the negotiations.

25 January: Despite Spada's hope that Bernini not get his way with the Fabbrica ("di non adherire al volere del Cav.re"), Sorrito withdraws "on the advice of Giovan Antonio de Rossi architect and friend of the cavaliere."

26 January: Alexander orders the negotiations closed *omni meliori modo*.

27 January: Bernini's capomastri make some concessions, the contract is written, and it is then read aloud twice *in congregazione*.

28 January: The minutes show that the contract is laid before the Fabbrica.[72] Spada learns that the capomastri are not pleased with the prices, and he urges that they be constrained to accept them.

29 January: The terms of the contract are accepted.

3 February: The issue of prices is taken up again, and Bernini expresses the hope of finishing the corridor in time for the procession of Corpus Christi.[73]

After nearly three weeks, on 21 February, a contract was drafted. The delay and the apparently superfluous discussion of 3 February may be explained by Alexander's desire to include the north and south corridors in the contract, at the same prices. This was agreed, the necessary emendations were made, and on 25 February the contract was presented and read aloud to the Fabbrica.[74] The work specified in the contract included the construction of the south colonnade and both north and south corridors. The contract was ratified and registered, backdated, to 29 January 1661, so that it would pertain to work on the corridor from that date.[75]

Later Phases in the Construction of the North Corridor

The contractual impasse explains the gap of a month and a half between 9 December 1660 and 22 January 1661 in daily notices regarding the progress of the north corridor. The new campaign took up where the old one left off, at the niches and pilasters of the wall nearest the palace.[76] A couple of days later, the foundations were begun for the exterior wall.[77] The building of the buttress niches against the palace was carried out through February and must have proved successful. At the end of the first week in March 1661, the vault of the armory was being dismantled as a first step in the destruction of the diagonal buttress wall.[78] As might be predicted, this work went slowly, and the last mention of the demolition of the vault appears on 29 April 1661.[79] This cleared the way for the full length of the outer wall to be continued.[80] The stone bases of the exterior order were set from 30 May, and on the interior from 11 June 1661.[81]

Because the dimensions of the north corridor were firmly established by this time, it was possible to excavate the foundations for corridor walls to be located in front (to the east) of the Ferrabosco clock tower and to assure their alignment with the walls rising near the basilica, even while the old palace entrance remained in use. Since the walls in front of the tower were located over the path of the stepped access ramp, they must have interrupted traffic on the piazza and entrance into the palace (the cordonata was still in use).[82] During feast days and Easter celebrations it was necessary to build temporary carriage paths across the piazza to negotiate the construction site.[83]

During the latter half of 1661, the area around the base landing was systematized. The walls of the staircase at the west end of the corridor, in front of the base landing, were finished in June 1661, and steps began to be installed.[84] On 18 October 1661, the stairs that appear next to the Scala Regia on the Bernini sketches were removed, and a day later the "piloni" around the base landing were continued while intrusive walls were demolished.[85] The bronze arms of Paul V were taken down from the wooden doors, the "Porta Scala Regia," that led to the basilica, and the doors were themselves "demolished," that is, temporarily removed. The operation of removing the doors was carried out from 20 October through 3 November 1661.[86]

The order of these operations recorded in the "diario dei lavori" gives us an insight into the construction procedure, which advanced incrementally along the corridor. From the west end of the corridor, the work progressed eastward for a time. Scaffolds were erected for building the vaults of the niches below the palace, and the four vaults built first were probably nearest the Cortile del Maresciallo, the area most critical to the stability of the whole enterprise.[87] The vaults were begun just days after the Ferrabosco curtain wall had been pulled down.[88] The last vault on the west end of the corridor was closed on Christmas Eve, 1661.[89]

When the vault behind the clock tower was closed, workers began dismantling the clock tower, in January 1662.[90] The demolition of the tower was accomplished in predictable fashion. First the mechanism was removed, and then scaffolding was erected to carry on the demolition of the tower.[91] With the help of the scaffolding, the bronze orb and cross at the summit of the tower could be removed, then the cap, or "pyramid," was demolished.[92] The clock was salvaged to be reinstalled over the piazza at the end of the diagonal wing projecting from the south end of the Logge (Fig. 117).[93]

In April 1662 Cavaliere d'Arpino's mosaic representing the Madonna flanked by Sts. Peter and Paul was detached from the wall above the Portone di Bronzo.[94] A series of notices makes it clear that a halt in the demolitions occurred due to the procession for the feast of Corpus Christi (Corpus Domini) in 1662. The scaffolding had to be dismantled for the occasion, and subsequently reerected to permit the demolitions to continue.[95] The traditional route of the Corpus Christi procession was thus important enough to warrant significant delays in construction. It is even conceivable that the delays had a symbolic importance, serving to emphasize the function of the new corridor for the procession. Eventually, the Portone di Bronzo itself was hoisted from its hinges and rolled to its new location where it was newly accommodated.[96] The columns of pavonazzo that flanked the portal in its earlier setting were removed but not reinstalled; in 1672 they were still to be found behind the basilica.[97]

The immediate prelude to the complete demolition of the clock tower was the work on the corridor vaults behind (west of) the clock tower and the corridor walls in front (east) of the clock tower in July 1662.[98] The clock tower was entirely demolished by August 1662 to make way for one of the last sections of the corridor to be completed.[99] The demolition of the "porta maggiore del palazzo, con la sua facciata, horologio, musaici, statue, e . . . altri musaici, et armeria" was recalled in Martinelli's guidebook, which is usually dated to the period 1660–62. Martinelli makes special mention of Bernini's reuse of the mosaics, the marble angels, and the bronze doors, and reports that the Navicella had been entirely dismantled without any firm plan for salvaging and displaying it elsewhere.[100] When the work in these areas was completed, attention again shifted to the west where the corridor joined the Scala Regia and the narthex of St. Peter's. To accommodate the new shape of the palace, the rooms between it and the Benediction Loggia above the narthex had to be reconfigured.

A good deal of work had already been undertaken in late 1661 and early 1662 in the area at the foot of the old Scala Regia around a doorway referred to as the Porta Vecchia or Porta Regia.[101] This work involved the removal of stairs, the demolition and reconstruction of a wall and, later, the demolition and reconstruction of an arch.[102] The documents do not permit us to identify the walls with certainty, but a reasonable guess is that the Porta Regia was composed of the bronze doors that lay between the base landing of the old Scala Regia and the portico of the basilica. A further reference to the "muro dell'Arcone in testa al Braccio" may pertain to work on the arch that terminated the west end of the corridor.[103] In March 1662, old walls were torn out and replaced with the imposts and the lunette over the Porta Regia.[104] Shortly thereafter, the vault at the end of the corridor near the foot of the Scala Regia was completed.[105] This was the vault nearest the base landing. The last wall slated for demolition in the west end of the corridor was torn down in April 1662.[106] The walls must have been consolidated by May or June 1662 to facilitate the procession of the Corpus Christi.

Figure 117. View of Vatican Palace entrance and St. Peter's from east (Photographic Archives, National Gallery of Art, Washington, D.C., Rene Huyghe Archive)

By September 1662, the structures over the base landing of the Scala Regia were being systematized between the Sala Regia and the Benediction Loggia. The large arch "of the window over the corridor" was being finished, as were the roofs over the vaults of the corridor, so that the stucco could be applied to the east-facing wall between the palace and the basilica (Plate 78).[107] This work had to be consolidated before excavations for the Scala di Costantino were begun. Our first notice of them appears in October 1662.[108] At the same time, work on the staircase proceeded from the top down, beginning with the grading of the Cortile del Maresciallo.[109] Similarly, the cordonata that connected the east end of the corridor with the Cortile di S. Damaso needed to be graded to meet the new corridor. The paving of the courtyard had to be lifted in October 1662, and significant excavations were required to join it to the new level of the corridor.[110]

We cannot determine exactly when the corridor was completed. On the basis of an avviso published by Pastor, Wittkower believed that the corridor was finished when the pope inspected the piazza on 18 November 1662.[111] The avviso does not refer to the corridor as Wittkower implied, yet the chronology may be accurate. The annular vault of the central passage through the north colonnade had been completed by October 1661.[112] A year later, on 9 November 1662, the last portion of the corridor vault was finished, thus completing the passage from the Borgo Nuovo through the north colonnade to the palace entrance at the Portone di Bronzo, and from there through the new corridor to the foot of the Scala Regia.[113]

The last page of the "diario dei lavori" is dated 13 December 1662. It indicates that eight workmen were still in the process of tearing down the clock tower which, by that time, must have been standing among the vaults of the new corridor.[114] Finally, a notice from 26 December 1662 states that Bernini brought finished drawings of the new Scala Regia for Alexander's review.[115] Thus began the final episode in the design and construction of a new entrance to the Vatican Palace.

Finalizing the Design

The *misura e stima* of the *muratori* for work accomplished between 21 February 1661 and December 1664 itemize and quantify the construction of the corridor in valuable detail.[116] From the document we learn that the roof over the entire corridor was 490 ⅓ palmi (109.5 m.) in length.[117] Twelve windows were provided for the corridor, eleven of them to overlook the piazza and one toward the rooms of the majordomo.[118] Included in these records are the removal of the statue of St. Peter to the Cortile dei Falegnami, the demolitions of the statue niche, the construction of new landings for the Scala di Costantino, and the eight steps of the first flight and forty-one steps of the second flight, which are the same numbers as are present today.[119] Another item is the document for disassembling and rebuilding of the roof over the finestrone of the base landing.[120]

The exterior of the corridor was supplied with twenty-four Doric capitals. To bring the Paul V wing down to the new level of the corridor required excavation along 334 palmi (76.6 m.), which is the distance from the entrance wall of the "porta dell'-Horologio" to the "foot of the Scala Regia" or more specifically, to the point where the wall of the wing touched the façade of St. Peter's.[121] To remove the massive wall of the armory required the demolition of its 153-palmi (34.18 m.) length.[122] To build the new corridor wall against the palace required the removal of masonry for a length of 290 palmi (64.78 m.), from the entrance wall of the clock tower to the older wall that supported one side of the Scala del Maresciallo.[123] All of these dimensions correspond to the features delineated on the corridor plan of 1660.

Perhaps the most complicated change in the arrangement of the corridor took place in finalizing the base landing. In Bernini's corridor plan, 17 steps join the base landing to the narthex of the basilica, whereas in execution only nine steps serve this function and they have remarkably low risers (Fig. 109).[124] Likewise on the drawing, 17 steps join the corridor to the base landing, but in execution this number was reduced to 13. The corridor elevation shows a rise of 11 palmi (2.45 m.) from both the corridor and the narthex to the base landing. As built, the change in elevation from the narthex to the base landing is just under 1.5 meters, and 1.95 meters between the corridor and the base landing. The lowering of the base landing brought it into a closer relation with the axes leading to it. In turn, this meant that stairs had to be added to the old Scala Regia.[125] In the event, this was easier than altering the passage from the narthex. By utilizing a greater number of steps between the base landing and the corridor, the pavement of the corridor could be inclined even more gently than the drawings had specified. (In execution, the west end of the corridor is about 23 cm. narrower and, at the east end, 26 cm. wider than anticipated on the corridor plan.)

In retrospect, so much of the corridor design seems the product of a meditative, hermetic evolution that we may be tempted to minimize the important stimuli provided by the counterprojects, Maderno's early essay on the theme of a new palace entrance, and the Bartoli piazza proposal. The counterprojects drew attention to the need to connect palace and piazza. This connection had been anticipated in Bartoli's engraving. And it is the precise coincidence of the demolitions foreseen on Maderno's drawing and those later executed by Bernini and Alexander VII that demonstrate how closely allied these two schemes were.

Maderno's plan was bold in concept, linking the structures and forms of one part of the palace to those of another, creating unity where none seemed apparent (Fig. 50). To realize this vision required one penetrating insight and two fundamental operations, which were also essential to Bernini's program a half-century later. First, Maderno envisioned an extensive east–west plane extending from the middle of the old Scala Regia, past the Scala del Maresciallo, to the wall joining the path of the Borgo Nuovo. This line prefigured the position of the north wall of Bernini's corridor. Next, the plan entailed demolishing the diagonal buttress. Maderno proposed replacing part of it to support a newly aligned stairs between the base landing and the Cortile del Maresciallo, whereas Bernini and Alexander were prepared to sacrifice the stairs to the logic of the axial entrance. Finally, to consolidate the alignment of the palace from east to west, Maderno foresaw the destruction of a bay on the southwest side of the Maresciallo. Maderno's scheme would have brought together the heterogeneous features of the palace that overlooked the piazza into a single, blocklike entity. He would have provided four floors of space for the offices of the curia displaced during the construction of the façade and nave of St. Peter's. And he would have imposed a definitive relationship between the palace and the basilica.

Ferrabosco profited from the scheme by robbing the most obvious advantage from it, while eschewing all of its difficulties. He constructed an entrance tower in front of existing foundations and simply built over and around obstructions like the diagonal buttress wall and the Cortile del Maresciallo. Superficially, the effect was the same and the cost was considerably less. By contrast, Bernini and Alexander VII cast aside most of Maderno's extensive program, culling from it an idea of the greatest aesthetic potential: an axial connection between the palace portal and the Scala Regia.

There is good reason to believe that Maderno had not conceptualized such an axis, although he had experimented with a similar composition at the Palazzo Mattei. Here, in a planning gesture unusual for Rome, Maderno aligned the entrance axis of the palace with the first flight of palace stairs. He thus created a vista from the portal through a vestibule and one side of the palace courtyard, to terminate at the principal staircase of the building.[126] Although this work was completed in 1606, a few years before his designs for the Vatican Palace, Maderno seems not to have aspired to the same goals there. The potential for realizing an axial relationship between the palace entrance and the Scala Regia was buried too deeply in the rest of the fabric. Thus, Maderno was concerned to express traditional forms in new ways, preserving the separation of the western and eastern routes to the upper palace while maintaining a loggia between them overlooking the piazza. The whole thrust of Maderno's concept was to extend and consolidate the imposing mass of the palace over the piazza.

This is where the influence of Bartoli's engraving must have insinuated itself, providing a model for the connection of piazza porticoes and palace stairs (Fig. 77). In Bartoli's idealizing vision, however, the messy reality of the palace had no part. It was left to Bernini and Alexander VII to invent a corridor to be a component of the piazza, a passage to the palace entrance, and the substructural border of the palace. Paradoxically, while the corridor conjoined piazza and palace, it removed the latter from the former, creating an impenetrable barrier of formality. Behind it, the irregular silhouettes of the palace could play upon themes of variety and formal diversity. The historic image of venerability would be retained, but with new reserve.

Perhaps most impressive is the fact that Bernini and Alexander were able to envision an uninterrupted axial route from the colonnade to the foot of the old Scala Regia by thinking through and ultimately building through the early seventeenth-century entrance and the buildings that lay behind it. In place of a clock tower, vestibule, courtyard, and cordonata leading up to the palace, Bernini and Alexander designed a broadly unified corridor, cohesive in plan and elevation. This resulted in a new majesty of image and function. The ceremony of entrance enforced by the new scheme was stately and processional rather than episodic and halting, for the visitor would have been firmly guided from the north colonnade to the foot of the old Scala Regia along a single uninterrupted axis.

The importance of this contribution, overlooked in discussions of the Scala Regia and Piazza S. Pietro, is underscored by the very cost of the operation. To build the north corridor, the Fabbrica di S. Pietro had to spend 28,643.76 scudi.[127] By contrast, the cost of the Scala Regia was a little more than half that sum, 16,591.67½ scudi, with an additional 1,418.19 scudi for decorative stucco work.[128] By incorporating the entrance portal, the Portone di Bronzo, within the more massive proportions of the colonnade and corridor, Bernini and Alexander obliterated all trace of the fortress-like character of the earlier entrance. For it, they substituted the more traditional aspects of a façade with columns and pilasters, a heavy unbroken entablature, and a balustrade crowned by statuary. The features of the palace entrance were subsumed in the scheme for the piazza. The design blurred the boundaries separating basilica, palace, and piazza, conflating the images of passage and border, and making them one in structure and meaning.

SIX

Bernini's Staircase, 1663–1666

CARLO Fontana's account of the new Scala Regia, written a generation after its construction, characterized the old "scala maestra" as a poorly lit, uninterrupted descent that challenged the courage of the pope and the endurance of his porters. In sum, it did little to enhance the dignity of the palace.[1] These concerns may have justified reconstructing and redecorating the staircase, whose proportions were not significantly different from those of the usual sixteenth-century palace, which is to say, about 10 or 12 palmi (2.23 or 2.68 m.) in width, similar to the upper flight of the present Scala Regia and to the Scala del Maresciallo. By contrast Bernini's Scala Regia is 5.21 meters between the columns and an impressive 8.29 meters between the walls at the base landing.

The new sense of spaciousness and grandeur was not lost on contemporaries. In 1670 Richard Lassels recorded how from "the Church of S. Peter you ascend into this Pallace by an easy and stately pair of stairs capable of ten men a brest."[2] This is certainly an exaggeration, since the width of the staircase between the columns at the double landing diminishes to just 3.85 meters, which cannot comfortably accommodate ten people. Lassels's reaction is nevertheless a useful measure of the impression the stairs made on contemporaries. The French architect De Cotte, for example, also made special note of the size of the stairs during his visit in the 1680s.[3] But these observations of size and capacity belie the complications that lay behind the creation of Bernini's masterpiece.

Perhaps more relevant than the limitations of the preexisting staircase is the fact that Bernini's Scala Regia was destined to have a more conspicuous role in the larger circulation network of the palace. When the north corridor replaced the Ferrabosco clock tower, a new palace entrance was created. The new Scala Regia was obviously built to complement this development in form and spirit rather than to resolve problems with the existing stairs.

Oddly enough, we have no indication as to when the new staircase was commissioned or approved. And unlike all other components of the piazza or the basilica, there is no recorded discussion of the design among members of the Reverend Fabbrica di S. Pietro. In fact, given the absence of documentary information in this regard, we may wonder if the work was ever officially sanctioned by the bureaucracy that administered its execution. To those members of the Congregation who objected to the vast expenditures on the piazza, the specter of a new project devoted to enhancing the grandeur of the palace and the glory of the papacy in the person of Alexander VII cannot have had a positive effect. Even from Alexander's point of view, there must have been some concern in promoting a project that had not been anticipated in the earliest phases of planning for Piazza S. Pietro. More will be said of these issues at the end of this chapter. Here it must suffice to emphasize that the design and construction of the Scala Regia followed the construction of the north corridor as part of the same enterprise, using the same workers, the same systems of contracts and accounting, and the authority of the Fabbrica to oversee the completion of the work.

130

Figure 118. Western buttresses of Scala Regia (Marder)

The lack of official sanctions for the Scala Regia from the Fabbrica di S. Pietro also hampers our effort to establish a firm chronology for the design process. As construction on the north corridor was coming to a conclusion in late 1662, the design of the new Scala Regia must have been well advanced. On St. Stephen's Day, 26 December 1662, Bernini brought some "finished drawings" for Alexander's review.[4] Whether these drawings offered differing solutions to rebuilding the staircase or a single solution presented in various aspects is unknown. Given the small number of extant drawings for the stairs, we might imagine a relatively short rather than a protracted period of design, but the vagaries of survival may be misleading. Nor is a documented chronology of construction much help in trying to grasp the process of thinking that culminated in the executed design.

Still, there is a good deal to be learned about the design and construction that, in turn, clarifies the nature of the Scala Regia. The evidence derives from a close reading of the drawings and documents, and from careful observations of the structure of the monument especially in areas that have been previously unexplored.

Physical Context for the Design of the Scala Regia

At the end of 1662, the old Scala Regia was still in place, incorporating the changes made by Maderno to the stairs laid out by Bramante and remodeled by Sangallo. It consisted of two unbroken flights of steps. The first flight began at the base landing and rose to the present level of the double landing, where the ascent required a 180-degree turn before continuing along its present path. As it has sometimes been said that the lower flight was encased in converging rather than parallel walls before Bernini's work, it deserves to be repeated (see Chapters 2 and 3) that this was not the case. The plans of Alfarano and Mascarino both show a stair hall of consistent width. And while neither plan has a reliable scale, their proportions conform to the dimensions of the risers that Maderno installed between existing walls in 1614–15 and to the dimensions of the preexisting situation represented on Bernini's corridor plan.

In addition to the graphic evidence, we should observe the structures on the west-facing exterior wall of the Sala Regia. Here are two buttresses that rise from the sides of the lower staircase, supporting the treads, walls, and vaults over the lower flights

131

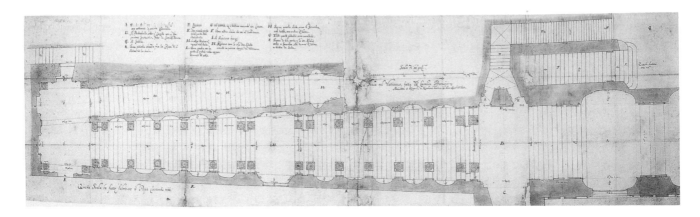

Figure 119. Plan of Scala Regia, drawing, Nicodemus Tessin (National Museum, Stockholm, CC 268)

(Fig. 118). The buttresses built by Bernini are kneed-in to conform to the converging side walls of the stairs below them. Before Bernini's work, the buttresses were parallel and more closely spaced. The north buttress was thus paired with a structure whose point of attachment can still be seen in the interrupted pattern of brick between the present supports. The tighter width conforms to our other evidence for the state of the monument before Bernini's intervention.[5] The archaeological evidence therefore gives every reason to suppose that parallel walls, supported by closely placed parallel buttresses, once enclosed the lower flight of the Scala Regia, just as they do at the upper flight.

This fact needs emphasis in view of repeated assertions in the literature to the effect that Bernini inherited rather than created the converging contours of the lower walls and thus had to compensate for the visual effects they produced. This false notion appeared in Panofsky's article of 1919, and has been revived by Evers and repeated by others.[6] Panofsky was perhaps misled by Fontana's text, which begins with the statement that the old stairs stood "in those same walls that limit the new Scala Regia."[7]

Evers's argument is based on two other pieces of evidence. The first is a conclave plan from the time of Paul V's election (1605), which shows the stairs within a trapezoidal shape. Given the notoriously diagrammatic character of the conclave plans and their unreliability in such details, however, the evidence is highly suspect. The plan for the conclave of 1655, also illustrated by Evers, proves the point, for here

the staircase is rendered as two parallel flights, but one side of the palace is flanked by Bernini's north corridor, which was not to be built for another five years. This conclave plan was evidently composed well after the time of the election and cannot be used for evidence of the palace in 1655. As is well known, the value of the conclave plans for accurate information about the shape and dimensions of the palace is mixed at best.[8]

Nor can Evers's claim of the prior existence of the converging walls be sustained by their supposed medieval origins.[9] We have studied the early history of the site in detail in Chapter 2, and found no indications for such a composition. Moreover, documents of the later 1660s prove that the walls date from the seventeenth century, and a physical inspection of them confirms the documentary evidence. As later passages in Fontana's text and observations of the masonry evidence make amply clear, the new shape of the stairs was for Bernini an especially arduous task and a praiseworthy accomplishment. The new stairs were indeed built into much of the older structure, as Fontana claimed, but not entirely. The lower and upper stairs shared a common wall, and, if our evidence is reliable, their axes were parallel when Bernini began work.

We must therefore imagine the preexisting axis of the lower stairs to have been about five degrees less than (i.e., rotated counterclockwise from) their present axis, as revealed on the plans of Tessin and Fontana (Figs. 119, 120). With this set of orientations in mind, the Letarouilly plan reveals how the new

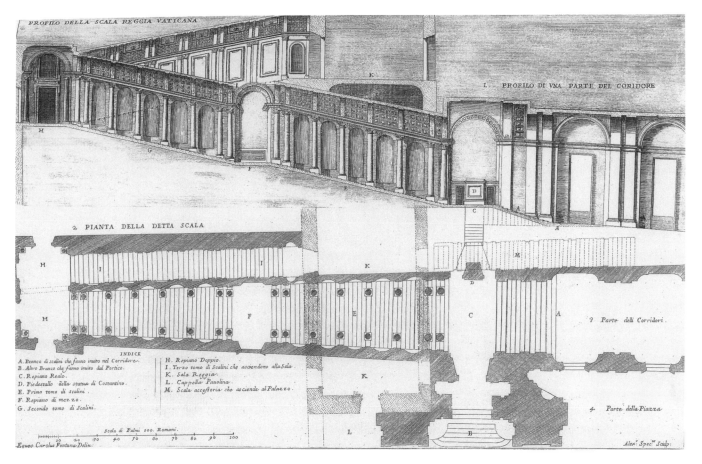

Figure 120. Plan and section of Scala Regia, engraving, Fontana 1694 (Marder)

south wall of Bernini's stairs interrupts the otherwise rectangular contours of the rooms of the palace to the south of the stairs (Fig. 121). Bernini's south wall cuts through these rooms diagonally in a manner that confirms the imposition of a new order upon a preexisting fabric of rectilinear spaces. A comparison with the Mascarino plans demonstrates that the disposition of rooms shown by Letarouilly must be dated to the period of Maderno's interventions (Figs. 34, 35). These features corroborate the evidence for the parallel path of the lower stairs before Bernini took a hand in their design.

In determining the shape of the stairs in the earlier seventeenth century, we can consider how they might have influenced the subsequent structure. For example, the former staircase had a vault nearly equal in height to that of the present barrel vault near the foot of the stairs. The height of the vault from the time of Paul V was about 44 palmi (9.829

m.) as indicated on Bernini's elevations of 1660 (see Chapter 5) (Figs. 107, 108). The present barrel vault, measured at the second bay from the base landing, is 9.8 meters, as indicated on a modern section drawing made by Vatican architects (Diagram B).[10] The congruence of these dimensions strongly suggests the spatial envelope within which the new stairs would be conceived. The image of grandeur perceived by Lassels was therefore achieved within dimensions that were not entirely dissimilar to those previously on the site. What had changed, apart from the crucial adjustment of axis, was a new system of support. This system resolved the disparity of dimensions between the broad new base landing and the much narrower passage of the uppermost flight. In this achievement, the uppermost flight of stairs, preserved from an earlier era, was brought into harmony with the new piazza and palace entrance.

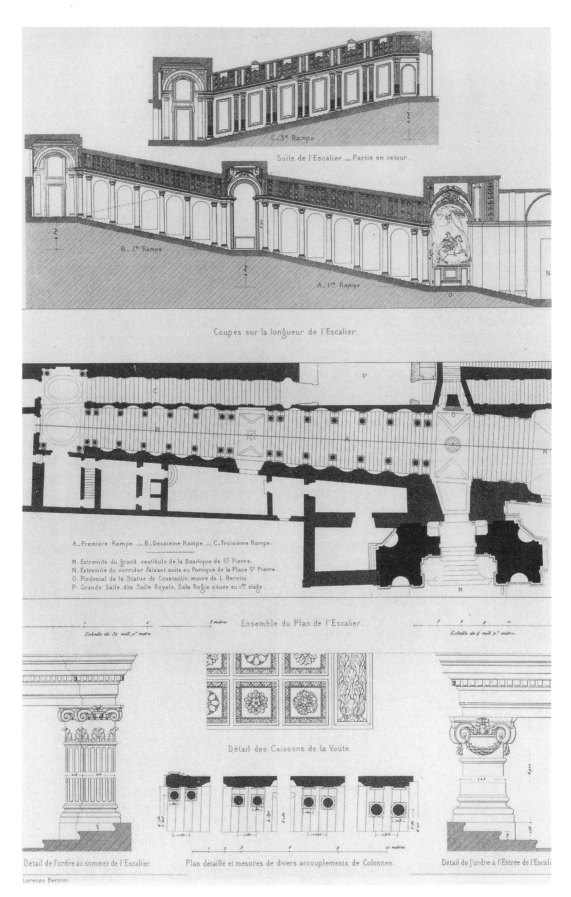

Figure 121. Section, plan, and details of Scala Regia, engraving, Letarouilly 1882 (Bibliotheca Hertziana)

Diagram B. Transverse section of the Scala Regia at the second bay from the base landing, showing the structure between the staircase vaults and floor of the Sala Regia above (drawing by Nora Onorato and Francesca Toffolo adapted from Vatican City Technical Services drawing H.4.4; SCV PLADO2)

Drawings and the Design Process

The first operations in designing the new Scala Regia must have included fixing a new axis of ascent and its perimeters, and determining the length of the lower stairs, which would now include an intermediate landing to break the monotony of the ascent. The position and orientation of the axis was a logical extension of the northern corridor axis, which had been established by 1660. The angle formed by this axis and the preexisting north wall of the stairs determined the location of the corresponding new south wall.

The intermediate landing for the lower stairs might have been positioned in a variety of locations, but a break near the midpoint in the ascent would obviously be desirable. To incorporate a window for the illumination desired by the pope, the landing would have to be situated where the exterior struc-

tures would permit a south-facing exposure. As with the disposition of the walls, the architect's options would have been limited by expense and practicality. The rooms to the south of the staircase, for example, were a necessary part of the structure and could not be sacrificed to improve the location of the window and the landing. This is where we may imagine the first drawing entering the story.

A perspective drawing in wash and chalk, now in Munich, is the earliest evidence of Bernini's efforts to systematize these features and constraints (Fig. 122). It was published by Voss in 1922.[11] The drawing offers a solution dominated by the presence of serlian arches located at the foot, the middle, and the top of the staircase. Each of the arches is borne

Figure 122. Preliminary project for Scala Regia, drawing, Carlo Fontana (Staatliche Graphische Sammlung, Munich, inv. 33864)

on pairs of freestanding columns with Composite capitals and Attic bases. The double column units are topped by sections of a projecting entablature. The section *en ressaut* at the intermediate landing is particularly prominent, for it spans two sets of column pairs.

From the arch above the base landing hangs the arresting image of two trumpeting figures of Fame bearing the papal escutcheon. This image may have been inspired by a similar group located at the foot of the stairs between the Sistine Chapel and the Cappella Gregoriana in the time of Sixtus V, although the motif is hardly unique to these examples. Unlike the narrow sacristy stairs, the composition of the Scala Regia was made to appear broad and spacious. The motif of the serlian arch was probably reintroduced from early planning phases when it appeared in projects for the arcades around the piazza (Fig. 86). At the Scala Regia, the motif assumed a more specific context when understood as a continuation of the shape of the colonnade vaults and a forecast of the window above the throne in the Sala Regia (Fig. 18). The motif also had an important structural function.

The Munich drawing provides the first graphic indication of walls that converge as the stairs rise. The walls are lined with pilasters, continuing the dominant motif of the corridor; and the spare, even severe, appearance of the barrel vaults lends an aura of spacious austerity that is consistent with the character of the corridor. At the same time, there is a distinct break from the architecture of the corridor, indicated in the more lavish architectural vocabulary of the column capitals, the decorative festoons of the lowest arch, and the animated figural sculpture.

Voss must have been prompted to attribute the drawing to Bernini because of its relationship to the Scala Regia as built. The signature in the lower left corner is certainly not autograph, and the drawing itself may be the work of the studio rather than Bernini's hand.[12] Nevertheless, there can be little doubt in the absence of other information that the ideas in the drawing bear his imprimatur if not his hand, because its features are in accord with the circumstances of the design history as we know it. Alexander had been concerned with problems of lighting, and the Munich drawing vividly emphasizes the bright illumination that was anticipated. On the drawing the shadows cast across the stairs by columns indicate strong sources of light from the portico at the base landing and from the intermediate landing. Moreover, we can imagine the sturdy arches on columns providing structural support for the walls of the Sala Regia, which run over the lower stairs.

According to Voss, the columns and arches at the foot of the stairs and those at the intermediate landing on the Munich drawing were conceived precisely to support these walls. This hypothesis can be confirmed where the second column on the Munich drawing is placed on the seventh step of the ascent. The seventh tread on the Fontana engraving also lies exactly under the east wall of the Sala Regia, whose weight would have been borne by the lowest diaphragm arch in the drawing (Fig. 120). Although Voss did not mention it, he must have realized that the number of treads between the lower sets of columns would result in the location of the second diaphragm arch (at the intermediate landing) under the west wall of the Sala Regia. He then suggested that the remaining arch (the highest in the drawing) was created to add symmetry to the design.

Voss's analysis of the drawing was, in part, a critique of Panofsky's discussion of 1919, which emphasized the visual effect of the Scala Regia and took no structural issues into account. Panofsky believed that the rows of columns that Bernini eventually set next to the walls were meant to counteract the visual effect of great depth that the converging walls would otherwise have had. Panofsky based this notion on a simple premise: since the rows of columns converged more slowly than the walls, the columns must have been intended to compensate for the swifter perspective effect of the walls.

In 1919, Panofsky did not yet know about the Munich drawing. He had been immersed in a series of articles on the theory and visual effect of perspective.[13] While writing about the Scala Regia, he did not enjoy the advantages of direct access to the monument and relied heavily on engraved representations, as he admitted.[14] These circumstances may explain his notion of a slowed (rather than an accelerated) perspective. In a rejoinder to Voss published in 1922, Panofsky maintained that the Munich drawing simply proved his point: for him, the column pairs placed ever closer to the walls along the ascent also had the effect of slowing the apparent speed of the perspective.[15] In 1931, Wittkower concurred with this notion, adding that the reduced width at the top of the lower flight brought its dimensions into conformity with those of the preexisting second flight of stairs.[16]

Panofsky and Wittkower assumed that the Munich drawing depicts a narrowing space. Panofsky went further in claiming that with the columns Bernini must have been intent on "slowing" the appearance of perspective imparted by otherwise undisguised walls. He was, of course, trying to explain how Bernini coped with the supposed challenge of preexisting walls that converged, yet we now can be certain that this convergence did not predate Bernini's intervention. In short, Panofsky was unaware of the constraints in design that were inherent in the site. Moreover, the argument of Panofsky and Wittkower presupposes that the four sets of columns in the drawing would have lined up in the visitor's eye so forcefully as to define the width of the staircase. Yet this supposition is hard to accept on the evidence of the drawing, where the presence of the walls dominates the isolated pairs of columns. The argument also presupposes that the columns in the drawing are set progressively closer to the walls as the stairs rise. Yet the uppermost columns in the drawing are not demonstrably closer to the walls than the columns of the intermediate landing. As a result of these observations, it seems very unlikely that the columns in the Munich drawing were intended to counteract the perspective reading induced by the walls.

It is axiomatic that observers see in a monument the features for which they are prepared, and there can be no doubt that Panofsky wished to see the evidence of perspective manipulation in Bernini's design. Yet the notion of the "counterperspective" effect of the columns as built cannot have been a consideration in the design process but rather, at most, a felicitous result of compositional logic. Had the rows of columns followed the contours of the walls in parallel fashion or been made to converge more swiftly than the walls, the progressive proportions of the serlian arches would have been unacceptably awkward. To maintain a relatively constant appearance of the serlian arch from the bottom to the top of the stairs, the height and width of the aisles must diminish in proportion to the progressive diminution of the main passage. Within the converging space of the walls, only a slower convergence of columns could preserve the

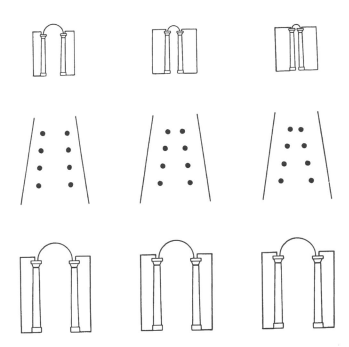

Diagram C. Schematic diagram showing how the arrangement of columns produces serlian arches with (left to right) diminishing, constant, and widening aisles, and openings of differing proportions from bottom to top. The example on the left is most like the Scala Regia, where the openings diminish proportionally as the stairs rise (drawing by Francesca Toffolo).

relative proportions of the aisles and main passage of the staircase along its ascent (Diagram C). In sum, Bernini merely followed a design procedure that could produce unified proportions along the ascending stairs.

The character of the Munich scheme was based principally on a structural solution, as Voss indicated. The lowest diaphragm arch was intended to support the east wall of the Sala Regia as already suggested, and the middle arch would have supported the west wall of the same room. The broad middle arch, which spans the intermediate landing, sits over four pairs of columns, the lowest of which are positioned on the twenty-seventh step of the stairs; on Fontana's engraving the west wall of the Sala Regia is located over the thirtieth step.[17] The correspondence of columns and vaults with the walls of the Sala Regia argues forcefully for the structural genesis of the Munich scheme. And there were other material considerations.

In the Munich drawing, the elaborate use of ink wash emphasizes the effects of light in the compo-

Figure 123. Exterior window for intermediate landing (lower left) and western buttress between Cappella Paolina and Sala Regia (right) (Marder)

indication of light from an east-facing window like the one eventually built above the base landing.

The intermediate landing required a large window with an extensive southern exposure unhampered by structures beyond the south wall of the staircase. Inevitably, the imposition of Bernini's stairs isolated some of these rooms, and they would have to be abandoned. Yet most were, and still are used. In the event, the necessary exposure for a large window at the intermediate landing could be gained only by moving the landing west of the midpoint of the staircase. Even in this position, the south-facing window of the landing is pushed flush against the rooms that precluded a more easterly location at the midpoint of the stairs (Fig. 123). The change in location of the intermediate landing also meant that the structural support offered by its columns and the broad transverse vault (shown in the Munich drawing) was removed by almost 10 palmi (2.234 m.) from a position underneath the wall of the Sala Regia. The relocation of the window and the landing thus necessitated a new solution for bearing the west wall and floor of the Sala Regia.

The solution was incorporated in the scheme shown on the preparatory drawing for the foundation medal of 1663 (Fig. 124). The drawing is located in the Vatican Library.[18] Strictly speaking, the

Figure 124. Preliminary design for Scala Regia foundation medal, drawing (BAV, Chigi J. VI, 205, fol. 264)

sition of the new stairs. Entirely bound on the north by the palace, the stairs would have to gain illumination from other exposures. This is the reason for the emphasis on light entering from the basilica narthex and from the intermediate landing, resulting in long diagonal shadows, from lower left to upper right and from upper left to lower right, cast by the columns. If sunlight was the source, the shadows at contrary angles must have been intended to demonstrate how the stairs would look in the morning and afternoon. The lower flight was particularly difficult to illuminate, and that is what the drawing emphasizes. The upper flight would have been adequately lit by a west-facing window, which is not depicted. These matters may help to account for the subsequent development of the design. It is notable that, at this stage in the design process, there is no

drawing was not part of the design process, and it may not even be by Bernini. It nevertheless serves to record a moment in the design process when aspects of his thinking had developed beyond the stage represented in the Munich drawing, after he had more thoroughly understood the constraints of the site. Bernini overcame these constraints with characteristic simplicity. He imposed lines of weight-bearing columns, broken only at the intermediate landing, to flank the walls of the staircase. A line of bearing columns permitted the intermediate landing to be located without regard for the structures above it, creating instead a broad system of support upon which the intersection of the Sala Regia, its walls, and its floor could be securely loaded wherever necessary. These structural functions were noted by Wittkower, who recognized them in the executed design even if he did not associate them with the preparatory drawing for the medal.[19]

While recalling the colonnade of the piazza, the peristyle also permitted the intermediate landing to be located in a position independent of the west wall of the Sala Regia. The paired columns, having lost their structural function, were temporarily forsaken, to be reintroduced only at a later moment for aesthetic purposes. Today the presence of the Sala Regia over the stairs is recalled only in the most innocuous details: the niches in the first, fourth, and fifth bays are shallower that those in neighboring bays. This can be seen on two plans of the Scala Regia drawn by Nicodemus Tessin the Younger, which are unique in representing these and other details (Figs. 119, 125). The extra wall mass behind the shallower niches helps to support the walls of the Sala Regia, as can be verified by comparing their location with the location of the walls depicted on Fontana's engraving.

Such features reveal the accuracy of Tessin's plans and his unfinished section drawing, the latter showing only the first five bays of the stairs, the base landing (with the equestrian lightly sketched), and the eleven steps to the corridor (Fig. 126). The plans give exact dimensions in palmi, oncie, and minuti. Together they are the most reliable records of the Scala Regia as originally built. By contrast, the details of the niches do not appear in Fontana's drawing of the plan, which, with just four rather than five bays between the base and intermediate landings, appears to rely on an intermediate stage in the

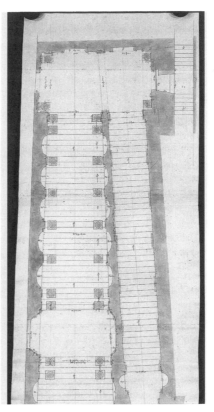

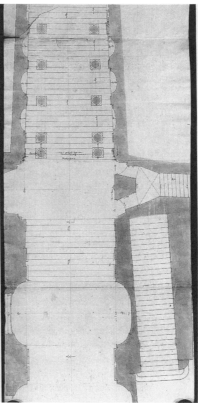

Figure 125. Plan of Scala Regia, drawing, Nicodemus Tessin (National Museum, Stockholm, THC 2172)

Figure 126. Longitudinal section of Scala Regia's lower flight, drawing, Nicodemus Tessin (National Museum, Stockholm, THC 2173)

development of the design, rather than the monument as built (Fig. 127).[20]

The south-facing window of the intermediate landing opens to a small courtyard, hardly more than a light well, that was part of the lower palace. To merge the dimensions of the window with the wider dimensions of the landing, Bernini inserted a perspective embrasure creating an apparent expansion of width where light enters (Plate 36). This means of connecting openings of different sizes is not unprecedented, although it does recall those used on the stairs of Palazzo Barberini and elsewhere in Bernini's work.[21] The result dramatizes a sequence of design decisions culminating in the invention of the rows of columns whose perspective effect is perhaps the most impressive aspect of the monument. The fact that Bernini utilized the motif to serve structural requirements only adds to the richness of the design concept as it was executed.

This analysis presumes that the columns have a structural function, as Voss and Wittkower assumed. The assumption heretofore based on circumstantial evidence can now be confirmed by direct observation. In the crawl space below the Sala Regia and above Bernini's Scala Regia (the space is marked in Fontana's engraving under the letter "K"), there are walls over the rows of columns as well as over the lateral walls of the stair hall (Fig. 120). Diagram B shows how these bearing walls are aligned above the

columns and the outer walls of the stairs to support the floor of the Sala Regia.

The isolated serlian arches resting on double columns in the Munich drawing were thus transformed into a continuous barrel vault in the drawing for the medal, whereas other features still bear the imprint of the earlier scheme. For example, the Composite columns reappear, as does the low vault over the base landing, where the groins of diagonal arches intersect. In execution, Ionic capitals were employed, and the vault was raised to a higher position. Because the size of the columns in the Munich drawing diminishes with the ascent, the same must be true of the scheme represented on the drawing for the medal, enhancing the effect of a receding perspective. The transverse arches of the barrel vault are also a strong presence on the drawing for the medal and serve to enhance the illusion of depth.

In the medal itself, a papal annual struck in 1663 for the feast of Sts. Peter and Paul (29 June), there are several important changes from the composition on the drawing (Fig. 128).[22] The perspective is emphasized by raising the figures of Fame and the papal stemma high enough to allow the full profile of the barrel vault to be seen, as Wittkower noted. In this position, the escutcheon overlaps the inscription, which is written on a banderole and rendered as though "nailed" to the pictorial field of the medal rather than isolated on the rim as on the drawing.

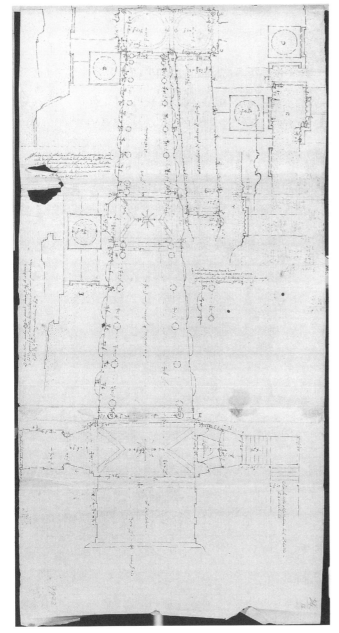

Figure 127. Preliminary plan of Scala Regia, drawing, Carlo Fontana (Windsor 9923, The Royal Collection; copyright Her Majesty Queen Elizabeth II)

In sum, the changes between drawing and medal make the illusionistic aspects of the perspective more insistent. I believe the effect of the changes betrays the spirit of the architecture.[23]

On the medal the trabeation of the corridor, absent in the preparatory drawing, provides a visual connection between the circumference of the coin and its central image. The cornices are interrupted above the base landing by a cross axis of lateral

arches, which are summarily drawn in the preparatory sheet. The level of the base landing is firmly indicated on the medal, and a distinction between the staircase and the base landing is reiterated by a change in the design of the trabeation: the medal appears to show a full architrave, frieze, and cornice over the columns rather than the contracted entablature ("cornice architravata") of the executed monument. It might be argued that the small scale of the medal precluded the representation of details like the break of the trabeation at the intermediate landing. Yet the scale of the medal was not too small clearly to represent engaged columns along the walls of the stairs rather than the pilasters that appear on drawings and the executed monument. By these means, the image on the medal offers greater depth and texture than does the preparatory drawing. In my opinion, these details reflect aspects of the design process and not simply the medalist's conception.

The drawing in Munich is difficult to date. Neither Voss nor Wittkower hazarded a guess in this regard, and our information does not supply much new insight. All are agreed that the scheme must have appeared before the preparatory drawing for the Scala Regia medal issued in June 1663. On the other hand, the Munich drawing cannot be earlier

Figure 128. Foundation medal for Scala Regia (BAV, Medagliere)

Figure 129. Putti drawn over preliminary section for lower flight of Scala Regia, drawing (chalk over graphite) (Museum der bildenden Künste Leipzig, inv. 7901)

Figure 130. Putti drawn over preliminary section for lower flight of Scala Regia (chalk over graphite), drawing (Museum der bildenden Künste Leipzig, inv. 7900)

than August 1660, when the reconstruction of the Scala Regia may have been first anticipated. Within this three-year period, it is most reasonable to date the drawings closer to December 1662, when we know that finished schemes did exist.

The preparatory drawing for the medal must be dated earlier than June 1663 and later than the Mu-

nich drawing, during a transitional period of design. This chronology is consistent with the use of the Munich scheme as a possible composition for the medal. As Courtright observed, the chalk circle drawn over the Munich sheet conforms to the placement of the stairs on the medal.[24] A transitional phase in design would also explain the changes be-

Diagram D. Tracing of preparatory longitudinal section of the Scala Regia drawn in graphite under chalk figural sketches (prepared by Nora Onorato from Leipzig 7900 and Leipzig 7901, figs. 129, 130)

tween the medal and the preparatory drawing for it. The medal itself represents a stage in the design process loosely fixed to a period before 29 June 1663.

The design process was advanced in a third drawing in Leipzig. The drawing, now cut in two pieces, is a longitudinal (that is, east–west) section of the lower stairs (Figs. 129, 130).[25] The section was drawn in lightly ruled pencil lines. On the verso of the original drawing, a study of ornamental moldings, looking much like a frame, was begun but not completed. Bernini later used the sheet to sketch putti for the Cathedra Petri in black chalk over the ruled lines. The sheet was subsequently cut, and a recomposition of the pieces in a photomontage illustrating the verso shows that the original dimensions of the paper were larger than the two existing parts.[26]

For our purposes, dealing with the original drawing (now drawings) is somewhat awkward, and a tracing of the section serves to isolate aspects relevant to our discussion (Diagram D). The section is a study of the most challenging portion of the structure, the first flight of the lower stairs that lies under the Sala Regia. This is the flight whose vaults had to rise under the Sala Regia and support its walls and floor. Wittkower pointed out where the floor and walls of the Sala Regia are indicated on the drawing. This observation can be verified by comparing the thicker west wall (on the left) with the slimmer east wall of the Sala Regia. The relative dimensions of these walls correspond to the thicker and thinner walls depicted in Fontana's engraving and on some of the early sixteenth-century plans

(Figs. 120, 28, 29). In these details we can better understand the great depth of the arch over the intermediate landing in the Munich drawing when compared to the narrower arch adjacent to the base landing.

The double column unit at the lower and upper part of the section drawing in Leipzig also corresponds to features on the Munich drawing, where the serlian arches are borne on column pairs. In the Leipzig section, there are also single columns between the lower, middle, and uppermost landings as on the medal. The Leipzig scheme thus combines design features of the two compositions, but also introduces new ones. The niches located in the walls between the columns are a new aspect of the design.[27]

In the Leipzig section, the paired columns have a common entablature arranged horizontally, as they do on the Munich scheme. Their capitals and bases are therefore at the same level. In execution, these details were modified where the entablature is horizontal only over the first column, and over the second column it is inclined.[28] The levels of the bases and capitals differ. The same holds true on the right of the drawing, where the entablature nearest the intermediate landing is horizontal and inclined over the stairs. The reason for the modification is inherent in the design: if the entablature remains horizontal over the paired columns at the top and bottom, it must climb at a steeper angle than the stairs. This in turn creates problems in proportions and visual effects, where a progressive diminution of scale is developed. The steep rise of the entablature would increase the height of the barrel vault even while its radius diminishes. The result would be a barrel vault whose proportions would be taller and narrower above the middle columns than above those at the bottom and top.[29]

The Leipzig section bears no scale, and the few dimensions indicated on it are rubbed, blurred, and mostly illegible. Next to the first column profile on the left, two numbers can be read: 51½ palmi and, above that, 4½ palmi. Without knowing precisely what features those numbers refer to, we can infer that their sum of 56 palmi (12.51 m.) corresponds to the 57-palmi height (12.73 m.) of the vault projected over the base landing. The dimensions also approximate the height of the same features in Fontana's engraving (55 palmi, 12.28 m.).

On Fontana's engraving the vault over the base landing is depicted only slightly higher than the vault over the corridor. Yet the vault is in fact considerably higher than the corridor (Plate 12). It would therefore appear that Fontana's engraving, like his preliminary plan, was based on an intermediate stage in the design process and not on the dimensions of the executed monument.[30] The approximate date of this design phase would position both the Leipzig drawing and the engraving more securely in relation to other evidence for the design process. We are consequently thrown back to the problem of dating the Leipzig section.

To begin, we must reiterate that the Leipzig section of the Scala Regia is drawn in graphite under, not over, the chalk sketches of the putti for the Cathedra Petri.[31] This is obvious from an examination of the drawing, and confirmed by simple logic: the chalk sketches of the putti make a reading of the finer architectural lines quite difficult, but the architectural lines do not disturb our reading of the figural sketches in chalk. Moreover, the graphite lines of the architectural parts appear on the front and back of the sheet, while the chalk sketches appear on the recto only. While the autograph aspect of the chalk studies is unquestioned, the most that can be said of the architectural drawing is that it represents Bernini's thinking, even if it is not from his hand. Other stylistically similar sheets of architectural studies may also be the work of a shop assistant.[32] It is easy to imagine the studio using the front and back of the sheet for thin-lined drawings and Bernini then using the front again for chalk sketches of the putti. Any other scenario involves a convoluted logic of events that also defies the evidence of the drawings as received. The artistic priority of the putti sketches (hence their succession to the finer architectural lines) was emphasized when the original sheet was cut and the pieces trimmed, no doubt by a later collector, to feature these bravura chalk performances.

If we accept that the sketches of putti came later, as the evidence indicates, the figures would provide a *terminus ante quem* for the architectural parts. Harris has dated the sketches of the putti to around 1660, presumably on the general basis of style, and Ostrow evidently concurs.[33] Because the planners were still working out the connection of the north corridor to the preexisting stairs in 1660, this date is unacceptably early for the architectural schemes.

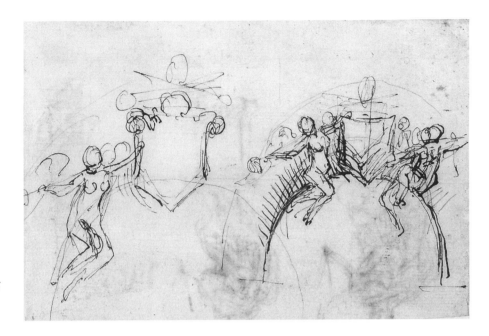

Figure 131. Studies for fames with coat of arms at base landing, drawing (Museum der bildenden Künste Leipzig, inv. 7852)

All writers agree that the chalk sketches are studies for the putti in the gloria surrounding the window above the Cathedra Petri.[34] The chronology of the Cathedra designs is uncertain, but the execution of the gloria is documented in payments from November 1663 to December 1665.[35] It is therefore possible that the sketches of the putti were done to guide the stuccoists as late as the second half of 1663. This provides a *terminus ante quem* for the architectural sketches. In my opinion, the Leipzig section drawing should be loosely dated after both the Munich drawing (around December 1662) and the medal design (well before June 1663) and therefore to the first half of 1663.

The Leipzig section does not represent the end of the design process. The definitive arrangement of the columns and wall niches, the position of the landings, and the dimensions of the plan are represented on Fontana's engraving, yet other features of the engraving differ from the executed monument. Some differences are relatively minor: he does not depict the skylights of the upper flight, there is no door in the west wall of the double landing to connect it to the Sistine staircase, the niches below the walls of the Sala Regia are not shallower than their neighbors (as previously mentioned), nor are there coffers in the narrow bay separating the base landing from the corridor (Fig. 120). Most important, Fontana's engraving does not illustrate the height or the shape of the vault as executed over the base landing.

Here Bernini built an extraordinary vault that expands upward from west to east, like a half-cone laid on its side with its outer surface nestled into the floor of the room located above it. The vault rises well above the roof of the north corridor in order to incorporate the large, east-facing window that lights the base landing (Plate 12). In fact, the pointed apex of the finestrone rises so high that it literally invades the room above it. On the exterior, the rising profile of the finestrone overlaps the horizontal course between two stories of the palace (Plate 78). On the interior, the vault is covered only by raising the floor over it in a series of steps leading to the rectangular window above the finestrone.[36]

In fact, the peak of the vault stands about 17 meters over the base landing.[37] This measurement translates into 76 palmi, which is 20 palmi higher than the configurations represented on our graphic evidence. That the drawings or Fontana's engraving simply erred in these details is unlikely. It is more likely that the Fontana engraving, like the drawings, represents a stage in the planning process rather than a record of what was built. This conclusion is consistent with additional graphic evidence.

This evidence is to be seen in a pen-and-ink sketch, also from Leipzig, in which Bernini further experimented with the position and size of the fames and the papal stemma relative to the arch to which they would be attached (Fig. 131).[38] Wittkower observed how the changes from the Munich drawing,

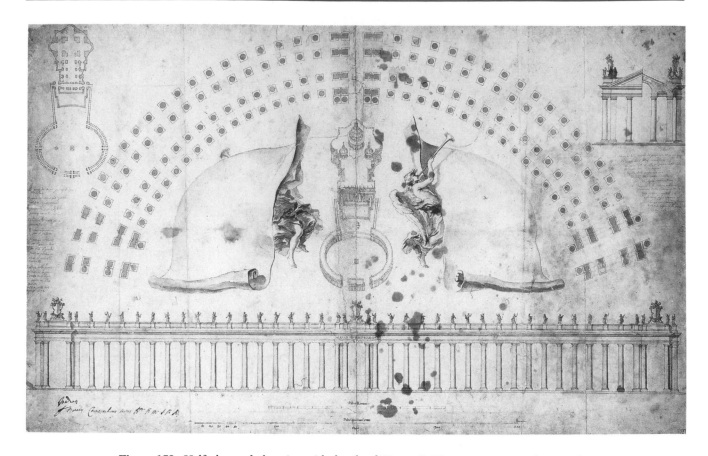

Figure 132. Half-plan and elevation with details of Piazza S. Pietro, preparatory drawing for engraving, G. B. Bonacina, 1659 (British Museum, Payne Knight Oo 3–5)

to the preparatory drawing for the medal, and subsequently to the execution of the medal, included changes in the figures of the fames and the papal stemma. The essential changes concern the size and position of the fames and the escutcheon relative to the arched opening. These matters continued to occupy Bernini in the pen-and-ink sketch from Leipzig.

I believe that Bernini began on the right of the sheet with small figures that are similar in proportion to those on the medal. These parts are lightly drawn. The pen then moved to a broader scale on the left of the sheet. Finally, returning to the right, Bernini canceled the original, lightly drawn profile of the arch and lowered it to encompass all but the tip of the escutcheon and the legs of much enlarged figures. In this process the upper profile of the arch assumes a taller aspect, while the lower profile has been set by stages ever lower against the figures. The apparent impatience with which the draftsman

realized this solution is betrayed by the quality of the pen lines. At the beginning the touch is light; it becomes more insistent on the left, and positively emphatic in the cancellations and the redrawn arch on the right.

Wittkower also pointed out that the fames on the Munich drawing were conceived to emphasize a strong three-dimensional circling motion around the escutcheon, with the left figure leaning forward and trumpeting to the left, and the right figure leaning back and trumpeting to the right.[39] This precarious choreography is forsaken in the Leipzig pen study where the figures face inward and their trumpets outward. Bernini used the motif in drawings for a number of projects such as the tombs of Giovanni Cornaro, Innocent X, and Alexander VII (Figs. 176, 177, 178).[40] It also appears in the preparatory drawing and the Bonacina engraving for Piazza S. Pietro, where the winged figures hold an inscription (Figs. 100, 132). The left figure is leaning back, and its upper body is hidden under the folds of the fictive parchment in a manner analogous to the pose of the right figure on the Munich drawing.

The partially hidden figure conveys the notion of movement suspended in space.[41] For the Scala Regia this figure was studied in three other pen sketches also in Leipzig.[42] Each of the sheets contains two studies. The first sheet of the series establishes the pattern of drapery around the bare leg emerging from the figure (Fig. 133). Two billowing folds appear to cushion the leg from below. These folds reappear on the second, related sheet where Bernini experiments with their position below the extended leg (Fig. 134). Here, an elaborate contrapposto (right leg forward, right arm back; left arm forward, left leg back) is complemented by the elegant path of a twist of drapery from the left leg, across the body, and around the right shoulder.[43] Turning the sheet of paper over, we see how Bernini briefly experimented with a different arrangement in the upper figure, where the drapery crosses the torso in a less elegant manner and terminates in a rather artificial flourish around the legs (Fig. 135). Finally in the lower figure on this page, the earlier configuration of the drapery is restored, wings are added with the indication of the trumpet, and the figure is designated as definitive by a circle and cross drawn on the lower edge of the sheet.

After so much study, it is surprising that the pose was not employed at the Scala Regia, but it was adopted for one of the angels (not a fame) bearing the papal escutcheon on the south side of the portico, where the equestrian figure of Charlemagne would be placed in the eighteenth century (Fig. 136). In this location, the concept of two winged figures flanking the Chigi escutcheon was purposefully repeated to emphasize the relationship with the north side of the portico. The fames are obviously appropriate for the palace entrance, and their iconographic importance would explain why a backward leaning, partially hidden pose would have been inappropriate: fames trumpeting the glories of Alexander VII at the palace entrance had to assume assertive, not reticent poses. On the south side of the narthex, the figures could be transformed into angels, and the pose of the partially hidden body could be thoroughly exploited.[44]

Courtright and Lavin have followed Wittkower in suggesting that the progressive changes in the po-

Figure 133. Preliminary study for fame at base landing, drawing (Museum der bildenden Künste Leipzig, inv. 7810)

Figure 134. Intermediate study for fame at base landing, drawing (Museum der bildenden Künste Leipzig, inv. 7809)

sitions of the fames, from the Munich drawing to the medal, served to incorporate the figures and the escutcheon more fully into the architecture. These authors maintain that the reason for raising the figures in relation to the extrados of the arch was to

Figure 135. Definitive study for fames at base landing, drawing (Museum der bildenden Künste Leipzig, inv. 7809)

reveal the uninterrupted continuity of the barrel vault. Lavin also pointed out that the "underpitched" vaulting above the base landing depicted in the drawings and the medal was raised to a much higher elevation in execution. This is an important new observation, and Lavin suggested that the increasingly elevated position of the fames was related to the raising of the vault during the design process.[45]

The relationship of these figural studies to the architecture of the vault is undeniable, but there are limits to this line of reasoning. For while the figures of Fame appear ever higher from one drawing to the next and highest in the medal, the height of the vault represented in these images does not change. When the vault was raised, employing a remarkable combination of structural features, the motivation was surely more pressing than the relocation of a pair of fames and a papal coat of arms. Presumably, the structural pyrotechnics were invented in response to the introduction of Constantine to the ensemble, for the tall vault and its window serve to wash the equestrian with dazzling brilliance and give it spiritual meaning.

Since neither the drawings nor the medal includes the statue of Constantine, the scale and position of the fames would have been initially adjusted for intrinsic aesthetic effects. Their incorporation on the extrados of the stairs later coincided with the raising

Figure 136. Angels and coat of arms at west end of south corridor (Marder)

and reshaping of the vault over the base landing. The primary purpose in raising the height of the vault was not to give the figures of Fame more space, but rather to incorporate the magnificent finestrone that illuminates the statue of Constantine.

Unfortunately, the evidence does not permit us to date this moment in the evolution of the design. A reasonable *terminus post quem* is indicated by the first notices about the Constantine during the pontificate of Alexander VII, datable to April 1662.[46] A firm *terminus ante quem* is provided only by Alexander's diary notation about the Constantine in July 1664, when the stairs were very nearly finished.[47] The pope's commitment to the Constantine by this time is confirmed in late 1664, in the planning and execution of the large window over the base landing designed to illuminate the statue. Between these dates there is only Alexander's diary reference to "disegni rifiniti" in December 1662, which may or may not correspond to the schemes on the Munich drawing or the foundation medal. My guess is that the drawing and the medal may be dated late in 1662, and that the medal was struck to commemorate the beginning of the work in early 1663 according to a design that was already superseded. The statue of Constantine, which required the structural adjustment of the base landing, would have been introduced into the ensemble by the beginning of 1663. With the resolution of this component, other matters

of construction could be engaged with the same ingenuity and a similar flair for dramatic resolution.

Before passing to issues of construction, we must briefly consider a drawing that entered the design process before a definitive scheme for the finestrone had been accepted. The drawing, from Bernini's workshop, depicts an angel holding a banderole with the words "IN HOC SIGNO VINCES" (Fig. 137). The project has been previously associated with the decoration of the pier niche over St. Helena at the crossing of St. Peter's.[48] Yet the extensive documentation for the crossing in the basilica offers no evidence of a design semicircular in shape for that portion of the piers.[49] Nor would the shape fit in the north aisle of the basilica, where the equestrian Constantine had originally been intended. On the other hand the luminous character of the representation would be quite consistent with a window decoration for the Scala Regia, much like the window design for the contemporary Cathedra Petri.

If my guess is correct, this project would have been generated during the planning process immediately after Bernini's Constantine was to be transferred to the Scala Regia and before the grand, east-facing window assumed its present profile. The drawings show a composition originally intended to be executed in the finestrone above Constantine. The massive wooden cross would have been mounted below or to the side of the window, much

Figure 137. Angel bearing inscription "IN HOC SIGNO VINCES" within lunette, drawing (BAV, Archivio Chigi 24915)

as it is today (Plate 12). The uninspired banderole of the present composition, so difficult to associate with Bernini's penchant for movemented forms, would have been a late substitution for the more evocative and expensive window, which nevertheless carried precisely the same message. Like the pointed profile of the finestrone, which is surely not intended to evoke associations of Gothic form, the clear glazing that was installed represented something of a compromise in execution rather than a distinctly new aesthetic impulse.[50]

Construction Procedure

The construction of the Scala Regia was Bernini's greatest technical triumph in architecture, an achievement hailed by contemporary biographers and later commentators for its daring. The architect himself thought it his most challenging accomplishment, as we learn from the account of his son Domenico:

> Although the work appeared of little note at first sight, it proved so challenging for the Cavaliere that he used to say that this was the most difficult task he had ever accomplished and that if, before beginning it, he had found it described by someone else, he would not have believed it. After supporting a large part of the Sala Regia and the Cappella Paolina on the walls of the stairs, it suited him to widen them, to demolish the walls and support these huge buildings on braces. On these he rested a great vault that he built over the new staircase which, necessarily broader at its base than its summit, freed it of any deformity with a most artful invention. When he raised two straight lines of columns on both sides, they made the middle equal in proportion and width [at the top and bottom] and at the same time they helped to fortify and provide a flank to the vault that sustains the weight of the exceedingly heavy construction.[51]

Domenico's description was rehearsed in abbreviated fashion in 1681 by Baldinucci, who understood the general importance of the monument as clearly as he misunderstood the method by which it was achieved.[52] In the biography of the architect's son, we have confirmation that the stairs were broadened at the base and that the composition of columns was managed in such a way as to preserve the proportions of the flanks and the middle passage

through their height. We also have confirmation of the structural function of the columns.

A still more vivid account of the operation is given by Carlo Fontana, an active participant in the project, who provided details that cannot be learned from any other source (Appendix). Fontana wrote a "nuts-and-bolts" description of construction that evokes images so compelling as to explain why Alexander VII wanted at least part of it recorded in drawings. At Bernini's instance, regrettably, none were made. We must therefore be content with Fontana's description, which elucidates the structure still visible above, below, and around the staircase.

On the Letarouilly plan of the Vatican Palace depicting the floor below the Sala Regia, there is a room (now room 32 of the Gallery of Modern Religious Art) recognizable by lines of groin vaulting and three piers as the old *marescalcia* (Fig. 19).[53] This room is the substructure for the north half of the Sala Regia, originally extending under its entire length. A computer tracing over the plan enables us to reconstruct the original extent of the space uninterrupted by the path of the Scala Regia (Diagram E). Confirming the impressive dimensions of this room in its original state are the remains of its vaulting, still visible (much damaged) in the crawl space over the Scala Regia and under the Sala Regia. (See Diagram F for locations of Figs. 138–52.)

We have mentioned this space with reference to Fontana's engraving under the letter "K" (Fig. 120). To call it a "crawl space" is only partially accurate. Although one must crawl on all fours to gain access to it, some areas are big enough to stand in. Because it is impossible to photograph in its entirety, one must imagine the space as composed, like the staircase, of a nave and flanking aisles. Here we can actually see bearing walls aligned above the rows of columns on the stairs. Holes in the walls averaging about 1.5 meters square permit access from one side of the crawl space to the other. Remains of the vaults that originally supported the Sala Regia floor reveal a concrete and tufa matrix coated with stucco and painted white (Figs. 138, 139). Most of this vaulting has been sliced away to accommodate the palace stairs, but we cannot be certain when this was first done. Across the east and west sides of the crawl space can be seen a series of massive brick arches which support the east and west walls of the Sala Regia (Figs. 140, 141). Near the apex of Bernini's

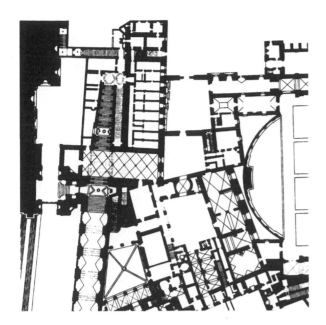

Diagram E. Computer restoration of the vaulted *marescalcia* located under the Sala Regia. The Scala Regia now occupies the left portion of the *marescalcia*, whose vaulting survives in ruins in the crawl space above the staircase (Figs. 138–144, 146–151). The portion to the right (north) of the Scala Regia survives as room 32 of the Gallery of Modern Religious Art (adapted by Nora Onorato from Letarouilly).

Diagram F. Detail of Diagram E showing the location of Figs. 138 (a), 139 (b), 140 (c), 141 (d), 142 (e), 143 (f), 144 (g), 146 (h), 147 (detail below b), 148 (i), 149 (j), 150 (k), 151 (detail above e), 152 (l). Dashes between letters on the diagram denote related images.

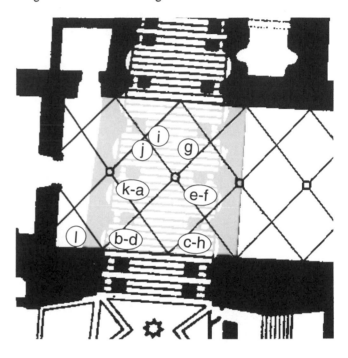

central vault is a reinforced pier that was originally one of the supports in the vaulted space below the Sala Regia (Figs. 142, 143). Also over the apex of Bernini's principal vault, but running east–west along its spine, hangs the remains of a wall that formerly ran parallel to the stairs (Fig. 144).

The vaults and walls directly over Bernini's Scala Regia are otherwise hidden under existing rooms. Over the path of the lower staircase beyond (to the west of) the Sala Regia presently lies the modern sacristan's rooms. They are entered directly from the Sala Regia and are stepped up from east to west to give space to the rising vault of Bernini's construction (Fig. 145). (It was once possible to see how the vault over the base landing was couched in the floor of a room above it in a similar way, but that floor was entirely changed in 1990, before I was able to

photograph it; see my comments, with dimensions, elsewhere in this chapter.)

There is no other datable, physical evidence of a staircase on the path of the present Scala Regia before the sixteenth century, although a staircase probably existed on this site as Chapter 2 suggests. In Bramante's time, there was such a stair, the Via Iulia Nova, and we know that Sangallo impressively rebuilt it. Thereafter, we have documents pertaining to changes made at the base of the stairs to accommodate the new level of Maderno's façade for St. Peter's. With this information, we can make some informed guesses about the visible remains.

The large brick arches at the east and west of the crawl space were probably built in the sixteenth century by Sangallo the Younger, who reinforced the walls of the Sala Regia when its height was

Figure 138. Crawl space above Scala Regia with Bernini's wall over south columns (left) and wooden strut and masonry (right) supporting remains of earlier vaulting (Marder)

Figure 139. Crawl space above Scala Regia with Bernini's wall over south columns (right) and masonry supporting remains of earlier vaulting; early sixteenth-century masonry in background (Marder)

Figure 140. Crawl space above Scala Regia with early sixteenth-century masonry between Bernini's walls (Marder)

Figure 141. Crawl space above Scala Regia with early sixteenth-century masonry between Bernini's walls (Marder)

increased (Figs. 146, 147). We cannot be certain whether Sangallo or Bramante was responsible for disrupting the vaults in the room under the Sala Regia, because we do not know the height of the stair hall in their day. Nor do we know if an earlier staircase stood on this site. We do know that the width of the Scala Regia before Bernini's intervention was about 16 palmi. The broken masonry that sits along the spine of Bernini's barrel vault may have been the southerly wall of this staircase. This conclusion would be consistent with the location of the exterior buttress that adjoined the west wall of the Sala Regia (Fig. 118). Ultimately, Bernini enlarged the path of the Scala Regia where, at the base landing, the width

Figure 142. Crawl space above Scala Regia with Bernini's wall over north columns (right) and wooden and iron struts supporting the remains of earlier vaulting (Marder)

Figure 143. Crawl space above Scala Regia with Bernini's wall over north columns (left) and wooden and iron struts supporting the remains of earlier vaulting (Marder)

Figure 144. Crawl space above Scala Regia with Bernini's principal vault (below) interrupting an early sixteenth-century wall (middle) previously supporting an earlier vaulting system (above) (Marder)

Figure 145. Rooms over lower flight of Scala Regia west of Sala Regia, with steps to accommodate the rising vault of staircase (Marder)

was 37 palmi (8.29 m.) between walls and 20 palmi (4.47 m.) between the lowest columns.[54]

Bernini's problem, as Fontana pointed out, was to rebuild the stairs without endangering the integrity of the Sistine Chapel, the Sala Regia, and the Cappella Paolina, whose structures were interdependent with that of the Scala Regia. Bernini's procedure was simple and effective. He built around existing structures. Making extensive use of wooden beams, he ensured that older vaults and walls would remain in place, and simply built new ones under, over, through, and to the side of preexisting masonry. Another set of timbers was used to support the shuttering for new walls and vaults and to brace them against the old ones. When the work was done and the masonry had cured, the inessential portions of the preexisting structure could be safely cut away. So, too, could most of the supporting beams.

Evidence of the process is still visible in the crawl space, where Bernini's vaults were cast right over

Figure 146. Crawl space above Scala Regia with details of sixteenth-century masonry (Marder)

Figure 147. Crawl space above Scala Regia with details of sixteenth-century masonry (Marder)

Figure 148 (left middle). Crawl space above Scala Regia with sawed-off stumps of temporary support beams (Marder)

Figure 149 (left bottom). Crawl space above Scala Regia with sawed-off stumps of temporary support beams (Marder)

Figure 150 (below). Crawl space above Scala Regia over southern aisle between Bernini's timber and masonry supports (Marder)

some wooden supports. When the vault was set, the beams were roughly sawed away, leaving only a small length in the core of the new masonry (Figs. 148, 149). Other wooden supports were installed to act as struts, primarily between new walls and old vaults. Without these struts the old vaults would collapse, endangering the integrity of both newer and older components and spaces (Figs. 142, 143, 150). In one place, a particularly large expanse of earlier vaulting is supported by iron tie rods. The rods are embedded in a travertine block in a new wall (it is located above the fourth column from the base landing on the north side), and they extend to support a broadly arching section of the fifteenth-century vault (Fig. 151). More numerous are the massive beams with their flat heads abutting older vaults and their lower ends footed deep in new walls. That this work dates from the pontificate of Alexander VII is indicated by chalk graffiti, including the Chigi emblems (Fig. 152).

Despite the appearance of great spaciousness in the lower run of Bernini's new stairs, the strengths and tolerances of the materials were not stretched beyond their traditional capacities. In determining the width between the columns under the axis of the Sala Regia (the fourth set of columns from the base landing), we find that Bernini used the same measurements that separate the piers in room 32 of the Gallery of Modern Religious Art, the old *marescalcia*.[55] In other words, Bernini continued the rhythm of the older support system under the southerly portion of the Sala Regia, so that the columns of the Scala Regia are never more widely spaced than the old piers under the Sala Regia. At the Scala Regia it was building technique, not technology, that was and remains remarkable among those familiar with that art.

This much of the building process can be certified in the visible remains on the site. Yet the problems posed by the older structures and their aging masonry were not over. After the work was begun, Fontana reported, it was discovered that the wall common to the upper and lower flights of the old stairs was largely in tatters, threatening the stability of the three major ceremonial spaces directly or indirectly connected with it. Again, Bernini seized upon the use of a system of wooden braces, struts, and jack stands so conceived and erected that they won the admiration of the *professori* as well as casual

Figure 151. Crawl space above Scala Regia with iron struts supporting earlier vaulting (Marder)

Figure 152. Graffiti with Chigi emblems in the vaults over the Scala Regia (Marder)

visitors. This was the triumph that Alexander VII wanted to record in drawings. Bernini's refusal, Fontana wrote, was based upon the fear that this very evidence could be turned against him, as it had been recently in the basilica. (The reference is to the bell towers for St. Peter's, which had to be demolished when cracks appeared in the foundations.) Should some problem arise at the Scala Regia, the architect would be forced to forfeit "the credit he had won with such difficulty."

In addition, there may have been another reason for Bernini's refusal to record the scaffolding in a drawing. We recall the claim reported by Domenico that the architect would not have believed such a structural feat possible had he not accomplished it himself. This assertion is so rich in meaning that it must be true, and it is supported by Fontana's account. Filled with terror at the sight of so great a fabric suspended in midair, he said, the fear "would have discouraged us from working below it, if we had not first carefully ascertained that this rigging of supports with diagonal chains was able to sustain it [the fabric]." Hence the real potential for disbelief and, incidentally, testimony to Fontana's subordinate role in the enterprise.

In truth Bernini's "disbelief" in his own accomplishment was a clever disguise for the fact that the achievement was due in part to a valued assistant. Here again, Fontana provides the crucial information: the system for bracing the crumbling walls was due to the "gran prattica, & intelligenza del Capo Mastro Simone Brogi." Indeed, Fontana credited Brogi, "questo esperto Professore," for working so carefully and so closely with Bernini that the reinforcements themselves gave "form and mass" to the new staircase, although Fontana firmly assigned the design itself to "the artifice of the above architect," namely Bernini. Here it is pertinent to recall the contractual squabbles of 1660 recounted in Chapter 5, when Bernini characterized his nominee, Brogi, as the "one of greater ingenuity," in contrast to Spada's candidate, who had greater experience. The record proves that Bernini's assessment was more than hollow partisanship. It was so accurate as to prove potentially embarrassing.

The only other features of the Scala Regia that required innovative building techniques were the skylights for the upper stairs. From the documentary evidence, it would appear that the design and con-

struction of the skylights had no precedent. They may have been among the last contributions to the architectural design, having been invented while building was under way. At least that would be a reasonable explanation for the information recorded in the documents.[56] First the preexisting vault had to be torn down and rebuilt.[57] This must have been done before the idea of the skylights came into being, because the new vault was itself dismantled and rebuilt, presumably to incorporate the skylights.[58] Alexander VII's diary offers some chronological indications for these events. In July 1664, after he and Bernini discussed the work at Ariccia, their thoughts turned to the windows of the upper stairs of the Scala Regia.[59] In the following month, Bernini, having already begun to design the Scala di Costantino, produced some trial designs ("saggi") for the windows.[60] This information corresponds to the nature of the execution recounted in the documents.

Bernini's skylights were built into the barrel vault some four meters over the upper flight of stairs.[61] The skylights were undoubtedly more troublesome than anticipated, as the wording of the payments suggests. Here we find records "for making the roof over one of the said skylights and then tearing it down"; for "an arch made under one of the said skylights, which was torn down"; "for . . . a piece of roof, and then tearing it down, and then returning to rebuild it, and break it down again . . . and walling it up."[62] The payments include notices for the building of a model, and there is every reason to believe that it was required to answer the need for what was, in essence, an untried architectural component.[63] This model or studies related to it were presented to Alexander VII on 31 August 1664.[64] Without these documents and an eighteenth-century mention of the six skylights in the upper stairs, we might still wonder whether the two existing skylights that appear in Letarouilly's section were invented later than the seventeenth century (Fig. 121).[65]

Thus, contrary to the notion of Bernini's redesigning and decorating an existing space, as the older literature would have it, the present Scala Regia gives ample evidence of his invigorating spirit in matters of structure and execution. And while the antiquated view of Bernini as a mere decorator has long been revised, it has been replaced by the belief that Bernini's talent as a sculptor overshadows his achievements as an architect. The truth of the matter is that Bernini's goal in every architectural commission was to achieve a richness of expressive content by controlling space and light to a greater degree that his classicizing architectural vocabulary might imply.

Building Chronology and Decoration

Construction of the Scala Regia followed immediately upon the completion of the north corridor. The corridor was essentially complete by December 1662, and in the following month Bernini and Alexander were busy planning the demolition of the old Scala Regia.[66] On 26 January 1663, the pope could still use the old Scala Regia to arrive at St. Peter's.[67] By March, he had to use an alternate route and chose to leave the palace by way of the newly graded cordonata from the Cortile di S. Damaso to the north corridor.[68] Work at the Scala Regia was then well under way. Long ago, Fraschetti published a notice of 9 April 1663 purporting to establish the beginning date of the Scala Regia. Fraschetti misunderstood and misdated the document yet, as luck would have it, the false date turns out to be surprisingly close to a chronology supported by more comprehensive documentation.[69] The earliest work in stone can be dated to April and May 1663.[70]

To maintain the dignity of the site while work was under way, a canvas was hung across the foot of the stairs, hiding the disruption to the palace and its new ceremonial entrance. The canvas was covered with gesso painted to resemble "the arch and cornices" that would eventually be erected at that spot.[71] The motif of a perspective representation at palace entrances was popular in the mid-seventeenth century, as we shall see in Chapter 9, and the canvas at the foot of the future Scala Regia no doubt depicted the fictive recession of space that the monument would evoke in three dimensions.

As time went on, the new construction continued to interrupt the usual patterns of ceremony and ritual. Such was the case when the work threatened the traditional observance of the Chinea at St. Peter's. The Chinea consisted of the Neapolitans' ritual presentation of a white horse to the pope as a sign of their fealty. The pope would receive the offering at St. Peter's. In June 1663, to the displeasure of

the Spanish (Naples was ruled by Spain), Alexander planned to hold the ritual at the Quirinal rather than the Vatican Palace. His reason was presumably related to the construction under way on the Scala Regia. Later, he wisely agreed to stage the event at the Vatican as usual, even though it required him to use the Sistine sacristy stairs rather than the Scala Regia to descend to the basilica to meet the throngs.[72]

It is curious that we have no report of a foundation ceremony for the Scala Regia. On 27 November 1663, the medalist Gaspare Morone was paid for ten copper medals with the image of the Scala Regia that had been "placed under the columns of the said stairs."[73] Perhaps a small ceremony did take place for symbolic purposes on 29 October 1663, the anniversary of Constantine's victory at the Milvian Bridge and triumphal entry to Rome. If so, the equestrian statue of Constantine would have been destined by this time to be placed at the foot of the stairs, although it was not included in the representation on the medal prepared well in advance. Gold versions of the medal also existed, and Alexander gave one to a visitor in February 1664.[74]

Alexander would not have missed the opportunity to stress the symbolic importance of the new ceremonial entry to the palace, even if the foundation ceremony was less than extravagant. But he was equally interested in the technical aspects of the work. Already in May 1663, he had probably paid a visit to the building site, and he did so again for certain in early December 1663 in the company of Bernini.[75] The later visit might have been the occasion for Alexander to suggest recording the construction process in drawings, a suggestion that Bernini declined, as we have seen.

In any case, the Scala Regia was still very much a construction site at the end of 1663, and the pope's visit may be understood as a supervisory inspection as well as a demonstration of his involvement with the project. At the time, raw masonry was still in evidence wherever new walls stood and new vaults enclosed them. Yet even before the columns were in place or the walls fully articulated, the new aspect of the lower stairs must have contrasted in a striking way to the traditional shape and proportions of Sangallo's upper stairs, which would remain undisturbed for several more months.

On 13 April 1664, Alexander again descended the

Scala Regia, this time in the *sede gestatoria* for the Easter ceremonies in St. Peter's. As was usual, he was raised on the chair in the Sala Ducale ("ubi sede gestatoria ascendio") and brought down the stairs under a baldachin ("sub baldachino descendia per schala magna . . . ad Porticus S. Petri").[76] By this time, the essential components had been systematized. The steps of the upper flight had been reset, and all of the columns of the lower staircase were "in opera."[77] The only temporary structure necessary at the time was to be found at the base landing, where a "ponte" was required for the papal entourage to enter the narthex of the basilica and then into the church itself.[78]

The unfinished state of the base landing is of some significance, given Alexander's propensity to extemporize in matters of architectural design. For, on the day after Easter, that is, 14 April 1664, he spoke to Bernini about two new ideas, no doubt inspired by the use of the stairs on the previous day. One was to employ the niches in the walls of the Scala Regia as places "for the use of pilgrims," in other words, posts of honor where favored visitors might observe papal processions of one sort or another. The other new idea was to make use of the space behind the present location of the Constantine to build another staircase connecting the Cortile del Maresciallo to St. Peter's.[79] The proposed stairs would reestablish the link between the Cortile del Maresciallo and the entrance of St. Peter's.

It is hard to believe that a feature like the Scala di Costantino, so fully integrated into the architectural composition of the site, would have made such a late entry in the design process, and yet that appears to be the case, judging from our sources. Indeed, with this information, the chronology of the documents falls easily into place. Three months after the Easter procession, on 13 July 1664, Alexander and Bernini were still discussing the resolution of the lower portion of the newly planned staircase around the "two openings where the statue [of St. Peter] is and where the Constantine will be located."[80]

In mid-November 1664, there are payments for the "scaletta nuova a piedi la Scala Regia," which must pertain to the lowest eight steps of the Scala di Costantino. From this document, we also learn that the stairs employed had been salvaged from the previous staircase on the site.[81] The work of arranging the new stairs required the removal of the old

statue of St. Peter, the demolition of the statue niche, the construction of new landings for the stairs, and the installation of 49 treads and risers, the same number as are in place today.[82] The chronology is consistent with the mention of the statue of St. Peter in Alexander's diary some months earlier, in July 1664.[83] Among the works documented from November 1664 is the installation of the pointed arch that accommodates the east-facing finestrone.[84]

Then in late March 1665, after an inspection of the Cathedra Petri and the new paving of the narthex, Alexander "ascended by the stairs to the cortiletto and through the [Sala] Regia to the Stanze."[85] This notice of the Scala di Costantino is the first to indicate that the staircase was finished. The chronology explains why the *misure* for the Scala di Costantino are among the last to be made for the Scala Regia enterprise. Only after this time could Bernini and Alexander turn their attention to the placement of Constantine, including fixing the design and location of the pedestal.

The use of the unfinished Scala Regia for the Easter celebrations in 1664 is but one indication of Alexander's eagerness to see the project completed. Other examples are to be found in the payments for "covering the rough masonry of the scala nuova for the procession of Corpus Christi in the years 1664 and 1665."[86] We may conclude that during the course of 1664 and 1665, the Scala Regia began fully to assume its new role within the circulation patterns and ceremonial functions of the Vatican Palace, by offering a spacious, well-lit connection between the palace and the basilica.

Brogi and his team were able to build the structure of the Scala Regia within the remarkably short period of two years, between January 1663 and December 1664.[87] The truth is that the construction time may have been even briefer, but we simply do not have a firm date of commencement on which to depend. To be sure, work remained to be accomplished in 1665 and 1666, as the list of subsequent payments attests, but this period of the enterprise was dominated less by construction than by embellishment. The records of the period include payments for stucco, glass, lettering, and coloring.

The most prominent of these decorations consisted of the papal escutcheon and the trumpeting figures of Fame. The escutcheon was produced by Pietro Sassi by June 1664.[88] The figures of Fame, carved by Ercole Ferrata, were paid for in three installments on 29 August, 10 October, and 14 November 1664.[89] Ferrata (1610–86) was among the most talented and trusted of Bernini's assistants, having worked for the master on the Pimentel Tomb at S. Maria sopra Minerva, the confessio at S. Francesca Romana, the decoration of the nave of St. Peter's, the decoration of S. Maria del Popolo, the Elephant and Obelisk monument at Piazza S. Maria sopra Minerva, the Cathedra Petri, the Cappella del Voto in Siena, and the angels at Ponte Sant'Angelo.[90] It is not surprising that Bernini chose him for the most conspicuous job at the Scala Regia. For his work on the two figures of Fame, Ferrata was paid a total of 130 scudi. The two wooden trumpets were turned on a lathe by Carlo Padredio.[91]

The other sculptors responsible for stuccoes at the Scala Regia were Lazzaro Morelli (1619–90) and Paolo Naldini (c. 1623–91), both regular members of Bernini's stable of assistants. At the Scala Regia, Naldini was paid a total of 145 scudi for his "figure e putti" between 30 January and 5 June 1665.[92] Morelli was less active at this commission, having been paid a total of just 40 scudi in two installments on 26 March and 24 April 1665.[93] Surprisingly, none of the documents indicates which artist was responsible for the relief medallions over the base landing, and this must remain for the moment an open question. Morelli was active in Bernini's work on the nave decoration of St. Peter's and at S. Maria del Popolo, as well as at the colonnade, the Cathedra Petri, Ponte Sant'Angelo, the tomb of Alexander VII, and the Tabernacle of the Holy Sacrament.[94] Naldini had worked for Bernini on the interior of S. Maria del Popolo, the statues of the colonnade, the interior of the church at Ariccia, and the Ponte Sant'Angelo.[95]

Apart from the figural decoration, the sculptural embellishment of the stairs was executed by the *capomastri muratori*. A long document published by Borsi and Quinterio in their book on Bernini, mentions every detail that belongs to this aspect of the ensemble and the price of its execution.[96] The list of features begins at the double landing and proceeds down to the base landing including all the accessible rooms in between. The document then records the work done at the summit of the Scala Regia, outside the door to the Sala Regia, and concludes with a list of the items required to complete the decoration of the Scala del Maresciallo. This *misura e stima* constitutes the most complete and concise account of decorative elements for any building by Bernini. It was presented to the Fabbrica and approved on 23 September 1667.[97] Payment was made on 9 December 1667.[98]

Of the other contributions to the decorative ensemble, the most noteworthy are due to painters, glaziers, and woodcarvers. In October 1663, at the order of Bernini, the glazier Andrea Haghe made a trial window on which the Chigi star was represented against a blue field, and this was redone the following month.[99] The windows for the double landing were executed only in the following year, and they were painted by Giovanni Paolo Schor.[100] In April 1665 Haghe submitted a bill for two new windows, each "fatti à fuoco di color turchino con la Stella."[101] Others of similar design were also contracted.[102] A bill for work done by Haghe beginning in April 1664 includes, under the date of 29 May, the sum of 79 scudi for redoing a large arch over the Scala Regia with its 529 pieces of glass.[103] If this work was accomplished to glaze the finestrone, as I believe, we have thus a likely date for the completion of the vault behind it. The vault and the window were raised to provide the light necessary to illuminate the equestrian statue of Constantine.

One of the most elaborate ornaments of the upper portion of the stairs was the pair of elegantly carved wooden doors on the double landing. This rich floral design, with opulent oak leaves surrounding the papal mounts, resembled the motifs employed in fabric designs for liturgical vestments and draperies for churches produced by the Bernini studio. In this case, Schor was the artist responsible, and his drawing is perhaps one that has been previously mistaken for a fabric design.[104] The leaves and branches were carved almost fully free of their relief and gilded.[105] Their effect may very well have been intended to evoke in three dimensions the silken hangings that were common furnishings in the basilica on the most sacred occasions. Although much deteriorated today, these doors must have been among the principal glories of the staircase.

Other parts of the staircase and its decoration that are monochromatic today were also painted, such as the medallions in the vault above the base landing and the figures of Fame and their trumpets. The wooden doors at the summit of the stairs, leading into the Sala Regia, were evidently carved as well as painted.[106] Finally, between 15 April 1665 and 15 November 1668, virtually all parts of the Scala Regia were whitewashed or painted "the color of travertine" as was common at the time.[107]

Responsibility for Design, Construction, and Embellishment

We have already remarked on the absence of notices for the Scala Regia in the minutes, resolutions, or decrees of the Congregation of the Fabbrica. Despite the fact that the Fabbrica kept all records of the enterprise and footed the bill for it, no presentation to this body by Bernini or anyone else was ever recorded. This fact is all the more striking in view of the objections to Piazza S. Pietro and the battles over its design as recorded in the meetings of the Fabbrica, in Alexander VII's diary, in Spada's literary remains, and in the drawings of the counterprojects. It may just be that these skirmishes had exhausted the participants, especially Bernini's principal patron. Another possibility is that Bernini, as architetto di palazzo during Alexander's reign, succeeded naturally to a task so intimately related to the functions of the palace.[108]

Among others in the papal court who would have had a lively interest in the Scala Regia, Virgilio Spada (d. December 1662) was a discriminating dilettante, a highly informed supervisor, and the one serious rival to Bernini's hegemony over the design of the piazza and its dependencies. He was devoted to architecture, a man of great knowledge in the art, and he had considerable experience in matters pertaining to the basilica, the piazza, and the Borgo. We have mentioned his plans for the Borgo and the spina, and his part in unraveling technical matters pertaining to the failure of Bernini's bell towers is well known.[109] We will not be surprised therefore to discover that wherever the dust was kicked up over aesthetic, financial, or practical issues at Piazza S. Pietro, his opinion was quick to be heard.

By nature extravagant in his scheming, Spada was also a remarkably tight-fisted administrator, who knew the value of a scudo in the architectural workplace. With Spada, however, Bernini's relations were often strained, their mutual suspicions fueled by a long history of manipulation and contrary in-

tervention.[110] It was he, for example, who had the most to say about Bernini's compensation for designing Piazza S. Pietro.[111] Spada's claim that he was never really opposed to Bernini and often supported him speaks eloquently for itself. While not necessarily disingenuous, it calls attention to a perception in the seventeenth century that was no doubt shared by Bernini.[112]

In truth, the case for Spada's influence on the piazza is perhaps stronger than has previously been supposed. Alexander chose him to announce the project and conferred with him frequently. We have seen that compositional features such as the paired order (ultimately forsaken) and the triple passage with an annular vault (retained) were probably due to Spada's influence. For his role in the design of the north corridor, there is little proof. He knew the problems, as his advice for resolving it ("like a slow fever") indicates, but for a contribution to the design there is no evidence. Nor is there evidence of a contribution by him to the design of the Scala Regia.

While Alexander sought the counsel of both Spada and Bernini, he was obviously aware of the friction generated by their creative personalities and never consulted them together. He preferred rather to nourish his faith in the talents of his artist and, separately, to rely on Spada's intimate knowledge of building. Anxious to realize an appropriately grand connection to the basilica and, by way of the corridor, to the piazza, Alexander VII may simply have discussed the project in private. This would have been easier after the death of the tireless Virgilio Spada. Late that month, we have the first notice of presentation drawings for the stairs in the pope's diary. The circumstances tend to rule out any significant contribution by Spada to the design of the Scala Regia as we know it, even though he was active in other architectural enterprises, such as the systematization of Piazza della Rotonda, until the eve of his death.[113]

What then of the pope's role in the design of the Scala Regia? In the person of Alexander VII was a unique combination of planner, builder, and client in the modern sense of those terms. In his youth he had made a study of Vitruvius and other sources of theory and composition.[114] His promotion of building projects all over Rome is legendary and his infatuation with the architecture and planning of churches and piazze is still evident throughout

Rome, Siena, Castel Gandolfo, and Ariccia. At the Vatican Palace and St. Peter's, his sympathy for building had special significance, for in these places he was primary occupant and chief celebrant, as well as principal patron.

In the contemporary accounts we have surveyed, the record of Alexander's participation in the realization of the Scala Regia is so rich that the terms of the question change. It is not a matter of whether but rather how the pope contributed to the design and execution of the monument. In my view, Alexander and Bernini carved out the essential building program as a team, reviewing together the possibility of aligning the north corridor with the old stair hall and eventually configuring and decorating the new one. Their work in these matters was so closely allied that one should hesitate to make more precise distinctions, even if we could make definitive attributions of the drawings to either man.

Nevertheless, the impetus for introducing certain features and the responsibility for realizing others may be hinted at in the sources. Domenico Bernini wrote that it was Alexander who recognized the stairs to be "inferior . . . to the majesty of the place from which they came and to which they led," painting a picture of Alexander as the commander and Bernini as his lieutenant. This approach appeals to common sense and it is underscored by Fontana's assertion that the pope found the ascent to be too narrow, steep, and poorly lit to complement its context. Alexander's diary is particularly revealing in its attention to matters of lighting as, for example, in the two notices from 1657 regarding his concern about the lights of the previous staircase.[115] Moreover, our analysis shows that he also inspired the skylights on the upper flight.

These preoccupations would have found ready acceptance in Bernini's view of architecture. From his earliest works, Bernini had been consistently concerned about the introduction of light into his buildings. We have already studied the impact of the intermediate landing on the larger design, the dramatic realization of the finestrone about the base landing, and the troublesome resolution of the skylights on the upper flight of the stairs. It may be indicative of the entire building process that, in all of this activity, Alexander is witness only to a model for the skylights. The circumstances reinforce Bernini's role as facilitator. Then, too, Alexander would

have been most concerned about functional and ceremonial routes and patterns of circulation in the palace. It is he who notes in his diary as early as 1657 the necessity of the cordonata as a connection between the piazza and the Cortile di S. Damaso.[116] This fact deserves some emphasis, as Bernini's meticulous corridor plan of about 1660 still does not include this feature, perhaps because the architect could find no convenient method of incorporating the old structure. Yet it eventually is included in the design and execution of the corridor.

In matters of structural design, on the other hand, Bernini must have been completely in charge. Even so rich a source as Alexander's diary contains no hint of Alexander's participation in this field, and Fontana's discussion repeatedly mentions Bernini's masterful direction of the works to which all documentary evidence bears consistent witness. It is worth recalling Fontana's report of Alexander's desire to have a drawn and written record of the most challenging aspect of the work, when the walls of the old stairs had to be shored up before the new construction could proceed. Such a request would have been unnecessary had Alexander been responsible for the scheme, nor could Bernini have dismissed Alexander's wish if the scheme were not entirely his own responsibility.

Fontana mentions his own activity at the Scala Regia so modestly that he can only have been one of the talented team of palace architects contributing their expertise to the success of the enterprise. That he did participate and have ready access to the workshop is amply certified by his detailed knowledge of the project, which is recorded in his account of the enterprise (Appendix). This narrative surpasses that of any other contemporary source in its thoroughness and precision. Nevertheless, Fontana gives no evidence and makes no claim that he himself had anything to do with the conception of the design.

The only other candidate eligible to share design honors with Bernini and Alexander would be the "ingenious" capomastro Simone Brogi. According to Fontana, it was Brogi's reserves of invention that rescued the operation from the potential disasters posed by the ruinous walls of existing structures. For how much more was he responsible? One possibility is that he, rather than Bernini, invented the two lines of columns that characterize the monument. In the discussion of the shoring up procedure, did Fontana refer to Bernini as "the architect" and Brogi as a "Professore"? In this account Brogi's reinforcing arches "almost give form and mass to the Scala Regia," wrote Fontana, referring to the form-giving aspect of structural components.[117] This is important, because later on, in describing Bernini's rebuilding of the stairs, Fontana claimed for "the virtue of the Professore" the inspiration to dress up its "unhappy framework" with Ionic columns, bases, and capitals all in travertine.[118] Whether "professore" refers to Brogi or Bernini will simply have to remain in doubt, as will the invention of the rows of columns. My own suspicion is that Fontana, well aware of Brogi's impact on the design, purposely encouraged our indecision to forestall a less than flattering image of the architect of the Fabbrica. If the great inventions came from the "aiutanti" and "professori," perhaps the role of "architetto" required some fostering protection.

The essential fact to emerge from so close a reading of the evidence is that a famous architect like Bernini could derive major design ideas from an assistant, as well as from the stimulus of a client. In these respects, the situation is similar to modern architectural practice. In the case at hand, there can be little doubt that the design process embraced stages of thought for which we have no record, and these would also influence our understanding of the creative process that led to the realization of the monument. Apart from information on the design chronology, however, we may not have lost much of crucial significance for the architecture. Most likely, our chief lacunae lie in the creation of the decoration. For it was, ironically, in the realm of decoration that the principal artist and his assistants had the broadest latitude for experimentation. Although the essential shape and structure of the Scala Regia were largely a response to necessities imposed by constraints of the site, this was not the case for the stucco and painted embellishment.

In matters of architecture, executors were necessary to realize the form and meaning of a design. With respect to a vast decorative program, the problem is more complicated and our conclusions must be more tentative. This much we know: the architectonic and figural sculpture of the Scala Regia was a product of Bernini's stable of sculptors and decorators, all of whom were simultaneously involved with other commissions under his authority. There can be no doubt that he hired these assistants because of their ability to realize his ideas faithfully, even if their style differed from his.

Although Alexander's diary offers no evidence of his involvement with the sculptural embellishment of the Scala Regia, his participation in the exaltation of the papacy must be assumed. Without Alexander's approval, the conspicuous display of his escutcheons would be unthinkable. Similarly, the Constantinian medallions in the vault over the base landing must have been part of a program Alexander approved and perhaps invented. While still a cardinal, Chigi had taken an active interest in the Constantine statue from the time of its commission in 1654 (see Chapter 8).

The many references in the iconography and individual motifs of the sculpture to themes in the Sala Regia, the Sistine Chapel, and the Cappella Paolina were no doubt the joint inventions of Bernini and Alexander, who had paid close attention to the decorative and ceremonial functions of these rooms in other contexts, as when they remodeled the Sala Ducale in 1656–57 (see Chapter 9).[119] The putti there forecast those later placed at the summit of the Scala Regia over the door into the Sala Regia, and the fictive cloth around them anticipates the drapery later arranged behind the equestrian statue of Constantine. For the experience of the visitor, of course, these features are presented in reverse chronological order, indicating how Bernini adjusted the vocabulary of the staircase decoration to anticipate conspicuous motifs in the ceremonial rooms of the palace. Other examples of the process have already been mentioned.

The strong community of style and form among Bernini's various works for Alexander also argues for the secondary importance of the assistants in matters of invention. The *ignudi* over the base landing and the intermediate landing are stylistically related to the figures over the windows at Sant'Andrea al Quirinale.[120] The figures of Fame appear in a study for the memorial inscription for Urban VIII at S. Maria in Aracoeli, as well as at Sant'Andrea and in a preliminary scheme for S. Maria del Popolo.[121] The Constantinian medallions over the base landing are similar to the medallions in the dome of S. Tommaso di Villanova at Castel Gandolfo.[122] The putti in the vaults of the double landing resemble those in the dome of S. Andrea, S. Maria dell'Assunzione at Ariccia, and the Fonseca Chapel in S. Lorenzo in Lucina.[123] Many other comparisons could be made to argue for the community of motifs employed by Bernini in his other commissions executed by various assistants.

The same considerations apply to the architectonic decoration, where individual forms and their combinations frequently appear in other commissions by Bernini. The motif of the coffered extrados, which appears behind the fames and the papal escutcheon on the medal for the Scala Regia, also appears on the arches over Bernini's *Noli Me Tangere* in SS. Domenico e Sisto and over his altar to the Blessed Ludovica Albertoni.[124] It was eventually employed behind the angels at the end of the south corridor in 1671 (Fig. 136). A system of decorated coffers and transverse ribs like those over the lower flights of the Scala Regia appears in the side reliefs of the Cornaro Chapel above the half-length portrait busts.[125] The motif of the floral garlands bound by ribbons that flutter over a coffered vault was incorporated in the dome of the Fonseca Chapel (Plate 31).[126] And we have already noted the double-voluted rib termination that appears inside the finestrone of the Scala Regia and in the dome of the church at Ariccia, as well as on a working drawing for the figure of Fame (Fig. 134).[127] Such comparisons bear witness to a common fund of decorative motifs repeatedly employed by the shop at Bernini's command or with his approval.

Results of the Design Process

In view of the short time between the earliest document for the Scala Regia in 1663 and the completion of its structure by the beginning of 1664, we may consider the possibility that some work was under way before the notices for it appear, and perhaps before a definitive design had been established. The circumstances encourage this hypothesis: once the width of the corridor was changed from 22 palmi (represented in the Vatican plan) to 38 palmi (represented in Bernini's large elevation and section) we can assume that a momentous change in thinking had taken place. The earlier dimension would have suited the width of the existing Scala Regia, but it would not have embraced the width of the staircase

immediately south of it, which appears in Bernini's façade elevation. The wider span of the new corridor design did precisely that.

As construction of the corridor progressed, the solution to the design of the new Scala Regia would have become increasingly obvious. It would also assume the shape of a tapered passage, with a wide opening joining the corridor at the base landing, and a narrower dimension where the staircase arrives at the double landing. The composition of the double landing was designed to feign a parity of the dimensions between the openings to the lower and upper flights of stairs. Bernini retained Sangallo's upper flight and the location of the double landing and, hence, the slope between them. The slope of the lower stairs was determined by the location of the base landing (on axis with the narthex) and the depth of the intermediate landing. With so many features preordained, it would be natural for the structure of the new staircase to anticipate a definitive design.

As Maderno's successor to the post of architect of St. Peter's, Bernini was in a unique position to appreciate the potential of his predecessor's projects for restoring the integrity of the Vatican Palace. The consolidation of the old Scala Regia along the same axis that defined the south front of the palace and the northern border of the piazza produced a new unity of form and functional purposes. For now, beyond the obvious cohesion of façades and spaces, the portions of the palace to the east of the stairs could be brought into geometric conformity with those west of the stairs, and their alignment gave form to a new monumental entrance to the palace.

This process entailed a historic reevaluation of the palace fabric and its public orientations. In the past, the visitor entered the palace through the Portone di Bronzo and ascended the cordonata to reach the Cortile di S. Damaso and the Palace of Sixtus V. The path of approach was characterized by frequent changes in scale and direction without any apparent motivation beyond that of realizing the traditional east-facing entrance to the palace. By contrast, the broad avenue of the north corridor provided a calculated transition between the straight streets of the Borgo and the axial organization that defined the expression of power in palatial architecture of the seventeenth century. At the end of the north corridor, the visitors began their ascent to the "Regia" mentioned in the inscription on the foundation medal. This ascent takes place entirely within the palace precinct. Because the perspective made the ascent appear long, the visitor must have seemed rocketed to the summit.

The effect of the lower flights, ensconced between columns of diminishing height to either side of a rising vault whose radius grows ever smaller, had a deliberate psychological effect. Even in the sixteenth century, Cortesi recommended stairs with turns and landings to discourage a full view of the ascent in the single glance. "For men," he wrote, "are clearly moved much more slowly to do those things which contradict nature. And it is, in fact, against nature for bodies to strive to reach high places, thus it is natural that men are less eager to ascend those stairs which their eyes tell them to be the steepest."[128] This, in a nutshell, is the situation cultivated by architect and patron at the Scala Regia with its deep treads and short risers stretching between converging rows of columns. That the space was clearly understood as a perspective is demonstrated in the writing of Nicodemus Tessin the Younger who termed "L'Escallier Pontifical au Peristyle . . . fort remarquable, tant par rapport à la quantité de Colonnes, que la belle diminution qu'il a observé selon la Perspective."[129] In the notes to his second trip to Rome, he mentions "die Treppe in Perspectiv" and "die perspectivische Treppe," which leaves no reasonable doubt about his understanding of the monument within the illusionistic tradition.[130]

In sum, the daunting challenge of the lower flight was a kind of sorcery brewed to surprise and edify visitors. All too quickly, they reached the double landing, from which it was but a short distance to the most magnificent hall of state in the palace. This route bypassed the extroverted sections of the palace, such as the Logge, and favored a more firmly controlled experience, which is the essence of ceremony. Even in descent, a program controls the passage as the inscription on the foundation medal states, "from the aula to the house of God" ("AB AULA AD DOMUM DEI").

SEVEN

The Design and Execution of
Bernini's Statue of Constantine 1654–1670

CRADLED in a tall but shallow niche at the foot of the stairs, the equestrian sculpture representing Constantine's Vision of the Cross provides a dynamic visual image where the ascent to the palace begins. In fact, there is little about the sculptural composition to betray its long and complicated history. The statue was originally commissioned for the interior of St. Peter's in 1654, during the pontificate of Innocent X Pamphili (1644–55). Upon the accession of Alexander VII, the stone was acquired, only to languish in the artist's studio until it was destined for its present location. Bernini's work on the statue continued through the pontificate of Clement IX Rospigliosi (1667–69), and the unveiling finally took place during the reign of Clement X Altieri (1670–76) in 1670.

Sixteen years in the making, the equestrian statue of Constantine is the only sculptural commission by Bernini to have been actively pursued through more than two pontificates – indeed no fewer than four. Little wonder that the complicated history of the work has never been fully described.[1] The purpose of this chapter is to follow the fortunes of the commission through drawings, documents, and sources, and to trace the path of Bernini's thinking for the commission that became the longest running drama of his career as a sculptor. In view of the time elapsed between the initial commission and its completion, the many elaborations of form and meaning to emerge from the evidence will hardly be surprising. So many meanings may be attached to the monument that a subsequent chapter will consider them at greater length.

Most modern visitors see Bernini's Constantine from the portico of St. Peter's, where the horse and rider appear against a backdrop of animated drapery (Plates 18, 19, 20). Constantine looks up in a glance of surprise and amazement reinforced by his outstretched arms and upturned hands (Plate 21). The action is directed toward a gilded cross in the upper reaches of the vaulted space (Plate 25). His horse reacts to the same stimulus with a turn of the head, flared nostrils, and an open jaw that evokes the animal's fright.

The sculpture rests on a pedestal incorporating two doors that lead to the Scala di Costantino concealed behind the statue. Above the horse and rider, the niche is terminated by a coffered arch whose profile is twisted to the right. The skewed aspect of the arch is entirely rectified when seen from the corridor connecting the staircase with the colonnades of Bernini's Piazza S. Pietro (Plates 10, 16).[2] This suggests that the commonly reproduced view from the narthex was not the only, or even the primary view of the ensemble. When seen during the morning hours from either the portico or the corridor, the horse and rider are washed by waves of natural light. Its source is the huge east-facing window whose peak soars high into the vault over the base landing.

Against the arched opening into the Scala Regia, the trumpeting figures of Fame hold between them the papal escutcheon of Alexander VII Chigi. Two roundels with reliefs depicting the baptism of Constantine and Constantine founding St. Peter's are set in the vault over the door to the portico and over the equestrian, respectively. Like those on Michelangelo's Sistine ceiling, and similar to their many Roman progeny, each roundel is borne by two *ignudi*. Pairs of sphinxes crouch above the moldings surrounding these portions of the vault (Plates 11, 14, 17). On the sill of the east-facing window, against the light, the Cross appears directly in line with Constantine's gaze. Below the Cross, a banderole bears the words "IN HOC SIGNO VINCES" ("in this sign you will conquer"), signifying the theme of the vision (Plate 12). In this ensemble, Bernini's goal was to create the momentary effect of Constantine's Vision of the Cross and to relate that event to the Constantinian heritage of St. Peter's and the papal palace.

The circumstances of Constantine's vision are known as follows. Having decided to challenge Maxentius's rule over the empire, Constantine entered Italy over the Alps and prepared his march on Rome. The enemies met at the decisive Battle of the Milvian Bridge on 29 October, A.D. 312. Maxentius was vanquished, and Constantine made a triumphal entry into the city. Some time before the triumph – sources do not agree as to where or when – Constantine had witnessed an apparition of the Cross that foretold his victory. As a result, when the battle was won, Constantine disbanded the Praetorian Guard, ordered a stay of Christian persecutions, and issued a new decree of religious toleration. Soon after, he founded the basilica over St. Peter's grave and founded the basilica of S. Giovanni in Laterano as well.[3]

The most widely known account of the apparition is that of Constantine's contemporary Eusebius (c. 260–c. 340) in his panegyric, the *Life of Constantine*.

> And while he was thus praying with fervent entreaty, a most marvelous sign appeared to him from heaven, the account of which it might have been hard to believe had it been related by any other person. He said that about noon, when the day was already beginning to decline, he saw with his own eyes the trophy of a cross of light in the heavens, above the sun, and bearing the inscription, CONQUER BY THIS. At this sight he himself was struck with amazement, and his whole army also, which followed him on this expedition, and witnessed the miracle.[4]

In his sleep that night, according to Eusebius, Constantine witnessed a second vision, this one of Christ, bearing "the same sign which he had seen in the heavens" and commanding Constantine to use it

in all encounters against his enemies.[5] This is the essence of a story told in many variations from the time of Lactantius in the fourth century to Jacob of Voragine in the thirteenth century and Baronius in the late sixteenth century.[6]

It is obvious that Bernini's representation pertains to the first vision or apparition and not the second. Despite any similarities to representations of a conversion and despite the frequent references to it as such, Constantine's apparition of the Cross was not a conversion.[7] Although the notion of a conversion is prevalent, the true subject of the equestrian group was made explicit by the artist in a letter of 30 December 1669 to the French minister Colbert contrasting the conception of the statue to that of Louis XIV. In that letter Bernini described his Constantine as "represented in the act of admiring the Vision of the Cross appearing to him."[8]

The Commission for St. Peter's

The relevant documents in the Archivio della Reverenda Fabbrica di S. Pietro, never previously gathered systematically, provide a full account of the commission for Bernini's statue of Constantine. Even before the first official record of the commission, Bernini was actively considering the equestrian, since on 5 September 1654, he paid a visit to Cardinal Fabio Chigi – the future Alexander VII – and showed him a design for the statue of the emperor.[9] The first official notation of the commission appeared on 29 October 1654. According to the terms, Bernini was to receive 100 scudi a month for work on a memorial to the emperor Constantine that was to be erected in the basilica and composed in a manner "similar" to the memorial for Countess Matilda.[10] On 30 October 1654, 300 scudi was allotted for the project.[11]

A list of expenses of the Fabbrica for March 1655 includes a provision to pay the stone supplier Filippo Frugone for two pieces of Carrara marble for "the statue of Constantine on horseback and its basrelief."[12] In fact, the 300 scudi originally set aside for the work was meant to pay for the stone, for that is the amount the supplier was to receive as advance payment on 7 April 1655.[13] We know this to be the cost of the marble from the contract for the "two pieces of Carrara marble on which would be carved the story of Constantine the Great by the Cavaliere Bernini to be put in St. Peter's."[14] According to the contract, the smaller piece of stone was to arrive in Rome within three months, by June, and the larger by December 1655. Both were to conform to *model-letti* mentioned in the document and provided by Bernini himself.[15]

Heretofore, it has been assumed that Bernini worked on the commission under Innocent X, but abandoned it upon the accession of Alexander VII.[16] Documents and circumstances enable us to refine these conclusions. When Bernini's contract was written in October 1654, Innocent X was already ailing. He died on 7 January 1655. As the stone was not expected in Rome until the end of 1655, Berni-ni's work for Pamphili would have been confined to drawings and models. An undated notice in the Chigi archives mentions a payment to Bernini of 400 scudi "beyond the 500 scudi received in the time of Innocent X."[17] If the artist did receive a hundred scudi a month for his work during the Pamphili pon-tificate, he would have been at the job for five months from September (or perhaps August) 1654 through the new year – a time frame that corre-sponds to the notice of his meeting with Cardinal Chigi to discuss the Constantine.

Chigi had a deep interest in the project, which, contrary to being abandoned, was given new life on the very day of his election, 7 April 1655, when the Fabbrica arranged to pay for the stone, as indicated above. (The contract was corrected and rewritten on 9 April 1655.) Since the members of the Fabbrica were papal appointees, we can assume that their res-olutions were consistent with the desires of the newly designated pope. All of these circumstances validate Domenico Bernini's much quoted passage describing how "the sun had not yet set on that happy day which saw the creation of a new Pontiff when the Cavalier was summoned by the Pope and treated by him with demonstrations at once appro-priate to his new dignity and to their old reciprocal affection."[18] By the spring of 1656, the impressive marble, weighing over 30 carrettate, arrived in Rome.[19]

Three drawings survive from the earliest period of design, presumably under Innocent X. One, now in the Academia de San Fernando in Madrid, is surely an autograph testimony of Bernini's ideas (Fig. 153). It was introduced by Wittkower, who

maintained that the monument is depicted in the niche of the first pier along the north aisle in St. Peter's, next to the tomb of Countess Matilda, which was installed in the second pier of the north aisle.[20] Whether this was the design that Bernini showed Cardinal Chigi we may never know, but the drawing does prove that the artist was thinking about the site in St. Peter's, as the dimensions of the equestrian and its setting would suggest.[21] Moreover, there are chronological and thematic reasons to subscribe to Wittkower's location of the intended monument on the first pier of the north aisle. From 1652 the vaults and domes of the north aisle were being embellished with mosaics under the direction of Pietro da Cor-tona.[22] The iconography of Constantine's Vision of the Cross in this area makes good sense as the Cap-pella della Pietà (first chapel on the north) was orig-inally dedicated to the passion of Christ and the Cross, and the mosaic depicting the mystery of the Cross dominates the vault of the aisle in front of it. (Michelangelo's *Pietà* was installed there only in 1736, and the dedication was changed in 1749.) Be-cause the Cappella S. Nicola (second on the north) was known as the Cappella del Crocifisso until 1626, there was a legacy of the Cross and its iconography here, too.[23]

The drawing in Madrid indicates how the com-position of the equestrian was initially conceived with both horse and rider twisting more vigorously than would be the case in the executed monument. A source for the emperor's pose is to be found, in reverse, in Raphael's fresco of the meeting of Leo the Great and Attila, which decorates the wall of the Stanza d'Eliodoro in the Vatican Palace (Fig. 154).[24] Here, the invader's hands are flung back and his gaze is turned upward in the opposite direction. The correspondence is surely not coincidental. Bernini's son and biographer stressed the study his father made of the frescoes in the Vatican by Raphael, Giu-lio Romano, and Michelangelo.[25] In this case it may be that Bernini intended to emphasize Constantine's surprise by quoting the reaction of Raphael's Attila to the same sort of heavenly sign.

In the Madrid drawing, the horse, more massively muscular than in execution, turns its head backward in avoidance. By contrast, the rider is transfixed by the apparition, while his shoulders and torso are turned to the viewer so that both of his hands are clearly visible. The startled gesticulations of horse

Figure 153. Study for equestrian statue of Constantine in St. Peter's, drawing, (Academia de San Fernando, Madrid)

Figure 154. Meeting of Leo the Great and Attila, fresco by Raphael, Stanza d'Eliodoro, Vatican Palace (Alinari/Art Resource, N.Y., AN1137)

Figure 155. Study for equestrian statue of Constantine, drawing (Museum der bildenden Künste Leipzig, inv. 7915)

and rider in the Madrid drawing seem to turn upon themselves, and these compressed movements respond to the constricted dimensions of the site in St. Peter's. The position of Constantine's hands, the violent turn of the horse's head, and the turn of the horse's body would have contributed to a dramatically physical conception in the relatively narrow width of the aisle of St. Peter's. The effect would have been more tactile and visceral, and less pictorial than the executed group.

A second drawing, now in Leipzig and certainly not autograph, reflects this early moment in the design process (Fig. 155).[26] It may be a copy of the Madrid drawing or a successive phase of design: the turn of the horse's head and the twist of the rider toward the viewer are nearly identical, although not as vigorous, the muscular energy of the horse has been diminished, and the rider's massiveness has been increased. A third drawing, also from Leipzig and associated with the early phase of the project, features a pair of putti (one with wings) raising a glowing cross in the midst of clouds (Fig. 156).[27] In the upper left corner is a head identified as a study for Constantine. The head has been traced through from the verso of the sheet, which had until recently

been pasted down (Fig. 157). Brauer and Wittkower believed that the cross and putti were intended for the location of the monument in St. Peter's, no doubt because they differ in composition from the Cross and banderole executed in the Scala Regia. In addition, the cross and putti mounted directly over the niche in St. Peter's would explain the pronounced torsion of the equestrian in the early phase of design and also provide a component analogous to the pair of putti above the "similar" memorial to Countess Matilda.[28]

For the second Leipzig drawing, the terms "recto" and "verso" are relative: while the sheet has been cut to feature the cross and the putti on the present recto, the verso may have been drawn first, because it contains a group of studies perhaps associated with the earlier Fountain of the Four Rivers (1647–51).[29] This raises the possibility that Bernini had been thinking about the Constantine much earlier than the date of the commission, at a time when he was involved with the fountain. In the end, however, it seems more judicious to imagine Bernini picking up an old sheet of studies – if that is what it was – and reusing the clean surface on the back for new purposes. Because the sheet has been cut, we do not

169

Figure 156. Study for putti with cross, drawing (Museum der bildenden Künste Leipzig, inv. 7806)

know the full extent of the drawings on either side and hence cannot speculate on the ways they might have served the shop in the interval between the planning of one monument and the commission for another.[30]

From St. Peter's to the Scala Regia

Domenico Bernini wrote that the Constantine statue had been no more than "sketched out" during the pontificate of Innocent X, and we now know that this process took place on paper and possibly in clay models but not in stone.[31] Throughout the period between the death of Innocent X and the transfer of the project to the Scala Regia, Bernini continued to ponder the monument. Evidence for this may be found in a number of important drawings and a terra-cotta *bozzetto*, which are closely related to aspects of both the Madrid drawing for the location in St. Peter's and the executed monument at the Scala Regia.

Figure 157. Studies for head of Constantine(?) with other studies, drawing (Museum der bildenden Künste Leipzig, inv. 7806v)

Figure 158. Studies for figure of Constantine, drawing (Museum der bildenden Künste Leipzig, inv. 7802)

A chalk sketch in Leipzig, in which the rider bears the heavy folds of a mantle slung across his chest, over his right shoulder, and upon his right leg, offers a case in point (Fig. 158).[32] As in the Madrid drawing the rider's head is turned and tilted precipitously to the left, but the emphatic presence of the heavily drawn mantle is new. The position of the arms has also been adjusted so that the right arm is forward rather than behind the body and the left arm appears to be located on the left side of the horse, as will be the case in the executed monument. In the *bozzetto* now in the Hermitage, St. Petersburg, the drapery is slung lower over the chest and behind the rider's thigh rather than over it, while the left arm (still intact) maintains the new forward position (Fig. 159).[33]

There are elements of the *bozzetto* that nevertheless suggest a relationship to the site of the original commission in St. Peter's.[34] Above all, the mass of horse and rider is compressed, as would befit a group intended for the niche drawn in the Madrid study. Compared to the executed monument, the horse rears higher and Constantine is more closely united with it; the space between the chest of the rider and the mane of the horse disappears. The transformation of forward movement into a vertical direction enables the artist to straighten the head of the horse so that its position more closely resembles the executed statue, with the mane now flung over the neck of the animal rather than flying in midair as depicted on the Madrid drawing. Because the *bozzetto* is damaged and Constantine's head is missing, we do not know whether its twist and inclination reflected an early or late state of Bernini's thinking. It is therefore difficult to place it confidently among the design studies for St. Peter's or for its eventual location at the Scala Regia.

An impressive black chalk drawing, now in Rome in the Corsiniana, depicts Constantine's upraised head and neck in profile (Fig. 160).[35] A sketch in the upper right corner of the sheet depicts the emperor's head as though seen from below. In both representations, the form of the beard is quite pronounced, unlike the less emphatic feature suggested in the drapery sketch and the Madrid study. The varying appearance of the beard has particular relevance to a passage copied from the *Church History* of Nicephorus Calixtus, VIII, 55, in the Bernini papers in Paris. The passage describes Constantine as

thinly bearded, and Wittkower maintained that the description, copied in Bernini's hand, demonstrated his concern for historical accuracy.

In fact, the excerpt is not in Bernini's handwriting, which is easily identifiable in other documents bound in the same volume.[36] And because the autograph drawing shows a long beard and the excerpt describes a short one, it is likely that someone other than Bernini was responsible for the citation from Nicephorus. This hypothesis finds support in the early eighteenth-century account of De Rossi. In it, we are told that Bernini wanted to provide the emperor with a long beard "all'orientale" to emphasize the attitude of the head looking up at the Cross, but the artist was discouraged by his patron Alexander VII, who preferred the short-bearded Constantine.[37] To judge from these sources, Bernini was drawing and Alexander was advising, one influenced by Eastern (presumably Byzantine) tradition, the other by literary sources like Nicephorus describing "il costume de i Latini," that is, the short-bearded type.

These observations are related to the role of the Corsiniana drawing in the design process. The emphatic profile suggests a view of the figure from the portico of St. Peter's, while the small sketch in the corner of the sheet suggests that the emperor's head is viewed obliquely from below, that is, from the corridor leading up to the base landing. In short, this drawing pertains to the figure of Constantine at the Scala Regia, rather than in the aisle of St. Peter's where the dominant views would not have emphasized these features.[38] The prominence of the emperor's beard suggests that the drawing was made shortly after the relocation of the figure at the Scala Regia, but before Alexander insisted on the short-bearded type. This moment occurred around April 1662, when the first notices about the equestrian appear during Alexander's pontificate.

Actually, Bernini began working the stone in the spring of 1662.[39] In early 1669, Bernini claimed that he had worked on the statue for seven of the fourteen years the stone had been in the studio, and these were probably the most recent.[40] In other words, the stone had arrived in 1656, but would not have been worked until 1662. This interpretation of the chronology corroborates Domenico Bernini's report that Queen Christina saw the artist at work on the equestrian during a studio visit that took place two months before a visit by Alexander VII. Since

Figure 159. Bozzetto for equestrian statue of Constantine, terracotta (Hermitage, St. Petersburg, inv. 673)

Figure 160. Study for head of Constantine, drawing (by kind permission of the Istituto Nazionale per la Grafica, Rome, FC127503)

we can date Alexander's visit (the first of two) to 19 June 1662, the queen would have seen the work in progress in April 1662.[41] To be sure, Domenico cannot be trusted in all details. He says, for example, that he was six when the pope first visited, but he was probably confusing this with the later papal visit, which took place in 1663.[42] And he is obviously incorrect, as Wittkower noted, in suggesting that the Constantine was finished upon that second visit.[43]

The reason for Domenico's confusion may be explained in a charming incident during Alexander's call on Bernini's studio. Preparing to leave after viewing every room in the studio, Alexander met the artist's wife with a young son on either hand. Then follows a marvelous exchange, in which the pope asked about the little *puttini* genuflecting at her sides. Addressing the younger one, Alexander teasingly inquired, "Which of you two is the meaner one?"

Without a moment's hesitation Domenico blurted out, "Checco, Signor Papa," referring to his older brother, Francesco. Whereupon the smiling pope turned to his majordomo, who from under his mantelletta handed him a necklace of gold worth 500 scudi. Putting it around little Domenico's neck, Alexander then responded, "To you goes the prize for being the good one." The necklace, Domenico later wrote, was even in his day kept in the house in memory of the occasion. He must have interpreted the gift, wrongly it turns out, as a reward to his father for completing the Constantine.

In sum, we can be reasonably certain as to when Bernini began work on the marble. What remains unclear is when the change in the location of the Constantine was determined. Was he working on the marble even before the equestrian was destined for the Scala Regia? Or might the new destination have inspired his activity on a neglected commission? The answer depends in part on the dating of the earliest schemes for the new staircase, but this, too, is an unresolved issue (Chapter 6). The Munich drawing and the representation on the foundation medal do not include the Constantine, but we cannot be absolutely certain whether they should be dated before or after the "disegni rifiniti" mentioned by the pope in December 1662. A reasonable *terminus post quem* for the choice of the new location would be April 1662, coinciding with the beginning of Bernini's seven-year effort to realize the statue. A *terminus ante quem* for the change in the location of the Constantine is provided by Alexander's mention of it in July 1664.[44] Whether later 1662, 1663, or early 1664, Bernini could afford to work slowly on the Constantine while construction on the Scala Regia advanced.

Completion of the Ensemble

On his visit to Paris, from April to December 1665, Bernini mentioned the Constantine as still unfinished.[45] During his absence, work on the staircase proceeded under the direction of his brother Luigi Bernini, who signed many of the Fabbrica documents in this period. Within a year of the return from France, a payment appears for a wooden model of the pedestal of the Constantine that had been hurriedly constructed *in situ*.[46] The document for the

model mentions chiaroscuro painting on the model and false doors on the sides, and so could refer to a temporary construction for a liturgical event or a trial design or both.[47] Beginning in midsummer of 1668 there appear payments for the stone of the pedestal, transport, and assembling the components on the site.[48] The final accounts in September 1668 indicate that the pedestal had no figural elements, although it was painted or gilded rather than simply bare as it is today.[49]

Before the statue of Constantine had been brought to the Scala Regia, Bernini experimented with the appearance of the ensemble *in situ* with the help of clay models. Three carrettate of clay were employed, about 5,400 pounds, which is a tenth of the weight of the marble ordered for the equestrian. The models apparently included the drapery hanging behind the equestrian.[50] Payments for the models late in 1668 suggest that Bernini was reworking some parts, presumably the composition of the drapery, even as the statue was reportedly finished in the studio in July of 1668. That was, in any case, the moment that Bernini showed the statue to Clement IX.[51]

In November and December 1668, payments were registered for work and materials necessary to transport the equestrian from the studio to the Vatican. There were wooden planks and beams for the statue, bales of hemp to wrap it, and skids to drag it.[52] Begun on 2 January 1669, the removal of the Constantine must have caused quite a stir.[53] At Bernini's house a wall of the studio had to be demolished to bring the statue to the street, either because the crated sculpture could not be tilted as the stone was when brought into the room or because it had been pieced (enlarged) in the studio.[54] In the street the statue was loaded onto a wooden sledge with the help of a winch and pulled through the city by two pairs of oxen. The scenario was played out over ten days, and the statue arrived at the Vatican Palace by 12 January 1669.[55] At the Vatican the Constantine was pulled up the northern corridor and over its western steps, and finally hoisted onto the pedestal with the help of two winches and no fewer than seven pairs of oxen.

These operations are described in the "stima della portatura e mettitura in opera della statua di Costantino Magno," on the basis of which the relevant payments were made.[56] In the process the Constantine was unharmed, but in its wake there was work to be done. The wall of Bernini's studio had to be rebuilt, and the damage to the street and Piazza S. Pietro by the sledge had to be repaired.[57] Since the work could only be accomplished in daylight, the Fabbrica had to pay two guards to watch over the statue by night. Evidently, there was some discussion about putting the name of the reigning pope in an inscription on the pedestal, but Clement IX refused the honor, attributing the commission to his predecessor, Alexander VII.[58] In view of the eventual criticism the statue received, this seems to have been a wise decision.

Documents indicate that the niche in which the statue is located was largely built around the sculpture. The marble was held in place by iron rods sunken securely into travertine supports.[59] At approximately the same time that these were fixed, "the new wall in the niche for the statue" was built.[60] Very likely, the construction continued through the night, for there are payments for candles for the "opera del Costantino" at exactly this time.[61] Work on the wall behind the equestrian continued from February into March 1669, by which time both the ornament for the coffered arch and the stucco for the drapery backdrop were in the process of being realized.[62] The sculptor Giovanni Rinaldo directed the execution of the drapery, assisted by Cosimo Rustichella.[63] Payments for the drapery appear through the summer of 1669, and they make it clear that the work interfered with events taking place in the palace.[64] In fact the scaffolding for the stucco work had to be entirely dismantled so that the procession of the Corpus Christi could pass with its usual banners in evidence.[65] By September 1669, the final payments for the stucco drapery appear along with those for the eleven coffers and their decorations in the soffit over the equestrian.[66]

From the late phases of design after Bernini's return from France, there is a large drawing showing the statue of Constantine in its eventual setting (Fig. 161). Architectural parts are rendered in thin graphite lines and figural elements in black chalk. The horse and rider are drawn in fine lines, while the drapery behind the figures has been depicted in more emphatic strokes. There are also random, that is to say virtually accidental, strokes of red chalk on the sheet. Heretofore the date and purpose of the drawing have not been discussed in light of docu-

ments, and whether the drawing is autograph remains in question.[67] A close examination of the evidence reveals its date, its place in the design process and, most important, the steps Bernini took to realize the ensemble.

Because the pattern of folds in the drapery behind the equestrian differs from that in the drawing and because the baldachin has not assumed its definitive form, the drawing ought to predate the final payments for stucco drapery in 1669. The pedestal was carefully drawn to include details like its deeply undercut cornice. On the other hand, it is located precisely on the vertical axis of the niche, whereas in execution the pedestal is placed to the left of this axis. Curves over the doors manage to disguise but do not completely hide the fact that the left side of the pedestal as built is narrower than the right side (Fig. 162).[68] These features of the drawing must have been set down sometime before the pedestal was built in the summer of 1668.

The pedestal was made asymmetrical and displaced to the left of the niche for a specific reason: to have it appear exactly centered within the width of the door to the basilica narthex (Plates 19, 20). The unequal curves on the flanks of the pedestal mask its asymmetry. And within the larger space of the niche, the angled face of the slurred pilaster on the right serves the same purpose, which is to urge a symmetrical reading of the statue within the niche when in fact the group had to be displaced to the left. The angled pilaster does not appear on the drawing but was, like the asymmetrical placement of the pedestal, invented later.

Very likely, the need to adjust the location of the ensemble became evident only when a model of the group was tried *in situ* in the summer of 1668. Such a discovery is precisely why full-scale models proved useful. The drawing is surely an earlier study of the installation. If we assume that Bernini studied this crucial matter personally, his return from Paris in December 1665 would provide a *terminus post quem* for the drawing which, if not autograph, was certainly done at his direction in anticipation of the model.[69] This procedure would have fostered an expeditious and economical study of the ensemble in anticipation of its transfer to the site.

Other evidence proposed for the design and execution of the equestrian cannot be accepted so readily. In favor of the authenticity of a terra-cotta

Figure 161. Study for equestrian statue of Constantine at base landing of Scala Regia, drawing (Museum der bildenden Künste Leipzig, inv. 7916)

bozzetto now in the Barockmuseum in Salzburg, little of substance can be said. Its features simply do not correspond with the design history of the monument as we know it from drawings, documents, and sources.[70] I suggest that another, fragmentary *bozzetto* for the horse, usually associated with Bernini's equestrian statue of Louis XIV, may be for the Constantine group, but this must remain a mere hypothesis (Fig. 163).[71] More curious is the case of a small

bronze figure of Constantine in the Ashmolean Museum in Oxford (Fig. 164). Wittkower suggested that it might be the work of a later sculptor using an early *bozzetto* by Bernini as a starting point.[72] This is an attractive possibility, for it would explain the long beard of the emperor, the massive cloak behind him, and the position of the left hand. None of these features correspond to the executed monument, but the evolution of all of them can be followed in the

Figure 162. Pedestal of equestrian statue of Constantine and flanking doors ((Bibliotheca Hertziana, D36880)

Figure 163. Bozzetto fragment for equestrian statue, terracotta (Museo Nazionale di Palazzo Venezia, Rome, inv. 13421, coll. Goya 208, neg. no. 156521)

graphic evidence and argumentation I have presented. Thus, Wittkower's suggestion still seems attractive, and Penny proposes that the changes in pose are due to later, critical reactions to Bernini's finished work (discussed in Chapter 8).[73] Here we must return to a documented chronology.

With the essential components of the Constantine in place, the project moved into a final phase. Surfaces of the statue had to be finished after its transport to the Scala Regia, but by this time Bernini's labors may have had another agenda. At the end of 1669, the artist was already thinking about a potentially grander and, from a political point of view, more conspicuous commission that might entirely overshadow the Constantine, namely the equestrian statue of Louis XIV. On the eve of Constantine's departure from the studio in December 1669, Bernini wrote to Colbert and emphasized how the statue of Louis XIV would be completely different from the Constantine. A small portion of this letter was already cited in relation to the subject of Constantine's vision, discussed at the beginning of this chapter; here Bernini's comments deserve to be presented in greater detail. "This statue," wrote Bernini of the Louis XIV equestrian, "will be completely different from that of Constantine, for Constantine is represented in the act of admiring the Vision of the Cross

Figure 164. Bronze statuette of Constantine, workshop of Bernini? (Ashmolean Museum, Oxford, no. 73, neg. no. NP 12)

appearing to him and that of the King will be in the attitude of majesty and command."[74]

In Bernini's conception, Constantine was intended to appear surprised and even humbled by the vision, whereas Louis XIV would appear majestic and commanding, grand and controlled, like the traditional *condottiere*. Thus, it may be that the finishing touches applied by the artist on the Constantine *in situ* were intended to dramatize the emperor's response to the vision and to deemphasize his stateliness. From late June through the summer of 1670, Bernini was hard at work on the Constantine, assisted by a laborer whose primary responsibility was to erect, break down, and reerect a scaffold enabling the artist to continue his labors.[75] Adjustments were also made to the composition of the drapery on the basis of models and full-scale drawings brought to and from the site.[76]

Kauffmann characterized the drapery as sort of inner frame for the equestrian, and his observation is well taken.[77] The folds of the drapery project strongly from the back surface of the niche, flowing over the architecture and virtually effacing the pres-

ence of a planar background. These protrusions of stucco are especially deep at the front and back of the equestrian, enhancing its vitality and blurring its nature as a relief (Plates 22–24). The horse is so deeply cradled in the fictive cloth that its anatomy appears implausibly bowed when viewed from below, its hind and forequarters projecting from a recessed midsection. In short, Bernini employed extraordinary means to produce unusual results. In effect, we are induced to forget that the equestrian is not a detached, freestanding sculpture.[78] The most active parts of the drapery, behind the tail and below the head, hide the places where the relief would be most apparent. The glittering, movemented pattern of gilt on the drapery contributes to these effects and contrasts with the smooth forms of horse and rider. The success of Bernini's strategy was mixed. On one hand there has been little recognition of the equestrian as relief sculpture among modern critics. On the other hand these and other effects of the relief drew withering criticism from contemporaries, as we see in the following chapter.

From autumn through December 1670, payments

were made to workers for the gilding applied to the drapery, the polishing of marble figures with abrasives, and the polishing of the pedestal in preparation for the transfer of the statue.[79] All this work must have related to matters of adjustment and repair rather than contributions to the process of design and execution, even if some of the payments for earlier services continue to appear in the documents.[80]

On 29 October 1670, in the presence of Clement X and a host of onlookers, the equestrian statue of Constantine was unveiled.[81] From the enthusiastic correspondent for the Duke of Modena came a letter responding to the dramatic qualities of the ensemble much as Bernini must have hoped, characterizing the vision itself as "a sparkling flame in the semblance of the Cross, with a heavenly voice that asserted to him how in this sign he would conquer the cruel tyrant Maxentius."[82] The date of the unveiling was an anniversary of Constantine's victory and, in a sense, of Bernini's too, for it also celebrated the anniversary of the initial commission.[83] Over a year later, on 14 December 1671, the Fabbrica paid Bernini a final installment of 2,100 scudi, bringing his compensation to an impressive total of 7,000 scudi for work on the Constantine.[84]

EIGHT

Meanings of the Constantine Imagery

IN the previous chapter the evolution of Bernini's equestrian statue of Constantine was traced from early designs for the location in St. Peter's through the long history of its execution for a new site at the foot of the Scala Regia. The story began under the pontificate of Innocent X in late 1654 and continued into the first years of Alexander VII's reign. During this time, Bernini's work was done largely on paper. In 1662 he began working on the marble, a process that was not completed until the unveiling of the ensemble in 1670.

Several problems arise in the circumstances of the statue's history, and we must attempt to address them in this chapter. Above all, why was the location of the sculpture changed? One of the new facts to emerge from our investigation of the commission is the active, indeed crucial role played by Fabio Chigi in the initial phase of the design and later, as Alexander VII, in its realization. As cardinal, Chigi surveyed an early design and, on the very day of his election, his ministers contracted the stone for St. Peter's. Yet his active patronage on behalf of the basilica makes it difficult to understand why he ordered the equestrian project resituated. Why did he do this, and how was the original conception of the monument altered when the ensemble was removed from the interior of the basilica? What was the significance of the Constantine ensemble in its new location at the northern tip of the basilica narthex, at the foot of the Scala Regia?

I would like to suggest that the eventual meaning of Bernini's equestrian group was adumbrated in his original conception, when the monument was intended for the aisle of the basilica. The iconographic associations developed within the basilica were enriched and extended when the statue of Constantine was relocated to the foot of the Scala Regia, where the connection of church and palace coincide. The change in site was complemented by an amplification in iconographic intentions that would now incorporate references to both edifices.

The Significance of the Equestrian

Fundamental to the course of Bernini's thinking about Constantine's Vision of the Cross was its conception as an equestrian monument. It is therefore surprising that only Kauffmann has recognized this issue.[1] Among the influences Kauffmann has considered are coin types showing the triumphant Constantine on horseback and alluding to the emperor's role as the *eques romanus*. Another includes the equestrians found inside and outside Western medieval churches and often identified as Constantine. Finally, there is the tradition of the *adventus divi* commemorating Constantine's victorious entry into Rome on October 29, which is the date Bernini's monument was commissioned and later unveiled.[2]

These associations raise several problems despite their obvious significance for a broad understanding of Bernini's statue. There is, for example, no representation in coinage of Constantine's Vision of the Cross, although there are representations of the Cross with a motto alluding to the vision.[3] Nor is there any generally accepted equestrian representation of Constantine's vision in Western medieval churches.[4] And while the ideas related to the *adventus*

Figure 165. Constantine's Vision of the Cross, fresco by Giulio Romano, Sala di Costantino, Vatican Palace (Musei Vaticani, XXIV. 23. 17)

theme may offer a suggestive association for the Constantine in its eventual location at the entrance to the Vatican Palace, the theme is only tangentially helpful to our understanding of the equestrian when it was intended for the interior of the basilica.[5]

A synthetic overview of the iconography reveals essentially two types of representations of Constantine's Vision of the Cross.[6] The more common iconography depicts the emperor standing before his soldiers in a pose resembling an *adlocutio*, but rather than addressing his troops the emperor acknowledges the Cross and the heavenly message of victory. Perhaps the most conspicuous example of this arrangement is the fresco by Giulio Romano in the Sala di Costantino at the Vatican Palace, of 1520–23 (Fig. 165).[7] The emperor stands on a podium, in front of his tents, in the midst of his troops. In the distance to the far right is the Ponte Sant'Angelo

situated so as to identify the Vatican as the location of the apparition.[8] Centered at the top of the composition is the Cross borne by angels and to the right of it, as though connecting the Cross with the bridge, is the Greek legend that accompanied the vision in the early accounts.

A similar composition was employed in the frescoes of the Sala di Costantino in the Lateran Palace, completed by Cesare Nebbia between 1585 and 1589 (Fig. 166).[9] Here the emperor stands on a low podium at the right of the composition. The view is more restricted than in the Vatican fresco, suppressing the possibility of a broad landscape and narrative details while emphasizing human reactions to the supernatural event. In a composition that mediates between these solutions, Giacinto Gemignani painted the same scene in fresco on a wall of the Lateran Baptistery in 1648 (Fig. 167). Here the Milvian

Figure 166. Constantine's Vision of the Cross, fresco by Cesare Nebbia, Sala di Costantino, Lateran Palace (Musei Vaticani, XXXIII. 19. 17)

Bridge is located in the geometric center of the composition. Bernini surely knew these conspicuous works of art, and the similarity of the gestures of Gemignani's Constantine and Bernini's statue is indeed remarkable.

In contrast to these representations in which the emperor stands in the midst of his troops, there is another type for Constantine's Vision of the Cross in which the emperor is depicted on horseback. One example may be seen in the Galleria delle Carte Geografiche, in the Vatican Palace (Fig. 168). The gallery, which occupies a long tract of the Cortile del Belvedere on the southwest, was frescoed between 1579 and 1583.[10] It shows the Vision of the Cross occurring as Constantine approaches the scene of battle at the Milvian Bridge. Resembling the iconography in the nearby Sala di Costantino, the event is depicted in a vast landscape, in which the Milvian Bridge is prominent. The scene is portrayed from a bird's-eye view to complement other landscapes painted in this room and to emphasize the universality of the drama. The equestrian type of Constantine's Vision of the Cross also appears in the frescoes of the Benediction Loggia at S. Gio-

vanni in Laterano between 1585 and 1590.[11] The artists in charge were Nebbia and Giovanni Guerra. Unfortunately, the fresco is too damaged to analyze the gestures of figures, but its present state is sufficiently preserved to indicate the emphasis on a vigorous battle portrayed as though its outcome were very much at stake (Fig. 169).

The vision with the emperor on horseback is not a common iconography, as far as I know, and it probably derives from Byzantine tradition. An early example is the manuscript illumination in a collection of the homilies of Gregory of Nazianus, now preserved in the Bibliothèque Nationale in Paris. The manuscript was dedicated to the family of the Byzantine emperor Basil I and has recently been dated to the years 879–883.[12] In the miniature, Constantine witnesses the vision in the midst of battle. With spear in hand he gallops toward Maxentius, runs him through, and thrusts him from the Milvian Bridge into the Tiber. Behind the crowned emperor flows his cloak, and above the head of his horse appears the Cross emblazoned with the Greek words for the motto "in this conquer" (Fig. 170).

It is thought that the illustrations of Constantine

Figure 167. Constantine's Vision of the Cross, fresco by G. Gemignani, Lateran Baptistery (Musei Vaticani, XXXII. 160. 1)

Figure 168. Constantine's Vision of the Cross, fresco, Galleria delle Carte Geografiche, Vatican Palace (Musei Vaticani XXXIII. 44. 14)

Figure 169. Constantine's Vision of the Cross, fresco by C. Nebbia and G. Guerra, Benediction Loggia, S. Giovanni in Laterano (Bibliotheca Hertziana, D9535)

Figure 170. Scenes from the life of Constantine, Byzantine illumination, MS Grec 510, fol. 440 (copyright cliché Bibliothèque Nationale de France, Paris)

in this manuscript derive from a larger cycle that is now lost. There are versions of the story in Greek, Syriac, and Latin from the eighth century onward, and while none survive that may be identified as a model for the miniature in question, there are sufficient variations on the theme to suspect that the illumination in the Bibliothèque Nationale was not unique.[13] A reflection of early Byzantine tradition may be seen in a fresco dating to 1466 in the monastic church of the Holy Cross at Agiasmati on Cyprus. Here two groups of mounted figures converge, looking into the sky where the Cross is evoked by stars and the vision is made plain in the usual Greek motto. The evocation of a Cross formed by stars reflects a variant of the Constantine legend known in an eighth-century manuscript from Sinai, which says that the inscription (rather than the Cross) was formed by stars.[14]

Curiously enough, the Byzantine miniature now in Paris may have had an unexpected influence in Italian art, since it was in Florentine collections throughout the sixteenth century.[15] The chances that Bernini was influenced at an early stage by an iconography derived from Byzantine art are thus less tenuous than they might at first seem. In any case the equestrian iconography for Constantine's vision was not unprecedented when Bernini planned the monument for St. Peter's. And if the iconography derives ultimately from Byzantine tradition, Bernini would have known more recent examples at the Vatican and the Lateran.

Bernini's conception of Constantine's Vision of the Cross differs from these precedents in the omission of narrative details that distract from the per-

Figure 171. Monument to Countess Matilda, Bernini, St. Peter's (Alinari/Art Resource)

sonal and spiritual dimensions of the event. Yet the horse is not essential to these aspects of the representation. After all, his statue of Longinus in the crossing of St. Peter's convincingly portrays a response to a miraculous event.[16] Obviously, then, we have more to explain in the unusual inclusion of Constantine's horse. By invoking the rare equestrian iconography, Bernini and his patrons must have had specific intentions. To understand them we must return to aspects of the documentary evidence.

The commission for the Constantine expressly called for a memorial that would be "similar to" (*ad similitudinem*) Bernini's tomb of the Countess Matilda of Tuscany in the right aisle of St. Peter's. The tomb was commissioned by the Fabbrica in 1633 and finished in 1644.[17] It consists of an over-life-size statue of Matilda and, below, a sarcophagus (Fig. 171). Matilda was the late eleventh- and early-twelfth-century ruler who came to the aid of Gregory VII during Emperor Henry IV's challenge to papal authority. With her help, the emperor's forces were defeated, a schism thwarted, and the emperor humiliated. His abjuration before Gregory VII took place at Matilda's fortress at Canossa, after the emperor had been forced to wait barefoot for three days in the snow. The scene of the emperor's submission is carved in relief on the front of the sarcophagus, where Henry IV is depicted kneeling before the enthroned Gregory VII, while Matilda observes from the right.

Ordered by Urban VIII, the tomb presents Matilda as an exemplum of the temporal leader dedicated to defending the papacy. To herald her example, Urban VIII had the remains of the countess exhumed from the abbey church of S. Benedetto Po, near Mantua, brought to Rome, and interred in St. Peter's.[18] In her new context the classicizing figure of the countess was conceived with the intention of presenting Matilda as an ideal model for relations between secular rulers and the papacy, while the tomb itself celebrated "a time-honored victory of the Church over the temporal power."[19] The same associations pertained to the so-called Apartments of Matilda, painted with her story by Gian Francesco Romanelli at about the same time. Here the popes entertained the "stranger princes" up to, and no doubt well after, the time of Bernini's intervention of the Scala Regia.[20]

From the documents and circumstances one might reasonably infer that the patrons of Bernini's Constantine had in mind a monument comparable to the tomb of Matilda in form and intention. This would in any case be likely from the fact that the two monuments would have been the only ones in St. Peter's that were not dedicated to a pope, a saint, or a martyr of the early church.[21] Although there is nothing in the early drawings to confirm it, indications in the documents of two pieces of marble for an equestrian and a bas-relief suggest the possibility of a large figural group over a relief, similar to the composition of the Matilda monument.

The remains of Constantine, unlike Matilda, were buried elsewhere, in the Church of the Holy Apostles in Constantinople. A passage from Nicephorus, one of the sources consulted in the design process, goes into detail on the subject.[22] The use of the term "memoria" in the Constantine documents may therefore denote a cenotaph, that is, a tomb monument honoring a person whose body is buried somewhere else.[23] For this, there is ample precedent in the form of an equestrian.

In discussing the executed monument at the foot of the Scala Regia, scholars have already compared Bernini's Constantine to equestrian funerary monuments in sculpture, such as Donatello's Gattamelata and Verrocchio's Colleoni. The draped baldachin in the niche above the Constantine also has a conspicuous role in fifteenth-century equestrian funerary monuments such as the tomb of Cortesia Sarego (1424–29, S. Anastasia, Verona) and other examples of the type (Fig. 172).[24] These monuments are found throughout Italy. As examples we can cite the monument to King Ladislaus by Marco and Andrea da Firenze (1428, S. Giovanni a Carbonara, Naples), the monument to Annibale Bentivoglio (with a rearing horse, 1458, S. Giacomo Maggiore, Bologna), the tomb of Girolamo Orsini (d. 1484, S. Maria delle Grazie, Monterotondo), and the tomb of Nicola Orsini (d. 1509, SS. Giovanni e Paolo, Venice).[25]

The type had its origins in medieval tomb monuments, such as the now-destroyed equestrian of Pietro Farnese (d. 1363), once located over the Porta del Campanile in the right aisle of the Florence Cathedral. The rearing equestrian was made of wood and papier-mâché; it had a wooden baldachin; and the hanging behind it was covered with Anjou lilies. All of these features offer close parallels to Bernini's monument at the foot of the Scala Regia.[26] We do not know whether the portal of the cathedral was included in the iconography of the Farnese tomb. There is a clear relationship, however, between the doors in the Constantine pedestal and the "doors of death" that appear at the foot of many funerary monuments, including Donatello's Gattamelata. Courtright observes that Constantine's horse, "rearing in an attitude of worldly triumph, could perhaps equally be interpreted . . . as triumphing over Death itself."[27] This seems to me a provocative and valuable perception, based on the triumphal associations of the rearing horse. A few points nevertheless deserve clarification.

In the original commission for St. Peter's we have no evidence of a pedestal and none for the drapery behind the figure. Because the term "memoria" may simply indicate a monument rather than a tomb, our first question is whether the evidence of the Madrid

Figure 172. Tomb of Cortesia Sarego, 1424–29, S. Anastasia, Verona (Alinari/Art Resource)

drawing will support the notion of a funerary association. I believe it does, inasmuch as freestanding equestrian sculptures do not appear in Italian churches except in this context, which does not depend on the presence of drapery motifs, sarcophagi, or related elements such as the doors of death. Just this kind of monument stood in old St. Peter's on the inside of the entrance wall to the basilica.[28]

The monument was dedicated to Roberto Malatesta (died 1482), and it must have been a well-

known feature of St. Peter's. Vasari made note of it, as did Alfarano, and Grimaldi depicted it *in situ* as a rearing equestrian on a low pedestal (Fig. 173, 174).[29] When the nave and façade of old St. Peter's were pulled down to make way for Maderno's additions in the early seventeenth century, the equestrian was brought to the Villa Borghese where it stood in the gardens.[30] The essential point is not that Bernini must have known this equestrian, which he certainly did, but rather that the tradition of the equestrian as a funerary monument was part of living memory at St. Peter's. Any equestrian planned in St. Peter's a few decades after the removal of the Malatesta monument would have recalled this familiar typology.

Although Bernini did not intend that his equestrian should be a funerary monument, its form alluded to that tradition. His strategy for the commission in 1654 was to imagine the Constantine as an equestrian in order to portray the vision of the Cross and, at the same time, recall the sepulchral tradition. By this means, he enhanced the allusive power of the figure in subtle ways. The essence of the *condottiere* funerary monument is that of a powerful animal dominated by its rider. In a calculated twist of meaning and intention, Bernini has altered this conception to emphasize a massive horse who reacts dazed and stunned, as does its rider, to the apparition. Thus Bernini's equestrian stresses values that are apparently paradoxical to the very essence and nature of the man and beast in the funerary association, in which the horse is usually maintained under tight control by the psychological and physical composure of its master.

By this kind of formal transformation, Bernini converted the traditional image of an equestrian funerary monument into a scene of compelling spiritual energy, as found in the many depictions of the conversion of Saul to Paul, such as those painted by Michelangelo, Caravaggio, and other artists. Presented in this way, Bernini's version of the theme takes on new significance as a triumphal motif. The horse rears, but not in triumph. The triumph in this vision belongs to the divine power that motivates the gestures of both horse and rider. As such, Bernini's conception of Constantine may well have been intended as a gloss on the passage from Eusebius, who interpreted the vision of the Cross as a triumph over death, as follows:

> But at the time above specified, being struck with amazement at the extraordinary vision, and resolving to worship no other God save Him who had appeared to him, he sent for those who were acquainted with the mysteries of his doctrines, and inquired who that God was, and what was intended by the sign of the vision he had seen. They affirmed that He was God, the only begotten Son of the one and only God: that the sign which had appeared was the symbol of im-

mortality, and the trophy of that victory over death which He had gained in time past when sojourning on earth.[31]

In the Christian church the triumph over death is the ultimate metaphor of spiritual efficacy, for which the Cross is the principal symbol. Bernini's presentation builds paradox on paradox, for the apparition that humbles the warrior also empowers him. Although the historic narrative is reduced to a single personal encounter, its implications assume universal dimensions by virtue of the divine origin of Constantine's strength and the implications of his victory. Constantine's victory over Maxentius becomes the triumph of the Cross, the chief emblem of the church over its enemies.

The Equestrian as Relief

The contract for Bernini's stone specified that the marble be comparable in quality to that of the stone "for Sant'Agnese." This is a reference to the marble for Alessandro Algardi's Miracle of St. Agnes, which was never executed for the church of S. Agnese in Piazza Navona because of the death of the artist in June 1654.[32] In the draft of the contract, a string of canceled words would have had Bernini's marble comparable to "l'historia di S. Leone Papa," a reference to the relief of the meeting of Leo and Attila. This altarpiece was carved by Alessandro Algardi for the southwest altar of St. Peter's. While such comparisons are common in contracts for stone and otherwise unremarkable, in this case they do stimulate some thought about Bernini's Constantine in relation to Algardi's work.[33]

Algardi's relief of the meeting of Leo the Great and Attila was commissioned in 1646, but the work went slowly.[34] Algardi received final payment in 1653, when the relief was unveiled on the site. From this moment the success of Algardi's work was assured. The deeply carved figures of Leo and Attila seem to rival the potential of freestanding sculpture in plasticity and freedom of movement, yet the composition in relief is carefully controlled to insure the formal unity of its parts (Fig. 175). The narrative composition is in fact so sensitively adjusted to the exposition of the theme that critics found in Algardi's altarpiece a new benchmark for the art of relief

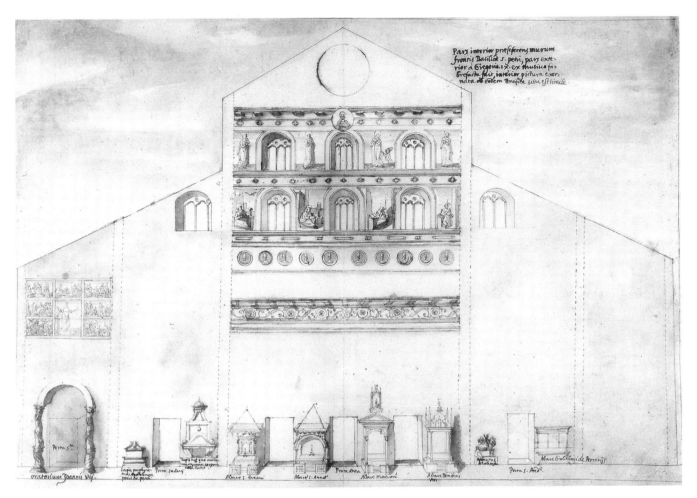

Figure 173. Grimaldi's view of interior façade wall of old St. Peter's with monument to Roberto Malatesta in St. Peter's, drawing (BAV, Archivio S. Pietro, A. 64 ter, fol. 18)

Figure 174 (right). Detail of monument to Roberto Malatesta in St. Peter's from previous figure

sculpture. It was against the high quality of this piece that later relief sculpture would be measured. Montagu cites Thomas Regnaudin to the effect that the relief "should be put on the level with the antique." This judgment has special resonance in 1672, two years after the unveiling of Bernini's Constantine.[35]

Leo's expulsion of Attila was historic proof of the ascendance of the spiritual authority of the pope over temporal might. The theme of divine over temporal authority is also fundamental to the conception of Constantine's vision of the Cross. It is possible that the critical success of Algardi's relief in 1653 encouraged the overseers of the Fabbrica to commission the equestrian statute of Constantine in the following year. In this case the theme would have assumed the added dimension of an artistic competition between the two leading sculptors of seventeenth-century Rome.[36]

Today we think of Bernini as the commanding genius of his time, but Montagu has recently demonstrated that contemporaries thought Algardi fully Bernini's equal.[37] In 1645 John Evelyn reported that among sculptors and architects "Cavalier Bernini and Algordi were in greatest esteeme," and shortly thereafter, in 1651, Richard Symonds was told that Algardi "far excells Bernino in statuary."[38] Similarly, Paolo Giordano Orsini, writing to Queen Christina before her arrival in Rome in 1654, named Bernini and Algardi the two leading sculptors of the day.[39] Cardinal Chigi himself acknowledged the competitive atmosphere between the two artists in 1652, when planning two statues for the Chigi Chapel at S. Maria del Popolo. "To improve the work by competition," he wrote, "I have destined one of them for Signor Bernini and the other for Algardi."[40] In the event, the statues were commissioned only after Chigi was elected pope, by which time Algardi had died. In this artistic atmosphere, however, there is good reason to understand Bernini's visit with Chigi in September 1654 to discuss the Constantine, and good reason to understand Chigi's interest in the sculpture.

Bernini's ambitions for Constantine's Vision of the Cross are evident from the beginning. In the account of his father's career, Domenico Bernini took the trouble to mention that for its size and quality, the stone for the Constantine was one of the rarest in Rome.[41] He was obviously well informed on this point, for he knew that the size of the stone was thirty carrettate, just as the documents tell us. When in Paris, Bernini himself boasted about the cost of the marble (3,700 crowns) for a work that was, he said, only to be a relief.[42] A marble of this size would be difficult to carve as a rearing horse and rider if it was not to be pieced. Moreover, the fact that it was to be a relief made the challenge of a naturalistic portrayal all the greater. Already, the inclusion of horses in the relief of the meeting of Leo the Great and Attila had been of grave concern to the Con-

gregation of the Fabbrica. On the other hand Bernini went out of his way, iconographically speaking, to include the horse in Constantine's Vision of the Cross. As we have seen, Raphael's example was important here, as it must have been to the composition of Algardi's relief.

The circumstances suggest that the invention of an equestrian relief on a colossal scale was Bernini's creative response to the competitive aspect of the commission. If the rearing horse was not a common aspect of the iconography of Constantine's Vision of the Cross, there was nevertheless a tradition to sustain it. That the equestrian was always intended to be a relief, as it was finally executed, would have made considerations of support a bit easier to resolve, as Hibbard has noted.[43] Nevertheless, on this scale, the equestrian statue of Constantine must have been consciously designed to take its place in the lore of the sculptor's medium for its sheer grandeur, and more particularly so as it was to be carved of a single stone rather than pieced or cast in bronze.[44]

Wittkower observed that Bernini's Constantine established "a type of Baroque equestrian monument which remained in vogue until Falconet's Peter the Great in Leningrad."[45] Wittkower went on to discuss the Constantine in the context of the equestrian Marcus Aurelius, the Gattamelata, the equestrians of Giovanni Bologna, Leonardo da Vinci, Pietro Tacca, and so forth. Of course, none of these examples is an equestrian in relief. What Bernini eventually did in the monument – and planned for the original site in St. Peter's – was to fashion a freestanding monument from the relief, thus answering the challenge posed by Algardi's Meeting of Leo the Great and Attila. In borrowing a gesture from Raphael's Leo and Attila, Bernini's initial thought (the Madrid drawing) was to demonstrate Algardi's failure to exploit this conspicuous precedent and build upon its power of expression.[46] With a change in location and the passage of years, however, this notion became irrelevant, although the general strategy with the medium succeeded brilliantly. For in matters of purely formal intention, Bernini transformed the stone into an image so strongly three-dimensional that its character as a relief has largely escaped modern comment.

Figure 175. Meeting of Leo the Great and Attila, marble altarpiece by Alessandro Algardi, St. Peter's (Alinari/Art Resource)

Old and New Associations with St. Peter's

Our best evidence for the transfer of these iconographic associations of papal authority and victory to the new location at the Scala Regia may be identified in features that we have already discussed, the pedestal and the drapery behind the equestrian. We have pointed out in the previous chapter how the

doors in the pedestal allude to the doors of death known from sepulchral design, and the formal evidence weighs heavily in favor of this association at the Scala Regia. Bernini used a similar pedestal design with curved sides flanking a central section on several earlier tomb monuments, and its use again here cannot have been casually intended. The same composition appears in Bernini's design for the tomb of Doge Giovanni Cornaro from the early 1650s, where the lateral curves bear inscriptions and a single door is placed between them, and in the project for the tomb of Innocent X, where the doors are located on the sides (Figs. 176, 177).[47] The motif of the door of death was also important to the designs for the tomb of Alexander VII of 1672 in St. Peter's, where the figure of Death presides over a door in the basilica (Fig. 178).[48] The iconographic relationship among these works is consolidated by the trumpeting fames bearing coats of arms, who also appear on the Beaufort catafalque of 1669 and, of course, the Constantine at the Scala Regia.[49]

Similar associations may be read in other parts of the composition of the Constantine. Just as the door connotes a passage from one reality to another, so too a curtain or an arch may allude to the borderline between two modes of being.[50] These observations have double relevance to the composition of the base landing of the Scala Regia, where the prominently coffered arch over Constantine may have sepulchral meanings and also allude to the transforming character of the ascent to the principal audience hall of the papacy.

The prominent stucco drapery that falls in great folds from the baldachin behind the figure of Constantine is a rich symbol, at once multivalent and specific in its references. Beyond their purely compositional functions, the stucco drapery and baldachin may allude to the tents of the emperor that appear in other versions of the apparition. The gilded drapery is perhaps also a cloth of honor; and it is certainly a theatrical device to suggest revelation, "the possibility of perceiving the truth, the *sensus spiritualis*, behind all things."[51] In this sense, the drapery may appropriately represent a true baldachin anticipating the furnishings of a papal reception in the Sala Regia.[52]

Then, too, the drapery may have been intended

Figure 176. Project for tomb of Doge Giovanni Cornaro, drawing (formerly Blunt Collection, London; photograph Courtauld Institute of Art neg. 289/68, 26)

mance of *Costantino Pio* in the Ottoboni theater bore a frontispiece by Juvarra that featured Bernini's equestrian so that, in time, the references between theater and the visual arts had come a full circle, the latter influencing perceptions of the former.[56] The drapery also recalled the custom of employing hangings on the route of the Corpus Christi procession and the related tradition of decorating the route of a triumphal procession.[57] Then, there is the image of the "tent of appearances," discussed later in this chapter. In all cases the striking image of Constantine becomes a tableau vivant, a living theater scene, much as was the famous Ecstasy of St. Teresa in the Cornaro Chapel.[58]

Figure 177. Project for tomb of Innocent X in S. Agnese in Piazza Navona, drawing (Windsor 5604, The Royal Collection; copyright Her Majesty Queen Elizabeth II)

to enhance allusions to the theater, as performances featuring the apparition of the Cross to Constantine are well documented.[53] It was in this vicinity of the old palace, most probably in the Cortile del Maresciallo, that a *sacra rappresentazione* of Constantine was performed during the Carnival season of 1484.[54] Other dramatic presentations of the Constantine and Sylvester story have been documented throughout the course of the sixteenth and into the seventeenth century in Rome, Florence, Siena, and Orvieto.[55] It is impossible that these performances were not known in Rome before, during, and after the reign of Alexander VII. In 1710 a libretto for the perfor-

Here as before, we must insist that while Bernini's concept for the original commission drew meaning from the tradition of funerary monuments, it was neither a tomb nor a cenotaph. In other ways, the sepulchral tradition gave poignance to the equestrian statue in the new location. Since the sixteenth century, there had been a plan to erect equestrian statues of the Most Catholic Emperor Charles V and the Most Christian King Francis I in front of the portico of St. Peter's. In this position the two monarchs were to be commemorated as "defenders of the faith" following their union against the Turks. This project was never realized, but it was also not forgotten in the long institutional memory associated with St. Peter's, and the existence of drawings must have been known to the community of interested patrons and artists in Rome. Guglielmo della Porta's study of the Charles V monument in fact shows a sarcophagus at the base of the equestrian.[59] The idea is to honor the ruler and his legacy to the church, a theme of obvious relevance to Bernini and his depiction of Constantine.

It is difficult to know if the sixteenth-century horsemen influenced Bernini's thinking about the Constantine as originally planned for the interior of St. Peter's. On the other hand, it is virtually impossible to deny their relevance when Bernini's equestrian was shifted to a site flanking the entrance to the basilica. In my view, the sixteenth-century scheme offered a precedent for relocating the ensemble in a position that would enlarge upon Constantine's role as protector of the church, similar to Matilda.

At St. Peter's, we know that grand plans such as the moving of the Vatican obelisk or the creation of a piazza with porticoes survived for centuries, finally to be executed long after they were proposed. Recollections of Charles V were found throughout the old basilica before its demolition and were known from the account of Alfarano, among others.[60] Moreover, the emperor's image had been a conspicuous part of the decorations of the palace entrance upon his visit in 1536.[61] Bernini was a great admirer of Guglielmo della Porta, a master of bronze casting, and Alexander VII was a cultivated patron surrounded by learned counselors. In these circumstances a knowledge of the sixteenth-century schemes must have encouraged the relocation of the

Figure 178. Project for tomb of Alexander VII in St. Peter's, drawing (Windsor 5603, The Royal Collection; copyright Her Majesty Queen Elizabeth II)

equestrian statue of Constantine to the north end of the narthex of St. Peter's. Eventually, the arrangement of twin protectors guarding the church entrance was consolidated in the eighteenth century when the equestrian figure of Charlemagne was commissioned and executed at the south end of the narthex between 1720 and 1725, as a pendant to Constantine.[62]

Associations with Basilica and Palace

The sixteenth-century source for equestrian figures flanking St. Peter's constitutes only one part of the story, for Bernini's Constantine was also associated with the entrance to the papal palace. Indeed, there is a long tradition of the sovereign protector on horseback depicted at the entrance to his buildings that should be associated with Bernini's Constantine. The best known example is the bronze equestrian Marcus Aurelius, formerly situated between the Lateran Palace and S. Giovanni, just as Bernini's equestrian is located between the Vatican Palace and St. Peter's.[63] In the 1530s the transfer of the equestrian, which was known as the "caballus constantini," from the Lateran to the Capitoline partook of this tradition.[64] Other examples of the type are legion.

From Constantinople the most apposite example was the equestrian image of Constantine painted in the vestibule of the Imperial Palace.[65] Other prominent examples of the theme are plentiful. Charlemagne had transported the equestrian of Theodoric from Ravenna to Aachen, where it was set near the imperial palace and the palace chapel. (As papal legate, Fabio Chigi had been stationed in Aachen.) An equestrian statue of Frederick II stood over a portal in a court of Castel del Monte. The so-called Regisole was removed from Ravenna to Pavia, where it stood in front of the cathedral of S. Siro and became a symbol of municipal authority.[66] The equestrian portrait of Niccolo D'Este III was set up in front of the ducal palace, facing the cathedral in Ferrara in 1441.[67] Leonardo's ill-fated Sforza monument (documented from 1489) was to be erected in front of the Milan Cathedral, and the clay model for it was set up in the courtyard of the ducal palace. With the growth of the idea of absolute monarchy from the sixteenth century on, as Janson explains, the equestrian monument had become "a public assertion of dynastic authority," from Giovanni Bologna's monument to Cosimo I De' Medici (commissioned 1587) and Pietro Tacca's equestrians of Philip III (1616) and Philip IV (1640) of Spain, to Francesco Mochi's Farnese dukes in Piacenza (unveiled 1623 and 1625) and Falconet's Peter the Great.[68]

The special tradition of rulers and horses at the entrance to their palaces is ancient in origin and would have been known in literary texts. Examples include the statue of Nero in the vestibule of his Domus Aurea (Suetonius, *Nero*, 31) and Septimius Severus before his palace (Cassius Dio 77, 11).[69] The Dioscuri on the Quirinal, erroneously believed to be the work of Phidias and Praxiteles, were also

involved in this tradition. Seventeenth-century antiquarians thought they were brought from Alexandria by Constantine to decorate his bath complex on the Quirinal, while Flaminio Vacca thought the horses were formerly in front of Nero's Domus Aurea. Sixtus V found the statues on the Quirinal and brought them to the front of the pontifical palace there. In the following century, Alexander VII projected a new architectural setting for them but never carried it out.[70]

In France, there is a medieval tradition of horsemen associated with churches and cathedrals, as has been mentioned in connection with the image of Constantine. Moreover, the tradition of "the equestrian at the portal" – for so it could be characterized – flourished at French châteaus throughout the sixteenth and seventeenth centuries. Examples of equestrians or projects for them conforming to the tradition can be cited from Blois, Chambord, Ecouen, Fontainebleau, Assier, Le Verger, the Luxembourg Palace in Paris, Château La Roche du Maine, and the Ducal Palace at Nancy.[71] Some of these monuments bear striking similarities to Bernini's Constantine. The statue of Louis XII at Blois is installed in a niche crowned by a baldachin. The statue of Pierre de Rohan at Le Verger is shrouded in a royal canopy whose form closely resembles Bernini's baldachin drapery for Constantine. The rider at the portal of Ecouen, who is the owner of the château, bridles a rearing horse (Fig. 179).[72]

These are variations of a well-established tradition of an owner or sovereign depicted at the entrance to his palace. Often the figure is presented within an entrance pavilion of the sort seen in the examples mentioned above.[73] With these features in mind, the planners may have intended several allusions in the location and symbolic referencing of the statue of Constantine and its architectural context. In discussing ancient Near Eastern practice, Smith suggests connections of domical entrance vestibules to the Roman, Byzantine, and medieval custom of marking a royal or divine reception by means of a ciborium, baldachin, or even "the Tent of Appearances under which the Kosmocrator can sit enthroned, like a god while receiving the acclamations, adoration, and supplication of his subjects."[74] Perhaps such imagery was known and evoked in raising

ESCOVAM
faces par le dehors

Figure 179. Entrance portico of Château d'Ecouen with equestrian statue of Constable Anne de Montmorency, engraving by du Cerceau 1579 (Marquand Library, Princeton)

the vault over the base landing to almost domical proportions and setting the equestrian against a rich cloth of gilded stucco drapery.

Smith has also traced the practice of setting up a king's throne at the city gate or palace of a ruler to the ancient Near East, and he accounts for the appearance of the ruler under a ceremonial canopy at the entrance to Roman and Byzantine palaces as an extension of this custom.[75] Knowledge of these traditions and customs may be hard to prove for the seventeenth century. But, given the circumstances, it is fair to assume that the cultivated and cosmopolitan Alexander VII and his artist were familiar with the most obvious aspects of the equestrian tradition when they relocated the Constantine to the entrance of the Vatican Palace. At this site the rep-

resentation of the miraculous apparition once again transcended its narrative character. More than the divinely inspired protagonist in a miraculous episode, Constantine assumed the roles of founder and guardian of the basilica and the palace.

Constantine was widely acknowledged as the founder of the early Christian basilica during the period of its reconstruction in the sixteenth and seventeenth centuries. During the demolitions in 1606, for example, when the atrium columns were being dismantled, Constantinian medals of gold and silver were recovered and heralded as proof of his part in building the basilica.[76] And because of its obvious association with the basilica, the early palace was also commonly considered the work of Constantine. Today we believe that Pope Symmachus established the earliest papal lodgings, the *episcopia* for the convenience of the bishops of Rome, somewhere in the midst of the basilica's fabric in the sixth century. Among sixteenth- and seventeenth-century writers, however, Constantine was given credit for this achievement. Alfarano made this point, and his view was reiterated by popular, frequently cited authors like Severano, Alveri, and Ciampini well into the seventeenth century.[77]

These associations help to explain the appearance of two images of Constantine included among the frescoes of other subjects on the entrance façade of the atrium at the original church. In the first scene, Peter and Paul appeared to the leprous emperor in a dream and counseled him to seek Pope Sylvester for a cure (Fig. 180). In the sequel, Sylvester proved the divine nature of Constantine's dream by presenting him with portraits of Peter and Paul even before the emperor had explained the circumstances of his visit (Fig. 181).[78] These images did not include the emperor's apparition of the Cross, but they did pertain to the theme of the superiority of divine over secular authority. This theme was appropriately located where the north flank of the atrium incorporated the lower palace. Although the popes did not live here, the lower palace did include an elaborate apartment known as the *camera imperatoris* for the use of visiting monarchs, emperors, and important ambassadors.[79] For them, the image of Constantine was intended as an exemplum of the ideal ruler.

The frescoes at the entrance to the atrium of old St. Peter's are thought to date from the third quarter

Figure 180. Sts. Peter and Paul Appearing to Constantine in a Dream, drawing after the atrium fresco in old St. Peter's (BAV, Archivio S. Pietro, A. 64 ter, fol. 46)

of the thirteenth century, and they are related to the appearance of Constantinian iconography on the twelfth-century mosaics of the portico of S. Giovanni in Laterano, where the Donation and Baptism of Constantine once appeared.[80] The scenes correspond to ceremonies involving the pope and secular monarchs that were performed in front of the entrances to the basilicas, as when the emperor kissed the pope's foot before entering the basilica and proceeding to the palace.[81] Bernini's statue of Constantine at the entrance to the palace may have been partly intended to recall these ceremonies. From numerous seventeenth-century drawings and reports, it is clear that representations of Constantine at the entrance to the early Christian basilica were widely known, long after the atrium was pulled down to make way for Maderno's nave and façade.[82] Under the aegis of Alexander VII, the emperor appears at the entrance to the palace as a demonstration of the divine origin of temporal authority.

Constantine as Monarchic Exemplum

In Chapter 3 we noted the fact that Bernini's Constantine replaced a statue of St. Peter situated at the foot of the preexisting Scala Regia. This statue had been taken from the Cappella Clementina of the basilica and set up by Paul V on the axis of the newly

built portico. The preference for the equestrian statue of Constantine over the existing statue of St. Peter may seem at first puzzling, given the central association of the church and the palace with the saint. The answer lies in the changing function of the Scala Regia.

From the early sixteenth century through Paul V's reign, the Scala Regia served exclusively to connect the basilica to the Sala Regia. This function is implicit in the figural iconography of the narthex, with its statues of 36 popes, and its connection to the base landing of the palace stairs where a statue of St. Peter, the first pope, was placed. Until Bernini's work, the staircase did not provide direct access to or from the piazza. From the early seventeenth century through the 1650s, one entered the palace from the piazza through Paul V's new wing and entrance tower. Under Alexander VII, the buildings of Paul V were demolished and replaced by the northern corridor that directly connected Piazza S. Pietro with the Scala Regia. The corridor transformed the Scala Regia into the principal entrance of the palace. The sculpture at the base landing would therefore welcome not only special visitors from the basilica but also those gaining entry from the city on their way to a papal audience.

The substitution of Peter, the apostolic image, by Constantine, the imperial archetype, was calculated to respond to the new function of the staircase. No

Figure 181. Pope Sylvester showing Constantine a portrait of Sts. Peter and Paul, drawing after the atrium fresco at Old St. Peter's (BAV, Archivio S. Pietro, A. 64 ter, fol. 40)

longer simply an extension of the basilica, the Scala Regia had become a link between the palace and the secular world. It was precisely for this new function that Bernini's Constantine was situated at the Scala Regia. At the entrance to the palace, Constantine's Vision of the Cross, by which he conquered and ruled, served as a historic reminder to all important visitors about the divine source of true power. The image of Constantine was an ideological overture to a papal audience in the Sala Regia, a hall decorated with variations on the theme of the ideal Christian ruler. Perhaps an allusion to the Imperial Palace at Constantinople was also intended, for there too, the entrance was dominated by an image of Constantine, as already mentioned.[83]

The notion of displaying to visitors the exemplary "deeds performed by emperors in a Christian manner," especially those of Constantine and Charlemagne, was a part of the Renaissance palace tradition in Rome, as we know from Cortesi's treatise on the ideal palace for a cardinal.[84] Vasari indicates that the original program for the Sala Regia under Paul III was to have included the depictions of six kings and their defense of the church.[85]

This theme survived in the seventeenth century, as is evident from the depictions of emperors and rulers in the saloni of Palazzo Mattei and Palazzo Spada.[86] At the Sala Regia, however, the ideal re-

lationship of *sacerdotium* and *imperium* (as Partridge terms it) was fully developed long before the decoration was completed. For under Pius IV (1559–65) the histories of sovereigns different from those depicted singly were to be shown in scenes of obedience to the pope. In a third stage of the program's development, the end wall with the papal throne was to be flanked with paintings representing "the submission due to the priesthood and the inferiority of temporal rule." The examples of possible subjects here included the submission of Abraham to Melchizedek, Alexander the Great to the high priest of Jerusalem, Constantine to Pope Sylvester, and Charlemagne to Pope Leo III. These depictions in the Sala Regia would have been consistent with the representation in the glass of Bramante's serlian window, above the throne, of the French king kneeling before the pope.[87]

The Constantinian reliefs in the roundels of the vault above the base landing elaborate these themes in significant ways (Plate 11). These reliefs were part of a decorative program no doubt redesigned in concert with the equestrian in 1662. By late 1664, Ferrata, Naldini, and Morelli were receiving payments for the trumpeting figures of Fame, the papal coat of arms, the roundel reliefs in the vault, and related embellishments, all of which were executed in stucco (Chapter 6). Between this time and September 1667 the entire sculptural ensemble within the vaulted landing at the foot of the Scala Regia would have been outfitted with all of its components.[88]

The two roundel reliefs are borne by *ignudi* performing the same function as do those on Michelangelo's Sistine Chapel ceiling, where the figures are also entwined by a thick vegetal garland (Plates 14, 16). Above the roundels are pairs of crouching sphinxes, which have been interpreted as imperial symbols or, alternatively, as a motif appropriate to thresholds. The first interpretation is based on the association of sphinxes with the heraldry of the Flavian emperors.[89] The alternative explanation depends on associations with the sphinx whose riddle Oedipus had to answer to pass into his land in safety.[90] To these we should add a third possibility, derived from the corpus of sixteenth- and seventeenth-century emblem books in which the sphinx represents ignorance, or more precisely the banishment of ignorance.[91] In any case all of these motifs, like others in the Scala Regia, recall the decorative and figural themes in the Sala Regia, the Sistine Chapel, and the Cappella Paolina. The roundel reliefs themselves elaborate the broader meaning of the Constantinian iconography.[92]

The relief on the north side of the vault, above the equestrian and closer to the palace, represents the baptism of Constantine by Pope Sylvester. The relief on the south side of the vault, located above the door to the portico of the basilica, represents Constantine founding St. Peter's.[93] The Baptism is dominated by the standing figure of Sylvester and the kneeling figure of Constantine. The emperor is depicted nude, hands clasped over his chest and head bowed before the pontiff. Other figures on the right hold his cloak and, in the background, his crown. Sylvester is depicted with the single-crown tiara that Constantine reputedly bestowed upon the pope to symbolize his investment with imperial powers.[94] In the Founding of St. Peter's the figure of Constantine plays the leading role. Placed almost on the axis of the composition, the emperor vigorously swings a pick into a pile of broken ground. Again, secondary figures on the right hold his cloak and his crown. On the left, Pope Sylvester, now wearing the sacral mitre rather than the tiara, invokes the presence of Peter and Paul, who appear above in a bank of clouds.

Bernini's composition of the Baptism of Constantine follows in general lines the model provided by the same scene in the Sala di Constantino. This formal relationship may be due as much to the prominent fresco in the Vatican Palace as to the mutual dependence of both representations on the ceremony of baptism itself. Quednau has shown how, for all its essential compositional features, the baptism in the Sala di Costantino depends on the description of the rite in Roman ceremonial.[95] The same is true of Bernini's relief (cf. Fig. 182).

The Foundation of St. Peter's also appears in the Sala di Costantino, where it occupies a section of the socle zone below the representation of the baptism.[96] The format of the scene on the socle is long and its narrative is elaborated in greater detail than on the roundel at the Scala Regia. But the fact that the entire socle of the Sala di Costantino provided the subject for a suite of engravings commissioned during the papacy of Alexander VII offers timely evidence of the popularity of these motifs in the seventeenth century.[97] Particular to Bernini's composition is the emphasis on Constantine's personal participation in digging the foundations for the new basilica. Presiding conspicuously over his labors are the dedicatory apostles Peter and Paul.[98]

The stories of the baptism and the founding of St. Peter's are not recounted by Eusebius or Lactantius, who are usually cited in relation to the vision of Constantine. Instead, the narratives are part of a biography of Pope Sylvester (314–55), called the *Acta Silvestri*, or *Vita Silvestri*, written in the second half of the fourth century.[99] The *Acta Silvestri* has two parts. The first is an account of Sylvester's life, and the second is devoted to the stories of Sylvester and Constantine, like that of Constantine's lapse of faith after his victory at the Milvian Bridge and the renewed persecution of Christians that ensued. The latter part of the *Acta* includes the legends that were illustrated in fresco on the atrium of the early Christian basilica and later in the seventeenth-century roundels of the Scala Regia.

From this source we learn that, as result of excessive pride and unwillingness to acknowledge his divine inspiration, Constantine was afflicted by leprosy and healed by Sylvester. Thus convinced of powers greater than his own, Constantine declared his full faith in Christ. He was healed of his leprosy, and seven days later was baptized by Sylvester. After another week of atonement, Constantine visited

Figure 182. Baptism of Constantine, fresco by Giulio Romano, Sala di Costantino, Vatican Palace (Alinari/Art Resource, N.Y., AL 7951)

the confessio of St. Peter, and there he founded the basilica of the apostle. He subsequently built S. Giovanni in Laterano and other basilicas for Christian worship. In a final gesture of thanksgiving, the emperor conferred his temporal authority upon the pope.

Pohlkamp has traced the stories of the *Acta* in some 350 Latin manuscript texts, in addition to Greek and Oriental versions.[100] Two printed editions of the *Acta* are known from the fifteenth century, and there are others from later periods.[101] Moreover, the stories in the *Acta Silvestri* are retold with some variations in the *Liber Pontificalis* of the seventh century, again in the famous *Constitutum Constantini* of the eighth century – the forgery better known as the Donation of Constantine – and in the thirteenth-century *Golden Legend* by Jacob of Voragine, the

fourteenth-century *Church History* of Nicephorus, and the writings of Cesare Baronius.[102]

Despite such a distinguished pedigree, particularly the baptism of Constantine raised significant historical questions, and the appearance of the scene in the vault of the Scala Regia must be understood as asserting the official papal view of a debated chapter in the history of the early Church. Already in the fourth century, Eusebius (*Vita Constantini*, IV, 61–62) wrote that Constantine had been baptized near the end of his life in the east, at Nicomedia, and this version of the baptism was adhered to by a number of early history writers, such as Ambrose, Cassiodorus, and Jerome.[103] Against these opinions, other writers such as the Venerable Bede, Isidor of Seville, Otto of Freising, Hugh of Fleury, and Vincent of Beauvais, supported the version of Constantine's baptism in Rome by Pope Sylvester. References to the Roman baptism in the Donation of Constantine, which Lorenzo Valla had identified as a forgery in the fifteenth century, further discredited the testimony of the *Acta*. Thus, Valla, Nicholas of Cusa, and Aeneas Silvius Piccolomini (the future Pius II) were among those who doubted Constantine's baptism in Rome.[104] Another critical approach was to reject large parts of the stories in the *Acta* and uphold others, including the baptism of Constantine in Rome by Pope Sylvester, as did Maffeo Vegio in his treatise on St. Peter's and Bartolomeo Platina in his history of the popes.[105]

We do not know how many literary sources Bernini and his patron Alexander VII consulted, but we have already recorded their interest in a citation from Nicephorus (regarding Constantine's beard, see the previous chapter), another early writer supporting the claim for Constantine's baptism in Rome.[106] More relevant than any early visual or literary source is the fact that by the sixteenth century the story of Constantine's baptism in Rome by Sylvester was an officially accepted event in the history of the church. The event was upheld in the authoritative *Annals* of Baronius and his edition of the *Roman Martyrology*.[107] It was represented in the Sala di Costantino and the Galleria delle Carte Geografiche in the Vatican Palace, and the Sala di Costantino and the Benediction Loggia at the Lateran.[108]

With reference to the scenes in the Sala di Costantino, it has been noted that both the baptism of the emperor and his founding of a basilica were represented together in the medieval Benediction Loggia at the Lateran.[109] Yet the iconography of the relief in the Scala Regia is more particular than has been generally acknowledged. Constantine is not laying the foundation stone, which has a separate iconography, but is assisting in digging the foundations of St. Peter's precisely as described in the *Acta Silvestri*.[110] The process involved the emperor's personal intervention in the foundation of the basilica, beginning with his breaking the ground and removing twelve baskets of earth "on his own shoulders."[111] The same story is recounted in the *Annals* of Baronius.[112] Bernini omitted the baskets in his relief, emphasizing instead Constantine's forceful swing of a pick into hallowed ground while the pope addresses his attention to Peter and Paul, who attend the event on a celestial bank of clouds.

Constantine's baptism by Sylvester and the emperor's personal participation in the construction of St. Peter's have obvious implications for the imperial character of the basilica and the sacred authority of the pope. Both themes underscore the importance of St. Peter's as a manifestation of the emperor's piety. The roundels support the legitimacy of the Roman baptism as opposed to the alternative tradition of Constantine's baptism in the East. Because Sylvester had performed the baptism in Rome, the papacy could claim responsibility for Constantine's conversion and his benefactions, in spite of the well-attested forgery of the Donation. Constantine's part in these events reinforced the heritage of the basilica as evidence of his piety and the primacy of papal rather than secular power.

Such representations were entirely consistent with the practice, recounted by Ugonio, of occasionally displaying at the high altar of St. Peter's the very image of Peter and Paul thought to have been shown by Sylvester to the ailing Constantine as recounted in the pope's *Acta*.[113] Normally, the miraculous image of Peter and Paul was kept in the sacristy of the basilica. There it was described in the seventeenth century by the English traveler Richard Lassels, who pronounced its history "both long and knowne: & if any man be ignorant of it, let him read it in Baronius."[114] De Sebastiani mentioned it in 1683, and in 1687 Carlo Bartolomeo Piazza's account of the liturgical calendar for St. Peter's described the image among the gifts Constantine donated to the church.[115] References to the baptism and the vision of the Cross also appear in the *Acta Sanctorum Bollandiana* of 1680.[116]

Common worshipers knew these stories in Bernini's time. Thus, for the Feast of St. Sylvester, on 31 December, one of the readings in the Roman breviary tells the whole story of Constantine's leprosy, the appearance of Peter and Paul, the search for Pope Sylvester, the healing of the emperor, and his baptism by Sylvester.[117] The images on the roundel reliefs therefore were not especially learned or erudite, but reflected the liturgical calendar as celebrated by every Catholic who attended devotions on the appropriate day.

It is uncertain whether the subjects of the reliefs in the vault of the Scala Regia were part of the proposed memorial ensemble to Constantine when it was intended for the interior of St. Peter's. That must remain a possibility, given the close relationship of the iconography to the history of St. Peter's. The hypothesis is encouraged by the documents, cited in the previous chapter, providing for a stone specifically intended to carry reliefs in a composition that would have resembled the tomb of Countess Matilda. In the present context, the subjects of the relief roundels enlarge upon the significance of Constantine's vision of the Cross. That event demonstrated the divine source of the emperor's authority, but it did not make him Christian nor did it consummate his association with St. Peter's. These facets of the history of the church were confirmed in the narrative reliefs of the roundels, taken from the *Acta Silvestri*, which linked the emperor's fate to the destiny of the pope. As such, the sculptural ensemble complements the theme of the ideal Christian ruler. The reliefs of the baptism and the founding of the basilica are emblems of imperial submission and spiritual regeneration, piety and good works, by which his divinely inspired authority was exercised.

By the time of Bernini's work, the iconography of Constantine had already been invoked many times at the Vatican Palace. We have already mentioned examples in the Sala di Costantino and the Galleria delle Carte Geografiche. A seated figure of the emperor also appears on the socle level of Raphael's Stanza dell'Incendio as one of the "benefattori della chiesa," with Charlemagne, Astulphus of England, Godfrey of Bouillon, Lothar, and Ferdinand of Spain.[118] And episodes from the life of Constantine were frescoed along with those from the lives of Charlemagne and Charles V in the Sala di Carlo Magno.[119] In all of these instances, Constantine serves as the exemplar of the Christian monarch, but nowhere is his divinely inspired power so dramatically emphasized as at the base landing of the Scala Regia. As a result, it is clear that the images of Constantine at the entrance to the palace composed a special message for visiting rulers and their emissaries about their relationship to the church.

The same message can be found in other, related circumstances. In 1625, on his first major diplomatic mission, Cardinal Francesco Barberini was sent to Paris to resolve the Valtelline crisis in which papal interests had suffered at the hands of French troops. Cardinal Francesco's mission failed, despite his cordial relations with Louis XIII, and upon the eve of Barberini's departure, the king left him a remarkable

gift: seven of the recently completed tapestries of the life of Constantine designed by Rubens.[120] One, the Baptism of the Emperor, was hung in Barberini's Paris apartment. It was surely meant to express the king's good faith toward the papacy and his submission to its spiritual authority. A later gift of five additional scenes completed the series. The power of these objects to suggest the adherence of the monarch to papal interests was unmistakable. In Rome, the tapestries were hung in the *salone* of the Palazzo Barberini, a showplace of the family palace.[121]

The formal influence of the Barberini tapestries on Bernini's work was probably slight. Constantine's vision of the Cross in the tapestry was patterned on the *adlocutio* composition, with the emperor standing on a podium in the midst of his troops.[122] In fact, the weakness of Rubens's figure of Constantine drew criticism from otherwise supportive observers, which explains why the Barberini commissioned Pietro da Cortona to design a new version of the scene to be made into a tapestry in the factory that the cardinal had subsequently established in Rome. This version, completed in 1633, was also based on the standing-emperor type.[123]

The monarchic associations of the tapestries were again demonstrated in December 1655, when Cardinal Francesco arranged to have the Barberini tapestries hung in St. Peter's for the arrival of Queen Christina of Sweden. Christina had renounced Protestantism and her throne to embrace the Roman Catholic Church, and as such her entire life became an exemplum for rulers of all nationalities who wished to maintain an allegiance to the papacy. In this instance, the scenes from the life of Constantine were intended to underscore the real importance of Queen Christina's abdication, which acknowledged and increased the glory and strength of the church. The spectacle of her entry into St. Peter's in many ways brought to life those virtues embodied in the acts of Countess Matilda on behalf of the church centuries earlier, a point not lost on contemporaries. During her visit to the basilica on Christmas Day of 1655, Alexander VII "was reminded of the German calumny against Gregory VII," so bravely opposed by that "most pious princess Matilda."[124]

In what is often termed the Age of Absolutism, such imagery assumed extraordinary powers of association. In a culture where no event was casual, Bernini's reception of Queen Christina at his studio in April 1662, while working on the statue of Constantine, was full of disguised meanings as well as the obvious and obligatory flattery. This was the first of several visits she made to his workplace, and it is significant that Bernini must have just taken up the Constantine at the time. According to Domenico's biography, Bernini greeted the queen dressed in his "coarse and rough" work clothes, saying it was the only worthy attire for a *virtuoso* of his station.[125] Immediately intuiting his meaning, Christina insisted upon touching them as a sign of her esteem for his art.

The subtext for this exchange is the disguised honor Bernini was paying her in his work on the Constantine and her acknowledgment of the power of his art to evoke this conceit. Ever attentive to the symbolic implications of his work for contemporary life, Bernini seized the opportunity of Christina's visit to bathe in the reflected glory of her majesty. By this means, both the artist and the queen could acknowledge the importance of her abdication and her embrace of the Catholic Church with reference to the empowering experience of Constantine's vision.

Imperial Imagery at the Basilica

Although Christina's abdication from the throne of Sweden, her conversion to Catholicism, and her arrival in Rome took place during the pontificate of Alexander VII, these events had been anticipated during the later years of the Pamphili pontificate, when Fabio Chigi was secretary of state to Innocent X.[126] Queen Christina's saga was a conspicuous instance of monarchic deference to the papacy, which may have encouraged the conception of the Constantine in the first instance. Because the same theme guided the conception of the tomb of Countess Matilda and because Bernini's statue of Constantine was to be patterned after it (according to the contract), we may even consider these monuments gender-related.

Conspicuous examples of a ruler portrait at the entrance to a basilica patronized by that monarch can be found in the early and late seventeenth century, in the statue of Henry IV of Navarre placed in the transept portico of the Lateran and the statue of Philip IV located in the portico of S. Maria Maggiore.[127] This practice was anticipated in the medieval representations of Constantine on the atrium of old St. Peter's and the portico of the Lateran basilica. But the associations of a ruler as benefactor of the entire mission of the church had very specific meanings for the decoration of new St. Peter's. This may explain why the original location of the statue of Constantine was eventually occupied by the monument to Queen Christina (Fig. 183). Her tomb was erected between 1696 and 1702 in the niche of the same pier that had been originally destined for Constantine, next to the tomb of Countess Matilda. And like Bernini's memorial for Constantine, the eighteenth-century contract for Christina's tomb specified that it be built "similar to that of the Contessa," that is, Countess Matilda.[128]

The theme of sovereigns in the service of the church reverberates in projects for St. Peter's related to Bernini's Constantine in the late seventeenth century. In a letter of 1693, a Polish Jesuit named Vota recalled how he had more than once suggested that a statue of Jan III Sobieski, one of the most faithful and successful of all imperial defenders of the Catholic Church, be put at the south side of the portico of St. Peter's, "vis-à-vis de celle de Constantin."[129] To accompany the new work, inscriptions would have been raised to make the relationship of the figures clear: "Constantinus dedit, Joannes servavit." The figure of Sobieski was to be standing rather than on horseback because of the difficulty of finding a whole and perfect piece of white Carrara marble. Evidently, the aura of Bernini's technical achievement in working with a single massive stone had not been forgotten. The proposal was scuttled, according to Padre Vota, because of competing plans to place a figure of the Countess Matilda or even a statue of Louis XIV in that location.

During the later years of the seventeenth century, a statue of Louis XIV would have been an unexpected presence in Rome, given the strains between the French crown and the papacy over the Jansenist controversy. This heretical movement advocated a form of predestination that minimized the efforts of the church to intervene on behalf of the faithful to attain salvation. Jansenism developed from the writings of the Belgian who gave the movement its name, but the principal threat to the papacy came from its success in France where so many bishops fell under its influence. Even the archbishop of Paris was prepared to embrace its tenets. The issue of Jansenism

Figure 183. Monument to Queen Christina, north aisle of St. Peter's (Alinari/Art Resource, N.Y., AL 5938)

threatened to undermine the major prerogatives of the church in matters of religious governance. In 1651 a special congregation was organized to deal with the heresy, in 1653 a papal constitution condemned it, and by 1654 the Inquisition's list of prohibited books included all works written or inspired by Jansenists.[130]

Beyond references to exemplary rulership, it is likely that in 1654 Constantine's Vision of the Cross was originally intended in part as an admonition to the French monarchy regarding the abrogation of powers traditionally belonging to the church. Through the end of the seventeenth and the begin-

ning of the eighteenth century, political tempers rose steadily until 1720, when the earlier bull *Unigenitus* (1713) condemning Jansenism was finally registered by the French parliament. This was the most important achievement of Clement XI Albani (1700–21) in foreign affairs, and it was commemorated, as Wittkower recognized, in the commission for the equestrian statue of Charlemagne located at the south end of the portico (Fig. 184).[131]

Like Constantine, Charlemagne was a model of the Christian ruler. The fountain in the atrium of the old basilica commemorated those provinces and cities that he had ceded to the church, their names

the sixteenth century, Charlemagne's extreme devotion to the church was exemplified in the story of his kissing each of the steps of St. Peter's on bended knee.[134]

The equestrian statue of Charlemagne was commissioned in 1720 from the young sculptor Cornacchini. It was destined for the location where Padre Vota had anticipated another statue of Countess Matilda, or the king of Poland, or the king of France. When Cornacchini's Charlemagne was unveiled in 1725, the two equestrians were hailed, in words that recall the conception of the sixteenth-century Charles V and Francis I, as "two grand, magnanimous, and invincible emperors, ready to guard and defend the Catholic Church."[135]

These events explain how the earlier sixteenth-century idea of an equestrian of Francis I flanking the portal of the basilica was ultimately realized in a statue of Charlemagne, which, in changed circumstances in 1725, alluded in turn to Louis XIV on the tenth anniversary of his death in 1715, or so I would like to think. Even then, the potent symbolism of imperial associations did not cease. In a reprise of the theme played earlier for Queen Christina's visit to Bernini's studio, the unveiling of Cornacchini's monument took place in the presence of another woman, the Bavarian princess Violante Beatrice, in 1725. In the midst of the ceremony, an observer was moved to exclaim that he could hardly determine whether the general applause of the audience was directed more at the statue or at its regal beholder.[136] Art and admirer were thus united by the common theme of the virtuous ruler.

Historical Contexts for Bernini's Constantine

Constantine's Vision of the Cross was planned as one of several major enterprises to embellish St. Peter's during the pontificate of Innocent X. The campaign included the decoration of the nave carried out to Bernini's designs between 1645 and 1648, the adornment of the north aisle beginning in 1652, and the commission of Algardi's Leo and Attila. In the nave, the floor and piers were decorated with colored stone, and on the piers, portraits of martyr-popes of the early church were depicted in relief medallions borne by pairs of putti. A pair of portraits

Figure 184. Equestrian statue of Charlemagne, west end of south corridor, St. Peter's (Marder)

inscribed on the bronze shafts of the fountain.[132] The coronation of Charlemagne by Leo III encapsulated the obedience and piety of the good king to the papacy. As the embodiment of French monarchic fealty, Charlemagne was shown with the features of the contemporary king Francis I, and Leo III assumed the likeness of Leo X in Raphael's depiction of the coronation in the Stanza dell'Incendio.[133] In

adorns the face of each pier, and between the portraits are putti bearing the papal tiara and keys. In the same campaign, allegories of Christian virtues were set in the spandrels of the nave.[137]

Bernini's designs for the piers recalled the decoration of old St. Peter's, whose nave was also lined with portraits of the early popes. This association, in turn, gave added emphasis to the connection between the early church and the new church, the first popes and those in living memory, including the reigning pontiff. The purpose and effect were to underscore the historical legitimacy of papal authority. The theme was expanded in the commission of Algardi's Meeting of Pope Leo and Attila. Here the powers of the pope were exercised not by means of superior physical might but by divine intervention. The vigor of the invading Hun and his army was entirely subdued, the enemy turned in its tracks and set fleeing by the hand of the pope aided by his spiritual allies and forebears Peter and Paul.

The interior decoration of St. Peter's would have been anticipated from the time of Paul V onward, and the idea for the Leo and Attila altarpiece dates from the same pontificate.[138] The involvement of Guido Reni, the Cavalier d'Arpino, and Giovanni Lanfranco in attempting to realize the Leo and Attila emphasizes the importance of the commission for the greatest artists of the day. Their charge was to recast in the basilica the theme so powerfully set forth by Raphael in the Vatican Stanze. Within the context of these works, the representation of Constantine's vision would have suggested similar connections between the early church and the papacy and illustrated the superiority of spiritual over temporal power. It was through Constantine that Christian and imperial power was united in the papacy and the exercise of papal prerogatives in the temporal realm was legitimized.

The Pamphili pontificate was not known for its lavish patronage of art in St. Peter's, and this is hardly surprising in view of the abstemious and unimaginative personality of Innocent X, who, earlier in his career, was dubbed "Monsignor No-Go" (Monsignor Non Va).[139] In fact the entire panorama of political events during the years 1644–55 would seem a bleak background for the assertion of papal primacy in the realm of temporal power. The Treaty of Westphalia in 1648 spelled "the definitive wreck of the Catholic restoration. . . . It set the seal on the system, first introduced by the Protestant party, of the prince's dominion over religion and conscience."[140] In Britain, the strength of the Protestants was signaled by Cromwell's rise and the ineffectual reign of Charles I, who was executed in 1649.[141] By 1653 Catholics were excluded from toleration there, and in 1655 the Catholic clergy had been ordered to leave. In France, there was the crippling issue of Jansenism. Wracked by European wars and subsequent developments that weakened the papacy as a political institution and a religious force throughout the Continent, the role of Innocent X was reduced to tending the precious image of his office in a period of decline.

Precisely these circumstances gave impetus to the commission of the equestrian statue of Constantine. Given the challenges facing the papacy in the last years and months of Innocent's reign, the assertive image was a calculated response and an exhortation to monarchs tempted to challenge the traditional powers of the church. The equestrian statue of Constantine witnessing an apparition of the Cross reasserted the orthodox relationship between temporal rulers and the true church, and demonstrated the historical power of its most potent symbol.

At the center of these political dramas was Innocent X's secretary of state Cardinal Fabio Chigi, the papal representative to the discussions at Westphalia, where papal prestige was so severely compromised. He had also been one of the protagonists in the early years of the Jansenist controversy.[142] After his papal election, Chigi moved the commission forward with a contract for the marble and an account of work already performed. At this time the monument was still intended for the basilica.

Among those at the papal court who may have advised on the transfer of the Constantine, Virgilio Spada would have had a special place. He was a member of the Fabbrica di S. Pietro, and as we have seen he participated in the design of Piazza S. Pietro from its inception. Moreover, he was in charge of the decorations for the interior of St. Peter's in the late 1640s. His death in December 1662 took place only as Bernini began to work the stone for the equestrian, which would help to explain why it is not recalled in Spada's memoirs.[143]

Another potential adviser to the project was Cardinal Francesco Barberini, who from 1633 served as archpriest of the Basilica, an office that normally included the role of prefect of the Congregazione della Reverenda Fabbrica di S. Pietro. He retained these positions until mid-1667, when he renounced the post as archpriest, but, rather exceptionally, he retained his position as prefect of the Fabbrica until his death in 1679.[144] Although his role as a patron of art is sometimes minimized, in fact he should be recognized in his role at St. Peter's as the most consistently powerful sponsor of individual works and vast programs of his century.

Cardinal Francesco had first-hand knowledge of the symbolic value of Constantinian imagery. He had received the Rubens tapestries portraying the events from the emperor's life and later loaned them for Christina's entry into St. Peter's. Cardinal Francesco was also responsible for the restoration of the mosaics on the Triclinium Leonianum at the Lateran in 1625, where the figure of Constantine is paired with that of Charlemagne. Here, in a portion of the decoration that may well date from the seventeenth-century restoration, the emperor is depicted with Pope Sylvester, and the pair is matched with Leo III and Charlemagne.[145] The francophile position of the Barberini is often pointed out in discussions of the period but rarely documented in the patronage of art. One example may be the relationship that the cardinal wished to restore at the Lateran of the French monarchic prototype, Charlemagne, with the first Christian emperor, Constantine.[146]

In the event, however, it is Alexander VII working with Bernini who deserves credit for the *concetto* of Constantine at the foot of the Scala Regia. Indeed, the historical circumstances impel us to appreciate the equestrian as much for its political relevance as for its significance to the long history of St. Peter's and the papal palace. Elsewhere I have explained how in 1660 the French foreign minister Mazarin tried to insult Alexander VII by proposing to erect an equestrian statue of Louis XIV on the slopes of the Trinità de' Monti.[147] It is an intriguing story, and here we need only recall the immediate inspiration for the project, the Peace of the Pyrenees, which was concluded to papal disadvantage in 1659. Mazarin and Fabio Chigi were old adversaries, and to celebrate the treaty in Rome was to rub French salt into papal wounds. These wounds were inflamed by French claims of territorial jurisdiction over the Trinità de' Monti. Bernini's project for it would have transformed the slope into a series of ramps and

grand stairs, in the midst of which was to be the equestrian of Louis XIV, secretly conceived and obviously symbolizing the concept of sovereignty.

These were but the most prominent debates between Paris and Rome. There was also Alexander VII's attempt to forge a league of Christian princes against the Turks, which Mazarin and the young Louis XIV opposed. Then the Créqui affair took place in August 1662, in which French troops stationed in Rome clashed with the pope's Corsican Guard. In the end Alexander had neither the military strength nor the political force to counter the French who dominated relations with Rome through the end of the pontificate.[148]

In the course of these conflicts, art was a weapon of choice. The project for the equestrian at Trinità de' Monti is strikingly like that of Constantine in pose and gesture (Fig. 185). As the centerpiece for his statement of sovereignty at Trinità de' Monti, Mazarin anticipated an equestrian directly modeled after the project for the Constantine in St. Peter's. For the French, Louis XIV would become the new Constantine who rears in confident triumph rather than surprise. When Mazarin's scheme collapsed upon his death in 1660, Alexander's response was measured but direct. Reappropriating the equestrian imagery, the figure was returned to its original form as the God-fearing emperor; this occurred about the time that Bernini began to work on the stone in 1662. Now, however, the commission carried a most explicit propagandistic message directed at the French monarch and, by extension, all temporal rulers.

These events may have helped to inspire the transfer of the statue of Constantine to its present location, yet the new configuration was undoubtedly encouraged by the sixteenth-century project calling for two equestrians, the Most Catholic Emperor Charles V and the Most Catholic King Francis I, to flank the basilica as protectors of the Church. In fact, the evidence suggests that Alexander VII and Bernini had themselves forecast a pendant for Constantine long before the figure of Charlemagne was erected in the eighteenth century.[149] The Chigi stemma, carved to Bernini's design for the south end of the basilica narthex and put in place in 1671, indicates that Alexander thought of the two ends of the narthex as parts of a whole. Preparatory drawings support this hypothesis, for the angel on the right assumes the pose Bernini had carefully studied

Figure 185. Equestrian statue of Louis XIV, detail of project for the Spanish Steps, drawing (National Museum, Stockholm, CC 790)

in figural drawings for the base landing of the Scala Regia, as we have seen in Chapter 6 (Figs. 135, 136). Then, too, the angels of the south narthex are placed against an arch with a coffer motif that derives from the scheme represented on the Scala Regia medal and is familiar from other commissions executed by Bernini.[150]

A fortunate archival discovery allows us to date the angels of the south corridor to 1671 and to attribute them securely to the hand of Giovanni Rinaldi.[151] Rinaldi had worked closely with Bernini in completing the equestrian statue of Constantine in 1669–70, and had obviously been given firm instructions, as well as Bernini's models, for the angels under the south narthex. The ensemble was prominent enough in the eyes of contemporary artists to have been drawn twice by Filippo Juvarra. He surely did so knowing it to be the design of Bernini carved by an executor.[152] Apart from the insight into workshop practice that these drawings offer, the interrelationships of figural motifs on the north and south sides of the basilica narthex suggest that they were conceived as part of a unified ensemble. The interchange of figural ideas on the drawings supports the notion that the ends of the narthex were viewed as pendants, rather than independent decorations. Alexander himself diagrammed the relationship.

A pencil sketch in Alexander's hand shows a triangle whose points are inscribed with the names "Petri" (at the top), "C. Magni" (at the left), and "Const." (at the right, Fig. 186). The configuration of these components in the sketch duplicates the positions of the two equestrians at St. Peter's.[153] In Greek letters above the triangle is the word "metamorphosis," suggesting a sort of mystical as well as a programmatic and historical relationship among the protagonists.[154] In his book on St. Peter's, Alfarano had described how Charles V won his victories as Peter's vicar.[155] In Alexander's configuration Constantine and Charlemagne had assumed the roles of Charles V and Francis I, which had been forecast as a guardian pair in the sixteenth century.

Alexander himself expressed the notion of metamorphic identities in the service of the church in 1655, upon the first visit of Queen Christina to the basilica. During the encounter, he approved her adopting the name Christina Alexandra, inasmuch as this was not his given name but the one in which he assumed the persona of St. Peter. For Alexander, Christina's new name was a sign of respect for the first pope, Peter, as well as for himself.[156] As late as

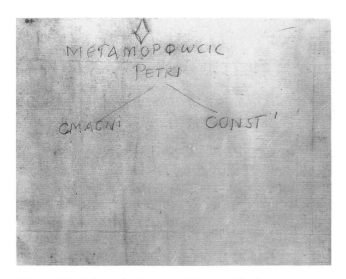

Figure 186. Schematic diagram of Peter—Charlemagne—Constantine triangle, drawing (BAV, Chigi a. I. 19, fol. 40v)

1671, losing hope of realizing the second equestrian but wishing to preserve the Petrine imagery, Bernini proposed moving the Navicella to the south portico.[157] Paradoxically, it was the critical response to his Constantine that prevented this proposal from being adopted.[158]

Alexander VII had unusually broad knowledge of Carolingian archaeology, lore, and legend, having been stationed as a papal nuncio at Charlemagne's historic capital in Aachen.[159] As the legendary successor to the first Christian emperor, Charlemagne had sponsored ecclesiastical benefactions that were recalled throughout the Middle Ages and the Renaissance in Rome. Even before the creation of Cornacchini's statue, the relationship between the emperors was expressed along the path of the Scala Regia. From a viewpoint halfway along the second flight of the Scala Regia, the fresco of the enthroned figure of Charlemagne in the Sala Regia is perfectly framed by Sangallo's doorway (Plate 66). Above the figure is an inscription explaining Charlemagne's significance: "CAROLUS MAGNUS IN PATRIMONII POSSESSIONEM/ROMANUM ECCLESIAM RESTITUIT." In rebuilding the Scala Regia, Bernini had preserved the dimensions and location of the second flight of stairs leading to the Sala Regia, so that the visual relationship between the frescoes and the stairs was also maintained.[160] It is almost unnecessary to repeat the fact that the scene and the text are part of a cycle in the Sala Regia featuring the temporal rulers whose benefactions had been essential to the church and examples for modern princes and rulers.[161]

Critical Fortunes of Bernini's Constantine

In the end the long creative process by which Bernini realized Constantine's Vision of the Cross became the stuff of legend. For a time, Bernini could manipulate the legend to good effect, vaunting the difficulties of the commission and exalting over the time he required to realize it. He did this with a coyness characteristic of his immense ego in 1669, when he complained about the fourteen years spent on the Constantine and claimed himself incapable of realizing the Louis XIV equestrian.[162]

The dark side of this long labor had yet to appear. For in the following year, the damage of this arduous history to Bernini's reputation was well enough known for Clement X to make light of it. In October 1670, shortly before the Constantine was unveiled, Clement X made a cutting remark in Bernini's presence about his tardiness in realizing an equestrian of the Altieri nephew. Referring to the commission for an equestrian of Louis XIV, Clement exclaimed, "with these horses of yours, neither the King of France will come to Rome, nor my nephew to Paris." The pope had discovered that, despite a sizable advance, the equestrian statue of Don Gaspare was still absent from the courtyard of the Altieri palace.[163]

There was more criticism even before the unveiling, as we learn from an avviso issued less than a month after the statue had arrived at the Vatican. In February 1669, it was being "censured by many."[164] In this context the anxious Colbert asked Bernini to make the equestrian statue of Louis XIV like that of Constantine, but not to copy it.[165] After the official inauguration late in 1670, Colbert might have phrased his request differently. For by then, it seemed nearly everyone had some fault to find with the Constantine: the pose was not convincingly naturalistic, Constantine appeared fearful, the horse had neither bridle nor stirrups, and without them the rider could surely not be expected to stay on such a restive steed.[166] Almost nothing good could be said of this "heap of errors."[167]

The criticism of Bernini's Constantine deserves

clarification. Apart from the comments in the avvisi and various guidebooks, whose positions vary from appreciative to qualified to disdainful, there are three principal statements on the statue. One is a critique dating from the time of the unveiling or just after it, around 1670–74.[168] The second is a response to this devastating critique, in sum, a defense of Bernini.[169] A third statement is a polemical tract whose points are obviously based on the first critique. The later criticism is longer and more casually organized than the earlier one, with frequent repetitions and biting criticisms made more incessantly throughout. Although this third statement is generally dated to 1670, it must have been composed after 1725, since it makes reference to the completed statue of Charlemagne in the south end of the basilica narthex.[170]

The criticisms are more revealing than previous accounts of them would suggest. Apart from the demonstration of literary talents at work, and occasionally overworked in these statements, there are at least two useful lessons to be learned from the two criticisms and the response of Bernini's defender. The first and most obvious is the degree to which Bernini's sculptural style in the equestrian was clearly out of step with contemporary expectations. This notion is conveyed in the almost endless satirical or ironic comments of the criticisms and the lamely defensive posture of the response. The second lesson to be gleaned from the evidence is, oddly enough, the degree to which the venomous criticism betrays a keen awareness of the history of the ensemble and Bernini's goals in realizing it. Thus, rather than the meretricious digs they appear to be, the stinging comments of the two critiques – and by extension, the document for the defense – betray a profound understanding of the formal and iconographic contexts within which the statue was realized.

In short, there is a subtext for these commentaries, which has remained previously unrecognized because it is disguised in overheated prose. The subtext, all but submerged in the plethora of classical references and exaggerated similes and metaphors, is this: the critics have understood Bernini's ambitions and his intentions and conclude that he has failed precisely because those ambitions and intentions are misdirected.

For example, the critics severely judged the attempt to make of the statue a "basso e mezzo rilievo"

immured in a wall, they said, like Neptune's trident in a rock or a centaur that is half horse, half man, and in the final analysis utterly beastly. Even Algardi, wrote the critics, had the sense to make whole figures of his two protagonists in the relief of the meeting of Leo and Attila. Then, too, Bernini has not decided whether to make the principal view from the narthex or corridor of the palace entrance. And why should the rider's pose be that of a St. Francis receiving the stigmata, when one doesn't see the Cross? Constantine is too youthful; although he wears a crown that looks like horns, he is but sparsely bearded. Presented with half a man and half a horse, wrote the critic, we are also confronted by a Constantine half shaven and half bearded. This then opens the door for the later critic to recall how it is claimed that unbearded youth are hardly safe from the sculptor's brother Luigi, even in the supposedly protective presence of the emperor.[171]

From what we have learned of the history of the commission it becomes obvious that the critics are referring to Bernini's efforts to work in relief and to challenge Algardi's achievement in the medium. The critics (unlike most modern historians) acknowledge the two principal views from which the statue was designed to be seen, from the narthex and the corridor, and pronounce the effort to achieve this double emphasis a failure. Among other problems, when viewing the equestrian from either the narthex of the basilica or the north corridor, the Cross remains invisible and Constantine's gaze is therefore unexplained. The crown, wrote the critics, is an all-too-crude symbol of the emperor's bestowing imperial powers on the papacy (the later writer refers specifically to the "donation," that is, the Donation of Constantine). And the critical references to the sparsely bearded face of Constantine reveals that Bernini's differences with Alexander on this historic matter were public knowledge. But worst of all was the compromise to Bernini's reputation that resulted from his brother Luigi's attack in 1670 on a young boy at the site.[172]

This last event was a brutal sodomy, probably committed behind the pedestal in the darkness at the foot of the Scala del Costantino. The young victim suffered sixteen broken bones, Luigi was forced to flee to Naples upon threat of arrest and punishment, and his possessions were seized. The papal family was angry, the Bernini name fell into disgrace, and the great artist's future was endangered. Forced to pay a fine of 2,000 scudi to the boy's father and 24,000 scudi to the public treasury, Bernini needed intercessors at court as never before. And here again, irony leads events, for among Luigi's defenders was Queen Christina, whose petition on his behalf was reported by the avvisi as a defense of sodomy. Minimizing Luigi's crime, the queen supposedly called for "protectors and defenders" of the practice of which the "princes" of the day were so enamored.[173] One doubts that this is truly what she claimed, but the words of the avviso clearly recall the iconographic associations to rulership that attached to the Constantine and obviously to the arguments attributed to her. Eventually, Luigi was pardoned and the sculptor's fine reduced.

At the beginning, in 1670, the public fires from the scandal burned intensely in the avvisi. By 1674 they merely smoldered. The first extensive critique of the Constantine was probably composed in this period. Against the claims of the critics, a response was composed to defend the statue and Bernini's conception of the monument on historical and aesthetic bases.[174] One of the criticisms was the awkwardness of the figures buried in the wall, which could not serve to evoke the location of the apparition. This was a sly reference to the programmatic intention of the sculpture to suggest the Vatican as the true location of the vision. To the critics' tongue-in-cheek pronouncement *non erat hic locus*, the simple response was the contrary, to wit *erat hic locus*, and the presence of the basilica of St. Peter's was construed as evidence to the effect that Constantine's vision had occurred at the Vatican. Obviously the critic was aware of the programmatic intention of the ensemble to espouse the Roman location of the apparition, a much debated historical matter. To the objection that the equestrian deserved to be modeled in the round, the defense responded that sculpture, like painting, is no more than an artifice. (The later critic will return to this theme, faulting the ensemble for appearing too much like a banquet sculpture of marzipan and meringue. (In fact, the references to Pegasus in the Constantine critiques actually match a sugar *trionfo* of Pegasus created by Bernini's assistant, G. P. Schor, for a banquet in 1667.)[175]

As to the sparsely bearded Constantine, wrote Bernini's defender, ancient medals and statues at the Campidoglio show him so. And the "lie that the head of Constantine is not accurate because it is not beautiful" was answered by reference to the arbitrariness of all portraits of Constantine, which were entirely invented by sculptors and painters to display their talents. Beauty, after all, consists of the proportions of the parts. If the head of Constantine resembles Habbakuk, as the critic maintained, then he has the head of a saint. If the crown resembles horns, Constantine has the face of a Moses.[176] In every case the critical posture of Bernini's defender was two-pronged, negating mere realism in favor of expressive naturalism and asserting the role of sculpture in the domain of artifice. If the lack of a bridle be cause for alarm, wrote Bernini's advocate, should we criticize the ancient sculptors of the Quirinal horses (then thought to be Phidias and Praxiteles) for omitting the same accoutrements? No, he concludes, "sculptors are imitators of nature and living nature was created without reins."[177]

In this last notion is the heart of the defense against all charges of ill proportions. Regarding the apparently exaggerated length of the horse, the curvature of the body (masked by the drapery, as we remember), the long neck, the immense tail dragging on the ground, the oddly shaped ears, and so forth, there is but one response. A horse can be depicted standing still or in movement, but in either case the "rules of nature" differ. A moving horse will literally change shape, and so too will his appearance.[178]

Bernini's goal was to represent the equestrian in motion, and this is where he ran afoul of his critics. Unlike other celebrated equestrian statues of the period, as Wittkower noted, Constantine's horse does not assume any of the classic positions, such as the curvet or pesade, popularized by European riding academies and the artists influenced by them. The same may be said of Bernini's equestrian of Louis XIV.[179] This fact was already recognized and faulted in the later of the two critiques, in which the anonymous author wrote that Constantine's horse is hardly comparable to the steeds of the famous Spanish Riding Academy.[180] As Wittkower wrote, "Bernini sacrificed correctness to the impression of rapid movement which he needed." But the most important consideration was the creation of a mode of expression that was not duplicated in the discipline of horsemanship or portraiture. As Constantine's Vision of the Cross was a miraculous, unworldly event, it was not meant to correspond to mundane eques-

Figure 187 (above). Statue of Louis XIV as Marcus Curtius, Versailles (Giraudon/Art Resource, N.Y., 19103)

Figure 188 (below). Medal of equestrian Louis XIV as Rex Christianissimus (BAV, Medagliere)

trian practice. The whole purpose of the ensemble was to evoke the sense of metaphysical, not physical experience. The same may be said of Bernini's equestrian portrait of Louis XIV.

In 1665, Colbert had approached Bernini with the idea of an equestrian statue of Louis XIV.[181] The project was vague, and for two years nothing ensued. Between late 1667 and early 1668 Colbert brought up the subject again, but Bernini had good reason to be wary. His plans for the Louvre had been rejected, and the payments of his pension from France were in arrears. Later still, in 1669 as we have mentioned, Bernini expressed his reservations on the basis of his experience with the Constantine. By mid-1669, however, the project was a reality,

211

with the marble for the commission having arrived in Rome in July 1669, purchased from royal funds already committed in May.

Upon the arrival of the stone in Rome, an avviso reported that the equestrian statue of the king was to be set at the Trinità de' Monti.[182] This rumor represents the revival of the old Mazarin project, perhaps under the auspices of the French correspondent in Rome, Abbé Elpidio Benedetti.[183] With the equestrian statue of Constantine (and its monarchic references) nearly completed and by now destined for its new location, perhaps Benedetti hoped to even the score.[184] In his letter of December 1669, Colbert asked Bernini to make the king's equestrian resemble that of the emperor, changing the head and poses enough to avoid the semblance of a copy. Bernini's reply, written when the Constantine was ready for transport to the Vatican, made it clear that emperor had been depicted in the act of witnessing a vision, while the king would be represented in majesty and command.[185]

When the equestrian of Louis XIV was finished, Bernini's great supporter the Jesuit Padre Giovanni Paolo Oliva wrote in a letter of 1673 that the work surpassed any equestrian monument in Rome, including the horses of Phidias and Praxiteles.[186] Under the circumstances, there could be no mention of Constantine, whose poor critical reception would have become already worrisome to the French. Symptomatic of the general response was that of the young French architect Robert De Cotte in the 1680s. He characterized the statue of Constantine as "une des plus mauvaisse ouvrage que le Bernin est faite."[187]

It is even possible that the unfortunate reception of Bernini's Constantine did as much to ensure the failure of the equestrian Louis XIV in France as other factors, like differences in taste, lack of appreciation for Bernini's *concetto*, or the professional jealousy of the French artists. The irony is that after so many years of planning and thinking about the Con-stantine, Bernini may have undermined his own efforts when the opportunity arrived to execute a truly dynastic monument. We may never know what the equestrian statue of Constantine looked like before it was finished *in situ*, but one guess is that it possessed greater formal power in Bernini's mind, and perhaps in the stone, before the artist began to distinguish its conception from that intended for the Sun King.

The statue of Louis XIV languished in Rome until 1684, when it was finally shipped to Paris. It was brought to the gardens at Versailles, moved once, and recarved in 1687 by Girardon to become a representation of Marcus Curtius leaping into the chasm of the Roman Forum. The French had taken exception to the horse's pose, the support carved as flags under its belly, the florid drapery style, and the smile on the king's face. Nevertheless, from 1687 to 1702 the equestrian Marcus Curtius commanded a prominent location in the gardens at the Neptune Basin, as Berger has demonstrated. It was removed to its present isolated location at the Bassin des Suisses only in 1702.[188]

Even in its present state, the monument in the gardens of Versailles bears a strong resemblance to the equestrian of Constantine (Fig. 187). The pose of the horses is nearly identical, and the position of the riders on their mounts is entirely comparable despite the differences in their gestures, attitudes, and the drapery. The similarities to the Constantine are equally obvious in the preparatory drawings, a terracotta bozzetto, and even the Travani medal with its legend on the reverse, "LUD. MAGN. REX CHRISTIANISSIMUS" (Fig. 188). That these similarities can be so readily perceived, even after Girardon's reworking of the Louis XIV, testifies to their similarity of conception. It is the most tangible evidence we have of the way Bernini hoped his Constantine would have been understood and its message appreciated by those who themselves commanded positions of temporal power.

NINE

Iconographic, Ritual, and Historical Contexts for the Ensemble

THE notion of a staircase to heaven, that of a Scala Santa or a Jacob's Ladder, are all relevant in some broad ways to an understanding of the Scala Regia. As stairs ascend they are intended to lift the soul as well as the body, and the Vatican Palace is hardly unique in combining an entrance with a rising processional path. The very existence of a staircase in these contexts establishes differing metaphoric and actual spheres of importance, in which the audience halls and rooms of reception embody references to the elevated position of the ruler. Nevertheless, the program of the Scala Regia is distinguished from other staircases because it belongs to the principal residence of the popes. Unlike the Scala Santa at the Lateran, which has its own Constantinian associations, the Scala Regia was not a shrine, and its function embraced both religious and temporal spheres of papal activity.[1] Within the range of meanings that evolve from its unique status and location, therefore, the Scala Regia should be understood as a formal entrance, a major connection between the palace and the basilica, and a conspicuous route of departure from the sacred confines of the apostolic precinct.

To some degree the shape of the Scala Regia is indicative of its singular function, for no similarly prominent staircase in the Western European tradition assumes the form of a narrowing trapezoidal ascent marked by architectural members that diminish in scale to resemble a coherent perspective construction. Embellishing this scheme and integral to its many meanings is the over-life-size equestrian statue of Constantine in a narrative context that presents his apparition of the Cross before the Battle of the Milvian Bridge. Complementing the ensemble are roundel reliefs with scenes from the life of the emperor, his baptism, and his foundation of St. Peter's, which illustrate his pious recognition of the power of the Cross. Other decorative features underscore the triumphal character of these events and their historical and topographical significance. Stucco ribbons overlapping architectural forms appear to wave in a breeze of vitalized space below a transverse arrangement of festoons and other vegetal forms that transform the lower flights of the stairs into a kind of bower.

Typologically, the staircase of the Scala Regia has an uncomplicated background. Joined at a double landing, the lower and upper flights of stairs climb along straight paths enclosed and vaulted between solid walls. The type was introduced into the vocabulary of Renaissance architecture at the Palazzo Medici in Florence around 1444.[2] For its grace and width, the most famous example from the early Renaissance in Italy was the staircase at the Palazzo Ducale in Urbino. Leonardo made special mention of it, as did Vasari and Daniele Barbaro.[3] In both palaces the treads were horizontal steps, although Alberti (bk. I, 13, 19) also described the use of inclined ramps, such as those used in the cordonate of the Vatican Palace. Alberti also advocated spacious dimensions and well-lit landings for important buildings, and these features also appear in the Scala Regia.

In Rome the enclosed, interior staircase with axial flights was introduced in the Palazzo Venezia in 1465 and reappeared at the Cancelleria around 1485.[4] Antonio da Sangallo the Younger gave the type its definitive Roman form in the designs for the Palazzo Farnese when the palace was remodeled after the election of Paul III in 1534. In the later seventeenth century, Bernini would use the same depth of tread at the Scala Regia and risers that were only slightly moderated in height. Sangallo's treads are about 55.5 centimeters deep, and Bernini's quite comparably between 53.2 and 56.5 centimeters. The staircase at the Palazzo Farnese is steeper than Bernini's, presumably because the available space did not permit a longer ascent with shorter risers supporting each tread. At the Palazzo Farnese the risers are 12.8 centimeters high, whereas those of the Scala Regia average about 11.5 centimeters high, creating a more gracious and stately rhythm.[5]

Sangallo should be seen as a true innovator in the design of gracious staircases. His work at the Vatican Palace in this regard must have represented a significant advance over the achievement of Bramante at the same location, for it was Sangallo whom Vasari repeatedly heralds in this regard. Vasari was particularly sensitive to good stair design, as we have seen from his comment about the "commodious" nature of the ascents to the Giberti apartment and to the Sala Regia (Chapter 2). Decades later he would compare a proposal for the Palazzo Vecchio to the Vatican stairs: "I am certain that Your Excellency will see not just a staircase but a miracle in that place, and that it will appear to you as if you were traversing the stairs that lead from the Sala Regia to St. Peter's in Rome."[6] For Vasari, the Sangallo staircase at the Vatican Palace was an achievement so remarkable that it appears not to have been equaled even by his own stair designs, themselves described as "so gentle and pleasant that going up is almost like walking on the level."[7]

From the early fifteenth century, then, staircases played a prominent role in palace design. Scamozzi particularly emphasized them in the early seventeenth century, and Tessin was obviously fascinated by the European examples he knew in the late seventeenth century. Given this heightened awareness of the typology, it becomes significant that Bernini engaged a traditional composition and altered its proportions by adjusting its dimensions. One of the curious aspects of the Scala Regia's proportions is how they subvert the intentions of modern visitors wishing to pass quickly either up or down. Because the risers are low and the treads deep, quick strides

are forcefully discouraged. Bernini's purpose was to forge physical, mental, and symbolic connections among the palace, the basilica, and the piazza in a way that both reinforced tradition and developed the ascent into a more stately and magnificent space.

The Scala Regia enhances the age-old function of the palace and the basilica in asserting the primacy of the pope in spiritual and temporal matters. The genius of the design, therefore, resides not merely in the evocative composition of structure, light, and space, but also in the ability of this ensemble to express the pretenses of papal authority. In this chapter I will argue that the real significance of the Scala Regia lies in its ability to project a coherent program appropriate to both a multitude of functions and a variety of specific ritual and historical contexts.

Scala Regia as Palace Stair: Colonnades and Garden Perspectives

The oldest and most frequent comparison to the Scala Regia is with the perspective colonnade in Palazzo Spada and for good reason (Fig. 189). Involved are conspicuous works by the two celebrated rivals of the period, Bernini and Borromini, building related perspective structures at nearly the same time. They must have been discussed so frequently in the eighteenth century that simple mistakes of chronology and precedence had infected the comparison. The two works are close enough in form and spirit that comparisons become inevitable, and in the climate of neoclassical taste it must have been easy to assume the priority of Bernini's sober style over Borromini's richly innovating vocabulary. In 1790, Francesco Cancellieri corrected the erroneous and apparently widespread notion that Borromini had developed the Spada perspective in competition with or, alternatively, in imitation of the Scala Regia by pointing out that Borromini's work came first.[8] Yet even the usually reliable Cancellieri erred in dating Borromini's work to the 1630s, during the pontificate of Urban VIII, a mistake that still appears in the modern literature.[9]

In a recent study, Leonello Neppi has established that the perspective colonnade at the Palazzo Spada was designed and built in the period 1652–53.[10] The documentation also makes clear that the mathematical calculations and the visual aspect of the per-

Figure 189. Borromini's garden colonnade, Palazzo Spada (Marder)

spective were determined in large part by the Augustinian architect Padre Giovanni Maria Bitonto, rather than Borromini. Moreover, during the construction process it was Padre Bitonto, not Borromini, who ordered changes in the design even while the little monument was taking shape. The collaboration between Bitonto and Borromini was very likely an easy and willing professional relationship, for they worked together in other situations that required the combined expertise of a mathematician

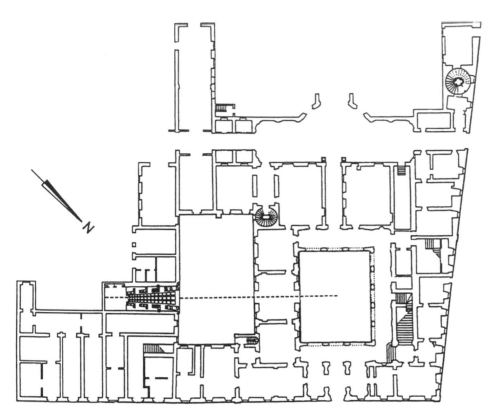

Diagram G. Schematic plan of the Palazzo Spada with its perspective colonnade in relation to Cardinal Bernardino's reception room and the central courtyard (drawing by Nora Onorato and Francesca Toffolo)

and an architect.[11] More important, the new information makes the Spada colonnade a more attractive precedent for the Scala Regia than formerly thought. According to the new chronology, the little colonnade appeared in Rome only ten years before Bernini began work on the Scala Regia, and not in the 1630s as previously believed. Moreover, the participation of Bitonto in collaboration with Borromini makes it easier to imagine Bernini's willingness to draw upon the work of his rival. We therefore have good reason to examine the history of the Spada colonnade more closely.

Cardinal Bernardino Spada acquired his palace, built around a rectangular courtyard, in 1632, but the colonnade rests on land purchased in 1652 to enlarge the property southeast of the palace nucleus (Diagram G).[12] On the wall of the new property Cardinal Bernardino had a false perspective painted to be seen across a garden court from his reception rooms and the central courtyard. This painted perspective covered an area approximately 20 palmi high and 16 palmi wide, or about 4.46 by 3.57 meters.[13] Fictive arches connected two lines of pilasters receding into illusionistic space. Its axis was aligned

with that of the cardinal's audience room on one side of the courtyard. Flanking the painted recession were chiaroscuro niches and statues, which may have recalled those on the sides of Raphael's School of Athens. Occupying the center of the perspective were two figures leaning against the hedge of a bosquet. Whether they served as repoussoirs or were represented in a more distant position is unknown, as no representation of the painted perspective survives.

This composition may have been designed by the architect Paolo Maruscelli, who signed the documents for its completion by the painter G. B. Magni in 1642. At the same time, the cardinal's rooms facing the perspective were remodeled. This coincidence of activity probably commemorated Cardinal Bernardino Spada's relationship with the Minim order at SS. Trinità de' Monti. The Minims were renowned experts in mathematics, geometry, and perspective representations. The learned Cardinal Spada, who no doubt shared the Minim passion for these pursuits, became the protector of the order in 1642. Two years later, the Minim Padre Emmanuel Maignan would design the famous Meridian Gallery, also painted by Magni, in another wing of the palace.[14]

Neppi has related the plantings in the painted perspective to the garden imagery that is recorded in a preparatory drawing for the built colonnade, leaving little doubt that the colonnade was the three-dimensional realization of the earlier, two-dimensional illusion (Fig. 190).[15] The drawing for the architecture was made by Francesco Righi, who often worked for Borromini, and the wall behind the three-dimensional version of the colonnade was again painted by Magni.[16]

Borromini's construction closely paralleled the original imagery. Although the end wall lacks the staffage and compositional elaboration in chiaroscuro, the architecture of the colonnade is composed of two files of freestanding Doric columns bearing a full entablature and a plain-coffered barrel vault. The columns recede in 12 pairs whose dimensions diminish progressively as the colonnade extends from the nucleus of the palace. Organized into four groups on either side, the columns were illuminated

Figure 191. Borromini's garden colonnade, detail, Palazzo Spada (Marder)

Figure 190. Elevation of Borromini's garden colonnade at Palazzo Spada, drawing by F. Righi (Albertina, inv. 1156)

by three light wells of which just one has survived (Fig. 191).

The diminishing size of the columns, their converging paths, the decreasing radius of the barrel vault, and the rising grade of the pavement combine to impart a prospect of great size in a space less than nine meters deep. An antique statue, placed on the axis of the vista about three and a half meters behind the colonnade, turns out to be surprisingly small in comparison to its appearance within the perspective colonnade. Positioned there in the eighteenth century, the statue provides a focal point to replace the deteriorated landscape once painted on the back wall as Righi depicted it.

The surprising effect of the false perspective at the Palazzo Spada may be felt even by visitors well prepared for the experience. It is certainly stronger

Figure 192. Interior view of north corridor leading to Scala Regia, engraving by G. B. Falda (Bibliotheca Hertziana, D19854)

documents of an existing structure than as the engraver's anticipation of them. It is significant that Falda envisioned the corridor and the staircase as a continuous perspective vista. On the engraving featuring the corridor, the vista terminates at a garden fountain. On the other engraving the vista is closed by a curved garden wall and slender trees (Figs. 194, 195).[18] In depicting a garden as the concluding element of the Scala Regia perspective, Falda responded to a tradition that was well established in seventeenth-century Rome.

The fictive landscape perspective was a conspicuous feature in Roman palace design, although it seems to have escaped much scholarly discussion. One example was to be found in Bernini's remodeling of the Palazzo Chigi at Piazza SS. Apostoli between 1664 and 1667, where a visual axis crossed the rooms of Cardinal Flavio Chigi on the piano no-

Figure 193. Imaginary view of Scala Regia, engraving by G. B. Falda (Bibliotheca Hertziana, D19855)

than the illusion imparted by Bernini's Scala Regia, but the difference is one of intention as well as effect. Magnificence is a principal feature of the Scala Regia, and its dimensions had to maintain a grandeur befitting its context. Moreover, Bernini's composition was constrained by structural necessities and formal relationships that had no equivalent at Palazzo Spada, where the goal was to provide amusement and delight. And if the dimensions were also limited at Palazzo Spada, they did not prevent the realization of an ideally conceived pictorial scheme.[17] Nevertheless, the long-standing comparison between the Spada colonnade and the Scala Regia betrays an inescapable unity of spirit. This unity belongs in part to an unexpected tradition.

When Giovanni Battista Falda engraved the two plates depicting the interiors of the north corridor of Piazza S. Pietro and the Scala Regia, issued in 1665, the stairs were still under construction (Figs. 192, 193). This makes the engravings less important as

Figure 194. Interior view of north corridor, detail of engraving by G. B. Falda (Marder)

bile. This line extended in a north–south direction through the doors of rooms aligned enfilade just within the main façade (Fig. 196). Under Bernini's direction the axis was carried through a window to terminate on the wall of a house across the street, the Vicolo del Piombo. Here a painter extended the view in a landscape featuring a distant scene of trees and woods, a river, boats and little figures, all framed by Doric pilasters.[19]

In the period 1671–76, a similar vista was arranged at the Palazzo Borghese, where Carlo Rainaldi rearranged the rooms and walls of Prince Giovanni Battista Borghese's ground-floor apartments. The prospect originated at the west entrance to the palace and extended north through no fewer than ten rooms and an outer wall of the palace, across an alley, through an adjoining palace belonging to the Borghese, and across the Tiber to the actual landscape of the Prati di Castello (axis beginning from room A2 through room A20, Fig. 197). The owner took great pride in this wondrous view and even interrupted the construction to show it to visitors.[20] No doubt Rainaldi and the Borghese were engaged in an expensive game of outshining the Chigi by creating a more marvelous palace vista

that terminated in a real rather than a fictive river landscape, where the boats and figures now actually moved across the river while real trees in the distance bent with the prevailing breeze. In this way, a natural vista was meant consciously to challenge the painter's art.

The remodeling of Palazzo Barberini in the years 1672–79 provides another example of a grand landscape axis, although it is of a different sort. For among the changes to the palace made at this time was the opening of a carriage path through the central axis of the palace at the level of the entrance portico, leading up a ramped avenue to the gardens at the back of the property (Fig. 198). The axis was terminated visually at a seated statue of Apollo bearing his lyre in one hand and gesturing to the approaching visitor with the other.[21] The perspective implications of the entrance are made explicit in illusionistically canted moldings located precisely where the new route was tunneled through the palace. At the summit of the entrance avenue illustrated in Specchi's engraving, the visitor turned back to the palace, whose garden façade became a principal entrance (Fig. 199). In this sequence of rises and turns

Figure 195. Imaginary view of Scala Regia, detail of engraving by G. B. Falda (Marder)

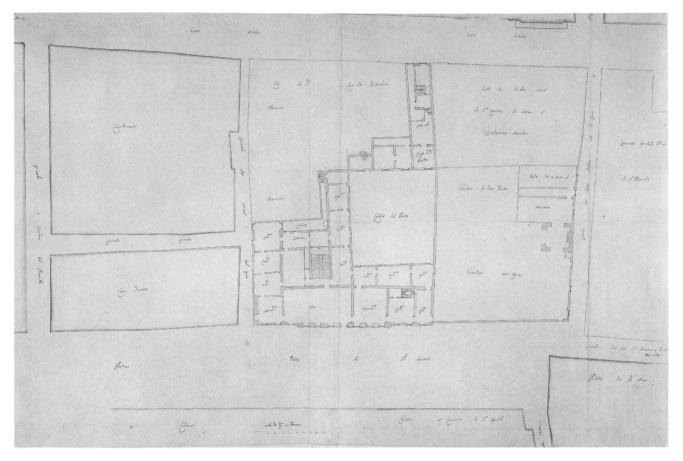

Figure 196. Plan of Palazzo Chigi, drawing (BAV, Chigi P. VII, 10, fol. 61v–62)

one may even recall the cordonata to the Cortile di S. Damaso at the Vatican.

These later seventeenth-century examples are undoubtedly related to the perspectives in earlier Roman gardens and villa *casini*. There is, for example, a perspective frame on a wall of the Hercules Gallery at the Villa Pamphili that may well have been painted with a garden scene to correspond to the real garden that lies beyond the doors on the opposite wall. A perspective frame on the north border of Scipione Borghese's hanging garden on the Quirinal probably surrounded a perspective similar in character to the one at the Palazzo Spada. The origins of these and many other examples of the period go back at least as far as the sixteenth century, when Michelangelo planned to extend the entrance axis of the Farnese Palace from the main portal, through the courtyard, across a bridge over the Tiber, to close at a fountain located in the gardens of the Farnesina on the opposite bank.[22] The key point is that

Bernini and Alexander surely understood the Scala Regia within this tradition when they envisioned a new entrance to the Vatican Palace.

The perspective at Palazzo Spada extended visually from the little colonnade through Cardinal Bernardino's reception room to the courtyard of the palace. The axis was fixed by a system of folding wooden shutters arranged at the courtyard to reveal and frame the perspective. Virgilio Spada described these features in his account of the life of his brother, Cardinal Bernardino, in the hopes that the aesthetic function of the ensemble would be preserved by their heirs.[23] Additional written evidence suggests a meaning for the arrangement.

In a letter of 1653 to James Alban Gibbs, the famous professor at the Sapienza and the cardinal's physician, Bernardino Spada discussed the perspective colonnade and its meaning. (Gibbs, a noted poet, had recently left Rome for the court at Modena.)[24] In the letter, Bernardino wrote of the "log-

tion across from the cardinal's audience chamber. The illusory nature of mundane perception was a fitting message and a reminder for the cardinal and his visitors.

To be sure, the Spada epigram was a flight of literary fantasy. Indeed the letter to Gibbs indicates that Cardinal Bernardino was answering an epigram by Gibbs with one of his own. Nevertheless, the conceit that inspired the literary production must have had some currency among contemporaries, as the verses written to the Barberini indicate. Because the Spada were particularly prominent and active at the court of the Chigi, it is fair to assume that Bernini and Alexander VII were familiar with the conceit. At St. Peter's, Virgilio Spada had played a role second only to Alexander and Bernini in designing the piazza and overseeing its execution, and he was active in many other building enterprises of the papacy.

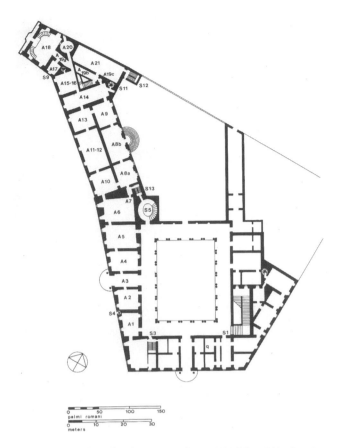

Figure 197. Plan of Palazzo Borghese (Waddy 1990, fig. 42)

Figure 198. Perspective diaphragm arch on ground-floor axis of Palazzo Barberini (Marder)

getta" he had constructed opposite his audience chamber. "And truly, for the small thing that it is," he wrote, "it forms a very long prospect, whence it gave occasion for a moral epigram, that I send you." The letter is located in the Spada archives, but Neppi found the corresponding epigram in the Barberini archives, addressed to a Barberini cardinal.[25] The epigram elaborates the theme of *grandezza*. In brief, it is a musing on the illusory nature of worldly things large and small. The metaphor developed in the epigram makes it clear that the colonnade was meant to inspire reflections on the same theme.

From the documentation we know that the field above the front arch of the Spada colonnade bore an inscription in verse with gold letters. Although the inscription has entirely disappeared, it likely referred to Spada's "epigrametta morale," and may even have included part of its text.[26] This being the case, the inscription would have spelled out the literary and visual *concetto* of the little monument, which would have been perfectly suited to its loca-

VEDVTA POSTERIORE DEL MEDEMO PALAZZO BARBERINO CON FACCIATA E SCALA CHE PORTA AL GIARDINO, ET AL PIANO DELLA SALA.
Architettura del Caualier Borromino.
1. Giardino con L'Obelisco antico verso le quattro Fontane .
Data in Luce da Domenico de Rossi dalle sue Stampe in Roma alla Pace con Priuil del S.P. e Licenza de Superiori .

Figure 199. View of east (garden) façade of Palazzo Barberini, engraving by Alessandro Specchi (BAV, Cicognara, V, 3865)

By the same token, Alexander VII and Bernini would have known the Spada palace well. Indeed, Bernini had long been consulted in its remodeling and decoration, including the renovation of the "scala nobile" in 1660.[27] Moreover, there were frequent contacts among the Barberini, the pope, and Bernini: Cardinal Francesco, to whom Bernardino's epigram may have been sent, served as prefect of the basilica and directed the Congregation of the Fabbrica, under whose authority and administration the Scala Regia was constructed. It is therefore reasonable to conclude that the conceit invented for the perspective colonnade at Palazzo Spada served also to enrich the metaphoric allusions of the Scala Regia ten years later. Quite possibly, the perspective imagery of the Chigi, Barberini, and Borghese palaces had the same intention of eliciting a contrast between worldly illusions and real grandeur.

A perspective illusion intended to charm and edify the visitor will have its greatest impact near the en-trance of a palace or close to its public chambers, and this explains the location of the vistas in the palaces we have discussed. In each case, the imagery is developed through a reception suite, and this is reflected in the position, form, and function of the Scala Regia. In fact, the approach to the papal audience provided the ideal setting for an exposition of the theme of *grandezza*, contrasting worldly illusions and spiritual realities. At the Vatican Palace the visitor was meant to understand that mundane appearances are deceptive and that a higher authority governs the realms of this residence.

Although the iconographic relationship between the form of the staircase and its real and symbolic meanings were made clear by association with a long-standing tradition, the most convincing evidence for a metaphorical interpretation of the Scala Regia derives directly from the monument (Fig. 200). From the base landing, the prospect of the ascent appears long and arduous. Yet climbing the

Figure 200. Early-twentieth-century view of Scala Regia (ICCD, D1755).

staircase turns out to be relatively effortless because the distance is shorter than it seems to be. In this experience, the unusually low risers and deep treads play an important role. But the key to the visitor's response lies in the realm of the concept. Visible expectations are denied and corrected by visceral experience. What seems at the beginning to be a distant goal turns out to be much closer than expected. Instead of a hard climb, the visitor is propelled to the double landing with remarkable ease and speed. On the Scala Regia, the illusion of sensory perceptions seems literally to dissolve as one leaves the outside world to ascend to the reception of the pope and his representatives.

This revelatory process was adumbrated in the depiction of the vision of Constantine, which asserts the superiority of spiritual over temporal power and perception. The stunned reaction of the emperor is explained only with reference to the power of the Cross to affect his destiny. Humbling the mighty and empowering the humble, the spiritual context transcends mundane perceptions.

Despite these features, there is a major difference in the effect of the Spada colonnade and the Scala Regia. At the little colonnade, one discovers that the landscape (or sculpture) at the end of the axis is smaller than anticipated. The visitor becomes a giant in the midst of a miniaturized architectural setting. By contrast, at the Scala Regia the visitor is initially dwarfed by the monumental scale of the architecture and over-life-size sculpture of Constantine. As the stairs rise, however, the architecture assumes a more normative character: though still quite large, the staircase becomes more like the scale of a typical large palace. In this process, the decorative sculptures are collaborating elements. The *ignudi* above the intermediate landing, for example, are life-size. At the top of the perspective axis, the architecture evokes a more comfortable scale, and the small size of the putti cavorting above the double landing in the saucer domes implies the growth of the visitor with the ascent. The architecture and sculpture of the Scala Regia inspire confidence and strength as visitors ascend to realize their true stature.

Crucial to this process is the bond that is progressively realized between the visitor and the setting. Precisely for this reason, and contrary to the folly at Palazzo Spada, human proportions never dominate the architectural setting at the Scala Regia.[28] Halfway along the uppermost flight of the stairs, where the path has narrowed, the enthroned image of Charlemagne frescoed on a distant wall of the Sala Regia floats above the door to the audience, a majestic successor to Constantine and a prelude to the vision of the reception (Plate 66). The revelatory experience culminates at the top of the stairs in the presence of the pope, where the order of a spiritual hierarchy on earth is revealed.

Ceremonies of Entrance, Ascent, and Descent

In a recent article, Shearman has traced the traditional entry into Rome for emperors and kings along the Via Triumphalis, branching off the Via Cassia about ten kilometers from the city.[29] The approach was regulated by formal ceremonial instructions, which entailed a stop outside the walls at Monte Mario, at a place called La Croce, where the approaching visitor first sees the city. Here curial dignitaries greeted royalty before proceeding to a fork in the road leading to the Porta del Popolo or the Prati di Castello, the Vatican, and St. Peter's.

Papal ceremonial specifies this entry exclusively for an emperor or king, who would be received at the steps of the basilica by the pope if he was to be crowned, or within the basilica if no coronation was involved. After the ceremony of greeting, the pope repaired to the palace, later followed by the emperor or king after paying appropriate homage at the tomb of St. Peter. A second reception then took place within the Sala Regia.[30]

From Monte Mario, the visitor obtained a dramatic first view of the city and, equally important on a symbolic level, a view to the old Milvian Bridge where Constantine had vanquished Maxentius. La Croce was in fact the spot where Constantine was reputed to have witnessed the vision of the Cross.[31] It was commonly acknowledged in the seventeenth century that Constantine eschewed the usual triumphal procession into the city after the victory and instead made his way directly across the Prati to the tomb of St. Peter, where he gave thanks for divine intervention and later built the basilica. This story is found in many authoritative sources, among which are the *Annals* of Baronius, Severano's account of the seven patriarchal basilicas, and Piazza's *Efemeride vaticana.*[32]

The meaning of these facts is at the same time simple and profound for our understanding of Bernini's interventions. By virtue of the provisions in papal ceremonial, the arriving emperor or king would see the site of Constantine's victory and then retrace the emperor's route through the Prati to the basilica of St. Peter. After visiting the tomb, the visitor, emulating Constantine's piety, would have been led to the papal audience. At the foot of the Scala Regia, the visitor would have been confronted by a monumental image of the apparition that forecast the historic victory and accounted for the basilica, which Constantine had built in thanksgiving. The basilica and the vision gave tangible proof of the efficacy of the Cross and the power of its protectors.

This sequence of events invested the arrival with layers of meaning that together composed the historical, topographical, and iconological prelude to a papal audience. Topographically, the ruler's advent was catalyzed where, historically, Constantine began, that is, with the vision of the Cross. Bernini's narrative cycle of the vision, the baptism, and the founding of St. Peter's illustrated the spiritual forces that shaped the destinies of the church and the papacy, emphasizing in these circumstances a string of associations that would have been retraced in the course of arrival.[33] In this process, visitors became a material accessory to the programmatic character of the palace entrance. Topography and history had conspired to define the nature of their status and, implicitly, the reason for their visit.

The arrival of dignitaries was entirely governed by ceremonial that in turn depended upon the rank of the visitor. For the emperor's reception in the palace, the usual protocol entailed an audience in the *aula prima* (Sala Regia), and then a progression of more intimate settings in the *aula secunda* and *aula tertia* (combined as the Sala Ducale by Bernini). For a king the regimen was much the same, although the ceremonial omits the progressive embellishment provided by the sequence of rooms following the large reception in the Sala Regia. The principal distinction between the entrance of an emperor, king, or queen and ranks of lesser royalty appears to be one of emphasis and precedence. Princes, dukes, ambassadors,

or envoys made their way directly to the palace, where they were greeted but not immediately presented. Ushered into the *capella parva S. Nicolai* (before the 1530s) or the Cappella Paolina that took its place, the visitor was meant to pray in private while the pope arranged himself in appropriate regalia. At the correct moment, then, the visitor was beckoned forth to find the setting transformed and magnified with symbols of papal splendor whose center was the pope himself. After the requisite three bows in approaching his presence and the possible exchange of a word of greeting, the visitor was then dismissed to be brought down into the basilica to venerate its chief relics.[34]

In the context of the symbolic value of Bernini's ensemble, it is worth remarking that princes, ambassadors, and envoys, indeed, any dignitary but an emperor or king, entered the city by way of the Via Flaminia and the Porta del Popolo, not over the Prati di Castello.[35] Thus, they did not retrace the route of Constantine's advent and would not have been susceptible to the intentions of the sculptural ensemble meant to address the visitor of imperial or regal status along the path that led from La Croce to the basilica, and from there to the narthex, which provided a progressively revealing scenario duplicating their own passage into the city.

These elaborations of pontifical ceremony found expression during Alexander's reign in the elaborate choreography arranged for the arrival of Queen Christina in December 1655. She arrived first at night, unofficially, three hours after Vespers, entering Rome by way of the Vatican gardens where she was given comfortable apartments but not greeted. The official entry required her to leave the city early the following morning in order to reenter through the Porta del Popolo. Ceremonial required this route, and her status would not have been flattered by any departure from the canonic procedures. The assembled cardinals then joined her entourage and accompanied her to the Vatican. Upon reaching Piazza S. Pietro, all of the cardinals save the two oldest deacons left her and came to the Sala Regia to do their *obbedienza.*[36]

With the two elder deacons flanking her, Christina was led to the basilica façade to be met by the canons of St. Peter's, brought to the high altar where the Sacrament was displayed and hymns were sung, and then conducted to "a stair by which the palace communicated with the temple," that is, the old Scala Regia. There she was met by the majordomo (as on the previous night's arrival), eight bishops of the *cappella pontificia*, and two cardinals who had left the *obbedienza* for this purpose. Together they ascended to the consistory in the Sala Regia to come before the pope. Ushered forward in this group, she and the two cardinal deacons knelt three times, at the entrance, the middle of the space, and in front of the throne. On the third occasion, she kissed the hand and foot of the pope, and after a brief exchange the ceremony was concluded.[37] The remarkable quality of this scenario, which was produced to accommodate a queen of Sweden who had renounced her throne, lies not in its peculiarities but in its entirely predictable character.[38] Every aspect conforms to regimens formulated in the late-fifteenth-century papal ceremonial.

Inevitably, the overriding importance of the Scala Regia within the constellation of various rituals and functions of the basilica and palace derives from the association with the popes themselves. This association was established on the very day of a papal election when, after paying homage to the new pope in the upper chapels of the palace, the cardinals accompanied him down the staircase. One of them led the procession, bearing a cross, an image that would have been magnified in significance after the installation of Bernini's Constantine.[39] During the descent, the two oldest sopranos from the choir of the Chapter of St. Peter's sang antiphonally, "Ecce sacerdos magnus." At the portico the new pope was received by the entire Chapter in the vicinity of the Constantine statue. His reception was then heralded by the choir singing "Tu es Petrus" while the procession made its way through the narthex to the central door of the basilica, directly under Bernini's relief of Christ's charge to Peter (1633–46).[40] The relief depicts Christ's lesson to Peter, emphasizing the words of the singers. Here the new pope delivered a brief oration and was carried into the church to be kissed hand and foot again, as in the palace moments before, by each of the cardinals.[41] In other words, we find in the themes and location of Bernini's art the resonance of rituals whose content similarly reverberates in his imagery.

On the third night after his death, the body of the dead pope was adored for the last time by the assembled cardinals as it lay in state in the Sistine Chapel. If the pope died elsewhere than the Vatican, his body was brought on a litter drawn by two white mules to the palace. At the base landing of the Scala Regia, the body was transferred from the litter to a coffin and carried up to the Sistine Chapel. It is no doubt from this practice that the staircase behind the statue of Constantine, the Scala di Costantino, took the name by which it is still more generally known, the Scala dei Morti. This passage provided the most direct route by which the body could be taken into the upper palace. On the fourth day of lying in state, the body was brought down the Scala Regia and into the basilica for the last time.[42]

Ecclesiastical Imagery: The Forty Hours Devotions

In the foregoing section, I have drawn a relationship between perspective illusions and palace architecture and their relevance to the Scala Regia. Yet the Scala Regia is not exclusively, or even primarily, a domestic staircase. It is therefore no surprise also to find significant formal relationships with aspects of ecclesiastical architecture. It was evidently Borromini's work on a decoration for a Devotion of the Forty Hours at the Vatican that inspired the transformation of the painted garden perspective at Palazzo Spada into three dimensions.[43] Moreover, a letter from Cardinal Bernardino Spada to his brother provides evidence of his enthusiasm for Carlo Rainaldi's perspective set for the Forty Hours Devotion held in the Gesù in 1650.[44] Two years later, construction of the little garden colonnade was begun in the family palace.

From this evidence it is clear that liturgical celebrations had a significant role in the development of perspective imagery in seventeenth-century Rome, enhancing a tradition of local palace architecture. It is likely that the Forty Hours Devotion and other, selected examples of religious imagery provided the common source for many experiments and achievements in perspective construction. Certainly the introduction of religious typologies and iconography into the web of formal and conceptual precedents and contexts for the Scala Regia is entirely appropriate to its location and various functions.

The Devotion of the Forty Hours involved the display and veneration of the Eucharist for forty consecutive hours.[45] The celebrations were held at Advent and Lent, but they might also be staged on a variety of other occasions, such as to celebrate the return to health of an important individual or in thanksgiving for a victory or the safe return of an important person. There were several variations in the relevant liturgy during the course of the sixteenth century in Italy, and in some cities the devotions were organized as a perpetual prayer staged from one church to the next. In Rome the devotions were held in separate churches but most consistently in the Gesù and S. Lorenzo in Damaso. The Forty Hours Devotion was also regularly held on the first Sunday of Advent in the Cappella Paolina at the Vatican Palace.

The sites of the Forty Hours were provided with a theatrical set embellishing the high altar and dramatizing the presence of the Host. Such sets, or *apparati*, generally consisted of flats painted to impart the illusion of deep space in the altar chapel. Centered and suspended within this space was a monstrance bearing the Host that was the spiritual and geometric focus of the entire celebration. Thousands of lamps and candles were employed, but their introduction was deftly controlled so that the sources of light were often concealed. As a result of the manipulation of directed and reflected light, the Eucharist "glowed as if it were the source of illumination for the entire scene."[46]

The celebration at the Vatican started with a mass in the Sistine Chapel, where the host was consecrated and then brought through the Sala Regia to the Cappella Paolina. The procession was led by the pope, whose adoration of the Eucharist was intended to be the inspiring example for cardinals, clerics, confraternities, and lay worshipers who visited the Cappella Paolina over the next forty hours to share in prayers, readings, songs, and sermons, all presented while the consecrated host was displayed upon the altar. In the case of confraternities and other religious groups that worshiped together, the devotions also entailed a formal procession to the site of the ritual.

The staging of the Forty Hours Devotion appeared in Rome as early as 1550, and by 1592 it was institutionalized by Clement VIII.[47] Rules at this time prohibited an ostentatious display of the Host,

and just six candles or lamps were permitted to illuminate the tabernacle with the Eucharist. Within three years, more sumptuous versions of the altar decorations appeared at the Gesù. A description of the apparatus from 1608 refers to an Ionic colonnade with three levels of arcades above it. Similarly splendid arrangements were made for the devotions in the Gesù in 1610, 1611, and 1623, and there is no evidence of any reversion to the simplicity originally mandated.

Bernini's involvement with the Forty Hours *apparati* dates from 1619, when he first used hidden light sources to illuminate the Host.[48] His later *apparato* for the Cappella Paolina in 1628 is considered a notable milestone in this regard, incorporating the hidden light generated by more than two thousand candles to illuminate a representation of the "Glory of Paradise" surrounding the Host.[49] Unfortunately, we have no representation of these works, or at least none that scholars can agree on. Lavin has suggested that the 1628 set appears in an engraving of 1787 by Francesco Piranesi, in which case the twisted columns and scrolled crown of the decorations would be closely related to the composition of Bernini's Baldacchino (1624–33) in St. Peter's (Fig. 201). Other scholars believe the engraving depicts an apparatus that Bernini erected in the Cappella Paolina much later, during the pontificate of Clement IX (1667–69).[50] Regardless of the date of the set, we can be certain that Bernini was involved in staging the celebration, and his name was associated with the sets from the early part of the century.[51]

In fact, the visual evidence for the *apparati* is limited. What does survive indicates that at least one type consisted of an assertively architectural environment evoked through the use of perspective arrangements. The first dated representation of a set for the Forty Hours Devotion in Rome, Pietro da Cortona's design in 1633 for S. Lorenzo in Damaso, is of this type (Fig. 202). It was sponsored by Cardinal Francesco Barberini and hence offers a connection to work at the Vatican. Cortona also produced the design for S. Lorenzo in Damaso in 1650.[52] From the same year, 1650, there also survives a large engraving of the set designed by Carlo Rainaldi for the Gesù (Fig. 203). The diarist Gigli characterized the Gesù celebration of 1650 as "an extraordinary feast day and more beautiful than usual" and certified that the set was widely visited.[53]

This helps us to understand why it had so impressed Bernardino Spada.

Both Cortona's set of 1633 and Rainaldi's of 1650 are dominated by architectural perspectives evoking deep space in the choir behind the high altar. The architecture is bilaterally symmetrical, and the illusory space is meant to be understood as an extension of the viewer's space. This theme is advanced by the use of freestanding columns grouped in pairs. In the case of both works, the illusion is opened within a diaphragm arch resting on projecting sections of entablatures that are supported by the column pairs. Rainaldi's scheme is particularly notable for its insistence on the repeating pairs of columns and projecting entablatures to convey the visual fiction of great space.

Precisely these features anticipate the composition and vocabulary of Bernini's earliest scheme for the Scala Regia, in Munich, where paired column units like those conceived by Cortona and Rainaldi provide the essential theme (Fig. 122). In the Munich drawing the coupled columns support projecting sections of entablature that, as in *apparati*, support diaphragm arches. In Cortona's arrangement, the motif opens a view to the distance; in Rainaldi's, it controls the spatial recession; in Bernini's, it opens, closes, and punctuates the receding space. The repetition of three sets of column pairs on both sides of the stair hall in the Munich drawing particularly serves to recall the Gesù scheme. Similarly, the gloria of clouds suspended in front of the first arch on the Rainaldi engraving and, to a lesser extent, the clouds in Cortona's drawing recall the location and conception of the figures of Fame who appear to hover above the base landing.

Given the great number of *apparati* for which there is no graphic evidence, it is not wise to insist on specific sets as the sources of Bernini's ideas. Our knowledge is simply too fragmentary to arrive at secure conclusions. On the other hand, we have the testimony of Virgilio Spada, cited above, that Borromini designed a Forty Hours set that influenced his palace colonnade, hence before 1652; and this may have inflected Bernini's thinking.[54] Another possible influence may have come from the work that engaged Bitonto in the Cappella Paolina in 1655, particularly since he was often consulted for his expertise in perspective.[55]

What we can insist upon is the cumulative influence of this imagery. In a stair hall whose walls narrow as they rise, such associations would have been inescapable, more particularly as the *apparati* were closely associated with the very rooms to which the Scala Regia leads, namely the Sistine Chapel, the Sala Regia, and the Cappella Paolina. While our knowledge of the celebrations in the Paolina is imperfect, we do know that visits to the Vatican Palace to participate in the devotions were institutionalized in the Roman religious calendar by the late sixteenth century.[56]

The physical circumstances surrounding the Scala Regia and the many formal associations between it and the sets for the Devotion of the Forty Hours make a compelling context for the design of the staircase. The relationships to the *apparati* reveal more than a set of formal influences on Bernini's design. Because the devotions were well-attended events, their imagery enjoyed wide recognition. By employing these familiar compositional elements, Bernini must have intended a meaningful relationship with the Scala Regia. The ease with which we associate the features of the devotional sets by Cortona and Rainaldi, as well as Borromini, with the preliminary drawing in Munich and the eventual staircase design underscores Bernini's desire to make this connection explicit.

Bernini employed an architectural arrangement that transformed the staircase into a processional prelude to the Cappella Paolina, the locale for the Forty Hours Devotion. He created a three-dimensional ideation of images seen in the *apparati* themselves. The intensity of this relationship reached its peak during the celebrations, but the residual strength of the associations adhered to the Scala Regia throughout the year. The result forever changed the staircase from a neutral avenue of circulation to a passage imbued with meaning. No longer a straight, uniform connection of utilitarian design, Bernini's Scala Regia reverberated with echoes of the "most resplendent Paradise" created in the Cappella Paolina and elsewhere in Rome during the Forty Hours Devotion.[57]

Before Bernini's intervention the architecture of the old Scala Regia bore no expressive content and its figural components added very little. The sixteenth-century fresco at the double landing, which depicted Christ and St. Peter walking on the waves, defined the spiritual bond between the two figures and, by extension, between the apostle and his papal

Figure 201. Forty Hours apparatus in the Cappella Paolina, attributed to Bernini, engraving by Francesco Piranesi (by kind permission of the Instituto Nazionale per la Grafica, Rome; CL2422)

Figure 203. Forty Hours apparatus for the Gesù, engraving after the design by Carlo Rainaldi, 1650 (Rome, Biblioteca dell'Istituto di Archeologia e Storia dell'Arte, Raccolta Lanciani, vol. 38, I)

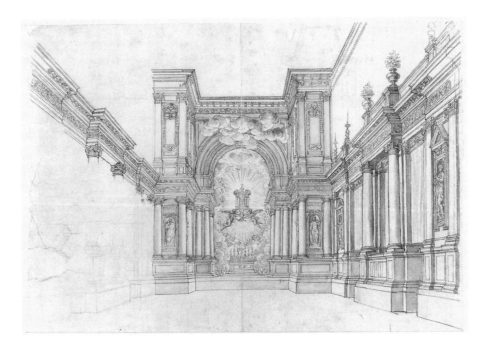

Figure 202. Forty Hours apparatus for S. Lorenzo in Damaso, drawing by Pietro da Cortona, 1633 (Windsor 4448, The Royal Collection; copyright Her Majesty Queen Elizabeth II)

successors.[58] (In the early seventeenth century Paul V had presented the identical message in a similar context by locating Giotto's Navicella at the entrance to the palace, near the cordonata di S. Damaso.[59]) With the new Scala Regia, this imagery was replaced by a three-dimensional ensemble whose visceral effects recalled and approximated visions of splendor and spirituality.

The path of descent along Bernini's staircase was also a calculated experience. For on the way down the reverse perspective of the staircase has the effect of telescoping distances and making the Cross of Constantine's vision appear more prominent than it would otherwise be. The sudden blaze of sunlight from the finestrone and the celestial presentation of the Cross has the same blinding effect on a viewer as it does upon the emperor, becoming a physical expression of the narrative.[60] During Holy Week this imagery extended into the basilica where the display of a brightly illuminated Cross, hung near the Baldacchino, provided a powerful addition to the experiential aspect of teh Scala Regia. (The scene was captured by painters and engravers through the eighteenth century.[61]) Although Constantine's mother, Helena, was associated with the finding of the True Cross, in the seventeenth century it was thought that the relic had been donated to St. Peter's by Constantine himself.[62] Such images and events consolidated the essential unity of palace and church iconography, which was conceived in a mutually reinforcing manner.

More Ecclesiastical Imagery: Fictive Choirs, Perspective Tabernacles, and the Feast of Corpus Christi

The letter of 1656, in which Cardinal Bernardino expressed his appreciation for Rainaldi's Gesù apparatus of 1650, goes on to recount his reception of the Cistercian historian and theologian Ferdinando Ughelli. Upon his reception in the cardinal's audience chamber, the visitor admired the newly built garden colonnade. In the ensuing conversation, the cardinal shared his fantasy (as he called it) of making a similar perspective in the apse of a Roman church.[63]

He may have had in mind something like Bramante's illusionistic choir built in Milan in the late fifteenth century at S. Maria presso S. Satiro, where

the constraints of the site made a real choir impossible to build.[64] In a depth of a few centimeters, Bramante painted a choir that appeared to be many meters in length. Whether from this or another precedent, Bernardino's meaning was clear to Ughelli, who brought up the possibility of S. Lorenzo in Lucina as a site for Spada's experiment, probably because a restoration of the church was then in progress. On the following day, the cardinal visited the church in the company of its officials with whom he tentatively confided his idea ("come una cosa molto rimota et in aria") for developing an illusionistic representation in the choir, based on the Gesù apparatus of 1650. From the correspondence, it transpires that Bitonto was charged with taking dimensions and Borromini with composing a plan. In the event, practical, liturgical, and symbolic prob-

Figure 204. Altar of S. Agnese in S. Agnese in Piazza Navona. Rome, engraving, Domenico De Rossi (Bibliotheca Hertziana, D20941)

lems overcame the cardinal's intentions at S. Lorenzo in Lucina. Other locations were then considered – S. Maria di Monserrato, S. Lorenzo fuori le mura, S. Giovanni in Laterano, and S. Pietro in Vincoli – but to no avail.[65]

This episode suggests an interest in ecclesiastical perspectives that can be traced elsewhere in contemporary Rome. At S. Agnese in Piazza Navona, Carlo Rainaldi designed a perspective behind the statue of St. Agnes in the right (north) transept in 1654 (Fig. 204).[66] In the 1660s, the young Carlo Fontana reflected the general interest in perspective effects for the windows and doors at the church of S. Rita da Cascia near the Campidoglio.[67] Indeed the circumstances go far to suggest that these compositions, the Forty Hours *apparati*, and the manifestations of perspective experiments in Roman gardens and palaces were all part of a broad revival of pictorial imagery whose inspiration can be traced back through the great Bolognese treatises to its invention by Brunelleschi.[68]

Figure 205. Tabernacle in S. Lorenzo. Florence, Desiderio da Settignano (Alinari/Art Resource, N.Y., AL2210)

Figure 206. Altar in S. Anna dei Lombardi, Naples, Benedetto da Maiano (Alinari/Art Resource, N.Y., AN25534)

Contributing to the fund of special knowledge on the subject in seventeenth-century Rome were the Minim scholars at Trinità de' Monti, whose specialty in the theory and practice of perspective enjoyed pan-European fame and recognition. While their relations with Cardinal Spada have already been mentioned, we should add that Bernini was himself not immune to the attractions of perspective theory, for in a letter of 9 January 1657, he made reference to the library at the Trinità de' Monti and the many "useful" ideas its books contained.[69]

The appearance of a perspective illusion in an ecclesiastical context therefore complements what we know of the association with palace architecture in Rome. Where they appear in churches, perspective motifs often have eucharistic associations. This is true of the examples Spada was proposing for the choirs, but also of the many altar tabernacles bearing perspective reliefs that date from the fifteenth and early sixteenth centuries.[70] The perspective tabernacle of

231

1450 by Bernardo Rossellino, now S. Egidio in Florence, and the tabernacle of 1461 for S. Lorenzo in Florence by Desiderio da Settignano are obvious examples (Fig. 205). A related type, exemplified in Benedetto da Maiano's tabernacle of the 1460s for S. Anna dei Lombardi in Naples, features the iconography of the Annunciation (Fig. 206). Lavin has already drawn attention to the possible relationship of such images to Bernini's work in the Cornaro Chapel, where low reliefs behind the family portraits on the side walls extend the illusionistic space laterally. The formal relationship of these reliefs to the tradition of perspective tabernacles with eucharistic associations serves, according to Lavin, to invest the Cornaro Chapel with the same values.[71]

Lavin has also related Bernini's perspective reliefs in the Cornaro Chapel with the design of Padre Bitonto's contemporary sacrament tabernacle for S. Paolo Maggiore in Bologna in 1647 (Fig. 207).[72] The altar was commissioned by Virgilio Spada. As Lavin

Figure 207. Tabernacle in S. Paolo Maggiore, Bologna, G. M. Bitonto (Archivi Alinari, Archivio Villani, neg. 26736)

points out, Bernini must have known of the tabernacle, for it was executed in Rome and Bernini had himself been personally involved in the design of the altar. Documents of 1634 refer to his model of the chapel, and drawings show that Bernini was commissioned to provide an architectural frame for the altarpiece, Alessandro Algardi's life-size Decollation of St. Paul. The figures were installed in 1643.[73] It is impossible that the tabernacle subsequently designed by Bitonto would have escaped Bernini's attention, given his personal contribution to this conspicuous enterprise.

Bitonto's gilt bronze tabernacle was composed as a barrel-vaulted nave flanked by aisles. The aisles have flat ceilings, and the bays along the outer walls have niches. Lavin has noted the compositional resemblance of these features to the scheme of the Cornaro Chapel perspectives, mentioned above, and he relates them to "transitional architecture" as represented by Antonio da Sangallo the Younger's vestibule in Palazzo Farnese and Bernini's Scala Regia.[74] I would go further in emphasizing a direct relationship between the perspective tabernacle tradition and the Scala Regia as transitional and even transforming architecture. This relationship was made visible whenever the stairs were viewed from below, but especially during the feast of Corpus Christi.

Corpus Christi is the principal feast in honor of the Eucharist in the Roman liturgical calendar.[75] Celebrated on the Thursday after Trinity Sunday, this holiday was marked by a popular procession. Since the reign of Paul IV (1555–59), it was customary for the pope to lead the procession from the Vatican Palace, through the Borgo, and back to St. Peter's. Along this route, the Host was carried under a canopy followed by the pope in pious worship.[76] While its ostensible purpose was to encourage the public display of piety, the evening procession developed into a festive occasion illuminated by candles and torches, and decorated with canopies and flags, banners, garlands, and precious cloth suspended from nearby houses and palaces.[77] Eventually, the procession filed past some of the most precious examples of textile art in the city, including the set of tapestries designed by Raphael for the Sistine Chapel.[78] Francesco Panini captured the setting in an engraving of about 1770, showing the Raphael tapestries hanging in the north corridor below the base landing of the Scala Regia (Fig. 208).

Figure 208. View of base landing and Scala Regia from north corridor, engraving by Francesco Panini (Bibliotheca Hertziana, B5950)

The Corpus Christi ritual began in the Sistine Chapel where the pope said mass. He processed then into the Sala Regia and, at the summit of the Scala del Maresciallo, prepared to walk or to be carried down the steps to lead the train out of the palace by way of the S. Damaso cordonata, through the Borgo Nuovo and the Borgo Vecchio, and then back to St. Peter's. The order of the groups in the procession was carefully controlled. The route and routine were followed with few modifications up to the time of Alexander VII and appear in contemporary paintings (Fig. 209).[79] The only variation I have found occurred in 1619, when the usual retinue met the pope at the palace entrance rather than processing with him from the Sala Regia. This procedure called attention to the new palace portal while permitting some finishing work to be done on the spaces inside it before being used. In the following year, 1620, the gathering of processors took place as usual in the ceremonial rooms of the palace

and left the palace as usual from the S. Damaso cordonata, and it appears this pattern was followed throughout the rest of the century.[80]

After Alexander VII, the processional route in the palace changed slightly to respond to Bernini's design for the piazza, corridors, and stairs. For now the pope descended from the palace by way of the Scala Regia and followed the north corridor to the colonnade, which brought the procession to the Borgo Nuovo, just as the south colonnade and corridor led back into the basilica from the Borgo Vecchio. Already in the seventeenth century, the procession was related to the design of the piazza, as we know from Carlo Fontana's account.[81] This relationship is validated by the specifics of the ceremony, where the junctures of each major portion of the design gave the porters a natural place for substitutions. The procedure allowing for the honor of bearing the pope and the Host to be spread among a group of conspicuously favored courtiers

233

Figure 209. View of St. Peter's and Vatican Palace on Feast of Corpus Christi, painting, anonymous (Museo di Roma, inv. 4216)

continued into the nineteenth century.[82] To participate and to be seen in the event was a signal privilege, as liturgical celebrations otherwise gave little opportunity for lay officials of the curia to publicize their status.[83] We must therefore think of the procession as a mobile tableau taking place against the changing scenography of the route with ever changing participants.

Among the most highly charged moments in the procession were those that took place in the palace, where the pope gathered and deployed the symbols that radiated his authority in clothing, precious furnishings, and gestures of piety and command. Alexander and Bernini must have had this notion in mind when they maintained the alignment of the Portone di Bronzo with the Borgo Nuovo, transmitting the extension of papal power from the palace through the length of the corridor and into the city along a single axis. The corridor provided the ideal setting for the display of ornament on the feast of Corpus Christi. In the eighteenth century a version in tapestry of Leonardo's *Last Supper* was hung near the statue of Constantine; later a copy was hung next to Charlemagne on the south side of the portico.[84] These juxtapositions emphasized the role of rulership in the dispensation of the Host and its efficacious effects. Eucharistic imagery was thus married to the ideals of temporal and spiritual power. At other times, as we saw, Raphael's Sistine tapestries were hung in the corridor for Corpus Christi, bringing together eucharistic imagery with the promise of the Old Dispensation and the New Dispensation in the Old and New Testament scenes depicted.

Perhaps the most potent image in Alexander and Bernini's scheme was one for which no visual evidence survives. For when the pope was brought down the Scala Regia, a living picture was created in unforgettable dimensions. Preceded by a monstrance bearing the Host, Alexander VII (and later popes) would have been enveloped in a barrel-vaulted space flanked on either side by lines of columns. The perspective effect would have rendered the pope somewhat distant at first but increasingly prominent as he descended the staircase. Adoring the Host, he would have given living form to the symbolic connection between Eucharist and papal authority. The presence of the Host in this context evoked the image of a eucharistic tabernacle in palatial dimensions.

The issue does not reduce to identifying who might have witnessed this tableau or whether it was recorded in any form. Its importance is entirely conceptual and ideological in the true sense of the word. Even for those whose observation point was deep in the urban fabric of the Borgo, the image of the pope as primary intercessor between the body of Christ and the faithful was real and potent. This mental image was incorporated in the reality of the pope's descent from the palace to the piazza. Along the path that led from the double landing of the Scala Regia to the base landing near Constantine, an image of the elevated Host and the adoring Alexander VII recapitulated the perspective imagery of innumerable altar tabernacles of the fifteenth, sixteenth, and seventeenth centuries. By these means Bernini and Alexander had composed a setting in which ritual could be transformed into a mimetic expression of art to reinforce the essential meaning of the event.

Other Rituals Involving the Scala Regia

Catalano, whose monumental compendium of papal ceremonial is based on ceremonial accounts from the late fifteenth- through the mid-eighteenth centuries, lists nearly 40 occasions in the liturgical calendar that call for a *cappella pontificia*, which is, as Gregory Martin defined it in 1581, a "Chappel day, when the Pope and al the Cardinalles are present together at divine service."[85] Many of these occasions would have been observed in St. Peter's. Those that were held in the basilica or required a procession would have used the Scala Regia: for example, the feasts of the Purification, Palm Sunday, Epiphany, Ascension, Pentecost, Last Supper; the saints' days of Peter and Paul, Stephen, Sylvester; All Saints' Day; Christmas; and the anniversary of a pope's election.[86]

On these occasions and many others too, therefore, the Scala Regia ensemble would have assumed special meanings and symbolic intentions. To account for each of them would require another volume, so that here we can do no more than test our understanding of the monument against a cursory mention of some rituals we know from papal ceremonial, Roman martyrologies, and accounts of the liturgical events observed in St. Peter's by Romans and visitors alike. For example, on 3 May, which is the feast of the Invention of the Cross, commemorating Helena's finding of the Cross on Golgotha (*inventus* = discovery), the Roman breviary rehearses the story of Constantine's apparition. C. B. Piazza's commentary for that day, in *Efemeride Vaticana per i Pregi Ecclesiastici...di S. Pietro in Vaticano* of 1687, reminds readers that a piece of the precious relic of the Cross was enshrined in a pier of the crossing of St. Peter's, having been donated to the basilica by Urban VIII in 1629.[87] Further, in retelling the story of Constantine's vision of the Cross, Piazza explains the meaning of the words "in hoc signo vinces." And while he does not argue the site of the apparition, he reflects contemporary opinion in quoting an earlier seventeenth-century source to the effect that the event took place in the Prati, at Monte Mario.[88] This belief, so pervasive in papal Rome, was consistent with the propagandistic intention of Bernini's eques-

trian, whose dramatic staging in the Vatican Palace was undoubtedly meant to imply that the apparition had occurred in the vicinity, and not before Constantine's arrival in the city, as some sources maintained (see Chapter 7).

Again, on the feast of the Exaltation of the Cross (14 September), Piazza refers to the vision of the Cross, although the breviary does not.[89] Finally, on 21 May, which is the feast of Constantine himself, Piazza refers to the emperor as the "Piissimo Fondatore di questa S. Basilica" who after the victory at the Milvian Bridge "by means of the sign of the Cross," came to venerate at the tomb of the apostles. There, eight days after his baptism, he laid the foundations of the basilica.[90] The story of Constantine's vision was thus well known to worshipers at St. Peter's, and no visitor would have missed the various associations the narrative presupposed. Nor could anyone have mistaken the significance of seeing its sculptural reenactment from the narthex of the basilica.

The associations of ritual and figural iconography also include the roundel reliefs in the vault above the base landing. For on the feast of St. Sylvester, on 31 December, one of the readings in the Roman breviary tells the whole story of Constantine's leprosy, the appearance of Peter and Paul, the search for Sylvester, the healing of the emperor, and his baptism by the pope.[91] Moreover, there was a reminder of the event in the sacristy of St. Peter's, where a painting of the apostles Peter and Paul, said to be the same image that Sylvester had showed Constantine, was preserved. The origins of the story in the *Acta Silvestri* have already been discussed in Chapter 8. It remains to emphasize that Piazza's account is proof of the currency of the stories deriving from the *Acta* at the end of the seventeenth century.[92]

All of these associations were reinforced on 18 November, when the Dedication of the Basilica of the Apostles Peter and Paul was celebrated. The feast was instituted by Urban VIII and is recorded in Baronius's *Martyrologium Romanum*, in which reference is made to the authority of the *Acta Silvestri*.[93] Among the many celebrations throughout the year, it must have been one of the most important in validating the Constantinian heritage of St. Peter's and, by extension, the sacred character of the Vatican Palace.

Piazza describes 18 November as a day to profess

one's faith through hymns and verse, which could be delivered from the steps of the basilica or even from private palaces. Participants included foreign princes or their representatives whose presence was the more conspicuous when they gathered around the altar of St. Peter, itself a memorial to the foundation of the basilica inasmuch as the beginning of Bernini's Baldacchino in 1624 commemorated the anniversary of the whole Constantinian fabric in 324.[94] On this day, according to Piazza, no foreign bishop was permitted to enter the basilica without first reciting the "Libello della Fede," from which grew the legend that "he who swears falsely before the Altar of St. Peter will be struck dead."[95] (The practice may well have something to do with the Jansenist controversy among bishops, which under Urban VIII developed into a serious problem by mid-century and may have encouraged the commission for the Constantine statue in the first instance, during another centenary for the basilica in 1654.) That the vision of the Cross, the foundation of the basilica, and the baptism of Constantine were all topics of current interest is only made more obvious by Lualdi's extensive and earnest attempts to sort the legends and the sources from the facts.[96]

Relationships of Iconography, Design, and Concept

The design of the Scala Regia was conceived in an ambience highly charged by concerns for ritual and meaning. Yet the ritual to which the stairs respond at any moment could change to suit the ceremony. The path of a rite, its conceptual tenor, and its significance for the palace or the basilica molded the use and meaning of the monument in countless ways. For these reasons the imagery of the ensemble was intended to be read from different vantage points and with different combinations of ideas depending on the occasion for which that imagery was relevant.

This constellation of associations could depend on illusionistic extensions of virtual space in palatial architecture, evocative recollections of ecclesiastical settings, or monumental fabrications of the tabernacles that contained the sanctified Host on special feast days. All of these relationships and endless others emphasize the inexhaustible multiplicity and es-

sential unity of the messages incorporated in the design and meanings of the Scala Regia ensemble. In all cases the purpose was to dignify the image of the pope as principal agent of the church. In truth, his presence and the authority he claimed were the catalysts that concretized an endless variety of meanings, ideas, and associations emerging from the monument in seemingly infinite combinations with the single goal of consolidating his spiritual and temporal jurisdictions.

Given these circumstances, we may wonder whether any aspect of the iconography had a determining influence on the design, or whether associative meanings were developed after the fact. Without explicit evidence we can only guess that structural issues, aesthetic concerns, and iconographic considerations developed simultaneously. As for the relationships with palace entrances, it is reasonable to suppose that Bernini and Alexander were encouraged to resolve the geometry of the lower stairs with reference to a perspective effect that had been so provocatively used at Palazzo Spada and in other palace and garden designs. Such inspirations were entirely in keeping with a staircase that brought visitors up to the palace chapels and down from the palace to the basilica, for perspective constructions were also deeply rooted in ecclesiastical traditions. I doubt whether the designers set out to have the Scala Regia resemble a container for the Host, yet we know on the basis of Carlo Fontana's statement that Bernini's Piazza S. Pietro was designed in part to enshrine the Corpus Christi processions. Because the Scala Regia is a part of the piazza campaign and its geometry, it would be hard to deny the stairs the same iconographical and functional associations. An interpretation of the design after the fact may therefore be entirely consistent with the way contemporaries understood the monument.

Bernini was certainly familiar with perspective effects and susceptible to their evocative power. He employed perspective constructions in the lateral reliefs of the Cornaro Chapel, in the Forty Hours apparatus later engraved by Francesco Panini, and in other large- and small-scale works. The splayed arch behind the monument to Countess Matilda in St. Peter's (1633–44), for example, suggests the emergence of the countess from her glorious place in history, that is, as a figure who moves triumphantly into St. Peter's through a threshold of time and space.[97] Bernini later used the motif in preliminary designs for the tomb of Alexander VII (1671–78).[98] In the Altieri Chapel (1671–75) at S. Francesco a Ripa, a splayed arch establishes a connection between the center of the chapel space and the altar of the Blessed Ludovica Albertoni.[99] A preparatory drawing of 1664 for Bernini's statue of the Spanish king Philip IV at S. Maria Maggiore in Rome shows a set of columns theatrically arranged to give the impression of a space sharply receding to focus on the figure of the king (Fig. 210).[100]

Yet it is in Bernini's involvement with the stage, design, and stage effects, that we find the most interesting connections with the Scala Regia. Stages like Palladio's Teatro Olimpico in Vicenza were commonly composed of inclined avenues and buildings whose façades converge into the distance to give the sense of spatial recession more extensive than the dimensions on which the sets are actually constructed. And while none that I know incorporates an axial stair hall like the Scala Regia, there are great numbers of theater designs for sets arranged as perspective scenes flanked by freestanding columns and incorporating staircases.[101] Bernini and Alexander VII must have known many such examples, and the artist may have even created some for his own productions. John Evelyn's remark in 1644 about Bernini giving "a Publique Opera . . . where in he painted the seanes, cut the Statues, invented the Engines, composed the Musique, writ the Comedy & built the Theatre all himselfe," is often cited as evidence for the universality of the artist's genius.[102] Unfortunately, we do not have extensive information about Bernini's "prospettive," although recently published documents support the extensive testimony of contemporary sources for his work in the genre.[103]

Of the datable productions we can associate with Bernini, it is interesting to note that all were produced for the Carnival festivities. As Carnival precedes Lent, we can assume that many of his theatrical images had resonance for subsequent liturgical settings as, for example, the Forty Hours Devotions. The "Fiera di Farfa" (1639), whose sets are now documented as Bernini's, was part of a secular opera presented by Cardinal Francesco Barberini together with a sacred opera and a Forty Hours apparatus.

The play of 1638 entitled *The Flooding of the Tiber*

Figure 210. Preliminary project of monument to Philip IV at S. Maria Maggiore, drawing (BAV, Chigi P VII, 10, fol. 45)

(*Inondazione del Tevere*) opened with a view of Rome featuring the Tiber, St. Peter's, Castel Sant'Angelo, and "many other buildings well known to a Roman inhabitant," according to a contemporary.[104] I suspect that the vista was intended to recall one of the most popular and frequently copied city views, or *vedute*, in the whole history of the genre. An example is illustrated in Figure 14. (It is a scene so frequently depicted in contemporary drawings, engravings, and paintings as to earn a full-length modern catalogue.)[105] Bernini's invocation of the well-known panorama allowed the spectator to recognize the theater as an emulation of art and to acknowledge its reciprocal association with daily life.

For a similar effect during the same performance, Bernini arranged for the Tiber slowly to rise and ultimately to overflow its banks. The effect was skillfully managed for maximum effect, as water ran over hastily set barriers and threatened to deluge the spectators, who were ultimately kept dry by a sluice directing the water harmlessly away from the stage at the last moment. The effect was noted by biographers and nearly all subsequent commentators. Theater historians have pointed out that the hydraulics involved in this operation were not new to the stage.[106] What deserves more general acknowledgment is the concept behind Bernini's machinations, which was to startle an audience into recollections of the Tiber floods during the Carnival of the previous year.[107]

In sum, Bernini applied conventional means to manipulate conventions of art and human experience. It was the familiar *veduta* and the real flood of 1637 that inspired these special effects. A later scene in the same performance took place in torchlight at "the portal that leads into the Palace of St. Peter," that is, the Vatican Palace under Paul V's clock tower. The setting was chosen in order to make a joke about the "owners" of the palace, the Barberini, not knowing who came and went through that entrance by night. As Lavin has explained, such ribald references to his patrons and his ambience "helped Bernini break through theatrical convention and establish links with the real world."[108] The episode at St. Peter's assumes special significance when it is recalled that Cardinal Antonio Barberini, in attendance at the performance, occupied the former Giberti apartments over the palace gate (Chapter 2). This fact, and hence the gist of the joke, was noted with appreciative enthusiasm by the Modenese ambassador, though it has since been largely forgotten.[109]

Since Bernini made no major innovations in stage design, his contributions to the theater must be sought in the content of the scripts and the meaning of his images rather than in his special effects. Bernini is himself quoted as having said that in matters of stage design, the smaller the expense and fuss the better, implying that the concept of a play was far more important than its machinery. He even spoke of writing a play whose theme was the constant malfunctioning of the set machinery, a remark that may allude to portions of an existing text that is his only surviving script.[110] Whether this was a topos of the period or the inspiration for later productions with the same theme is still uncertain.[111] The point of Bernini's theatrical illusions was not to fool his audience

by their lifelike aspect, for this would have destroyed all recognition of the artifice that was their principal recommendation. In a passage characteristic of Bernini's themes, one of his actors says that "when a thing looks truly natural, there's got to be some craft behind it."[112]

The audience was meant to derive pleasure from this recognition and its manifestation in Bernini's creations. Beecher and Ciavolella have revealed this aspect of his theater, which is profoundly indicative of his work in the other genres. "Out of situation, character, and convention," they write, "Bernini creates not a meaning so much as a process that is designed to hide itself from the audience, yet tease it into discovering the play's essence. The theatrical process becomes a metaphor in action, preoccupied with the meanings implicit in the modes of its own existence and its relationship to the audience."[113] The scheme of artifice is therefore a shared creation, imparting the pleasures of recognition to the beholder and intimacy with the creator.

As the aesthetician Emanuele Tesauro wrote in 1655, the result is "the double pleasure of him who forms a witty concept and him who hears it. For the former takes pleasure in giving life, in another's intellect, to a noble birth of his own, and the latter rejoices in abducting with his own wit what the other's wit stealthily hides, for no less sagacity is required in comprehending than in composing such ingenious emblematic designs."[114] Lavin has cast the same idea in simpler language, explaining that Bernini unexpectedly involves the audience, which is made to be a participant in the "happening" on stage. In turn, this makes the beholder aware of a new level of existence or, we might add, new possibilities of association. "The relevance of this awareness," writes Lavin, "lies in a series of interlocking conceits which link the theater and art on a level that can only be described as metaphysical."[115] For Bernini theatrical place-making was the means to an end, and the simplicity of a solution must have been its principal recommendation. This would have been especially true wherever the setting had to serve multiple functions.

If the evidence for the Scala Regia points to the reciprocal influence of image and meaning in the process of design, we may also wonder about the intended public for these theatrical pictures. Who was intended to witness and appreciate them? The question is not easily answered without the explicit testimony of viewers. Nevertheless, on the conceptual level that guided the planning and programs of the stairs, we may recall that in his diary Alexander VII identified the wall niches of the Scala Regia as appropriate for the use of pilgrims.[116] This notation alludes to the fact that viewers were expected for the various events and rites that took place on the Scala Regia. The ten niches on each side of the lower stairs serve no structural function, and they were achieved only with difficulty and in slightly irregular fashion (Chapter 6). Given the circumstances, it hardly matters whether they were ever used as Alexander had described, for their existence implies the presence of viewers that he anticipated.

Here we have arrived at a level of interpretation that suggests a symbolic understanding even of seemingly inconsequential parts of the composition. Like so many facets of architectural iconography, the niches signify viewers and attendants whether or not they are present. From this we may speculate on the possibility that the effect of the iconography does not depend on the viewer's physical presence. Where palace ceremonial so firmly governed the rites and rituals of ecclesiastical life, the viewer or witness to any particular event can be said to exist on a virtual level of reality in which participants, regardless of their location, knew the route of the Corpus Christi procession, or the Forty Hours Devotions, or the arrival of a king or an ambassador, and could easily conjure up the imagery brought to life along a path of previously dormant symbols. Oleg Grabar has ventured such notion with regard to Islamic tradition by suggesting "in a theme like the palace [in its most general sense] that it is the metaphysical memory and vision that ruled the physical reality. A magician architect could always change any stage into a new setting."[117]

This metaphoric symbolism, which exists in memory as well as in fact, is particularly relevant at the Scala Regia for several reasons. One is the relatively exclusive nature of access to the monument during the very rituals that gave its form special meanings, since a truly public event could not be achieved without devaluing the power and specificity of the ensemble's messages. Another reason for the reliance on metaphoric symbolism lies in the fact that the pictures of meaning evoked by the monument were not literal re-creations of imagery but approxima-

tions, visual similes whose relevance lies in their fluid and allusive character. Finally, the virtual rather than physical presence of the viewer serves as the vehicle for communicating meaning in the design because of its dimensions and its chameleon-like nature, necessarily adaptable to successive events and situations requiring varying symbols, like different sets in a theater but without a truly mobile array of scene flats or stage furniture with fixed associations.

For Bernini's contemporaries the relationship between material fact and emotive suggestion informed the Scala Regia in much the same way that meanings were construed for colonnades, stairs, and perspectives in the science of optics, moral conceits, and the visionary power of nature. In 1646, the Jesuit Athanasius Kircher, friend of Alexander VII and intimate at court, published a book with a chapter on supernatural visions ("magia rappresentativa").[118] Among his reports was an account of the mirages that had been described to him while crossing the Straits of Messina some ten years earlier. The apparitions included "buildings, palaces, and castles, with infinite numbers of columns arranged according to the principles of perspective."

Because Kircher believed this and other visions of the Morgana di Reggio to be divine manifestations, the perspective imagery of the hallucination assumes special meaning. Since the time of Brunelleschi and Alberti, linear perspective was used to render the divine in an apparently tangible way, mediating the realms of the mundane and the spiritual.[119] Kircher understood the visions as such, and although he does not identify the purpose of perspective imagery in this regard, its function is and was self-evident. The vision of Paradise, similarly suggested in the sets for the Forty Hours Devotions, was made explicit in contemporary descriptions and later commentaries.[120] In another of Kircher's accounts a fellow Jesuit described an apparition in Reggio of "royal castles in abundance . . . and all of a single form and finish" hovering above "more than 10,000 pilasters of equal length." Here, too, Kircher attributed the natural phenomenon to divine power.[121] In the seventeenth-century imagination, columnar perspectives were associated with palace imagery and with supernatural and even divine forces. The Scala Regia and its decorations express these relationships and carry them beyond the realm of magical revery to a level of spiritual revelation about the importance of place (site of a vision and of St. Peter's legacy), the nature of time (Constantine's and that of the palace), and the continuities between historical recollection and living emblems of authority.

The arrangement of columns in compelling perspectives served as visual cues to other realities, which might be encapsulated in the significance of a theater production, a garden folly or palace vista, a liturgical celebration, or the decoration of churches or their furnishings. In any one of these cases, the design evokes a world beyond mundane appearances. In the end, therefore, it would be a mistake to interpret the visual effects of the Scala Regia according to a single set of traditions, typologies, ceremonies, or iconographic associations. Rather, we should envision a loose conceptual framework within which the composition of the Scala Regia reverberates with echoes of secular theater and church ritual, palatial grandeur and poetic illusion, vaporous space and tangible structure. Only by these means could a monument with functions as obvious and diverse as this one be transformed into an appropriate setting each day of its existence. Put another way, we must think of the Scala Regia as a polymorphic symbol, with as many layers of meaning and intention as there were occasions for its use. In this way meanings were intended to unfold progressively to complement a variety of circumstances and transform them into ritual. From this point of view, the inimitable success of the Scala Regia resided and still resides in a rich symbolic texture and formal cohesion capable of assuming specific identities to suit papal, that is to say ideological, requirements.

Alexander's Administrative Personality

However sophisticated a design and its meanings, a monument is realized only when it promises to fulfill the aspirations of its patron. Without them, there is no monument. Thus, Vasari's praise of the predecessor to the Scala Regia in the sixteenth century poses for us the challenge of explaining why Alexander VII should have been disposed to rebuild that part of the palace a century later. In short, the new construction must have responded to a stimulus more compelling than a set of functional, ceremonial, or aesthetic requirements. That stimulus, condi-

tioned by historical developments, was embodied in the personality of Alexander VII and the context of the Chigi pontificate (1655–67).

Descended from Sigismondo Chigi, brother of Agostino who had been banker to Julius II, Fabio Chigi (b. 1599) was intensely aware of a distinguished family heritage whose luster had been compromised by financial pressures in the later sixteenth century.[122] He studied theology in his native Siena, where he developed humanist interests, especially in art.[123] He arrived in Rome in 1629, and was shortly sent to Ferrara as vice-legate, then to Malta (1634), and finally as papal nuncio to Cologne where he spent 13 years from 1639 to 1642. In 1643 he was named nuncio extraordinary to discussions that led to the Treaty of Münster, and he represented the papacy at the Peace of Westphalia in 1648. In 1651 he assumed the office of secretary of state under Innocent X, who made him a cardinal the following year.

Throughout his career Fabio Chigi was a consummate bureaucrat, the creation of a papal foreign office whose goals in the mid-seventeenth century were destined to be dashed repeatedly by circumstances beyond its control. Teased and belittled by false hopes for a rejuvenated papal state, he suffered the fate of presiding over a reorientation of political power that challenged papal authority and the strength of the church, frequently relegating it to impotence in matters of pan-European importance. It is usually assumed that in these circumstances, he found increasing consolation in matters of palace ritual, sacred ceremony, secular scholarship, poetry, art, and architecture. For these he was indeed well prepared by his earliest studies in Siena, his broadly cosmopolitan professional experiences, and his lineage.[124] But this explanation may be too simplistic.

By all accounts Chigi's career was as brilliant as it was ultimately unsuccessful. He had won the support of influential cardinals like Giulio Sacchetti, Francesco Barberini, and Bernardino Spada. Even his nemesis, the French minister Mazarin, offered grudging praise when the two met in Cologne, Mazarin predicting that Chigi would soon be elevated to the purple and perhaps elected pope. But if the scenario came to pass, the minister opined in 1651, "it will be the weakest pontificate since St. Peter."[125] At the conclave of January 1655, Chigi was indeed a compromise candidate whose election on 7 April came after a tortured 80-day session and Sacchetti's unsuccessful bid for leadership.[126] The new pope assumed the name of his Sienese predecessor, Alexander III, no doubt building as his artists did, on the association with the Greek Alexander.[127] In the realm of politics, it was an ironic choice.

Rosa characterizes Alexander VII as "formed by diplomatic and curial life, a good executor," but not without the faults deriving from the administration of others' policies rather than the development of his own. In the campaign against Jansenism and at the Peace of Westphalia, for example, his principled rigidity prevailed over any intuitive or creative impulse in the face of certain defeat.[128] Not given to extemporizing papal policy, he could not perceive the inevitability of new political alignments destined to compromise the authority of the church. In these regards his performance conforms to Partner's delineation of career curialists whose bureaucratic training emphasized financial and papal-state administration over the duties of representing the spiritual powers of the papacy.[129] By disposition and circumstance Alexander VII evolved into a superb micromanager, reordering the papal chancery with new *regulae*, reactivating the various governing *congregazioni*, reinvigorating the traditional decorum of the *cappella pontificia*, and reviving the practice of frequent papal audiences. In the unforgettable words of Pasquino, he became "Maximus in minimis, minimus in maximis."[130]

His contemporary and friend Padre Sforza Pallavicino recounted how Alexander spent as much as six or seven hours a day in public audiences, usually in two shifts, in addition to the usual Sunday morning appearance for the poor. The pope would hear as many as a hundred petitioners at a sitting, frequently conversing in various foreign languages. The pope was also a stickler for reading all *memoriali* in their entirety and making corrections in his own hand. By the end of the week, Pallavicino calculated that Alexander had heard from more people and signed and sent more orders than his predecessors had in two months.[131] Although previously overlooked by art historians, the constant contact with large audiences had a significant expression in Bernini's only other major intervention at the Vatican Palace, the creation of the Sala Ducale as a single large chamber from two previously discrete rooms that composed the *aula secunda* and the *aula tertia*.

This was achieved in 1656–57 by demolishing the wall separating the rooms and hiding the remnant of dividing structure under billows of gilded stucco drapery, the papal escutcheon, and cavorting putti.[132] The result deeply impressed Tessin.[133]

In the reforms of the papal chapel (*cappella pontificia*) Alexander was adamant in excluding all non-participatory observers, concretizing the roles of subdeacons and acolytes in services, formalizing the dress of the pontifical chaplains, and making certain that they, not the barons or nobility, marched closest to the cross in processions. Mere courtiers were banished from services, complete silence was ordered of participants, and grooms and attendants were required to dress formally in all public appearances.[134]

As part of this campaign of orthodoxy, Alexander revived the visits of the *cappella pontificia* to the principal basilicas in Rome, often delivering an extemporaneous sermon in Latin on these occasions.[135] His grand manner also extended to personal matters as, for example, in his own impeccable dress ("inarrivabile" wrote the Venetian ambassador), his sumptuous table, and the inexplicable habit of keeping all audiences on their knees, with the exception of cardinals and ambassadors, for as many as two and three hours. He was said to have chosen one thousand soldiers from the infantry especially to attend him in solemn cavalcades, and otherwise to be posted in the city to be marshaled whenever he passed. Two cavalry regiments fully dressed in cuirass with holstered arms and drawn swords accompanied him on official business in the city, while in the countryside he indulged a penchant for being transported and attended in a sedan chair.[136]

All of this and more are conveyed by the eyewitness account of Philip Skippon from 1663:

> One day we saw the pope Alex. VII coming out from a chapel where he had said mass: before him went several gentlemen; a priest in a blue habit with a gold cross: and when he came out into a presence-chamber, many kiss'd his toe; and one German priest, after he had saluted the shoe, begg'd aloud, an indulgence for himself and 20 of his friends. The pope gave his benediction, by lifting up two of his fingers. He went into his sedan, and was follow'd by some cardinals in coaches, and bishops on mules; next came his light horsemen, about 20; every one with a lance and a banner on it; then three trumpets and a kettledrum before a troop of cuirassiers all in armour; round about the sedan went a guard of Switzers in their red and yellow

liveries; a company of musketeers stood nigh the palace, who all were in a ready posture, and kneeled as the pope went by. He had a red habit over a surplice, and a gold tippet; his hat was red, and plaited.[137]

Alexander's reforms, particularly those pertaining to ceremony, were broadcast in foreign courts with as much emphasis as the pope's remarkably astute appointments to curial posts.[138] Described by the Venetian ambassador as absolutely punctilious in the observance of every rite, Alexander insisted on pomp and circumstance as an antidote to flagrant abuses, and this extended to the prohibition of services at night, reform of church music, reform of the orders, strictures on admission to the prelature, and eventually the publication of a new Index of prohibited books.[139] If his responses occasionally bordered on the compulsive, his policies were at least well defined. In the days of Innocent X, even for the papal chapels, grooms and *servitori bassi* were often seen only partly uniformed, whereas Alexander VII had them outfitted "so buffed and formal and . . . so perfectly accountable that some have judged it excessive."[140]

From these and other reports there emerges a paradox between love of indulgent ceremony on one hand and humble religiosity on the other. Chigi's letter of 1644, written while he was still a cardinal, described with pride the months required to build his coach, which was decorated in black velvet and ornamented with four bronze bowls "full of fruit falling out as though from a basket" and sprays of wheat and flowers.[141] Yet after his election, he still ate from majolica dishes rather than silver, and even made an effort to cancel the traditional procession of the *possesso* by which the popes were ceremonially invested. He slept in a bed that was no more than a bare board, at the foot of which was a casket, and he was said to have surrounded himself by other reminders of death like the skull Bernini had cast for him in bronze or the skeleton traced in the bottom of his silver drinking cup. His meditations on the writings of Francis de Sales (whom he beatified in 1661 and canonized in 1665) are well known, and each morning after mass he spoke to his confessor.[142] Perhaps the contradictions were best encapsulated in the preciousness and morbidity of "a neat clock, made by Campani, wherein a death walks with a flaming sword at the striking of every hour."[143]

Alexander's piety may have been conditioned by his own fragile constitution. A sickly child, he was once expected to die but went on to make a modest recovery.[144] Among other ailments, he suffered throughout his life from gallstones. For these he had undergone painful, life-threatening surgery in 1642 while nuncio in Cologne, attributing his survival to an effigy of the Savior there.[145] The operation was not successful, and years later the Venetian ambassador nastily repeated the rumor that Alexander VII still bore an oozing fistula.[146] True or not, the medical problem was never resolved. Indeed, one reason for insisting on a sedan chair in the countryside may have been to avoid the road bumps and brusque movements that produced excruciating pain while riding in a carriage.[147]

It is even possible that Alexander's reported "horror" about descending the old Scala Regia (Appendix), may well have expressed a matter of unseemly physical rather than emotional distress. Bernini's design made the descent better illuminated and provided an additional landing that would ease Alexander's concerns and quite possibly his bodily discomfort while he was carried in the sedan chair. In this way, his architectural intervention at the Scala Regia could be justified in a code that was quite plain to the knowing and perfectly reasonable to those who were not so well informed.[148]

That Alexander's afflictions interfered with his duties was apparent early in the pontificate, at the Corpus Christi procession in 1655. Suffering from the stones, Alexander nevertheless insisted on being carried through the procession behind the Host. Apart from his ill-health, this was unexceptional, for other popes had made the circuit in a seated position while carrying the monstrance with the Host or having it carried in front of them. For the event, however, Alexander commissioned Bernini to design a *talamo*, a processional float upon which the pope could kneel rather than sit, to lessen the strain on his lesion. The *talamo* replaced the usual chair with a decorated support like a faldstool, which allowed the pope to complete the entire length of the customary processional route in a minimum of distress.[149] The monstrance was fixed on its own support directly in front of the pope, who was thus positioned to adore it on bended knee.[150]

From surviving descriptions we know that Bernini's *talamo* for Alexander VII was unusually ornate. At the pope's feet, ample folds of red velvet

Figure 211. Alexander VII Carried in Procession on feast of Corpus Christi, painting, G. M. Morandi (?) (Musée des Beaux-Arts, Nancy, inv. 37)

concealed the appurtenances enabling Alexander to take the weight off his knees and minimize his discomfort. In this position the pope processed through the piazza and Borgo, remaining virtually motionless in a pose of exceeding reverence. As Gigli noted in wonder and admiration, "the pope was carried not in a chair, but kneeling with his head uncovered, holding the Blessed Sacrament in his hand with great devotion, moving neither his eyes nor body and appearing so immobile that people thought him an apparition."[151] Through these means Bernini transformed a medical necessity into a liturgical spectacle whose effect was more visionary for the immobility it enforced upon the pope. That Alexander's piety was induced by stones seems to have passed unremarked by all save Pasquino again, who exclaimed that a bed would have served better than a *talamo*, and a bier better than a bed.[152]

Imparting the image of Alexander VII in pietistic reverence as never before, Bernini's invention was commemorated in prints and paintings, and later on the papal annual medal of 1664, which depicts on its reverse the image of the pope in humble adoration of the Host (Figs. 211, 212).[153] Whitman and Varriano have emphasized the "unprecedented choice of this subject for an annual medal" especially in view of Alexander's preference for architectural im-

Figure 212. Medal depicting Alexander VII carried in procession on Feast of Corpus Christi, engraving, Bonanni 1706 (Bibliotheca Hertziana)

ages in this format, and they underscore the importance Alexander placed on architecture and papal ceremony.[154] The medal also bears witness to Alexander's devotion to the Eucharist, the significance of which was strengthened by the fact that he was elected in the particularly long and contentious conclave after a Palm Sunday display of the Holy Sacrament in the Cappella Paolina, as discussed in Chapter 1.[155]

It remains only to remark upon the date of the medallic issue, some nine years after the creation of the *talamo* in 1655 but only a year after the annual medal of 1663 featuring the Scala Regia. The architecture of the Scala Regia was essentially finished when the pope used the staircase at Easter of 1664 (Chapter 6), and several months later the image of the kneeling pope appeared on the new annual medal. The timing of these events underscored the interrelationship of ceremony and architectural design, possibly even alluding to a specific connection between the eucharistic imagery of the Corpus Christi procession and the architecture that encompassed its path between the palace and the city. Certainly other papal annual medals were devoted to nonarchitectural themes, but none have so close a relationship to major architectural enterprises. By choosing to have himself depicted holding the Host at Corpus Christi, Alexander may have intended to emphasize the essentially religious function of the Scala Regia and Piazza S. Pietro in the face of mounting criticism over his architectural extravagances.[156]

The medal and the *talamo* stress Alexander's keen interest in the perception of his office projected through ritual and its accoutrements. An English visitor to S. Maria Maggiore was appropriately impressed by such imagery, remarking on the pope's triple crown, his embroidered *media* borne by twelve men in scarlet flanked on either side by "a great fan made of white peacock's tails," the maces, mitres, and cross-bearers, and the trumpet blasts sounded at his entrance followed by the cardinals marching two by two.[157] In the words of a later English traveler, the pope on his sedan chair appeared "to sail forward . . . like a celestial being."[158] This was precisely the intended effect. To enhance the image of the pope in this manner was to stress the essential nature of his office, a goal served most conspicuously by the ensemble at the Scala Regia. Alexander reveled in ritual, and the new staircase admirably served his taste for the formal display of his authority. Yet the enterprise has a programmatic, as well as a personal element that is related to political circumstances.

Alexander's Political Dilemmas

The pivotal event of Alexander VII's pontificate actually took place six years before his election. The Treaty of Westphalia of 1648 put an end to the Thirty Years' War, but it also relegated the Papal States to a minor position among European powers and – oddly for a war initially sponsored by religious differences – demoted the importance of Catholic–Protestant frictions as a defining force in international politics. The Spanish and Austrian Hapsburg alliance was effectively compromised, and the dreams of a united empire that were nourished through the sixteenth century were forever dashed. Meanwhile, France and Spain continued to do battle, as the Papal States remained unable to influence the outcome. German princes confirmed their independence from the emperor and their right to religious self-determination. Eventually, Protestant Sweden dominated the Baltic, limited only by Dutch maritime interests, and the Restoration monarchy in England was more inclined to the French than to the papal court.[159]

The inability of the Roman Catholic Church to influence the new political alignments was clear when the treaty was negotiated at Osnasbrück and signed at Münster (24 October 1648). As the nuncio extraordinary there, Fabio Chigi was unsuccessful in opposing those articles damaging to the church. Especially compromising was the idea that the dominion of rulers would determine the religion of their subjects. The result weakened the authority of the church and broke the power of Germany, which would no longer be a threat to France. Even in subsequent decades, when the German princely houses changed their faith from Lutheranism to Catholicism, their people did not always follow suit. (This will explain Alexander's solicitous reception of the German princes hailing from the lands of his former nunciature.)[160] Upon the death of Ferdinand III in 1657, there was even the threat of a Protestant succession to the Holy Roman Empire. Although Alexander campaigned vigorously on behalf of Leopold of Hapsburg, these activities had negligible effect on his eventual election.

The goal of Mazarin to nullify papal influence in political matters reached its zenith in the Peace of the Pyrenees concluded between France and Spain in 1659. The negotiations were carried on without the knowledge of Roman authorities, much less representation. The result consolidated the *status quo*. With it Mazarin had brought about the end of Spanish domination in Europe and the threat to France of an allied Spanish and Austrian empire. Even more conspicuous than the weakness of Spain was the humiliation of the Holy See. Symptomatic of the situation were two articles of the treaty promising support by the kings of France and Spain for the dukes of Modena and Parma against the papacy. The equestrian statue of Louis XIV, planned by Mazarin for Trinità de' Monti, was only the most pungent of artistic initiatives in this situation (see Chapter 8). That the statue was never realized hardly compromised the effect of the insult, which was general knowledge among visitors for several years.[161]

With the election of Emperor Leopold in 1657, Alexander felt compelled to aid in the defense of the Holy Roman Empire against Turkish incursions along the Danube. This responsibility encouraged the pope to organize a coalition against the Turks, a defensive proposition that Mazarin feared might compromise the hold he had imposed upon the empire. Mazarin died in 1661, and it was ostensibly to work out the details of this alliance that the young Louis XIV sent the Duke of Créqui to Rome. Créqui's embassy arrived in June 1662, to be housed by the Duke of Parma in Palazzo Farnese.

From all of the circumstances it is obvious that Créqui's embassy was designated to complicate rather than resolve the tensions between France and Rome.[162] For eleven years, the Most Christian King had posted no official ambassador to the city. Now, among other demands upon his arrival, Créqui wanted to extend the privileges of diplomatic immunity to the blocks around his residence, a matter of particular sensitivity, as it lay along the daily route of the pope's Corsican Guard. On one of its routine marches between the Corsican barracks and the Vatican in August 1662, words were exchanged, a member of the guard was knocked to the ground, and the Corsicans shrouded the palace in a hail of gunfire. A volley was fired when Créqui appeared at a window, and his wife barely managed to escape upon her return from church, although one of her pages was killed. Eventually, Créqui and his wife found refuge with Cardinal D'Este and Alexander

called his Corsican Guards to task, but the damage had been done.

The French demand for papal remedy was predictably immoderate and unfulfilled.[163] The French seized Avignon, and prepared an army in Piedmont to march upon Rome. Through the intervention of Ferdinand II de' Medici, Grand Duke of Tuscany, a settlement was affirmed in Pisa in 1663. In the following year Alexander's nephew, Flavio Chigi, was sent to Paris to make amends under humiliating circumstances. And while Pastor suggested that Cardinal Flavio successfully demonstrated the pope's greater dignity, Créqui's reassignment to Rome in 1664 is more indicative of the unrepentant French attitude over the affair.[164] Only the agreement signed at Pisa brought the episode to an end, although a monument in the form of a "a small pyramid in an obscure place not far from Palazzo di Farnese" remained for all to bear witness to the unpleasant affair.[165]

Then, too, the issue of Jansenism plagued Alexander's tenure. Already as a nuncio, Chigi had written against the heresy first enunciated in Cornelius Jansen's *Augustinus* (1640).[166] According to this belief, summarized in the famous "five propositions," the operation of God's will was a matter of preordained grace. As this view questioned the very power and efficacy of the church to intervene on behalf of its faithful, Innocent X condemned the propositions as heretical. But the debate was inflamed by new questions regarding papal infallibility. Alexander VII issued an apostolic constitution, in 1656, in support of his predecessor's condemnation. Another decree of 1665 in turn bolstered the earlier two, but with no effective result in France, where the heretical views were most strongly held.

In this matter the support of Louis XIV was entirely unpredictable. On the issue of Jansenism, Louis XIV wished to back the pope but had also to consider the influence of his bishops, who were as reluctant as Parlement to promulgate Alexander's bull. On the matter of infallibility, the king vacillated conspicuously. In early 1662, he defended the doctrine at the Sorbonne, but by September of the same year he had come to consider the notion of papal infallibility more threatening to his absolute rule than Jansenism.[167] As Sonnino infers, "It would almost seem, therefore, that the King's ideas of absolutism required contempt for the power of the Holy

See as an alternative to admitting a limitation on his own authority."[168]

Nor was Louis XIV alone in his antipapal ambitions. In June 1662, sponsored by the perception that the Holy See was abusing its influence in Germany, the Elector of Cologne (the seat of Chigi's former nunciature!) contacted the French with a proposal for allying against the papacy. On the same account, the French contacted the Elector of Mainz in September 1662. Only mutual suspicions, it seems, prevented the development of these exchanges.[169] Even where the papacy was not involved, other European heads of state had similarly ambitious programs to establish absolutist rule, as did Charles Emanuel II of Savoy.[170] In his case the ruler's ambitions were consolidated in an equestrian of his illustrious forebear Victor Amadeo I, located on a landing of the staircase at the Royal Palace in Turin.[171] The position of the work is comparable to that of Constantine at the Scala Regia, which serves related purposes of referring to the ancestry of the ruler's power.

Alexander was also unfortunate in arenas other than international politics. He had inherited a national debt of significant proportions, and his efforts to cut it by devaluing the interest on papal bonds was both unpopular and unsuccessful. In 1655 there was shortage of grain, and by the time it was resolved a year later, Rome was in the grips of the plague. Between May and August 1657, the population of the city was dramatically reduced, falling to a little over 100,000. An extensive report on the administration of the Papal States composed by Cardinal Giulio Sacchetti in 1663 called for reforms, but these were not well received.[172] Whether because of physical frailty or lack of workable policies or the ever present concern for micromanaging, Alexander VII could not strengthen the material well-being of the state he governed. On the other hand, as Krautheimer has noted, the pope was able and motivated "to give Rome in the course of a mere twelve years a new face and to provide her with a new image."[173]

Each of these circumstances gives resonance to the imagery of the Scala Regia and Alexander's urge to reaffirm the spiritual and temporal dominions of his office just when both seemed so much at risk. To build an image of authority and historic preeminence, he relied in part on the expressive power of architecture. In short, the notion of a world-worn leader retiring to the activities of a dilettante misrepresents the entire process. Under Alexander VII the dignity of the papacy would be reflected as much in the configuration of the palace as in the policies that emanated from it. His challenge was to find appropriate venues and a suitably expressive language for his goals, for which the Scala Regia was admirably suited.

Palace Imagery and Papal Authority

The invention of the Scala Regia by Bernini and Alexander VII prioritized a single route of arrival and departure for the Vatican Palace. It enforced an axial geometry on both events, dissolving the capricious turns and fragmented avenues of access created during the course of the sixteenth century, and substituting for them a boldly controlled thoroughfare. The character of this refashioning of the palace fabric may therefore be seen as an architectural expression of authority in the age of absolutism, as previously hinted (end of Chapter 6). Yet the realities were more complicated and more richly endowed with meaning. For just as the design of the staircase cannot be explained exclusively with reference to groups of typological parallels and influences, neither can its existence be completely understood with reference to the personality of its patron or the political problems of his pontificate.

There can be little doubt that Alexander VII reveled in the display of formality and the observance of time-honored protocols. Yet this proclivity also served the requirements of his office within the immediate context of pan-European events, which challenged the authority of the papacy in every crucial sphere of its activity. The adumbration of ritual and pomp also responded to the broader ambitions of the papacy for more than two centuries. With the background of Alexander's tumultuous pontificate in mind, every contribution to the exaltation of his office becomes an affirmation of his rule over the obstacles of contemporary events. His sponsorship of the Scala Regia and its decorative ensemble expresses the millennial objective of the popes to assert their spiritual and temporal power, uniquely construed from the charge to St. Peter and Constantine's beneficence to the early modern present.

In these circumstances, Alexander's special interest in the celebration of Corpus Christi is particularly revealing. A recent study of the feast in relation to the topography of the Borgo in the Renaissance has stressed the symbolic importance of the pope's role. "Although the subject of Corpus Domini was the body of Christ," Ingersoll suggests, "the real sign vehicle was the body of the pope, who was invested with charismatic symbols."[174] The monstrance that he carried and alone worshiped through the entire path of the procession sent a special message about papal prestige. "The image of the pope as the vehicle for the sacrament," writes Ingersoll, "was an archetypal embodiment of papal supremacy. Corpus Domini projected the ideal of papal absolutism within the controlled atmosphere of the Borgo. The pope at the center with the Eucharist attained an equilibrium from seemingly contradictory expressions of pomp and humility."[175] In the case of the Corpus Christi procession, while humility may appear to undermine the concept of temporal power, in fact it endows the stature of a secular ruler with the piety of a holy man.[176] These facts are consistent with Alexander's creative interest in the feast day and with aspects of his administrative and religious personality.

It is necessary to reemphasize that the pope is the primary beneficiary of the Corpus Christi procession, in the sense that he alone is a fixed participant with an unchanging role in the pageant. In the changing constellation of players, the pope was cast as the principal instrument through which the Eucharist was extended to the faithful. He alone directed the arbitration and extension of grace to the flock of onlookers.[177] This explains exactly why Alexander VII welcomed the opportunity to stage the event and ultimately to enshrine it in the permanent paths of Piazza S. Pietro and the Scala Regia. While a procession is essentially a mobile event, the Corpus Christi celebrations bore a number of permanent images. Chief among these at the Scala Regia was the columnar perspective and, among figural representations, the Vision of Constantine. These features left no doubt of the legacy – Christian, Petrine, and imperial – to which the papacy was heir.

The story of Constantine and its importance for the papacy is so intertwined with the palace that the relocation of the equestrian, which was originally meant for the basilica, may seem inevitable in hindsight. In his sponsorship of the Portone di Bronzo, Paul V had already made allusion to the Imperial Palace at Constantinople and the Bronze Gate at its entrance (Chapter 3). The placement of the image of Constantine at the Vatican Palace underscores the notion of the ruler represented at the portal to his residence, to which we have already alluded. An ideological overture to a papal audience in the Sala Regia, itself decorated with variations on the theme of the ideal Christian ruler, the statue of Constantine alluded perhaps also to the figures at the entrance of the Imperial Palace at Constantinople, which was also dominated by an image of the emperor (Chapters 2, 3, 8).[178]

These references would be consistent with the old tradition for associating the papal palace to the Palace of the Emperors on the Palatine Hill.[179] Even the prominent use of columns as the motif most obviously defining the Scala Regia could be viewed in this regard. Colonnades were said by Suetonius to connect the Temple of Apollo to the ancient *Palatium*, for example, and a conjectural reconstruction of colonnades is still recognized in the archaeological literature as leading to its aula regia.[180] Nor can we rule out an association with the peristyle located in front of the Golden Court, close to the *aula regia*, whose columns were reputedly known since Alexander VII's day.[181] The association of a columnar hall with an audience chamber was well established in the seventeenth century, as the illusionistic decorations of Palazzo Pitti in Florence and Palazzo Spada in Rome attest. Both were frescoed by Agostino Mitelli and Angelo Michele Colonna, and both glorify imperial precedents.[182]

On the broadest level of interpretation, the Constantine imagery at the Scala Regia called to mind the role of the emperor in conferring on the papacy its jurisdiction in temporal realms and the pope as the modern "priest-king." The idea of the church as the *imperium* and of the pope as its imperial overseer is centuries old. In Renaissance funeral orations, both Pius II and Julius II were characterized as restoring the *imperium* of their office to its ancient splendor.[183] Other popes of the period and in medieval times were similarly described.[184] In the Middle Ages, Ullmann observed, the pope needed "to live in a place which suitably brought into relief his monarchic function." During the course of the ninth century, the residence of the popes at the Lateran was termed the *sacrum palatium*, projecting their sacerdotal authority and their regal-imperial functions.[185]

The ostensible source of the popes' imperial jurisdictions at that early date was the Donation of Constantine, the eighth-century forgery that purported to recount how Constantine had conferred upon Sylvester the garments, insignia, and symbols that made him heir to all imperial realms and privileges. Not surprisingly, the forgery appeared during a period of conflict between the pope and the Holy Roman Emperor.[186] By the time Valla had proved the document a forgery in the fifteenth century, however, its basis in the more venerable *Acta Silvestri* was well established, and the latter was the source that inspired the figural iconography of Scala Regia, as we have seen. With the transfer of the papal residence under Nicholas V from the Lateran to the Vatican came also the tradition of the *sacrum palatium*.[187]

The tradition of the *sacrum palatium* continued to be reinforced at the Vatican Palace well into the seventeenth century. Both the figural iconography (with images of Peter and Paul flanking the Madonna and child) and the architectural composition of the Portone di Bronzo (recalling the Imperial Palace at Constantinople) under Paul V alluded to the heavenly authority of the ruler of this place, conforming brilliantly to Smith's characterization of a palace portal as a "ideogram" of the divine wisdom of the state.[188] Similarly, the entrance fountain would have been construed as its lavacrum and the crowning loggia (never built) of the new entrance wing as its place of royal appearances.

Also under Paul V, the statue of St. Peter placed at the foot of the staircase between basilica and palace made explicit the extension of Petrine authority from basilica to palace (Chapter 3). By its very location the image stressed the dual nature of the papal mandate as sacerdotal and temporal. The substitution of Constantinian for Petrine imagery during the pontificate of Alexander VII reinforced this idea. Recollections of the emperor's Roman baptism and his founding of St. Peter's underscored the very aspects of the Sylvester legend developed in the Donation forgery, namely the favor shown the pope by the emperor and, consequently, the ascendance of papal over secular powers. For, despite the revelation of the forgery, the basis of its fiction resided in a trusted source, the *Acta Silvestri*, which continued to enjoy wide acknowledgment and legitimacy

as expressed in the writings of Baronius and the substance of the Roman breviary (Chapter 8). As Ullmann has pointed out, the author of the eighth-century Donation clearly grasped the aim of the *Acta*, which was to legitimize the superiority of Sylvester's authority over that of Constantine.[189]

In the *Acta*, Constantine's authority was symbolized by his crown, a feature that plays so prominent a part in Bernini's composition that it merited the censure of his critics (Chapter 8). Its conspicuous role in the ensemble is not fortuitous. The *Acta* states that for his baptism, Constantine put aside his crown and prostrated himself before the pope.[190] In the representation of the scene in the roundel relief, the bare head of the emperor is contrasted with the crowned Sylvester. In the context of the emperor's apparition, the theme of papal preeminence over imperial pretensions is unmistakable. Its meaning at the entrance to the *sacrum palatium* serves to emphasize the dual roles and jurisdictions of the pope.

The concept of the pope as the embodiment of both secular and religious power has a long and complex history, extending far back into the Middle Ages.[191] In a recent book, Prodi has suggested that over the course of two centuries, between 1450 and 1650, the papacy underwent a profound metamorphosis, evolving a secular bureaucracy that could serve the Papal States governed by a single priest-king.[192] Rietbergen argues that the idea is perhaps the central motivation in papal politics within and beyond the Papal States. The whole notion begins with the memorable formulation by Kantorowicz that "under the *pontificalis maiestas* of the pope, who was styled also 'Prince' and 'true emperor,' the hierarchical apparatus of the Roman Church tended to become the perfect prototype of an absolute and rational monarchy on a mystical basis, while at the same time the State showed increasingly a tendency to become a quasi-Church or a mystical corporation on a rational basis."[193] That seventeenth-century historians and theologians acknowledged the dual nature of papal authority is amply proved by citations from contemporary sources. Even the French kings before Louis XIV were viewed as endorsing the temporal aspects of papal power, which was traced to Constantine.[194]

Many commentators criticized the power assumed by the popes and the concomitant diminution of influence of cardinals and the papal court on the direction of the state in the seventeenth century. But no one doubted or questioned the role of the pope as "un Prencipe misto," enjoying temporal and ecclesiastical rule over what was characterized as an "Ecclesiastical Monarchy."[195] Current thinking on this issue revises the previous, generally held belief that the Papal States languished as a political entity during the emergence of the great nation states of the early modern era. Far from the usual view of the papacy generating one reform after another culminating in the Counter-Reformation, scholars like Prodi and Rietbergen envision the trajectory of papal politics as paralleling the evolution of the absolutist states of Europe and, in some sense, providing a model for them.[196]

This thesis has received widespread acceptance.[197] What has not been given adequate consideration is the fact that the evolving concentration of power in a "sovereign prince and pastor" took place during the two centuries that the papal residence at the Vatican assumed its definitive form to give physical shape to the concept. From the time that Nicholas V designated the Vatican Palace rather than the Lateran as the principal apostolic dwelling, every artist, iconographer, planner, and architect working there must have been dedicated to the task of conditioning the new *sacrum palatium* for its traditional roles. Few features of the palace better document this goal over the centuries than the principal entrance and staircase of the palace.

In the twelfth century the tower stairs of the *turris scalarum* gave notice of the Vatican's emulation of north Italian rulers' palaces. By the mid-fifteenth century, the project for Nicholas V's double-towered gate matched the most magnificent image of entry conceived anywhere on the peninsula. Subsequent contributions from the time of Pius II to Innocent VIII, Julius II to Paul III, and Paul V to Alexander VII, glorified the experience of arrival at the palace in a manner that is consistent with the continuing assertion of papal hegemony in the political sphere. From this point of view, it is hardly accidental that the Vatican staircases of Bramante and Sangallo were the model and envy of Italian nobles, princes, and duchies, as Vasari's comments prove and the monuments repeatedly demonstrate.[198] The same will have been true of Bernini's Scala Regia.

The evolution of the royal staircase in Europe is too extensive a topic to be investigated here, yet it bears some consideration that many of the most impressive works in the genre postdate Bernini's Scala Regia, whether at Turin or Caserta, Versailles or Hampton Court. The unique aspect of the principal staircase at the Vatican Palace is the way that it complemented the growth of the fabric as a whole, in keeping with the ideology of its primary occupant and the office that he represents. The fact that Alexander preferred the Quirinal Palace to the Vatican, as already mentioned, supports this notion forcefully. One was a residence, the other primarily a symbol. Like his predecessors over the millennia, but especially during the previous two centuries, Alexander conceived of the Vatican Palace as the principal representation of his authority. To argue this point further, it is necessary to reflect on the process by which Alexander VII transformed the Scala Regia from a palatial thoroughfare into a new ritual space.

A New Focus of Ritual

It may seem paradoxical that the final step in the transformation of the Vatican Palace entrance should have taken place in the ebb of papal power in Europe. Why was the last substantial contribution to the Renaissance palace fabric made at a moment of such vulnerability to the office it enshrined? As this chapter should prove, there is no single fact, circumstance, or symbol to explain adequately the invention or meaning of the Scala Regia. Yet more than anything else, Alexander VII and Bernini must have understood the Scala Regia as the real and conceptual nexus by which the *sacrum palatium* was related to the Christian cult and the secular world. This fundamental aspect of the Scala Regia distinguishes it from the staircases and entrances of other palaces, such as the great family or ducal residences to which its form and embellishment are otherwise comparable in many ways.

The difference in character between the Scala Regia and other palatial staircases may also be summarized by distinctions of use. For the palaces of high clerics and low, monarchs, and princes, recent scholarly investigations have stressed the importance of the staircase as a stage for the demonstration of etiquette. Itself the outgrowth of the consolidation of power and, ultimately, the development of the absolutist state, the requirements of civilized behavior in matters of social interaction became codified with increasing rigidity from the sixteenth to the seventeenth century. Where residential architecture was concerned, the focus of events lay beyond the stairs at the room or rooms of reception. Along this path, the staircase was the great divider of realms, so that a guest greeted there by a host had been done a great honor. The further a host descended in acts of greeting, the greater the honor to the guest, all such deference being clearly defined in etiquette books of the day.[199]

Similar matters pertaining to the papal court were codified in official ceremonial and widely circulated handbooks explaining, for example, how the visitor would ascend accompanied or unaccompanied, depending on status, to the audience of a pope, or how many bows to make in his presence and from what distances. But with the creation of the Scala Regia, Alexander VII and Bernini transformed the stairs into a new focus of papal ritual, endowing it with unique programmatic significance. In this transformation the space of the staircase became something more than it had been.

The impetus for this operation resided partly in Alexander's desire to extend the vision of the piazza to the palace, and partly in his hope of providing a fitting expression for the link between palatial and church estates. Alexander may have been inclined to pursue this project because of some small advantage to his physical infirmities, but the overwhelming inspiration must lie in his perception of the palace entrance as a field of ritual. He designated this field to define his claim and that of all popes to exercise the dual role of absolute monarch and infallible priest.

Instead of a gentle but barren flight of stairs, Alexander VII and Bernini conceived of a space that would be infused with distinct architectural forms, figural sculpture, and decorative devices that resonate with programmatic intention. This effect was not coincidental or haphazard. Both artist and patron profoundly understood the transforming power of architectural and figural imagery to enhance the prestige of the pope and his office. These men did more than reconstitute the shape or even the visceral experience of climbing or descending a staircase. They transformed it into a theater for stylized behavior that was intended to authenticate papal power according to a seemingly endless variety of scripts offered by liturgy and ceremonial, and enacted through ritual.

Ritual structures beliefs and endows them with legitimacy. While it generally alludes to more than it may explicitly specify, collective ritual usually serves to perpetuate tradition or to traditionalize new perceptions. Moreover, ritual has the capacity to evoke and concretize ideas and symbols. Anthropologists call this process transformation, a state of mind or moment "when symbol and object seem to fuse and are experienced as a perfectly undifferentiated whole." Etiquette does not have the same capacity, nor is it necessarily related to a pressing ideology. For these reasons, the enactment of sacred ritual becomes far more significant to our understanding of the Scala Regia than the demonstration of etiquette.[200]

The goal of ritual is to compose and legitimize ideologies, and its enactment is an assertion of order that implies acceptance and permanence among the celebrants. Ritual operates on emotional and perceptual more than strictly intellectual levels, and its effect discourages questioning. As Moore and Myerhoff put it, ritual is "a message stated in a form to render it unverifiable, separate from standards of truth and falsity."[201] And because it conveys messages as though they were unquestionable, ritual is the most effective way of asserting those very precepts that are most in doubt.[202]

In Alexander's relations with Louis XIV, Charles Emanuel II of Savoy, the German electors, the Grand Duke of Tuscany, or the dukes of Parma and Modena, may be found more than ample reason for the dynamic assertion of the pope's imperial sovereignty and sacred mandate. In this respect the equestrian image of Constantine, clearly shown in the vision as a captive of divine imperatives, may symbolize the Duke of Modena, the French king, the Hapsburg emperor, or the English monarch, all of whom (like other rulers) had been characterized as a modern Constantine in their own courts.[203] The columnar context of the vision, itself the embodiment of an archetypal visionary palace, was designed to evoke both mental and physical responses to the illusion of mundane perceptions.

These notions lead us back to the issue raised earlier in this chapter regarding the intended audience. To what extent can those excluded from the space of the Scala Regia be said to participate in its shaping of church ritual, and how could this possibly effect a change in perceptions among those adherents (or adversaries) far removed from the papal court? On this issue Burke has anticipated some of my conclusions with eloquence and conviction.[204] First, he alludes to the "connoisseurs of ritual" who were prepared to know what they could not always see on a given occasion. Moreover, the knowing and the less erudite would have had access to books or pamphlets describing and sometimes illustrating events. Such booklets sometimes appeared at an event and other times after its conclusion. In all cases, they could be and often were widely circulated throughout the Papal States and Europe.[205] Then, too, as Burke suggests, one did not need to know precisely what a ritual meant in order to be impressed by it. The essence of collective ritual is to establish rather than justify a common purpose or goal.

Burke terms the position of a pope an "amphibious state," uniting the dignified with the efficient and the charismatic with the bureaucratic in his official capacity of imperial priest.[206] This oddly embracing metaphor captures best what papal ritual intends to achieve. Of the two roles of the pope, the one most in doubt in the seventeenth century was his monarchic identity, and this is often what rituals most emphasize. The very act of kissing the foot of the pope as the Holy Roman Emperors were to do illustrates the concept by emphasizing the pope as an absolute, imperial monarch.[207] The kiss of the foot was a requisite aspect of every papal audience, as the ceremonials make clear.[208] The adoration of the Eucharist during the Corpus Christi feast had the same effect, for the devotion that participants showed the processing Host represented by extension a reverence for its chief administrator, the pope.

The disdain and occasional contempt that European governments showed the papacy cannot have been unmitigated. The circumspect mediation of the Grand Duke of Tuscany in the Créqui affair, the secrecy involved in the contacts between the Elector of Cologne and Louis XIV, and the waffling position of the French king on the issue of Jansenism all suggest that the Holy See retained the power of independent action that could limit the authority of absolute rulers in realms significant to them.[209] In this light we can imagine that papal ritual served as

a "polemical instrument," a means of persuasion aimed at demonstrating the power and authority of the pope exactly when secular rulers were advancing their own claims of sovereign ambition throughout Europe.[210]

In the end the use of ritual, and of art and architecture to enhance it, speaks most eloquently of their patron rather than of their fluid intentions, presumed meanings, or results. For more than two centuries, the papacy had been building a bureaucracy to support age-old claims of sovereignty in matters of state and spirit. By the seventeenth century the result was clearly perceived. One writer of the period described the appearance of a "sacred double-edged sword . . . between the divinity of spiritual and temporal authority . . . the weapon sent to the popes from the highest skies."[211] Others expressed the same notion in different ways. Queen Christina reportedly wrote that God "has willed that the government of His Church should be a monarchical one; He has communicated His infallibility to the Pope, not to the Councils: the Pope is everything; they are nothing without him. How can a man be Christian if he is not a Catholic? And how can one be a Catholic if one refuses to the Pope the submission that is due to him?"[212]

During the pontificate of Alexander VII, the challenges to his hegemony were real and perceptible. Even the domestic and intramural challenges of rulership must have given cause for dramatic gestures to reaffirm the stability of papal governance in the face of near constant obstacles and apparently insurmountable problems. These circumstances cannot be separated from Alexander's enthusiasm for bureaucratic rectitude, spiritual orthodoxy, and demonstrative ritual. Nor can the animation of these passions be separated in turn from his patronage of monuments like the Scala Regia. Alexander's response to his situation was one for which he had been well prepared by birth, training, and disposition – the simulation of his office by the evocation of historical precedent and cultural referents. If the result was the creation of a new Rome, the basis for its imagery was the assertion of Alexander's office in the very moment of its decline. In this regard, the Scala Regia represented his ambitions historically, encapsulating a policy in which perceptions were pitched against realities.

Appendix

Carlo Fontana, *Templum Vaticanum et Ipsius Origo* . . . , Rome, 1694, pp. 233–237.

Libro IV, capitolo XIII: *Dell'antica Scala maestra, che conduce all Sala Regia*

In quell'istessi muri, che restringono la nuova Scala Regia, risiedeva già l'altra antica costrutta di cattiva forma, e divisa già in due Tomi non uguali: ciascheduno de'quali era composto di numerosi Scalini. Per quella longhezza che era più di palmi 300, rendevasi la medesima molto oscura: non essendo bastante quel solo lume, che in faccia aveva per illuminarla più del primo Tomo, e però era tenebroso il secondo, come quello, che riceveva in pochissima quantità il lume, per essere da esso molto lontano. Da queste cause procedeva, che volendo i Sommi Pontefici passare dal Palazzo al Tempio, portati nella Sedia Ponteficia alquanto eminente, ricevevano orrore in vedere frà quelle oscurità un pendio continuato di Scalini, senza riposo di ripiano, seguendone anche grande incommodo per quelli che portavano li Sommi Pontefici; onde pareva poco decoroso, che per quelle Scale, per tali difetti, & anco per quello richiedeva la dignità Ponteficia, si dovesse passare in quelle solenni funzioni Pontefice con l'accompagnamento di tanti Porporati, & altri degnissimi Personaggi. Questi inconvenienti fecero risolvere subito Alessandro VII di rinovare la detta Scala, ordinatone il disegno al Cavalier Bernino per l'essecuzione dell'opera.

Non possiamo tralasciare prima di descrivere la magnificenza della nuova Scala, di palesare le grandissime difficoltà, e pericoli, che incontrò questo celebre Architetto nell'innovazione di questa fabrica, e gl'impedimenti di porre in opera pensieri molto più nobili, e vasti, da esso partecipateci, à cagione di quei muri vecchi, che di presente circondano anche la Scala nuova. E di quegli Edifizij, che sono sopra di essa, cioè la Sala Regia, Cappella Sista, e l'altra dove s'espongono le 40. ore, detta la Paulina. Per essere queste immutabili rendevano ad esso non solo scarsezza di lume, ma di più l'obligavano à non uscire da quei limiti; Perciò fù necessitato à deporre ogni suo vasto pensiero, & investigare altri ripieghi adeguati alla necessità di quel luogo; e con tanta applicazione si accinse à questa impresa, che stabilì i disegni per dar forma alla Scala presente. Ma non quì terminarono all'Architetto le difficoltà, e pericoli: poiche dopo principiata l'opera con gran fervore, nel [p. 234 begins:] rompere in alcune parti quei muri, che s'inalzavano sin alla cima degli Edifizij, si scuoprì, che la grossezza di quel muro, che divide le Scale dalla Sala Regia, era nel mezzo piena di rovine. Onde si prevedeva il totale pregiudizio della muraglia, e con essa la distruzione de medesimi Edifizij. Impiegò in tal caso il diligente Architetto tutto il suo valore in trovare modo per assicurarsi, e difendere da così strano accidente, con industriosi sostegni di Puntellature validamente armate, senza investire la propria rovina, poste in opera dalla gran prattica, & intelligenza del Capo Mastro Simone Brogi. Quelle Machine erano di travi così ben ordite, e tessute, che rappresentavano un ripartito Squadrone di legnami, e rendevano stupore per la loro tessitura non tanto à gli Spettatori, che à i Professori.

Informato pienamente di sì bella invenzione il Papa Alessandro VII, mosso dalla curiosità, ordino à Noi, che con ogni diligenza il tutto delineassimo, e descrivessimmo insieme col Bernino. Questo con sentimento di gran dolore essagerava con Noi l'infausto caso, conoscendolo forsi atto à risvegliare nelle menti l'altro, che seguì nelli tempi passati poco lontani da questo, e vicino al Tempio; mentre quei casi potevano fargli perdere il credito, che con tante fatiche si acquistò. Veramente apportò anche à Noi sì gran terrore, in vedere per aria così gran fabrica, che non averessimo avuto, l'animo di pratticarvi sotto, se prima non ne fossimo fermamente accertati, che quell'armamento di puntelli con incatenature diagonali fosse stato abile à sostenerla.

Finalmente operò con tanta accuratezza, & assistenza, questo esperto Professore, nel rinforzare i muri con sostruzioni d'Archi, che quasi anche danno forma, e massa alla Scala nuova, che rese sicuri li rovinosi Edifizij. Non può alcuno à bastanza distinguere, e conoscere quanto industrioso, e stimabile sia stato l'artificio del predetto Architetto, in sapere porre rimedio à rovine tanto evidenti, e rendere con maraviglia universale la Scala sì luminosa, e magnifica, con ornamenti tanto nobili. E chì non hà veduto il funesto spettacolo, che rappresentavano quelle muraglie à guisa di Caverne, gli parerà un Iperbole, mentre quelle facevano concepire negli animi di tutti un fermo timore della loro rovina.

[p. 235 begins:] Capitolo XIV. *Della nuova Scala Regia Vaticana che conduce al Palazzo Ponteficio*
Saggiamente scrive Leon Battista Alberti [lib. I, cap. 13], esser le Scale la più difficil parte, e di maggior briga di tutte l'altre, da disporsi negli Edifizij; atteso che, conviene dar ad esse illuminazione, publico, e nobile Ingresso, & uscita con più adagiata elevazione, secondo la loro qualità, nel modo, e forma che riferisce Vitruvio. Cioè, che sotto la norma, che assegna Pitagora [lib. 1, cap. 2], deve lo Scalino avere le sue misure proporzionali, secondo quella figura triangolare ortogonia. Deve dunque costare di trè parti di questa l'elevazione della fronte dello Scalino, il piano di quattro, e l'Ipotenusa, che dà il pendiò, di parti cinque. E benche voglia detto Autore, che questa sia la più rigorosa misura geometrica, per la situazione del natural passo: tuttavia riusciranno sempre migliori le Scale, quando si faccino di men'elevato pendiò.

Di quest'elevata pendenza appunto trovasi la Scala Regia, mentre li Gradini nella loro fronte sono minori della proporzione assegnata dal detto Pita-

gora, ma maggiori ne' loro Piani, e per conseguenza l'Ipotenusa più inclinante, il tutto è ben disposto, e vi si trova la docilità, che gli conviene stimata tanto necessaria anche dallo Scamozzi [lib. 2, cap. 34] mentre dice, che le Scale Regie debbino essere disposte agiatamente.

Sono grandi le difficoltà, che nascono tanto nel disporre il numero de' Branchi, per assegnare fra quelli il necessarij Ripiani per il riposo de' Popoli: da quali vengono continuamente frequentate, quanto nella collocazione delli forami. Et in specie quando per ottenere la sufficienza del lume, viene uno obligato à mendicarlo dalle pareti, quali anche procedono nella disposizione; & alle volte s'incontrano tali intoppi, che non ammettono, per le loro situazioni vestitura d'ornati, seconda richiedono le buone Regole, & i vasti pensieri, che partorisce l'Architetto simetriatamente, nel modo che il sudetto Scamozzi [lib. 11, cap. 34] l'espone.

Se bene trovasse il Bernino il sito della Scala antica, nella quale hà sostrutta l'altra nuova, scarsezza di sito, e di lume, angustezza di muri, infelice Ingresso, & ignobile uscita; non di meno tanto operò col valore [p. 236 begins:] del suo talento, che portò alla vista del Publico questa sontuosa Scala, con verle procacciato industriosamente quelle parti, delle quali era priva. La rese anche molto commoda nello scendere, e salire, & in specie per quelli, che portano li Sommi Pontefici. Mercè l'agevolezza de' suoi Scalini frà quali Repiani, che l'interrompono, con avere tolto anco quell'orrore; che dall'antica, si ritraeva; e le diede un nobile Ingresso, che contiene la larghezza degli Ambulatorij, con abondanza di lume ottenuto artifiziosamente dalla Volta del secondo Tomo, à segno che rendesi la medesima luminosissima. Mà quello che fà stimabile la virtù del Professore, è l'avere con mirabile artefizio, e legiadria vestita quell'infelice ossatura d'ornati di Colonne d'ordine Ionico, con sue Basi, e Capitelli di Pietra Tiburtina; quali fù obligato à disporre non parallele, ma concorrenti al punto. E benche siano distanti alquanto dalle Pareti, con tutto ciò non scemano quella larghezza del tutto di essa Scala. Procede anche da tale situazione un buonissimo contorno elevato, con gli ornamenti della Cornice architravata, che in pendio ricorre con li sotto Archi, che sopra il vivo di esse Colonne s'inalzano arcuatamente con quelle Rose nobilmente intagliate; che sembrano à punto uno Scenico, ornato di tale nobiltà, che apporta sommo godimento, rispetto anche à quell'Arme d'Alessandro VII. poste in quel lato, che fà principal imbocco. Queste sono sostenute eminentemente da due gran Fame campeggianti in quegli ornati d'intagli, col ricorso di sedici Colonne per lato, e con altri, che vestono li Repiani, e sostegono la Volta. Quelli intagli sono disposti con varij ornamenti di Putti, Festoni, e Stelle, che fanno vago intreccio, sin dal principio, al fine. Onde si gode una sì stimabile vaghezza che infonde à ciascheduno la curiosita di salirvi, e fà conoscere a' Riguardanti, che prima si siano disposti gli ornamenti, e poi le Pareti, e che non abbi avuto l'Architetto alcuna obligazione à quelle muraglie, ma abbia trovato il sito aperto, & avuta libertà di fare li disegni di suo proprio capriccio, e non secondo richiedeva la necessità del luogo, senza che impedissero quello Pareti l'essecuzione d'altri spaziosi pensieri. Incontrò finalmente Bernino non solo la piena sodisfazione d'Alessandro VII; come di genio nobile, e grande, ma l'applauso commune di tutto il Popolo, col felice esito di quest'opera. Onde cagionò motivi al medesimo Pontefice d'ornare maggioremente quell'altro lato del sontuoso Ingresso di essa Scala, che riguarda il Portico, e la Loggia contigua al Tempio, coll'intiera Statua equestre di fino Marmo di Carrara, di grandezza quasi di due naturali, che rappresenta il Magno Costantino à Cavallo [p. 237 begins:] in quell'atto, che gli apparve la Croce fatta dal di lui famoso Scalpello. Risiede questa sopra un eminente Piedestallo, ne' lati del quale sono obliquamente due Ambulazioni, che tendona alla Scala inferiore. Fù in vece di Nicchia arrichita questa Statua di nobile Padiglione, che la ricopre, facendo, coll'unione di quelle simbrie, Medaglie, & intagli, che ornano la Volta di esso Ingresso, una magnifica, & imperiale comparsa, rispetto all'Ambulazioni avanti il Tempio. Il tutto più chiaramente scorgerassi dalla delineata Pianta, e Profilo.

Notes

Abbreviations

AFSP Archivio della Fabbrica di San Pietro, Vatican City
ASV   Archivio Segreto Vaticano, Vatican City
ASR   Archivio di Stato, Rome
BAV   Biblioteca Apostolica Vaticana, Vatican City

INTRODUCTION

1. Among English-language references, see Wittkower 1985, 192–93; *Macmillan Encyclopedia of Architects* 1982, I, 197; Fleming, Honour, and Pevsner 1974, 34 (with the quotation); Pevsner 1966, 251; Held and Posner 1972, 40–41; Jordan 1969, 204–5; de la Croix and Tansey 1986, 715–16.

CHAPTER ONE. A Tour of the Monument

1. Lassels 1670, 49.
2. "One must look under the colonnade of St. Peter's for the door that leads to it," he continued. Stendhal 1957, 55 (1827), 106 (1828).
3. Cf. Fontana 1694, 191; Bonanni 1696, pl. 72; Letarouilly 1882, II, pls. 107, 112, 113, 114 (originally pls. E.3, F.2, F.3, F.4).
4. Scamozzi 1615, I, 316: "I gradi delle Scale deono [*sic*] esser dispari . . . come vuole Vitruvio."
5. Taja 1750, I, 1. The preface (p. 25) explains that Taja wrote the MS in 1712; it was edited in 1748.
6. On the symbolism of the gate, see Smith 1956, 10.
7. The frame and the cornice of the Doric order are stone, as can be seen in the breaks between pieces, but much of the surface has been treated in faux marble, falsely suggesting stucco.
8. Fontana 1694, 195; Briccolani 1828, 19.
9. This is the theme of Birindelli 1982; but it was adumbrated

in his earlier volume on Piazza S. Pietro, 1981, 2–3, fig. II, 82 (schema 5), 116 (schema 10).
10. Fokker 1938, 208; Berra and Rosso 1938; also Birindelli 1981, 222–23, n. 4.
11. Stendhal 1957, 55 (1827). The opening of the spina had been discussed periodically since the pontificate of Sixtus V (1585–90), and even by Bernini.
12. The Chigi monti in the glazing at the double landing have been replaced by the different designs seen in photographs from various epochs. Bonanni's engraving shows the original scheme, conforming to the documentary evidence. Barbier de Montault 1870, 4, already mentions the "deux vitraux modernes" in this location.
13. Jestaz 1966, 174: "Le dedans de ces galleries son voultée aveq des ars doubleau sur des pillastre et entre iceux pillastre des croisé dans cul-de-four; cela est d'un méchant goût."
14. ASV, Sacro Palazzo Apostolico, titolo X, 119, art. I, fasc. 4, contains relevant documents.
15. Stendhal mentions the use of gas illumination in St. Peter's in 1827 (Stendhal 1957, 68).
16. Leti 1675, III, 534–36.
17. ASV, Sacro Palazzo Apostolico, titolo X, 119, art. I, fasc. 4.
18. The width across the corridor between pilasters inside the Portone di Bronzo is 6.87 m., whereas the width between the last pilasters at the west end of the corridor is 8.03 m., an increase of 1.16 m.
19. Birindelli 1981, 119.
20. At the Portone di Bronzo the risers are 15.5 cm. and the treads 48.5–50.5 cm.; here they are 14.5 and 56–58 cm. respectively.
21. Wittkower 1966, 251.
22. Wittkower 1966, fig. 35. The inscription above the niche with St. Helena and the True Cross bears the alternative motto "IN HOC VINCES."
23. See Bernini 1713, 107; and the end of Chapter 8 for a description of the imagery and its effect at the inauguration of the monument in 1671. Keyssler 1751, 549, attests to the

presence of the cross in his day. From the mid-eighteenth and late-nineteenth century, however, comes evidence for an alternate inscription from Isaiah 60,3: "AMBULABUNT GENTES IN LUMINE TUO ET REGES IN SPLENDORE ORTUS TUI" ("Gentiles shall come to thy light, and kings to the brightness of thy rising"). See the anonymous *Descrizione del Palazzo Vaticano* 1724–30, fol. 4, with contractions in the inscription); and Barbier de Montault 1870, 4 ("la fenêtre ogivale est accompagnée de cette belle inscription: 'Ambulabunt gentes in lumine . . . ' "). As other sites under Alexander VII's patronage bear inscriptions with verses from Isaiah and Psalms, the citation cannot be dismissed. Perhaps this was a second citation in the glazing of the window that was lost when the glass was replaced. We simply cannot be sure.

24. Taja 1750, I, 2–3, wrote of its appreciation by "persone intendenti d'architettura; perchè da un sito disadatto, ed irregolare, per l'opportuna apertura delle due porticelle nel piedestallo di graziosa, e di utile centinatura, si cava leggiadra novità alla vista, e comodità allo sfogo di questo luogo, ch'è di così gran uso." Taja was obviously responding to Bernini's critics also in his praise of the "egregia statua, per se stessa di maniere feroce, e di movenza mirabile." Taja's participation in the aesthetic debates of the day is also evident in the comments on Fabio Cristofani's mosaic of Cavaliere d'Arpino's composition over the Portone di Bronzo, where Taja praised the lack of disturbing reflections on the glassy surface. The effect obviously contrasted with the mosaic altarpieces then being erected in St. Peter's.

25. Cancellieri 1784, 78–79, claims that campanili columns were used at the Scala Regia and the façade portico of S. Andrea al Quirinale, but probably not at the twin church on Piazza del Popolo.

26. Birindelli 1982, 122.

27. I have measured the 5.21 m. dimension between the lowest columns of the Scala Regia. Bonanni's engraving (Fig. 5 above) indicates a dimension of 23 ⅓ palmi (5.21 m.) between the columns of the central passage of the colonnade.

28. For the imperial symbolism in connection with the motif on the sixteenth-century Tower of the Winds in the Cortile del Belvedere, see Courtright 1990a, 88–89. For a useful explanation of the motif at Palazzo Pamphili (1646) and S. Maria in Via Lata (1662), see Joseph Connors in *Macmillan Encyclopedia of Architects* 1982, I, 463–64, "Cortona."

29. My thanks to Henry Fernandez for this observation. The notion could be expanded if we credit Bramante with ambitions to achieve a perspective effect, as does Bruschi 1969, 424–25.

30. Birindelli 1982, makes this observation.

31. Barbier de Montault 1870, 4, also records the same 78 steps on the perspective flights.

32. See Bernini's tomb of Countess Matilda in St. Peter's (Wittkower 1966, fig. 38); the upper story of Palazzo Barberini and niches in the north staircase (Waddy 1990, figs. 139, 155); and the foot of the staircase at Palazzo Mattei (Hibbard 1971, fig. 42a). Bernini may have had a hand in the design for the Palazzo Barberini.

33. Birindelli 1982, 18–19.

34. Birindelli 1982, 19–20.

35. Varriano 1986, 144–45.

36. See, for example, the drawing of the vault in Windsor Castle, Royal Library 5565, which was certainly made after the monument, but not necessarily by a member of Bernini's studio (pace Blunt and Cooke 1960, 21, cat. 43).

37. Worsdale 1981, 260. There are many other examples.

38. Erler 1995.

39. Pastor 1923–53, XXXI, 1–9.

40. References to the election and the events of Palm Sunday have apparently been overlooked in the secondary literature since Gattico 1753, 353–359, and no one has previously related these events to the palms that decorate Alexander's commissions.

41. The risers vary between 12.5 and 13 cm. and the treads between 57 and 59 cm. These steps are therefore one or one and a half cm. taller and as much as 2.5 cm deeper than those of the lower flights.

42. Laugier 1765, 112–13: "Les ordres d'Architecture ne conviennent point dans les parties rampantes. On les a employés à Scala Regia du Vatican, & ils y font un très-mauvais effet. Un entablement rampant ne peut être supporté par un chapiteau dont le tailloir est nécessairement horizontal."

43. Scamozzi 1615, I, 312 and 316, repeatedly recommends the use of "abundant" natural light in stairs. He also suggests using skylights: "si può anco prendere il lume da qualche apritura, ò lanterna artificiata ad alto; il quale lume venendo dal puro Cielo, e non potendo esser impedito da cosa alcuna, & in tanta quantità, che si diffondi fino à basso."

44. Brunelleschi's first panel of the Florentine Baptistry seen from the cathedral included a burnished silver sky that would provide the viewer with a reflection of the real sky and moving clouds. In the second panel, of Piazza della Signoria, the skyline was cut out so that a direct view of sky and clouds resulted when the beholder took the appropriate position in front of the image.

45. The thought is inspired by Campbell 1977, 157, with additional literature.

46. On the drawing for the glazing of the Pantheon's oculus, see Marder 1989, 630. On Bernini's awareness of the effects of light falling from the oculus of the Pantheon, see the diary of Chantelou 1985, 147, entry for 24 August 1665, paraphrasing an observation in Serlio's Book 3.

47. The inset must be an editor's posthumous addition to the engravings by Letarouilly (died 1855), as Patricia Waddy reminds me.

48. Servi 1861; Redig de Campos 1967, 248. The stairs were inaugurated on 27 December 1860. The full enclosure was emphasized in Barbier de Montault 1870, 24.

49. Barbier de Montault 1870, 3–4, mentions the twenty travertine steps at the entrance to the corridor and describes the

corridor "éclairé par dix grandes fenêtres que Pie IX a fait vitrer."

50. ASV, Sacro Palazzo Apostolico, titolo X, 119, art. I, fasc. 2, for Vespignani's project of 1890-91, including a drawn plan of alternative sites and a characterization of those who compromised the formality of the setting: "persone civili e mascalzoni in manica di camicia, e dame e servette con fagotti diplomatici e sguatteri, e i fieri studenti della Biblioteca ed i pacifici impiegati di Palazzo, e gente fumante il sigaro e cocchieri masticanti la paglia di tabacco." Pius IX ordered another extensive restoration of the Scala Nuova in 1897.

51. The risers of the Scala del Maresciallo vary between 12.8 and 14 cm. and treads between 50.5 and 53 cm.

52. Tantouche 1623, 58.

53. Mola 1663, 47-48.

54. Both Mola 1663, and Baglione 1642, 16-17, mention other frescoes by Donato in Vatican staircases.

55. ASV, Sacro Palazzo Apostolico, titolo X, 119, art. I, fasc. 4, for the brick viewing stand proposed in 1840 and built by January 1842.

56. For examples pertaining to the Sala Regia, see Figs. 34, 35, and 43 ("Sala de Re").

57. Gattico 1753, 463 ("per scalas magnas").

58. BAV, Vat. lat. 12332, fol. 150v (13 April 1664), cited also in Chapter 6.

59. Fraschetti 1900, 318, n. 3. On Alexander's interest in Corpus Christi, see Chapter 9.

60. Gattico 1753, 422. On this occasion the procession began in the Sistine Chapel, continued through the Sala Regia, descended the Scala Regia halfway to the double landing, and progressed to the stairs of Sixtus V, leading to the Sacrament Chapel of St. Peter's.

61. The descent took place "per scalam versus portam principalem Palatii recta via da fontem, inde in transversum quasi usque ad tabernas, inde recta via ad fontem per scalas S. Petri ad Basilicam" (Gattico 1753, 431).

62. The account of 18 July 1623 refers to the two conclave rotas and conclave portal at the top of the stairs: "in capite Scalarum apud Aromatarium, & portam Conclavis in capite scalarum contra portam magnam ante Aromatarium" (Gattico 1753, 352).

63. Gattico 1753, 416. Here the new pope could be associated with the seated statue of St. Peter at the foot of the steps (Chapter 3).

64. Respectively, Battaglia 1943, doc. 191; Borsi and Quinterio 1980, 356; AFSP, Piano II, ser. 4, vol. 5, fols. 229-30, the last a glazier's bill for work "sopra la scala grande dove cala il Papa p. andare in chiesa" (see Chapter 6 for more documentation).

65. Cf. Borsi and Quinterio 1980, 257-58; and Fraschetti 1900, 318, n. 1.

66. Lualdi 1644-55, II, fols. 11v-12, quoted in Chapter 2. The two stairs are discussed in Chapters 2 and 3. The marble statue of St. Peter is discussed in Chapters 2 and 9.

67. Alveri 1664, II, 143, 154. The imprimatur for the second volume was granted on 13 June 1663, and Alveri refers to Bernini's design as in the course of construction.

CHAPTER TWO. **The Palace Entrance and Stairs During the Renaissance**

1. On Heemskerck, see Egger 1911, 23, pl. 17; Huelsen and Egger 1913-16, II, 68; and Filippi 1990, 25. These discussions are superseded by Carpiceci 1987; Veldman 1977; and Veldman 1987.

2. For the plan, later engraved by Natale di Bonifazio da Sebenico in 1589-90, see Cerrati's introduction to Alfarano 1914, xxvii-xlii; and now Silvan 1992.

3. Cf. my citations of Severano 1630, Alveri 1664, De Sebastiani 1683, and Ciampini 1693 in Chapter 8.

4. The essential introduction to the history of the Vatican Palace is Redig de Campos 1967, and newer literature is incorporated in Pietrangeli et al. 1992. Aspects of the early history of the palace were surveyed in Ehrle and Egger 1935.

5. See Ehrle and Egger 1935, 13, 29; Redig de Campos 1967, 21; Steinke 1984, 11-17, 23-25; and Radke 1988, 192-193.

6. D'Onofrio 1978, 92-97.

7. D'Onofrio 1978, 128-146.

8. See Ehrle and Egger 1935, 50; and Redig de Campos 1967, 21-25, for the older notion that the tower belongs to the period of Innocent III and the double-nave hall to a later era.

9. Steinke 1984, 32-51; Pistilli 1991, 19-21; and Mancinelli in Pietrangeli et al. 1992, 33, 34.

10. To Steinke 1984, 49-51; and Pistilli 1991, 19-21, with comments on the masonry; one must add the remarks of Radke 1988, 193 (kindly brought to my attention by Patricia Waddy).

11. The divergent axes are visible in Figs. 29 and 43. In the period between the execution of these drawings, the opening between the rooms was moved from the south to the center to create a visual axis through the Sala Regia to the door into the Sistine Chapel.

12. See the indications of grade above sea level in Magnuson 1958, pls. 1A, 2; and for the geology of the Vatican, De Angelis D'Ossat 1953.

13. Redig de Campos 1967, 25-33; D'Onofrio 1978, 218-224; Steinke 1984, 51-66; Shearman 1986, 25; Shearman 1990, 21.

14. For the *aula prima, secunda,* and *tertia,* see Ehrle and Stevenson 1897, 10-13.

15. Partridge and Starn 1990, 27.

16. Ehrle and Stevenson 1897, 11; Ehrle and Egger 1935, 69-70; Frommel 1964, 41-42; Shearman 1971, 6; Frommel 1984, 125; and now Partridge and Starn 1990, with the most recent bibliography. For descriptions of the decorations, see Taja 1750; Chattard 1762-67; and Pistolesi 1829-38, VIII, 88-117.

17. Frommel 1984, 118-119; Quednau 1979; Shearman 1972. Again see Taja 1750, 76; Chattard 1762-67; and Pistolesi 1829-38, VIII, 83-88, for the decorations of the rooms.

18. Skippon 1663-64, 662.

19. Redig de Campos 1967, 32, and his reconstruction on p. 38.

20. For the tradition of the spring and literature on the Algardi

fountain commemorating it, see Montagu 1985a, 87–90, cat. 191.

21. On the *turris scalarum*, see Ehrle and Egger 1935, 65–66, 81, 82, 111–112; Redig de Campos 1967, 37; Marder, 1996.

22. Previously, the inscription had been interpreted as a reference to the predecessor of the Sistine Chapel on the west side of the Sala Regia. See Steinke 1984, 83–112; Shearman 1986, 22–36; Radke 1988, 193; and Shearman 1990, 19–28. The *capella parva* had been dated as late as 1433 (Heydenreich and Lotz 1974, 42, fig. 15, and n. 19, where its older origin is hinted), but more generally to some unspecified period after 1280. See Ehrle and Stevenson 1897, 22–23; Ehrle and Egger 1935, 103–39; Redig de Campos 1967, 37–41; and Redig de Campos 1982, 91.

23. On the *capella parva*, see Ehrle and Stevenson 1897, 22–23; Ehrle and Egger 1935, 103–39; Redig de Campos 1967, 37; Steinke 1984, 83–96 and passim.

24. This was already intimated (and subsequently overlooked) in Ehrle and Egger 1935, 81. See Marder 1996.

25. The notion of dating the *capella magna* to the period before or just after the Avignonese exile is Shearman's.

26. Pagliara 1992, 256–65. The door was discovered in 1989 in connection with the cleaning of the frescoes and is referred to in Shearman 1990, 21, as a door or window. The implications of the door were discussed at length by Pagliara at the Convegno Internazionale di Studi "Michelangelo: La Cappella Sistina," Vatican City, 26–31 March 1990 (included in Pagliara 1992).

27. An illustrated miniature of 1457 suggests that a staircase between the Sala Regia and the basilica did exist by the mid-fifteenth century. The miniature illustrates the upper palace seen from the northwest, with the *capella magna* and the *aula magna* at right angles on the right side. Frommel suggests that a small roof on the south side of the reception hall may have covered a staircase rising from the atrium of the old basilica. Cf. BAV, Vat. lat. 2224, fol. 98, first published by Ruysschaert 1968, 263, n. 121; and subsequently by Frommel 1984c, n. 331; Frommel 1984a, 120; Maddalò 1987, 57, fig. 26; and Cavallaro and Parlato 1988, 55, fig. 12.

28. Alfarano 1914, 114, wrote that the portal was later restored by Julius II: "A sinistro porticus latere, qui est ad aquilonem, in angulo contra orientem, est magna porta a Iulio II restaurata, per quam introitur ad aliam porticum ab Innocentio octavo restauratam, qua per plures gradus ad augustum et sacrum Palatium Apostolicum ascenditur, in quo sunt aula magna Regia, sacella Sixti IV et Pauli III eximia."

29. Pagliara 1992, 257, and n. 14.

30. Ehrle and Egger 1935, 62.

31. Ehrle and Egger 1935, 61–62, 65, 111. Flavio Biondo's account of the papal mint located between the medieval bell tower and the *porta palatii* during the pontificate of Eugene IV (1431–47) gives proof that the *atrium helvetiorum* was closed before the time of Nicholas V (Ehrle and Egger 1935, 92).

32. Ehrle and Egger 1935, 57, 61–62.

33. Ehrle and Egger 1935, 61, n. 1.

34. Ehrle and Egger 1935, 62, 65; Egger 1928, 13–17, who posits that the surface of the *helvetiorum* may have sloped down from west to east, following the general contours of the Mons Vaticanus.

35. Ehrle and Egger 1935, 57 ("hostium scalarum palatii domini pape"), 66, 81.

36. Ehrle and Egger 1935, 66, 111–12, for the term *curia superior*.

37. Catalano 1750–51, 15; Ehrle and Stevenson 1897, 24.

38. Regarding date and authorship, see Magnuson 1958, 55–64; Westfall 1974, 167–84 (supporting the attribution to Alberti); Burroughs 1982, 197–207 (dating the idea of the Borgo scheme late in the pontificate); and Tafuri 1992, 50–67 (arguing against Alberti's participation).

39. Magnuson 1958, 73, quoting from Manetti's text: "Per intermediam vero ab area prima usque ad mediam praedictae basilicae quinque januis distinctae portam iter per rectam lineam dirigebatur. Per secundam autem, quae a dextris prominebat, recto tramite ad portam palatinam ibatur. At per tertiam a laeva versus Tiberim ad eum locum tendebatur, ubi nunc ingens ille et altissimus obeliscus exstat, et ubi in nova apostolicae ecclesiae reformatione domestica pro sacerdotibus canonicis cubilia designabantur, quae vulgo dormitoria appellantur."

40. Magnuson 1958, 78.

41. Magnuson 1958, 129. Manetti described the gate as a "porta cum fornice triumphali . . . , unde in palatium introibatur."

42. Westfall 1974, 145–47. For the comparison to Castel Nuovo, see Magnuson 1958, excursus I, 157–59; Hersey 1973, 32. For the gate at Naples, see also Kruft and Malmanger 1977.

43. In either case, we may be certain that the new portal was to be integrated in the system of fortifications built by Nicholas V within an older wall built by Boniface IX (1389–1404) joining the palace and the Porta S. Petri. For these features see Ehrle and Egger 1935, 87–89; Lewine 1969, 28, 33–34, 37–38; Westfall 1974, 144. Magnuson first suggested the eastern location, which he describes as near the present Portone di Bronzo. For the history of the Tower of Nicholas V, see Frutaz 1956.

44. Magnuson 1958, 130.

45. Magnuson 1958, 131, located the spiral stairs at the *turris scalarum*, in the northwest side of the courtyard. Westfall 1974, 152, envisioned the stairs immediately north of the "porta prima."

46. Westfall 1974, 150–51. Fagiolo 1985, 90–91, relates the towered gate to the double-towered loggia at the ducal palace at Urbino, which has also been discussed as a Solomonic palace.

47. Battisti 1957; Lewine 1993, 44, 66–67, 68–69 (with additional literature).

48. Courtright 1990a, 91–96, gives references on the *cochlea* with respect to the spiral stair located in the Tower of the Winds at the Vatican Palace.

49. The point is made by Frommel 1984a, 120.

50. Frommel 1983, especially 124–25, where a document of

January 1462 is cited for the cornerstone of the new tower and the ramped steps leading to it; and subsequent documents to 1464 are cited. See also Müntz 1878–82, 260, 270, 276.

51. Frommel 1983, 124. Egger 1928, 13, noted eight sections of the ramp on the Heemskerck drawing. On Fig. 22, Alfarano denotes with the letters "LL" the ramp that was *amplificata* by Pius II.

52. As Peter Day of the Devonshire Collections kindly reminds me, the drawing is now attributed to "Anonymous artist B," along with others by the same hand previously attributed to Heemskerck (Veldman 1977, Veldman 1987, Carpiceci 1987, Filippi 1990). The stone drinking trough for animals seen in many of the old views was hauled away in the early seventeenth century and now stands behind the basilica, next to the church of S. Stefano in Abyssinia. My thanks to architetto Ercadi of the Servizi tecnici in the Governatorato, Vatican City, for pointing out the present location of the trough.

53. Documentation on the ramp and the fountain, some of which was known to Müntz 1878–82, has recently been amplified in Frommel 1983, 124–25. Thoenes 1963, 100, notes that the fountain was recorded as early as the reign of Symmachus (498–514).

54. Frommel 1983, 125, 131–32.

55. Frommel 1983, 132, for references, including Grimaldi's description: "Porta autem palatii ab ipso Paulo [*sic* for Pius] quadra constructa inde ab Innocentio in meliorem formam mutata." A conspicuous example of another square-topped portal from the Piccolomini era is located between the Cortile del Maresciallo and the Cortile del Pappagallo (Redig de Campos 1967, 53 and fig. 26). The square portal at the palace entrance is also depicted in an anonymous sixteenth-century view of Rome at the Palazzo Ducale in Mantua (illustration in Westfall 1974, fig. 75). On the eve of the destruction of old St. Peter's and the palace in the early seventeenth century, Grimaldi, a notary and canon of St. Peter's, composed extensive notes illustrated with drawings by Domenico Tasselli. This material has been published in the facsimile of Grimaldi 1972.

56. Frommel 1983, 131; and Frommel 1984, 121, citing Müntz 1878–82, II, 40, 327.

57. Stevenson 1887, 12, 24.

58. Stevenson 1887, 13, citing Vasari 1568, II, 471–72, who wrote of "le logge di trevertino con tre ordini di colonne; la prima nel piano da basso, dove sta oggi il Piombo ed altri uffizj; la seconda di sopra, dove sta il Datario ed altri prelati; e la terza ed ultima, dove sono le stanze che rispondono in sul cortile di San Piero, le quali adornò di palchi dorati e d'altri ornamenti." Vasari attributed this work to Giuliano da Maiano and attributed the Benediction Loggia at St. Peter's and the Palazzo di S. Marco to Giuliano da Sangallo, although we now know the last two buildings to be the work of Francesco del Borgo.

59. ASV, Fondo Gonfalonieri 74, fols. 10–11, as in n. 96.

60. BAV, Vat. lat. 10742, 423v (from a palace description written about 1620 and before Bernini's interventions): "Era in

questo loco prima, una Torre con alcune abitatione ove era sopra il Orologio fabricato da Paolo II Venetiano." I am unable to confirm the attribution of the clock in Bonanni 1696, 212, to Joannis Antonius Castillionaeus during the pontificate of Calixtus III in 1455.

61. See Egger 1928, 17; Ehrle and Egger 1935, 111–12.

62. See Frommel 1984a, 121–22, who likens the composition to the system of corridors that Paul II had built at the Lateran Palace. Müntz 1879–82, II, 40, already remarked on the importance of connecting the Benediction Loggia and the Maresciallo arcade (the latter referred to in documents as "la logia . . . in su la piaza del pozo del palazo").

63. Frommel 1984a, 121, cites the diary of Antonio de Vasco of 1483.

64. Stevenson 1887, 14.

65. Frommel 1983, 132 and fig. 14. He associates it with the style of Baccio Pontelli, without further argumentation.

66. See the older bibliography in Kitao 1974; Madonna 1981; Madonna 1985, 127–31; Ingersoll 1985; Cambedda 1990; and Gigli 1990. My thanks to Jesús R. Escobar for the last two references.

67. Ackerman 1954, 43; and Bruschi 1969, fig. 282, for the portal. The alignment with the street can be seen on the 1577 map of Duperac and Lafrery (Fig. 42).

68. For the most important discussions, see Frommel 1984b, 360–62, and 337 (color illustration); Frommel 1984a, 122–23; Frommel 1977, 63–64; Shearman 1972, 25, n. 5; and Ackerman 1954, 199–200 (with the older literature). The attributions have shifted from Bramante to Peruzzi, then to Sangallo the Younger and back to Bramante.

69. Frommel's identification of this plan with Bramante's schemes is based on the statement by Vasari 1550, 576, that Bramante "rifece un disegno grandissimo per restaurare et dirizzare il palazzo del papa."

70. Frommel 1984b, 360–61.

71. Shearman 1972, 4, who suggests the stairs were inspired by those of the papal palace at Avignon, where Julius II had been stationed as a legate.

72. Connections between the palace and the plans for rebuilding the basilica are generally overlooked. See Frommel 1994, 402, 599–605 (cats. 280, 283, 286, 288, 289), with recent bibliography on the early longitudinal plans.

73. Shearman 1972, 4, and 25–26, n. 6, published the references for 1505, 1506, and 1507.

74. Frommel 1976, 73, n. 16; Frommel 1984a, 127.

75. Shearman 1972, 26, n. 6.

76. Alfarano 1914, 114, as quoted in n. 28 above. BAV, Vat. lat. 10742 (early seventeenth century), fol. 212, includes a diagram of the Constantinian atrium, with an indication of the "Porta del palazzo ristaurata da Giulio 2.o" (no. 121).

77. These dimensions depend on a reading of the recto and verso of Uffizi A 119, which I have studied with the help of notes made by Christof Thoenes for the Sangallo corpus of architectural drawings. I am very grateful to Professor Thoenes for sharing his research with me. Since the breadth of the double landing that joins the upper two flights was 35 palmi (7.82 m.), the wall between the second and the

last flights of the ascent could have been as much as 3½ palmi (0.78 m.) thick.

78. The taper from 19½ palmi to 16 palmi (4.356 m. minus 3.574 m.) is 0.782 m. The width from the lower to the uppermost column bases in the central passage of Bernini's Scala Regia tapers approximately 1.11 m. The outer walls of Bernini's Scala Regia narrow even more radically from 8.30 m. to 4.82 m., a reduction of 3.48 m. The dimensions and the circumstances should dispel the recurrent but incorrect notion that Bernini inherited a space with tapering walls whose effect he sought to minimize. The interpretation of the Sangallo drawing must remain open, because there is no later evidence for risers 19½ palmi wide.

79. Tuttle 1983. My thanks to the author for this reference. Julius II was in Bologna with Bramante for three months in the winter of 1506–7 and for five months in 1510–11. There is now fuller documentation in Hubert 1993 (kindly brought to my attention by Christof Thoenes).

80. Redig de Campos 1967, 100–2; Shearman 1972, 8, 30, n. 27; Frommel 1984a, 127–28, with references, and H. Fernandez and B. E. Shapiro in Frommel, Ray, and Tafuri 1984, 136–47, for an exhaustive analysis of Bramante's transformation of the medieval structures, Raphael's completion of the project, and the nineteenth-century imposition of conventional steps under Pius VII in 1816 and 1822. For a summary of the Logge chronology, see Borsi 1989, 291–94.

81. Ackerman 1954, 38–39, 45, 62; Redig de Campos 1967, 98–100.

82. Ehrle and Stevenson 1897, 11, quote Burchard's notations for 21 May 1506, when Julius II attended mass in St. Peter's and returned to the palace: "Ita quod exivit per portam palatii, ubi solet custodia seu guardia teneri; eo quod scalam, per quam soliti fuerunt pontifices descendere, demoliverant pro nova facienda, tali scilicet quod eques ire posset ex aula regali usque ad S. Petrum" (later quoted in part by Shearman 1972, 25, n. 6). Frommel 1984a, 121, n. 13, gives a differing version from Burchard for the same day: "intravimus per portam palatii ubi fit guardia, et ascendimus per viam qua cardinales ascendere solent, quando ad palatium equitant; ante scalam papa licentiavit cardinales antiquiores; tamen ascenderunt ad cameram paramenti." See also Shearman, in Pietrangeli et al. 1993, 16.

83. For examples, see Vasari 1568, V, 532; Martin 1969, 100; Ehrle and Stevenson 1897, 10, 11, 24 (n. 5), 26; Orbaan 1920, 8–9; Egger 1929, 21; Frommel 1964, 6, 10; Frommel 1984a, 119; Frommel 1983, 132.

84. See Frommel 1985 for comparisons.

85. Ackerman 1954, 20, 38.

86. Frommel 1984b, 362; Borsi 1989, 295. Frommel attributes the pentimenti to Bramante on the basis of a comment in Vasari's 1550 edition cited above. It should be mentioned that the relevant passage in the 1568 edition of Vasari (IV, 160) substitutes the verb "fece" in "rifece un disegno grandissimo." The first edition thus implies that Bramante redid an existing design. I do not see pentimenti on the drawing that may be interpreted as a staircase.

87. Redig de Campos 1967, 109–15; Pietrangeli et al., 1984, 205–7, 232–41; Frommel 1984b, 363–69.

88. Redig di Campos 1967, 114–15.

89. Redig de Campos 1967, 120; Borsi 1989, 293–95. The design is similar to Bramante's rusticated portal at the lower Belvedere. Curiously, the doubts of Sangallo's contribution expressed by Giovannoni 1959, 171–72, and figs. 129–30, have not been resolved.

90. Quoted by Ackerman 1954, 43.

91. For the previous state of research, see Frommel in Gombrich et al. 1989, 126, 129–30, 298–99 (illustrations, a reconstruction of the apartment's location, and a bibliography).

92. Martin 1969, 87–88.

93. Vasari 1568, V, 532: "Messer Giovanmatteo Giberti, che fu poi vescovo di Verona, che allora era datario di papa Clemente, fece far a Giulio, che era molto suo dimestico amico, il disegno d'alcune stanze che si murarono di mattoni vicino alla porta del palazzo del papa, le quali rispondono sopra la piazza di San Piero, dove stanno a sonare i trombetti, quando i cardinali vanno a concistoro; con una salita di commodissime scale, che si possono salire a cavallo ed a piedi."

94. Frommel in Gombrich et al. 1989, 299, raises the suggestive possibility that "some portions of the ramped stairs praised by Vasari may have been integrated into the lower part of the wide horse stairs of Sixtus V," although I find no compelling reason to date the cordonata to the pontificate of Sixtus V.

95. ASV, Fondo Borghese, ser. III, vol. 114 b/c, fols. 4–65, "Rolo delli appartamenti et stantie del palazzo di San Pietro in Vaticano distribuiti al tempo di Papa Clemente Ottavo": "Passato questo s'entra nel primo Cortille dove à mano dirita vi è un Arco, dove principia la salita per andare al Cortile della Conserva ò vero Dispensa" (fols. 42–44v). The Borghese version of the "Rolo" was cited by Orbaan 1913, 7; again by Orbaan 1920, 50, n. 1, and 457; and recently by Ruysschaert 1990, 358–59. Incidentally, the Loggia dei Trombetti was decorated with gilded stucco and painted grotesques (Ackerman 1954, doc. 89 dated 1552). The various rooms located off the cordonata in the nineteenth century are enumerated in Pistolesi 1829–38, III, 28, n. 5

96. ASV, Fondo Gonfalonieri 74, fols. 4–17, "Ruolo degli appartamenti e delle stanze nel palazzo Vaticano al tempo di Clemente VIII (1594)," was published by F. C. Colnabrini (pseudonym for Fr. Ballerini), 1895; and cited in Orbaan 1920, 457; and Ruysschaert 1990, 358–59. The Gonfalonieri "Ruolo," fol. 17, describes "la lumaga che va all'appartamento dell'Ill.mo Morosini e al megnaletto dove sonano li trombetti." The Borghese "Rolo," fols. 43–44, characterizes "una lumaghetta che cala ad una Portone che riesce nanti la Porta principale del Palazzo" from the same location.

97. Cf. Martinelli's diary (1660–63) published by D'Onofrio 1969, 331: "Il disegno delle stanze, che si murorono di mattoni, vicino alla porta del palazzo, et vicino al detto Torrone, le quali rispondevano sopra la piazza di S. Pietro, e dove stavano à suonare i trombetti quando li Cardinali andavano al Concistoro, con una salita di comodissime scale, che si

possono salire à cavallo, et à piedi, nelle quali stanze habitò il Card. Antonio Barberino, et ultimamente il Card. Rospigliosi, fù di Giulio Romano." D'Onofrio makes no mention of the context that I have tried to elucidate here.

98. Moryson 1617, I, 279, traveled in 1591–95.

99. See Connors and Rice 1991, 30, for the account of the anonymous French visitor, who thought the gentle slope of entrance hardly foreshadowed the grandeur of papal power. Keyssler 1751, 569, describes the palace entrance from the Portone di Bronzo to the Cortile di S. Damaso. See Chapter 1 for the late nineteenth century. As Stendhal informs us, the glazing of the Logge was installed only in the early nineteenth century: "When King Murat came to Rome, in 1814, he was astonished that the paving and the sides of the portico where Raphael's masterpieces are, were exposed to the rain, and he had windows installed" (Stendhal 1957, 108).

100. BAV, Vat. lat. 10742, fol. 424v (early seventeenth century): "Et qui alla destra si entra per un altro Portone rustico et magnifico che rende una fortezza amirabile dal aspetto et con grandezza seguitando l'Antica salitta piacevolissima."

101. E.g., Gombrich et al., 1989, 39, 42, 195, 298, 299, 496.

102. Skippon 1663–64, 663, described the Cappella Paolina as "the little chapel, where the pope says mass every morning, (when he lodges at the Vatican) and hears a second mass said by his chaplain. On holy Wednesday noblemen, etc. receive the host from the pope's own hand at this place."

103. Giovannoni 1959; Redig de Campos 1967, 124–32; Partridge and Starn 1990, especially 54–56, with extensive bibliography on the Sala Regia. For the Cappella Paolina, see Frommel 1964. Now in press, the new corpus of Sangallo drawings edited by C. L. Frommel and N. Adams should augment the following notes; as will Kuntz 1996.

104. For a discussion of this entrance and its importance for papal ceremony under Paul III, see Kuntz 1996. I have merely related the story of the entrance under Paul III to the previously unremarked aspirations of earlier pontificates.

105. The Duperac-Lafrery map appears to depict four arches on the west side, not three as in the drawing. See also Egger 1928, 21; and Redig de Campos 1967, 53–54, 131.

106. Frommel 1964, n. 48, noted the keystones.

107. Egger 1928, 20–21, dated the staircase to 1546–47 on the basis of payment documents for the marble door into the Sala Regia, but as the Sala Regia was already being decorated by 1541 (Mancinelli in Pietrangeli et al. 1992, 74), I presume that the new stairs leading to it were already completed.

108. Cf. Vasari 1550, 825; and Vasari 1568, V, 465–66, quoted here. "Fu con ordine del medesimo rifondato quasi tutto il palazzo apostolico, che, oltre quello che si è detto, in altri luoghi molti minacciava rovina; ed in un fianco particolarmente la cappella di Sisto, dove sono l'opere di Michelangelo, e similmente la facciata dinanzi; senza che mettesse un minimo pelo: cosa più di pericolo che d'onore. Accrebbe la sala grande della detta cappella di Sisto, facendovi in due lunette in testa quelle finestrone terribili, con sì mar-

avigliosi lumi e con que' partimenti buttati nella volta e fatti di stucco tanto bene e con tanta spesa, che questa si può mettere per la più bella e ricca sala che infino allora fusse nel mondo: ed in su quella accompagnò, per potere andare in San Pietro, alcune scale così comode e ben fatte, che fra l'antiche e moderne non si è veduto ancor meglio: e similmente la cappella Paulina, dove si ha da mettere il Sacramento, che è cosa vezzosissima e tanto bella e sì bene misurata e partita, che per la grazia che si vede, pare che ridendo e festeggiando ti s'appresenti."

109. See Frommel 1964, 6, for this interpretation.

110. Sernini's letter of 1538 includes the following statement: "La capella vecchia [capella parva] serve per scala a corrispondenza di quella, che va in San Pietro, o vien a punto a filo a ricontro d'essa, e scenderà come prima nel Cortile, dove smontano gli Cardinali, li quali puoi a suo piacere potranno venire a cavallo in detta sala, e quell'altra scaletta vecchia di marmo, si lieva" (from Frommel 1964, 6).

111. ASV, Fondo Borghese, ser. III, vol. 114 b/c, "Rolo," fol. 55v, describes the route from the Cortile di S. Damaso to the Maresciallo, "dove scavalcano li Ambasciatori per andare in Consistoro, al piede delle Scale che vano in Sala Regia, dove à mano dirita è un andito che passa dal sud.o Cortile al Cortille della Libreria Vecchia [Cortile del Pappagallo]." See also the same source, fol. 54v: "Ritornati nell Cortile dove scavalcano gl'Ambasciatori salito, le scale s'entra un sala Regia, dove voltati a mano dirita in faccia vi è la Capella di Sisto Quarto."

112. BAV, Vat. lat. 10742, fol. 434: "In questo vengono a smontare e cavalcare, tanto tutti Prencipi, Inbassatori... quando fanno Cavalcata et sagliono per la scalla... che e sboca in la Salla Reggia."

113. Writing in the early eighteenth century, Taja 1750, I, 8, discusses how Sangallo "raddirizzò la Regia scala nel modo, che era prima, che dal Bernini fosse abbellita." Earlier, Taja (p. 4) paraphrases Domenico Bernini's biography about the difficulty of the new work as "la più difficile, che facesse [G. L. Bernini] in architettura; massimamente [Taja adds] in considerazione di ciò, che era l'antico disegno del Sangallo."

114. Wasserman 1962.

115. Redig de Campos 1967, 192, emphasized the private aspect of the stairs. See also Mandel 1993.

116. BAV 10742, fol. 433v: "SIXTUS V PONT MAX PORTAM APERVIT VESTIBULUM ESTRUXIT SCALAS INTUS SUBSTRAVIT SACRORUM COMMODITATI AN MDLXXXVI. PONTIFIC. P.O."

117. ASV, Fondo Borghese, ser. III, vol. 114 b/c, "Rolo," fol. 55v: "Andando qui [the Sala Regia] per le scale che calano in San Pietro, calato la prima scala in faccia vi è una Porta grande ch'entra nella scala che cala dalla Sacristia alla Capella Gregoriana, fatta dalla fe. me. di Papa Sisto Quinto." The corridor is labelled "vicolo morto" and "vicolo novo" on Mascarino's drawings at the Accademia di S. Luca, suggesting that the passage was projected under Sixtus's predecessor, Gregory XIII.

118. ASV, Fondo Borghese, ser. III, vol., 114 b/c, "Rolo," fol.

55v: "Al Rifianco di questo Piano e la Istoria ove S. Pietro che dicese della Barca camina sopra l'acqua."

119. Evelyn 1955, II, 297.

120. See Mola 1663, 47–48; and Baglione 1642, 16–17; cited in Chapter 1.

121. See again ASV, Fondo Borghese, ser. III, vol. 114 b/c, "Rolo," fols. 42–63, and here specifically, fol. 43: "Prima nell'Intrare della Porta principale del Palazzo dove sta la Guardia delli Svizzari à mano dirita vi è una ritirata dove si fa il focco con una stantia contigua che serve per Dormire, a mano manca in faccia un altra stantia, serve per tenere l'Armatur[illegible]."

122. Egger 1928, 14, n. 4, warned against using the Alfarano plan as an accurate indication of the contours of the *atrium belvetiorum*, which I take as criticism of Voss 1922, who reproduced the plan on large scale.

123. Egger 1951.

124. Cf. BAV, Vat. lat. 10742, fol. 424v, quoted above in n. 100.

125. My thanks to Joseph Connors for the reference to Quarenghi's drawing in Angelini 1967.

126. Partridge and Starn 1990, 25.

127. Kuntz 1996; Martin 1969, 99–100.

128. Cf. the inscriptions, right to left, on Uffizi A 572: "Strada Cup(er)ta," "Via che discende al Cortile grande di palazzo," and "Porta che va ale stalle di palazo." The passage under the north – south portion of the old Via Iulia Nova is indicated by a break in the staircase on the Ferrabosco-Costaguti and the Alfarano engravings. One of the Mascarino drawings (Accademia di S. Luca G. 108) shows an "andito" in precisely this place.

129. ASV, Fondo Gonfalonieri 74, "Ruolo," fols. 4–17, ed. Colnabrini 1895, 22: "A mano diritta di detto cortille [*atrium belvetiorum*] per andare alle scale che vengono di San Pietro, vi è una scaletta che saglie tra una scala e l'altra" [that is, between the Scala Regia and the *turris scalarum*]. See also ASV, Fondo Borghese, ser. III, vol. 114 b/c, "Rolo," fols. 56v–57: "In faccia alle scale che vengono dalla Sala Regia vi è un'altra scala, che salisse al Cortille [del Maresciallo], dove scavalcano l'Ambasciatori, dove a mano dirita vi è una scaletta che cala nel primo Cortille [the *belvetiorum*]."

CHAPTER THREE. Paul V's New Palace Entrance

1. Hibbard 1971, 155–188 (169 for the model of 1608); important revisions and additions in Thoenes 1992 and Wazbinski 1992. Already in September 1607, Paul V with his *famiglia* and a cavalcade of gentlemen came from the Quirinal Palace to review a model of the façade at St. Peter's.

2. Orbaan 1919, 63, 72, with notices for the destruction of the *dataria* in August 1607 and a payment for its demolition in January 1609. The whole palace is mentioned at the same time: "Hoc anno 1609, die 19 Januarii fabricatores coeperunt diruere palatium Innocentii VIII in atrio basilicae."

3. Hibbard 1971, 156–64.

4. Bonanni 1696, 212. Bonanni 1706, 508–9, claims the first portal (the provisory solution?) was designed by Maderno, the subsequent portal by Ferrabosco, and the ornamentation of the portal by Vasanzio. In Martinelli's guide of the early 1660s (D'Onofrio 1969, 331), their work is described as follows: "La porta maggiore del palazzo con la sua facciata, horologio, musaici, statue, e per entro fonti, altri musaici, et armeria furono opere principiate da maestro Martino architetto, e poi compite da Giovanni Vansantio fiammingo." Baglione 1642, 176, gives early mention of Vasanzio ("ha . . . adornata la Porta del Palagio Pontificio con bella facciata") but makes no mention of Ferrabosco. G. B. Mola attributed the palace façade to Flaminio Ponzio (Mola 1663, 43). So far as I know the attribution of the clock tower design does not rely on building documents, and neither the literature on Ferrabosco (e.g., Muñoz 1911, Beltrami 1926) nor on Vasanzio (Hoogewerff 1928, 1942, 1943) clarifies the situation. Documents in Muñoz 1911, 90, do not mention Ferrabosco, while Ferrabosco documents published by Orbaan 1920, for the pontificate of Paul V pertain exclusively to his work as a fountain expert in and around the Vatican Palace. Ferrabosco himself claimed credit for the design in BAV, Vat. lat. 10742, fol. 370, as follows. "Per reedificare questa nuova machina [St. Peter's] fù necess.o buttar à terra gran parte del Palazzo Vaticano, e particolar.te quela fatta da Paolo II et Innoc. VIII, ch'era contigua alla Chiesa, e riguardava sopra la porta di esso Palazzo, e prospetto della piazza, la qual porta, e prospetto fù raccommodata da Paolo V.o con mio disegno." Again, on fol. 372, Ferrabosco wrote, "Paolo V.o ultimam.te accommodì l'entrata, e prospetto del Palazzo, che risponde verso la Piazza del Tempio con disegno dell'autore aggiuntovi molte stanze."

5. After claiming credit for the design of the entrance portal (quoted above), Ferrabosco discussed the destruction of the lower palace as follows (BAV, Vat. lat. 10742, 370–70v). "Questa parte del Palazzo comprendeva le stanze per il corpo di guardia de Svizzeri, Dataria, Seg.ria de Brevi, loro ministri, et offitiali, Archivii di Scritture, habitationi, et altre molte commodità p. i sommi Pontef.i, Corte, e loro famiglie, che dovendosi accommodar altrove, et essendo Mons.r Gio. Batta Costaguta Magiordhomo, e foriero magg.re di Paolo V.o a cui toccava la cura occupato in moltiplicità de negotii p. avanzar tempo, e poter di camera proveder alli sud.i bisogni, et altri che occorresero alla giornata, fece far la pianta del restante compresovi l'habitat.e de soldati della guardia, de Svizzeri, e Cavalli leg.i inclusovi la Basilica di S. Pietro, e tutti i siti de luoghi contigui." On this manuscript and Costaguti's career, see Borino 1947, 184–88; Pastor 1923–53, XXVI, 482; Thelen 1967b, 36–37; Lavin 1968, 45–46; Niggl in Grimaldi 1972, 505, n. 2; and Mancinelli et al. 1984, 149–50. Christof Thoenes has kindly alerted me to a copy of Ferrabosco's 1620 edition in the Bibliotheca Hertziana (see Thoenes 1990, 49).

6. For Maggi's view, see Ehrle 1914. For a convenient illustration of the whole print, see Morello 1993, 108–9.

7. Egger 1928, 15–16; Egger 1929, 15–21; Redig de Campos 1967, 206.

8. The painting (173 × 118 cm.) is a good deal smaller than the mosaic, and details (Paul's drapery, the curtain at the top) are different. Herwarth Röttgen has suggested a date of about 1606 according to Eliot Rowlands, who brought the work to my attention and kindly shared with me his museum catalogue entry, now in press, *European Painting in the Nelson-Atkins Museum of Art*, vol. 1, *Italian School*. The entry contains new documentation superseding Egger 1929, 17, 19–20; and an analysis of X rays that suggests the new picture was made after the lost cartoon and the mosaic.

9. Much of the documentation was published by Egger 1929, who nevertheless did not associate its early date with the date of the provisory design. For the sculptors' work, see Egger 1929, 18–19; and now Pressouyre 1984, 385–88.

10. Rowlands in MS cited in note 8. The precedent would be the Peter and Paul scenes commissioned by Paul III in the Cappella Paolina as Margaret Kuntz reminds me.

11. Pressouyre 1984, 386.

12. Egger 1929, 90; Rowlands in press, with citation of ASR, Camerale I, Fabbriche, Registro 1540; and Röttgen 1973, 119–22, with information on the work in St. Peter's between 1603 and 1612.

13. Magnuson 1982–86, 152–59. See Ostrow 1996.

14. Thoenes 1963, 118. The option of a south-facing portal appears on Maderno's Uffizi A 6728, which may date from this time.

15. "Processio non exivit extra portam Palatii propter ruvinam fabricae." Orbaan 1920, 10; again in Orbaan 1919, 96, citing the diary of the master of ceremonies, ASV, Misc. arm. XII, tom. 43, fol. 548b (latter cited in Egger 1928, 16).

16. BAV, Vat. lat. 12429, fol. 224r/v (8 January 1613) tells us that the bishop's residence was a palace "in Burgo veteri apud S. Jacobum Scossa Caballi." His route to the consistory is described as follows: "Venit ad Palatium per viam Burgi veteris versus Castrum S.ti Angeli, et deinde per Burgum Novum, et descendit in fine Scalarum Aulae Regiae."

17. Ferri and Pini 1885, 152. Egger 1928, 22, n. 3, indicates that Carlo Pini inscribed Maderno's name on the drawing. See also Thoenes 1963, 112–18.

18. Thoenes 1963, 113 and n. 104, noting the formal similarities to Borromini's project for the obelisk fountain at Piazza Navona that was superseded by Bernini's Four Rivers Fountain.

19. Egger 1928, 22.

20. Hence the title of Egger's article of 1928 and inclusion of the drawing among "piazza projects" by Hibbard 1971, 162–63. Egger's photo shows only the upper half of the drawing. The whole drawing was first illustrated in Thoenes 1963, 110.

21. Thoenes 1963, 115–16.

22. Brauer and Wittkower 1931, 66, n. 2. The flaps are now detached.

23. Smith 1956, 31–33, 36: "The crowning arcade was traditionally a mark of heavenly authority, because it was the distinguishing feature of the *Sacrum palatium*."

24. This staircase should not be confused with the *lumaghetta* mentioned in the previous chapter.

25. Cf. the spiral stairs in the Cortile del Pappagallo and the Torre dei Venti in Mascherino's drawings of the Vatican (Frommel 1984a, 143; Courtright 1990b, fig. 9), at the sixteenth-century Quirinal Palace and at Scipione Borghese's nearby Casino dell'Aurora (Hibbard 1971, 192–94), and in Maderno's designs (before 1628) for the Palazzo Barberini and the Ludovisi Palace (1622–23) on Piazza SS. Apostoli (Waddy 1990, 212–17, 293–99).

26. In 1550, this door in the Sala Regia was called the "porta custodiae primae Reverendiss. DD. Episcoporum" (Ehrle and Egger 1933, tav. I, plan for conclave of 29 November 1549–8 February 1550). The door on the opposite side of the Sala Regia leading to the druggist was called the "porta aromataria."

27. For the typical seventeenth-century apartment and Maderno's style, see Waddy 1990, 3–13, and 235–37.

28. Cf. Ehrle and Stevenson 1897, 24–26; Ehrle 1914, 12; Ehrle and Egger 1935, 64, 66; Egger 1951, 498, for the visits of Charles IV in 1368, Ladislaus of Naples in 1404 and 1408, Frederick III in 1452 and 1468–69, Roberto di S. Severino in 1485, Ercole d'Este in 1487, Prince Djem (brother of Sultan Bajazet) in 1489, Charles VIII of France in 1489, the Prince of Capua in 1492, Prince Federico of Naples in 1494, and Francesco Gonzaga in 1496.

29. Grimaldi, Barb. lat. 2733, fol. 241b, discussed the third floor of the Curia Innocenziana, with its "aula nobilissima cum multis cubiculis laqueribus aureis et picturis ornatis, quibus olim Carolus Quintus [et] alii magni principes excepti sunt."

30. Grimaldi, Barb. lat. 2733, fol. 241 b (quoted by Orbaan 1919, 63, n. 1); additional references in Duchesne 1902, 419.

31. Measured on a scaled drawing by Sangallo (Uffizi A 715), the width of the old Curia Innocenziana was 48–50 palmi. The width of Maderno's projected wing is just less than 51 palmi. The Curia Innocenziana measured some 385 palmi from the stairs at the rear corridor to the front of the Benediction Loggia. Maderno's wing is 530 palmi in length.

32. Hibbard 1971, 162.

33. Thoenes 1963, 134.

34. Thoenes 1963, 114, reinterpreted the significance of the fresco that had been previously thought to correspond to the provisory solution (cf. Paeseler 1941, 79–81, fig. 60). See Taja 1750, 457; and Forcella 1869–84, VI, 131, with the fresco's inscription and date.

35. The plan to display the Navicella "a sinistra della facciata nuova di San Pietro nella parete del palazzo Vaticano" is announced in an avviso of 28 July 1610 (Orbaan 1920, 175).

36. Hibbard 1971, 170–75.

37. "Papa . . . redivit ad palatium Apostolicum apud Sanctum Petrum . . . descendit ad basilicam . . . ascendit superius ad

suas cameras per viam Sanctae Martae in lectica vectus usque ad portam Panattariae" (29 March 1613; Orbaan 1920, 13).

38. See Hibbard 1971, 67, for a diagram of the old and new position of the façade.

39. AFSP, Piano I, ser. 1, vol. 14, no. 27, fols. 94–94v (19 June 1614); no. 29, fols. 98–98v (1 July 1614); vol. 15, no. 10, fols. 2v–3v (26 August 1615). These documents were brought to my attention by Margaret Kuntz. The number of steps mentioned in the documents is confirmed in the palace description of c. 1620 (BAV, Vat. lat. 10742, fol. 433v).

40. On Mascarino's drawing of the lower stairs (Fig. 34), 60 risers are indicated along the flight between the base landing and the double landing. This evidence suggests the addition of about 12 risers in Paul V's work, but one must be cautious about accepting such minute evidence on the drawing without corroborating information.

41. Appendix (Fontana 1694, 233).

42. BAV, Vat. lat. 10742, fol. 433v.

43. "PAULUS V PONT MAX SCALAS QUAE E REGIORE SUNT GRADIBUS AUXIT ET ORNAVIT A MDCXV PONT X." See BAV, Vat. lat. 10742, 433v.: "Doi repiani interposti a quella [Scala Regia] et nel 30 ove risvolta la scalla si trova in Testa un Portone [to the Sala Regia]." The "doi repiani" refer to the place where Bernini's double landing is today, and where 30 steps rose to the Sala Regia (instead of the 46 presently in situ).

44. Inexplicably, the documents of 1614–15 in the AFSP account for 37 steps while the description of c. 1620 mentions only 32.

45. AFSP, Piano I, ser. 1, vol. 15, no. 10, fol. 3v, also indicates another discrepancy regarding the number of stairs, recording 26, not 24 steps as mentioned in the description of c. 1620.

46. Number 175 on the plan: "Scala sotto al campanille che unisce con la vecchia che sale nel palazzo."

47. Egger 1929, fig. 2, published the engraving which he considered to be a proof engraving at the Albertina in Vienna. The engraving is now lost.

48. BAV, Vat. lat. 10742, fol. 433v; and Baglione 1639, 48: "E da un lato di questo portico [the basilica's narthex], che per una scala guida al palagio Pontificio, vedesi dentro ad una nicchia una statua di marmo di S. Pietro Apostolo con le chiavi nella mano destra, e nella sinistra tiene un libro, ed è di frammenti fabricata."

49. Cf. Michelangelo Lualdi, "Memorie istoriche, e curiose del tempio, e palazzo Vaticano raccolte, e confusamente MSS. in tre volume," Corsiniana 31.D.16–18, vol. II, fols. 11v–12, finished between 1644 and 1653, as follows. "Nelle faccie laterali a destra, et a sinistra il Portico [of St. Peter's] ha due uscite, dalle quali si entra sotto li campanili, e si fa per uno di questi passaggio nel Palazzo Pontificio Vaticano. E troverai dopo che sarai uscito dal piano del Portico e del campanile in faccia una nicchia con la statua di marmo di S. Pietro, e quivi due reggie scale a destra e sinistra per le quali vi si da il Tragitto all'augustissima Reg-

gia Vaticana." In the same source, vol. III, fol. 33: "Essendo il Palazzo Pontificio quasi contiguo alla Basilica Paolo V. l'unì con continuare la volta del portico nel fine di cui dopo la salita di alcuni gradi vi ha in faccia una nicchia con la statua di marmo di S. Pietro e quindi a destra e sinistra si diramano due longhe scale che portono nella sala reggia." On this manuscript, see Pélissier 1889, 421–422. I am dating Lualdi's account on the basis of his mention of the election of Innocent X and his failure to mention Algardi's Attila relief (1653) in an otherwise scrupulous account of the interior of St. Peter's. For additional notices of the statue of St. Peter, see notes 50 and 51 below and references in Chapters 6, 7, 8, 9.

50. Krautheimer and Jones 1975, no. 765; and Morello 1981b, 337 (13 July 1664): "con l'Allatio e col Favoriti, poi col Bernino per render la scala dal cortiletto in S. Pietro con due bocche, ove è la st(atu)a, e dove sarà messo il Costantino."

51. Hibbard 1971, 70, n. 5; D'Onofrio 1969, 156 (with the reference to the Sala Regia misspelled "Scala Regia"): "V'era una statua di S. Pietro [in the Cappella Clementina of St. Peter's], che da Carlo Maderno architetto fu levato per metterla a vista del portico di S. Pietro in un tabernacolo nel principio delle scale per le quali s'ascende alla Sala Regia del Palazzo Pontificio; la quale nel pontificato di Nostro Signore Alessandro VII e stata levata." If D'Onofrio is correct in dating the manuscript guide between 1660 and February 1663, Martinelli must have known of the removal of the statue of St. Peter in anticipation of the fact.

52. Bonanni 1696, 213; and Bonanni 1696, 175, commemorate the works as follows: "Porta restituta, ut Vaticanum Palatium adiri à Romanis Pontificibus ex dignitate posset, & antiquis scalis sublatis, novas è Vaticanis aedibus è Tyburtino lapide Paulus curavit, quae ex templi porticu primum assurgentes praeclarum è marmore statuam sancti Petri ab eodem Pontifice erectam obviam habuerunt, indè bipartito excurrentes flexu, altera, quae ad orientem vergit in Vaticani atrium, altera verò, quae ad occidentem in Regiam, quam dicunt aulam deferebat, qua vero flectebatur Pontificia spectabantur insignia cum hoc elogio." (There follows the inscription given here in my text.) Jack Freiberg has kindly informed me that the same information is found in BAV, Barb. lat. 2353, fol. 14v.

53. For this tradition and the problematic identification of the statue, see Guarducci 1991, 95–102, with bibliography.

54. Duchesne 1886–92, II, 14; and Valentini and Zucchetti 1953, IV, 402. Cited in Guarducci 1991, 95–98.

55. Cf. Alfarano 1914, 18, 116, 195; Grimaldi 1972, 180; and no. 132 on the Ferrabosco plan. For these and other references to the problem of the various statues of St. Peter in the basilica, see Carloni 1980; D'Onofrio 1990; and Guarducci 1991.

56. Grimaldi 1972; Lualdi 1644–53, II, fols. 11v–20; Bonanni 1696, 169, for the iconography.

57. Briganti 1962b, 16–23; Hibbard 1971, 194–97; Borsi 1974, 76–87.

58. Ferri and Pini 1885; Egger 1928, 16, Taf. VII; Brauer and Wittkower 1931, 89, n. 1; Thoenes 1963, n. 130; Hibbard 1971, 162–163.
59. Egger 1928, 16 and Taf. VII where the caption provides the dates. See also Brauer and Wittkower 1931, 89, n. 1; Thoenes 1963, 114 and n. 130. Egger 1929 does not discuss the drawing.
60. Hibbard 1971, 162–63.
61. Cf. BAV, Chigi, P VII, 9, fols. 25v–26, from the Bernini workshop; and the description of Paul V's entrance wing made c. 1660 during its destruction in BAV, Chigi P VII, 9, fol. 12.
62. Birindelli 1981, 8, is too cautious in claiming that the Ferrabosco portal aligned "more or less" with the axis of the Borgo Nuovo, as does Maderno's in the drawings.
63. For comments on Ferrabosco's drawing style, see Jacob 1975, 55–56.
64. Egger 1929, 1, 6, 29, 36; Orbaan 1920, 252, 331; Pastor 1923–53, XII, 693; Brauer and Wittkower 1931, 66; Thoenes 1963, 116–19; Redig de Campos 1967, 208–9.
65. Orbaan 1920, 251 (26 July 1617): "Il Pontefice hiermattina se ne passò da Monte Cavallo al Vaticano, ove restò a pranzo et si compiacque di vedere la fabrica del portone et nuova clausura del Palazzo, ordinata da Sua Beatitudine, che la sera se ne tornò a Monte Cavallo."
66. On 12 July 1619, Giovanni Battista Soria *falegname* was paid 2785.7 scudi for "lavori di legname fatti per servitio della fabrica nova della porta principale et membri attinenti ad essa del palazzo Vaticano et per diversi altri lavori di rappezzi" (Orbaan 1920, 330–31). Baglione 1642, 213, reported on "la Porta di bronzo del palagio Vaticano sotto l'Orologio, e anche suo gettito" by Orazio Censore (Orbaan 1920, 345). The payment to Carlo Bonamici *calderaro* for "li rami novi dati per coprire la porta del palazzo Vaticano, croce, banderola et campaniglio di detta porta et altro" was part of this work (18 July 1619; Orbaan 1920, 331). For a mention of Domenico Ferrerio in this connection, see D'Onofrio 1969, 331.
67. Lualdi 1644–53, III, fols. 3–3v: "Sopra il frontispicio della colonne due grandi angeli di marmo . . . il piede sopra di capitelli e con le destre invitano le curiose . . . a fissare lo sguardo in una Imagine della Vergine che con il Puttino nel seno si asside in un trono cui laterali assistono S. Pietro e S. Paolo. . . . E sopra vi si lege Paulus V Pont. Max. anno 13." See also Forcella, VI, 145, n. 532; and Egger 1929, 71.
68. For the topic in general, see Salomi 1992.
69. On the doors and the vision at Constantinople, see Grabar 1957, 150–52.
70. For the long tradition of bronze doors, including St. Peter's itself, see Matthiae 1971 and Mende 1983. See Mango 1959, 12–19, 21–35, and passim for the Bronze Gate at Constantinople. Knowledge of the Imperial Palace at Constantinople was available through the explorations of Pierre Gilles (1544–50) and literary sources known in Rome from the sixteenth century, e.g., the Constantino-

politan Book of Ceremonies, discussed in Guilland 1969, I, 217–18, 250–52, 530. For the relationship of Gregory XIII's Tower of the Winds to architecture at Constantinople, see Courtright 1990b, 122–23.
71. Egger 1910, 10–11; Egger 1929, figs. 10–13.
72. Egger 1929, figs. 8–9.
73. The Israel Silvestre engraving shows Bernini's south tower and the beginnings of the north tower, and so dates to the early 1640s. The drawing in the Staatliche Kunstbibliothek, Berlin no. 3840, usually attributed to Ferrabosco, may not be by him. See Egger 1910; Egger 1911, I, 26, Taf. 23; Egger 1928, 25 and pl. VIII; Egger 1929, 99, fig. 15; Brauer and Wittkower 1931, 89, n. 1; Ehrle and Egger 1933, 29, n. 2; Frutaz 1956a, tav. XLV; Thoenes 1963, 12, fig. 18; and Jacob 1975, 55–56, no. 192, who questions the traditional attribution to Ferrabosco on the basis of style. Some minor mistakes in the rendering of the palace would support her skepticism. For our drawing by Della Bella, see Viatte 1974, 57–58, who dates it to the artist's first Roman trip, 1633–39.
74. Egger 1929, fig. 13 (his Project E). For the Ferrabosco drawing, see below. For the drawing attributed to Della Bella, see Egger 1929, figs. 3, 15.
75. On the campanile, see Egger 1935.
76. I have been unable to consult Rocca 1612, whose interests must have been piqued by the Vatican bells.
77. Millon 1962. The drawing of 1641 shows Bernini's south tower of St. Peter's.
78. "We remarked in Italy, and especially in Rome, that there are almost no bells at all for the service of the Church, and less in Rome than in the smallest village in France." (Montaigne 1983, 78, January 1581). Lualdi 1644–53, III, fol. 3v: "Fornisce la vaga torre in uno horologgio sopra cui vani campane percorse l'hore, e li quarti ne additano;" and fol. 4: "Prima di entrare a vagheggiare la Basilica non sarà se non curioso fissare lo sguardo nella torre dove il metallo Vaticano
    Con il suo suon l'hore fugaci addita
    Et ad entrar ne la Gran Reggia invita."
79. Bonanni 1706, 505–9, nn. VIII, IX; Egger 1929, 13–14, figs. 4, 5; Bartolotti 1967, E. 618; Whitman and Varriano 1983, 56–57 (with further bibliography); Varriano 1984, 72.
80. The proof engraving is mentioned above. See Chapter 5 for the drawings by Spada and Bernini.
81. "Porta principale del Vaticano sotto alla Torre dell'Orologio dove resiede la Guardia di Svizzeri fatta et ampliata da Nostro Signore Paolo Quinto" (Egger 1929, 78).
82. Egger 1929, 77, quotes Grimaldi.
83. Cf. Egger 1910 and 1929, as well as the reference in Haus 1970, 5, and the *Enciclopedia dello spettacolo*, IX, 1962, tav. LXXIV, t. 18a (cited by Haus 1970, 5).
84. They were manned by "the Swicers" (Martin 1969, 88, 104).
85. Orbaan 1920, 323, and n. 2.
86. Lualdi 1644–53, III, fol. 3: "Si alza nel p.o ingresso una gran Torre con due pretiose colonne di marmo laterali alla

gran porta di bronzo, che dalla parte sinistra e destra ha feritore, che mostrano l'artigliaria di dentro."

87. Lualdi 1644–53, III, fol. 3: "Haveva questa prima entrata del Palazzo una Piazza d'arme con la sua artiglieria et ad uso guerriero la fabricò Innocenzo VIII. Mà il tempo deteriorandola tanto piu ch'era priva della maniere allettatrici della moderna Architettura Palazzo la demolì, et in questa forma da fondam.ti la rinovò."

88. Egger 1929, 8: "Loggia in faccia alla Porta dove resiede la monitione dell'artiglieria per la guardia." See Lualdi 1644–53, III, fol. 21.

89. Weil-Garris and D'Amico 1980, 76–79, where Cortesi recommended a vaulted room close to the entrance (preferably east-facing, as at the Vatican Palace) for the armory, so that "arms will be ready to hand . . . and the entrance of the house will be safer and easier to defend."

90. Egger 1929, 5–7, corrected the faulty transcription in Bonanni on the basis of Grimaldi's notations for the inscription location "in primo atrio Helvetiorum."

91. Egger 1929, 8. For the armory, see Pollak 1928–31, I, 377–80 (1625–38); Redig de Campos 1967, 217; Magnuson 1982–86, I, 224–25.

92. BAV, Vat. lat. 10742, fol. 371 speaks of the "Armeria ripiena d'arme da paolo V.o per armare molte migliaia di persone."

93. Egger 1929, 8, no. VII: "Fonte della guardia eccell.te ornata e scolpita tutta di Marmo," and fig. 16. It is described for us by Lualdi 1644–53, III, fol. 3 (text interrupted and continued on fol. 16).

94. See Freiberg 1991a, who generously shared his information with me before publication. The location of the fountain and other aspects of the new wing are described in BAV, Chigi P. VII. 9, fol. 12, which mentions the battered wall built of brick "con sua cimasa e feritoie di travertino . . . e dietro, vi era l'Arsenale dell'Artiglierie con un Portichetto avanti, so.a il quale vi era la Navicella di musaico. Seguiva doppo d.o Portichetto sino all'horologio un cortile scoperto con una fontana fatta da Papa Paulo V. con varij ornamenti di marmi, quali si sono conservati, che stava incontro la Cordinata, che si è abbassata che va nel cortile grande di Palazzo." Quoted in Freiberg 1991a, 841, n. 44, with references. On pp. 842–43, Freiberg associates Alexander VII's donation of the fountain with his interest in restructuring the hospital. The transfer took place beginning in 1664 under the auspices of Monsignor Francesco Maria Febei, director of the hospital from 1662 to 1680. I suspect the donation had been arranged by Febei's predecessor Virgilio Spada, hospital director from 1660 to 1662 (cf. Eimer 1971, II, 444).

95. Documentation in Freiberg 1991a, 835–36.

96. Documents of 1619 in Freiberg 1991a, 840, nn. 36 and 37.

97. Freiberg 1991a, 840–41.

98. My idea comes from Smith 1956, 28–30, who discusses the lavacrum, where purification precedes a triumphal entry in both the Eastern and Western traditions. Smith suggests

that the *pinea aurea* in the atrium of old St. Peter's performed this function.

99. See the avviso of 26 May 1618, in Orbaan 1920, 254, with reference to Piazza S. Pietro "dove ultimamente si è data l'acqua alle due fontane nuove fatta l'una dentro, l'altra fuori del cortile nuovo del palazzo Apostolico et foderato di metallo il portone del medesimo cortile, dove li svizzeri fanno l'ordinario corpo di guardia." Orbaan mistook this to refer to the older fountain standing in the midst of the piazza.

100. Freiberg 1991a, 839, n. 33, cites Grimaldi 1972, 424, for the inscription, "PAULUS V. PONT. MAX. ANNO PONTIF. SUI XIIII." The fourteenth pontifical year (May 1618 – April 1619) corresponds to the date of the avviso cited above.

101. BAV, Chigi P VII 9, fol. 12, from c. 1660, in n. 94 above.

102. Boorsch 1982–83, 18–19, gives a convenient illustration of the mosaic in its original location. For its removal, see the notice of 17 July 1610 in Orbaan 1919, 85; Paeseler 1941, 79; and note 103 below.

103. Paeseler 1941, 78, cited from Orbaan 1920, 175 (28 July 1610): "Nostro Signore . . . diede ordine, che la pittura della Navicella di San Pietro di musaico, che, come si è detto, si deve levar in 3 pezzi dalla facciata di dentro del palazzo del archipresbiterato, si debba collocare a sinistra della facciata nuova di San Pietro nella parete del palazzo Vaticano." In the documents, the "left" of the basilica façade is always the north and the "right" is the south.

104. Citations from Orbaan 1919, 86–95, in Paeseler 1941, 78.

105. Orbaan 1919, 21, for the notice of May 1612, cited in Paeseler 1941, 79, n. 165.

106. Orbaan 1920, 252 (28 October 1617): "Il Pontefice se ne passò in visita delle 7 chiese et tornò a pranzo poi a Monte Cavallo, sendosi in San Pietro compiacciuto dare alcuni ordini intorno alla fabrica del nuovo portone de svizzeri et di resarcire il musaico della Navicella di San Pietro, collocata nella fabrica del nuovo muro di detto portone verso il palazzo Vaticano." Contemporary sources report the damage that took place in the process of the transfer; the subsequent restoration was directed by Marcello Provenzale (further literature in Paeseler 1941, 81, 83). On 21 October 1625, G. B. Calandro received payment for "lavori di mosaico . . . al ornamento attorno ciborio dove a da stare il S.mo Sudario et ala Navicella difora dela faciata de S. Pietro fatti de diversi smalti minuti . . . p.aver restaurato la vela dela navicella nela cima dove e il fregio" (AFSP, Piano I, ser. 1, vol. 16, no. 43).

107. Orbaan 1920, 254 (10 March 1618): "(Hieri) . . . il dopo pranzo Sua Beatitudine se ne passò al Vaticano, di dove calò alla solita Statione in San Pietro, nella piazza della qual basilica per la prima volta fu scoperta la Navicella di musaico, ch'era prima nel palazzo archipresbiterale, posta hora nella parete d'un muro del palazzo Apostolico."

108. Cf. Torrigio 1618, 91; Bavinck 1620, 11; and *Le cose maravigliose dell'alma città di Roma*, Rome, 1621, 13 (cited by Paeseler 1941, 81–82 who also lists visual sources).

109. Published by Mehnert 1981, 14, with the date c. 1640, the drawing should instead be dated 1623–28, given the presence of the Barberini bees of Urban VIII at the base of the mosaic and the fact of its transfer in 1628 to a different location.

110. "PAULUS V. PONT. MAX. FLUCTUANTIS NAVI-CULAE SACRUM MONUMENTUM EX RUINIS ATRII VATICANAE BASILICAE SERVATUM PO-SUIT ET ORNAVIT AN. SAL. M.DC.XIIX PONT. XIII" (recorded by Bavinck 1620, 11, and Grimaldi 1972, fol. 148v; see Paeseler 1941, 83, for further citations).

111. On 14 January 1630, Bernini received payment of 100 scudi for the "collocamento" of the Navicella (AFSP, Piano I, ser. 3, vol. 160, 24v). Other references in Pollak 1928–31, II, 159–67; Paeseler 1941, 84–87; Thelen 1967a, C 37–39, 48–53; Thelen 1967c, 9–10; Hibbard 1971, 183; Heimbürger Ravalli 1977, 206–207; Francia 1989, 162.

112. Thelen 1967a, 52 and n. 10. Lualdi 1644–53, II, fol. 258v–60v, should not be overlooked, as he gives the whole story as follows: "Volendo Paolo V demolire l'antico Portico [of old St. Peter's] . . . pensò al modo di conservare intero con li suoi tesselli il musaico della Navicella, che quivi si custodiva. E Somministrò al pietoso Pontefice l'industria l'ordegno per cui tutto intero calato nel piano, l'alzò di nuovo e lo collocò l'anno 1617 in un'ampia e bella cortina di muro del Palazzo Vaticano dove questi al tempio si unisce, e fà mostra di se avanti del nuovo portico. Ma quivi la navicella esposta di nuovo alle pioggie alle turbini e procellosi venti faceva di nuovo ma con irreparabile ruina naufraggio, onde N. S. acciò memoria così insigne del Vicario di Cristo in oblivione non andasse, dallo aperto loco rapito la tutta intera la sottrasse alle ingiurie di tempi e la collocò il 1629 dentro la Basilica Vaticana sopra la porta maggiore l'appoggio sopra il cornicione che raggira attorno il tempio e sotto l'arco della gran volta, e da ambi i lati gli apri fenestroni perche meglio con la copia de raggi potesse essere vagheggiata."

113. Information in Paeseler 1941, 86, which is overlooked in Thelen 1967a, Thelen 1967c, Heimbürger Ravalli 1977, and others, despite Virgilio Spada's participation. See now Köhren-Jansen 1993, 29 (kindly brought to my attention by Christof Thoenes), and, more generally, Lisner 1994.

114. See the report by Francesco Maria Torrigio (1580–1650) transcribed in Güthlein 1981, 224–25.

115. For which see Borsi and Quinterio 1980, 313.

116. Gigli describes the location "nel primo cortile incontro alla Porta del Palazzo del Papa dove sono l'Imagini di S. Paolo et di S. Pietro pur di mosaico, ma moderne, le quali fece fare Paolo V per ornamento di quell'edificio da lui fatto di novo" (Paeseler 1941, 86).

117. Paeseler 1941, 86, quotes the *Ritratto di Roma moderna*, Rome, 1652, 18.

118. Mola 1663, 43. Mola's guide was originally composed by 1660 and updated three years later, a chronology that accords precisely with his text: "La Navicella di Musaico tanto famosa e de Giotto, oggi di novo levata p seguitare d.o porticale [the palace entrance], (ora non è più)." The

entrance was pulled down to make way for Bernini's north corridor in 1660.

119. From his discussion, it is clear that Paeseler 1941, 86, was thinking of the west side of the new *atrium helvetiorum*, although he speaks of "die östliche Schmalseite des Hofes."

120. BAV, Chigi P VII 9, fol. 12, has been cited by Brauer and Wittkower 1931 and more recently in Freiberg 1991a (neither mentioning the problem of the location of the Navicella).

121. See the account of the destruction of the Paul V wing in Chapter 5 below.

122. AFSP, Piano I, ser. 1, vol. 11, no. 22, fol. 300 (12 August 1662): "Benedetto Drei soprastante della R. Fab.a di S. Pietro. . . . Darete il Portone dell'Arsenale dell'Arteglierie, che stava sotto la Navicella di mosaico al S.r Card. Ginetti. . . ."

123. AFSP, Piano I, ser. armadi, vol. 348, fol. 4 (1 January 1665): "Cosimo Bartoli à conto de disegni, che fà p. la navicella . . . scudi 8."

124. The "counterproject" drawing illustrated in Wittkower 1975, figs. 94, 95, records the idea.

125. See AFSP, Piano I, ser. armadi, vol. 348, fol. 147 (1673), for payment of 120 scudi to the painter Oratio Manenti for "cartone à olio della Navicella di S. Pietro, conf.e la lista del S.r Cav.r Bernini Arch.o." Alternatively the cartoon may have been used to test the eventual location of the mosaic within the narthex entrance.

126. Avviso of 28 March 1671: "Nella Congregatione della Reverdenda Fabbrica giorni sono espose il Cavalier Bernino, che nel portico già terminato à fronte del suo poco applaudito Costantino si dovesse metter la Navicella di San Pietro, la quale per le tante scosse, si è ritirata in un angolo del Vaticano, questo suo pensiero ha riportato l'applauso; acciò si veda à fronte d'un opera si degna, ed antica il cumulo degli errori, che si osserva nella sua opera nuova, e moderna del Gran Costantino" (Rossi 1940, 58).

127. Paeseler 1941, 87. Ferrabosco and Costaguti 1684, XIV, were aware that the new location of the Navicella was "dove era situato nel Portico antico."

128. See Egger 1928, 24–25; Redig de Campos 1967, 114–15. The Loggetta is still accessible, encased as a mezzanine in the second floor of the eastern wing of the courtyard.

129. Ferrabosco and Costaguti 1684, XII, enumerate the facilities displaced by the demolitions, which "comprendeva le Stanze per il Corpo di Guardia de'Suizzeri, Dataria, Segretaria de'Brevi, Archivi de Scritture, Abitazione, con altre molte commodità per i Sommi Pontefici, Corte, e loro Famiglie."

130. The Segretaria Apostolica was moved to new offices near the Tower of Nicholas V in 1608–9. See the inscription from May 1608-April 1609 over the entrance: "SEG-RETARIA APOSTOLICA PAULO V PONT MAX PROVIDENTIA OPORTUNIORIBUS SEDIBUS COLOCATA AEDIFITIO AUTA INSTRUCTA ET ORNATA PONTIFICATUS ANNO IV" (BAV, Vat. lat. 10742 [description of c. 1620], fol. 442v). The datary was installed in the new apartments at the north side of the

Cortile di S. Damaso in 1609–10 (pace Hibbard 1971, 198, with a date of 1608). See the inscription recorded in BAV, Vat. lat. 10742, fol. 441: "PAULUS V PONT MAX DATARUM EX INNOCENTIO VIII PALATIO AD BASILICAE AMPLIATIONEM EXCISO, HUNC IN LOCUM TRANSTULIT PONT ANNO V."

131. Pastor 1923–53, XXVI, 481, wrote that Paul V devoted some 235,000 scudi to the palace. Of this work Hibbard 1971, 198, believed that "nothing of importance can be given securely to Maderno."

132. Redig de Campos 1967, 208.

CHAPTER FOUR. Bernini's Designs from Colonnade to Corridor, 1656–1659

1. My divisions differ from the three phases described in Brauer and Wittkower 1931, 88–96, which pertain only to the corridors and the Scala Regia and reflect a substantially different point of view. In brief, Wittkower, who wrote this section, did not investigate the introduction of the corridors into the piazza scheme and did not emphasize the role of the north corridor as part of the palace, whereas I see the introduction of the corridor as the first step in the creation of a new monumental entrance. In addition, I believe that the evolution of the corridor design ultimately betrays the intention to rebuild the Scala Regia, whereas Wittkower left the significance of this evolution unexplained. And finally, I understand the designs for the corridor and especially the Scala Regia as responses to a variety of structural requirements to a greater extent than did Wittkower.

2. Thoenes 1963, 102–4.

3. Ehrle 1928, 33–34, n. 155; Thoenes 1963, 105–7 and 139, n. 64. For an illustration of the fresco, see also Ackerman 1964, pl. 58.

4. Voss 1922, 3–4.

5. Brauer and Wittkower 1931, 66, n. 6; and Wittkower 1939–40, n. 76, with the suggestion that the engraving of the scheme was ordered later, about 1620, by Bartoli's nephew.

6. BAV, Chigi P VII 9, fol. 43.

7. Brauer and Wittkower 1931, 67, 97–99, correctly described the scheme as five-sided (pace Kitao 1974, 86, n. 31). Fasolo 1961, 212–17, believed the drawing resembles the style of Carlo's father Girolamo, but the traditional opinion is maintained by Thoenes 1963, 120–21; Kitao 1974, 86; and Kieven 1993, 162–63, cat. 55.

8. Ehrle 1928, 29–30, 36, 42, suggested a date of 1651, or at least before 1656, for these projects which he related to the documentary evidence for clearing the spina in that year. I will explain my reasons for dating two drawings after Innocent's death at the end of this chapter. From Baldinucci 1681–1728, V, 329–30, we learn that Rainaldi made four "modelletti di rilievo" for Innocent X in the early 1650s. One was in the form of a perfect square, another a circle, a third an oval, and the fourth a hexagon. Baldinucci indicates that all were to have the same eleva-

tion, with apartments above a portico. Apartments on the north side were for the conclavists; those on the south for the servants of the palace; and the Swiss Guards were to occupy the rooms closest to the palace. In 1696 Bonanni illustrated two schemes by Rainaldi, one hexagonal and the other a long oval in an engraving that accompanied a discussion of the design of the piazza (p. 188). Both schemes were to have had the same two-story elevations as described above, the lower arcaded and the upper enclosed. Baldinucci explains that the drawings were requested for study by the successor pope Alexander VII, but does not say when. Baldinucci does say that the drawings were returned to the architect's studio where they were much admired ("ed oggi recano non minore abbellimento allo studio di lui, che diletto ad ogni amatore di quest'arte, che si porta a verderli"). This is confirmed by Titi 1686, 2–3, who saw Rainaldi's drawings and recommended them to students ("à Virtuosi di pascer anche in questi l'intelletto con vederli in sua Casa").

9. The fundamental guide to the chronology of the piazza is by Del Pesco 1988. The best synthetic account of the design process is provided by Menichella in Martinelli et al. 1987, 3–20. Rietbergen 1983a and 1983b (pp. 295–356) give an extensive account of the administrative and economic aspects. Modern research is based on Fraschetti 1900, 307–26; Ehrle 1928, especially 33–44; and the pioneering discussion in Brauer and Wittkower 1931, 66–102 (the portion on Piazza S. Pietro, which forms the basis for all later research, was written by Wittkower: see their p. 5). Other outstanding contributions to the topic include Krautheimer 1985; Birindelli 1981; Kitao 1974; Guidoni Marino 1973; and Thoenes 1963.

10. AFSP, Piano I, ser. 3, vol. 163, fol. 86, originally published by Ehrle 1928, 34; Del Pesco 1988, 41. As elsewhere, Ehrle also provides the corresponding citation ("indice 233") from Fortini's index to the minutes of the Fabbrica meetings. In 1992, Sarah McPhee identified this index in the Archivio della Fabbrica and kindly brought it to my attention.

11. On the institution of the Fabbrica and its records, see Vespignanio 1762; the anonymous *Compendio* of 1793; Moroni 1840–61, XVI, 199–206; Ehrle 1928, 19–20; Del Re 1969; Rietbergen 1983a, especially 121–29; Basso 1987–88 (with convenient lists of the officers and financial resources over the centuries); and the bibliography by A. Anselmi in Contardi and Curcio 1991, 278, n. 5.

12. Ehrle 1928, 28–33; Hager 1968, 312, n. 23, with the modern citation of the relevant document from the Fabbrica; Heimbürger Ravalli 1977, 209–13; Güthlein 1981, 228–30. Hager 1968, 313–14, n. 59, provides an interesting notice from Valesio's diary entry of 25 June 1725 regarding Bernini's involvement as follows: "Mandò S. Stà a chiamare Paolo Bernino fig.o del celebre Cav.re Lorenzo architetto credendo che egli avesse fatto un disegno del Colonnato di S. Pietro con sopra le stanze per il Conclave desiderando S. B. di formarne uno stabile siccome avea pensato anche Innocenzo XII [sic, for Innocent X] ma quello rispose che

il disegno di ciò era stato del Borromini. S. B. mandò a Casa Chigi che gliene fu mandato uno abbozzo che avevano, ora dicesi che voglia fabricarlo nel Patriarchio di S. Giovanni."

13. Diary entry of 9 August 1656; Del Pesco 1988, 41.

14. Del Pesco 1988, 41.

15. Brauer and Wittkower 1931, 69. In Spada's plan, "si chiuderà [tha piazza] per linea retta, formando Bisquadro cen[tina]to con la facciata" (references n. 12 above).

16. AFSP, Piano I, ser. 3, vol. 163, fol. 89; quoted in Ehrle 1928, 34, n. 156; Del Pesco 1988, 42 (with citation of the same record in BAV, Chigi H II 22, fol. 96).

17. The new passage through the Vatican Palace wall was to join the existing cordonata, probably at an opening which appears on Maderno's plans (Figs. 50, 57). The relationship of these features implies a most interesting survival of Paul III's concern for developing an approach to the palace from the east.

18. There has been considerable doubt about the date and attribution of the plan on BAV, Chigi P VII 9, 32–33. Del Pesco 1988, 46–47, relates the drawing to a reference in the avviso of 8 September 1656 to a design "not by Bernini." This opinion is consistent with Kitao 1974, 12 and 91, n. 47, who does not believe Bernini produced a rectangular plan. The drawing was engraved in Fontana 1694, pl. 185, with an indication that the rectangular plan was by someone other than Bernini. Bonanni 1699, tav. 68, also published an engraving of the drawing with the legend "Idea Porticus quam Eques Berninus moliri meditabatur." Ehrle 1928, 43, 44, 72, suggested that the circular plan was drawn over the rectangular scheme. Brauer and Wittkower 1931, 66 (n. 1), 70–71, 76 (n. 1), 97, reject the attribution to Bernini of the circular scheme drawn over the rectangular plan. Borsi and Quinterio 1980, 67, fig. 68, 75, refer to the rectangular and circular plans as contemporaneous.

19. On Alexander's meeting with the librarian to discuss "i portici doppij degli antichi," see the pope's diary entry for 28 August 1656 in Del Pesco 1988, 46; and for Holstenius and the history of the report generally, pp. 11–38.

20. The drawing showing the single and double portico on BAV, Chigi P VII 9, fol. 34, was surely produced later than "il disegno de' portici doppi" that Bernini brought to the pope on 15 October 1656. Bernini's visit was recorded in the pope's diary; Del Pesco 1988, 47. In the caption to a photograph of fol. 34, Menichella in Martinelli et al. 1987, fig. 2, has the date 15 October 1656 with a question mark. The drawing is more likely to have been made to discuss the issues of climate control raised by Spada on 19 March 1657; see the parenthetical statement in my text immediately below.

21. Del Pesco 1988, 48–49, for the Fabbrica meeting of 17 March 1657. Brauer and Wittkower 1931, 71, bring out Bernini's role as both the chief designer and courtier who attributes the design to the pope.

22. See Morello 1992, and the testimony of the pope himself, writing in the third person: "Studiò architettura e gnomonica esattamente, oltre l'intender Euclide, e far le pra-

tiche del compasso, lavorò, di sua mano, con scalpello, e con lima" (Incisa della Rocchetta 1964, 442).

23. Pallavicino 1839–40, II, 182.

24. There must have been at least five exchanges between Alexander and Bernini before the meeting of March 1657. The first would have taken place before the initial announcement of the project; the second through the medium of Flavio Chigi (mentioned above); the third in connection with the design for the double portico (again mentioned above); the fourth on 4 February 1657 ("son da noi il P. Virgilio Spada, e poi il Bernino a lungo circa il portico di S. Pietro," mentioned in Alexander's diary, Del Pesco 1988, 47); and the fifth shortly after 12 March 1657 ("e si dica al Bernino che si parlerà de' portici ancora," again mentioned in the diary, Del Pesco 1988, 47).

25. BAV, Chigi P VII 9, fol. 35, is discussed by Brauer and Wittkower 1931, 72–73, Taf. 161 a. Menichella (caption to her fig. 1) attributes the drawing to Lazzaro Morelli without discussion but possibly in connection with payments made to him for "disegni" in 1657 (Menichella in Martinelli et al. 1987, 271). Wittkower believed the drawing was by the same hand that drew the transverse sections of the single and double porticoes; and since the proportions of the arcade in the latter are smaller, he believed it to be the earlier drawing. The comparative sections were illustrated, Wittkower thought, in response to some of the objections to the oval scheme registered on 19 March 1657 (see below). This seems plausible, but I believe Wittkower erred in dating the broad portico elevation much later, after the Ferrabosco clock tower was destined for destruction. He based this conclusion on the erroneous belief that the full 950-palmi length of the portico on the scaled elevation could not have fit into the north side of the piazza without the destruction of the clock tower. In fact, it would have fit very neatly into the space of the north colonnade, which was well in front of the clock tower and the old site of the Portone di Bronzo. The relevant dimensions can be compared in the reconstruction drawing in Kitao's fig. 5. (I am comparing the 950-palmi length of the portico to the inner circumference of the colonnade, illustrated in Kitao 1974, by using the formula ½ circumference = ½ pi × diameter. This method will only approximate the dimensions, but the correspondences are convincing.)

26. Menichella in Martinelli et al. 1987, 6; Del Pesco 1988, 53; and for Bernini's use of models, Bauer 1982 and Bauer 1983.

27. For the citation, see n. 43. The portal leading to the barracks of the Swiss Guard is illustrated in my Figs. 66, 71.

28. E.g., Brauer and Wittkower 1931, 73; Krautheimer 1985, 171; Del Pesco 1988, 51.

29. "Aggiongo ch'essendo questi piccoli vani di transito, coperti da un'architrave in piano, il dritto di questi col curvo degli archi, mi pare che apporterebbe quel più di bellezza, che desiderare si possa in cosa tale." The meaning of this passage, quoted from the full memorandum in BAV, Chigi H II 22, fols. 105–6, has not been previously explained. Spada's memorandum has been published almost com-

pletely, in two parts, by Brauer and Wittkower 1931, 71–72 (who did not identify the author); Güthlein 1979, 189–90 (second part only); Borsi and Quinterio 1980, 347–48; and Del Pesco 1988, 49–53, who is the first to consider these two parts as one document.

30. BAV, Chigi H II 22, fol. 106: "Dubitarei anche, che la commodità si rendesse minore, poichè essendo uno dei fini di tali portici il dar commodità a tante carrozze, che si radunnano al Vaticano o per bisogno de' Canonici che tutto l'anno vi vanno due volte il giorno, ò de' Cardinali, Prelati, Prencipi e Corteggiani, che concorrono colà quando vi risiede S. S.tà a fine che in tempo di pioggia, ò di sole possino stare al coperto, et all'ombra."

31. Skippon 1663–64, 648, continues a bit loosely: "From hence a double row of pillars [he means paired pilasters] lead up to the entrance of the vatican palace, whence there is a long gallery to the castle S. Angelo." Someone must have indicated the alignment with the Borgo Nuovo down which the Castel Sant'Angelo was visible. Skippon began his voyage in April 1663 and he was still in Rome in 1664.

32. Pallavicino 1839–40, II, 181.

33. Barozzi and Berchet 1879, 218–19. Later (p. 320) the ambassador disparaged the design of the piazza "con notabili difetti nell'architettura . . . che . . . renderà per sempre disabitata la città Leonina, o sia Borgo."

34. Alexander's diary for 20 May 1657; Menichella in Martinelli et al. 1987, 6–7; Del Pesco 1988, 54.

35. The diary entry for 3 August 1657 reads "Diamo a fare la medaglia pel portico ovato di S. Pietro, e fermiamo le parole pel rovescio di essa" and the inscription is given there as well (Del Pesco 1988, 56). Incidentally, Alexander did consider using the piazza as the design reverse for the papal annual medal on 17 June: "Card. Chigi = medaglia di q[uest]o anno che si mostri al cav. Bernino, et a noi, se li dica di q[uel] del Port[ic]o di S. Pietro" (diary entry in Del Pesco 1988, 55). The papal annual medal is traditionally issued each year on 29 June.

36. The sketch and letter in BAV, Chigi R VIII c, fol. 11, was first cited in Wittkower 1975, 281, n. 62; and subsequently in Morello 1981a, 318, and Morello 1992, 202–3. Del Pesco 1988, 55, located it chronologically.

37. "E quando la S.tà di N.ro Sig.re approvasse questo pensiero, non sarà difficile il trovar modo, che il Cav. Bernino ne divinisse l'Autore, acciò non li dispiacesse che altri volessero perfettionare i suoi disegni" (BAV, Chigi H II 22, fol. 105; Del Pesco 1988, 51).

38. Letter to Cardinal Leopoldo de' Medici from his agent Leonardo Agostini of 1 September 1657, discovered by Mercantini 1981, 27. Other citations from Alexander's diary in Del Pesco 1988, 56–57. Regarding the medal itself, see the literature cited in Del Pesco 1988, 57; and Whitman and Varriano 1983, 99–101.

39. Brauer and Wittkower 1931, 73, 74, connected the decision to demolish the Ferrabosco tower with the development, over the summer of 1657, of the double-column scheme. Krautheimer 1985, 171, dates the decision somewhat earlier, to 20 May 1657, assuming the design

at that time reflected the design of the medal produced in August.

40. Del Pesco 1988, 58.

41. The letter of Spada to Leonardo Agostini of 15 September 1657 was discovered by Mercantini 1981, 29–30. A portion of the letter appears in Del Pesco 1988, 57.

42. Mercantini 1981, 29: "Il disegno de portici si è variato, e si varia ogni giorno[.] Il p.o fu disegnato semplice con Pilastri, e membretti dal V.o Cav.re Bernino; N. S.re lo volse doppio, p.che ne restasse sempre illeso dall'ingiurie de tempi, si come è stata constante S. S.tà in no volervi altra fabrica sopra, dicendo che queste devono formare la picciola corte, e che restino servi del Palazzo, e della fabrica di S. Pietro, e no. emulatori, e così restorno delusi i pensieri di quelli, che vi designavano sopra la Canonica, et il Conclave."

43. Mercantini 1981, 30: "Ma non si è anche resoluto, se le Colonne habbiano ad essere a doe a doe o vero ad una ad una ornando solo le loro testate co colonne cioè dove è la porta della guardia dei Svizzeri, e dove resta aperta la strada di borgo novo ch'è la strada corr.te di Castello." On the other hand it had been determined to enlarge the columns from the 5 – palmi diameter mentioned in the second design to 6 ½ to 7 palmi in the third design, with the smallest columns on the interior perimeter and the largest on the exterior of a radial arrangement. It was noted that the size of the columns were intended to be comparable to those of the Pantheon.

44. Published by Mercantini 1981, 14–15, fig. 13, who mentions the importance of the drawing for the Scala Regia. Menichella in Martinelli et al. 1987, 17, n. 22, attributes the drawing to Lazzaro Morelli without discussion and dates it to the period before 2 September 1657, when Bernini presented a study of the portico with single columns; however, Spada's letter of 15 September clearly indicates that paired and single columns were still under consideration.

45. Menichella in Martinelli et al. 1987, 7, nn. 51 and 53, and 269–70 (documentation); Del Pesco 1988, 60–61.

46. The error in reading the Doric frieze as Ionic has been commonly made from Brauer and Wittkower 1931, to Menichella in Martinelli et al. 1987, 7, and persists in the textbook accounts.

47. Documents from Menichella in Martinelli et al. 1987, 269–70.

48. ASV, Avvisi 105, fol. 34, records the visit. The critical comments are recorded in BAV, Barb. lat. 6367, avvisi diversi, fol. 777v (Haus 1970, 124; Del Pesco 1988, 61). The latter reads in part: "Fù osservato, e sintende pare che Sua Beat.ne non ne resti con quella soddisfattione da desidera e che si era figurato sopra di che anche da molti li vien date varie eccettioni et errori di buona architettura non corrispondendo particolarmente il disegno della facciata di S. Pietro, e la spesa è immensa poichè sin'hora in modelli solo si è speso molte migliaia di scudi." Menichella in Martinelli et al. 1987, 7 and n. 55, doubts the veracity of the report.

49. Haus 1970, 124; Krautheimer 1985, 178; Del Pesco 1988, 66–67.

50. ASV, Avvisi 107, fol. 106 (Haus 1970, 125; Del Pesco 1988, 67).

51. ASR, Cartari-Febei, b. 191, fol. 13v (Haus 1970, 125; Del Pesco 1988, 70).

52. Avviso in Fraschetti 1900, 314, n. 2; Del Pesco 1988, 42–43. These objections must be understood in the context of the plague that appeared in Rome in May 1656, as Patricia Waddy reminds me.

53. "Il disegno de' portici da far a S. Pietro si è intorbidato perchè il disegno non era del Bernini, al quale si crede habbi fatto far de'mali offitii"; avviso of 8 September 1656 (Del Pesco 1988, 46, who relates this notice to the circular scheme discussed above). Regarding the activities of competitors, we also have the title of Bonanni's engraving of the circular and rectangular scheme (tabula 68): "Idea Porticus quam Eque Berninus moliri meditabatur in Area Vaticana."

54. Busiri Vici 1893.

55. Their character as critiques of Bernini's scheme was brought out in Brauer and Wittkower 1931, 98–100 (with earlier bibliography) and studied more fully in Wittkower 1939–40, republished in Wittkower 1975, 61–82, and notes on 280–82, from which the following citations are taken. The previous state of research is summarized by Ehrle 1928, 36–38. Kitao 1974, 133, n. 260, has pointed out how Italian authors, slow to relinquish the attribution to Bernini in the later 1930s, were influenced by the drawings in developing projects for a closed Piazza S. Pietro rather than the open spina that was eventually built.

56. BAV, Vat. lat. 14620. Busiri Vici 1973 explains the donation of the drawings, whose provenance is additionally recounted in newspaper articles pasted to the cover leaf of the volume.

57. Wittkower 1975, 74, considered the series of drawings "only intelligible in connection with a treatise which in all probability it was meant to illustrate," and gave historical examples of this type of verbal-and-graphic criticism.

58. Wittkower 1975, 76.

59. Menichella in Martinelli et al. 1987, 7–9.

60. Entry from Alexander's diary for 21 June 1659: "Il P[adre] Virg[ili]o Sp[ad]a è stato da noi a 19 ho[re] sopra la Cong[regazion]e dela Fabr[ic]a di hieri contro il Cav. Bern.o, che stamattina a 14 ho[re] è da noi e vi torna anco a 21 ho[re]" (Del Pesco 1988, 70–71).

61. The most famous example in architectural history is surely A. W. N. Pugin's *Contrasts* of 1836, in which the "beauties" of Gothic architecture are pitted against the "dry and sterile" forms of classicism on facing illustrations with little or no text.

62. Wittkower 1975, 63–65, ill. 87.

63. Wittkower 1975, 65–66, ills. 89, 81. I refer to the modern folio numbers, which are stamped on the lower right of each of the 14 leaves. In this way we avoid the confusion that arises in Wittkower's account when there is no older number written on the upper right of the individual drawings. (Almost needless to say, the lack of such numbers argues against some of Wittkower's basic premises regarding the nature of the drawings.)

64. The strong resemblances of some features on the counterprojects to Papirio Bartoli's scheme do not convince me that Bartoli's nephew was their author, as argued by Wittkower 1975, 82. Nor is Bartoli known to be related to "Constanzo de Paris inventore" who signed one of the drawings (mentioned by Wittkower 1975, 76). While the Bartoli engraving presumably had a wide audience, the influence of other piazza schemes are evident in the counterprojects.

65. Diary for 13 August 1656, specifies "senza fabrica sopra ma co' balustri e con statue ad ogni pilastrino" (Del Pesco 1988, 41).

66. Letter of 15 September 1657, from Mercantini 1981, 29; Del Pesco 1988, 45–46, 57. It was also Spada who criticized Bernini's use of single pilasters for being too weak visually and suggested doubling them (note 29 above and Del Pesco 1988, 51). The serlian motif embodies double vertical supports for the arcade.

67. Brauer and Wittkower 1931, 85, 100; Wittkower 1975, 63–65, 73–74, ill. 86; Kitao 1974, 120, n. 200. Worsdale 1986, 39, suggests that the drawing is by Alexander VII, but I cannot agree.

68. The two-story arcade drawn with dotted lines on the right of the sheet is a formulaic rendition of the old alternative scheme and does not have to be dated before 13 August 1656 when the pope essentially ruled out the use of more than one story.

69. BAV, Chigi H II, 22, fol. 109v. Text of the characterization in Brauer and Wittkower 1931, 70 n. 1; Wittkower 1975, 281, n. 66; Kitao 1974, 40. Discussed in Wittkower 1975, 79–81, the passage is generally ascribed to Bernini; but Morello 1992, 199–200, has recently suggested that it may be attributed to the son, Domenico Bernini. For another anthropomorphic image among the counterprojects, see Wittkower 1975, 73–74, ill. 85.

70. On "Bramante ruinante" see Ackerman 1970.

71. Wittkower 1975, 63.

72. Brauer and Wittkower 1931, 71; Wittkower 1975, ill. 97.

73. Wittkower 1975, 70.

74. Wittkower does not comment on the chalk underdrawing on the unfinished left side of the sheet. It depicts a colonnade arm that is three bays wide and, like the executed design, the flanking bays are covered by flat ceilings and the central bay is covered with a continuous annular vault. In my opinion, this composition reflects a passage in the Spada memorandum referring to "piccoli vani di transito, coperti da un'architrave in piano, il dritto di questi col curvo degli archi." Del Pesco 1988 dates the memorandum to 19 March 1657 (pp. 49–52, for text and argument).

75. Wittkower 1975, 65, ill. 89.

76. Wittkower 1975, 66–68, ill. 92.

77. Wittkower 1975, ill. 93 left. The correspondence with the previous drawing is imprecise: the stairs are separated by

different numbers of bays, so the schemes may be said only to approximate one another.

78. Wittkower 1975, 67–68, ill. 93 right.

79. For this type of staircase, see Wilkinson 1975.

80. A statement hidden in a footnote is relevant to the entire discussion here: "To make the Scala Regia Bernini took the bold step of connecting his corridor . . . with the old staircase, and thereby gave the palace its superb entrance in direct line with the Borgo Nuovo. It was an arrangement of great ingenuity which was probably planned after the critic's counterproject" (Wittkower 1975, 280, n. 11).

81. Wittkower 1975, 68, ill. 96.

82. Wittkower 1975, 72–74, ill. 100.

83. Wittkower 1975, 68, discussed this feature in relation to suggested changes to the basilica façade.

84. The foregoing analysis should explain why I disagree with Wittkower's characterization (1975, 73) of the little sketch above Bernini's perspective as emphasizing "the isolation of Bernini's entrance to the palace." It is precisely the lack of its isolation that is criticized in the counterproject. Here as elsewhere (e.g., 1975, 70), Wittkower assumed that the counterproject (of 1659!) was reaching back to criticize an early Bernini project, an exercise that would hardly make sense after the foundation medal was cast and the scheme known from the Bonacina engraving.

85. Wittkower 1975, 71, ill. 98.

86. Del Pesco 1988, 58, for the diary entry.

87. This was one of the problems the oval scheme was intended to alleviate. See Brauer and Wittkower 1931, 70, n. 1; and Kitao 1974, 89–90, n. 40.

88. Del Pesco 1988, 58, for the quote from Alexander's diary (note 40 above).

89. Del Pesco 1988, 60 ("Entrata al cop[erto] ale scale di pal[azz]o dal portico della piazza.").

90. BAV, Chigi a I 19, fol. 26; Del Pesco 1988, 60.

91. Del Pesco 1988, 60–66.

92. Entry in Alexander's diary for 28 March 1659 notes that "al Colonnato si lavori più a furia" (Del Pesco 1988, 71).

93. The completed elevation is reported to the Fabbrica in AFSP, Piano I, ser. 3, vol. 163, fol. 140v (Haus 1970, 15; Del Pesco 1988, 72). The 47 columns are mentioned in BAV, Chigi H II 22, fol. 162 (Brauer and Wittkower 1931, 81; Del Pesco 1988, 72).

94. Mortoft 1659–59, 79.

95. Wittkower 1975, 62, characterized the criticisms as "led by a particularly ruthless critic who probably belonged to the most reactionary ecclesiastical circle of the time."

96. Wittkower 1975, 280, n. 11, as quoted in note 80 above.

97. Brauer and Wittkower 1931, 100, n. 3.

98. See my discussion in Chapter 2 and the discussions in Brauer and Wittkower 1931, 97–98; Wittkower 1975, 78.

99. See Marder 1983b and 1986.

100. Wittkower 1975, ill. 91. See also the painted veduta in his ill. 108.

CHAPTER FIVE. Bernini's Designs for the North Corridor, 1659–1662

1. This dimension is taken from the scaled plan in Fig. 109. The plan shows that the portal stood about 600 palmi (134.04 m.) west of Maderno's fountain.

2. Payment discovered by Haus 1970, 15, 125; Del Pesco 1988, 72–73.

3. The differences between the drawing and the engraving are summarized in Kitao 1974, 111–12, n. 154. As we know from the monogram, the drawing once belonged to Sir Joshua Reynolds.

4. It should be noted that the numbers of corridor bays do approximate the 18 bays on each colonnade quadrant.

5. Brauer and Wittkower 1931, 76, n. 1; 80, 83, 88–90, 92.

6. See Kitao 1974, 38–41; 43; 78–79, n. 6; 81–82, n. 16; 112, n. 158; 115, n. 174.

7. The trial addition of the tetrastyle portico must be related to Bernini's making "i disegni del Portico" on 18 May 1659, the "disegno del Vestibolo del portico di S. Pietro" on 26 June 1659, and the "disegno del Portico" on 15 August 1659 (citations in Del Pesco 1988, 71, 73). I make this conclusion on the basis of the consistent use of the term "portici" to signify the colonnades, which are never referred to in the singular. These notices do not affect Wittkower's dating of the Vatican plan, to which the tetrastyle was added, perhaps much later, as Kitao 1974, 112, n. 158, pointed out.

8. "Larghezza della corsia di mezo pal. 22 ½" is the dimension inscribed on the Bonacina engraving. See also Kitao 1974, 113, n. 163. Later, in Fontana's engraving, we see that the width of the central passage was increased to 23 ½ palmi.

9. To be precise, I have taken the measurements from the inner face of the north side of the north bell tower. This feature provides a fixed reference point that remained unaltered after Maderno's construction of the façade in the early seventeenth century.

10. Brauer and Wittkower 1931, 89, nevertheless emphasized that the corridor wall must have been meant to join that of the old Scala Regia. It is unclear how they arrived at the latter conclusion.

11. Brauer and Wittkower 1931, 90. Because the uneven grade level represents the south rather than the north corridor, this sketch may record a later thought for the exterior articulation.

12. In the Falda engraving, the Piazza Retta is stepped up to the level of the basilica on three terraces. Apart from this detail the engraving is consistent with the plan of autumn 1659.

13. Questions about the nature of the sketchbook to which the small drawing belongs have been raised in other contexts (references in Marder 1991b, 288, n. 88; and Morello 1992, 205–7). Particularly baffling in this little volume is the remarkably uniform style and scale of drawings depicting buildings that are widely separated in time and circumstances. We cannot rule out the possibility that Chigi

a. I. 19 is a record of design ideas made long after the fact and pertaining to various commissions of special interest to the pope.

14. Brauer and Wittkower 1931, 90, 91, 93, 103, n. 3.

15. Brauer and Wittkower 1931, 92.

16. The last dimension, measured from base to capital, is given on Bonacina's engraving.

17. Brauer and Wittkower 1931, 90, 91, 93, 103, n. 3.

18. It should be observed that the distance between the northern edge of the basilica's façade and the north wall of the north corridor is the same in Bernini's plan, the façade elevation, and the Vatican plan when measured at a corresponding location.

19. On the basilica elevation, the height of the dividing pilaster to its "capital" is about 36 palmi. Add to this measurement the radius of the arch above the old Scala Regia (half of its 16-palmi width = 8 palmi), and the result is 44 palmi.

20. References to the citation in Del Pesco 1988, 80.

21. The critical reader may have noted an apparent problem where the dimensions of the corridor width and its distance from the basilica façade do not correspond in the Vatican plan (22 palmi + 22 palmi) and the façade elevation (11 ½ palmi + 37 palmi). The 4-½-palmi difference in the sums is explained by the greater distance between the façade and the corridor at the back (west) of the former than at the front (east).

22. Brauer and Wittkower 1931, 90–93, 103, n. 3.

23. Brauer and Wittkower 1931, 90. On this sheet Bernini also experiments with a new path for the cordonata and a vaulting system to join the colonnade.

24. Brauer and Wittkower 1931, 90.

25. Brauer and Wittkower 1931, 80, n. 1, referred to the gentle curve across the upper right of the sheet as an "undeutbare Zeichnung" and suggested that the palace was not drawn by Bernini. Perhaps Bernini turned the sheet 90 degrees and drew the curved line to trace the path of the Borgo Vecchio across the façade of a palace, approximating the juxtaposition of the street shown curving in front of the Palazzo dei Penitenzieri in the principal image of the drawing.

26. Brauer and Wittkower 1931, 90, 92.

27. Brauer and Wittkower 1931, 91.

28. Jestaz 1966, 175: "L'on y monte d'une pente douce et tournant, les carrosse y peuve aller mais dificilement à cause du tournan."

29. See Waddy 1990, 61–66.

30. For the sixteenth century the Palazzo Farnese may serve as an example (Waddy 1990, 62). For the seventeenth century there is the project for the Palazzo Barberini cited in Waddy 1990, 362, n. 12: "La prima loggia . . . si farà larga palmi 33. overo 34. acciòche possano voltarsi le carrozze, e condurre li padroni sino alle scale, e starvi in maggior numero à coperto, et acciòche riesca anche tal larghezza capace della fronte delle scale; ma l'altre tre loggie, che non hanno da usarsi per tal bisogno saranno un terzo men larghe, cioè palmi 22. o 23. ò poco più, nelle quali potranno

tuttavia andare due carrozze al pari" (BAV, Barb. lat. 4360, fol. 11).

31. Ost 1981, 236, n. 13 (quoting a document of 6 July 1656); and Krautheimer 1985, 47–53.

32. Note how the streets vary from 22 to 28 palmi in the design process sketched by Connors 1989, 279–93.

33. Pallavicino 1839–40, II, 181–82, observes of the palace, "non é fornito di cortile se non remotissimo dalle comuni scale, in cui possano trattenersi le carrozze."

34. Del Pesco 1988, 79. Del Pesco believes that the "corridor" refers to the central passage of the colonnade porticoes, but the terms "corridore" and "braccio" are used absolutely consistently in the documents to refer exclusively to the corridor.

35. Brauer and Wittkower 1931, Taf. 68b and 69c.

36. Brauer and Wittkower 1931, 90–91, n. 2, with reference to Ferrabosco and Costaguti 1684, tav. 18, wrote that Bernini had built the staircase into one of the "connecting rooms" systematized by Ferrabosco between the narthex of the church and the old landing of the Scala Regia.

37. Under Paul V, a double portal was also built between the Sala Regia and Cappella Paolina at the Quirinal Palace (Hibbard 1971, 194–98, and fig. 82b). In 1648, Borromini devised a double portal leading from the Lateran Palace to S. Giovanni in Laterano (Connors in Wilton-Ely and Connors 1992).

38. AFSP, Piano I, ser. 4, vol. 29 (Diario dei lavori dei portici circolari, 4 September 1659–13 December 1662). It was compiled by Carlo Drei.

39. Haus 1970, 128; Martinelli et al. 1987, passim. Some of their citations reappear in Del Pesco 1988.

40. Documents in AFSP, Piano I, ser. 4, vol. 29, fols. 116 (16 February 1660) to 127 (1 March 1660) discuss the completion of the pilasters at the end of the four rows of columns "nell'ingresso di palazzo."

41. This is the entry in Alexander's diary referred to above: "È da noi il Cav. Bernino per sfilar quello corridoro" (Del Pesco 1988, 79).

42. AFSP, Piano II, ser. 4, vol. 1, fols. 111–12 (1660). Del Pesco 1988, 79.

43. For Alexander's diary, Del Pesco 1988, 79.

44. Del Pesco 1988, 79: "Doppo pranzo ordiniam al Cav. Bernino il Corritoro, poi é da noi M. V. Spada e il Cardinale a 20 hore."

45. Diary entry for 30 March 1660; Del Pesco 1988, 79.

46. It is still visible at the top of the stairs where it has a thickness of about 1.40 m.

47. Brauer and Wittkower 1931, 66, n. 5, and 91, n. 3, for citation of BAV, Chigi P VII 9, fol. 12, an account of this portion of the work. The four rooms on each floor are easily identified on the plan in BAV, Vat. lat. 10742, fol. 243a, and on an early-seventeenth-century plan, unpublished, that Arnold Nesselrath kindly showed me.

48. AFSP, Piano I, ser. 4, vol. 29, fol. 164 (19 April 1660): "Il Restante degl'homini sono andati a demolire le stanze del Palazzo prossime alla facciata di S. Petri p. non essere sassi di porre in opera." Later, on 16 October 1660, there was

a report of work interrupted by rain: "Li scarpellini hanno proseguito li soliti lavori e li muratori non han potuto [these last two words are canceled] lavorato esendo piovuto" (fol. 311). Such notices can be found intermittently throughout the building process.

49. AFSP, Piano I, ser. 4, vol. 29, fol. 160 (14 April 1660): "Si è principiato a scoprire il tetto delle stanze che sono attaccate alla facciata che si devono demolire." The next day the work continued: "Si seguono a scuoprir le stanze del Palazzo da demolirsi" (fol. 161, 15 April 1660).

50. AFSP, Piano I, ser. 4, vol. 29, fol. 163 (17 April 1660): "Si sono principiato a demolire le stanze del Palazzo vicine all facc.ta di S. P.ro." Also the *misura e stima*, fol. 39v, which itemizes "tagliature di diversi massicci grossi" including a wall "sop.a il braccio log. dalla facciata di S. Pietro a Quella di Palazzo p. 57 [12.73 m.] at.o dal piano del Cortile vecchio sino al fine p. 84 [18.76 m.]." The dimensions correspond to the L-shaped space from the south front of the west apartments to the wall joining the basilica (13.1 m. and 19.2 m. respectively: the differences correspond to the measurements of the buildings before and after the work).

51. AFSP, Piano I, ser. 4, vol. 29, fol. 192 (28 May 1660): "Si segue a sfondar la Volta e muri delle Scale delle Stanze demolite del Palazzo che scendano in S. P.ro." These notices appear through 8 June 1660 (fol. 201). The documents thus reveal a previously unknown connection from the west apartments directly to the basilica. The state of our previous knowledge is summarized in Brauer and Wittkower 1931, 90.

52. The importance of the wall at the Scala del Maresciallo for determining the width of the corridor was noted in Brauer and Wittkower, without emphasizing the crucial fact that this wall is also the north side of the old Scala Regia. My guess is that the western end of the corridor was determined by a staircase that served the west apartments of the Maresciallo. Today, on the story above the vault of the base landing, the stairs end in a hall with a steeply inclined ceiling, where they once continued down to a lower floor that stood in front of the present "finestrone."

53. This is confirmed in the unpublished drawing that Arnold Nesselrath kindly shared with me (note 47).

54. AFSP, Piano I, ser. 1, vol. 9, fasc. 8, fol. 40v: "Per tagliatura del muro dell'Arsenale dell'Artiglieria che faceva Anima, con la scala demolita log. p. 153 [34.1 m.]." The 153 palmi specified here corresponds exactly to the unbroken surface of the diagonal buttress wall drawn under the preliminary scheme for the corridor in Fig. 109.

55. AFSP, Piano I, ser. 4, vol. 29, fols. 195–201 (1–8 June 1660): "Si seguono a demolir le scale." For the discovery of medals from the time of Paul II, see Martinelli in D'Onofrio 1969, 332.

56. 23 June 1660: "circa il gettito pel Corritore" (Del Pesco 1988, 80).

57. AFSP, Piano I, ser. 2, vol. 29, fol. 256 (18 August 1660): "Si cava a Cottimo la Terra dove s'ha da fare il Braccio del Portico che va à Palazzo." The information corresponds with the notice in the pope's diary for 31 August 1660: "M. Dondini = passi dal Bernino, si spedisca a fondar il gettito del braccio = si parli all'Appiani se lo vuol pigliar a cottimo = quanto gli resta al portico" (Del Pesco 1988, 80). Excavations continued on 30 August 1660: "Si segue a Cavar la Terra p. il fondamento da fare del Portico verso S. P.ro" (AFSP, Piano I, ser. 2, vol. 29, fol. 266). The work continued to 6 September 1660 (fol. 272). For the work of excavation from 5 September 1660 to 6 May 1661, we have a *misura e stima* of Giuseppe Boccimazza "cavatore di terra" in AFSP, Piano II, ser. 4, vol. 2, fols. 161–164v.

58. Diary entry for 1 September 1660: "Il C.a Bernino per cominciar il fondamento del braccio martedì prossimo" (Krautheimer and Jones 1975, no. 424; Krautheimer 1985, 173; Del Pesco 1988, 80).

59. AFSP, Piano I, ser. 4, vol. 29, fol. 266 (30 August 1660): "Si segue a Cavar la Terra p. il fondamento da fare del Portico verso S. P.ro." Similar notices appear through 6 September 1660 (fol. 272). The chronology is affirmed in the *misura e stima* for earthmoving and *breccie* from 5 September 1660 to 6 May 1661 in AFSP, Piano II, ser. 4, vol. 2.

60. On 7 September 1660 appears the first notice in the builder's diary "ad empir il fond.o" (AFSP, Piano I, ser. 4, vol. 29, fol. 273). On 15 September 1660: "Si seguono ad empire e cavare li fond.nti del Portico da farsi verso S. P.ro" (fol. 279). These notices continue through 29 November 1660 (fol. 329).

61. A notice on 29 October 1660 refers to the making of "li ponti p. demolir la navicella," and these references continue through 8 November 1660 (AFSP, Piano I, ser. 4, vol. 29, fols. 311–15). The removal takes place from 10 November ("S'è principiata a demolir la navicella") through 23 November 1660 ("S'è finita di demolire il Musaico della Navicella e si fa il ponte p. demolire il Muro di d.a"), as in fols. 316–25. The work "p. levare li travertini del orna.to della navicella" is referred to from 24 November 1660 to 13 January 1661 (fols. 326–56).

62. AFSP, Piano I, ser. 4, vol. 29, fols. 533, 536, 539, for the following notices from the "diario dei lavori": "Si demolisce la fontana della Cortina" (22 October 1661); "Seg.e demolir la fontana" (25 October 1661); "Finita demolire la font.a" (31 October 1661). These notices correspond to undated entries in the *misura e stima* as follows: AFSP, Piano I, ser. 1, vol. 9, fasc. 8, fol. 38: "Per hav. levata d'opera la fontana di fuori con tazza ovata resaltata, con Chocchiglia Delfini, et Ape e portatura dall'altra parte delle Scale" and "Per hav. levata d'opera calata nel Cortile e portata nel Cortile dell Armeria l'Arme di marmo di In.zo X, che stava sop. la Navicella." Apparently there were separate images of St. Peter and St. Paul below that of Giotto's work: "Per hav. tagliato il muro, e levato d'opera l'Imagine di musaico di S. Pietro e S. Paolo, che stavano sotto la Navicella" (fol. 39v).

63. AFSP, Piano I, ser. 4, vol. 29, fol. 325 (23 November

1660): "S'è principiato ad empire il fondam.a sinistra del Portico verso S. Pietro nel Casone dove erano l'Artegliere." On 9 December 1660: "S'è finito d'empire quella parte di d.o fondamento dover era l'Arsenale dell'Artiglierie, e s'è principiato a tirar su il muro a mano con lo scompartim.to de Pilastri" (fol. 335). On 22 January 1661: "Si seguita a murare sopra alli pilastri e Nichioni che sonno nel bracio del Portico della parte verso palazzo" (fol. 363).

64. AFSP, Piano I, ser. 4, vol. 29, fol. 395 (8 March 1661): "Si demolisce la Volta dell'Arsenale ecc. p. il Braccio." The work continued for over a month, after which we find no further mention of the arsenal foundations (cf. fol. 429; 29 April 1661). BAV, Chigi P VII, 9, fol. 12, mentions a portion of the preexisting wing used for the new corridor and measuring 289 ½ × 57 palmi, and those are the dimensions of the wing from the façade of the basilica to the clock tower.

65. AFSP, Piano I, ser. 4, vol. 29, fol. 365 (24 January 1661): "S'è principiato adempire il fondam.to del m.o esteriore del Braccio del Portico."

66. The *misura e stima* of the *cavatore* Giuseppe Boccimazza, cited above, for work dating between 5 September 1660 and 6 May 1661, brought the work of earthmoving to a halt. This corresponds with the notices in the "Diario."

67. "So che N.ro Sig.re vorrebbe prima vedere inviato il braccio, al quale hoggi si lavora; ma a' questo braccio sarà lavoro longo assai, come ho sempre detto non potendoci lavorare che poca gente e convenendo lasciai far presa a' I muri per non far periculare il palazzo contiguo, e però la fattura del braccio bisogna considerarla, come una febre lenta et haver patienza, con andarla medicando a' poco a' poco." Published by Del Pesco 1988, 80–81; Güthlein 1981, 236; and Borsi and Quinterio 1980, 349. The relevance of the letter and Spada's memorable image to the problems of the corridor has not been previously remarked.

68. AFSP, Piano I, ser. 4, vol. 29 (18 November 1660): "Si è principiata à guastar la selciata e demolir il muro dell'Arcipretato del S. P.ro li fondam.ti dell'altra parte del Portico a sinistra della piazza." This notice is confirmed by the diary of Cartari-Febei, busta 191, quoted by Haus 1970, 126–27, n. 84. For the purpose of the current discussion, I have not included the chronology of the south corridor and the south side of the colonnade, except where it affects that of their northern counterparts.

69. The edict is mentioned in the eventual contracts, cited below.

70. This and the following, rather lengthy, scenario are drawn from BAV, Vat. lat. 7939, fols. 311–13, known since the discussion of Prinzivalli 1899, and the reference in Pastor 1923–53, XXXI, 292–93. It has not otherwise been discussed in the literature, although the relevant passage has been published by Morello 1981a, 318–19; and Del Pesco 1988, 82–86 (drawn from the Morello transcription). Güthlein 1981, 236–38, published the same document from the Spada Archives.

71. This is mentioned by Spada. Bernini's preference for piecework was verbalized on his visit to Paris (Chantelou 1985, 222). According to Spada's account, Alexander and Bernini were encouraged by the contract they had negotiated with the *scarpellini* for the south colonnade and hoped to save 40,000–50,000 scudi on the cost of masonry by the same method. For references to the contract for the stone of the south colonnade and corridor, see Del Pesco 1988, 81; and Borsi and Quinterio 1980, 350; both without date. The contract is dated 12 November 1660 and entered in the minutes of the Fabbrica for that date (AFSP, Piano I, ser. 3, vol. 164, fol. 57).

72. AFSP, Piano I, ser. 3, vol. 164, fol. 77.

73. AFSP, Piano I, ser. 3, vol. 164, fol. 77.

74. AFSP, Piano I, ser. 3, vol. 164, fols. 87–90.

75. ASR, 30 Notai Capitolini, officio 38, Giustinianus, anno 1661 (former vol. 39), fols. 105, 106, 151, and fols. 107, 150 (drafts of 29 January 1661); fols. 153, 154, 209, 210 (with notice of the inclusion of the corridors); fols. 155, 156, 207. The contract was also copied *in extenso* into the minutes of the Fabbrica cited above.

76. AFSP, Piano I, ser. 4, vol. 29, fol. 335 (9 December 1660): "Si segue Cavar la Terra p. il fond.to del P.o verso Palazo, e s'è finito d'empire quella parte di d.o fondamento dove era l'Arsenale dell'Artegliere, e s'è principiato a tirar sù il muro à mano con lo scompartim.to de Pilastri." And fol. 363 (22 January 1661): "Si seguita a [murare?] sopra alli pilastri e Nichioni che sonno nel bracio del Portico della parte verso palazzo."

77. AFSP, Piano I, ser. 4, vol. 29, fol. 365 (24 January 1661): "S'è principiato adempire il fondam.to del m.o esteriore del Braccio del Portico dove unito all Portico delle grande [colonne?]."

78. AFSP, Piano I, ser. 4, vol. 29, fols. 371–92 (notices for 4, 5, 9, 15, 21, 28, 29 February and 1–2 March 1661 pertain to the niches); fol. 395 (8 March 1661 for the demolition of the vault of the armory).

79. AFSP, Piano I, ser. 4, vol. 29, fol. 429 (29 April 1661).

80. AFSP, Piano I, ser. 4, vol. 29, fol. 461 (14 June 1661).

81. AFSP, Piano I, ser. 4, vol. 29, fol. 451 (30 May 1661): "Seg.e . . . ad empire il fond.o del Braccio e si pongono in opera li Zoccoli e Basi di d.o ecc." And fol. 459 (11 June 1661): "Seg.e le Base e Pilastrini esteriori, e principiate le Basi e Zoccoli dell'Interiori del Braccio."

82. AFSP, Piano I, ser. 4, vol. 29, fol. 325 (23 November 1660): "S'è principiato a Cavar il fond.o d. m.o nella Cordonata avanti l'Horologio." This cordonata refers to the outdoor ramp from the piazza to the main portal under the clock tower.

83. AFSP, Piano I, ser. 1, vol. 9, fasc. 8, fol. 56: "Per haver mossi e scanzati diversi pezzi di Trevertini p. la Piazza p. fare cinq. strade da traversare le Carrozze p. le feste di Pasqua, et in altri tempi."

84. AFSP, Piano I, ser. 4, vol. 29, fol. 460 (13 June 1661): "S'è finito il muro della Scala dietro il frontesp.o e principiate a porre in opera li scalini."

85. AFSP, Piano I, ser. 4, vol. 29, fol. 529 (18 October 1661):

"E levar li scalini della porta a piedi la Scala Regia." And fol. 531 (19 October 1661): "Si seguano à Murare li Piloni del Braccio, e demolir il muro avanti la Porta vecchia à piedi la Scala Regia."

86. AFSP, Piano I, ser. 4, vol. 29, fols. 531v ("S'è calata l'Arme di Paolo V sop.a il Portone"), 532–36.

87. AFSP, Piano I, ser. 4, vol. 29, fol. 543 (7 November 1661: "Ponti e Armat.re p. la Volta del braccio"); fol. 544 (8 November 1661: "Si lavorano le Volte delle Nicchie sotto il Palazzo incontro le finestre. Si demolisce la Cortina p. porre in opera l'Architrave e Cornice del Braccio"); fol. 553 (18 November 1661: "Si son tirati sopra la Cortina 4 Archi del Braccio").

88. AFSP, Piano I, ser. 4, vol. 29, fol. 548 (14 November 1661) is the last mention of the curtain wall being pulled down. Compare this to the chronology outlined in note 87.

89. AFSP, Piano I, ser. 4, vol. 29, fol. 580 (24 December 1661): "S'è chiusa la Volta del Braccio attutto l'ultimo finstrone sotto Palazzo."

90. AFSP, Piano I, ser. 4, vol. 29, fol. 586 (5 January 1662): "Si leva la terra a piedi la Cordonata dell'Horologio. Si fanno li ponti p. demolir l'horologio."

91. AFSP, Piano I, ser. 4, vol. 29, fol. 585 (4 January 1662): "E levata la machina dell'horologio." And fol. 586 (5 January 1662, quoted in note 90 above).

92. AFSP, Piano I, ser. 4, vol. 29, fol. 589 (10 January 1662): "Ponti horologio e levata la Croce e pall di q.llo." And fol. 590 (11 January 1662): "Seg. li ponti e principiata demolir la piramide."

93. AFSP, Piano I, ser. 4, vol. 29, fol. 600 (26 January 1662): "Seg. l'horologio et accomodar la mostra nella testa d'una habit.e di Palazzo." Relevant notices continue through 10 February 1662 (fol. 612). Accompanying the transfer of the clock were the three bells that rang the hours. When reinstalled on the wing of Paul V, the face of the clock was modernized. AFSP, Piano I, ser. 1. vol. 9, fols. 45–46, for items pertaining to the "Horologgio Novo," including the notice "per la fodera di matt. . . . p. quan.o tiene la mostra di d. horologgio di Diametro p. 20 [4.46 m.] incollata sopra, che è dipinto a fresco." This information can now be added to the account of the Vatican clocks and bells in Corbo 1978.

94. AFSP, Piano I, ser. 4, vol. 29, fol. 659 (15 April 1662): "S'è calata la Madonna di musaico dell'horol.o."

95. AFSP, Piano I, ser. 4, vol. 29, fol. 688 (25 May 1662): "finita la terra à piedi la Scala e fatta la salita p. la processione"; fol. 697 (6 June 1662): "Si sono guasto I tuti i ponti del Braccio per la pricisione [processione]"; fol. 698 (9 June 1662): "Si sono fati li ponti dove pasava la pricisione. Si è ricomiciato ad dimolire la arlogio."

96. AFSP, Piano I, ser. 4, vol. 29, fols. 25v–28v. A caption to a recent photograph of the Portone di Bronzo gives the date of its installation as 1667, which would seem a misprint for 1661 (cf. Redig De Campos 1982, figure on p. 37).

97. AFSP, Piano I, ser. 4, vol. 29, fol. 38v.

98. AFSP, Piano I, ser. 4, vol. 29, fol. 718 (5 July 1662): "Si

è finita la volta ditro all'arlogio"; fol. 720 (7 July 1662): "Si seguono a fare le nicie avanti all'arlogio"; fol. 724 (12 July 1662): "Si è comicata la volta grande al atacho del Braccio avanti all'arlogio."

99. Notices in AFSP, Piano I, ser. 4, vol. 29, fols. 742, 748, 752 (5, 14, and 21 August 1662). Cf. fol. 754 (23 August 1662): "Seg.e a tagliare la platea dell'horologio" and "Si segue à tagliare il m.o del med.o p. l'ultima Nicchia del Braccio"; fol. 763 (4 September 1662): "Si è finito cavare il fondamento soto all'arlogio che è l'ultimo pezzo del Braccio." A mysterious and tantalizing exception to these conclusions is provided on the last folio of AFSP, Piano I, ser. 4, vol. 29, fol. 830 (13 December 1662), which pertains to the demolition of the clock itself. The subsequent volume with notices beginning on 14 December 1662 is lost.

100. D'Onofrio 1969, 331.

101. AFSP, Piano I, ser. 4, vol. 29, fols. 529, 531, 541.

102. For the latter, AFSP, Piano I, ser. 4, vol. 29, fol. 557, 560, 564, 586, 589.

103. AFSP, Piano I, ser. 4, vol. 29, fol. 593 (16 January 1662): "m.ro dell'Arcone in testa al Braccio."

104. AFSP, Piano I, ser. 4, vol. 29, fols. 635–36: "Si lavora l'Arco che fa della lunetta della Volta sopra la P.a a piedi la Scala Regia e si tagliano l'imposte dell'altro incontro."

105. AFSP, Piano I, ser. 4, vol. 29, fol. 637 (16 March 1662) and fol. 641 (21 March 1662): "S'è chiusa tutta la Volta in testa al Braccio à piedi la Scala Regia."

106. AFSP, Piano I, ser. 4, vol. 29, fol. 664: "Si taglia l'ultimo muro in testa al Braccio."

107. AFSP, Piano I, ser. 4, vol. 29, fols. 771, 772, 774, 775, 776, 780, 786.

108. AFSP, Piano I, ser. 4, vol. 29, fol. 788 (7 October 1662): "Si e comicato a levare la terra et chalcinaccio soto all Braccio per trovare il piano." The landing is probably the one that connects the shorter lower flight with the longer upper flight of stairs.

109. AFSP, Piano I, ser. 4, vol. 29, fol. 798.

110. AFSP, Piano I, ser. 4, vol. 29, fols. 806, 807, 809, 822, 826. This is also mentioned in BAV, Chigi P. VII. 9, fol. 12. Brauer and Wittkower 1931, 90, n. 3, suggested that Maderno had moved the lower end of the cordonata 15 palmi west of its original location and that Bernini had removed it eastward again.

111. Brauer and Wittkower 1931, 93, cite the Italian edition of Pastor, which corresponds to Pastor 1923–53, XXXI, 294, n. 7.

112. AFSP, Piano I, ser. 4, vol. 29, fol. 515.

113. AFSP, Piano I, ser. 4, vol. 29, fol. 813 (9 November 1662): "S'è finito l'ult.o pezo di volta del Braccio."

114. AFSP, Piano I, ser. 4, vol. 29, fol. 830 (13 December 1662): "Seg. a demolir l'horologio con otto homini."

115. 26 December 1662: "Il Cav. Bernino ha portati a veder I disegni rifiniti della Scala Regia che mette nel braccio" (Morello 1981b, 334; not cited in Del Pesco 1988).

116. AFSP, Piano I, ser. 1, vol. 9, fasc. 8.

117. AFSP, Piano I, ser. 1, vol. 9, fasc. 8, fol. 1.

118. AFSP, Piano I, ser. 1, vol. 9, fasc. 8, fol. 2.

119. AFSP, Piano I, ser. 1, vol. 9, fols. 50–53v (22 October 1664): "Scaletta, che dal repiano dove stava la statua di S. Pietro và nel Cortile di Sala Ducale" and "Per hav. levati d'opera li conci della Nicchia di S. Pietro Stipiti soglia, et Architrave, e membretti con sua Cimasa, e frontispitiio dritto."

120. AFSP, Piano I, ser. 1, vol. 9, fol. 56v: "Per la fatt., e disfattura di un pezzo di tetto a padiglione à capo il braccio dove si è fatto il finestrone a terzacuto log. p. 39 ½ [8.82 m.] lag. p. 45 [10.05 m.]"; and then on the same folio: "Per la fattura, e disfattura di un'altro pezzo di tetto fatto à secco sop.a detto mentre si lavorava il detto terzacuto log. p. 47 [10.5 m.] lag. p. 26 [6.06 m.]." The pointed arch of the finestrone has a maximum width of about 7.5 m., which would be easily covered by the dimensions of the rebuilt roof that is referred to here.

121. AFSP, Piano I, ser. 1, vol. 9, fasc. 8, fol. 40.

122. AFSP, Piano I, ser. 1, vol. 9, fasc. 8, fol. 40v.

123. AFSP, Piano I, ser. 1, vol. 9, fasc. 8, fol. 40v.

124. Most of the risers in this flight are 9.5 or 10 cm. high, and none is greater than 11.5 cm. in height.

125. AFSP, Piano I, ser. 4, vol. 29, fol. 460 (13 June 1661): "Sè finito il muro della Scala dietro il frontesp.o e principiati a porre in opera li scalini."

126. Hibbard 1971, 44–47 (with ground plan), 127–29. The palace was begun in 1598, and the stairs were built in 1606.

127. AFSP, Piano I, ser. 1, vol. 9, fasc. 8, covering expenses approved on 28 March 1665 ("Misura e stima de lavori diversi di muro . . . nella Costruttione del novo Braccio, che dal Portico Ovale guida alla Scala Regia, e cala nel Portico della medema Chiesa [St. Peter's]").

128. See respectively, AFSP, Piano I, ser. 1, vol. 2, no. 37, covering expenses approved on 28 March 1665 ("Mis.ra, e stima de lavori diversi di muro fatti nella Scala Regia, e Appartamento della Spetiaria, et altro sopra detto"); and no. 38, covering expenses approved on 23 September 1667 ("Mis.ra, e stima dell'opera di muro, et altro fatto p. servitio della R. Fab.a di S. Pietro p. ornare la scala che da Sala Reggia scende nel Cortile d.to della Floreria, et altri lavori di stucco nelli repiani della Scala Reggia p. finimento di d.o fatto doppo la mis.ra spedita di d.a Scala").

CHAPTER SIX. Bernini's Staircase, 1663–1666

1. Appendix, with text from Fontana 1694. Braham and Hager 1977, 13, 35–38, maintain that Fontana was composing the book in 1680, and its text was essentially complete in 1687.

2. Lassels 1670, 49.

3. Jestaz 1966, 174. De Cotte described the staircase as *large*.

4. Alexander's diary for 26 December 1662: "Martedì il Cav. Bernino ha portati a veder i disegni rifiniti della Scala Regia che mette nel braccio" (Krautheimer and Jones 1975, 643; Morello 1981b, 334).

5. These features are visible from the roofs of the Scala Regia, which I visited and discussed with Joseph Connors. Our exchanges helped formulate a part of this argument. The

new air conditioning for the Sistine Chapel in this area may now obscure a view of these parts of the palace.

6. Panofsky 1919, especially 242–43, 246–48; Evers 1967, especially 191–93, 197; Fagiolo 1967, cat. 197.

7. Appendix; Fontana 1694, 233.

8. Cf. Ehrle and Egger 1933.

9. Evers 1967, 197.

10. The diagram is taken from a drawing made in the late 1980s to study the feasibility of renovating the neglected spaces of the old palace to the south of the stairs. I wish to thank engineer Ercadi and architect Facchini for showing me this and other materials, and both Dr. Constantini and Dr. Stoppa for permission to publish them.

11. Voss 1922, 12–14, fig. 5. Later literature is cited below.

12. Kieven 1993, 172–73, cat. 59 (with color illustration) attributes the drawing to Carlo Fontana. This suggestion is plausible on the basis of style and circumstance, given that Fontana did work at the Scala Regia. Although he is not mentioned by name in documents, his detailed analysis of the construction process supports his own claim to being part of the crew (Fontana 1694, 234, and Appendix).

13. For a list of Panofsky's writings on perspective and a brief discussion of them, see Veltman 1980.

14. Panofsky 1919, 244. These are some of the reasons for the strength of Voss's analysis, as noted already by Thoenes 1977, 324 and 327.

15. Panofsky 1921–22.

16. Brauer and Wittkower 1931, 95 and n. 3.

17. Voss 1922, 12, points out that the intermediate landing on the Munich drawing is located after the 27th step. The west wall of the Sala Regia intersects the stairs at the 30th step on Fontana's engraving. These observations presume steps of equal dimensions.

18. Published by Brauer and Wittkower 1931, 95–96, as autograph. Regarding attribution, Harris 1977, xxii, cat. no. 79, considers this "a little more mechanical" than other drawings for medals generally attributed to Bernini. In *Bernini in Vaticano* 1981, 300, no. 304, Worsdale argues that the drawing is autograph and that the subject accounts for its mechanical aspects. Whitman and Varriano 1983, 105, no. 86, consider the drawing "so dryly linear that it must be from the hand of an assistant rather than by Bernini himself." Having seen other drawings for medals attributed to Bernini (illustrated in Harris 1977, xxii, cat. 79) I doubt that the Scala Regia medal drawing is autograph, but I do believe it reflects Bernini's design process, as does Worsdale 1986, 103.

19. Brauer and Wittkower 1931, 95.

20. Braham and Hager 1977, 36, no. 4. The discrepancies in design and dimensions when compared with the monument or Tessin's drawings have not been noted.

21. See Frommel 1985, figs. 222, 224. See Waddy 1990, 242, for Bernini's use of the motif at Palazzo Barberini, which offers just one conspicuous example among many of a staircase lined, like the Scala Regia, by columns.

22. For the medal see Brauer and Wittkower 1931, 95; Bartolotti 1967, 67, E. 63; *Bernini in Vaticano* 1981, 300–1, n.

305 (with bibliography); Whitman and Varriano 1983, 105, no. 86 (with bibliography); Varriano 1984, 72. For literature on Bernini and papal medals, see Varriano 1987.

23. On the basis of these observations, I do not believe that the medalist Gaspare Morone was responsible for the changes between the drawing and the medal, as Whitman and Varriano suggest.

24. Courtright in Lavin et al. 1981, 245, n. 6.

25. Published by Fischer 1928, 26; and subsequently in Brauer and Wittkower 1931, 95, n. 1, and 109. More recent literature includes Harris 1977, xxi, cat. nos. 75–76; Mehnert 1981, 33, no. 44, and 34, no. 46; Ostrow in Lavin et al. 1981, 180 (bibliography on p. 175, cat. nos. 41 and 42); Birindelli 1982, 66–67, n. 7, and 69, n. 8.

26. The photomontage appears in Lavin et al. 1981, 343, fig. D.

27. The floral molding on the verso may be a study for the moldings of the vault above the base landing, the intermediate landing, or the moldings of the coffers in the barrel vault, but the verso could also pertain to a different commission.

28. Birindelli 1982, 66, n. 7.

29. I cannot follow Birindelli's (1982) discussion, 69, n. 8, when he tries to explain how the freehand sketches of diagonal lines and equilateral shapes in the upper right of Leipzig 7901 represent a working out of the transition between horizontal and inclined trabeation. It is an important point because Birindelli maintains that the transition involves only one serliana, not two, and hence represents a solution closer to the final one than the section depicts.

30. This observation may qualify the conclusion (Kitao 1977, 85) that Fontana did not have access to Bernini's designs.

31. Ostrow has a parenthetical question mark on this point in Lavin et al. 1981, 175, cat. nos. 41 and 42. His caution is not necessary.

32. Birindelli 1981, 66, n. 7, and 69, n. 8, considers them autograph.

33. Harris 1977, xxi, cat. nos. 75 and 76 (the date is given in the relevant captions to the illustrations); Ostrow in Lavin et al. 1977, 180, who speaks of the drawings for the putti in relation to a final enlargement of the Cathedra Petri scheme c. 1660–61.

34. In my opinion Ostrow has correctly identified the putto in Lavin et al. 1981, 175, cat. no. 41, in the upper right of the gloria. The identification of others are, for me, less clear.

35. Battaglia 1943, 176–78, for payments to Lazzaro Morelli, Pietro Sassi, Antonio Raggi, and Paolo Naldini for work in wax, stucco, and metal, for work on angels, putti, drapery, and clouds. The terra-cotta bozzetto allegedly for the Cathedra Petri has found so little acceptance in the literature that we do not consider it here. See Rossacher 1967b; and the objections raised by Arnoldi 1971, and Wittkower 1985, 525, n. 25.

36. The hall outside of this room, now called the Camera Sanitaria, is two steps (16 cm. and 20 cm.) above the floor level of the Sala Regia. The room is three steps above the

hall (each of these steps is 18 cm.) At the window of the palace directly over the finestrone there is a final step (25 cm.) inserted in the thickness of the wall. A 1.15-m. gain in height over the level of the Sala Regia floor thus helps to encase the remarkable height of the vault over the new base landing.

37. Measuring such heights with modest means (hand-held infra-red beam, balloons, telephoto lens) is susceptible to a range of error that I have tried to correct by repeating the measurements and averaging the results.

38. Published by Voss 1922, 15, Abb. 7; and subsequently in Mehnert 1981, 44, cat. no. 71; Brauer and Wittkower 1931, 96; Courtright in Lavin et al. 1981, 241–46. For the verso, see Klinger in Lavin et al. 1981, 248–52; and now Ostrow 1991, 82.

39. Brauer and Wittkower 1931, 96.

40. For the projects see Blunt 1967, Preimesberger 1978, and Zollikofer 1994, respectively.

41. The backward-flying angel is a related type, for which see Lavin 1980, fig. 183 and Brauer and Wittkower 1931, Taf. 183, for the Cornaro Chapel and the tomb of Alexander VII, respectively (Courtright in Lavin et al. 1981, 246, n. 12).

42. The identification of Leipzig 7809r and v, and 7810r, was made in Brauer and Wittkower 1931, 96, n. 2; but the reading of the drawings is mine.

43. The architectural motif in the upper left of Leipzig 7809 verso is the terminal molding of the arch around the finestrone. Bernini used the same motif at the ends of the ribs in the dome at Ariccia. The motif appears in the church and in preparatory drawings for it; see Brauer and Wittkower 1931, 125 and Taf. 97a, 169c, 174b. The hexagonal coffers on the rectos of Leipzig 7809 and 7810 also suggest that these sheets were consulted when the Ariccia dome was being designed. The figures of Fame do not appear at Ariccia.

44. The figures on the south side of the narthex are discussed again in Chapter 9.

45. See Brauer and Wittkower 1931, 96; Courtright in Lavin et al. 1981, 243 and 245, nn. 10, 11 (with acknowledgments to Lavin).

46. See Chapter 8.

47. Cited in Chapter 3, note 50, in connection with the replacement of the statue of St. Peter and in Chapter 8 in relation to the issue discussed here.

48. For BAV, Chigi, inv. 24915 and 24927, see Brauer and Wittkower 1931, 23, n. 3; *Bernini in Vaticano* 1981, 104–5; Morello 1993, 91 (color plate), 164 (cat. 61).

49. Cf. Pollak 1928–31, II, 426–508; Lavin 1968, 19–37, for the history of the piers.

50. Given the shape of the drawing, I do not believe it could have been part of the Constantine iconography for the north aisle of the basilica.

51. Bernini 1713, 101–2. Domenico composed the *Vita* before his father's death, as D'Onofrio 1966, has demonstrated.

52. Baldinucci 1682, 109. For an English version of this account, see the translation of Baldinucci's *Vita* by Catherine

Enggass, with introduction by Robert Enggass, University Park, 1966, 43.

53. For its origins, see Chapter 2. Pietrangeli et al., 1992, 40, has an illustration.

54. The dimensions on Tessin's plans correspond to measurements I have taken at the site.

55. For the record, the distance between the centers of the isolated piers in the gallery is 4.85 m. The distance between the centers of the fourth set of columns is 4.94 m.

56. For what follows, see AFSP, Piano I, ser. 1, vol. 2, no. 37, a *misura e stima* for work between 21 February 1661 and 31 December 1664 (unpublished). Individual entries are not dated.

57. AFSP, Piano I, ser.1, vol. 2, no. 37, fol. 1r: "Per hav. disfatto il Tetto sop.a d.a Scala, che pigli aria sop. tutti due li branchi" and "Per hav. tornato à refare il sud.o Tetto p. essersi rialzato l'Appartam.to."

58. AFSP, Piano I, ser. 1, vol. 2, no. 37, fol. 1v: "Per hav. tornato, à desfare, e refare parte di d.o tetto p. dar lume al 2.o branco di Scale, che entra in Sala Regia" and "Per haver refatto il tetto sop.a il 2.o branco della Scala Regia dove sono li Lucenarii."

59. Alexander's diary for 6 July 1664: "Col Bernino per l'Ariccia, e pe'lumi del 2. branco della scala regia, fà aria fresca" (fol. 317, col. 2; Morello 1981b, 337). Mention of "aria fresca" may indicate operable windows or, more likely, simply windows onto the open air.

60. Alexander's diary for 31 August 1664: "il Cav. Bernino mostra i saggi de vetri pel cielo della seconda branca della Scala regia" (fol. 323v, col. 2; Morello 1981b, 337).

61. AFSP, Piano I, ser. 1, vol. 2, no. 37, fol. 2r: "Per la mett.a in opera di n.o 7 paradossi sotto li sud.i Lucenarii log. p. 17 [3.79 m.] con il costo di tre di d.ti messi con scommodo."

62. AFSP, Piano I, ser. 1, vol. 2, no. 37, fols. 5, 5v: "Per la fattura del tetto sopra uno di detti Lucenarii, e poi disfatto"; "M.o di un arco fatto sotto uno delli sudetti Lucenarii . . . quale è disfatto"; "Per hav. fatto un pezzo di tetto, e poin disfatto, e poin tornato à refare, e ridisfare . . . e murato n. sei bugi di arcareccie."

63. AFSP, Piano I, ser. 1, vol. 2, no. 37, fol. 5v: "Per hav.r fatto un modello di d.o Lucenaro à posticcio p. poter fare tutti l'altri son andate n.o 16 giornate d'homini." The historical precedent was surely Michelangelo's unexecuted skylights for the Laurentian Library vestibule (my thanks to John Pinto for the reference to Ackerman 1964).

64. Alexander's diary for 31 August 1664: "Il Cav. Bernino mostra i saggi de vetri pel cielo della seconda branca della Scala regia" (Morello 1981b, 323v, col. 2).

65. Chattard 1762–67, II, 11–12, is our eighteenth-century source.

66. See Alexander's diary for 20 January 1663: "Il Cav. Bernino è da noi à 22 ho. col disegno della Scala Regia, e sopra il gettito" (Morello 1981b, 264, col. 2).

67. Alexander's diary entry for 26 January 1663: "Scendiamo per la Scala Regia in S. Pietro" (Chigi O VI 58, fol. 517v; previously unpublished).

68. Alexander's diary entry for 30 March 1663: "Co' nostri scendiamo per la cordonata, passiamo a piedi tutto il Portico, e poi ci poniamo in sedia" (Morello 1981b, 270, col. 1; Del Pesco 1988, 91).

69. In fact, the notice published by Fraschetti 1900, 317, pertains to the stairs of the Palazzo Ludovisi (Palazzo Montecitorio) and dates from 1653. It is a report from Giulio delli Oddi, who served as the Modenese ambassador in Rome only until 1654. The document is to be found in the Archivio di Stato in Modena, Cancelleria ducale, ambasciatori e correspondenti estensi, Roma, busta 262, 9 April 1653. The document was also published in Borsi et al. 1972, 59; and subsequently in Borsi and Quinterio 1980, 315. The latter references cite the Archivio di Stato, Modena, Dispacci ambasciatori, Roma, b. 218, and do not make reference to Fraschetti's earlier publication, its erroneous date, or its association with the Scala Regia.

70. AFSP, Piano II, ser. 4, vol. 4, fol. 104, is the "Lista delli mesi aprile e maggio 1663" which is part of the "Giustificazione della Lista Spedita li p.o Giug.o 1663." It should be recognized that this *giustificazione* is the basis for the payment of 1 June 1663, the earliest document published in Borsi and Quinterio 1980, 356. The lack of references in Borsi and Quinterio 1980, to the appropriate *giustificazioni* and the inexplicable omission of notices in volumes consulted by the authors compromise their gathering of archival material. This first payment was made to the capomastri: "A m.ro Gio. Andrea appiano e compagni acconto delli lavori de tevertini che d.o fanno p. la nova scala che si fa."

71. AFSP, Piano II, ser. 4, vol. 4, fols. 248–248v, partially published in Borsi and Quinterio 1980, 356 (not included in Borsi and Quinterio 1984): "Per haver dato di gesso con colla alle tele che fingono l'arco, e cornicione a piedi alla Scala, che sale alla Paulina." The payment dates for the work are May and October 1663.

72. Archivio di Stato, Modena, Cancelleria ducale, avvisi e notizie dall'estero, busta 55, 30 June 1663, reads as follows: "Volevano i Spag.li p. mantenimento della loro gravità che la Chinea fosse riceuta al Vaticano conforme al solito, e se bene tal volta è ciò seguito al Quirinale è stato p. qualche Indisposit.ne de Papi, mà la bontà del Card.le d'Aragona restò appagata p. che Sua S.tà gli disse che si contentasse cosi p. questa volta à Causa della fabbrica della nuova scala che si fà al Vaticano p. andare alla Sala Regia passando hora il Papa p. la scala segreta della Cappella del Sacram.to non era dovere che a(?bassa) alla porta venisse alla Porta della Chiesa p. tal ricevim.to e poi tornasse indietro."

73. "Pagamento fatto a Gaspare Moreni [*sic*] di scudi 3 per 10 medaglie di Rame con l'impronta della scala Regia poste sotto le colonne della medesima scala" (Fraschetti 1900, 318, n. 1, citing AFSP, arm. IV, vol. 219, p. 23).

74. Krautheimer and Jones 1975, 221, no. 731; Morello 1981b, 336 (14 February 1664). In addition, in reporting a papal visit to the stairs, an avviso of 19 April 1664 speaks of the medal in the past tense: "Martedì al S.tà sua se ne tornò (dal Vaticano) à stantiare al Quirinale, mà prima andò considerando la fabrica della nuova, e magnifica scala che hà

fatta improntare nelle medaglie col motto, Est scala ad au-lam, quae ducit ad coelum" (the variant legend must be an inaccuracy; Archivio di Stato Modena, Cancelleria ducale, avvisi e notizie dall'estero, b. 55; Rossi 1939, 376).

75. A notation in Alexander's diary for 23 May 1663 reads: "scale che stian bene" (Morello 1981b, 276, col. 1). See also the entry for 2 December 1663: "Doppo pranzo siamo col Cav. Bernino a lungo fino alle 21 ho. che siamo alle 40 ho., poi per la Scala Regia caliamo in S. Pietro, ove anco vediamo la Cattedra col C. Barber.o e pel braccio, e pe-'portici e per Parione" (Morello 1981b, 336, fol. 292v, col. 2).

76. BAV, Vat. lat. 12332, fol. 150v (13 April 1664).

77. AFSP, Piano II, ser. 4, vol. 5, fols. 5, 7 (Borsi and Quinterio 1980, 356): "Al d. [Giacomo Balsimelli fattore] . . . ad un murat.re che hà lavorato a rimett.re in op.ra li scalini del 2.o banco della Scala Regia" and "Al detto [Balsimelli] . . . p. mancia p. haver por.e in opera, tutte le colonne della Scala Regia p. ord. del Cav.re [Bernini]."

78. Cf. the painter's payment for "il ponte a piedi la Scala Regia e la tenda della loggia della Bened." in AFSP, Piano II, ser. 4, vol. 5, fol. 9 (Borsi and Quinterio 1980, 356, with mistaken reference to fol. 9v).

79. Alexander's diary entry for 14 April 1664: "Cav. Bernino = un altra scala per scender in S. Pietro dal Cortile della Cisterna – le Nicchie della Scala Regia stiano nel piano per uso de'pellegrini" (Morello 1981b, 336, fol. 308, col. 2).

80. See Chapter 3, note 50.

81. AFSP, Piano II, ser. 4, vol. 5, fol. 25: "P. tassa pagato à quattro scarpellini, che hanno lavorato à ritoccare li scalini vecchi p. la scaletta nuova a piedi la Scala Regia." The older stairs were taken from the extensive flights that connected the former base landing to both the Maresciallo and its west apartments.

82. AFSP, Piano I, ser. 1, vol. 9, fols. 50–53v, for the entries following the date of 22 November 1664. These include works on the "Scaletta, che dal repiano dove stava la statua di S. Pietro và nel Cortile di Sala Ducale." Included are notices like the following: "Per hav. levato d'opera la Statua di S. Pietro di marmo at.o p. 14, e portata nel Cortile delli falegname; Per la mettitura in opera di n.o otto scalini del p.o branchetto; Per la mettitura in opera di n.o 41 scalino nella Scala che rivolta sim.e alli sud.i."

83. Morello 1981b, 337 (13 July 1664) as in note 47 above.

84. ASFP, Piano I, ser. 1, 9, fol. 56v: "Per la fatt., e disfattura di un pezzo di tetto a padiglione à capo il braccio dove si è fatto il finestrone a terzacuto log. p. 39 ½ [8.82 m.] lag. p. 45 [10.05 m.]," and then on the same folio: "Per la fattura, e disfattura di un'altro pezzo di tetto fatto à secco sop.a detto mentre si lavorava il detto terzacuto log. p. 47 [10.5 m.] lag. p. 26 [6.06 m.]."

85. Alexander's diary for 31 March 1665: "Vediamo la Cattedra, e la Armi, la silicata del Portico, la scala pel cortiletto, e per la Regia sagliamo alle Stanze" (fol. 345 v, col. 1; Morello 1981b, 338).

86. "1666. Decreto della Congregazione di pagare a Pietro Girelli gli apparati pel portico e cuopire il rustico della scala nuova per la processione del Corpus Domini negli anni 1664 e 1665 per questa sola volta" (Fraschetti 1900, 318, n. 3, citing AFSP, arm. VIII, vol. 47, p. 569).

87. The *misura e stima* of Brogi, Agustone, and Ustino includes work datable, at least in theory, between 21 February 1661 and the end of December 1664. See AFSP, Piano I, ser. 1, vol. 2, no. 37: "Mis.ra, e stima de lavori diversi di muro fatti nella Scala Regia, e Appartamento della Spetiaria, et altro sopra detto p. servitio della Rev.da Fabrica di S. Pietro detti lavori fatti à tutte Spese, e fattura delli Capi Mas.ri Muratori Simone Brogi, Gio. Albini Agustone, e Pietro Ustini Compagni." The work itemized in this document can have been executed only after a definitive plan for the Scala Regia had been established, and we know that Alexander VII was still perusing designs in December 1662. The early date on the document enabled the payments to be made according to the contract established with the Fabbrica in January and February 1661. Reimbursements for this *misura e stima* were approved for payment by the Fabbrica only on 28 March 1665. This date is confirmed by a payment in AFSP, Piano I, ser. armadi, vol. 353. Fraschetti 1900, 318, n. 2 (citing AFSP, arm. IV, vol. 219, p. 23), offers a document of June 1665 to the effect that the stairs and the colonnade were finished, but I have not located this source.

88. AFSP, Piano II, ser. 4, vol. 5, fols. 11, 114: "A m.ro Pietro Sassi per fare di stucco l'arme di N.S.e sopra l'entrata della scala."

89. AFSP, Piano II, ser. 4, vol. 5, fols. 19, 22v, 25: "Al Sig. Ercole Ferrata . . . a conto delle due statue di stucco, che fa p. reggere l'Arme di N.S.; Al Sig. Ercole Ferrata . . . p. le due statue di stucco che reggono l'arme di N.S. nella nuova scala." These payments correspond to *giustificazioni* on fols. 204, 210, and 235, respectively (partially published in Schiavo 1981, 61). From the last page we learn that the two figures were 16 palmi high: "Per prezzo e saldo delle due statue du stuccho di palmi sedici alte quale rappresentano due Fame . . . sopra l'ingresso della scala."

90. See Wittkower 1966, cat. nos. 45, 47, 56, 58, 61, 63, 71, 72. Ferrata may also have worked on a portrait in the Cornaro Chapel (cf. Lavin 1980, 200). For Ferrata's role in the Bernini workshop, see the references listed in Tratz 1988, 483, s.v.

91. AFSP, Piano II, ser. 4, vol. 6, 25v: "A Carlo Padredio scudi Tre e 40 m.ta, sono p. haver fatto, e fornito à tutta Sua robba doi Trombe di abeto sottile p. le fame à piedi la Scala Regia." A turner perhaps by avocation, Padredio also published an accurate seventeenth-century guide plan to St. Peter's.

92. AFSP, Piano II, ser. 4, vol. 6, fols. 2, 7, 12, 19, 26 (some fols. referenced in Schiavo 1981, 61). All of these notices resemble the first (fol. 2): "Al S.r Paolo Naldini Scultore scudi Trenta m.ta à c.o delle figure, e Putti, che d.o fà di Stucco nella Scala." They correspond to the list of expenses (*liste*) on fols. 76, 109, 145, 165, 196.

93. AFSP, Piano II, ser. 4, vol. 6, fols. 12, 19 (partially published in Schiavo 1981, 61, and cited in *Bernini in Vaticano*

1981, 145). Second payment similar to the first: "S.re Lazzaro Morilli Scultore scudi Venti m.ta à c.o delli lavori di Scoltura di Stucco che d.o fa p. la Scala." They correspond to the *liste* on fols. 145 and 165.

94. See the biography and references compiled by Falaschi in Martinelli et al. 1987, 219–21, as well as her comments on Morelli's special role in arranging for the statues of the colonnade (pp. 28–30). Cf. also the references in Tratz 1988, 483.

95. See the biography with extensive references by R. Carloni in Martinelli et al. 1987, 221–23; and the references in Tratz 1988, 483.

96. AFSP, Piano I, ser. 1, vol. 2, no. 38: "Mis.a, e stima dell'opera di muro, et altro fatto p. servitio della R. Fab.a di S. Pietro p. ornare la scala che da Sala Reggia scende nel Cortile d.to della Floreria, et altri lavori di stucco nelli repiani della Scala Reggia p. finim.to di d.o fatto. Il tutto fatto dalli Mas.ri Simone Ambrogi, Gio. Albino Agustone, e Pietro Ustini Comp.i Capo Mas.ri mu.ri." It was signed by Bernini and his brother Luigi and Bendetto Drei, the soprastante. Payments were approved on 23 September 1667. The document is almost entirely published by Borsi and Quinterio 1980, 357–359 (document omitted in the Eng. ed., Borsi and Quinterio 1984).

97. Borsi and Quinterio 1980, 357, gives the date incorrectly as 13 September 1667.

98. AFSP, Piano I, ser. armadi, vol. 353 (Giustificazione dei mandati, unpaginated). The payment includes 16,591.67 scudi "per una mis.a della Scala Regia" and 1,487.19 scudi "per altra mis.a p. resid.o della Scala Regia." The first figure refers to our previously unpublished AFSP, Piano I. ser. 1, vol. 2, n. 37; the second figure refers to AFSP, Piano I, ser. 1, vol. 2, n. 38, cited by several authors.

99. AFSP, Piano II, ser. 4, vol. 6, fols. 74–75v: "Conto della R.da Fab.a di S. Pietro de lavori fatti da me Andrea Haghe Vetraro . . . p. servitio della Nuova Scala Regia." The earliest work is dated 14 August 1664. Work on 3 October 1664 was "p. ha. fatto la prova della stella, e colore torchino . . . e ripresa . . . p. ordine del S.r Cavall. Bernini." He was also paid "p. hav. fatto di nuovo una fin.ra di vetri dipinti torchini fatti à fuoco con le Stelle, tre p. sportelli . . . tra tutti tre sportelli," work done on 18 November 1664. The bills were all submitted on 30 January 1665.

100. AFSP, Piano II, ser. 4, vol. 5, fols. 229–230 is a bill of Andrea Haghe for the windows. The document for Schor's payment of 22 scudi "p. haver dipinto con Azuro oltramarino li due vani grandi, che danno lume il secondo braccio della Scala, che va in Sala Regia" is dated 10 December 1664 (fol. 27).

101. AFSP, Piano II, ser. 4, vol. 6, fol. 205.

102. Cf. payment to the painter Francesco Spagna in AFSP, Piano II, ser. 4, vol. 6, fol. 18 (24 April 1665): "P. spesa fatta p. un Sportello di vetro dipinto à foco p. la Scala Regia."

103. AFSP, Piano II, ser. 4, vol. 5, fols. 229–230: "Adi 29 d.o [May 1664] p. haver fatto di novo un'arco grande che stà sopra la scala grande dove cala il Papa p. andare in chiesa sono di n.o 17 sportelli de vetri quadri che fanno tutti li 17 sportelli n.o 529 vetri quadri compreso li mezzi à scudi 15 l'uno . . . 79.35 scudi."

104. Worsdale 1981, 245, for the comparison to fabric designs in general; and Battaglia 1943, tav. III, and doc. 191 for the payment to Schor, "per aver fatto un'altro cartone delli fogliami che sono nelle porte finte della scala che va in Sala regia scudi tre." I strongly suspect the "cartone" is the drawing formerly thought to be a fabric design, reproduced in *Bernini in Vaticano* 1980, 241–42, cat. no. 241, ill. 241 (Istituto Nazionale per la Grafica, Rome, F.C. 137506).

105. The carpenter Antonio Chiccari began to collect payment for his work on 26 June 1665, recorded in AFSP, Piano II, ser. 4, vol. 6, fol. 32: "A m.ro Ant.o Chiccari falegname . . . à bon conto delle Porticelle con fogliame, et altro p. erv.o del ripiano della nuova scala" (with corresponding *liste* on fol. 271). For the gilding see Borsi and Quinterio 1980, 357.

106. AFSP, Piano II, ser. 4, vol. 7, fol. 5: "A Marcant.o Inverni Indorat.e . . . di haver dato la Colla, gesso, biacca, et tinto li due portoni Intagliati à Capola Scala, che va in Sala Regia."

107. AFSP, Piano II, ser. 4, vol. 10, fols. 177–183v, is the *misura e stima* for the "lavori d'Imbiancature, e Coloriture di Trevertino" submitted by Mastro Antonio Martiani Imbiancatore.

108. Worsdale 1981, 231, mentions Bernini's appointment as the palace architect in 1655 (BAV, Chigi B. I. 12).

109. Borsi and Quinterio 1980, 303–7.

110. To put their relationship in perspective, one need only refer to the negotiations in the 1630s over the Spada Chapel intended for S. Andrea della Valle, for which see Montagu 1985b, 34–37.

111. Cf. the lively discussion in the 17 March 1657 meeting of the Fabbrica (Del Pesco 1988, 48–49).

112. Connors 1989b.

113. On Spada at Piazza della Rotonda, see Marder 1991b, 289.

114. Morello 1992.

115. Krautheimer and Jones 1975, 325, nos. 143, 144 (November 6 and 9, 1657); Morello 1981b, 324.

116. Krautheimer and Jones 1975, 206, no. 142 (see items 7 and 9); Morello 1981b, 324.

117. Fontana 1694, 234 (Appendix).

118. Fontana 1694, 235 (Appendix).

119. Illustration in Borsi and Quinterio 1980, 213, fig. 282.

120. Borsi 1967, pls. 16, 18, 28, 29; Borsi and Quinterio 1980, 112–13, fig. 147.

121. See Courtright in Lavin et al. 1981, 72–77; Lavin 1983; Wittkower 1966, 241, fig. 98; Borsi 1967, fig. 20, pls. 16, 18, 29; and the drawing in Lavin et al. 1981, 342. fig. B (study for the entrance wall of S. Maria del Popolo, Leipzig 7875v).

122. Illustrations in Borsi and Quinterio 1980, 119–21, figs. 158–60.

123. Illustrations in Borsi 1967, pls. 21, 23; Wittkower 1966, 240, fig. 95; Borsi and Quinterio 1980, 146–47, figs. 202–

3. It should be noted that the Fonseca Chapel was a private commission.

124. Wittkower 1966, 223, fig. 71; and pl. 120; Borsi and Quinterio 1980, fig. 255.

125. Wittkower 1966, 217, fig. 65.

126. Borsi and Quinterio 1980, 147, fig. 203.

127. The drawing is Leipzig 7807v. The motif at Ariccia is illustrated in Wittkower 1966, 240, fig. 95; it appears at the Scala Regia in my Plates 18, 20, 25.

128. Weil-Garris and D'Amico 1980, 80–81.

129. *Traité de la decoration intérieure des maisons royales et autres, tant à la ville, qu'à la campagne par M.r le Comte Nicodeme Tessin . . . 1717*, manuscript in the State Archives, Stockholm. In a printed *Catalogue des livres, estampes & desseins, du Cabinet des beaux arts, & des Sciences, appartenent au Baron Tessin*, Stockholm, 1712, 17, there are listed "Duoi disegni della Scala, fabricata in prospettiva nel Vaticano dal Cavaliere Lorenzo Bernini." My deep thanks to Guy Walton for both of these references.

130. Sirén 1914, 156, 157.

CHAPTER SEVEN. The Design and Execution of Bernini's Constantine

1. For the current state of research, see Kauffmann 1970, 278–89; Courtright in Lavin et al. 1981, 136–48; Schiavo 1981; and Marder 1991a and 1992.

2. Fagiolo and Fagiolo dell'Arco 1967, 68; and Birindelli 1982, 14. I discussed this issue in a paper summarized in Marder 1983a.

3. In general, see Baynes 1929, and for arguments on where the vision took place, especially pp. 398, 402–3.

4. *Vita Constantini* I, 28. Eusebius probably wrote the vita between Constantine's death in A.D. 337 and his own death in A.D. 340. The vita and Eusebius's *Ecclesiastical History* were composed in Greek and available in Latin translation from the sixteenth century. Thus the motto "In hoc signo vinces" is a Latin translation from the Greek. I have used the English versions edited by Ernest Cushing Richardson in Schaff and Wace 1961. For a modern discussion of the quoted passage, see Tartaglia 1984, 59–61. More bibliography is found in Baynes 1929, 397; and De' Cavalieri 1953.

5. Eusebius, *Vita Constantini* I, 29 (Schaff and Wace 1961).

6. For the standard sources, see Aufhauser 1912. A summary of early literature is gathered in Baynes 1929, 396, and Vogt 1957.

7. Wittkower 1966, 24, wrote of an apparition; but on p. 246, he indicated that the group represents Constantine "at the moment of his conversion." Hibbard 1965, 166, also erred in this regard.

8. Wittkower 1961a, doc. 24; translation from Wittkower 1966, 255.

9. Diary of Cardinal Fabio Chigi, BAV, Chigi a. I. 8 (k), fol. 5v (5 September 1654): "E dà me il Cav.r Bernino col disegno del Costantino." Published by Rossi 1939, 176, who is cited by Wittkower 1966, 251. At this time, Bernini frequently saw the cardinal, as for example, on 26 August 1654 (fol. 4v), 27 August 1654 (fol. 5), 23 October 1654 (fol. 10v), 10 November 1654 (fol. 12v), 6 December 1654 (fol. 14v), 16 December 1654 (fol. 15v), 31 December 1654 (fol. 17v).

10. AFSP, Piano I, ser. 3, vol. 163, fol. 30: "Eques Laurentius Berninus ponatur in lista pro scutis 100 quolibet mense ad beneplacitu. Sac. Congregat.nis pro erigenda memoria Constant.o Magno Imp.ri sibi fieri demandata ad similitudinem alterius eiusdem artificio collocata in Sacro Sancta Basilica Vaticana in memoria Comitiss. Matilde." Partially published in Schiavo 1981, 51–54. Copy in AFSP, Piano I, ser. 2, vol. 74, fol. 635. Fraschetti 1900, 318, n. 4, published the document in Italian with a reference I cannot trace. Brauer and Wittkower 1931, 103, n. 1; and Wittkower 1966, 251, simply cited Fraschetti. It should be explained that the Archivio della Fabbrica has been moved and renumbered over time, and citations in earlier literature are not always traceable in the current arrangement of volumes.

11. Information from a second version of the initial document. See AFSP, Piano I, ser. 4, vol. 27, fol. 169, with wording identical to the document in the previous note and marginal notations of a payment of 300 scudi: "fattoli m(andat)a a di 30 Otte. 1654." A draft of the document has the amount of 500 scudi canceled throughout and replaced by the figure of 300 scudi (Piano I, ser. 2, vol. 74, fol. 649).

12. The disbursement was registered on 6 April 1655. AFSP, Piano I, ser. 3, vol. 28, fol. 123, "lista del mese di marzo 1655, adi 6 Aprile," reads as follows: "Al port. Filippo Frugone acconto delli dui pezzi di marmo che devono servire p. far la statua di Costantino a cavallo e suo basso rilievo." Cited in Fraschetti 1900, 318, n. 4; Brauer and Wittkower 1931, 103, n. 2; and Schiavo 1981, 54, none of whom mentions the reference to a bas-relief. For Frugone, see Olszewski 1986 and Montagu 1989, 23, with additional references.

13. ASR, 30 Notai capitolini, Officio 38, vol. 34, fol. 122 (7 April 1655): "Filippus Frugonus ponatur in lista pro sc. 300 monete que sibi dantur pro arra duos lapidum Marmoreor. . . . Pro sculpen. historia Constantini magni per Eq. D. Lauren. Berninum elaboran. et in S. San.ta Vaticana Basilica collocan" (Brauer and Wittkower 1931, 103, n. 2).

14. The contract is to be found in ASR, 30 Notai capitolini, Officio 38, vol. 34 (Roverius), fols. 121, 126 (9 April 1655), with a copy on fols. 145 and 180. At this time, as the contract specifies, Frugone had already received the 300 scudi, which he was to return to the Fabbrica in the event the terms of the contract were not successfully met. AFSP, Piano I, ser. 3, vol. 28, fol. 126, published by Schiavo 1981, 54, is a draft of the contract with Frugone, in Italian, with cancellations and corrections. For other mentions in the documents, see AFSP, Piano I, ser. 3, vol. 163, fol. 73 (6 March 1655, corresp. to Piano I, ser. 3, vol. 176, fol. 53; and Wittkower 1966, 253); fol. 38 (6 March

1655, corresp. to Piano I, ser. 3, vol. 176, fol. 24); fol. 78 (21 April 1656, corresp. to Piano I, ser. 3, vol. 176, fol. 59); fol. 96v (20 January 1657, corresp. to Piano I, ser. 3, vol. 176, fol. 74); and Piano I, ser. 3, vol. 165, fol. 297 (30 February 1672).

15. I have been unable to trace the payment to the *provisore* Frugone on 13 August 1654 cited in Brauer and Wittkower 1931, 103, n. 2. For the function of *modelletti* and the development of a sculpture from design to execution, see Montagu 1986.

16. Wittkower 1966, 251.

17. BAV, Chigi H. II, 22, 61 (Fraschetti 1900, 320, n. 1; Brauer and Wittkower 1931, 103, n. 2; Wittkower 1966, 251, dating it August 1657 for unspecified reasons).

18. Bernini 1713, 95 (transl. by Bauer 1976, 36).

19. The delivery was obviously late by the terms of the contract. AFSP, Piano I, ser. 3, vol. 163, fol. 73 (6 March 1656; Wittkower 1966, 253.) There is more on carting the material from 21 April 1656, fol. 78. Olszewski 1986, 663, explains the "carrettata" as a volumetric measure related to the dimensions of a block expressed in cubic palmi. Klapsich-Zuber 1969, 72, points out that the "carrata" (or carrettata) was not a fixed unit, but differed from city to city and changed over time, depending on the size and strength of the carts used by the transporters. It is therefore uncertain whether the 30 carrettate included one block or two.

20. See Pérez Sánchez 1965, no. 1; Pérez-Sánchez 1967, 26 (with earlier bibliography); Wittkower 1966, 252–54; Harris 1977, xx, cat. no. 61; Courtright in Lavin et al., 1981, 138; Martinelli 1982, xxix.

21. Bernini 1713, 107, introduces some doubt about the location in St. Peter's: "Haveva Innocenzo destinato questo Colosso per la Chiesa di S. Pietro; mà non gli haveva determinato luogo." But his statement defies common sense, for how could an expensive equestrian monument, to be patterned on the Matilda memorial, have been commissioned by the Fabbrica for a site as yet undetermined in the basilica? See the convincing arguments about the intended location in Wittkower 1966, 253, whose measurements of the monument and the niche behind it I have independently verified. If we assume that the horse was to be positioned on a south wall of the basilica, advancing toward the apse, the only other sites in 1654 would have been opposite the second pier of the south aisle (now occupied by the monument to Pius X) or opposite the first pier of the south aisle (now occupied by the monument to Maria Clementina Sobieska). Neither of these locations would be as conspicuous as the first pier in the north aisle, and neither would support a pendant relationship with the tomb of Countess Matilda. Kauffmann 1970, 283, n. 37, raised the possibility that the setting in the Madrid drawing corresponds to the niche at the foot of the Scala Regia as depicted on Fig. 107, before Bernini's interventions there. But only St. Peter's has niches with the flanking columns represented on the Madrid drawing.

22. The work was not finished until well after his death. Briganti 1962a, 252–53; DiFederico 1983, 61.

23. Galassi Paluzzi 1975, 171, 259; Delfini Filippi 1989, 62–66.

24. Kauffmann 1970, 282, and fig. 153.

25. Bernini 1713, 14.

26. Brauer and Wittkower 1931, 103; Kauffmann 1970, 284; Mehnert 1981, 45–46, cat. no. 74; Courtright in Lavin et al. 1981, 143, n. 9.

27. Brauer and Wittkower 1931, 104; Kauffmann 1970, 281; Mehnert 1981, 46; Courtright in Lavin et al. 1981, 136.

28. The analogy with the Matilda monument was brought out by Courtright in Lavin et al. 1981, 138.

29. Brauer and Wittkower 1931, 104, n. 1, recognized the existence of the drawings on the verso. When the drawing was detached from its mount, the verso studies were variously identified as belonging to the Constantine by Mehnert 1981, 46; and to the Four Rivers Fountain by Courtright in Lavin et al. 1981, 136–37 and 143, nn. 7, 8. Ann Harris does not think the verso studies should be connected with the fountain and does not consider them autograph (opinion kindly conveyed by letter of 25 August 1992).

30. My arguments are presented in Marder 1992, 283, nn. 19, 20.

31. Bernini 1713, 95, described "il gran Colosso dell'Imperador Costantino a Cavallo, che essendo stato solamente abbozzato nel Pontificato d'Innocenzo," was inherited by the subsequent pope, Alexander VII.

32. For different readings of this drawing, see Brauer and Wittkower 1931, 104; Wittkower 1966, 254; Kauffmann 1970, 283 (whose sequence of the drawings is closest to mine); Mehnert 1981, 46, and Courtright in Lavin et al. 1981, 139.

33. See the catalogue entry by Nina K. Kosareva in Androsov 1991, 64–65, for a color illustration and bibliography.

34. Matzulevitch 1963, 71–73, believed the bozzetto belonged to the first phase of planning. This view has been dismissed without stated reasons in the subsequent literature. See Wittkower 1966, 254; and Kauffmann 1970, 283–84 (who believes, unlike Wittkower, that the bozzetto follows the drapery study in Leipzig and, like Wittkower, that the piece belongs to the second phase of work on the monument).

35. Brauer and Wittkower 1931, 104; Kauffmann 1970, 284; Martinelli 1982, pl. 30.

36. Paris, Bibliothèque Nationale ms. Italien 2084, fol. 195, ("Niceph.s lib. 8. cap. 55") is said to be in Bernini's own hand by Wittkower 1966, 254; and Wittkower 1985, 171. In truth, the excerpt is not in Bernini's hand, whose characteristics can be clearly seen on fol. 176 of the same volume, again on ms. Italien 2083, fol. 163r and v (formal letter of July 1665, presenting his Louvre drawings), and also on countless pages of the *giustificazione* and *liste* in the Archivio della Reverenda Fabbrica di San Pietro. The following words of the transcribed passage are underlined in original ink on the MS folio in Paris:

"barba mediocritur tenuis et rara, neq. admodum demissa erat." The *Church History* of the Byzantine historian Nicephorus (c. 1256–c. 1335) was translated into Latin by 1555, and there is a Greek text with the original Latin translation in a two-volume edition by F. Ducaeus, Paris, 1630.

37. De Rossi 1704, 12–13: "La figura è mirabile nell'espressiva, ed è perfetta in tutte le sue parti; ben è vero, che avendole fatto lo scultore da principio una fota, e lunga barba all'Orientale, ed essendo poi piaciuto al Pontefice Alessandro, che ella si levasse, per imitare più tosto il costume de i Latini, anno alcuni creduto esser difettosa la sveltezza, che dimostra, del collo, necessaria al primo intento del suo autore, particolarmente che vi concorre l'azione di guardar in alto con attenta osservazione." Kauffmann 1970, 284, n. 43, referred to De Rossi without discussing these issues.

38. Kauffmann 1970, 284–85.

39. Wittkower 1966, 251, has the correct date but his argumentation is incomplete.

40. Letter of Girardon to Colbert reporting on a visit to Bernini (4 February 1669): "Il nous dit sur ce sujet [the equestrian of Louis XIV] qu'il ne croyet pas pouvoir faire cet ouvrage pour le Roy; que le Constantin qu'il a faict a été catorze ans chez lui sur le chantie, et auquel il a travaillé sept années sans discontinuer." Francastel 1928, 45–46, cited by Wittkower 1966, 252.

41. Bernini 1713, 102–4, describes the visit of the queen. On p. 104 he says that Alexander made the first of two studio visits just two months later. The diary of the pope confirms two visits on 19 June 1662 and 5 June 1663. See Krautheimer and Jones 1975, no. 570 (19 June 1662) and no. 691 (5 June 1663). The avvisi reporting the two papal visits make no mention of the statue of Constantine. Cf. ASV, Avvisi 111; mentioned without citation in Pastor 1923–53, XXXI, 294, n. 6, and 301, n. 6; and Wittkower 1966, 251.

42. Domenico Stefano Bernini was born in Rome on 3 August 1657, the last of eleven children of Gianlorenzo Bernini and Caterina Tezio. If he were six years old at the time, the first papal visit would have occurred between August 1663 and July 1664, which cannot be the case given the evidence of the pope's diary and the avvisi. Domenico probably confused the first visit of Alexander with the second, the latter taking place when the boy was *almost* six. For biographical details, see *Dizionario biografico degli italiani* IX, 364–65.

43. Wittkower 1966, 251–52.

44. Cited in Chapter 3, note 50 in connection with the replacement of the statue of St. Peter.

45. Chantelou 1985, 260.

46. AFSP, Piano II, ser. 4, vol. 7, fol. 60 (3 December 1666, payment of 6.40 scudi); Borsi and Quinterio 1980, 357. The document mentions the carpenters' work done at night and over holidays. Piano I, ser. 3, vol. 4a, no. 14 (31 December 1670), lists a payment of 15.70 scudi for a wooden model of the pedestal.

47. AFSP, Piano II, ser. 4, vol. 8, fol. 80 (15 December 1666). Brauer and Wittkower 1931, 103, n. 7.

48. AFSP, Piano II, ser. 4, vol. 9, fol. 41 (13 July 1668), fol. 48 (24 August 1668), identical to the reference in Wittkower 1966, 252?); and fol. 55 (28 September 1668). The stonecutter Carlo Piervisani was paid 150 scudi on the basis of an assessment for the period 5 June – 4 August 1668 (Piano I, vol. 362, unpaginated; corresp. to Piano I, vol. 349, fol. 65).

49. AFSP, Piano II, ser. 4, vol. 9, fol. 55 (28 September 1668); and Piano II, ser. 4, vol. 10, 9v (20 February 1669). These are the final payments to Piervisani for work totaling 303.76 scudi on the marble pedestal. His work was completed by 27 September 1668 (the document gives the erroneous date of 1669). The payment corresponds to a detailed *giustificazione* in vol. 10, fol. 126. The *giustificazione* makes it clear that all exposed sides of the pedestal were flat and polished, and a payment of 6.70 scudi to the gilder Marcantonio Inverni "per diverse tinture fatte . . . nel Piedestallo del Constantino" indicates that the stone of the pedestal was at least partially gilded or painted.

50. AFSP, Piano II, ser. 4, vol. 9, fol. 64 (28 November 1668), contains a payment for three carrettate of clay "for the models of the Constantine" and for fifty swaddling bands (*fasci di lavoro*) for the models. A corroborative document for the three carrettate of clay appears in Piano I, ser. 3, vol. 4a, no. 14 (7 December 1668).

51. An avviso of 28 July 1668, recounts how Clement IX visited the Ponte S. Angelo and then "fù nell'officina del detto Caval.r Bernino à veder la statua, che questo hà fatto del Gran Costantino Imperatore da porsi incontro al portico di detta basilica" (Rossi 1939, 543; Pastor 1923–53, XXXI, 334, n. 3). Wittkower 1966, 252, cited a payment to Bernini of 1,000 scudi dated 13 July 1668, when the statue was described as *fatta*. See AFSP, Piano I, ser. armadi, vol. 348, fol. 15 left. AFSP, Piano I, ser. armadi, vol. 362 (unpaginated), has a reference to the "conto della soprad.a scoltura [Constantine] fatta." Additional payments to Bernini were registered on 19 November 1668 (2,000 scudi; Piano I, vol. 348, fol. 74), 9 February 1669 (1,000 scudi; AFSP, Piano I, ser. armadi, vol. 366, unpaginated), and 14 December 1671 (2,100 scudi; AFSP, Piano I, ser. armadi, vol. 369, unpaginated). Together the sum equals 6,100 scudi, which, with the early payments totaling 900 scudi, brought Bernini's stipend to 7,000 scudi.

52. AFSP, Piano II, ser. 4, vol. 9, fol. 62 (28 November 1668), "per fare li Curli da condurre la statua del Costantino," corresponding to the "Liste delle spese minute" in vol. 10, fol. 78); fol. 71 (14 December 1668, "per far Curli, et il Strascino de Travi, e Tavoloni per condurre la statua del Costantino"). Also Piano I, vol. 366 (unpaginated, 12 December 1668, for "sei Balle di Canepa in un Canapo . . . p. mettere in opera la statua del Costantino"); Piano I, vol. 362 (unpaginated, 14–19 December 1668, payment for the "scandaglio del lavoro . . . p. caricare et armare la statua del Costantino da condursi a S. Pietro"); Piano I, vol. 366 (unpaginated, 20 December 1668–12 January 1669, pay-

ment for the "scandaglio del lavoro . . . nella condottura della statua del Costantino a S. Pietro nel sud.o tempo").

53. AFSP, Piano I, ser. 3, vol. 4a, no. 14 (11 March 1669), for the *stima* of expenses for the transport and collocation of the statue, and for the beginning date of the procedure, 2 January 1669.

54. I have found no evidence of piecing on the monument. It would be useful to know if the original 30 carrettate were composed of one piece of marble or two. For the history of the house and studio, see Borsi, Luchinat, and Quinterio 1981.

55. Pastor 1923–53, XXXI, 334, n. 4, avviso of 12 January 1669: "Dalla casa del S. cav. Bernino famoso scultore è stata portata nel Palazzo Vaticano la statua di marmo a cavallo dell'imperatore Constantino magno, ch'egli ha fatto d'ordine di Papa Alessandro VII da collocarsi a piè della scala Regia dirimpetto al portico della basilica." Within the following ten days the sculpture would have been set upon its pedestal. See AFSP, Piano I, vol. 348, fol. 105 (23 January 1669: "c.to di caricare, armare, condurre ecc. la statua di Costantino . . . condotta dallo studio del Cav.r Bernini, e collocata sop.a il suo Piedestallo a piedi la Scala Regia" for work of 23 December – 23 January).

56. AFSP, Piano II, ser. 4, vol. 10 (1669), fols. 2v–3 and 80–80v (14 December 1668–19 January 1669). Corroborative documents in Piano I, ser. 3, vol. 4a, no. 14 (bearing the same dates).

57. AFSP, Piano II, ser. 4, vol. 10 (1669), fol. 8v ("selci, e Calce per accommodare le selciate rotte per la conduttura di detta Statua"), and documents in the notes above.

58. Rossi 1939, 544 (12 January 1669): "S. Stà non vuole che nell'inscrittione da farsi nel piedestallo di Costantino s'incida nepure una lettera del suo nome, mà quello ben sì del Predecessore di cui vuole sia la gloria." The tenor of this gesture is consistent with an avviso of a year earlier, in January 1668, "La statua di Costantino à cavallo opera del Cav.re Bernino si porrà sopra le scale della Basilica Vaticana nel luogo assignatoli da Papa Alessandro VII al quale si darà l'honore di tanta magnificenza" (Rossi 1939, 543).

59. AFSP, Piano II, ser. 4, vol. 10 (1669), fol. 35v, is a payment to Carlo Piervisani corresponding to the more explicit *misura e stime* on fols. 292–300, which, in turn, list a payment for "trevertini per il posamento de ferri, che reggono la Statua di Costantino" (fol. 298v, 20 February 1669). See also Piano I, vol. 369 (unpaginated), for payments to the ironmonger Ascentio Latini on 18 June, 5 July, and 27 August 1670, for his work on the Constantine.

60. AFSP, Piano II, ser. 4, vol. 10, fol. 8 (20 February 1669). On the same date there is a payment for fourteen carrettate of pozzolana "per li muri della statua del Constantino" (fol. 8v). On 27 March 1669, there is another payment for work on the wall "dietro la statua di Constantino" (Piano II, ser. 4, vol. 10, fol. 16, corresponding to the *giustificazione* on fol. 162 for work done between 21 January and 16 February 1669 "con ordine delle Sig. Cavaliere Bernino").

61. AFSP, Piano II, ser. 4, vol. 10, fol. 124 ("spese . . . dali 26 di Gennaro a tutto li 16 Febraro 1669"). Here there is a payment of twenty baiocchi "per Candellette di Cera servite per l'opera del Costantino."

62. AFSP, Piano II, ser. 4, vol. 10, fol. 23 (8 May 1669): payments for work on the wall and the vault behind Constantine and for the stucco; also fol. 24 (carting of lime "per li stucchi del Constantino, e suo muro"); fol. 24 (for pozzolana for the same purpose).

63. Rinaldo was first paid on 8 May 1669 (AFSP, Piano II, ser. 4, vol. 10, fol. 24v, corresponding to fol. 210, and to Piano I. vol. 348, fol. 111). Rinaldo was paid on contract for the "ornamento di stucco, che detto fa nella nicchia, dove è collocato il Constantino." Cosimo Rustichella, on the other hand, was paid (fol. 25) for "sue giornate, che ha lavorato di stucco all Panno del Constantino," that is, on a daily basis.

64. For payments, see AFSP, Piano II, ser. 4, vol. 10, fol. 32 and 33v, (both 10 July 1669); 43 (21 August 1669); 50 and 50v (both 11 September 1669).

65. AFSP, Piano II, ser. 4, vol. 10 (1669), fol. 32 (10 July 1669): payment "per disfare li Ponti, e steccato del Constantino per il Parato della Processione del Corpus Domini, e poi rifarli."

66. AFSP, Piano II, ser. 4, vol. 10, fol. 50v (11 September 1669): payment to Cosimo Rustichella *stuccatore* "per saldo, et intiero pagamento d'una misura, e stima de lavori di stucco fatti . . . nell'ornamento di Rose nel sottarco del Constantino." The payment corresponds to the *misura* of 3 September 1669 (fol. 365). A minor payment for contract labor was registered on 2 October 1669 (fol. 55). Piano I, ser. 3, vol. 4a, no. 14, includes similar information for Rustichella with the date 30 September 1669 (this in Schiavo 1981, 56).

67. See Brauer and Wittkower 1931, 104, n. 2 (implying that the drawing is the autograph sheet listed in the 1706 inventory of Bernini's possessions); Kauffmann 1970, 286–87 (also accepting the drawing); Harris 1977, xxiii, cat. no. 90 (1669–70, only the drapery is autograph); Mehnert 1981, 46 (with a date of 1666/68 and "possibly" before Bernini's voyage to Paris); and Courtright in Lavin et al. 1981, 142 (restoring the attribution to Bernini).

68. Noted by Taja 1750, 2–3.

69. In the absence of full documentation, Courtright in Lavin et al. 1981, 139 and 142, has some prescient observations about the drawing, to which we should add that the horse in the drawing does not correspond exactly to the executed group. In fact, the left hind leg of the horse differs so markedly as to suggest the contribution of a studio hand. Among the drawings where Bernini may have studied figural motifs on architectural elements rendered by another draftsman, one should add Leipzig 7864 (Lavin et al. 1981, 149, cat. no. 30) and Leipzig 7900r–7901r (originally one drawing, Lavin et al. 1981, 175, cat. nos. 41 and 42), the latter with architectural drawings for the Scala Regia and chalk drawings for putti on the Cathedra Petri. In short, while I have no doubt that the drawing represents Berni-

ni's thinking, too much remains conditional for me to be fully persuaded that the work is fully autograph.

70. On the basis of photographs, Wittkower 1980, 525, n. 22, called it "suspect." Nevertheless, see Rossacher 1967a.

71. Barberini 1991, 49. My thanks to Dr. Maria Giulia Barberini for showing me the piece and discussing with me the possible association with Constantine.

72. Wittkower 1966, 254, and fig. 109.

73. Penny 1992, 15, agrees with Wittkower and points out that the bronze corresponds with the Hermitage bozzetto in details like the cuirass.

74. Wittkower 1961a, doc. 24; translation from Wittkower 1966, 255.

75. AFSP, Piano II, ser. 4, vol. 11, fol. 22 (23 July 1670): payments for work during the period 23 June through 19 July "per assistere un Manuale di Continuo al Constantino, ad effetto di fare, e disfare li Ponti, et altro mentre si finisce di scolpire dal S.r Cav.re Bern.i."

76. AFSP, Piano II, ser. 4, vol. 11, fols. 23v and 30 (23 July and 3 September 1670: payments to Cosimo Rustichelli for "più delle sue giornate per havere lavorato al panno di stucco del Constantino," with corresponding *giustificazioni* on fol. 160 and fol. 174). Also fols. 29v and 39 (3 September and 1 October 1670: payments to Michelangelo Marullo *pittore* for "spolveri e ombregiamento che detto fa per l'ornamento del Constantino" and for "il disegno in grande, spolverato, et ombrato, che detto hà fatto nell'ornamento di stucco per la statua del Constantino"; with corresponding *giustificazione* on 194r); fol. 37 (1 October 1670: payment "per altro manuale che nel sudetto tempo [1–27 September] ha assistito al Constantino, per fare, e disfare Ponti, portar modelli, et altro mentre si è finito di scolpire, et indorato l'ornamento di stucco").

77. Kauffmann 1970, 286, seems to be refining Wittkower's point (1985, 160) about the drapery serving to enlarge the figural group within the dimensions of the niche.

78. We should remember that the tomb of Cardinal Pimentel in S. Maria sopra Minerva, similarly conceived in relief, dates from about the same time as the origin of the Constantine statue in 1654. See Wittkower 1966, 227–28.

79. AFSP, Piano II, ser. 4, vol. 11, fol. 29v (3 September 1670, payments to Marco Antonio Inverni and Vincenzo Coralli *indoratori* "per lumeggiare d'oro alcuni ornamenti per la statua di Constantino," corresponding *giustificazione* on fol. 172r). See also fol. 30 (3 September 1670, payments to a manual laborer "che ha assistito all'Indoratori che mettono d'oro alli fogliami del Panno del Constantino in tre giorni di festa" and for the cost of "pelle di Pesce per pulire il Panno del Constantino"); fol. 39 (1 October 1670, "per un soffietto per il polverare il Panno del Constantino," corresponding *giustificazione* on fol. 198); and fol. 53v (17 December 1670, payments to "i due lustratori, che hanno pulito il piedestallo del Constantino, e ripulito il Cavallo del medesimo à loro pomice"). Piano I, ser. 3, vol. 4a, no. 14, (15 July 1682) includes a very late payment of 76.25 scudi for gilding of the drapery behind Constantine and the cross among other unrelated items.

80. For examples of repairs, see AFSP, Piano II, ser. 4, vol. 13, fols. 24 and 314v (22 June and 5 December 1672), which are payments "per tagliare il massiccio, e fare l'astrico per l'ammattonato tagliato sotto il Piedestallo di Constantino" and "per l'Ammattonato rotato e tagliato in piano fatto nelli repiani delle due porte sotto la statua del Constantino," both of which operations were probably done in connection with the paving of the corridors in progress at this time. For examples of later payments for services rendered in the midst of the initial building process, cf. Piano I, ser. 3, vol. 4a, no. 14, dated (correctly?) 15 July 1682, which is a payment of 76.25 scudi to the gilder Inverni for gilding the drapery and the cross.

81. Avviso of 1 November 1670: "Martedi dopo desinare Sua Santità si trasferi (dal Quirinale) in segetta à visitare la Basilica di San Pietro, e poscia diede una vista à piedi della contigua scala regia del Palazzo Vaticano alla statua dell'imperatore Costantino Magno con la sua inscrittione fatta d'ordine pontificio dal Cavaliere Bernino famoso scultore dove era accorsa quantità di popolo" (Rossi 1940, 57). Originally published and correctly interpreted by Fraschetti 1900, 318, the date of the avviso was later mistaken by Wittkower 1966, 252, for the event.

82. Fraschetti 1900, 318, n. 5, quotes from a letter of 1 November 1670 in the Cancelleria Ducale, Archivio di Stato, Modena: "Martedi il Pontefice con la sua Beatifica Vista consolò il Popolo nell'andare che fece dal Quirinale al Vaticano, con ottimo aspetto di buona salute et alla porta del famoso tempio, il Cardinale Carlo Barberino li diede l'Ostensorio. Doppo si portò a piedi della Nobil Scala che conduce alla Sala Regia ove li fu scoperto la nuova statua di Costantino il Magno a Cavallo nell'atto quando stupido rimirò in aria una scintillante fiamma in sembianza di Croce, con voce Celeste che gl'affermò che in virtù di cotal segno vincerebbe il fiero tiranno Massentio il cui Eccel.te lavoro è opera del famoso Cav.re Bernino, e d'indi la santità sua se ne tornò al quirinale." An avviso for 1 November 1670 offers the same information as the letter quoted above, but in a more prosaic manner (Rossi 1940, 57).

83. Wittkower 1966, 252, incorrectly mistook the date of the letter for that of the unveiling. Kauffmann 1970, 289, n. 64, pointed out that the "Martedi" in the Modenese ambassador's letter must have been 29 October 1670, thus an anniversary of the original commission.

84. Wittkower 1966, 252, provides a citation I have been unable to trace. A corroborating notice of the total payment may be found in Piano I, ser. 3, vol. 4a, no. 14 (7 January 1672), which mentions the 7,000 scudi "pagati al Sig.e Cav.re Gio. Lorenzo Bernini per Conto e final pagamento di sua recognitione cosi arbitrata dalla Sag. Congregazione sotto li 2 Decembre 1671 et approvata dalla Santità di Nostro Sig.re per la scoltura dell'opera del Costantino da lui fatta." From this it is clear that the total represents payment for Bernini's work, exclusive of the cost of marble and related expenses.

CHAPTER EIGHT. **Meanings of the Constantine Imagery**

1. Kauffmann 1970, 281.
2. Kauffmann 1970, 278, 281–82, 288–89.
3. See Alföldi 1939, for the coin type of c. A.D. 350, with a motto bearing the words "HOC SIGNO VICTOR ERIS." On this basis Alföldi, subscribing to the account by Lactantius, maintained that the vision appeared with these words rather than the more usual "in hoc vince" or "in hoc signo vinces." Interestingly, this medal was known as early as 1615, according to Busiri Vici 1893, 24.
4. The argument of the Bamberg Rider as Constantine is by no means universally accepted, but see Traeger 1970a. Against the identification of the numerous Romanesque equestrians as Constantine, see the recent contributions by Seidel 1976a; 1976b; and 1981, 6–7, 16, 56–57. I want to thank Elizabeth McLachlan for steering me to Seidel's work.
5. Despite the promising title of Jörg Traeger, *Der reitende Papst* (1970), see the critical review by Elisabeth Garms-Cornides in *Art Bulletin* LX (1973), 451–56, who disproves that the horse is a symbol of papal power.
6. See the entries by Elena Croce in *Bibliotheca Sanctorum*, (1968), IV, cols. 238–48; Künstle 1926–28, II, 535–38; Pigler 1974, I, 489; J. Traeger in Kirschbaum 1968–76, II, cols. 547–51. These citations and a list of Constantine cycles before 1600, with bibliographies, are given in an appendix in Freiberg 1988, 595–624. With the important exception of Traeger's, as my note 12 explains, these discussions do not consider the problem of the equestrian that I am presenting here.
7. Here the term "adlocutio" appears in the inscription on Constantine's podium. Recent bibliography is in Gombrich et al. 1989, 256–57. Among earlier studies, see especially Quednau 1979.
8. Weil 1974a, 89–91.
9. Epp 1988, 62–66; Freiberg 1988, 620–21; Freiberg 1995, 28.
10. Ackerman 1954, 102–9; Freiberg 1988, 618–19; Cheney 1990; Schütte 1990, 98–99 (kindly brought to my attention by Christoph Frommel); and Gambi and Pinelli 1994, I, 416, II, 442 (color illustration). None of these references make note of the equestrian iconography.
11. Freiberg 1988, 622–24. The representation of Constantine on horseback is noted in Epp 1988, 66–68.
12. For Bibliothèque Nationale, ms grec 510, fol. 440r, see Omont 1929, 10–12, 31; Der Nersessian 1962, 197–228; Brubaker 1985, with citations from recent literature. There are also references to the miniature in Weitzmann 1942–43, 87–91 and 126–28. Traeger 1970a, 8, n. 41, mentions the illustration as one of only two representations he knows of Constantine's vision with the emperor on horseback. His other example is an engraving by the Netherlandish artist and architect Alaert du Hameel (c. 1449–c. 1509). He does not mention the examples in the Lateran Benediction Loggia, the Vatican Galleria delle Carte Geografiche, or Bernini's Constantine.
13. In an otherwise useful discussion, Stylianou 1971 makes no distinction between the two visions of Constantine described by Eusebius, one occurring before the battle and the other later, in the emperor's sleep.
14. Stylianou 1971, 67–68. The relationship of this depiction of the vision of Constantine with yet another example, painted in St. Nicholas Dabarski, Banja Pribojska (1571; Stylianou 1971, 64) might be significant, given the location of the scene in the narthex of the church and its relationship to the location of Bernini's sculpture. But the poor condition of the fresco makes further comparison impossible. The textual source for the iconography that includes the stars in the vision was apparently introduced by the fourth/fifth-century Byzantine author Philostorgius (Cecchelli 1954, 81–82).
15. The manuscript was brought to the west at the end of the fifteenth century, and a nephew of Leo X, Cardinal Nicholas Ridolfi, owned it at the beginning of the sixteenth century. After he died, Pietro Strozzi (d. 1558) bought it, and from him it came into the possession of Catherine de Medici. In 1594, after her death, it came into the collection of Henry IV of France. See Omont 1929, 10–12.
16. Kauffmann 1970, 281, introduced the comparison to Longinus.
17. Wittkower 1966, 201–202; Scott 1985, 119–27.
18. The church served the abbey of Polirone, founded by the rulers of Canossa and largely completed by Matilda. Between the right transept and the sacristy of the church, a "tomb" of Matilda of Canossa is still to be found.
19. Wittkower 1966, 17, for the quotation; Scott 1985, 125.
20. See Skippon 1663–64, 663.
21. Scott 1985, 119, makes this point for the Matilda tomb.
22. The passage from Nicephorus, bk. 8, chap. 55, discussed below, contains details of Constantine's death and burial in the Church of the Holy Apostles.
23. Du Cange 1840–50, V, 335 (s.v. "memoria"), provides the following definitions: monumentum, sepulchrum, ecclesia, sacellum, altare, loculus.
24. Kauffmann 1970, 287, cites Pope-Hennessy 1964, I, 366–69, with references to the tomb of Cortesia Sarego, the monument to Francesco Spinola in Genoa, and the monument of Marchese Spinetta Malaspina (now in the Victoria and Albert Museum, London).
25. *Courtauld Institute Illustration Archives*, Archive 2 (15th- and 16th-Century Sculpture in Italy), pt. 4, 2/4/79; pt. 7, 2/7/1–3. The Orsini tomb was kindly brought to my attention by Jack Freiberg. In Italy there are, of course, hundreds of equestrian tomb monuments without the drapery, which might be lost over time, given the frequent use of impermanent materials for the purpose. See now Wegener (1989).
26. Seiler 1989. I am grateful to Peter Seiler for calling my attention to his discussion of the Farnese monument.
27. Courtright in Lavin et al. 1981, 141, cites Bialostocki 1973. On pp. 141 and 145, nn. 37, 38, Courtright also suggests that the wreaths around the relief tondi in the vault con-

tribute to the funerary associations of the executed monument.

28. Arnoldi 1963, incorrectly locates the statue in the portico of St. Peter's. I want to thank Jack Freiberg for bringing this reference to my attention.

29. Vasari 1568, II, 650 ("una statua d'un uomo armato a cavallo, che oggi è per terra a S. Pietro, vicino alla cappella di S. Andrea"); Alfarano 1914, 70 ("In quo etiam loco [inside the entrance wall] fuit translata marmorea statua equo insidens Comitis Anversae [Sixti IV] S.R.E. Generalis huis Urbis atque Basilicae contra Saracenos acerrimi defensoris"); Grimaldi 1972, fols. 120v–121. In his edition of Alfarano 1914, Cerrati, 70, n. 2, and 188, provides further references to Malatesta and the monument, which appears as no. 55 on Alfarano's plan. Knowledge of the monument in the late seventeenth century is attested in Ciampini 1693, tab. XIX, letter P. None of these sources, apart from Vasari, are cited in Arnoldi 1963.

30. Cerrati's note to Alfarano 1914, 70, n. 2, gives evidence that the work was removed to the villa in 1616.

31. *Vita Constantini*, I, 32; translation in Schaff and Wace 1961, 491.

32. For the Miracle of S. Agnese, see Montagu 1985a, 152–56, 351–53.

33. For the common method of insuring quality by specifying a comparable marble, see Montagu 1989, 25.

34. Montagu 1985a, 138–46 and 358–64, gives a full discussion.

35. Montagu 1985a, 146.

36. A pair of works whose conception appears similarly related may be seen in Bernini's altar for the Cornaro Chapel in S. Maria della Vittoria (1647–52) and Algardi's high altar of S. Nicola da Tolentino (1651–54), for which see Montagu 1985a, 146–50.

37. Montagu 1985a, 205–6, for the following information.

38. Montagu 1985a, 205, points out that Symonds seconded his own judgment in describing Algardi's statue on the high altar of S. Paolo in Bologna as by "ye best sculptor now living."

39. Di Bildt 1906.

40. Montagu 1985a, 205.

41. Bernini 1713, 107.

42. Chantelou 1985, 260 (6 October 1665), cited by Wittkower 1966, 252.

43. So far as I know, Hibbard 1965, 166 and 209, is the only commentator to have remarked on the Constantine as a relief.

44. On the superiority of carving over casting, especially on a colossal scale, see Bush 1976, 23–31. Hibbard 1965, 209, maintained that the medium of relief "allowed Bernini to carve the rearing horse that had tantalized previous sculptors of freestanding monuments from Leonardo da Vinci to his own day." For an introduction to the massive bibliography on equestrians, see Liedtke 1989, 103–6.

45. Wittkower 1966, 23.

46. My thanks to Louise Rice for an exchange of ideas on this point.

47. Wittkower 1966, 217, dated the project for the family chapel in S. Nicolò da Tolentino, Venice, to a period after the Cornaro Chapel in Rome (finished 1651); and Blunt 1967, 231, to the early 1650s. A derivative scheme appears in the base of the tomb of Cardinal Pimentel of 1654, for which see Wittkower 1966, 227–28; and Blunt 1967, 231–32, who both remark on the relationship to the tomb projects now identified as belonging to Innocent X (Preimesberger 1978).

48. Wittkower 1966, 259–60; Courtright in Lavin et al. 1981, 145, n. 38.

49. Wittkower 1966, 218, associated the fames but did not extend their sepulchral meaning to the Scala Regia. Figures of Fame were also mounted inside the entrance wall of Bernini's S. Andrea al Quirinale (1658–76) and S. Tommaso at Castel Gandolfo (1659–61).

50. Bialostocki 1973, 17–18.

51. The quotation is from Eberlein 1983, 68. The tent is visible in nearly all the representations of Constantine's Vision of the Cross.

52. Such a baldachin was projected for the Benediction Loggia of St. Peter's in a drawing by Sangallo, Uffizi A 72 (see Frommel 1994, 619). See also Wittkower 1985, 160.

53. The point is made by Freiberg 1988, 181–83, for the Constantinian iconography at the Lateran transept. Also in Freiberg 1995, 125.

54. The man in charge of the play was a Genoese, born and educated in Constantinople. The play was performed "in pontificie atrio, ubi cardinales in curiam venientes ab equis descendunt," while the pope looked on from his windows above. See Carusi 1904, 130 (2 March 1484), for the interpretation of which my thanks to David Marsh.

55. Cioni 1961, 112–14; D'Ancona 1891, I, 289, 379, 381; D'Ancona 1872, II, 187–234 (references from Freiberg 1988, 182, 435).

56. Juvarra's borrowing was succeeded in 1729 by Nicola Michetti's frontispiece for a performance of *Carlo Magno*, which represented Cornacchini's equestrian of 1725. See Pinto 1980, 295–96.

57. Freiberg 1988, 185, 438, n. 206; Freiberg 1995, 127–29.

58. On the Cornaro Chapel, see Lavin 1980, passim; and especially Weil 1990.

59. Kauffmann 1970, 281, briefly cites Gramberg 1964, 81, no. 141. Gramberg 1964, 76–78, 81–84, 117–20, notes that the Charles V monument is the source for Bernini's Constantine and traces the survival of the project and related ones in the sixteenth century.

60. Alfarano 1914, 115, 121, 124, 152, 195, 196.

61. Podestà 1878, 312–13, and Forcella 1885, 49, for descriptions of the palace ornaments in honor of Charles V, including images of the emperor over the entrance portal.

62. Wittkower 1961b; and Enggass 1976, 200–2. Wittkower does not mention the connection with the schemes discussed by Gramberg 1964, 81, who was apparently the first to recognize the historic continuity concluded in the

equestrian figure of Charlemagne at the south end of the portico.

63. Among recent discussions, see especially Herklotz 1985, and Seiler 1989.

64. Ackerman 1957; Buddensieg 1969.

65. Eusebius, *Vita Constantini*, III, 3, was noted by Courtright in Lavin et al. 1981, 141.

66. Frugoni 1984, 32–70; Seiler 1989.

67. Vasari 1568, II, 386; Venturi 1914.

68. Janson 1973. On the political associations of equestrian figures in sculpture, see Keller 1971 and Frugoni 1984.

69. Grabar 1957, 150, n. 36.

70. For the antiquarian literature, see De Rossi 1704, 13–14; and Brauer and Wittkower 1931, 134–35.

71. Prinz and Kecks 1985, 247–62, figs. 284, 286, 287, 289, 294, and 333. The authors, p. 260, maintain that these equestrians symbolize the ideas of the State, Triumph, Apotheosis, and Light. They trace the iconography to Italian sources without citing specifics.

72. For the equestrian at Ecouen, see Liedtke 1989, 190, who attributes the work to Jean Goujon, architect to the owner, Anne de Montmorency.

73. See Whitman 1987.

74. Smith 1956, 42–43.

75. Smith 1956, 17–19; and for the imperial or royal ciborium symbolized by a tent, pp. 107–29.

76. Documents in Orbaan 1919, 52–53, mention "molte medaglie d'oro et di argento con l'impronta di Costantino imperatore, primo fondatore di quella sacrosanta basilica." The discovery was also recorded by Grimaldi 1972, 176. It would be interesting to know if any of these objects bore an image of the Cross, such as those illustrated in the anonymous "Dissertation Historique sur la vision de la Croix" (1681).

77. Alfarano 1914, 23: "Sed hinc inde a dextris et a sinistris extra quadriporticum, et Basilicae parietes duo etiam magna Episcopie a Constantino extructa fuere pro habitatione Summorum Pontificum." Severano 1630, I, 43: "Dall'una, e l'altra parte delle Scale fuori del Quadriportico, e delli muri della chiesa, Costantino edificò ancora due Episcopie, cioè habitationi per li Pontefici." De Sebastiani 1683, 9; and Ciampini 1693, cap. 4, give the same information. From the time of Alexander VII comes the account of Alveri 1664, II, 142: "Fù da Costantino Imperatore quivi fatta fabricare l'habitatione Pontificia, benche vogliono alcuni in luogo più alto, & in sito vario da questo, nel quale di presente si trova, che n'andò sempre avanzandosi, havendolo primieramente Simaco Papa molto accresciuto."

78. Hueck 1969.

79. Mentioned with references in Chapter 3.

80. Waetzoldt 1964, 36; and Herklotz 1989, 48 and 88.

81. See Wirth 1963 and Elze 1960 for this ceremony.

82. Waetzoldt 1964, 66–67. Letarouilly 1882 also includes a depiction of Constantine on horseback on the triumphal arch of St. Peter's, but there is no archaeological evidence for its authenticity.

83. Courtright in Lavin et al. 1981, 141. See Grabar 1936, 43–

44, on the painted image of Constantine in the vestibule of the imperial palace. The iconography is also related to Paul V's new palace entrance, for which see Chapter 3.

84. This is the recommendation of Paolo Cortesi in the sixteenth century, when he suggests such subjects for the courtyard of the ideal cardinal's palace. "For what is more admirable than to see how Constantine showed his deference to papal authority when he gave up Rome, which is the leader of all nations, and transferred the seat of the empire to Thrace? Or what is more pleasing than to see how Charlemagne was summoned by the advice of the College of Cardinals to wrest from the Lombards their possession of Italy, and how . . . he was made Emperor on the advice of the Pope?" To decorate the great hall of the palace, similar to the Sala Regia at the Vatican, Cortesi recommends representations of those who tried and failed to overthrow the rule of the Pontifex Maximus. See Weil-Garris and D'Amico 1980, especially pp. 91–95.

85. Vasari 1568, VII, 57. See Partridge and Starn 1990, n. 51.

86. Panofsky-Soergel 1967–68, and Neppi 1975.

87. Partridge and Starn 1990, 27, 31.

88. Borsi and Quinterio 1980, 357–59, for the *misura e stima* dated 23 September 1667 (AFSP, Piano I, ser. 1, vol. 2, no. 38).

89. Haus 1970, n. 255.

90. Worsdale 1986, 36, likens the sphinxes to those that appear over some doors at Palazzo Barberini. In fact, sphinxes also appear in the friezes of some rooms of the piano nobile there, and even more conspicuously below the cornice of the west-facing (main) façade.

91. In discussing the relevant emblem literature in relation to Bronzino's Luxury of about 1545, Moffitt 1993, 297, points out that the sphinx appears with wings only in 1621.

92. Wittkower 1966, 245–46, offers passing reference to the medallions. Only Grimme 1961, 19, has suggested that the reliefs belong to an iconographic ensemble, but he takes the argument no further. His attribution of the reliefs to Lorenzo Ottone (born 1648) finds no support in available evidence.

93. Freiberg 1988, 413, n. 114, emphasizes that the scene does not depict Constantine "laying the foundation stone" as described in Wittkower 1966, 246, and in most subsequent literature. See also Freiberg 1995, 104–7.

94. The same observation was made by Montagu 1985, 140 (citing Moroni 1840–61, LXXI, 29–38), for the figure of Leo the Great in Algardi's relief. For further information, see Ladner 1979.

95. Quednau 1979, 399, for the scene of the Baptism; and 407, for the ceremonial, which specifies the participation of a deacon with alb and dalmatic assisting to the right of the pope (left in the composition); a subdeacon with alb and tunicle assisting to the left of the pope (right in the composition); a subdeacon or "capellanus" with the book of readings; a subdeacon bearing the crucifix; a bishop (wearing a mitre) in the procession; and so forth.

96. Quednau 1979, 481–84, for the fresco.

97. *Monocromata in constantiniana vaticani aula, ab artefice summo Iulio Pippio Romano . . . Petrus Sanctes Bartolus à se delineata*, undated but bearing a dedication to "Illustriss. ac Reverendiss. D.D. Iacobo Ninio Senensi S.D.N. Alexandri VII. Pontificii Cubiculi Praefecto, D.no ac Moecenati benignissimo." Jacopo Nini was the papal *maestro di camera* and was made a cardinal in 1664.

98. The representation of the founding of St. Peter's in the vault of the Galleria delle Carte Geografiche is, like that in the Sala di Costantino, only distantly related to Bernini's composition.

99. The texts for the *Acta* were studied extensively by Levinson 1924. The previously held agreement about the fifth-century dating of the *Acta* has been recently revised by Pohlkamp 1983. The *Acta* have been referred to in a number of recent art historical studies among which can be mentioned: Walter 1970, especially 170; Lavagne 1977; Herklotz 1985, 41, n. 237; Freiberg 1988, 110–12; Herklotz 1989; Freiberg 1995, 222, n. 23.

100. In some copies of the *Acta*, there is a third section consisting of a purported exchange of letters between Constantine and Helena having to do with the search for the True Cross. See Pohlkamp 1984, 357 (for the texts, with references to the latest bibliography), and 359–60 (for the letters).

101. Pohlkamp 1984, 358, n. 2, refers to the Milanese edition of Boninus Mombritius, *Sanctorum seu Vitae Sanctorum*, and a second edition from Brussels, 1478; a Latin text in Laurentius Surius, *De Probatis Sanctorum Historiis*, Cologne, 1581, 1173–87; and Greek and Latin texts in Francesco Combefis, *Illustrium Christi Martyrum Lecti Triumphi Vetustis Graecorum Monumentis Consignati*, Paris, 1660, 258–336. There is also a modern, two-volume edition of Mombritius published in Paris, 1910. Freiberg 1988, 518–35, gives some excerpts from Mombritius with an English translation, but these do not include the account of Constantine's vision.

102. Duchesne 1886–92, I, cxiii; Fuhrmann 1968; Voragine 1969, 72–82. See also Nicephorus, bk. VII, chap. 29 (Constantine's vision), chap. 33 (the baptism by Sylvester), chap. 35 (refutation of the variant tradition of the baptism), chap. 46 (foundation of churches). For Baronius, see, for example, his monumental *Annals* (1738–46). In vol. III, anno 315, x, xiv, xv, xvii, there are cautions about the *Acta* (Freiberg 1988, 388, n. 19; Freiberg 1995, 223, n. 27 and 228, n. 67).

103. Webb 1981, thoroughly discussed the debate, with relevant bibliography.

104. Webb 1981, 96.

105. Webb 1981, points out that Jacob of Voragine was of two minds on the matter. On the feast of St. Sylvester (31 December), he upheld the testimony of the *Acta*, but he discounted it in the discussion of the feast of the Invention of the Holy Cross (3 May). See Voragine 1969, 74 and 271–72. Precisely this sort of approach to history no doubt contributed to the remarkable fall from popularity of the *Golden Legend* in the counterreformatory period. For a study of its critical fortunes, see Reames 1985, who points out that the book had 156 editions in different languages between 1470 and 1500, and that its publishing history virtually ends in the first decade of the seventeenth century. Its rehabilitation as a source for iconographers dates only from 1890, with the publication of Emile Mâle, *L'Art religieux du XIIIe siècle en France*. The circumstances suggest that Jacob of Voragine should be used with caution in discussions of Baroque art.

106. Nicephorus 1566, Lib. VII, cap. 33, pp. 239v–241r (from a copy formerly in the Chigi Library, BAV, Chigi V. 1839).

107. Baronius 1738–46, III, anno 324, 40; and Baronius 1630, 411–13, 634–35. Ciampini 1693, 30, cites the *Acta* in Baronius on the foundation of St. Peter's. The Roman baptism of the emperor is no longer officially accepted, and the current position is reflected in *Butler* 1956, IV, 644–45. For the suggested influence of the *Annals* on the decorative projects in St. Peter's, see Chappell and Kirwin 1974, especially 123.

108. See Freiberg 1988, 595–624, with mention of other examples in Rome and elsewhere (e.g., Camposanto, Pisa; S. Silvestro, Tivoli; Villa Montalto, Rome; SS. Quattro Coronati, Rome; Bardi Chapel, S. Croce in Florence; Palazzina della Viola, Bologna; Abbey of S. Silvestro, Nonantola). Also Freiberg 1995, 32.

109. Quednau 1979, 483, without mention of Bernini's reliefs. The Benediction Loggia of Boniface VIII, dated to the last years of the thirteenth century, included three frescoes: the baptism of Constantine, the founding of the Lateran basilica, and Boniface blessing the people. See Mitchell 1951. The loggia was dismantled by Domenico Fontana between 1585 and 1590.

110. See note 93 above. Similarly the scene in the Stanza di Costantino is not a "Grundsteinlegung von Alt-St. Peter," as Quednau 1979 styles it. For the related but distinct iconography of Constantine laying a foundation stone, see the transept fresco in St. John the Lateran discussed by Freiberg 1988, 145; and Freiberg 1995, 104–7.

111. Freiberg 1988, 528–35, for the text of the *Acta* and an English translation.

112. Baronius 1738–46, III, anno 324, p. 50. Scavizzi 1987, 43, comments on Baronius's reliance on the *Acta*.

113. Ugonio 1585, 4, wrote of the "quadretto, il quale si mette ne i giorni festivi di detta chiesa sopra l'altar grande, & è quello che lui [S. Silvestro] mostrò à Constantino, quando gli domandò chi erano questi Pietro e Paolo che gli erano apparsi, e chi vuol vedere questa historia, legga la vita di S. Silvestro."

114. Lassels 1670, 43–44. Sarah McPhee kindly brought the reference to my attention.

115. De Sebastiani 1683, 8; Piazza 1687, 290.

116. Maii I (4 May), 445.

117. I am using the *Breviarium romanum* of 1658 from the Archive of the Chapter of S. Pietro in Vaticano (BAV, Stampati, 446), 230–32 (31 December).

118. Jacoby in Frommel and Winner 1986, and Jacoby 1987.

119. Redig de Campos 1967, 213–14.

120. The commission dates from 1622, its patron Marie de' Medici. See Dubon 1964, Krüger 1989, and Zurawski 1989.

121. Dubon 1964, 16.

122. Unlike the Baptism, the Vision was not one of the scenes brought from Paris by Cardinal Barberini. Coolidge 1966, refers to Constantine's Vision of the Cross as "The Adlocutio." Krüger 1989, 162–66, 180–85, points out that the emperor gestures toward the vision with both arms rather than raising just one arm, as would be the case in a proper *adlocutio*.

123. Dubon 1964, 19; and Nesselrath in Mancinelli et al. 1984, 194–97.

124. Pallavicino 1839–40, I, 377.

125. Bernini 1713, 104.

126. This was a fact known to Domenico Bernini, 102.

127. See Klinger in Lavin et al. 1981, 248–50, where the statue of Henry IV, dedicated in 1608, is identified as the source for the statue of Philip IV.

128. The words describing the tomb to be built for Queen Christina are: "a somiglianza di quello della Contessa." See Braham and Hager 1977, 56–60; Enggass 1976, 68–69.

129. I owe this information and many kindnesses to Professors Juliusz Chroscicki of the University of Warsaw (who brought the letter to my attention) and Mieczyslaw Morka of the Instytut Sztuki, Polska Akademia Nauk, Warsaw. See Morka 1986, 129; Karpowicz 1974, 22; and Brahmer 1939, 140, for the relevant text of the letter of 6 June 1693, as follows: "J'ai dit cent fois, et même au pape 'incidenter', que je m'étonne qu'on n'ait pas placé une statue à VM [Votre Majesté, i.e., Jan III] dans le sommet du grand théâtre de S. Pierre, vis-à-vis de celle de Constantin, ouvrage de Bernino, avec ces inscriptions allusives à Rome: 'Constantinus dedit, Joannes servavit' ou bien 'asservit'. Je ne sais en quelle manière il faudrait habiller VM. Je crois qu'elle devrait être armée et avec des brodequins à la romaine, et quelque marque à la polonaise. Il serait nécessaire d'avoir un schizzo de toute la figure en son entier, fait par la main virtuosa de M. George [J. E. Szymonowicz-Siemiginowski] qui représente au natural la taille pour la hauteur, grosseur etc. Pour les linéaments du visage, ils sont fort bien exprimés par un pastel de M. George chez M. le cardinal Barberin, et on s'en pourrait servir ici. Elle ne sera pas à cheval, car on a trop de peine à trouver ici une pièce entière de marbre blanc de Carrare et parfait. Et de le bien venir, cela porterait trop de temps. Et cependant, inter os offam multa caderent. Mons. Giori n'a pas encore déterminé où il faut la placer. Car vis-à-vis de Constantin, place qui me plaisait infiniment et que j'ai envisagée, on a résolu de mettre la fameuse comtesse Matilde, qui donna le patrimoine de S. Pierre, sive partem Tusciae, à l'Eglise, comme Constantin lui a donné Rome. Le dit M. Giori la veut placer vis-à-vis d'une qu'il veut faire aussi au roi Louis Le Grand. Mais le lieu où ces statues seront, n'est pas encore fixé. Le prélat montre son beau génie qui ne saurait souffrir la nonchalance pour ne pas dire l'ingrati-

tude des Romains envers VM, qui ne se doivent pas contenter de l'inscription à son honneur qui est au Capitole."

130. Pastor 1923–53, XXX, 215–350.

131. Wittkower 1961, 464–73; Johns 1993, 62–64. For another example of monumental art inflected by the Jansenist controversy at precisely this time, see Marder 1984.

132. Ferrabosco and Costaguti 1684, pt. X, citing Baronius who recounts Frederick Barbarossa's destruction of the fountain in 1167.

133. Wittkower 1961, 466. For the Stanza dell'Incendio, see the contributions of J. Guillaume, F. Mancinelli, and A. Nesselrath in Frommel and Winner 1986, 159–81; and Pietrangeli et al. 1992, 130.

134. Partridge and Starn 1990, 47–48: "Et della singular pietà di quel Prencipe e Cristianissimo [Carlo Magno] sono piene le historie, ma particolarmente è degno di memoria, quello che di lui si legge, che per divotione baciò ad uno per uno tutti i gradi delle scale di San Pietro."

135. Quoted by Wittkower 1961, 466, from the *Relazione della Statua Equestre di Carlo Magno*, Siena, 1725.

136. Quoted by Wittkower 1961, 473, without the present context.

137. Brauer and Wittkower 1931, 43–45; Wittkower 1966, 215–16; Enggass 1978; and Montagu 1989, 128–34.

138. Montagu 1985a, 138–39.

139. Pastor 1923–53, XXX, 14.

140. Pastor 1923–53, XXX, 122.

141. Pastor 1923–53, XXX, 150.

142. Albert 1988.

143. On Spada's role in St. Peter's, see Montagu 1989, 129; and Güthlein 1979, 184–87.

144. At this time his nephew Carlo, already appointed archpriest of the Basilica, assumed the role of prefect. See Del Re 1969, 301, n. 41.

145. The figure of Peter with Charlemagne and Leo III is thought to have appeared on the right of the apse, and in the restored section on the left side of the apse Christ is shown bestowing the vexillum on Constantine and the keys on Sylvester. See Waetzoldt 1964, 40, n. 226; and the newer literature in Herklotz 1989, 81, n. 194. The fact that the appearance of Constantine can be attested at the triclinium only from the seventeenth century and may well date from the restoration should not trouble us. If nothing else, the situation proves the strength of his symbolic presence at the time and his role as the pendant for Charlemagne. As a pair, Sylvester and Constantine were analogous to Leo the Great and Charlemagne.

146. In a public lecture at the National Gallery of Art, Washington, D.C. (December 1992), Professor Marc Fumaroli suggested the influence of the early Christian Barberini ivory upon the composition of Bernini's equestrian statues of Constantine and Louis XIV. The ivory had been given to Cardinal Francesco in France in 1625 by the French archaeologist and literato Nicholas-Claude Fabri de Peiresc; see *Byzance* 1992, 63–66, with bibliography.

147. Marder 1980 and 1984; Lavin 1987, especially 447–51.

148. Magnuson 1982–86, II, 134–37. See also Chapter 9.

149. On the basis of the famous critique of Bernini's Constantine (Chigi, J. VII, 270) which mentions Charlemagne, Haus 1970, n. 377, has already suggested that the second equestrian was anticipated by Alexander VII; but this conclusion is not warranted by the critique, which dates from the eighteenth century and not from the time of the unveiling of the Constantine as Haus believed (see his n. 336).

150. The coffer motif also appears over the altarpiece of the Altieri Chapel in S. Francesco a Ripa and over the window of the Alaleona Chapel in SS. Domenico e Sisto.

151. AFSP, Piano I, vol. 348, p. 111 left and right, record payments totaling 120 scudi made on 8 July, 26 August, 23 September, and 2 December 1671 to "Monsù Gio. Rinaldo scult.re . . . à conto delle due Statue di stucco, che reggono l'Arme di Papa Aless.ro 7." The payments were approved by Bernini "p. il lavoro di due statue di stucco grandi p.mi 15 ½ l'una, che tengono l'Arme della S.t. me. di Aless.ro 7o . . . sotto il Braccio verso Cesi." Rinaldi frequently worked for Bernini.

152. The better known example is in the Metropolitan Museum of Art and is catalogued by Millon 1984, 188, pl. 25, inscribed "Bernino nel portico del Vaticano nel Latto sinistro oposto ala gran Scala Reggia." A second drawing by the young Juvarra in the Vatican Library has been recently published by McPhee 1993, 349, fig. 61. (My thanks to Sarah McPhee for sharing this discovery before its publication.) Juvarra's interest was no doubt related to his project of 1714 for a new sacristy for St. Peter's, to be entered through the south corridor (see Birindelli 1986, 21–46).

153. BAV, Chigi a. I. 19, fol. 40v, now published by Menichella in Martinelli et al. 1987, 15, fig. 25; and Morello 1992, 206, but without the associations I have made.

154. Alexander had used the term "metamorphosis" in his diary to describe his own transformation from cardinal to pope. Cf. BAV, Chigi a. I. 8: "Et eligerunt summum pontificem Cardinalem Chisium, qui vocari iussit Alessandrum Septimum – Metamorphosis" (cited in Rossacher 1971, 12–13). Rossacher 1986, used the term again in a modern critical context without citing sources and published a drawing that he identified as a study by Bernini for an equestrian statue of Charlemagne. The stylistic evidence for an attribution to Bernini is not convincing to me.

155. Alfarano 1914, 115, 152.

156. Pallavicino 1839–40, I, 377.

157. Avviso of 28 March 1671, quoted in Chapter 3, note 126.

158. See Chapter 3.

159. Chigi was in Aachen in 1649–50; see Pastor 1923–53, XXX, 127.

160. There is a similar relationship between ruler image and the stairs of approach at the Scala del Maresciallo, from which Gregory IX may be seen, as Margaret Kuntz explains in a forthcoming publication drawn from Kuntz 1996.

161. There is no architectural history of the Sala Regia to which the reader may be referred. See Redig De Campos 1967, 127. The most succinct iconographic description is in Taja 1750, 9. For a study of the frescoes, see Davidson 1976. The iconography is discussed by Röttgen 1975.

162. Letter of Girardon to Colbert cited in Chapter 7, note 40. The disingenuous tenor of this remark is comparable to Bernini's initial reluctance to carve the portrait bust of Francesco d'Este (Montagu 1985a, 157–60).

163. Avviso of 11 October 1670 in Rossi 1940, 57; and Martinelli 1959, 207: "Si portò Sua Santità giovedi doppo pranzo in lettica à vedere la propria fabrica del nuovo palazzo al Giesù, dove pensando veder nel cortile di esso la statua di D. Gasparo suo nepote à cavallo, conforma di già era stata ordinata al Cav.re Bernini con lo sborso un pezzo prima del denaro, non ebbe questa sodisfattione, e voltatosi al Cav.re che costi si trovava, si dolse con esso di questa tardanza, quale volendo humilmente scusarsi, proseguì sorridendo il Papa: Crediamo che con questi vostri cavalli, ne il Rè di Francia verrà à Roma, ne mio nepote si portarà à Parigi." Quoted in Martinelli 1959, 207.

164. Rossi 1939, 544 (9 February 1669): "Il Cav.re Bernino hà finalmente terminata la statua di Costantino, quale vien censurata da molti."

165. See Wittkower 1966, 254–55.

166. Rossi 1940, 58 (13 December 1670, cited in Wittkower 1966, 254): "Resta scoperta la statua di Costantino Magno sopra le scale, per andare alla Cappella Ponteficia del Vaticano, lavorata dal Bernino, e ciascuno vi assegna la sua pecca, e particolarmente, che non paia atto naturale, che stando egli à cavallo ripieno di spavento, senza briglia, e senza staffe, et anco tutto imbizzarrito resti inalborato à segno tale, che stimasi per impossibile, che un'huomo senza ritengo alcuno possa sostenersi sul dorso d'un cavallo simile; del resto in quanto al lavoro, non puol'esser fatto con maggior perfettione."

167. See Rossi 1940, 58, for the discussion on 28 March 1671 of Bernini's placement of the Navicella, with references to "suo poco applaudito Costantino," and "il cumulo degli errori, che si osserva nella sua opera nuova, e moderna del Gran Costantino" (again Chapter 3, note 26).

168. BAV, Vat. lat. 8622, fols. 134–35 ("Del Costantino del Cav.re Bernini"), printed in extenso by Fraschetti 1900, 321–24; not mentioned in Wittkower 1966. The writer describes the Charlemagne in the future tense, hence the date of the tract before 1720: "Se a fronte nell'altro lato de' portici (come esigge ogni dritto) si ponga una altra statua equestre a Carlo Magno è da sperarsi che non vi mancherà artefice che lo superi." The defense of Bernini cited in the following note suggests the critique was issued during the artist's lifetime, and other issues noted below would suggest a dating of c. 1670–74.

169. BAV, Vat. lat. 8622, fols. 154–57 ("Osservazioni contro il Constantino del Bernini e risposte"), referred to by Fraschetti 1900, 324, but not transcribed. It is not mentioned in Wittkower 1966. Berger 1985, 73–74, misinterpreted it as additional criticism of Bernini's work.

170. BAV, Barb. lat. 4331, fols. 1–23 ("Il Costantino Messo alla Berlina ò la Porta di San Pietro"), published with extracts by Previtali 1962, who is cited by Wittkower 1966, 254,

and in the subsequent literature. Bauer 1976, 46–53, published excepts in English translation. My dating is based on the mention, on fol. 17v, of the completed statue of Charlemagne in the south narthex ("a fronte nell'altro fianco de Portici già terminati un altra statua equestre à Carlo Magno"). Haus noted this reference but concluded that it meant Alexander VII was responsible for the second statue.

171. See the transcription of BAV, Vat. lat. 8622, fols. 134–35 in Fraschetti 1990, 321–324; and the original text of BAV, Barb. lat. 4331, fols. 1v, 2v, 3–3v, 3v–4, 5–5v, where the same points are made with several new ones.

172. The reference in the earlier critique is veiled by allusions to the broken and punctured Acqua Vergine; that in the later critique is quite direct in naming Luigi and describing his misdeeds.

173. According to an avviso, her argument was that "si come la Sodomia hoggidì non è più boccone fiorentino, ma ben si universale, e cibo specialmente da Prencipi, così li Sodomiti particolarmente in Roma hanno d'Protettori e Defensori grandi, sendo boccone che in Roma piace a' Piccoli e a' Grandi" (Martinelli 1959, 209).

174. Fraschetti 1900, 324, correctly understood BAV, Vat. lat. 8622, fols. 154–57, as a response to fols. 134–35, but made no attempt at interpretation. Berger treated fols. 154–57 as additional criticism, rather than "risposte." He notes the difficulty of reading the author's handwriting, which indeed is challenging enough to suggest why Fraschetti did not deal with it.

175. For an illustration and discussion of Schor's Pegasus and its appearance at the banquet, see Montagu 1989, 197, and figs. 268, 269. A drawing that I believe may be related to Schor's *trionfi* and to the Constantine, and hence to the criticism, is illustrated in Rossacher 1986, fig. 24.

176. "E bugia che la testa di Constantino non s'assomgli al vero perche non e bello. E fu sempre in arbitrio de scultori e Pittori variare a suo talento i sembiansi. E la bellezza consiste nella proportione delle membra. . . . Se v'è sembra il capo d'Abacu. egli ha faccia di santo, e se la Corona e simile alle Corne egli ha faccia di Mosé."

177. "I scultori sono imitatori della natura e la natura de viventi fù creata senza freno." See De Rossi 1704, 13–14, for the attribution to Phidias and Praxiteles. The comparison was not casual: an avviso of 30 November 1680, written two days after Bernini's death, described him as "the Praxiteles of our day" ("Spirato finalmente sabbato sera il Praxitele de nostri tempi Cavalier Bernino"; Martinelli 1959, 226). Notes in Skippon 1663–64, 657, prove that the horses were thought to be Greek in Bernini's day: "At Monte Cavallo stand the stately and curious statues of two men holding two horses, the workmanship of Phidias and Praxiteles."

178. "Il moto e la quiete: Della pausa lo mantiena nella sua giusta positura. Il moto ò il Corso lo distende se dunque assela al moto, non è contro la natura, che paia un poco qui disteso. E cosi le gambe sono p. misura giustissime, e per proportione adeguate, ma la curvatura le fà vedere al quanto attrate. . . . Dite che la coda è troppo lunga. Ma

[word illegible] la proportione secondo la regola del Moto e della quiete di viene in Bilancia giustiss.ma. Poi considerando quel Pestriero nel moto naturale mentre marcia à galoppo ed alza à piedi anteriori, il tergo s'abassa e la coda casca in terra onde ingegnosam.te affasciata dall'Artefice, si allontana dal tocco del Suolo e si rende più nobile sostenuta."

179. Wittkower 1961a, 502, n. 13, referred to a curvet. Berger 1985, 70–71, refers to a pesade. The differences are irrelevant to our purpose except to demonstrate the intentional ambiguity of the poses in Bernini's work.

180. BAV, Barb. lat. 4331, fol. 7v, has a reference to the "Cavalli Spagnuoli."

181. Wittkower 1961a, for the material of this paragraph. Newer literature in Berger 1985, 50–63; and Lavin 1993, 166–85.

182. Wittkower 1961a, 521, doc. 21.

183. Marder 1980, 1984.

184. According to rumor, Benedetti was to sell his villa on the Janiculum to finance the Trinità de' Monti project. The idea that the equestrian might end up there was still current in May 1671 as the report of the Modenese ambassador indicates (Wittkower 1961a, 523, doc. 33).

185. Wittkower 1961a, 521, docs. 23, 24. Bernini wrote that he would make a clay model himself and assist the young French pensioners with the actual carving.

186. Letter of 27 November 1673; Wittkower 1961a, 527, doc. 60. Berger 1985, gives evidence that the students of the French Academy worked on the Louis XIV equestrian from 1671 to 1677.

187. Jestaz 1966, 175.

188. See Berger 1985, for this and the following details of the history of the equestrian of Louis XIV.

CHAPTER NINE. Iconographic, Ritual, and Historical Contexts for the Ensemble

1. The Scala Santa of the medieval papal palace at the Lateran is supposed to have been used by Christ, having been taken from the praetorium of Pontius Pilate. Helena, Constantine's mother, brought the stairs from Jerusalem to Rome, as was well known in the seventeenth century (Freiberg 1991b, 82–83, citing Panciroli's handbook of 1600).

2. Frommel 1973, 60–66. On the topic in general, see Cousins 1992, Gambardella 1993, Ludwig 1939, Templer 1992a, Templer 1992b, and Wilkinson 1975.

3. Heydenreich 1967, 3, points out that the width of the Urbino staircase even exceeded the dimensions (unexecuted as such) that Pius II envisioned for the Palazzo Piccolomini in Pienza.

4. Frommel 1973, 60; superseded by Frommel 1985.

5. My measurements for the Scala Regia pertain to the lower flights. Those from the Palazzo Farnese are included in Frommel 1985, 142. By comparison, the steps of the north stairs of the Palazzo Barberini were 15 palmi (3.35 m.) wide and 2 ⅔ palmi (0.59 m.) deep as originally built. My

thanks to Patricia Waddy for the relevant information from documents

6. Satkowski 1993, 53.

7. Vasari 1568, IV, 451.

8. Cancellieri 1790, 10.

9. Cancellieri 1790, 10, dated the Spada colonnade to the pontificate of Urban VIII (1623–44). Similarly, Portoghesi 1970, 98 and 541; and Wittkower 1985, 225, still suggest a date shortly after 1635.

10. Neppi 1975, 175–88, especially 176, with documentation for land acquisition and construction.

11. Neppi's views on the attribution of the colonnade are clarified in Neppi 1983, especially 110–16.

12. Neppi 1975, 122, 176, for the original purchase and the subsequent acquisition, respectively.

13. The measurements are those of the width of the perspective field and the height of the tallest order (Neppi 1975, 146–47; and Neppi 1983, 107).

14. Neppi 1975, 127 and 189, mentions Bernardino as protector of the Minims. In discussing the Meridian Gallery, Neppi 1975, 189, mentions the fundamental work of the Minim student of Maignan, Jean-François Niceron, whose *Perspective curieuse ou magie artificiele des effets merveilleux de l'optique* was published in 1638. The connection to the Minims has also been made by Connors 1990.

15. Neppi 1975, 177; Neppi 1983, 107.

16. Neppi 1975, 177, n. 17, provides documentation suggesting that Magni's new painting on the garden wall in 1653 was repainted in 1659.

17. Neppi 1983, 111, offers evidence that Bitonto had hoped to build a perspective whose central vault would have been flanked by aisles with flat ceilings as was his tabernacle for the high altar of S. Paolo Maggiore, Bologna. The basis of the composition would thus have been the entrance of the Palazzo Farnese in Rome, with associations discussed in Lavin 1980, 97.

18. Details of the engravings indicate that Falda was guided by fragmentary information and his imagination rather than the architect's drawings, yet there may have been a scheme to transform the double landing of the staircase into a loggia with a view toward the papal gardens.

19. Waddy 1990, 291–320, with additional bibliography and, on p. 416, n. 159, the following *misura* for the painter Vincenzo Corallo: "Per haver dipinto a fresco il Muro incontro detta finestra . . . dipintoci, un ordine d'architettura con doi Pilastri dorici dalle parti con sua basa, Capitello, con Cornice Architravata sopra con doi risalti che termina il Vano dov'è il Paese dipinto con suo piedestallo sotto con cimasa, e basa con havere s . . . to finto attorno le due finestre e dipintovi à una l'impannata finta e dipintovi il Paese à fresco colorito con distanze, arbori, boscaglie, e figurine barche, e fiumi il quale ornamento è longo palmi 25 alt. reguagliato palmi 24, scudi 30."

20. Waddy 1990, 112–16, provides specifics and further bibliography. Hibbard 1962, 75–76, already mentioned the relationship of the Borghese vista to Borromini's perspective at Palazzo Spada but saw no wider context for the motif.

21. Waddy 1990, 251–71 (especially 257–58, for the statue), attributes the design of the renovations to the patron Cardinal Francesco Barberini and his house architect Angelo Torrone, rather than to Bernini as has been done in the past.

22. See Ackerman 1964, for the project described by Vasari 1568, VII, 224.

23. Neppi 1975, 289–90. In the same description, Virgilio also mentions that it was possible to see a perspective from the staircase on the opposite side of the central courtyard, but I am uncertain whether he is referring to the colonnade. For this and the shutters, see Neppi 1983, 106.

24. In Rome, Skippon 1663–64, 650, knew "Dr. Gibbs, who formerly practiced physick, but now devotes himself to poetry, and is lately made professor of humanity in the Sapienza. He hath told us he hath equal skill in making Greek, Latin, Italian, Spanish, French, and English verses. He also writes exactly like printing, and makes coats of arms, fregi, etc. with his pen very curiously." Somewhere Skippon obtained a list of English visitors in Rome since 1651 "to the number of 349."

25. Neppi 1975, 280, nos. 36 and 37; and Neppi 1983, 116, n. 2 and fig. 23. The epigram addresses a Barberini cardinal ("Vostra Eminenza"), who Neppi believes might have been Francesco Sr. (1597–1679), Antonio Jr. (1608–71), or Carlo (1630–1704). It runs as follows:

> Mole sub exigua spectatur porticus ingens;
> Cernitur in spatio semita longa brevi:
> Quoque magis distant tanto maiora videntur
> Quae sunt in proprio corpora parva loco.
> Artis opus mirae; mundi fallentis imago;
> Magna suis offert ipse pusillus, inops.
> Magna, sed in speciem, capienti parvula fiunt;
> Grandia sub coelo non nisi spectra manent.
> (Barb. lat. 1005, fol. 102)

26. Neppi 1975, 178; Neppi 1983, 105–6.

27. Neppi 1975, 168–73 and doc. 44. See also pp. 125 (Bernini's work for Bernardino's villa at Tivoli), 131 (the contacts with Bernardino regarding the crossing of St. Peter's, the campanili, and the high altar of S. Paolo in Bologna), and 140–43 (Bernini's decoration of a room in Palazzo Spada in 1636–39).

28. Pace Worsdale 1986, 103, who maintains that "the pope seems twice as tall as his real height" when he appears at the top of the stairs.

29. Shearman 1983.

30. Dykmans 1980–82, 93–117, 122–28, 147–50, 190–210.

31. Dykmans 1968, 598, n. 4, quotes the reference of Torrigio 1618 (new edition 1635, 546) to Monte Mario "dove forse apparse la Croce al pio Constantino."

32. Lualdi 1644–53, I, provides a whole disquisition on the site of the vision and its appearance. Baronius, *Annals*, 516–17, describes the entry through the "Prata Neronis." Severano 1630, 34, emphasizes that Constantine, "riconoscendo la vittoria di Dio mediante il seguito della croce, che gl'era apparso, volse per rendimento di gratie venerar ancor'il detto sepolcro di S. Pietro suo Vicario in terra." Severano

is cited in Haus 1970, n. 255, who suggests a parallelism between Constantine and the pope to which I cannot subscribe. Piazza 1687, 289, follows Severano's account almost exactly: "Ritornando da Ponte Molle per il Prati Quinzii passò per il Vaticano, e riconscendo la vittoria da Dio, mediante il segno della Croce, che li era apparso, volle per rendimento di grazie, venerar ancora il detto Sepolcro di S. Pietro suo Vicario in Terra."

33. On the *adventus* theme, see Kantorowicz 1944 and Smith 1956. Kauffmann 1970, 278, has suggested a relationship between Constantine's historic advent on 29 October and the date of Bernini's commission for the equestrian (29 October 1654; remarked in my Chapter 7), as well as to the notation of the Adventus Divi in the Calendar of 354. To these powerful associations I believe we should add the foundation date of the basilica, in the seventeenth century commonly held to be A.D. 324, and celebrated every year from the time of Urban VIII's accession.

34. In addition to the passages in Dykmans 1980–82 cited in note 30, see Catalano 1750–51, I, 358–70.

35. Catalano 1750–51, I, 368–70; Dykmans 1980–82, 204–10.

36. Pallavicino 1838–40, I, 377.

37. Pallavicino 1839–40, I, 377.

38. Compare the description of Montaigne's audience with the pope on 29 December 1580 (Montaigne 1983, 74–75).

39. See Dykmans 1980–82, 27–52 and 98–108, for the election ceremonial.

40. Wittkower 1966, 202–03, for the history of the relief that was initially placed over the portal just inside the basilica and transferred to its present location in the narthex in 1649. We should recall that after Paul V the "Tu Es Petrus" would have been sung in the presence of the seated statue of St. Peter that Bernini replaced with his Constantine.

41. See the accounts in Moroni 1840–61, VIII, 160; and Dykmans 1980–82, 51–52.

42. Moroni 1840–61, VIII, 186; Dykmans 1980–82, 221–37. According to modern verbal tradition, the Scala dei Morti is so named because each pope uses it only once, in a coffin carried from the palace to the basilica, although I have no evidence for this practice.

43. Neppi 1975, 175–76, cites his doc. 47 (misprinted as 48), the "Minute de' capitoli della vita del card. Bernardino Spada" written by Virgilio Spada in 1662: "E s'ingegnò [Cardinal Bernardino] di ricevere da un vicino certo sito accanto ad un giardinetto segreto per fare in tal sito una prospettiva di materia conforme che haveva veduto per opra del Cavaliero Borromino architetto nell'oratione delle quarantore di Palazzo [Vaticano], e riuscì cosa molto vaga, ma il costo eccedé di assai il gusto."

44. Recorded after the fact in a letter of 17 September 1656, published by Neppi 1975, 176, n. 5, and doc. 39.

45. See De Santi 1919, and the more recent wave of literature after Weil 1974b, such as Fagiolo dell'Arco 1976, Fagiolo dell'Arco and Carandini 1977–78, Noehles 1978, Noehles 1982, Weil 1982, Noehles 1985, and now Hammond 1994, 151–56.

46. Weil 1974b, 219.

47. Weil 1974b, 222–27, for this and the following information.

48. Noehles 1969, 204, n. 43, cites a mention of Bernini's "lumi ciechi, e coperti" without identifying the location of the set.

49. Described in an avviso first noted by Hibbard 1965, 163; and subsequently by Weil 1974b, 227; Fagiolo Dell'Arco and Carandini 1977–78, I, 75; Lavin 1980, 96. Lavin relates the hidden light of 1628 to the 1619 illumination by Bernini cited above.

50. Lavin 1980, 96, n. 18, associates the engraving with the earlier apparatus because of the formal relationship with the Baldacchino. For the literature on the Piranesi engraving, whose inscribed legend attributes the set to Bernini, see Weil 1974b, 243, n. 73 (with no opinion on the date of the apparatus); and Fagiolo dell'Arco and Carandini 1977–78, I, 253–55 (dating the apparatus to the pontificate of Clement IX for unspecified reasons but comparing it to a *macchina processionale* of 1686 designed by G. Ruggeri, not Bernini). To my mind the available evidence for dating is inconclusive, although I contribute to the hypotheses later in this chapter.

51. Caetano 1691, 131, described the Forty Hours celebration held in the Cappella Paolina in 1675, with its sepulchre "ornato di gran quantità di lumi, fregiato d'oro, à chiaro, e scuro, con molti angeli attorno, e argentaria, disegnato da Cavalier G. Lorenzo Bernino" (Worsdale 1981, 232).

52. Cf. the many examples mentioned in Weil 1974b (with a catalogue of descriptive pamphlets); and Fagiolo dell'Arco and Carandini 1977–78. For the 1633 apparatus and that of 1650, see Fagiolo dell'Arco and Carandini 1977–78, I, 82–83, 153–54.

53. Fagiolo Dell'Arco and Carandini 1977–78, I, 138–40, with quotation of Gigli's assertion that all the cardinals, the confraternities, and nobility were invited to participate, "le quali vi andorno processionalmente di modo che vi fu un concorso di Popolo grandissimo."

54. I would not rule out the possibility that Spada was referring to the set depicted on the Piranesi engraving. We have noted Bernini's name on the legend and formal similarities to the Baldacchino, and Borromini was unhappy with his credit on the design of the latter monument. This was also a problem between the architects in the design of the Palazzo Barberini (1626–33). The circumstances of shared (or disputed) authorship would be particularly compelling if we could date the engraved scheme to 1628, when the problems between the protagonists were developing.

55. In a letter of 30 October 1655 written to Cardinal Bernardino Spada concerning Borromini's refinements on the garden colonnade, Bitonto complained of poor health which he attributed to his work on the Cappella Paolina: "La cappella paulina mi ha consumato." Bitonto died in 1659, according to an avviso of May 10: "E qui passato all'altra vita con universale sentimento il P. Fr. Giov. Maria da Bitonto Agostiniano soggetto celebre nell'Architettura, e Disegno, con aver fatto diverse macchine in tempo di cinque Pontefici" (Rossi 1940, 322).

56. Kuntz 1996.
57. Fagiolo dell'Arco and Carandini 1977–78, I, 75.
58. See Chapters 1 and 2.
59. See Chapter 3.
60. See Plates 12, 20, and 21.
61. For examples, see Den Broeder 1991, 144–45, cat. no. 64 (Francesco Panini, "The Interior of Saint Peter's Illuminated"); 200–01, cat. no. 90 (Louis-Jean Desprez, "The Interior of St. Peter's Illuminated").
62. De Sebastiani 1683, 7–8, mentions "una parte del Sagro Legno della Croce, che donò Costantino à S. Silvestro."
63. The letter of 17 September 1656 begins as follows: "Mercordì, se mal non mi ricordo, discorrendo col P.re Abbate Ughelli nella mia camera dell'audienza incontro alla prospettiva del giardino segreto, con occasione ch'egli lodava la detta prospettiva io venni dicendogli il pensiero che qualche volta m'era passato per fantasia di farne una in qualche chiesa e come che il poterla fare in testa d'una nave principale aiuterebbe assai, e per la grandezza e per altro, la nobiltà e singolarità dell'opera, andassimo ricercando se alcuna ve ne fusse opportuna et ottenibile per la effettuatione." Quoted from the longer letter published by Neppi 1975, 176, n. 5, doc. 39.
64. The date of Bramante's project for the fictive choir may be 1479–80, as more recent critics propose, or 1482–87, as earlier scholars have suggested. The earlier literature is summarized in Bruschi 1969, 122–41, 171–73, 751–57. Stefano Borsi's catalogue in Borsi 1989, 173–77, provides a synthesis of scholarly opinions.
65. Letter of 19 September 1654, from Cardinal Bernardino to Virgilio, quoted in Neppi 1975, doc. 39, 281–82.
66. The perspective was not realized until 1664, following the construction of a full-scale model, the commission and completion of Ercole Ferrata's statue of St. Agnes, and the installation of the angels over the saint. Documentation in Eimer 1971, II, 484–87, 495–98, who remarks upon the perspectives only in passing (pp. 355, 358–59).
67. See Varriano 1986, 151–52, fig. 91.
68. For the treatises and the literature on perspective, see Kemp 1990.
69. Paris, Bibliothèque Nationale, ms. Italien, 2082, fol. 90.
70. See Freiberg 1974, including a corpus of 78 examples of the type. Kristen van Ausdall of Rutgers University is preparing a dissertation on the Renaissance tabernacle.
71. Lavin 1980, 95–98, 102–3. For a different opinion, see Montagu 1982, 242.
72. Lavin 1980, 97, n. 20, with citation of Neppi 1975, 125, 176 (making the connection with the Forty Hours sets); and Heimbürger Ravalli 1977, 53–55.
73. The contract for the sculpture was worked out from 1633 to October 1634, when Algardi signed it. Bernini's involvement with the altar dates from February 1634, and his drawings for the architecture can be dated between April and September 1634. Because the drawings give no clear indication of the sculpture, Jennifer Montagu suggests that Bernini was unaware of the negotiations for the sculpture

and hoped to gain the commission for himself – a circumstance fostered by Virgilio Spada, whose devious behavior toward Bernini can be documented in a related context. See Montagu 1985a, 51–53, 369–72 (with extensive bibliography); and Montagu 1985b, 34–37, with literature in her note 75.
74. Lavin 1980, 97.
75. Moroni 1841, 280–99; and Rubin 1991, with extensive bibliography.
76. Rubin 1991, 243, and figs. 12, 14, 16.
77. Rubin 1991, 248, 267.
78. Shearman 1972, 141–42.
79. Cf. Catalano 1750–51, II, 297–99, "De festo Corporis Christi." Two paintings of the procession include the image reproduced in Krautheimer 1985, fig. 48 (Museo di Palazzo di Venezia, n. 3261, deposito n. 120) and the picture illustrated here (Museo di Roma, n. 4216). My thanks to Lucia Cavazzi at the Museo di Roma for information on the location of these works.
80. BAV, Vat. lat. 12429, fols. 137v, 160v, 184–184v, 211v, 240, 259, 283, 327, 352v–353, 384–384v, 416v–417, 457–457v, are notices from Paul V's master of ceremonies between 1609 and 1620. Other searches have not turned up variations.
81. Fontana 1694, 243; and Krautheimer 1985, 63–68.
82. In 1818 the changing points for the porters occurred at the Sistine Chapel, the Portone di Bronzo, the end of the north colonnade arm, Piazza Rusticucci ("avanti la fontana"), the end of the south colonnade arm, the entrance to the south corridor, the statue of Charlemagne, and at the confessio of the basilica. See ASV, Sacro Palazzo Apostolico, titolo XI, 133, 4, art. II, fasc. 15.
83. See Ingersoll 1985; Worsdale 1986, 32, n. 10; and Rubin 1991, 263.
84. Moroni 1841, 285. Significantly, the tapestry had been given to Clement VII by Francis I as a sign of fealty.
85. Catalano 1750–51, II, 404–5; Martin 1969, 99.
86. In addition to Catalano 1750–51, see Moroni 1840–61, VIII, 142, 161. Martin 1969, 99, mentioned these "many solemne dayes in the yere, namely among the rest, every Sunday in Advent, and lent, Ashewenesday, Goodfryday, Holy Thursdaye, and so forth, which solemnitie is for the most part kept within the Palace in the Popes Chappel ... but upon the more principal feastes, as Christmas, Twelfthday, Easter, Ascension, Whitsunday, S. Peters day, in S. Peters Chappel within his Churche, joyning to the Palace beneth."
87. I am using the *Breviarium Romanum* of 1658 from the Archive of the Chapter of S. Pietro in Vaticano (BAV, Stampati, 446), 958–65; and Piazza 1687, 250–52 (3 May). On the transfer of the Cross to St. Peter's, see Scavizzi 1989, 42, with comments (p. 36) on sixteenth-century discussions of Constantine's vision. The influence of the relic on the design of the crossing piers is discussed by Lavin 1968, 20. Lindner 1975, 67, makes reference to Constantine's vision in the breviary.
88. Piazza cited Torrigio 1618 (edition of 1635, 546), who

himself was not insistent on referencing the location (note 31 above).

89. Piazza 1687, 543–46. The Invention of the Cross was originally celebrated in the Greek Church on 14 September (Cross 1957, 698). This fact is of some interest in conjunction with the celebrations of the Exaltation in the Greek Church, where Constantine's vision is also recalled.

90. Piazza 1687, 288–90.

91. *Breviarium Romanum* 1658, 230–32 (31 December, "in secondo nocturno lectio iiii"). A *Martyrologium Romanum*, Rome, 1651, from the Chigi collection reminds us on 31 December, "Romae natalis sancti Silvestri Papae, qui Magnum Constantinum Imperatorem baptizavit . . ." (p. 398; BAV, Chigi IV. 124).

92. Piazza 1687 (see discussion for 3 May, 21 May, 14 September, 18 November, and especially 31 December). On p. 290, Piazza describes the many gifts Constantine made to the basilica, including the picture of Peter and Paul. References to the baptism and the Vision of the Cross also appear in the *Acta Sanctorum Bollandiana*, Maii I (4 May), Antwerp, 1680, p. 445.

93. Baronius, *Martyrology*, 566–68. The same information appears in the *Martyrologium Romanum*, Rome, 1651.

94. The Baldacchino was commissioned by Urban VIII who instituted the feast of the foundation.

95. Piazza 1687, 673–77.

96. Lualdi 1644–53, I, passim, and fols. 121–124v for the celebration of 18 November.

97. The association of the splayed arch and an entrance derives from the conventional use of the form in palaces where stairs join courtyards as at Palazzo Farnese or Palazzo Mattei (respectively, Frommel 1985, figs. 222, 224; and Hibbard 1971, 127–29). The same allusion was recalled at the east-facing balcony on the exterior of the Cortile del Belvedere, as well as the motif on the upper loggia of the Palazzo Barberini.

98. Wittkower 1966, 259–60; Bernstock 1988; and now Zollikofer 1994.

99. Perlove 1990, pls. 3, 19.

100. Ostrow 1991, 96–97, and fig. 3, relates the workshop drawing to the Scala Regia and has suggested a date of 1664 for the scheme, corresponding to an appropriation of money presumably intended for the statue's execution. The dating is corroborated by an autograph pen sketch for the statue on the verso of the sheet that Bernini used for designing his fames and the papal escutcheon, executed in 1664, for the Scala Regia. The statue of Philip IV was executed by Bernini's pupil Girolamo Lucenti in 1664–66, unaccompanied by the columnar trappings of the early design.

101. See the illustrations in Bjürstrom 1962, 83, 139, 155, 173, 208, 224, 225, 227, 253, 255, 256, 257. Carandini 1990, with extensive bibliography, is a useful guide to Italian theater and spectacle in the seventeenth century. For an introduction to theaters and theater sets, see Pinelli 1973; and Fagiolo 1973.

102. Lavin 1980, 146–57. For discussions of Bernini and the theater, with additional bibliography, see Beecher and Ciavolella 1985; Hammond 1985; and Carandini 1990, 241–43.

103. Hammond 1985, 117, 119. For an introduction to Bernini's work in the theater, see D'Onofrio 1963 (intro. and app.); Lavin 1980; Beecher and Ciavolella 1985; and Hammond 1985.

104. See Lavin 1980, 150; and Hammond 1985, 118. The play is mentioned by Domenico Bernini 1713, 55; and described in a letter of the Modenese ambassador of 13 February 1638 (Fraschetti 1900, 264–65).

105. Krönig 1972.

106. Cf. Fraschetti 1900, 265; Beecher and Ciavolella 1985, 64.

107. For the flood, see Frosini 1977, 177–78.

108. Lavin 1980, 149–50.

109. "Fù pur anche detto che molti sotto il nome di tutela assassinavano chi confidava in loro. Fò nominato il portone che conduce nel palazzo di S. Pietro e fu essagerato che se i Patroni sapessero quello ch'entra et esce di notte, per il detto Portone, restarebbero maravigliati, e pure il Cardinal Barberino era presente all Comedia" (Fraschetti 1900, 264–65; D'Onofrio 1963, 98).

110. Beecher and Ciavolella 1985, 66, 68.

111. Jander 1969, 95–96, discusses the prologue to Francesco Cavalli's *Il Novello Giasone* of 1671, with designs by Carlo Fontana, in which the set collapses in ruins and the players blame the architect.

112. Beecher and Ciavolella 1985, 72, and passim for a fuller development of this theme.

113. Beecher and Ciavolella 1985, 74.

114. Beecher and Ciavolella 1985, 74. See Lavin 1980, 157, n. 31, for bibliography on Tesauro 1655.

115. Lavin 1980, 154–55.

116. From Alexander's diary for 14 April 1664 comes the notation "le Nicchie della Scala Regia stiano nel piano per uso de' pellegrini" (Morello 1981b, 308).

117. Although we arrive at the same idea from different evidence, I have obviously been influenced by Grabar 1990.

118. For Kircher's *Ars Magna Lucis et Umbrae*, Rome, 1646, see Carandini 1990, 216–17; and Rivosecchi 1982.

119. Rosand 1990, 148.

120. Noehles 1985, 91.

121. Rivosecchi 1982, 93–94.

122. References in Incisa della Rocchetta 1964. In addition to Rosa 1960, I have depended on Pastor 1923–53, XXXI; Magnuson 1982–86, II, 121–41; and Krautheimer 1985, 8–14; as well as the references cited below.

123. Cf. Pastor 1923–53, XXXI, 13–14; Bacci 1939.

124. For extensive bibliography, see Rosa 1960.

125. After the meeting of 1651, Mazarin characterized Mgr. Chigi as "homme d'espirit, bien intentionné, et d'une grande probité, et même sainteté de vie." But if his election were to succeed, "ce sera le plus faible pontificat qui ait été depuis Saint-Pierre." Sonnino 1966, 12–13.

126. Pastor 1923–53, XXXI, 1–9; and Rosa 1960.

127. See Krautheimer 1985, 10.

128. Rosa 1960.

129. Partner 1985; and now Partner 1990.

130. Romano 1932, 63.

131. Pallavicino 1839–40, I, 280–81; Pastor 1923–53, XXXI, 17.

132. Documents first published by Ozzola 1908, 16. The literature has been assembled by Westin 1978, 76–77, 149–50, 234–35. In the early sixteenth century the door between the two rooms was located next to their common wall on the south (Uffizi A 287, our Fig. 29). In 1521, the door was moved to be aligned with passages to the Sala Regia and the Logge, on the long axis of the rooms, as in our Fig. 28 (Shearman 1972, 25).

133. Sirén 1914, 157–58: "Man hat auss zweijen zimbern einss gemacht, undt umb die deformitet dess Gewelbess zu cachiren hat man diese decke gemacht, welche sehr artig gefallen ist, undt mit grau in weiss ohne viel arbeit bemahlet in ein gross muster, wie sie auf ihnen damasch inss gemein machen, mit weitleüfftigen branchissagen, undt den zeijchen dess wapens. Der grundt wahr gelb angestrichen darzwischen undt mit lichtbraun abgesetzt hinter dem laubwerck. Hernacher wahr das gelbe über raijret midt goldt, auf jede seite wahr in der mitten ein Kindt, so einen Schildt hielte, dar aber nicht viel facon an wahr; auf jeden seiten wahr wieder ein Kindt, so den teppicht aufhielte, welche aber alle sehr artig actioniret wahren; wiewohl an eine stelle 2 Kinder wahren. Die Schilde mit den Kindern wahren alle weiss wom gibst gelassen, die helffte von der tappeten sahe man auf jede seite aber alternativement wie eine guardine in falten hirunter hengend anfangen."

134. Rasmussen 1983, explains the papal chapel in detail.

135. Pallavicino 1839–40, I, 340, 411.

136. Barozzi and Berchet 1879, 243–44.

137. Skippon 1663–64, 651–52.

138. Pallavicino 1839–40 I, 263–66; 334–40; Barozzi and Berchet 1879, 222–24, 243–44; Incisa della Rocchetta 1964, 456–57.

139. Pastor 1923–53, XXXI, 124–29.

140. Barozzi and Berchet 1879, 243–44.

141. Ciampi 1878, 151.

142. Pallavicino 1839–40, I, 267; Ciampi 1878, 151, 214; Pastor 1923–53, XXXI, 16; Rosa 1960.

143. Skippon 1663–64, 652, wrote of the "neat models" he saw in the Quirinal Palace, including "the vatican palace with their gardens; and the roofs of them might be lifted up, and all the rooms discovered[,] a model of the pantheon, and one of the domo of Siena; a death's head in marble, rarely done by Bernini; a neat clock, made by Campani, wherein a death walks with a flaming sword at the striking of every hour." Skippon (1663–64, pp. 657–58) later visited "Signior Gioseppe Campani," the maker of fine lenses and clocks.

144. Pastor 1923–53, XXXI, 13, citing Pallavicino 1839–40, I, 27. On matters of Alexander's health, see Pastor 1923–53, XXXI, 17, 115, 116, 117, 121.

145. Pallavicino 1839–40, I, 267, recorded Alexander's request for the effigy, which was directed to his Jesuit friend there, Padre Goswin Nickel, who later became the general of the order and a promoter of Bernini's S. Andrea al Quirinale (Marder 1990, 110, n. 6; 112, n. 9).

146. The ambassador reports the pope's own observation that half of Rome and the majority of those outside believe his wound had not healed (Barozzi and Berchet 1879, 244).

147. My thanks to Drs. Joseph Cohn and Joseph Zullo for medical information on the rigors of bearing stones anywhere in the body, as much now as in the seventeenth century.

148. A still more restricted circle would have been privy to Alexander's autopsy, which justifies his own frustration over the treatment of his malady. "Fu aperto il corpo di N. Signore. Non vi si è trovata pietra alcuna; ma bensì il reno manco pieno di marcia bianca, non puzzolente, che ha così contaminata la punta di un de' polmoni, e la milza ancora. Da ciò si accendeva la febre. Il dolore che tanto lo martirizzava nasceva dal calare dell'urina, dal reno infocato e guasto alla vescica. Dentro la vescica vi erano tre grandole; dentro pure si è trovato grasso impastato. Il suo male principiò da una cascata, che fece a Castello Gandolfo, che offese il finaco. Sempre diceva, che il suo male non era pietra, e li medici, stimando il contrario, l'hanno medicato alla rovescia." Text in Pastor 1923–53, XXXI, 121. The fact that no stone was found in the autopsy does not mean that Alexander did not have one at some earlier time.

149. In 1625, the architect Orazio Torriani had designed a "talamo per la processione del Rosario" carried by forty men and bearing an image of the Madonna and child within a composition of four twisted columns topped by angels, joined by an architrave, and covered by a crown strongly resembling Bernini's design for the Baldacchino. See Fagiolo dell'Arco and Carandini 1977–78, I, 69–70; with reference to Lavin 1973. Another talamo designed by Bernini himself in 1639 for the church of the Madonna di Loreto assumed the form of a huge cloud that engulfed and effectively hid the men who carried it. The images on the cloud consisted of eleven "angels" carrying the Santa Casa di Loreto over the sea, while another four young angels provided instrumental and sung accompaniment in the procession from the Pantheon to the church near Piazza del Popolo. See Fagiolo dell'Arco and Carandini 1977–78, I, 119. The procession was repeated in 1640, and was anticipated by a similar one in 1637.

150. Moroni 1841, 280–99; and Incisa della Rocchetta 1932. Moroni cites a drawing of the talamo of 1655 by Carlo Ceci, but it has not been found.

151. Gigli's diary entry for 27 May 1655 is cited in Whitman and Varriano 1983, 120, without mention of the pope's illness.

152. "Perchè chiamarlo talamo? / Meglio sarebbe: letto / E al più presto possibile, / Magari cataletto" (Romano 1932, 56).

153. Worsdale 1986, fig. 14, has attributed the Procession of Corpus Christi with Pope Alexander VII Being Borne on a Litter (Musée des Beaux-Arts, Nancy, inv. 37) to the painter Giovanni Maria Morandi. The legend on the medal reads: "PROCEDAMUS ET ADOREMUS IN SPIRITU ET

VERITATE." Bonanni 1706, II, 665–85, provides a history of the feast of Corpus Christi from 1447. Bernini's *talamo* was used again by Clement IX in 1668, Clement X in 1670, Clement XI in 1706, Innocent XIII in 1722, Clement XIII in 1730, Benedict XIV in 1740, Clement XIV in 1769, Pius VI in 1775, and Pius VII in 1800 (Moroni 1841, 283).

154. Whitman and Varriano 1983, 119–20.

155. Gattico 1753, 353–59, for the circumstances of the scrutiny after Palm Sunday.

156. Indicative are the contemporary remarks of the Venetian ambassador (Barozzi and Berchet 1879, 245): "Ben è vero che Roma accrece di fabbriche e manca di abitatori, essendo rimarcabile la diminuzione di essi e patente ad ognuno, mentre nel corso e nelle strade più frequentate non si vedono, per così dire, se non case vuote e colla iscrizione: locanda." Against this opinion were the practical arguments, as for example, Pallavicino 1839–40, I, 181, regarding the feast of Corpus Christi.

157. Skippon 1663–64, 671.

158. Cited in Burke 1987, 169–70, 173.

159. Again the reader is referred to the summaries of the pontificate by Magnuson 1982–86, II, 121–41; Krautheimer 1985, 8–14; Pastor 1923–53, XXXI, 78–268; and the broader histories in Carsten 1961; Koenigsberger 1987; and Sonnino 1966 (the last kindly brought to my attention by Kathleen Doornbosch).

160. Remarked in Krautheimer 1985, 194, with further bibliography.

161. Skippon 1663–64, 676: "The boat fountain in Piazza d'Espagna, below this convent [Trinità de' Monti] was made upon the taking of Rochel. Cardinal Mazarine would have made a stately ascent thence up to Trinità del Monte, if the pope would have suffered the erecting of the French king's statue."

162. For the Créqui incident and its aftermath, see Pastor 1923–53, XXXI, 91–115; and Sonnino 1966, 29–67.

163. A similar event had occurred in London in October 1661, when a dispute over precedence between the Spanish and French ambassadors erupted in a brawl between their retainers. In that instance, Louis XIV decided on immediate and severe punishment of the offenders to the detriment of Philip IV's interests, and the same fate lay in store for the pope. Sonnino 1966, 31.

164. Pastor 1923–53, XXXI, 110–12.

165. Observed by Skippon 1663–64, 651, the pedestal for the pyramid bore the date 1664.

166. On Fabio Chigi and Jansenism, see Pastor 1923–53, XXXI, 171–268; Legrand and Ceyssens 1957; Ceyssens 1963–65; Albert 1988.

167. Sonnino 1966, 44, and passim, with the circumstances.

168. Sonnino 1966, 15.

169. Sonnino 1966, 44–45.

170. Carsten 1961, 469–70.

171. Lavin 1993, 175, with bibliography.

172. Rietbergen 1983b, 16–50.

173. Krautheimer 1985, 14.

174. Ingersoll 1985, 162–63.

175. Ingersoll 1985, 165.

176. See Burke 1987, 176.

177. Rubin 1991, 263, emphasizes that, despite specified orders and hierarchies, "the story of Corpus Christi processions is also one of disorder, of lawsuits . . . , of disputes over precedence and riots."

178. Courtright in Lavin et al. 1981, 141; and Grabar 1936, 43–44, on the painted image of Constantine in the vestibule of the imperial palace. Another line of research might begin with the association of Constantine with the Scala Santa through his mother, Helena, who brought the True Cross to Rome from Jerusalem (cf. Freiberg 1991b, 82–83).

179. "What Biondo had written about the Imperial Palaces, now could we say the same about the Papal Palace" (Marliani, *Antiquae Romanae Topographia*, 1534, III, 7; from Campbell 1977, 163). The thought has special meaning at the beginning of Paul III's pontificate.

180. Campbell 1977, 163, cites Suetonius, *Lives of the Caesars*, II, xxix, 3. For the reconstructions, see MacDonald 1965, 52, and pl. 40; and Coarelli 1975, 148.

181. Lanciani 1888, 110–11, describes the columns with Danaids between and equestrian statues of their husbands in front of them.

182. Campbell 1976.

183. McManamon 1976, 42, 49.

184. Ullmann 1955, passim; Wilks 1963, 254–87 (both cited by McManamon).

185. Ullmann 1955, 325; and Elze 1952.

186. Ullmann 1955, 74–86.

187. Westfall 1974, 6–7, 19–20; Courtright 1990a, 98–99. The history of this process deserves further investigation.

188. Smith 1956, 10.

189. Ullmann 1955, 78.

190. Citations in Ullmann 1955, 79. From the early Middle Ages the supremacy of Christian rulers was demonstrated in a ceremony in which a pope or bishop confirmed the dominion of the monarch. Kings were anointed, and emperors were crowned. By the ninth century these distinctions were replaced by a single ceremony of coronation (Bouman 1957, ix). As for the coronation of the pope, the origins were said by many to go back to Constantine, who made a present of his imperial crown to Pope Sylvester; others contended that the crown was sent to Rome by the king of France in 550 (Leti 1675, III, 372–73).

191. Kantorowicz 1944; Ullmann 1955, 1–44.

192. Prodi 1982.

193. Prodi 1982, 16–17, quoting Kantorowicz 1957, 193–194.

194. Cf. the title of Jean Morin's *Histoire de la delivrance de l'eglise chrestienne par l'empereur Constantin et de la grandeur et souveraineté temporelle donnée à l'eglise Romaine par les Roys de France*, 1630. The title page features the entroned pope gesturing to the French king, left, under the words "Gloria Pontificum." To the right are the forces of the emperor with a cross in the sky and the words "in hoc signo vinces." See Morin 1630, 12, for an account of the

vision of Constantine; and pt. 1, chap. XII for the argument that Constantine had been converted in France by French bishops.

195. Leti 1630–1701, 6–7: "Questa Corte è dominata da un Prencipe misto, perche essendo Ecclesiastico, gode anco nel temporale un gran stato, e con l'occasione dell'uno, si fà poi Arbitro del tutto; e così è necessario procurare, che nessun Prencipe così Temporale, come Sprituale se le opponga. . . . Ne tempi passati il Papa assieme con i Cardinali governavano questa Ecclesiastica Monarchia. . . . Hora s'è mutato, e il Papa governa solo, e a' Cardinali non hà lasciato altro, che l'apparenza."

196. O'Malley 1983 puts it succinctly: "In an age when royal absolutism advanced under the impetus of the powerful alliance of throne and altar, the papacy offered a first model of the modern priest-king." Some reviewers have noted Prodi's casual methodology but to my knowledge none have seriously disagreed with his conclusions by offering others. Rietbergen 1983b is more thorough in its archival foundations and computer analyses, and more specific in focus, but his results are essentially similar.

197. While O'Malley 1983 and Partner 1985 have merely remarked on the paucity of specific documentation to an otherwise convincing thesis, Gross 1985 has questioned whether Prodi's evidence amounts to an absolute papal monarchy or simply the elaborated machinery of governance. This issue seems to me less important for our purpose than the aspirations of governance that Prodi characterizes.

198. A stimulating talk by Alice Jarrard has demonstrated the extent to which staircases were elaborated in the context of the increasing demands of etiquette in later-sixteenth-century Florence and Parma, and seventeenth-century Modena and Turin (Italian Art Society, College Art Association, February 1994).

199. See Waddy 1990, 3–13, for examples.

200. For the anthropology, see Moore and Myerhoff 1977, from whose introduction I have drawn extensively.

201. Moore and Myerhoff 1977, 18.

202. See Moore and Myerhoff 1977, introduction.

203. See Chapter 8; Southorn 1988, 32; and Krüger 1989, 35, 37, 39, 40, 41, 46, 47, 58, 71, 115 (n. 2), 134–35.

204. Burke 1987, 176.

205. Mitchell 1990, 3–11, gives the background for reports of pageants, which ranged in form from the specially prepared *livret*, to brief avvisi to foreign courts, to private letters.

206. Burke 1987, 168, and more generally 168–82.

207. Burke 1987, 175, cites Wirth 1963.

208. Dykmans 1980–82, 98–99, and 561–62 for other references.

209. This is the theme of Sonnino 1966, with regard to Louis XIV.

210. See Burke 1987, 181.

211. Prodi 1982, quoted from the English edition, p. 23.

212. Pastor 1923–53, XXXI, 76–77.

Bibliography

Ackerman, J. S. (1949–51), "Bramante and the Torre Borgia," *Rendiconti della Pontificia Accademia Romana di Archeologia* XXV–XXVI, 247–65.

(1954), *The Cortile del Belvedere* (Studi e documenti per la storia del Palazzo Apostolico Vaticano 3), Vatican City.

(1957), "Marcus Aurelius on the Capitoline Hill," *Renaissance News*, X, 1957, 69–75.

(1964), *The Architecture of Michelangelo*, 2 vols., London.

(1970), "Notes on Bramante's Bad Reputation," *Studi bramanteschi: Atti del convegno internazionale*, Rome, 339–50.

Albert, Marcel (1988), *Nuntius Fabio Chigi und die Anfänge des Jansenismus, 1639–1651* (Römische Quartalschrift, suppl. Heft 44), Rome.

Alfarano [Tiberii Alpharani] (1914), *De Basilicae Vaticanae Antiquissima et Nova Structura* (Studi e testi 26, Documenti e ricerche per la storia dell'antica basilica vaticana 1), ed. Michele Cerrati, Rome.

Alföldi, A. (1939), "Hoc Signo Victor Eris. Beiträge zur Geschichte der Bekehrung Konstantins des Grossen," *Pisciculi: Studien zur Religion und Kultur des Altertums*, ed. Theodor Klauser and Adolf Rücker, Münster, 1–18.

Alveri, Gaspare (1664), *Di Roma in ogni stato*, 2 vols., Rome.

Ancel, R. (1908), "Le Vaticane sous Paul IV," *Revue bénédictine* XXV, 48–71.

Androsov, Sergej O. (1991), *Alle Origini di Canova. Le terrecotte della collezione Farsetti*, Venice.

Angelini, S. (1967), *I cinque album di Giacomo Quarenghi nella Civica Biblioteca di Bergamo*, Bergamo.

Arnoldi, Francesco Negri (1963), "Il Monumento di Roberto Malatesta per la Basilica di S. Pietro, oggi al Louvre," *Palatino* VII (nos. 1–4), 2–4.

(1971), "Iconologo allo sbaraglio," *Paragone-arte* 251 (January), 83–89.

Aufhauser, Johann Baptista (1912), *Konstantins Kreuzvision in ausgewälten Texten* (Kleine Texte für Vorlesungen und Ubungen 108), ed. Hans Lietzmann, Bonn.

Bacci, P. (1939), "L'elenco delle pitture, sculture e architetture di Siena compilato nel 1625–26 da Mons. Fabio Chigi poi Alessandro VII secondo il MS Chigiano I. 1. 11," *Bollettino senese di storia patria* n.s. X, 197–213.

Baglione, Giovanni (1639), *Le nove chiese di Roma*, ed. Liliana Barroero, Rome.

(1642), *Le vite de' pittori scultori et architetti*, Rome.

Baldinucci, Filippo (1681–1728), *Notizie dei professori del disegno da Cimabue in qua*, 7 vols., Florence (reprint ed. F. Ranalli, Florence, 1847).

(1682), *Vita del Cavaliere Gio Lorenzo Bernino scultore, architetto, e pittore*, Florence (new edition, ed. S. Samek Ludovici, Milan, 1948).

Barberini, Maria Giulia (1991), *Sculture in terracotta del barocco romano. Bozzetti e modelli del Museo Nazionale del Palazzo di Venezia* (exhibition catalogue, Museo Nazionale del Palazzo di Venezia), Rome.

Barbier de Montault, X. (1870), *Musées et galeries de Rome*, Rome (reprinted in *Oeuvres complètes de Mgr. X Barbier de Montault*, vol. II, *Le Vatican*, Poitiers, 1889).

Baronius [Cesare Baronio] (1630), *Martyrologium Gregorii XIII Pontificis Maximi Iussu Editum, et Urbani VIII Auctoritate Recognitum . . .*, Venice.

(1738–46) *Annales Ecclesiatici Auctore Caesare Baronio . . . Una cum Critica Historico-Chronologica P. Antonii Pagii* [Antoine Pagi 1624–1699], 19 vols., Lucca.

Barozzi, Nicolò, and Guglielmo Berchet (1879), *Le relazioni della corte di Roma lette al Senato dagli ambasciatori veneti nel secolo decimosettimo*, vol. II (Relazioni degli stati europei lette al Senato dagli ambasciatori veneti nel secolo decimosettimo, ser. III, Italia, Relazioni di Roma), Venice.

Bartolotti, F. (1967), *La medaglia annuale dei romani pontefici da Paolo V a Paolo VI, 1605–1967*, Rimini.

Basso, Michele (1987–88), *I privilegi e le consuetudini della Reverenda Fabbrica di San Pietro in Vaticano (secoli XVI–XX)*, 2 vols., Rome.

Battaglia, Roberto (1943), *La cattedra berniniana di San Pietro*, Rome.

"Battesimo" (1887), ["Il Battesimo di Costantino Magno e le Prevenzioni del Baronio"], *La Scuola Cattolica* XV (29 April) 355–71.

Battisti, Eugenio (1957), "Il significato simbolico della Cappella Sistina," *Commentari* VIII, 96–104.

Bauer, George, C. (1976), *Bernini in Perspective*, Englewood Cliffs.

(1982), "From Architecture to Scenography: The Full-Scale Model in the Baroque Tradition," *La scenografia barocca* (Atti del XXIV Congresso Internazionale di Storia dell'Arte 5, Bologna, 1979), ed. Antoine Schnapper, Bologna, 141–49.

(1983), "Bernini e i 'modelli in grande'," *Gian Lorenzo Bernini architetto e l'architettura europea del sei-settecento*, ed. Gianfranco Spagnesi and Marcello Fagiolo, Rome, 279–90.

Bavinck, Hermannus (1620), *Undericht und Wegweiser, wie ein Teutscher in und ausserhalb Rom, die . . . Kirchen . . . mit gebuhrlicher Andacht besuchen kan*, Rome.

Baynes, Norman H. (1929), "Constantine the Great and the Christian Church," *Proceedings of the British Academy* XV, 341–442.

Beecher, Donald, and Massimo Ciavolella (1985), "A Comedy by Bernini," *Gianlorenzo Bernini. New Aspects of His Art and Thought*, ed. Irving Lavin, University Park, 63–77.

Beltrami, Giuseppe (1926), "Martino Ferabosco Architetto," *L'arte* XXIX, 23–37.

Berger, Robert W. (1985), *In the Garden of the Sun King. Studies on the Park of Versailles under Louis XIV*, Washington.

Bernini, Domenico (1713), *Vita del Cavalier Gio. Lorenzo Bernino*, Rome.

Bernini in Vaticano (1981) (exhibition catalogue, Braccio Carlo Magno, Vatican City), Rome.

Bernstock, Judith (1988), "Bernini's Tomb of Alexander VII," *Saggi e memorie di storia dell'arte* XVI, 167–90.

Berra, F. L., and G. B. Rosso (1938), "La sistemazione dei borghi e il cavalier Gianlorenzo Bernini," *Arte Cristiana* XXVI, 57–82.

Bialostocki, Jan (1973), "The Door of Death: Survival of a Classical Motif in Sepulchral Art," *Jahrbuch der Hamburger Kunstsammlungen* XVIII, 7–32.

Bibliotheca Sanctorum (1961–70), 12 vols., Rome.

Birindelli, Massimo (1981), *Piazza San Pietro*, Bari (originally published as *La macchina heroica. Il disegno di Gianlorenzo Bernini per piazza S. Pietro*, Rome, 1980).

(1982), *La strada nel palazzo. Il disegno di Gianlorenzo Bernini per la Scala Regia*, Rome.

(1986), *Architettura come modificazione. Bernini all'Ariccia, e un'addizione di Juvarra*, Rome.

Bjürstrom, Per (1962), *Giacomo Torelli and Baroque Stage Design*, Stockholm.

Blunt, Anthony (1967), "Two Drawings for Sepulchral Monuments by Bernini," *Essays in the History of Art Presented to Rudolf Wittkower*, ed. D. Fraser, H. Hibbard, and M. Lewine, London, 230–232.

Blunt, Anthony, and Hereward Lester Cooke (1960), *The Roman Drawings of the XVII and XVIII Centuries in the Collection of Her Majesty the Queen at Windsor Castle*, London.

Bonanni, Philippo (1696), *Numismata Summorum Pontificum Templi Vaticani Fabricam*, Rome.

(1706), *Numismata Pontificum Romanorum quae a Tempore Martini V usque ad Annum MDCXCIX*, 2 vols., Rome.

Boorsch, Suzanne (1982–83), "The Building of the Vatican: The Papacy and Architecture," *Metropolitan Museum of Art Bulletin* XL, 3–64.

Borino, J. B. (1947), *Codices Vaticani Latini Codices 10701–10875* (Bibliothecae Apostolicae Vaticana Codices Manuscripti Recensiti), Vatican City.

Borsi, Franco (1967), *La chiesa di S. Andrea al Quirinale*, Rome.

(1974), *Il Palazzo del Quirinale*, Rome.

(1989), *Bramante*, Milan.

Borsi, F., et al. (1972), *Montecitorio. Ricerche di storia urbana*, Rome.

Borsi, Franco, Cristina Acidini Luchinat, and Francesco Quinterio (1981), *Gian Lorenzo Bernini. Il testamento, la casa, la raccolta dei beni*, Florence.

Borsi, Franco, and Francesco Quinterio (1980), *Bernini architetto* (text by Borsi and catalogue and documents by Quinterio), Milan.

(1984), *Bernini* (text by Borsi and catalogue and documents by Quinterio), English transl. by Robert Erich Wolf, New York.

Bouman, C. A. (1957), *Sacring and Crowning. The Development of the Latin Ritual for the Anointing of Kings and the Coronation of an Emperor before the Eleventh Century* (Bijdragen van het Instituut voor Middeleeuwse Geschiedenis der Rijks-Universiteit te Utrecht 30), Groningen.

Braham, Allan, and Hellmut Hager (1977), *Carlo Fontana. The Drawings at Windsor Castle*, London.

Brahmer, M. (1939), *Powinowactawa polska-wtoskie*, Warsaw (2nd edition, 1980).

Brauer, Heinrich, and Rudolf Wittkower (1931), *Die Zeichnungen des Gianlorenzo Bernini* (Römische Forschungen der Bibliotheca Hertziana 9), Berlin.

Breviarium Romanum (1658) (from the Archive of the Chapter of S. Pietro in Vaticano, BAV, Stampati, 446), Rome.

Briccolani, Vincenzo (1828), *Descrizione della sacrosanta basilica vaticana*, Rome.

Briganti, Giuliano (1962a), *Pietro da Cortona o della pittura barocca*, Florence.

(1962b), *Il Palazzo del Quirinale*, Rome.

Brubaker, Leslie (1985), "Politics, Patronage, and Art in Ninth-Century Byzantium: The Homilies of Gregory of Nazianus in Paris (B.N. Gr. 510)," *Dumbarton Oaks Papers* XXXIX, 1–13.

Bruschi, Arnaldo (1969), *Bramante architetto*, Bari.

Buddensieg, Tillmann (1969), "Zum Statuenprogramm in Kapitalsplan Pauls III," *Zeitschrift für Kunstgeschichte* XXX, 177–228.

Burke, Peter (1987), *The Historical Anthropology of Early Modern Italy*, Cambridge.

Burroughs, Charles (1982), "A Planned Myth and a Myth of Planning," *Rome. The City and the Myth*, ed. P. Ramsey, Binghamton, 197–207.

Bush, Virginia (1976), *The Colossal Sculpture of the Cinquecento*, New York.

Busiri Vici, Andrea (1893), *La piazza di San Pietro in Vaticano nei secoli III, XIV, e XVII*, Rome.

(1973), "Una interessantissima udienza pontificia di dieci anni fa," *Strenna dei romanisti* XXXIV, 104–9.

Butler (1956) [*Butler's Lives of the Saints*], ed. Herbert Thurston and Donald Attwater, New York.

Byzance (1992) [*Byzance, l'art byzantin dans les collections publiques françaises*], Paris.

Caetano, R. (1691), *Le memorie de l'anno santo MDCLXXV*, Rome.

Cambedda, A. (1990), *La demolizione della spina dei Borghi*, Rome.

Campbell, Malcolm (1976), "The Original Program of the Salone di Giovanni da San Giovanni," *Antichità viva* XV, no. 4, 3–25.

(1977), *Pietro da Cortona at the Pitti Palace. A Study of the Planetary Rooms and Related Projects*, Princeton.

Cancellieri, Francesco (1784), *Sacrestia vaticana eretta del regnante pontefice Pio Sesto*, Rome.

(1790), *Descrizione delle cappelle pontificie e cardinalizie di tutto l'anno*, Rome.

Carandini, Silvia (1990), *Teatro e spettacolo nel seicento*, Bari.

Carloni, Rosella (1980), "Documenti relativi alla statua marmorea di S. Pietro in Vaticano," *Alma Roma* XXI, 49–57.

Carpiceci, Alberto Carlo (1987), "La basilica vaticana vista da Martin van Heemskerck," *Bollettino d'arte* LXXII, nos. 44–45, 67–128.

Carsten, F. L., ed. (1961), *The New Cambridge Modern History*, vol. V, Cambridge.

Carusi, Enrico (1904), "Il diario romano di Jacopo Gherardi da Volterra . . . 1479–1484," in L. A. Muratori, *Rerum Italicarum Scriptores*, ed. G. Carducci and V. Fiorini, vol. XXIII, pt. 3, Città di Castello.

Catalano, Josepho (1750–51), *Sacrarum Caeremoniarum Sive Rituum Ecclesiaticorum Sanctae Romanae Ecclesiae*, 2 vols., Rome.

Cavallaro, Anna, and Enrico Parlato (1988), *Da Pisanello alla nascità dei musei capitolini. L'antico a Roma alla viglia del Rinascimento* (exhibition catalogue, Musei Capitolini), Rome.

Cecchelli, Carlo (1927), *Il Vaticano*, Milan and Rome.

(1954), *Il trionfo della croce. La croce e i santi segni prima e dopo Costantino*, Rome.

Ceyssens, L. (1963–65), *La fin de la première période du jansénisme: Sources des années 1654–1660* (Bibliothèque de l'Institut Historique Belge de Rome, XII–XIII), 2 vols., Rome.

Chantelou, Paul Fréart de (1985), *Diary of the Cavaliere Bernini's Visit to France*, ed. Anthony Blunt and George C. Bauer, transl. Margery Corbett, Princeton.

Chappell, Miles L., and Chandler W. Kirwin (1974), "A Petrine Triumph: The Decoration of the Navi Piccole in San Pietro under Clement VIII," *Storia dell'arte* VI, 119–70.

Chattard, G. P. (1762–67), *Nuova descrizione del Vaticano o sia del Palazzo Apostolico di San Pietro*, 3 vols., Rome.

Ciampi, Ignazio (1878), *Innocenzo X Pamphili e la sua corte*, Rome.

Ciampini, Joannis (1693), *De Sacris Aedificiis a Constantino Magno Constructis*, Rome.

Cioni, Alfredo (1961), *Bibliografia delle sacre rappresentazioni*, Florence.

Coarelli, Filippo (1975), *Guida archeologica di Roma*, Verona.

Colnabrini, F. Cesare (1895), *Ruolo degli appartamenti e delle stanze nel Palazzo Vaticano al tempo di Clemente VIII (1594)*, Rome.

Compendio (1793) [*Compendio di teorica e di pratica ricavato dalli decreti e resoluzioni originali della sagra congregazione della Reverenda Fabrica di S. Pietro*], Rome.

Connors, Joseph (1989a), "Alliance and Enmity in Roman Baroque Urbanism," *Römisches Jahrbuch für Kunstgeschichte* XXV, 207–94.

(1989b), "Virgilio Spada's Defense of Borromini," *Burlington Magazine* CXXXI (February), 76–90.

(1990), "Ars Tornandi: Baroque Architecture and the Lathe," *Journal of the Warburg and Courtauld Institutes* LIII, 217–36.

Connors, Joseph, and Louise Rice, eds. (1991), *Specchio di Roma barocca. Una guida inedita del XVII secolo*, Rome.

Contardi, Bruno, and Giovanna Curcio, eds. (1991), *In Urbe Architectus. Modelli, disegni, misure. La professione dell'architetto a Roma 1680–1750*, Rome.

Coolidge, John (1966), "Louis XIII and Rubens: The Story of the Constantine Tapestries," *Gazette des Beaux-Arts* LXVII, 271–92.

Corbo, Anna Maria (1978), "Campane, orologi e campanili della Basilica Vaticana. I. Le campane; II. Gli orologi," *Commentari* XXIX, 217–41.

Courtright, Nicola (1990a), *Gregory XIII's Tower of the Winds in the Vatican*, Ph.D. diss., New York University.

(1990b), "The Vatican Tower of the Winds and the Architectural Legacy of the Counter Reformation," *I.L. 60: Essays Honoring Irving Lavin on His Sixtieth Birthday*, ed. Marilyn A. Lavin, New York, 117–44.

Cousins, Windsor F. (1992), "Filippo Juvarra and the Baroque Staircase," in *An Architectural Progress in the Renaissance and Baroque. Sojourns in and out of Italy* (Papers in Art History from The Pennsylvania State University 8, Essays in Architectural History Presented to Hellmut Hager on His Sixty-sixth Birthday), ed. Henry A. Millon and Susan Scott Munshower, University Park, 624–53.

Cross, F. L. (1957), *The Oxford Dictionary of the Christian Church*, London.

D'Ancona, Alessandro (1872), *Sacre rappresentazioni dei secoli XIV, XV, e XVI*, 3 vols., Florence.

(1891), *Origini del teatro italiano*, 3 vols., Turin.

Davidson, Bernice (1976), "The Decoration of the Sala Regia under Pope Paul III," *Art Bulletin* LVIII, 395–423.

De Angelis D'Ossat, Guglielmo (1953), *La geologia del Monte Vaticano* (Studi e documenti per la storia del Palazzo Apostolico Vaticano, I, no. 1), Vatican City.

De' Cavalieri, Pio Franchi (1953), *Constantiniana* (Studi e testi 171), Vatican City.

De la Croix, Horst, and Richard G. Tansey (1986), *Gardner's Art through the Ages* (8th edition), 2 vols., New York.

Delfini Filippi, Gabriella (1989), *San Pietro, la basilica, la piazza* (Guide del Vaticano, 1), Rome.

Del Pesco, Daniela (1988), *Colonnato di San Pietro. "Dei portici antichi e la loro diversità". Con un'ipotesi di cronologia*, Rome.

Del Re, N. (1969), "La Sacra Congregazione della Reverenda Fabbrica di San Pietro," *Studi romani* XVII, 288–301.

Den Broeder, Frederick A. (1991), *Old Master Drawings from the Collection of Joseph F. McCrindle* (exhibition catalogue, Princeton University), Princeton.

Der Nersessian, Sirarpie (1962), "The Illustrations of the Homilies of Gregory of Nazianus, Paris Gr. 510," *Dumbarton Oaks Papers* XVI, 197–228.

De Rossi, Domenico (1704), *Raccolta di statue antiche e moderne data in luce sotto i gloriosi auspicj della Santità di N. S. Papa Clemente XI*, Rome.

De Santi, Angelo (1919), *L'orazione delle quarant'ore e i tempi di calamità e di guerra*, Rome.

Descrizione del Palazzo Vaticano (1724–1730) [Descrizione del Palazzo Vaticano fatta nel pontificato della S. M. di Bened.[etto] XII [1724–1730], Archivio di Stato, Rome, Biblioteca 496.

De Sebastiani, Pietro (1683), *Viaggio sagro e curioso delle chiese più principali di Roma*, Rome.

Di Bildt, C. (1906), "Cristina di Svezia e Paolo Giordano II," *Archivio della Società Romana di Storia Patria* XXIX, 5–32.

DiFederico, Frank (1983), *Mosaics of St. Peter's. Decorating the New Basilica*, University Park.

Di Salvo, Andrea (1988), "L'imagine di Cangrande della Scala nell'opera di Ferreto Ferreti," *Bollettino dell'Istituto Storico Italiano per il Medioevo e Archivio Muratoriano* XLIV, 123–53.

"Dissertation Historique sur la vision . . . de la Croix" (1681) ["Dissertation Historique sur la vision que Constantin eut de la Croix de N.S. . . . confirmée par des medailles antiques tirées du Cabinet de Saint Geneviève de Paris"], *Journal des scavans* XI (14 April 1681), 121–31.

Dizionario biografico degli italiani (1960–), vols. I–, Rome.

D'Onofrio, Cesare (1963), *Gianlorenzo Bernini. Fontana di Trevi. Commedia inedita*, Rome.

(1966), "La priorità della biografia di Domenico Bernini su quella del Baldinucci," *Palatino* X, 201–8.

(1969), *Roma nel seicento*, Florence.

(1978), *Castel S. Angelo e Borgo. Tra Roma e papato*, Rome.

(1990), *Un popolo di statue racconta. Storie, fatti, leggende della città di Roma antica, medievale, moderna*, Rome.

Dubon, David (1964), *Tapestries from the Samuel H. Kress Collection at the Philadelphia Museum of Art. The History of Constantine the Great Designed by Peter Paul Rubens and Pietro da Cortona*, London.

Du Cange, Charles Du Fresne (1840–50), *Glossarium mediae et infimae latinitatis*, Paris.

Du Cerceau, Jacques Androuet (1579), *Les plus excellents bastiments de France*, Paris.

Duchesne, Louis Marie Olivier (1886–92), *Le Liber Pontificalis*, 3 vols., Paris.

(1902), "Vaticana. Notes sur la topographie de Rome au moyen-âge," *Mélanges d'archéologie et d'histoire* XXII, 3–22.

Dykmans, Marc (1968), "Du Monte Mario à l'escalier de Saint Pierre de Rome," *Mélanges d'archéologie et d'histoire* LXXX, 547–98.

(1980–82), *L'Oeuvre de Patrizi Piccolomini ou le cérémonial papal de la première renaissance* (Studi e testi 293–94), 2 vols., Vatican City.

Eberlein, Johann Konrad (1983), "The Curtain in Raphael's Sistine Madonna," *Art Bulletin* LXV, 61–77.

Egger, Hermann (1910), *Architektonische Handzeichnungen alter Meister*, Vienna.

(1911), *Römische Veduten*, 2 vols., Vienna.

(1928), "Carlo Madernas Projekt für den Vorplatz von San Pietro in Vaticano," *Römische Forschungen der Bibliotheca Hertziana* VI, 11–31.

(1929), "Der Uhrturm Pauls V," *Mededeelingen van het Nederlandsch Historisch Instituut te Rome* IX, 71–110.

(1935), "Turris Campanaria Sancti Petri," *Mededeelingen van het Nederlandsch Historisch Instituut te Rome* XV, 59–82.

(1950), "Quadriporticus Sancti Petri in Vaticano," *Papers of the British School in Rome* XVIII, 101–3.

(1951), "Die päpstliche Kanzleigebäude im 15 Jahrhundert," *Mitteilungen des Österreichischen Staatsarchivs* III, 487–500.

Ehrle, Franz (1914), *La grande veduta Maggi-Mascardi (1615) del tempio e del palazzo Vaticano*, Rome.

(1928), "Dalle carte e dai disegni di Virgilio Spada," *Atti della Pontificia Accademia Romana di Archeologia*, ser. III, memorie II, 1–98.

Ehrle, Franz, and Hermann Egger (1933), *Die Conclavepläne* (Studi e documenti per la storia del Palazzo Apostolico Vaticano 5), Vatican City.

(1935), *Der Vatikanische Palast in seiner Entwicklung bis zur Mitte des XV. Jahrhunderts* (Studi e documenti per la storia del Palazzo Apostolico Vaticano 2), Vatican City.

Ehrle, Franz, and Enrico Stevenson (1897), *Gli affreschi del Pinturicchio nell'appartamento Borgia del Palazzo Apostolico Vaticano*, Rome.

Eimer, Gerhard (1971), *La Fabbrica di S. Agnese in Navona. Römische Architecten, Bauherren und Handwerker im Zeitalter des Nepotismus*, 2 vols., Stockholm.

Elze, Reinhard (1952), "Das 'Sacrum Palatium Lateranense' im 10. und 11. Jahrhundert," *Studi Gregoriani* IV, 27–54.

(1960), *Die Ordines für die Weihe und Krönung des Kaisers und der Kaiserin*, Hannover.

Enggass, Robert (1976), *Early Eighteenth-Century Sculpture in Rome*, University Park.

(1978), "New Attributions in St. Peter's: The Spandrel Figures in the Nave," *Art Bulletin* LX, 96–108.

Epp, Sigrid (1988), *Konstantinszyklen in Rom. Die päpstliche Interpretation der Geschichte Konstantins des Grossen bis zur Gegenreformation*, Munich.

Erler, Mary C. (1995), "Palm Sunday Prophets and Processions and Eucharistic Controversy," *Renaissance Quarterly* XLVIII, 58–81.

Evelyn, John (1955), *The Diary of John Evelyn*, ed. E. S. de Beer, 6 vols., Oxford.

Evers, H. (1967), "Zur 'Scala Regia' des Vatikans," *Rendiconti della Pontificia Accademia Romana di Archeologia* XXXIX, 190–215.

Fagiolo, Marcello (1985), "Architettura e città nel "piano" di Niccolò V," in *Roma 1300–1875. La città degli anni Santi. Atlante*, ed. M. Fagiolo and M. L. Madonna, Rome, 88–91.

Fagiolo, Marcello, and Maurizio Fagiolo dell'Arco (1967), *Bernini, una introduzione al gran teatro del barocco*, Rome.

Fagiolo dell'Arco, Maurizio (1973), *La scenografia dalle sacre rappresentazioni al futurismo*, Florence.

(1976), " 'Quarant'hore, fochi d'alegrezza, catafalchi, mascherate e cose simili.' Dall'effimero alla struttura stabile in Roma barocca," *Ricerca di storia dell'arte* I–II, 45–70.

Fagiolo dell'Arco, Maurizio, and Silvia Carandini (1977–78), *L'effimero barocco. Strutture della festa nella Roma del '600*, 2 vols., Rome.

Fasolo, Furio (1961), *L'opera di Hieronimo e Carlo Rainaldi 1570–1655 e 1611–1691*, Rome.

Ferrabosco, Martino, and Giovanni Battista Costaguti (1684), *Architettura della basilica di S. Pietro in Vaticano . . . da Martino Ferrabosco, e posto in luce l'anno M.DC.XX. Di nuovo dato alle stampe da Mons. Gio. Battista Costaguti . . .*, Rome.

Ferri, Nerino, and Carlo Pini (1885), *Indice geografico-analitico dei disegni di architettura civile e militare esistenti nella R. Galleria degli Uffizi in Firenze*, Florence.

Filippi, Elena (1990), *Maarten van Heemskerck Inventio Urbis*, Milan.

Fischer, W. G. (1928), "Die Handzeichnungen aus dem römischen Barock in der Leipziger Stadtbibliothek," *Zeitschrift für bildenden Kunst* LXII (no. 3), 25–28.

Fleming, John, Hugh Honour, and Nikolaus Pevsner, eds. (1974), *The Penguin Dictionary of Architecture*, Harmondsworth.

Fokker, Timon (1938), *Roman Baroque Art*, Oxford.

Fontana, Carlo (1694), *Templum Vaticanum et Ipsius Origo*, Rome.

Forcella, Vincenzo (1869–84), *Iscrizione delle chiese e d'altri edifici di Roma fino ai nostri giorni*, 14 vols., Rome.

——— (1885), *Tornei e giostre, ingressi trionfali, e feste carnevalesche in Roma sotto Paolo III*, Rome.

Francastel, Pierre (1928), *Girardon*, Paris.

Francia, Ennio (1989), *Storia della costruzione del nuovo San Pietro da Michelangelo a Bernini*, Rome.

Fraschetti, Stanislao (1900), *Il Bernini*, Milan.

Freiberg, Jack (1974), "The *Tabernaculum Dei*: Masaccio and the 'Perspective' Sacrament Tabernacle," M.A. thesis, Institute of Fine Arts, New York University.

——— (1988), *The Lateran and Clement VIII*, Ph.D. diss., New York University.

——— (1991a), "Paul V, Alexander VII, and the Fountain by Nicolò Cordier Rediscovered," *Burlington Magazine* CXXXIII (December), 833–43.

——— (1991b), "The Lateran Patronage of Gregory XIII and the Holy Year 1575," *Zeitschrift für Kunstgeschichte* LVII, 66–87.

——— (1995), *The Lateran in 1600. Christian Concord in Counter-Reformation Rome*, Cambridge.

Frommel, Christoph L. (1964), "Antonio da Sangallos Cappella Paolina: Ein Beitrag zur Baugeschichte des Vatikanischen Palastes," *Zeitschrift für Kunstgeschichte* XXVII, 1–24.

——— (1973), *Der Römische Palastbau der Hochrenaissance*, 3 vols., Tübingen.

——— (1976), "Die Peterskirche unter Papst Julius II. im Licht neuer Dokumente," *Römisches Jahrbuch für Kunstgeschichte* XVI, 57–136.

——— (1977), "Bramantes 'Disegno grandissimo' für den Vatikanpalast," *Kunstchronik* XXX, 63–64.

——— (1983), "Francesco del Borgo: Architekt Pius' II und Pauls II, I. Der Petersplatz und weitere Römisches Bauten Pius' II Piccolomini," *Römisches Jahrbuch für Kunstgeschichte* XX, 107–54.

——— (1984a), "Il Palazzo Vaticano sotto Giulio II e Leone X. Strutture e funzioni," in Carlo Pietrangeli et al., *Raffaello in Vaticano* (exhibition catalogue, Vatican City), Milan, 118–35.

——— (1984b), "Lavori architettonici di Raffaello in Vaticano," in *Raffaello architetto*, ed. C. L. Frommel, S. Ray, and M. Tafuri, Milan, 357–78.

——— (1984c), "Francesco del Borgo II. Il Palazzo Venezia und San Marco," *Römisches Jahrbuch für Kunstgeschichte* XXI, 73–164.

——— (1985), "Scale maggiori dei palazzi romani del Rinascimento," in *L'Escalier dans l'architecture de la Renaissance*, ed. A. Chastel and J. Guillaume, Paris, 135–44.

——— (1994), "St. Peter's: The Early History," in *The Renaissance from Brunelleschi to Michelangelo. The Representation of Architecture*, ed. Henry A. Millon and Vittorio Magnago Lampugnani, Milan, 399–423, 598–633.

C. L. Frommel, S. Ray, M. Tafuri, eds. (1984), *Raffaello architetto*, Milan, 1984

Frommel, Christoph L., and Matthias Winner, eds. (1986), *Raffaello a Roma. Il Convegno del 1983*, Rome.

Frosini, Pietro (1977), *Il Tevere. Le inondazioni di Roma e i provendimenti presi dal governo italiano per evitarle*, Rome.

Frugoni, Chiara (1984), "L'antichità: Dai 'Mirabilia' alla propaganda politica," *Memoria dell'antico nell'arte italiana*, I, *L'uso dei classici*, ed. Salvatore Settis, Turin, 5–72.

Frutaz, A. P. (1956), *Il Torrione di Niccolò V in Vaticano*, Vatican City.

Fuhrmann, Horst (1968), *Das Constitutum Constantini (Konstantinische Schenkung): Text* (Fontes Juris Germanici Antiqui in Usum Scholarum ex Monumentis Germaniae Historicis Separatum Editi 10), Hannover.

Galassi Paluzzi, Carlo (1975), *La basilica di S. Pietro*, Bologna.

Gambardella, Cherubino (1993), *L'architettura delle scale. Disegno, teoria e tecnica*, Genoa.

Gambi, Lucio, and Antonio Pinelli (1994), *La Galleria delle Carte Geografiche in Vaticano*, 3 vols., Modena.

Gattico, Giovanni Battista (1753), *Acta Selecta Caeremonialia Sanctae Romanae Ecclesiae*, Rome.

Gigli, Giacinto (1994), *Diario di Roma 1608–1644*, ed. Manilio Barberito, 2 vols., Rome.

Gigli, Laura (1990), *Rione XIV: Borgo*, Rome.

Giovannoni, Gustavo (1959), *Antonio da Sangallo il Giovane*, 2 vols., Rome.

Gombrich, Ernst, et al. (1989), *Giulio Romano* (exhibition catalogue, Mantua), Milan.

Grabar, André (1936), *L'Empereur dans l'art byzantin*, Paris.

——— (1957), *L'Iconoclasm byzantin. Le dossier archéologique*, Paris (2nd edition, 1984).

Grabar, Oleg (1990), "From Dome of Heaven to Pleasure Dome," *Journal of the Society of Architectural Historians* XLIX, 15–21.

Gramberg, Werner (1964), *Die Düsseldorfer Skizzenbücher der Guglielmo della Porta*, 2 vols., Berlin.

Grimaldi, Giacomo (1972), *Descrizione della basilica antica di S. Pietro in Vaticano. Codice Barberini latini 2733*, ed. Reto Niggl, Vatican City.

Grimme, Ernst Günther (1961), "Novus Constantinus. Die Gestalt Konstantins des Grossen in der imperialen Kunst der mittelalterlichen Kaiserzeit," *Aachner Kunstblätter* XXII 7–20.

Gross, Hanns (1985), review of P. Prodi 1982, *Journal of Modern History* LVII, 576–77.

Guarducci, Margherita (1991), *San Pietro e Sant'Ippolito: Storia di statue famose in Vaticano*, Rome.

Guidoni Marino, Angela (1973), "Il colonnato di Piazza S. Pietro: Dall'architettura obliqua di Caramuel al 'classicismo' berniniano," *Palladio* XXIII, 81–120.

Guilland, Rodolphe (1969), *Etudes de topographie de Constantinople byzantin* (Berliner Byzantinisch Arbeiten 37), 2 vols., Berlin.

Güthlein, Klaus, (1979), "Quellen aus dem Familienarchiv Spada zum römischen Barock. I," *Römisches Jahrbuch für Kunstgeschichte* XVIII, 173–247.

(1981), "Quellen aus dem Familienarchiv Spada zum Römischen Barock II," *Römisches Jahrbuch für Kunstgeschichte* XIX, 174–243.

Hager, Hellmut (1968), "Progetti del tardo barocco per il terzo braccio della Piazza S. Pietro," *Commentari* XIX, 299–314.

Hammond, Frederick (1985), "Bernini and the 'Fiera di Farfa'," in *Gianlorenzo Bernini. New Aspects of His Art and Thought*, ed. Irving Lavin, University Park, 115–178.

(1994), *Music and Spectacle in Baroque Rome*, New Haven.

Harris, Ann Sutherland (1977), *Selected Drawings of Gianlorenzo Bernini*, New York.

Haus, Andreas (1970), *Der Petersplatz in Rome und sein Statuenschmuck. Neue Beiträge*, Ph.D. diss., Freiburg-im-Bresgau.

Heimbürger Ravalli, Minna (1977), *Architettura, scultura e arti minori nel barocco italiano. Ricerche nell'Archivio Spada*, Florence.

Held, Julius S., and Donald Posner (1972), *17th and 18th Century Art. Baroque Painting, Sculpture, and Architecture*, Englewood Cliffs.

Herklotz, Ingo (1985), "Der Campus Lateranensis im Mittelalter," *Römisches Jahrbuch für Kunstgeschichte* XXII, 3–43.

(1989), "Der mittelalteriche Fassadenportikus der Lateranbasilica und seine Mosaiken. Kunst und Propaganda am Ende des 12. Jahrhunderts," *Römisches Jahrbuch der Bibliotheca Hertziana* XXV, 25–95.

Hersey, George (1973), *The Aragonese Arch at Naples 1443–1475*, New Haven.

Heydenreich, Ludwig H. (1967), "Federico da Montefeltro as a Building Patron," *Studies in Renaissance and Baroque Art Presented to Anthony Blunt*, London, 1–6.

Heydenreich, Ludwig, and Wolfgang Lotz (1974), *Architecture in Italy 1400–1600*, Harmondsworth.

Hibbard, Howard (1962), *The Architecture of the Palazzo Borghese* (Memoirs of the American Academy in Rome 27), Rome.

(1965), *Bernini*, Harmondsworth.

(1971), *Carlo Maderno and Roman Architecture 1580–1630*, London.

Hoogewerff, G. (1928), "Giovanni Van Santen architetto della Villa Borghese," *Roma* VI, 1–12, 29–64.

(1942), "Giovanni Vansanzio fra gli architetti romani del tempo Paolo V," *Palladio* VI, 49–56.

(1943), "Architetti in Roma durante il Pontificato di Paolo V Borghese," *Archivio della Società Romana di Storia Patria* LXVI, 135–47.

Hubert, Hans W. (1993), *Der Palazzo Comunale von Bologna. Vom Palazzo della Biada zum Palatium Apostolicum*, Köln.

Hueck, Irene (1969), "Der Maler der Apostelszenen im Atrium von Alt-St. Peter," *Mitteilungen des Kunsthistorisches Institutes in Florenz* XIV, 115–44.

Huelsen, Christian, and Hermann Egger (1913–16), *Die römischen Skizzenbücher von Marten van Heemskerck*, 2 vols., Berlin.

Incisa della Rocchetta, Giovanni (1932), "La processione papale del Corpus Domini nel 1655," *L'illustrazione vaticana* III, 498–500.

(1964), "Appunti autobiografici di Alessandro VII," *Studi e testi* CCXXXVI, 439–57.

Ingersoll, Richard (1985), *The Ritual Use of Public Space in Renaissance Rome*, Ph.D. diss., University of California, Berkeley.

Jacob, Sabine (1975), *Italienische Zeichnungen der Kunstbibliothek Berlin. Architektur und Dekoration 16. bis 18. Jahrhundert*, Berlin.

Jacoby, Joachim W. (1987), *Den Päpsten zu Diensten. Raffaels Herrscherzyklus in der Stanza dell'Incendio im vatikanischen Palast*, Hildesheim.

Jander, O. (1969), "The Prologues and Intermezzos of Alessandro Stradella," *Analecta Musicologica* VII, 87–111.

Janson, H. W. (1973), "The Equestrian Monument from Cangrande della Scala to Peter the Great," in *Sixteen Studies*, New York, 157–88.

Jestaz, Bernard (1966), *Le voyage d'Italie de Robert De Cotte*, Paris.

Johns, Christopher M. S. (1993), *Papal Art and Cultural Politics. Rome in the Age of Clement XI*, Cambridge.

Jordan, R. Furneaux (1969), *A Concise History of Western Architecture*, London.

Kantorowicz, Ernst H. (1944), "The 'King's Advent' and the Enigmatic Panels on the Doors of Santa Sabina," *Art Bulletin* XXVI, 207–31.

(1957), *The King's Two Bodies. A Study in Mediaeval Political Theology*, Princeton.

Karpowicz, Mariusz (1974), *Jerzy Eleuter Siemiginowski malarz polskiego baroku*, Wroclaw.

Kauffmann, Hans (1970), *Giovanni Lorenzo Bernini. Die figürlichen Kompositionen*, Berlin.

Keller, Ulrich (1971), *Reitermonumente absolutischer Fürsten. Staatstheoretischen Voraussetzungen und politische Funktionen*, Munich.

Kemp, Martin (1990), *The Science of Art. Optical Themes in Western Art from Brunelleschi to Seurat*, New Haven.

Keyssler, Johann Georg (1751), *Neueste Reisen durch Deutschland, Böhmen, Ungarn, die Schweitz, Italien, und Luthringen*, Hannover.

Kieven, Elisabeth (1993). *Von Bernini bis Piranesi. Römische Architekturzeichnungen des Barock*, Stuttgart.

Kirschbaum, Engelbert, ed. (1968–76), *Lexikon der christlichen Ikonographie*, 8 vols., Rome and Freiburg.

Kitao, T. K. (1974), *Circle and Oval in the Square of Saint Peter's. Bernini's Art of Planning*, New York.

——— (1977), "Carlo Fontana Had No Part in Bernini's Planning for the Square of Saint Peter's," *Journal of the Society of Architectural Historians* XXXVI, 85–93.

Klapisch-Zuber, Christiane (1969), *Les Maîtres du marbre Carrare, 1300–1600*, Paris.

Köhren-Jansen, Helmtrud (1993), *Giottos Navicella. Bildtradition, Deutung, Rezeptiongeschichte*, Munich.

Koenigsberger, H. G. (1987), *Early Modern Europe 1500–1789*, London.

Krautheimer, Richard (1985), *The Rome of Alexander VII 1655–1667*, Princeton.

Krautheimer, Richard, and Roger B. S. Jones (1975), "The Diary of Alexander VII: Notes on Art, Artists, and Buildings," *Römisches Jahrbuch für Kunstgeschichte* XV, 199–233.

Krönig, Wolfgang (1972), "Storia di una veduta di Roma," *Bollettino d'arte* LVII, 165–98.

Kruft, Hanno-Walter, and Magne Malmanger (1977), *Der Triumphbogen Alfonsos in Neapel. Das Monument und sein politische Bedeutung*, Tübingen.

Krüger, Peter (1989), *Studien zu Rubens' Konstantins-zyklus*, Ph.D. diss. University of Tübingen, Frankfurt.

Künstle, Karl (1926–28), *Ikonographie der christlichen Kunst*, 2 vols., Freiburg-im-Breisgau.

Kuntz, Margaret (1996), *The Cappella Paolina in the Vatican Palace*, Ph.D. diss., New York University.

Ladner, Gerhart B. (1979), "Der Ursprung und die mittelalterliche Entwicklung der päpstlichen Tiara," in *Tainia. R. Hampe zum 70. Geburtstag*, ed. H. A. Cahn and E. Simon, Mainz, 449–81.

Lanciani, Rodolfo (1888), *Ancient Rome in the Light of Recent Discoveries*, Boston.

Lassels, Richard (1670), *The Voyage of Italy . . . in Two Parts*, London.

Laugier, M. l'Abbé (1765), *Observations sur l'architecture*, Paris.

Lavagne, Henri (1977), "Triomphe et baptême de Constantin. Recherche iconographique à propos d'une mosaïque médiévale de Riez," *Journal des Savants* (July – September), 164–90.

Lavin, Irving (1968), *Bernini and the Crossing of Saint Peter's*, New York.

——— (1973), "Letter to the Editor," *Art Bulletin* LV, 475–76.

——— (1980), *Bernini and the Unity of the Visual Arts*, 2 vols., New York.

——— (1983), "Bernini's Memorial Plaque for Carlo Barberini," *Journal of the Society of Architectural Historians* XLII, 6–10.

——— (1987), "Le Bernin et son image du roi-soleil," in "*Il se rendit en Italie.*" *Etudes offertes à Andre Chastel*, Rome, 441–78.

——— (1993), *Past-Present. Essays on Historicism in Art from Donatello to Picasso*, Berkeley.

Lavin, Irving et al. (1981), *Drawings by Gianlorenzo Bernini from the Museum der Bildenden Künste Leipzig, German Democratic Republic*, Princeton.

Legrand, A., and L. Ceyssens, eds. (1957), *La correspondance antijanséniste de Fabio Chigi nonce à Cologne plus tard Alexandre VII* (Bibliothèque de l'Institut Historique Belge de Rome 8), Rome.

Letarouilly, Paul (1882), *Le Vatican et la basilique de St.-Pierre de Rome*, 3 vols., Paris.

Leti, Gregorio (1667), *Il nepotismo di Roma*, Amsterdam.

——— (1675), *Itinerari della corte di Roma ò vero teatro historico, cronologico, e politico della sede apostolica, dataria, e cancelleria romana*, 3 vols., Valenza.

——— (1630–1701), Istruzione agli ambasciatori che assisteranno nella corte di Roma per la Maestà Catolica, et il modo che devono tenere per escercitar la loro ambasciaria, n.d., no city cited.

Levinson, W. (1924), "Konstantinische Schenkung und Silvesterlegende," *Studi e testi* 38, 159–247.

Lewine, Carol F. (1993), *The Sistine Chapel Walls and the Roman Liturgy*, University Park.

Lewine, Milton (1969), "Nanni, Vignola, and S. Martino degli Svizzeri in Rome," *Journal of the Society of Architectural Historians* XXVIII, 27–40.

Liedtke, Walter (1989), *The Royal Horse and Rider. Painting, Sculpture, and Horsemanship 1500–1800*, New York.

Lindner, Amnon (1975), "The Myth of Constantine the Great in the West: Sources and Hagiographic Commemoration," *Studi medievali* XVI, 43–95.

Lisner, Margrit (1994), "Giotto und die Aufträge des Kardinals Jacopo Stefaneschi für Alt-St.-Peter. I. Das Mosaik der Navicella in der Kopie des Francesco Berretta," *Römisches Jahrbuch der Bibliotheca Hertziana* XXIX, 45–95.

Lualdi, Michelangelo (1644–53), "Memorie istoriche, e curiose del tempio, e palazzo Vaticano raccolte, e confusamente MSS. in tre volume," Biblioteca Corsiniana 31. D. 16–18, Rome.

Ludwig, Rudolf Martin (1939), *Die Treppe in der Baukunst der Renaissance*, Kassel.

MacDonald, William L. (1965), *The Architecture of the Roman Empire*, vol. I, New Haven.

Maddalò, S. (1987), *Appunti per una ricerca iconologica-imagine di Roma*, Udine.

Madonna, Maria Luisa (1981), "La via Alessandrina," in *Le arti a Roma sotto Alessandro VI*, ed. M. Calvesi, Rome, 4–9.

——— (1985), "L'architettura e la città intorno al 1500," in *Roma 1300–1875. La città degli anni santi. Atlante*, ed. M. Fagiolo and M. L. Madonna, Rome, 126–32.

Magnuson, Torgil (1958), *Studies in Roman Quattrocento Architecture* (Figura 9), Stockholm.

——— (1982–86), *Rome in the Age of Bernini*, 2 vols., Stockholm.

Mancinelli, Fabrizio, et al. (1984), *Raffaello in Vaticano*, Milan.

Mandel, Corinne (1993), "*Felix Culpa* and *Felix Roma*: On the Program of the Sixtine Staircase at the Vatican," *Art Bulletin* LXXV, 65–90.

Mango, Cyril (1959), *The Brazen House. A Study of the Vestibule of the Imperial Palace of Constantinople* (Archaeologisk-Kunsthistoriske Meddelelser. Det Kongelige Danske Videnskobernes Selskab 4, 4), Copenhagen.

Marder, T. A. (1980), "Bernini and Benedetti at Trinità dei Monti," *Art Bulletin* LXII, 286–89.

——— (1983a), "Bernini's Scala Regia: Fresh Light on Constantine,"

Abstracts of Papers. Seventy-first Annual Meeting of College Art Association of America, February 17–19, 1983, Philadelphia, 105.

(1983b), "La chiesa del Bernini ad Ariccia," in *Gian Lorenzo Bernini architetto e l'architettura europea del sei-settecento*, ed. Gianfranco Spagnesi and Marcello Fagiolo, Rome, 255–77.

(1984), "The Decision to Build the Spanish Steps: From Project to Monument," in *Projects and Monuments in the Period of the Roman Baroque* (Papers in Art History from The Pennsylvania State University 1), ed. Hellmut Hager and Susan S. Munshower, University Park, 82–99.

(1986), "Palladio e Bernini: Il Tempietto di Maser e la Rotonda di Ariccia," *Bollettino del Centro Internazionale di Studi di Architettura A. Palladio* XXIII (1981), 17–26.

(1989), "Bernini and Alexander VII: Criticism and Praise of the Pantheon in the Seventeenth Century," *Art Bulletin* LXXI, 628–45.

(1990), "The Evolution of Bernini's Designs for the Façade of Sant'Andrea al Quirinale: 1658–76," *Architectura* XX, 108–32.

(1991a), "Bernini's Equestrian Statue of Constantine," *Abstracts and Program Statements. College Art Association Seventy-ninth Annual Conference, February 21–23, 1991*, Washington, 95–96.

(1991b), "Alexander VII, Bernini, and the Urban Setting of the Pantheon," *Journal of the Society of Architectural Historians* L, 273–92.

(1992), "Bernini's Commission for the Equestrian Statue of Constantine in St. Peter's: A Preliminary Reading," in *An Architectural Progress in the Renaissance and Baroque. Sojourns in and out of Italy* (Papers in Art History from The Pennsylvania State University 8, Essays in Architectural History Presented to Hellmut Hager on His Sixty-sixth Birthday), ed. Henry A. Millon and Susan Scott Munshower, University Park, 280–306.

(1996), "The Turris Scalarum: Its Date in Relation to the Medieval Fabric of the Vatican Palace," *Monumenti, Musei e Gallerie Pontificie, Bollettino* XVI (in press).

Martin, Gregory (1969), *Roma Sancta (1581)*, ed. George B. Parks, Rome.

Martin, Michel (1986), *Les Monuments équestres de Louis XIV. Une grand entreprise de propagande monarchique*, Paris.

Martinelli, Valentino (1959), "Novità berniniane 3: Le sculture per gli Altieri," *Commentari* X, 204–27.

(1982), *Bernini Drawings*, transl. Katherine Asbury Giacheti, Florence.

Martinelli, Valentino, et al. (1987), *Le statue berniniane del colonnato di San Pietro*, Rome.

Matthiae, Guglielmo (1971), *Le porte bronzee bizantine in Italia*, Rome.

Matzulevitsch, Giannetta (1963), "Tre bozzetti di G. L. Bernini all'Ermitage di Leningrado," *Bollettino d'arte* XLVIII (nos. 1–2), 67–74.

McManamon, John M. (1976), *The Ideal Renaissance Pope: Funeral Oratory from the Papal Court*, New York.

McPhee, Sarah (1993), "A New Sketchbook by Filippo Juvarra," *Burlington Magazine* CXXXV (May), 346–50.

Mehnert, Karl-Heinz (1981), *Gianlorenzo Bernini. Zeichnungen* (Kataloge der Graphischen Sammlung 5, Museum der bildenden Künste Leipzig), Leipzig.

Mende, Ursula (1983), *Die Bronzetüren des Mittelalters: 800–1200*, Munich.

Mercantini, Maria (1981), *Due disegni inediti berniniani per Piazza S. Pietro*, Città di Castello.

Millon, Henry A. (1962), "An Early Seventeenth-Century Drawing of Piazza San Pietro," *Art Quarterly* XXV, 229–41.

(1984), *Filippo Juvarra. Drawings from the Roman Period 1704–1714* (Corpus Juvarrianum, Accademia delle Scienze di Torino), pt. I, Rome.

Mitchell, Bonner (1990), *1598. A Year of Pageantry in Late Renaissance Ferrara*, Binghamton.

Mitchell, Charles (1951), "The Lateran Fresco of Boniface VIII," *Journal of the Warburg and Courtauld Institutes* XIV, 1–6.

Moffitt, John F. (1993), "A Hidden Sphinx by Agnolo Bronzino, *ex tabula Cebetis Thebani*," *Renaissance Quarterly* XLVI, 277–307.

Mola, Giovanni Battista (1663), *Breve racconto delle miglior opere d'architettura, scultura et pittura fatte in Roma . . . 1663* (published as *Roma l'anno 1663 di Giov. Batt. Mola*, ed. Karl Noehles), Berlin.

Montagu, Jennifer (1982), review of Lavin 1980, in *Burlington Magazine* CMXLIX (April), 240–42.

(1985a), *Alessandro Algardi*, New Haven.

(1985b), "Bernini Scultures Not by Bernini," in *Gianlorenzo Bernini. New Aspects of His Art and Thought*, ed. Irving Lavin, University Park, 25–61.

(1986), "Disegni, Bozzetti, Legnetti and Modelli in Roman Seicento Sculpture," in *Entwurf und Ausführung in der europäischen Barockplastik*, ed. Peter Volk, Munich, 9–30.

(1989), *Roman Baroque Sculpture. The Industry of Art*, New Haven.

Montaigne, Michel Eyquem de (1983), *Montaigne's Travel Journal*, transl. Donald M. Frame, San Francisco.

Moore, Sally F., and Barbara G. Myerhoff, eds. (1977), *Secular Ritual*, Amsterdam.

Morello, Giovanni (1981a), "Documenti berniniani nella Biblioteca Apostolica Vaticana," in *Bernini in Vaticano*, Rome, 313–20.

(1981b), "Bernini e i lavori a S. Pietro nel "Diario" di Alessandro VII," in *Bernini in Vaticano*, Rome, 321–40.

(1992), "I rapporti tra Alessandro VII e Gian Lorenzo Bernini negli autografi del Papa (con disegni inediti)," in *Documentary Culture. Florence and Rome from Grand-Duke Ferdinand I to Pope Alexander VII* (Villa Spelman Colloquia 3), ed. Elizabeth Cropper, Giovanna Perini, and Francesco Solinas, Bologna, 185–207.

(1993), *Vatican Treasures. 2,000 Years of Art and Culture in the Vatican and Italy*, Milan.

Morin, Jean (1630), *Histoire de la delivrance de l'eglise chrestienne par l'empereur Constantin et de la grandeur et sovveraineté temporelle donnee a l'eglise Romaine par les Roys de France*, Paris.

Morka, Mieczysław (1986), *Polski Nowozytny Portret Konny i Jego Europejska Geneza*, Wroclaw.

Moroni, Gaetano (1840–61), *Dizionario di erudizione storico-ecclesiastica*, 39 vols., Venice.

(1841), *Le cappelle pontificie, cardinalizie e prelatizie*, Venice.

Mortoft, Francis (1658–59), *Francis Mortoft: His Book Being His Travels through France and Italy 1658–59* (reprint ed. Malcolm Letts, London, 1925).

Moryson, Fynes (1617), *An Itinerary Containing His Ten Yeeres Travell through the Twelve Dominions of Germany, Bohmerland, Sweitzerland, Netherland, Denmarke, Poland, Italy, Turky, France, England, Scotland, and Ireland* (reprint ed. James MacLehose, 4 vols., Glasgow, 1907–08).

Muñoz, Antonio (1911), "Martino Ferabosco architetto," *Vita d'arte* VII, 83–103.

Müntz, Eugène (1878–82), *Les Arts à la cour des papes pendant le XVe et le XVI siècle* (Bibliothèque des Ecoles Françaises d'Athènes et de Rome 4, 9, 28), 3 vols., Paris.

Neppi, Leonello (1975), *Palazzo Spada*, Rome.

(1983), "Punti di vista sulla prospettiva Spada," *Bollettino d'arte* LXVIII (no. 22), 105–18.

Nicephoros [Nicephori Callisti Xanthropuli] 1566, *Scriptoris Vere Catholici, Ecclesiasticae Historiae Libri Decem et Octo*, Paris.

Noehles, Karl (1969), "Architekturprojeckte Cortonas," *Münchner Jahrbuch der bildenden Künste* XX, 1969, 171–206.

(1978), "Visualisierte Eucharistietheologie. Ein Beitrag zur Sakralikonologie im Seicento Romano," *Münchner Jahrbuch der bildenden Künste* XXIX, 92–116.

(1982), "Scenografie per le quarant'ore e altari barocchi," in *La scenografie barocca* (Atti del XXIV Congresso Internazionale di Storia dell'Arte 5, Bologna, 1979), ed. Antoine Schnapper, Bologna, 151–55.

(1985), "Teatri per le quarant'ore e altari barocchi," in *Barocco romano e barocco italiano. Il teatro, l'effimero, l'allegoria*, ed. Marcello Fagiolo and Maria Luisa Madonna, Rome, 88–99.

Olszewski, Edward J. (1986), "Giovanni Martino Frugone, Marble Merchant, and a Contract for the Apostle Statues in the Nave of St. John Lateran," *Burlington Magazine* CXXVIII (September), 659–66.

O'Malley, John W. (1983), review of P. Prodi 1982, in *American Historical Review* LXXXVIII, 1016–17.

Omont, Henri (1929), *Miniatures des plus anciens manuscrits grecs de la Bibliothèque Nationale du VIe au XIVe siècle*, Paris.

Orbaan, J. A. F. (1913), "Un viaggio di Clemente VIII nel Viterbese," *Archivio della Società Romana di Storia Patria* XXXVI, 113–45.

(1919), "Der Abbruch Alt-Sankt-Peters 1605–15," *Jahrbuch der k. preuszischen Kunstsammlungen* XXXIX, Beiheft, 1–139.

(1920), *Documenti sul barocco in Roma* (Miscellanea della R. Società Romana di Storia Patria), Rome.

Ost, Hans (1981), "Studien zu Pietro da Cortonas Umbau von S. Maria della Pace," *Römisches Jahrbuch für Kunstgeschichte* XIII, 231–85.

Ostrow, Steven F. (1991), "Gianlorenzo Bernini, Girolamo Lucenti, and the Statue of Philip IV in S. Maria Maggiore: Patronage and Politics in Seicento Rome," *Art Bulletin* LXXIII, 89–118.

(1996), *Art and Spirituality in Counter-Reformation Rome: The Sistine and Pauline Chapels in S. Maria Maggiore*, Cambridge.

Ozzola, Leandro (1908), "L'arte alla corte di Alessandro VII," *Archivio della Società Romana di Storia Patria* XXXI, 5–91.

Paeseler, Wilhelm (1941), "Giottos Navicella und ihr spätantikes Vorbild," *Römisches Jahrbuch für Kunstgeschichte* V, 49–162.

Pagliara, Piernicola (1992), "Nuovi documenti sulla costruzioni della Cappella Sistina," in *La Cappella Sistina. La volta restaurata: Il trionfo del colore*, ed. Pierluigi De Vecchi, Novara.

Pallavicino, Sforza (1839–40), *Della vita di Alessandro VII*, 2 vols., Prato.

Panofsky, Erwin (1919), "Die Scala Regia im Vatikan und die Kunstanschauugen Berninis," *Jahrbuch der preussiszchen Kunstsammlungen* XL, 241–78.

(1922), "Zu Hermann Voss: 'Bernini als Architekt an der Scala Regia und den Kolonnaden von Sankt Peter.' Eine Ergänzung," *Kunstchronik* XXXIII, ii (no. 36), 599–602.

Panofsky-Soergel, Gerda (1967–68), "Zur Geschichte des Palazzo Mattei di Giove," *Römisches Jahrbuch für Kunstgeschichte* XI, 109–188.

Partner, Peter (1985), review of P. Prodi in *English Historical Review* C, 173–75.

(1990), *The Pope's Men: The Papal Civil Service in the Renaissance*, Oxford.

Partridge, Loren, and Randolph Starn (1990), "Triumphalism and the Sala Regia in the Vatican," in *"All the World's a Stage..." Art and Pageantry in the Renaissance and Baroque* (Papers in Art History from The Pennsylvania State University 6), ed. Barbara Wisch and Susan Scott Munshower, University Park, 22–82.

Pastor, Ludwig von (1923–53), *The History of the Popes*, 40 vols., London.

Pélissier, Lèon G. (1889), "Un Inventaire des manuscrits de la Bibliothèque Corsini a Rome," *Mélanges d'archéologie et d'histoire* IX, 389–429.

Penny, Nicholas (1992), *Catalogue of European Sculpture in the Ashmolean Museum 1540 to the Present Day*, Oxford.

Pérez Sánchez, Alphonso E. (1965), *Veintiséis dibujos boloñeses y romanos del siglo XVII*, Madrid.

(1967), *Catálogo de los dibujos. Real Academia de Bellas Artes de San Fernando*, Madrid.

Perlove, Shelley (1990), *Bernini and the Idealization of Death*, University Park.

Pevsner, Nikolaus (1966), *An Outline of European Architecture*, Harmondsworth.

Piazza, Carlo Bartolomeo (1687), *Efemeride vaticana per i pregi ecclesiastici d'ogni giorno dell'augustissima basilica di S. Pietro in Vaticano*, Rome.

Pietrangeli, Carlo, et al. (1984), *Raffaello in Vaticano* (exhibition catalogue, Vatican City), Milan.

(1986), *The Sistine Chapel. The Art, the History, and the Restoration*, New York.

(1990), *Michelangelo e la Sistina. La tecnica, il restauro, il mito* (exhibition catalogue, Vatican Museums and the Biblioteca Apostolica Vaticana), Rome.

(1992), *Il Palazzo Apostolico Vaticano*, Florence.

(1993), *Raffaello nell'appartamento di Giulio II e Leone X*, Milan.

Pigler, Andor (1974), *Barockthemen: Eine Auswahl von Verzeichnissen zur Ikonographie des 17. und 18. Jahrhunderts*, 2nd edition, Budapest.

Pinelli, Antonio (1973), *I teatri. Lo spazio dello spettacolo dal teatro umanistico al teatro dell'opera*, Florence.

Pinto, John A. (1980), "Nicola Michetti and Ephemeral Design in Eighteenth-Century Rome," in *Studies in Italian Art and Architecture, 15th through 18th Centuries* (Memoirs of the American Academy in Rome 35), ed. Henry A. Millon, Rome, 289–322.

Pistilli, Pio Francesco (1991), "L'architettura tra il 1198 e il 1254," in *Roma nel duecento: L'arte nella città dei papi da Innocenzo III a Bonifacio VIII*, ed. Angiola Maria Romanini, Turin, 1–71.

Pistolesi, Erasmo (1829–38), *Il Vaticano descritto ed illustrato*, 8 vols., Rome.

Placzek, Adolf K., ed. (1982), *Macmillan Encyclopedia of Architects*, 4 vols., New York.

Podestà, B. (1878), "Carlo V a Roma nell'anno 1536," *Archivio della Società Romana di Storia Patria* I, 303–44.

Pohlkamp, Wilhelm (1983), "Tradition und Topographie: Papst Silvester I. (314–335) und der Drache vom Forum Romanum," *Römische Quartalschrift* LXXVIII, 1–100.

(1984), "Kaiser Konstantin, der heidnische und der christliche Kult in den Actus Silvestri," *Frühmittelalterliche Studien* XVIII, 357–400.

Pollak, Oskar (1928–31), *Die Kunsttätigkeit unter Urban VIII*, 2 vols., Vienna.

Pope-Hennessy, John (1964), *Catalogue of Italian Sculpture in the Victoria and Albert Museum*, London.

Portoghesi, Paolo (1970), *Roma Barocca. The History of an Architectonic Culture*, Cambridge, Mass.

Preimesberger, Rudolf (1978), "Das dritte Papstgrabmal Berninis," *Römisches Jahrbuch für Kunstgeschichte* XVII, 157–81.

Pressouyre, Sylvia (1984), *Nicholas Cordier: Recherches sur la sculpture à Rome autour de 1600*, 2 vols., Rome.

Previtali, Giovanni (1962), "Il Costantino messo alla berlina o bernina su la porta di San Pietro," *Commentari* XIII, 55–58.

Prinz, Wolfram, and Ronald Kecks (1985), *Das französische Schloss der Renaissance*, Berlin.

Prinzivalli, V. (1899), "Il Colonnato di S. Pietro e Lorenzo Bernini," *Catholicum* I (January), 6–9.

Prodi, Paolo (1982), *Il sovrano pontefice: Un corpo e due anime, la monarchia papale nella prima età moderna*, Bologna, 1982 (*The Papal Prince. One Body and Two Souls: The Papal Monarchy in Early Modern Europe*, trans. Susan Haskins, Cambridge, 1987).

Quednau, Rolf (1979), *Die Sala di Costantino im Vatikanischer Palast*, Hildesheim and New York.

Radke, Gary M. (1988), review of Steinke 1984, in *Journal of the Society of Architectural Historians* XLVII, 192–94.

Rasmussen, Niels Krogh (1983), "Maiestas Pontificia: A Liturgical Reading of Etienne Dupérac's Engraving of the Capella Sixtina from 1578," *Analecta Romana Instituti Danici* XII, 109–148.

Raymond, John (1648), *An Itinerary Contayning a Voyage Made through Italy in the Yeare 1646, and 1647*, London.

Reames, Sherry L. (1985), *The "Legenda Aurea." A Reexamination of Its Paradoxical History*, Madison.

Redig de Campos, Deoclecio (1967), *I Palazzi Vaticani*, Bologna.

(1982), "The Apostolic Palace," in *The Vatican. Spirit and Art of Christian Rome*, New York, 91–147 (reprint of author's essay in *The Vatican and Christian Rome*, Vatican City, 1975, 95–129).

Rietbergen, P. (1983a), "A Vision Come True: Pope Alexander VII, Gianlorenzo Bernini and the Colonnades of St. Peter's," *Mededelingen van het Nederlands Instituut te Rome* XLIV–XLV (nos. 9–10), 111–63.

(1983b), *Pausen, Prelaten, Bureaucraten. Aspecten van de Geschiedenis van het Pausschap en de Pauselijke Staat in de 17e Eeuw.*, Nijmegen.

Rivosecchi, Valerio (1982), *Esotismo in Roma Barocca. Studi sul Padre Kircher*, Rome.

Robertson, Clare (1992), *"Il Gran Cardinale." Alessandro Farnese, Patron of the Arts*, New Haven.

Rocca, Angelo (1612), *De Campanis Commentarius*, Rome.

Romano, Pietro (1932), *Pasquino e la satira in Roma*, Rome.

Rosa, M. A. (1960), "Alexander VII," in *Dizionario bibliografico degli Italiani* II, Rome, 205–15.

Rosand, David (1990), " 'Divinità di cosa dipinta': Pictorial Structure and the Legibility of the Altarpiece," in *The Altarpiece in the Renaissance*, ed. Peter Humfrey and Martin Kemp, Cambridge, 143–64.

Rossacher, Kurt (1967a), "Berninis Reiterstatue des Konstantin an der Scala Regia: Neues zur Werkgeschichte," *Alte und Moderne Kunst* XII (no. 90), 2–11.

(1967b), "Das fehlende Zielbild des Petersdomes: Bernini's Gesamtprojekt für die Cathedra Petri," *Alte und Moderne Kunst* XII (no. 95), 2–21

(1971), "Die Metamorphose der Kaiserdalmatika und Bernini's Konzept für S. Pietro," *Alte und Moderne Kunst* XVI (no. 119), 2–13.

(1986), "Der Aufruf der Seligen zum Elysium als Konzept von Neu-St.-Peter," *Pantheon* XLIV, 61–71.

Rossi, Ermete (1939), "Roma ignorata," *Roma* XVII, passim.

(1940), "Roma ignorata," *Roma* XVIII, passim.

Röttgen, Herwarth (1973), *Il Cavalier d'Arpino* (exhibition catalogue, Museo Nazionale del Palazzo di Venezia), Rome.

(1975), "Zeitgeschichtliche Bildprogramme der katholischen Restauration unter Gregor XIII, 1572–1585," *Münchner Jahrbuch der bildenden Künste* XXVI, 89–122

Rubin, Miri (1991), *Corpus Christi. The Eucharist in Late Medieval Culture*, Cambridge.

Ruysschaert, Jose (1968), "Miniaturistes romains su Pie II," in *Papa Pio II, Atti del convegno del V centenario della morte*, ed. D. Maffei, Siena.

(1990), "La Bibliothèque et la typographie vaticanes de Sixte

V," *Miscellanea Bibliothecae Apostolicae Vaticanae IV* (Studi e testi 338), Vatican City, 343–63.

Salomi, Salvatore, ed. (1992), *Le porte di bronzo dall'antichità al secolo XIII* (Istituto dell'Enciclopedia Italiana, Acta Enciclopaedica 15), Rome.

Satkowski, Leon (1993), *Giorgio Vasari Architect and Courtier*, Princeton.

Scamozzi, Vincenzo (1615), *L'idea della architettura universale*, 2 vols., Venice.

Scavizzi, Giuseppe (1987), "Storia ecclesiastica e arte nel secondo cinquecento," *Storia dell'arte* LIX, 29–46.

(1989), "The Cross: A 16th-Century Controversy," *Storia dell'arte* LXV, 27–43.

Schaff, Philip, and Henry Wace (1961), *A Select Library of Nicene and Post-Nicene Fathers of the Christian Church*, ser. 2, vol. 1 (Eusebius) (1st edition 1890), Grand Rapids.

Schedel, Hartmann (1493), *Liber cronicarum cum figuris et ymagibus ab inico mundi*, Nuremberg.

Schiavo, Armando (1981), "La Scala Regia e l'imperatore Costantino," *L'urbe* (March/April), 49–62.

Schütte, Margret (1990), *Die Galleria delle Carte Geografiche im Vatikan. Eine Ikonologische Betrachtung des Gewölbeprogramms*, Ph.D. diss., University of Bonn.

Scott, John Beldon (1985), "Papal Patronage in the Seventeenth Century: Urban VIII, Bernini, and the Countess Matilda," in *L'Age d'or du mécénat (1598–1661)*, ed. Roland Mousnier and Jean Mesnard, Paris, 119–27.

Seidel, Linda (1976a), "Holy Warriors: The Romanesque Rider and the Fight Against Islam," in *The Holy War* (Conference on Medieval and Renaissance Studies 5, Ohio State University, 1974), ed. Thomas Patrick Murphy, Columbus, 33–77.

(1976b), "Constantine and Charlemagne," *Gesta* XV, 237–39.

(1981), *Songs of Glory. The Romanesque Façades of Aquitaine*, Chicago.

Seiler, Peter (1989), *Mittelalterliche Reitermonumente in Italien. Studien zu Personalen Monumentsetzungen in den Italienischen Kommunen und Signorien des 13. und 14. Jahrhunderts*, Ph.D. diss., University of Heidelberg.

Servi, Gaspare (1861), *La nuova scala al Vaticano opera dell'architetto Cav. Filippo Martinucci*, Rome.

Severano, Giovanni (1630), *Memorie sacre delle sette chiese di Roma*, Rome.

Shearman, John (1971), "The Vatican Stanze: Functions and Decoration," *Proceedings of the British Academy* LVII, 1–58.

(1972), *Raphael's Cartoons in the Collection of Her Majesty the Queen and the Tapestries for the Sistine Chapel*, London.

(1983), "A Functional Interpretation of Villa Madama," *Römisches Jahrbuch für Kunstgeschichte* XIX, 315–27.

(1986), "The Chapel of Sixtus IV," in Carlo Pietrangeli et al. (1986), *The Sistine Chapel. The Art, the History, and the Restoration*, New York, 22–91.

(1990), "La storia della cappella Sistina," in Carlo Pietrangeli et al. (1990), *Michelangelo e la Sistina. La tecnica, il restauro, il mito* (exhibition catalogue, Vatican Museums and Biblioteca Apostolica Vaticana), Rome, 19–28.

Silvan, Pierluigi (1992), "Le origini della pianta di Tiberio Alfarano."*Rendiconti della Pontificia Accademia Romana di Archeologia* LXII, 3–23.

Sirén, Oswald (1914), *Nicodemus Tessin D. Y's Studieresor i Danmark, Tyskland, Holland, Frankrike och Italien*, Stockholm.

Skippon, Philip (1663–64), *An Account of a Journey Made thro' Part of the Low Countries, Germany, Italy, and France* (reprinted in *A Collection of Voyages and Travels . . . in Six Volumes* VI, ed. A. Churchill and J. Churchill, London, 1732).

Smith, Earl Baldwin (1956), *Architectural Symbolism of Imperial Rome and the Middle Ages*, Princeton.

Sonnino, Paul (1966), *Louis XIV's View of the Papacy (1661–1667)*, Berkeley.

Southorn, Janet (1988), *Power and Display in the Seventeenth Century. The Arts and Their Patrons in Modena and Ferrara*, Cambridge.

Stappleford, Richard (1978), "Constantinian Politics and the Atrium Church," in *Art and Architecture in the Service of Politics*, ed. Henry Millon and Linda Nochlin, Cambridge, Mass., 2–19.

Steinke, Katharina B. (1984), *Die mittelalterlichen Vatikanpaläste und ihre Kapellen. Baugeschichtliche Untersuchung anhand der schriftlichen Quellen* (Studi e documenti per la storia del Palazzo Vaticano 5), Vatican City.

Stendhal (1957), *A Roman Journal*, transl. Haakon Chevalier, New York.

Stevenson, Enrico (1887), *Topografia e monumenti di Roma nelle pitture a fresco di Sixto V della Biblioteca Vaticana*, Rome.

Stinger, Charles L. (1985), *The Renaissance in Rome*, Bloomington.

Stylianou, Andreas, and Judith A. Stylianou (1971), EN TOΨTΩ NIKA. *In Hoc Vinces. By This Conquer* (Publications of the Society of Cypriote Studies 4), Nicosia.

Tafuri, Manfredo (1992), *Ricerca del rinascimento. Principi, città, architetti*, Turin.

Taja, A. M. (1750), *Descrizione del Palazzo Apostolico Vaticano*, 3 vols., Rome.

Tantouche, F. (1623), *Traicté de tout ce qui s'observe en la Cour de Rome tant par nostre sainct Pere, que par Messeigneurs les Illustrissimes Cardinaux*, Paris.

Tartaglia, Luigi (1984), *Eusebio di Caesarea. Sulla vita di Costantino*, Naples.

Templer, John (1992a), *The Staircase. History and Theories*, Cambridge, Mass.

Templer, John (1992b), *The Staircase. Studies of Hazards, Falls, and Safer Design*, Cambridge, Mass.

Tesauro, Emanuele (1655), *Il cannocchiale aristotelico: O sia idea delle argutezze heroiche vulgarmente chiamate imprese*, Venice (reprinted Turin, 1670).

Thelen, Heinrich (1967a), *Francesco Borromini. Die Handzeichnungen*, 2 vols., Graz.

(1967b), *Zur Entstehungsgeschichte der Hoch-altar von St. Peter in Rom*, Berlin.

(1967c), *Francesco Borromini, mostra di disegni e documenti Vaticani*, Vatican City.

Thoenes, Christof (1963), "Studien zur Geschichte des Petersplatz," *Zeitschrift für Kunstgeschichte* XXVI, 97–145.

(1977), review of T. K. Kitao 1974, *Zeitschrift für Kunstgeschichte* XL, 324–27.

(1990), "Zur Frage des Maßstabs in Architekturzeichnungen der Renaissance," *Studien zur Künstlerzeichnung. Klaus Schwager zum 65. Geburtstag*, ed. Stefan Kummer and Georg Satzinger, Stuttgart, 38–55.

(1992), "Madernos St.-Peter-Entwürfe," in *An Architectural Progress in the Renaissance and Baroque. Sojourns in and out of Italy* (Papers in Art History from The Pennsylvania State University 8, Essays in Architectural History Presented to Hellmut Hager on His Sixty-sixth Birthday), ed. Henry A. Millon and Susan Scott Munshower, University Park, 170–93.

Titi, Filippo (1686), *Ammaestramento utile e curioso di pittura, scultura et architettura nelle chiese di Roma, palazzi Vaticani, di Monte Cavallo, et altri*, Rome.

Torrigio, Francesco Maria (1618), *Le sacre grotte Vaticane*, Viterbo (new edition, Rome, 1635).

Traeger, Jörg (1970a), "Der Bamberger Reiter in neuer Sicht," *Zeitschrift für Kunstgeschichte* XXXIII, 1–20.

(1970b), *Der reitende Papst*, Munich.

Tratz, Helga (1988), "Werkstatt und Arbeitsweise Berninis," *Römisches Jahrbuch für Kunstgeschichte* XXIII–XXIV, 395–483.

Tuttle, Richard J. (1983), "Julius II and Bramante in Bologna," in *Le arti a Bologna e in Emilia dal XVI al XVII secolo* (Atti del XXIV Congresso Internazionale di Storia dell'Arte, 1979), ed. A. Emiliani, Bologna, 3–8.

Ugonio, Pompeo (1585), *Le cose maravigliose dell'alma città di Roma*, Rome.

Ullmann, Walter (1955), *The Growth of Papal Government in the Middle Ages. A Study in the Ideological Relation of Clerical to Lay Power*, London (2nd edition reprinted with minor corrections, 1965).

Valentini, Roberto, and Giuseppe Zucchetti (1940–53), *Codice topografico della città di Roma*, 4 vols., Rome.

Varriano, John (1984), "The Architecture of Papal Medals," in *Projects and Monuments in the Period of the Roman Baroque* (Papers in Art History from The Pennsylvania State University 1), ed. Hellmut Hager and Susan S. Munshower, University Park, 69–81.

(1986), *Italian Baroque and Rococo Architecture*, New York.

(1987), "Alexander VII, Bernini, and the Baroque Papal Medal," in *Italian Medals* (National Gallery of Art, Studies in the History of Art 21), ed. J. G. Pollard, Washington, 249–60.

Vasari, Giorgio (1550), *Le vite de' più eccellenti architetti, pittori, et scultori italiani...*, Florence (reprint, ed. Luciano Bellosi and Aldo Rossi, Turin, 1986).

(1568), *Le vite de' più eccellenti pittori scultori ed architettori...*, Florence (reprint, ed. Gaetano Milanesi, 9 vols., Florence, 1906).

Veldman, Ilya M. (1977), "Notes Occasioned by the Publication of the Facsimile Edition of Christian Hülsen and Hermann Egger, *Die römischen Skizzenbücher von Martin van Heemskerck*," *Simiolus* IX, 106–13.

(1987), "Heemskercks Romeinse Tekeningen en 'Anonymous B'," *Nederlands Kunsthistorisch Jaarboek* XXXVIII, 369–82.

(1980), "Panofsky's Perspective: A Half Century Later," in *La prospettiva rinascimentale. Codificazioni e trasgressioni* I, ed. M. Dalai Emiliani, Florence, 565–84.

Venturi, Adolfo (1914), "Un'opera sconosciuta di L. B. Alberti," *L'arte* XVII, 153–56.

Vespignanio, Johanne Carolo (1762), *Compendium Privilegiorum Rev. Fabricae S. Petri*, Rome.

Viatte, Françoise (1974), *Dessins de Stefano della Bella, 1610–1664* (Inventaire général des dessins italiens II, Musée du Louvre, Cabinet des Dessins), Paris.

Vitruvius (1956), *Vitruvius on Architecture* (Loeb Classical Library), ed. Frank Granger, Cambridge.

Vogt, Joseph (1957), "Constantinus der Grosse," in *Reallexikon für Antike und Christentum* III, Stuttgart, cols. 306–79.

Voragine, Jacob of (1969), *The Golden Legend*, transl. G. Ryan and H. Ripperger, New York.

Voss, Hermann (1922), "Bernini als Architekt an der Scala Regia und an den Kolonnaden von St. Peter," *Jahrbuch der preussischen Kunstsammlungen* XLIII, 2–30.

Waddy, Patricia (1990), *Seventeenth-Century Roman Palaces. Use and the Art of the Plan*, Cambridge, Mass.

Waetzoldt, Stephan (1964), *Die Kopien des 17. Jahrhunderts nach Mosaiken und Wandmalereien in Rom* (Römische Forschungen der Bibliotheca Hertziana 18), Vienna.

Walter, Christopher (1970), "Papal Political Imagery in the Medieval Lateran Palace," *Cahiers archéologiques fin de l'antiquité et moyen age* XX, 155–76.

Wasserman, Jack (1962), "The Palazzo Sisto V in the Vatican," *Journal of the Society of Architectural Historians* XXI, 26–35.

Wazbinski, Zygmunt (1992), "Il Cardinale Francesco Maria del Monte e la fortuna del progetto buonarrotiano per la basilica di San Pietro a Roma: 1604–1613," in *An Architectural Progress in the Renaissance and Baroque. Sojourns in and out of Italy* (Papers in Art History from The Pennsylvania State University 8, Essays in Architectural History Presented to Hellmut Hager on His Sixty-sixth Birthday), ed. Henry A. Millon and Susan Scott Munshower, University Park, 146–69.

Webb, Diana M. (1981), "The Truth about Constantine: History, Hagiography and Confusion," in *Religion and Humanism* (Ecclesiastical History Society, Studies in Church History 17), ed. Keith Robbins, Oxford, 85–102.

Wegener, W. J. (1989), *Mortuary Chapels of Renaissance Condottieri*, Ph.D. diss., Princeton University.

Weil, Mark S. (1974a), *The History and Decoration of the Ponte S. Angelo*, University Park.

(1974b), "The Devotion of the Forty Hours and Roman Baroque Illusions," *Journal of the Warburg and Courtauld Institutes* XXXVII, 218–48.

(1982), "Ludovico Burnacini and the Migration of the Forty Hours Style from Rome to Vienna," in *La scenografie barocca* (Atti del XXIV Congresso Internazionale di Storia dell'Arte 5, Bologna, 1979), ed. Antoine Schnapper, Bologna, 157–62.

(1990), "The Relationship of the Cornaro Chapel to Mystery Plays and Italian Court Theatre," in *"All the World's a Stage..." Art and Pageantry in the Renaissance and Baroque* (Papers in Art History from The Pennsylvania State University 6), ed. Barbara Wisch and Susan Scott Munshower, University Park, 458–86.

Weil-Garris, Kathleen, and John D'Amico (1980), "The Renaissance Cardinal's Ideal Palace: A Chapter from Cortesi's *De Cardinalatu*," in *Studies in Italian Art and Architecture 15th through 18th Centuries* (Memoirs of the American Academy in Rome, 35), ed. Henry A. Millon, Rome, 45–123.

Weitzmann, Kurt (1942–43), "Illustration for the Chronicles of Sozomenos, Theodoret, and Malalas," *Byzantion* XVI, 87–134.

Westfall, Carroll William (1974), *In This Most Perfect Paradise. Alberti, Nicholas V, and the Invention of Conscious Urban Planning in Rome, 1447–55*, University Park.

Westin, Robert (1978), *Antonio Raggi: A Documentary and Stylistic Investigation of His Life, Work, and Significance in Seventeenth-Century Roman Baroque Sculture*, Ph.D. diss., Pennsylvania State University.

Whitman, Nathan T. (1987), "Fontainebleau, the Luxembourg, and the French Domed Pavilion," *Journal of the Society of Architectural Historians* XLVI, 356–73.

Whitman, Nathan T., and John L. Varriano (1983), *Roma Resurgens. Papal Medals from the Age of the Baroque* (exhibition catalogue, University of Michigan, Ann Arbor), Ann Arbor.

Wilkinson, Catherine (1975), "The Escorial and the Invention of the Imperial Staircase," *Art Bulletin* LVII, 65–90.

Wilks, M. J. (1963), *The Problem of Sovereignty in the Later Middle Ages*, Cambridge.

Wilton-Ely, John, and Joseph Connors (1992), *Piranesi Architetto*, Rome.

Wirth, Karl-August (1963), "Imperator Pedes Papae Deosculator: Ein Beitrag zur Bildkunde des 16. Jahrhunderts,"

Festschrift für Harald Keller, ed. H. M. von Erffa and E. Heiget, Darmstadt, 175–221.

Wittkower, Rudolf (1939–40), "A Counter Project to Bernini's Piazza S. Pietro," *Journal of the Warburg and Courtauld Institute* III, 88–106 (reprinted in Wittkower 1975).

(1961a), "The Vicissitudes of a Dynastic Monument: Bernini's Equestrian Statue of Louis XIV," in *De Artibus Opuscula XL. Essays in Honor of Erwin Panofsky*, ed. M. Meiss, Princeton, 497–531.

(1961b), "Cornacchinis Reiterstatue Karls des Grossen in St. Peter," *Miscellanea Bibliothecae Hertzianae* (Römische Forschungen der Bibliotheca Hertziana 16), Munich, 464–73.

(1966), *Gian Lorenzo Bernini, the Sculptor of the Roman Baroque*, London.

(1975), *Studies in the Italian Baroque*, London.

(1985), *Art and Architecture in Italy 1600–1750*, Baltimore, (3rd edition).

Wohl, Hellmut (1992), "New Light on the Artistic Patronage of Sixtus V," *Arte Cristiana* LXXX, 123–34.

Worsdale, Marc (1981), "Bernini Inventore," in *Bernini in Vaticano*, Rome, 231–78.

(1986), "Eloquent Silence and Silent Eloquence in the Work of Bernini and His Contemporaries," in *Vatican Splendour. Masterpieces of Baroque Art* (exhibition catalogue, National Gallery of Canada), Ottawa, 29–40.

Zollikofer, Kaspar (1994), *Berninis Grabmal für Alexander VII. Fiktion und Repräsentation*, Worms.

Zurawski, Simone (1989), "Connections between Rubens and the Barberini Legation in Paris, in 1625, and Their Influences on Roman Baroque Art," *Revue Belge d'Archéologie et d'Histoire de l'Art* LVIII, 23–50.

Index

Padredio, Carlo, 159, 282 n91
Palace of Sixtus V (Vatican), 4, 53, 54, 80, 96, 97, 101, 163
Palatine, 25, 247
palatium Caruli, 31
palatium inferiore (lower palace), 31
palatium novum, 33
palatium superiore (upper palace), 33
Palazzo Barberini, 24, 140, 201, 219, 258 n32, 291 n90, 295 n5, 297 n54, 299 n97
Palazzo Borghese, 62, 219
Palazzo Chigi at Piazza SS. Apostoli, 218–19
Palazzo dei Penitenzieri, 61
Palazzo Farnese, 214, 220, 232, 245, 295 n5, 296 n17, 299 n97
Palazzo Ludovisi, 281 n69
Palazzo Massimo alle Colonne, 91
Palazzo Mattei, 129, 197, 258 n32, 299 n97
Palazzo Senatorio, 34
Palazzo Spada, 197; perspective colonnade, 214–18, 220–2, 224, 247
Palazzo Venezia, 213
Palladio, Andrea, 94, 237
Pallavicino, Sforza, 88, 89, 241
Pallotto, cardinal Gianbattista, 91
Palm Sunday, 23, 24, 244, 301 n155
Panini, Francesco, 47, 232, 236, 298 n61
Panini, Giovanni Paolo, 5
Pantheon, 25, 258 n46, 300 n149
Paris, Louvre, 211
Parma, duke of, 245, 250
Pasquino, 241, 243
Paul II, pope, 38, 39, 40, 50, 51, 57, 61, 67, 78, 79, 122
Paul III, pope, 27, 28, 34, 43, 50–3, 67, 78, 103, 197, 214, 249, 263 n104, 271 n17
Paul V Borghese, pope, 4, 8, 9, 17, 37, 38, 48, 55, 56, 58, 64, 66, 67, 69, 71, 75, 76, 77, 78, 80, 90, 97, 104, 106, 107, 118, 121, 126, 128, 132, 133, 196, 238, 247, 248, 249, 275 n37, 278 n93, 291 n83, 298 n80
Peace of the Pyrenees, 206, 244
Peace of Westphalia, 240, 241
Pellegrino, Antonio del, 41, 42
Pelle, Giacomo, 124, 125
Pentecost, 43
Peruzzi, Baldassare, 43, 91
Phidias, 194, 210, 212, 295 n177
Philip IV, king of Spain, 301 n163
Philostorgius, 289 n14
Piazza del Popolo, 23
Piazza della Rotonda, 160, 283 n113
Piazza, Carlo Bartolomeo, 200, 225, 235, 236
Piazza S. Ignazio, 117
Piazza Scossacavalli, 59
Piazza S. Maria della Pace, 117
Piazza S. Pietro, 4, 5, 6, 9, 20, 22, 25, 26, 28, 30, 31, 34, 36, 37, 46, 47, 48, 53, 54, 55, 56, 60, 61, 81, 82, 83, 84, 98, 105, 107, 108, 109, 110, 113, 115, 117, 129, 130, 139, 160, 165, 175, 196, 225, 236, 247; Bartoli plan, 84; Bonacina engraving, 107; construction chronology, 101–3;

counterprojects, 91–101; early design chronology, 85–90; foundation medal, 89, 95, 101; fountains, 63, 76, 107; later design chronology, 90–1; models, 88, 107, 120; Piazza Obliqua, 111; Piazza Retta, 111; Piazza Rusticucci, 10, 94, 298 n82; project with sight lines, 104; projects before Bernini, 83–5; terzo braccio, 107, 111
Piervisani, Carlo, 286 n48, n49, 287 n59
Piranesi, Francesco, 227
Pisa, Camposanto, 292 n108
Pisa, treaty of, 245
Pius II, pope, 37, 42, 69, 247, 249
Pius IV, pope, 83, 197
Pius IX, pope, 25, 26
plague, 273 n52
Platina, Bartolomeo, 200
Ponte S. Angelo, 159, 286 n51
porta curie palatii, 36
Porta del Popolo, 225
Porta, Guglielmo della, 193
Porta Iulia (Cortile del Belvedere), 42, 46, 47
porta palatii, 43, 44, 260 n31
Porta Pertusa, 47
porta prima, 36, 48
porta S. Petri, 30, 36
Porta Vaticana, 47
Porta Vecchia (Porta Regia), 126
Portone di Bronzo, 6–9, 11, 12, 15, 69, 71, 76, 82, 87, 104, 107, 108, 111, 116, 117, 126, 127, 129, 163, 247, 248, 257 n18, n20, 258 n24, 271 n25, 278 n96, 298 n82
Prati di Castello, 219
Praxiteles, 194, 210, 212, 295 n177
Pugin, A. W. N., 273 n61

Quarenghi, Giacomo, 54
quattuor custodia, 36
Quirinal Palace, 63, 67, 77, 88, 91, 117, 157, 249, 275 n37

Raggi, Antonio, 280 n35
Rainaldi, Carlo, 85, 103–5, 106, 219, 226, 227, 228, 231
Raphael, 4, 30, 31, 34, 42, 44, 45, 167, 168, 190, 201, 204, 205, 216, 232
Regnaudin, Thomas, 189
Reni, Guido, 205
Reverenda Fabbrica di S. Pietro, 29, 56, 66, 85, 86, 88, 91, 92, 95, 96, 124, 125, 129, 130, 160, 166, 167, 174, 175, 179, 190, 205, 274 n93, 285 n36
Reynolds, Sir Joshua, 274 n3
Ricci, G. B., 63, 64, 67, 77
Ridolfi, cardinal Nicholas, 289 n15
Righi, Francesco, 217
Rinaldi, Giovanni, 175, 207, 287 n63, 294 n151
Romano, Giulio, 48, 50, 167
Rossellino, Bernardo, 231
Rossetti, Cesare, 57
Rossini, Luigi, 47, 48, 54
Rubens, Peter Paul, 201

Rucellai, Giovanni, 66
Rustichelli, Cosimo, 175, 287 n63, n66, 288 n76

Sabbatini, Lorenzo, 34
Sacchetti, cardinal Giulio, 240, 241, 246
sacrum palatium, 61, 248, 249
Sala di Carlo Magno, 201
Sala di Costantino, 198, 200
Sala Ducale (*aula secunda* and *aula tertia*), 27, 31, 34, 35, 51, 158, 162, 225, 241, 282 n82
sala pubblica, 48
Sala Regia (*aula prima* or *aula regia*), 4, 6, 19, 20, 24, 25, 27, 29, 31, 34, 35, 36, 43, 44, 46, 50–4, 59, 61, 62, 63, 64, 127, 136, 137, 139, 140, 143, 145, 150–3, 155, 162, 197, 198, 208, 224, 225, 226, 233, 259 n56, n60, 280 n36, 291 n84, 294 n161, 300 n132
Sale Paoline, 63
Salviati, Francesco, 34
Sangallo the Younger, Antonio da, 21, 34, 43, 44, 47, 50, 52, 53, 54, 63–4, 131, 151, 152, 157, 163, 213, 214, 232, 249
Sansovino, Jacopo, 94
Sassi, Pietro, 158, 280 n35
Scala del Maresciallo, 27, 36, 50, 52, 54, 59, 62, 63, 120, 121, 128, 130, 159, 233, 259 n51, 276 n52, 294 n160
Scala di Costantino, 18, 19, 26, 27, 31, 66, 122, 123, 127, 128, 156, 158, 165, 209, 226
Scala Nuova, 25–7
Scala Regia, and ceremonies, 224–6; and ecclesiastical imagery, 226–36; base landing, 15–19; *cavalcatori*, 66; colonnades and garden perspectives, 214–24; construction procedure, 150–7; construction chronology, 157–60; costs, 129; design responsibility, 160–3; double landing, 22–4; drawings, 14, 19, 55, 132, 135–50, 171, 174, 175, 176, 228; figures of Fame, 16–17, 140, 145–8, 158–9, 162, 165, 197, 228; finestrone, 28, 145, 148–50, 158, 159, 161, 163; fresco of Christ and St. Peter walking on water, 27–8, 54, 228; graffiti, 155; *ignudi*, 17, 18, 22, 23; intermediate landing, 21–2; lower stairs, 19–21; medal, 19, 138–9, 140, 141–3, 145–6, 148–9; new focus of ritual, 249–51; physical context, 131–5; relief medallions, 17, 74, 79, 140–3, 272 n35, n38, 276 n55; skylights, 24, 25, 145, 156, 161; sphinxes, 162, 197, 198, 200; statue of St. Peter 66, 128, 158, 196, 248, 280 n47; term "Scala Regia," 28; upper stairs, 24–5; wall niches, 239
Scamozzi, Vincenzo, 19, 20, 214, 258 n43
Schedel, Hartmann, 35
Schor, Giovanni Paolo, 159, 210, 283 n100, 295 n175
secunda custodia, 36
Semprevivo, Ranuccio, 57
Septimius Severus, emperor, 194
Sernini, Nino, 52

Plates

Plate 1. Exterior, Portone di Bronzo (Bibliotheca Hertziana, C37043)

Plate 2. Exterior, Portone di Bronzo, Madonna enthroned with Christ and Sts. Paul and Peter, mosaic design by Cavaliere d'Arpino (Bibliotheca Hertziana, U.Fi.DI, 160f)

Plate 3. Exterior, Portone di Bronzo, angel on pediment (south), Ambrogio Bonvicino and Nicolò Cordier (Bibliotheca Hertziana, U.Fi.DI, 160d)

Plate 4. Exterior, Portone di Bronzo, angel on pediment (north), Ambrogio Bonvicino and Nicolò Cordier (Bibliotheca Hertziana, U.Fi.DI, 160e)

Plate 5. Interior, north corridor, looking west toward Scala Regia (Bibliotheca Hertziana, C37044)

Plate 6. Interior, Portone di Bronzo, papal escutcheon under vault of north corridor (Bibliotheca Hertziana, D36874)

Plate 7. Bay of north wall in north corridor (Bibliotheca Hertziana, D36875)

Plate 8. Detail of pilaster bases, north corridor (Bibliotheca Hertziana, D36877)

Plate 9. Detail of pilaster capitals, north corridor (Bibliotheca Hertziana, D36878)

Plate 10. Angle view of base landing, equestrian statue of Constantine, and Scala Regia from north corridor (Bibliotheca Hertziana, C37047)

Plate 11. Axial view of base landing and Scala Regia from north corridor (Bibliotheca Hertziana, C37046)

Plate 12. View of finestrone, cross, and banderole over base landing, looking east down north corridor from Scala Regia (Bibliotheca Hertziana, C37045)

Plate 13. Figures of fame and papal escutcheon over base landing at entrance to Scala Regia (Musei Vaticani XXII. 7. 43)

Plate 14. View into vault of base landing, south side (Bibliotheca Hertziana, D36886)

Plate 15. Medallion relief of Constantine Founding St. Peter's, vault of base landing, south side (Bibliotheca Hertziana, D36887)

Plate 16. View into vault of base landing, north side (Bibliotheca Hertziana D36884)

Plate 17. Medallion relief of Baptism of Constantine, vault of base landing, north side
(Bibliotheca Hertziana, D36885)

Plate 18. Equestrian statue of Constantine and base landing looking north (Bibliotheca Hertziana, C37048)

Plate 19. Equestrian statue of Constantine from narthex of St. Peter's looking north (Bibliotheca Hertziana, C37049)

Plate 20. Equestrian statue of Constantine (Bibliotheca Hertziana, D36879)

Plate 21. Equestrian statue of Constantine, detail of rider's head, torso, and arms (Marder)

Plate 22. Equestrian statue of Constantine, detail of front of horse and drapery from below (Bibliotheca Hertziana, D36881)

Plate 23. Equestrian statue of Constantine, detail of drapery and forelegs of horse (Bibliotheca Hertziana, D36883)

Plate 24. Equestrian statue of Constantine, detail of drapery and hind legs of horse
(Bibliotheca Hertziana, D36882)

Plate 25. View of vault over base landing (Bibliotheca Hertziana, C37050)

Plate 26. Axial view of Scala Regia (Bibliotheca Hertziana, D36888)

Plate 27. Detail of capitals, lower flight of Scala Regia, north side (Bibliotheca Hertziana, D36893)

Plate 28. Detail of base, lower flight of Scala Regia, north side (Bibliotheca Hertziana, D36892)

Plate 29. View of vault over Scala Regia next to base landing (Bibliotheca Hertziana, D36890)

Plate 30. View of vault over Scala Regia between decorated tranverse arches (Bibliotheca Hertziana, D36891)

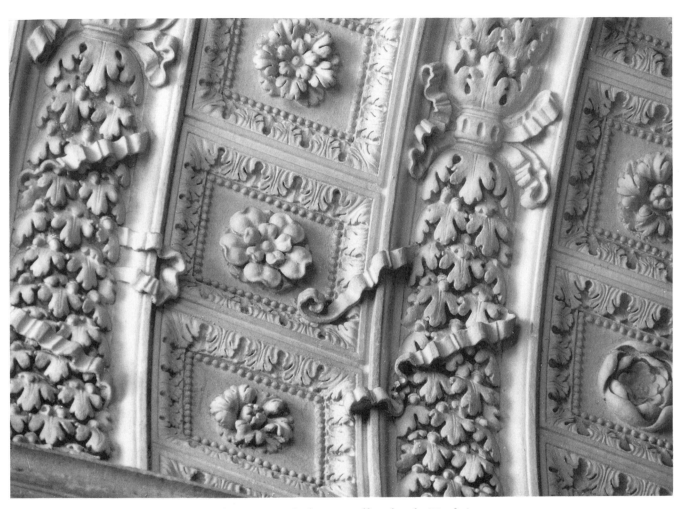

Plate 31. Detail of stucco soffits of vault (Marder)

Plate 32. View into side aisles of Scala Regia (Marder)

Plate 33. Detail of column and pilaster bases in side aisles of Scala Regia (Marder)

Plate 34. View of narrowing coffers over first section of side aisles of Scala Regia (Bibliotheca Hertziana, D36894)

Plate 35. View of narrowing coffers over last (highest) section of side aisles of Scala Regia (Bibliotheca Hertziana, D36895)

Plate 36. Intermediate landing, south wall (Bibliotheca Hertziana, D36896)

Plate 37. Intermediate landing, north wall (Bibliotheca Hertziana, D36897)

Plate 38. View into vault over intermediate landing (Bibliotheca Hertziana, D36898)

Plate 39. View into vault over south side of intermediate landing (Bibliotheca Hertziana, C37053)

Plate 40. View into vault over north side of intermediate landing (Bibliotheca Hertziana, C37054)

Plate 41. View down Scala Regia and north corridor from double landing (Bibliotheca Hertziana, C37052)

Plate 42. Double landing looking southeast (Bibliotheca Hertziana, C37060)

Plate 43. Detail of double landing at southeast corner (Bibliotheca Hertziana, D36900)

Plate 44. Double landing looking south (Bibliotheca Hertziana, C37059)

Plate 45. Double landing looking west (Bibliotheca Hertziana, C37057)

Plate 46. Double landing looking north (Bibliotheca Hertziana, C37058)

Plate 47. View into vaults of double landing (Bibliotheca Hertziana, C37061)

Plate 48. View into south vault of double landing (Bibliotheca Hertziana, C37063)

Plate 49. Putti in south vault of double landing, northwest pendentive (Bibliotheca Hertziana, D36908)

Plate 50. Putti in south vault of double landing, southwest pendentive (Bibliotheca Hertziana, D36907)

Plate 51. Putti in south vault of double landing, southeast pendentive (Bibliotheca Hertziana, D36904)

Plate 52. Putti in south vault of double landing, northeast pendentive (Bibliotheca Hertziana, D36902)

Plate 53. View into north vault of double landing (Bibliotheca Hertziana, C37062)

Plate 54. Putti in north vault of double landing, southwest pendentive (Bibliotheca Hertziana, D36909)

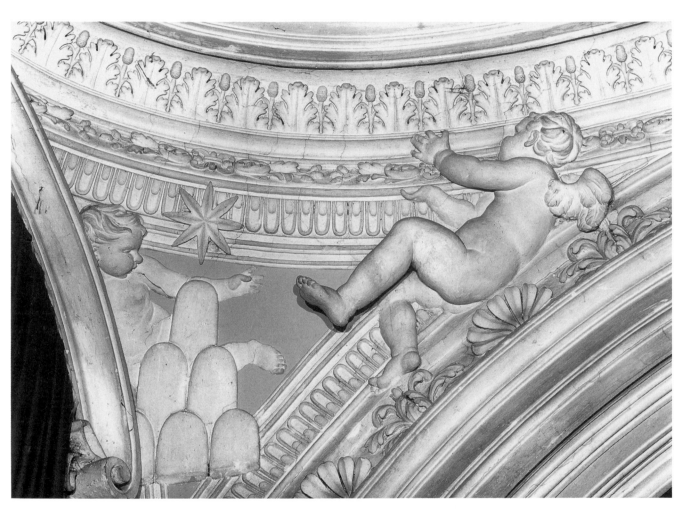

Plate 55. Putti in north vault of double landing, northwest pendentive (Bibliotheca
Hertziana, D36903)

Plate 56. Putti in north vault of double landing, northeast pendentive (Bibliotheca Hertziana, D36906)

Plate 57. Putti in north vault of double landing, east side (Bibliotheca Hertziana, D36901)

Plate 58. Putti in north vault of double landing, west side (Bibliotheca Hertziana, D36905)

Plate 59. Upper flight of Scala Regia looking east (Bibliotheca Hertziana, C37055)

Plate 60. Upper flight of Scala Regia, north wall (Bibliotheca Hertziana, D36913)

Plate 61. Detail of pilaster capitals, upper flight of Scala Regia (Bibliotheca Hertziana, D36915)

Plate 62. Detail of pilaster bases, upper flight of Scala Regia (Bibliotheca Hertziana, D36914)

Plate 63. View into vault of upper flight of Scala Regia (Bibliotheca Hertziana, C37055)

Plate 64. Papal escutcheon and wooden doors of Sala Regia at summit of Scala Regia
(Bibliotheca Hertziana, D36910)

Plate 65. Papal escutcheon at summit of Scala Regia (Bibliotheca Hertziana, D36912)

Plate 66. View of fresco of Charlemagne enthroned in Sala Regia, seen from the upper flight of the Scala Regia (Bibliotheca Hertziana, D36911)

Plate 67. Base of Scala di Costantino with doors leading to base landing of Scala Regia
(Bibliotheca Hertziana, D36934)

Plate 68. Scala di Costantino (Bibliotheca Hertziana, D36933)

Plate 69. West portico of Cortile del Maresciallo with arches of Scala del Maresciallo and Scala di Costantino (Bibliotheca Hertziana, D36929)

Plate 70. West portico of Cortile del Maresciallo looking south, with arches of Scala del Maresciallo and Scala di Costantino (Bibliotheca Hertziana, C37064)

Plate 71. Scala del Maresciallo looking west from Cortile del Maresciallo (Bibliotheca Hertziana, D36922)

Plate 72. Detail of pilaster capital and entablature, Scala del Maresciallo (Bibliotheca Hertziana, D36928)

Plate 73. Detail of pilaster base, Scala del Maresciallo (Bibliotheca Hertziana, D36926)

Plate 74. Scala del Maresciallo looking east from Sala Regia (Bibliotheca Hertziana, D36924)

Plate 75. Lunette at foot of Scala del Maresciallo, Christ Washing the Apostles' Feet, fresco by Donato da Formello (Bibliotheca Hertziana, D36925)

Plate 76. West side of Cortile del Maresciallo (Bibliotheca Hertziana, C37065)

Plate 77. East side of Cortile del Maresciallo (Bibliotheca Hertziana, C37066)

Plate 78. Finestrone over base landing of Scala Regia located between the façade of St. Peter's (left) and apartments of Cortile del Maresciallo (right) (Bibliotheca Hertziana, D37051)